BODIE & BROCK
THOENE

Take This Cup

Jerusalem Chronicles, Book Two

 ZONDERVAN®

ZONDERVAN

Take This Cup

Copyright © 2014 by Bodie Thoene and Brock Thoene
This title is also available as a Zondervan ebook.
Visit www.zondervan.com/ebooks.
This title is also available in a Zondervan audio edition.
Visit www.zondervan.fm.
Requests for information should be addressed to:
Zondervan, *Grand Rapids, Michigan 49530*

ISBN 978-0-310-33599-3 (hardcover, jacketed)

Library of Congress Cataloging-in-Publication Data

Thoene, Bodie, 1951-
    Take this cup / Bodie & Brock Thoene.
        pages cm. -- (Jerusalem chronicles ; Book Two)
    ISBN 978-0-310-33598-6 (softcover)
    1. Jesus Christ--Fiction. 2. Lazarus, of Bethany, Saint--Fiction. 3. Bible. New Testament--
History of Biblical events--Fiction. I. Thoene, Brock, 1952- II. Title.
    PS3570.H46T23 2014
    813'.54--dc23   2013041150

Cover design: Kirk Douponce

Cover photography or illustration: Robin Hanley

Interior illustration: Ruth Pettis

Interior design: Katherine Lloyd, The DESK

Editing: Ramona Cramer Tucker, Sue Brower, Bob Hudson, Anna Craft

Printed in the United States of America

17 18 19 /RRD/ 23 22 21 20 19 18 17 16 15 14 13 12 11 10 9 8 7

For my prayer warrior stars, with love from Bodie

Every Friday at 5 o'clock we toast one another with these words:

"Here's to the women who went before us, to
those who will come after us, and to us . . ."

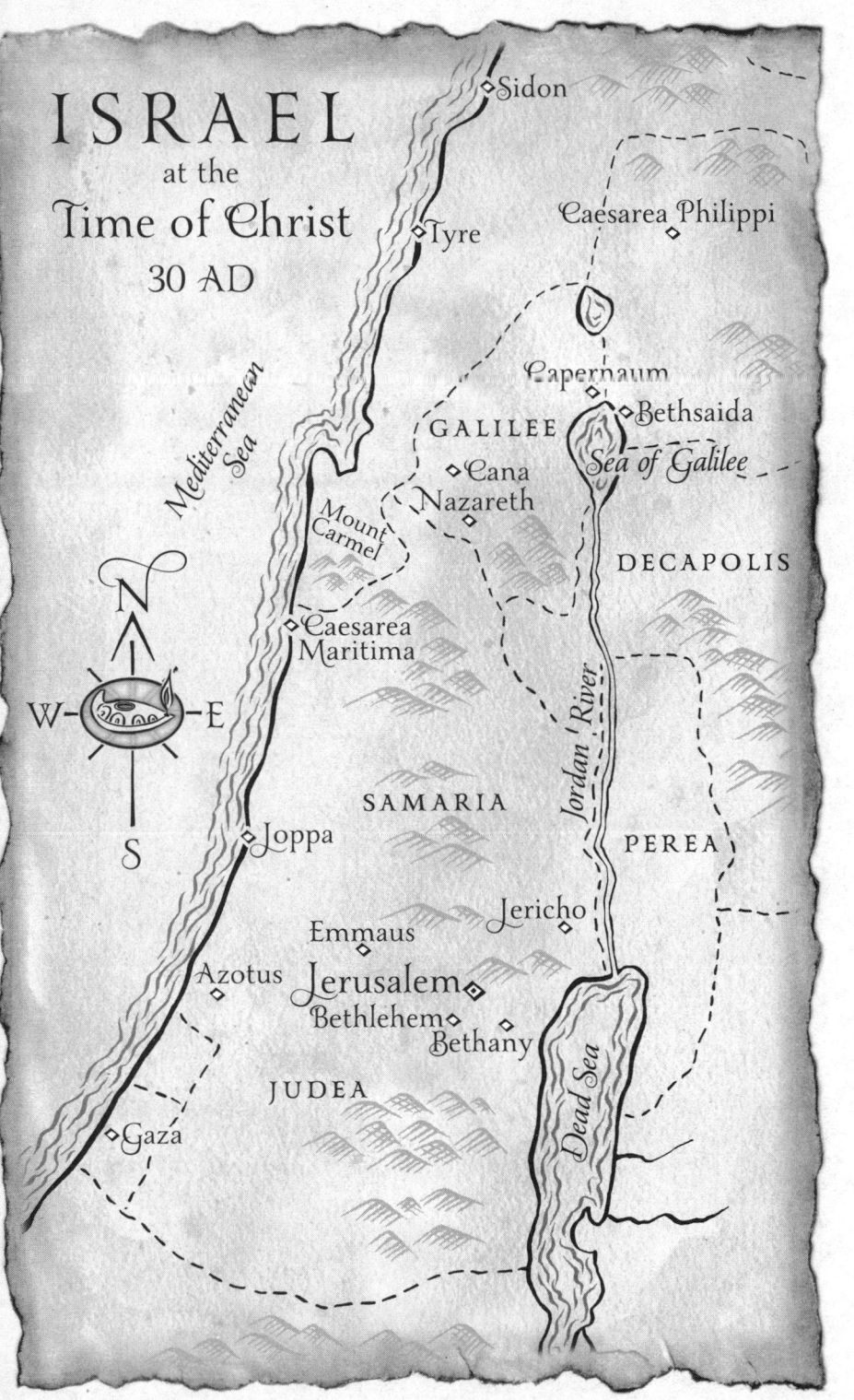

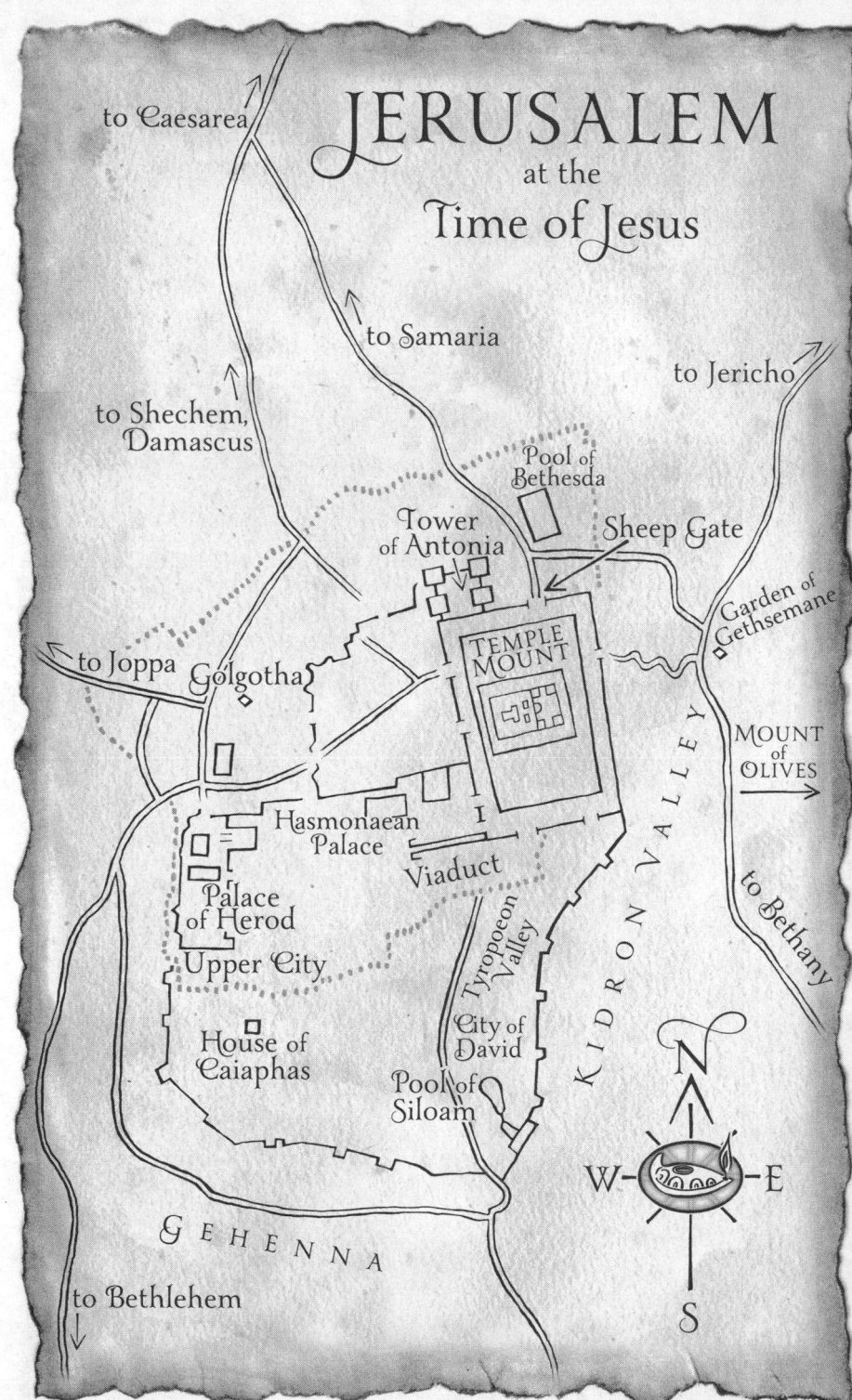

JERUSALEM
at the
Time of Jesus

to Caesarea

to Samaria

to Jericho

to Shechem, Damascus

Pool of Bethesda

Tower of Antonia

Sheep Gate

Garden of Gethsemane

to Joppa

Golgotha

TEMPLE MOUNT

Hasmonaean Palace

MOUNT of OLIVES

Viaduct

Palace of Herod

Upper City

Tyropoeon Valley

KIDRON VALLEY

to Bethany

House of Caiaphas

City of David

Pool of Siloam

GEHENNA

to Bethlehem

N
W — E
S

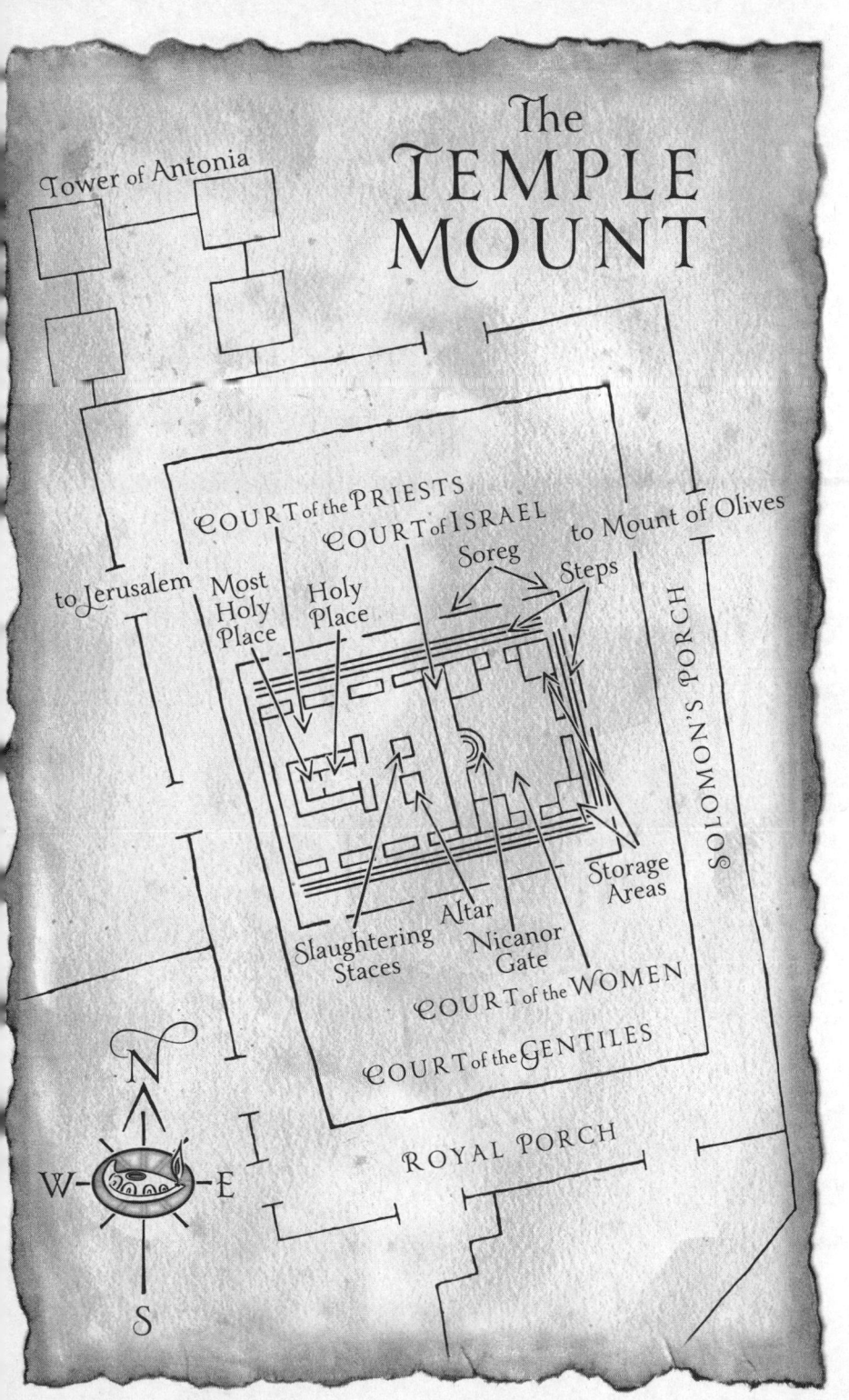

The
TEMPLE MOUNT

Tower of Antonia

to Jerusalem

COURT of the PRIESTS

COURT of ISRAEL

to Mount of Olives

Soreg

Steps

Most Holy Place

Holy Place

SOLOMON'S PORCH

Slaughtering Staces

Altar

Nicanor Gate

Storage Areas

COURT of the WOMEN

COURT of the GENTILES

N
W — E
S

ROYAL PORCH

Part One

As a deer pants for water,
so my heart longs for you, O Lord.

PSALM 42:1[1]

Chapter 1

My mother's name was Sarah. She was the fifth daughter of Boaz, a weaver of fine wool prayer shawls in Jerusalem. Sarah was taller than most men, ample hipped and heavy-set, with thick, curly hair, and wide green eyes in a square, practical face. Her teeth were straight and strong. Such things as teeth mattered.

Sarah's weaving of prayer shawls was skilled, her work meticulous. Her shawls were worn by the Temple priests and pilgrims alike.

Sarah's one flaw was that she walked with a limp. But her father was quick to remind everyone that Sarah was a cheerful, loving girl and a hard worker. She would bless any man in search of a good helpmate.

One after another, Sarah's older sisters married. There were, however, no suitors for Sarah. Her limp, though not severe, was problematic. It was not easy for her to ascend and descend the hundreds of steps in Jerusalem. The streets were steep, and a woman's duties of shopping in the souk and fetching water would surely be hindered by her handicap. And men desiring to be head of a household did not want the head of a woman taller than their own.

Year after year she hoped and prayed. But there was not one man in all of Israel who asked for Sarah's hand in marriage.

Sarah resigned herself to remaining an unmarried virgin in her father's house. Content with her life, she helped her mother and father in the little shop, located fourth from the high end of the Street of the Weavers.

Sarah's place was at the entrance of the shop. There, she and the loom were a sort of fixture on the street. Sarah played the loom like an instrument. She sang in perfect rhythm with the movement. Passersby gathered in a half circle to watch and listen as she performed.

Sarah was twenty-three, well past marriageable age, the morning her mother's distant cousin Lamsa ben Baruch entered the shop and fixed his steady gaze upon her as she worked.

"May I help you, sir?" Sarah's mother asked as she braided and tied the knots on the four corners of the prayer shawl.

"Aye. If you are Rebekah, wife of the weaver Boaz, then I am your cousin Lamsa . . . here from the land of Gan Eden."

Sarah's mother squealed with delight and laid aside her work. "Boaz! Boaz! It's my cousin Lamsa! Lamsa, from beyond the four rivers of Eden!" She rushed to embrace him.

"You've gotten plump, Rebekah," Lamsa drawled in his Eastern dialect. "But you are still pretty!"

The *thump, thump, thump* of Sarah's loom continued as she observed the reunion through the screen of warp and woof.

My grandfather, Boaz, rushed from the back room and clasped Lamsa's arms. "Lamsa! And you've gotten lazy! Fifteen years or more since you delivered your wool to Jerusalem personally! Sent a steward to Jerusalem to us every year but now . . . look at you!"

Sarah observed Lamsa. He was tall and strong, but not as tall as she. Lean and muscled, he clearly did not live a life of ease. Though she knew he was in his early forties, his grizzled beard and weathered skin made him appear older than he was. Yet his brown eyes, quick and observant, took in details of the shop.

His expression was pleased as he observed bolts of fine woolen fabric. A rainbow of colors and constellations of patterns filled two walls. Prayer shawls of intricate weaving were priced for rich or humble, a variety of sizes neatly folded on shelves. Finally, he took in the loom and Sarah and grinned.

"My flocks would be flattered that their wool has become such a fine and holy covering. I will tell them next season when they are shorn."

Sarah smiled shyly and looked downward but did not break the rhythm of her labor.

A lock of wild black hair spilled from beneath Lamsa's turban and across his brow like the forelock of a horse.

"There is no wool like the wool of Lamsa's sheep," Boaz praised. "It is the fleece of Eden—that is what I tell our customers. Nothing so thick and yet silky. No fleece like it in the world."

Rebekah clapped her hands in delight. "But you are here with us! How's the family? Your sons? Three of them, yes? And your wife?"

"My sons are well and strong. Ten, twelve, and fifteen." His smile faltered. "But my beautiful Jerusha flew away last spring, trying to give me our fourth child, and I am without my great companion."

Boaz and Rebekah clucked their tongues and wagged their heads in unison at the news.

"Oh, Lamsa!"

"Poor Lamsa!"

"So sorry to hear your news!"

" . . . very sorry. May she rest in peace."

" . . . in peace."

"What's a man without a wife . . ."

" . . . a wife."

"Only half . . ."

"What's life without a woman?"

Boaz's eyes glanced furtively at his daughter. His lower lip extended. Eyebrows rose and fell as he turned his face slightly to one side as a thought passed through his mind and out his ear. "Rebekah, go fetch your cousin something to eat quickly. He has come a long way to see us."

Sarah thought her father made it sound as though Lamsa had not eaten in a thousand miles and that he had come all the way from Eden just to share a meal. Sarah saw that her father and mother had invisibly tattooed the word *widower* across Lamsa's forehead.

Lamsa bowed slightly as Sarah's mother hurried off to fetch refreshment.

"The dust of Eden remains on our mountains." Lamsa laid out his wares on the fabric table to show samples of this year's wool and fine, thick fleeces from his flocks in the North beyond Babylon. "And the glory of Adonai remains in our high mountain pastures. My sheep drink in the memory of it from the waters, and even the grass they graze translates the vision of Adam into this . . ." He swept his hand proudly over the wool.

Boaz ran his fingers over the miracle produced by Lamsa's flock and closed his eyes in pleasure at the quality. "Nothing like this wool anywhere."

Lamsa added, "Ah, brother, you should taste the meat of my lambs. Nothing has such flavor. I dream of it when I am away."

"You must be hungry! Where is that woman?" Then Boaz called to Rebekah, "Wife, where are you? Hurry! Bring the wine and cheese and bread for Lamsa."

Rebekah bustled in with a tray of food and a jug of wine. "I must go prepare a feast for you, Lamsa. So many years since we have served you! Our daughter, Sarah, will help me. She is a good cook. Sarah?"

Sarah tried to maintain her smile but was well aware her mother had already mentally discarded the word *widower* and substituted the phrase *potential husband for lame, too-tall Sarah, twenty-three-year-old spinster daughter.*

Rebekah motioned to Sarah, and the thump of the loom fell silent. She stepped from her chair and towered over the room.

"This," Boaz said, smiling, "is our daughter Sarah. She was a child when last you were here."

Lamsa did not say, "My, how you've grown," but Sarah saw the thought in his expression.

Sarah stepped forward and curtsied. "Cousin Lamsa, I know you by the beauty of the wool I weave, sir."

Lamsa kissed her on both cheeks. "Cousin Sarah, you play the loom as if it were David's harp." He gestured at her father's wares. "And here is the poetry and the melody and the music of your effort."

It was a kind thing for him to say, and a true thing as well. Sarah bowed her head slightly, then left with her mother so Boaz and Lamsa could conduct business.

Sarah limped after her mother through the curtain into the back room of the shop. Rebekah lingered to eavesdrop. Sarah, disgusted, waited, hands on hips. The voices of the two men drifted to her.

"It's a long way for you to travel, Lamsa."

"I wanted to see you. I remembered you have five beautiful daughters."

"Yes. Yes. The four oldest are married with families of their own now. They weave for me in their homes."

"Sarah is a skilled weaver," Lamsa remarked.

Sarah wanted to cover her ears. Her mother was almost vibrating as she panted and wrung her hands at the curtain.

"Mother," Sarah hissed. "Come on. Please! We have to go to the Street of the Butchers before they close." Sarah plucked at her mother's sleeve.

Rebekah came to her senses as Sarah tugged her out the back door of the shop into the late afternoon air. "We must have the butcher prepare a haunch of lamb for us," Rebekah decided.

"Not lamb, Mother. You heard what Lamsa said about his lamb. Anything but his own will be sawdust in his mouth."

"Oh, Sarah, you are so clever. Such a clever girl! Why you have never married . . ."

They trudged up the alley toward the open corridor leading to where butcher shops lined the street known as "Shambles."

Sarah rolled her eyes. "Mother. The man is not looking for a wife!"

"He most certainly is!" Rebekah would not be swayed.

"He's not looking for me."

Rebekah glanced up at Sarah. "And why not you? Why, I ask?"

"And I am not looking for a husband. Not one who lives a thousand miles away."

Rebekah pinched her cheek. "Look at you. Pretty girl. Pretty green eyes. Your eyes are your best feature. What's wrong with you? Such a place he lives. A rich man. Eden . . ."

"I'm no Eve. What's for dinner?"

Rebekah was drawn back to the problem of inferior lamb. "Beef," she declared.

"The best pieces will be gone by now."

"Fish."

"Too late in the day. No fresh fish."

"Then what?"

"A chicken," Sarah answered. "We'll have the butcher slaughter a chicken. Fresh enough."

Rebekah snapped her fingers. "You're so smart, daughter. Yes, you can make that . . . that . . . wonderful dish your father enjoys so much."

And so the chicken was slaughtered, plucked, and roasted as Lamsa hurried to the public baths and returned in time for a sumptuous meal prepared by Sarah. Wine flowed. The best wine. Lots of it.

Lamsa reclined happily and patted his belly. "There are wild pheasant in the hills. Practically pick them up without a snare. But my boys do love to hunt. Imagine pheasant cooked like this."

Rebekah simpered, "Sarah can cook anything. Can't you, Sarah? Tell him your secret."

"Garlic," Sarah replied without elaboration.

Lamsa nodded slowly. "Ah, yes. Garlic. We have garlic. And rosemary and thyme grow wild on our hills." He pressed his fingers together and formed a tent shape. "Two mountain ranges border our grazing lands like this. Climbing and climbing to impossible heights. The snowfall on the peaks never fully melts. On the lower slopes it melts into ten thousand waterfalls and is the source of the Tigris and Euphrates rivers. Eden. You see? And at the very north of the mountain ranges, where my fingers meet, is Ararat, a volcano with two great peaks, where

9

Noah and his ark came to rest. Noah opened the door of the ark and out they came . . . all the animals. So our mountains and valleys abound with wildlife."

Sarah questioned, "And your flock grazes on the wild spices? Perhaps that is why your lamb is superior in taste to any other." She meant this as a joke.

Lamsa continued to nod as he considered such profound wisdom. "That must be it. Such a clever girl. That has to be it." Sarah smiled slightly. "It could be nothing else."

"All fruit trees grow wild there. Except orange trees. But every spice grows wild. And asparagus. Just stroll out of your door. Vegetables . . . all kinds . . . wild."

Sarah replied too pleasantly, "A miracle. And so the lamb is seasoned before it is cooked, and vegetables are perfectly ripe and ready on the hillside. A woman has no need to go to the souk . . ."

Lamsa broke his bread and placed a piece on Sarah's plate. "We are never without variety, and every day is beautiful. My town is called Amadiya. It is built of stone and is as old as Jerusalem, they say. Abraham would have known it. Built on a high plateau that overlooks river valleys. Beautiful. A fortress. A safe place for our wives and children. Only one way up. A steep staircase cut in the side of the mountain. Protection for our families from raiders while we shepherds move our flocks from meadow to meadow."

Sarah considered her lame foot and wondered if there were more steps leading to Amadiya than there were in Jerusalem. "But what if the women and families wish to go with their husbands?" she asked.

Lamsa replied, "Then they come. And live in tents among the flocks. Seven or eight months of the year is a long time to stay alone in a stone house in the village. Many families come along with the men. All work together. Children. Women. But only if they do not wish to stay in a fine stone house in the village." He smiled. "It is pleasant. If Father Abraham would come upon us, he would not know how many centuries had passed. The descendants of Noah's wild deer often follow our flocks as we move from pasture to pasture. They drink with the sheep in the dry season. It is written, 'As a deer pants for water, so my heart longs for you, O, Lord.'"[1]

"I have heard something like that." Sarah drizzled honey on her morsel.

"Perhaps it is not the exact quote. But I know the truth of it."

Rebekah, as if fearing that Lamsa would catch on to Sarah's amusement, suddenly interrupted, "Come now, daughter, finish your meal. Lamsa and your father have things to discuss. Business."

The women cleared the table.

Rebekah heated water for washing. "Sarah," she chided, "he is a good man."

Sarah lifted a brow. "He's had too much wine and talks too much."

"Your father knows how to conduct business."

"Business! Do you think I don't know . . ." Sarah exhaled heavily. "Mother, I am content to be who I am and wish to remain where I am. Amadiya! How many steps up the face of a mountain to reach the village? Stop plotting. Not one more word!" Sarah warned.

They cleaned up the rest of the dishes in silence.

Immediately afterward, Sarah retreated to her bedchamber on the rooftop. Storm clouds gathered, and the half-moon shone through the silver vapor. She had been in bed an hour when Boaz and Rebekah rapped softly at her door.

"Enter."

Rebekah's expression was wistful, hopeful, as she blinked at Sarah. Boaz's lower lip protruded as it did when he was negotiating a sale.

"Daughter, are you asleep?" Rebekah whispered hoarsely.

"Not now." Sarah sat up.

"Good." Boaz pulled up a stool and, sucking his teeth, sat down slowly. "The chicken tonight was . . ."

"Just a chicken, Father."

"Lamsa enjoyed it very much." Rebekah leapt in too quickly.

Sarah did not reply at first, but a sense of dread filled her. "Father? What have you done?"

Her parents exchanged a guilty glance. Boaz cleared his throat. "You're no spring chicken."

"Not slaughtered and plucked quite yet, you mean, Father? Not stewed or roasted?" Sarah covered her face with her hands. "Just tell me."

"It's good news, really." Rebekah stroked her back. "He . . . Lamsa . . . likes you."

Sarah sighed. "Mother, everyone here likes me. I have only friends here. I have sisters and nephews and nieces who like me. Who love me. Strangers stop to watch me weave. They like me. I love my work."

Boaz cleared his throat. He smelled of too much wine. "Here's the bargain. Lamsa came here looking for a wife. Here. I mean, to this house. My house. He remembered that I had five daughters. He is looking for a wife, you see, from Jerusalem. He is not finished having children, and he wants a wife from Jerusalem, which will add stature and authority to his descendants, since his people did not return from exile when the captivity ended. He came looking . . . for you."

"No, Father! Not for me. I am the leftover daughter. The only one of five who is unmarried."

"That may be, but that made his choice easier."

"His choice?" Tears welled in Sarah's eyes.

Rebekah glanced nervously at Boaz. "Yes. He is a good man. A rich man."

"He lives eight months in a tent with sheep," Sarah protested. "Is this what you want for me?"

"Here is the bargain," Boaz reasoned. "His choice of my five daughters is you. No matter that your sisters are married. Lamsa chooses you. He came here for you. But he says . . ."

Silence hung in the air like a large spider suspended from a web. Sarah looked from Rebekah to Boaz, then back again. "What?"

Boaz continued cautiously. "Lamsa says he will not force you to marry him. Will not force you to leave your family and go back to Gan Eden unless you are certain you want to go."

Sarah blurted, "Then it's settled. The answer is no!"

Rebekah clasped her hand. "Sarah, your last chance . . ."

"No, Mother."

Boaz drew himself up. His eyes simmered in anger. "He is a fair man. He says you should pray on the matter and ask the Lord if there is some way you might be happy. That is what Lamsa says, and I command you to pray!"

Tears spilled. "What about my work?"

Boaz's chin lifted slightly. "Lamsa will take your loom to Amadiya. You will weave there. Your fabric, your prayer shawls, will be returned here to be sold in Jerusalem. I could not lose my most skilled weaver. For Lamsa, it is less raw wool to be caravanned. Thus, more economical."

"What about my limp? The mountains? Walking?"

"He says you may have your own donkey to ride. I would have nothing but the best for my daughter. He is a wealthy herdsman."

Sarah could not utter another word. All the details for a marriage contract had been worked out.

So, she pondered, *this is how marriage happens. A distant relative in need of a woman walks through the door, and a bargain is struck. With the one caveat, I must agree.* "All right, Father, Mother. I will consider his . . . business arrangement."

"And pray?" Rebekah clasped her hands in a desperate pantomime of prayer.

"Yes, Mother. I will pray. I promise. I will."

The two scuttled like crabs out of her room and closed the door.

Sarah rose and leaned her chin against her hand on the windowsill. Male voices drifted up.

"My daughter says you are a most excellent man. She considers herself unworthy. You stride the mountains like a lion. She is lame and only useful at her loom."

Lamsa's rich, deep voice replied, "When I was a boy, I owned a pet ewe who was lame. She gave me many lambs. Her wool was the finest grade. Yes, I have many donkeys for Sarah to use. She may choose her own. And I will carry her home riding on my own camel . . . if she will come. But I do not wish for an unhappy companion. It is a long way to my high mountain valleys. She will not likely see her family again."

And so, that night, Sarah prayed about the proposed match. Could she like this man? Could she live in tents among the sheep for eight months of the year? Like the Abraham and Sarah of old, Lamsa's fathers were among those in Israel who stayed behind in Babylon when Nehemiah the prophet returned to rebuild the walls of Jerusalem.

Sarah reminded God that she was happy without a husband. Lamsa was a distant relation, a wealthy Jewish herdsman who lived in the land of ancient Babylon. He was not handsome.

"Abba, God of Abraham, Isaac, and Jacob, you hear my prayers. I do not wish to leave my pleasant life and leave Jerusalem for exile in a wild land unless you have some greater purpose for me. But if I was to have a son, I would dedicate him to serve you. And then I would be pleased to leave my home and kin." She stopped and thought, then continued speaking aloud to God. "If Lamsa says he will stay for a while in Jerusalem, and not leave until after the rainy season, Lord, then I will know. Just after the end of the rains. Tell me, please, Lord, what is your will?"

In that instant, as she finished praying, a flash of lightning split the sky. It divided like forked antlers, and the clouds lit up in the shape of a giant hart. A thunderclap followed, shaking the house. The heavens opened and rain bucketed down, sluicing off the eaves and into the street.

Sarah returned to her bed and lay for a while listening to the pleasant drumming of rain on her roof. Then she went to sleep, believing the Lord would give her a sign.

In the morning over breakfast, Lamsa and Sarah's father spoke about the weather.

Lamsa did not look at Sarah. "Last night I saw a bolt of lightning like the antlers of a great white hart in the sky. And such a rain followed."

Sarah paused. "I saw it too. A great hart in the eastern sky. Beautiful."

Lamsa smiled. "When there is thunder in our mountains, we say it is the sound of two great harts doing battle. The hart is a symbol for us who wander in distant land. Adam's great hart, strong and wise. We will one day all be gathered here in Eretz-Israel, because the Lord promised that even the land where I dwell will be Israel when Messiah comes. I am waiting for that day."

Sarah blinked down at her plate of eggs and bread. "I am also waiting for Messiah. He must come soon."

"When we see him as conqueror, it is written that it will be as lightning flashes from east to west."[2]

"Yes." Sarah swallowed hard as the answer came to her. "We will all see him at the same time. Jerusalem and your precious mountains and pastures."

Lamsa leaned forward slightly and studied her face. "You would love my mountains, I think."

Sarah nodded once. "Yes. I think. I think . . . I will. Yes. I would like to go see such a sight. Asparagus growing on a mountaintop . . . and such things. Thunder."

Lamsa leaned back and laughed loud and hearty. He patted his chest. "Oh, my heart! My happy heart!"

Sarah laughed with him. "All right, then."

Boaz and Rebekah embraced. "Praise be to God! Praise be!"

When things quieted down, Lamsa instructed, "Have the *Ketubah* drawn up, Boaz. I think it would be wise that we would marry here and stay here in Jerusalem with you until the rainy season is over. Sarah, would this please you?"

All was well. The matter was settled over breakfast, and by dinner the contract was signed.

The wedding took place in Jerusalem that very next week. From the first night, Sarah was happy with her husband. He was gentle with her, and she was cherished by him. It was a good match.

By the time the rainy season ended, Sarah had intricately woven her husband a beautiful prayer shawl. She was more than content; she was in love. When the rains were over and the camels packed for their return journey to Eden, Sarah told her parents a secret: "I am carrying Lamsa's child. I will send word when the baby is born."

So my mother, with her loom and carrying me, left all her family behind and traveled a thousand miles east and north by caravan.

Chapter 2

$\mathcal{A}$ll in the encampment tending my father's herds were asleep, except for the watchmen posted around the flock.

A chorus of summer breezes curled down from the heights, filling the valley with whispers of tall pines and the creaking sighs of yews and junipers.

My mother, heavy with me, had chosen to follow the grazing sheep with my father, rather than stay behind in a stone house in the fortress town of Amadiya to await my birth. There was a midwife in the shepherds' camp and an elderly rabbi named Kagba, a wise man, who knew the secrets of *Torah* and taught the children. If I turned out to be a boy, Kagba would perform the circumcision.

Sarah stood framed in the dark entrance of their tent. Her arms tenderly embraced me, dancing in her womb. "Your father is tending the flocks tonight, my little lamb."

Watch fires had burned to embers that winked and sparkled on the improvised stone hearth. The pleasant sharpness of wood smoke scented the air. Shepherds and vigilant herd dogs ringed the meadow. A psalm of the shepherd boy David came to her: *"The LORD is my shepherd; I shall not want."*

Beyond the circle of guardians, an outer hoop of cedar trees protected the lush grazing grounds. A herd of a dozen roe deer cropped the grass at the near edge of the meadow. For a moment Sarah thought she saw the ghost-like form of a white hart watching from the shadows.

The words of the psalmist continued, *"He makes me lie down in green pastures."*

The crescent of a waning moon climbed over the peaks, and a myriad of stars reflected on the surface of a small, pristine lake. *"He leads me beside still waters."*[1]

Night birds called from the rushes lining the shore. In the middle distance an owl hooted fitfully.

There seemed no separation between earth and sky. Sarah caught a glimpse of Rabbi Kagba standing on a low hill, surrounded by her three stepsons and a half-dozen other children attending his astronomy class. He pointed out constellations and the movement of the stars.

She had never really thought about the constellations or the names of stars when she lived in her lonely rooftop bedchamber in Jerusalem. But now she enjoyed the bits of information in the rabbi's lessons.

"A man will not be lost in the wilderness if he learns the path of the stars," the rabbi told his students.

Sarah whispered, "Stars above and stars shining up from beneath the surface of the water."

Turning, she followed the direction indicated by the silhouette of the teacher's outstretched arm. He traced a waterfall of glittering stars spanning the breadth of the heavens. Kagba's voice drifted across the pond: "The Great Sky River! Other peoples name it 'The Celestial Way.' It is said that when Messiah comes, his authority will stretch . . ."

The breeze reversed its direction, and Kagba's words swirled away toward the west.

A meteor streaked across the sky, followed by another and another as they had done for three nights. Kagba had earlier explained these shooting stars were called the Perseids. They appeared for a month around the same time each year in late summer.

I shifted slightly in my mother's womb, and she smiled.

"You're late arriving, I think, my bright star. Can you hear me? We all wait for you to join us here beneath the stars that shone above Eden."

As if in reply, a brilliant streak flashed across the horizon, and I answered with a rhythmic tapping beneath her right ribs.

"Soon. Is that what you are saying?" She rubbed the bulge. Was it elbow, knee, or behind? "The midwives say you are a big baby. A son, they say . . . ready to be born. Late summer while the Perseids rain down, they told me. Why do you wait? What you have to look forward to . . . You will love living here, little lamb. As I do. I never knew there could be a place on earth so beautiful. Beauty beyond what your father described."

A triangle of mountain ranges framed the valley. There was an opening at the bottom of the triangle so the rivers that watered Eden could flow into the plain. Jagged peaks reared up on her right and left—peaks so stony and so tall they scraped the clouds and pierced the heavens. Waterfalls tumbled from the heights into pools as blue as the eyes of angels.

"Hurry, little lamb, so your eyes will see stars touch earth. You will hear the bleating of your papa's sheep. Oh, when I think . . . what I might have missed if I had not come to Paradise!"

"He restores my soul. He leads me in paths of righteousness."[2]

Sarah knew the path she had taken was the right one. She had not realized how empty her life had been until she fell in love with Lamsa. Her stepsons had accepted her without question and loved her generously. Occasionally the youngest boy, Ezra, spoke to Sarah about his mother. He was the quiet one of the three. How he missed her! She had been a beautiful, fragile woman, and both she and a baby died in childbirth. This fact clearly troubled little Ezra when Sarah's condition became unmistakable. He had lost his beloved mother. Would he also lose Sarah?

Sarah had done her best to assure Ezra that she was as strong as an ox, never sick a day. Lamsa said she was made to bear children with ease. And Lamsa should know such things, since he had spent his life helping the ewes give birth.

The sheep of Lamsa's peaceful flock shone silvery in the moonlight, like a vast field of new-fallen snow. For months since her arrival, she had witnessed the miracle of life as ewes gave birth to lambs in the fields of summer. Sarah was ready now, and unafraid of labor and childbirth.

"Though I walk in the valley of the shadow of death, I will fear no evil, for you are with me."

Sarah had sung the psalm of David daily in Jerusalem as she plucked the strings of her loom, but she had never understood the meaning of the poetry until now.

"Your rod and your staff, they comfort me."[3]

She whispered, "Only let the baby come soon, Lord. So I can send word to my family in Jerusalem before the weather turns bad and none can travel to the west. My mother will worry all next winter if she does not hear!"

As if in answer to her prayer, three meteors drifted slowly from the heart of the constellation. The muscles of her abdomen suddenly tightened in the first sign of labor.

Sarah laughed, gazed up in awe, and stroked her belly. "Well! That was not so bad," she said aloud. Glancing toward the nearby tent of Hepzibah, the head midwife, she wondered if she should fetch her now or let her sleep. Sarah decided she would wait awhile. Hepzibah, who had become her good friend, had explained that labor usually took several hours before a baby was ready to be born.

Sarah returned to her soft fleece bed and propped herself up with pillows so she could view a patch of sky through the open tent flap. She saw the constellation of Perseus with his sword upraised. A meteor shot from the warrior's head. She wondered if her mother could see the same flash of light in far-off Jerusalem. Her eyes brimmed with tears at the thought. For an instant she was filled with longing for her mother. Rebekah had, after all, been present at the births of all the grandchildren. This was one she was going to miss.

Sarah shook herself free from sadness. She counted the Perseids between contractions. About one shooting star every minute. When there were four meteors between contractions, Sarah's water broke. The intensity of the pain suddenly increased.

So this is it, she thought as her belly became rock hard, held for a minute, and then slowly relaxed. *Not so bad. I must tell Ezra not to worry. Not at all.*

Sarah said aloud, "Hmmm. So my sisters exaggerated their pain. Probably to impress their husbands."

Sarah rose from her bed. Yet another contraction seized her. This was much stronger. She groaned and gripped the tent pole for support, panting until it passed.

All right . . . then . . . all right . . . So maybe they were not exaggerating all of it.

Stepping outside the tent, she cupped her hands and called cheerfully, "Hepzibah, wake up, my sister! You'd better hurry. I need your help, Hepzibah. Our little one says he wants to see the dawn with his own eyes this morning!"

Chapter 3

$\mathcal{I}$ was born shortly before sunrise. They tell me I was a large, angry, big-voiced baby, with a full head of dark hair and fists that made my father proud. I had an appetite to match my size.

"He's going to be a big fellow." My father smiled down tenderly at me. "A fighter, I think."

According to the tradition of our family, my name would not be revealed until the circumcision on the eighth day. My mother guessed that surely Father would call the boy something that honored a warrior ancestor. She mentioned a dozen names, but my father did not respond to her suggestions.

"Can't you tell me?" my mother asked him the day before my circumcision.

"The Lord has not revealed the boy's name to me yet, wife. Tonight, as is my tradition, I'm going to the waterfall for a *mikvah*. I will pray and ask the Lord to tell me what I should call my son. A name is so important. It sets the course for a life. I will bathe beneath the waterfall and immerse myself in the pool. Then I'll listen for the voice of the Lord. Adonai will speak to me. He will tell me who my son is meant to be." Father gathered clean clothes and a blanket and struck out in the dark up the path to bathe in the cold snow melt.

Mother lay in the tent with me at her side. She says I nursed and then slept. A trickle of milk escaped my full lips. She wrapped my fingers around her thumb, kissed my forehead, and whispered, "I know who you are. Though your father will name you for a mighty man, a great man, you are my little lamb. You will always be that to me."

My father returned at daybreak. With his hair swept back from his face, he looked like a young man as he stood over Mother and me.

"Well?" she asked.

"He is to be a servant of the Most High. The Lord has revealed it to me."

She patted the edge of the bed, eagerly inviting my father to sit. "Tell me."

He grabbed a jug of cold milk and took a long swig, wiping his mouth with the back of his hand. Then he sank down beside her.

Father took her hand. "Nehemiah. That is his name. Like the one who rebuilt the walls of Jerusalem. Look at those hands. The hands of a wall builder, don't you think?"

"Nehemiah. Does this mean our son will return to Jerusalem?" my mother ventured.

"The Lord has spoken. On behalf of all in my family who remained in exile, our son will return . . . for some mighty purpose, it will be. The Lord has spoken this to me clearly."

"For a mighty purpose. Then I will be content."

On the eighth day of my life, my father lifted a calloused palm and squinted toward the brightening eastern horizon. The sun had not yet appeared above the peaks of the Bersheesh range, but he studied the fading stars carefully. When he could no longer distinguish Regulus, the Little King star marking the paw of the Lion of Judah, he muttered, "It's time." Raising his voice he called toward our tent, "Sarah! Bring the child."

My mother, cradling me, stood with Hepzibah in a circle that included my three brothers, a brace of shepherds, and Rabbi Kagba. A chorus of *"Baruch HaBa . . .* Blessed is he who comes," greeted me.

Even though it was the Sabbath, when all ordinary work was prohibited, this particular ceremony was not only allowed to continue, it was required.

Rabbi Kagba explained: "The eighth day . . . always. We stand here in the shadow of Bersheesh, which we remember is the same expression as the first word in *Torah*. Here, beside the Mountain of Beginnings, beneath the same crags that witnessed the dawn of creation, we continue an unbroken obedience to that commitment. A special blessing attaches to a son of Abraham who is joined by covenant to the Almighty on his Sabbath day. Such a one, it is said, is selected by the Lord of the Sabbath for a divine anointing, because the Almighty breaks his own law of Sabbath rest to welcome the newcomer into our people. Please give the child to his eldest brother to hold, on this, the ordained eighth day."

When Mother detached me from her breast, I gave a full-throated yelp of protest.

The rabbi smiled. "In fact," he added, "the only time we do not circumcise on the eighth day is if there is risk to the health of the child. Clearly," he said, indicating how I brandished two clenched fists, "such is no concern today!"

Ezra, my youngest brother, stifled a yawn, and this action spawned a wave of similar motions among the shepherds newly come from the night watches.

"And," Rabbi Kagba instructed, "we perform this ceremony early in the day, because we should always rush to complete a *mitzvah*, a duty, and never delay it or put it off."

A rough-hewn wooden bench had been padded with a fleece and topped with a woven woolen cloth for the ceremony. The group drew nearer together to witness as the rabbi opened a leather case and withdrew a small, sharp blade. My eldest brother unfolded the swaddling from around me.

Without speaking, Rabbi Kagba delivered a message by upraised eyebrow to Hepzibah and received a nod in reply. The midwife stepped slightly behind my mother. The rabbi had seen more than one mother faint at the sight of her son's blood and always made sure someone was prepared to catch her.

"Blessed are you, Adonai, King of the Universe," Kagba intoned, "who has sanctified us with your commandments and commanded us in the ritual of circumcision."

While the last syllable of the blessing still hung in the morning air, the rabbi flicked the knife in its duty and the act was complete. They tell me that, instead of crying out, I frowned and tightened my jaw. This stoicism brought expressions of approval to the faces of the shepherds.

While Kagba staunched the blood, Father loudly bellowed, "Blessed are you, Adonai our God, King of the Universe . . ." When he realized that his shouting was not needed to cover any crying, he moderated his tone and continued, "King of the Universe, who has sanctified us with your commandments and commanded us to make him enter into the covenant of Abraham, our father."

And the witnesses responded, "As he has entered into the covenant, so may he be introduced to the study of *Torah*, to the wedding canopy, and to good deeds." As yet still unnamed, I was rewrapped and cradled by my brother.

Eber, one of the shepherds, poured a cup of wine from a goatskin bag and handed it to the rabbi, who raised it aloft.

"Each time we welcome a son of the covenant," Rabbi Kagba said, "we prepare our hearts for Messiah. 'Blessed is he who comes,' we proclaim, renewing our hope that the Anointed One is coming." Then he added, "And I have seen him."

This announcement caused a stir among the onlookers.

Unwilling to interrupt the ritual, Kagba waved away the buzz of questions. Instead of answering, he prophesied over me, "This son of Abraham will, with his own eyes, see Messiah in Jerusalem. It is time for the blessing of the wine."

When *Kiddush* had been said for the fruit of the vine, Kagba touched his finger to the liquid and placed a drop on my lips. Mother says I sucked the dark red fluid thoughtfully.

"Now," Kagba demanded of Father, "what is his name?"

"He shall be called . . . Nehemiah."

"Nehemiah," Kagba repeated with approval. "Cupbearer to the king and rebuilder of walls. Very good. So, Creator of the Universe, may it be your will to accept this act of circumcision as if we had brought this child before your glorious throne. And in your abundant mercy, through your holy angels, give a pure and holy heart to Nehemiah, son of Lamsa, who was just now circumcised in honor of your Great Name. May his heart be wide open to comprehend your holy law, that he may both learn and teach, keep and fulfill, all your laws. Amen!"

I was returned to my mother and tucked next to her heart. I'm sure I gave a man-sized sigh and snuggled contentedly closer to her.

Though it was barely past sunrise, the feast in honor of my circum-cision began. A large tent, its sides rolled up, had been arranged on the grassy plain as a pavilion. It was sizable enough to contain all the herdsmen not on duty. They reclined in a great circle on heaps of hides.

Platters and trays loaded with food were carried around and cups splashed with wine. It was, after all, another *mitzvah* to celebrate the life of the newest member of the covenant, even if I, the guest of honor, was fast asleep.

"So, now, Rabbi," Father demanded, waving a green onion for emphasis, "you must tell us your tale. You say you have seen the Messiah?"

Scratching his beard, Kagba leaned back and stared toward the southwest. "I met him just months after his birth," he said. "By now he would be a grown man, in his twenties. He is some-where, learning, studying, listening . . . waiting for the call of the Spirit that will prompt him to reveal himself. I'm sure of it."

"Don't be so vague!" Father insisted. "Tell us plainly, who is he?"

"He is called Jesus, the son of Joseph, whose father was named Jacob."

"Like Jacob the Patriarch was the father of Joseph the Dreamer," Mother murmured.

"Just so," Kagba agreed approvingly. "I noticed that con-nection as well."

"And why haven't we heard of him before?" my father inquired. He counted on his fingers in thought. "If he was born in the time of Old Herod of despicable memory, why are we only now learning of him?"

The rabbi sat up straighter at that. "It is *because* he was born in the days of the Butcher King that you haven't heard of him," he suggested. "But let me tell my story in its proper order."

Father shushed the other conversations around the meal. "Fill your plates," he said, "but listen to the learned rabbi."

The shepherds needed no urging to load their platters with heaps of rice and lamb stewed with tomatoes. Then they settled back to be entertained.

"You know I have some knowledge of the stars," Kagba said modestly. "Many years ago I located something in the fourth book of the law. You all have heard it: 'A star shall come out of Jacob.'[1] Now, many teachers believe this foretells the coming of the Messiah. But I, and others, wondered if his birth was linked to the sight of an actual star in the heavens.

"For many years I studied and pondered, searching the night sky for clues and struggling with ancient texts by day. I was not alone in my quest. There was a great man of our people named Balthasar who lived"—Kagba gestured toward the east—"over the mountains, in Ecbatana. We wrote to each other, sharing knowledge and anticipation.

"And then one spring, we saw it: the wandering star the Romans call Mars, that we call Ma'adim, the Adam. It was joined to the Atonement star that resides as the heart of the virgin. You remember? 'The virgin shall conceive and bear a son'?"[2]

Kagba paused to scoop up some lamb with a piece of flat bread and munched before continuing. "I will not try to recount all that I witnessed over the next year or so, but let me say that there were wondrous sights in the skies: the Righteous King star joined to the Lord of the Sabbath, over and over again, until I became convinced the birth of Messiah must be at hand.

"I traveled from Tarsus, where I had carried out my

studies, to Damascus, and who do you think I found there? My old friend Balthasar, come all the way from Parthia on the same errand as myself. Other scholars assembled too—from Ethiopia, from India—all with the same goal: to greet the newborn king.

"The stars led us to Jerusalem, where Herod was ruling, but he claimed to have no knowledge of a newborn king of the Jews. He said he wanted us to continue our research so that he might worship this child too.

"We were led on to Bethlehem, of which the prophet Micah wrote, and there we found him: a small child, born to parents from Nazareth, but living for a time in Bethlehem. We worshipped him there—Old Balthasar, the others, and myself. We gave him gifts of gold, frankincense, and myrrh."

"But you still haven't told us why no one else knows of him," Father insisted.

Kagba looked grim. Turning toward my mother, he said, "Sarah, child, I wonder if you would see if there are some pomegranates? I'd love to have one."

When Mother rose obligingly, passing Nehemiah to Hepzibah, and was out of earshot, the rabbi explained. "One of our number was warned in a dream that Herod meant to harm the child. So we did not return to Jerusalem, but fled the country a different way. It was right after that when Herod . . ."

Father's eyes saddened as he recognized the tale. "Murdered the boy babies of Bethlehem. I remember hearing of it!"

"But Jesus and his parents, warned by us, escaped into Egypt. Thereafter I lost track of them. But I know," Kagba said forcefully, "that he lives and must be revealed. It is my goal to seek him out and to see him again before I die."

"When? Now?"

Kagba shrugged. "It may not be for years. But I will know when it's time, just as I knew those two decades and more ago. Then I will find him again. And the Lord revealed to me this: your newborn son will play a special role."

Chapter 4

The Perseid meteor shower came around the fourth summer after my birth, marking again my birthday. I had, by then, shortened my name to Nehi, and would answer to nothing else.

My father often remarked that I was a strong child—strong of will and body. I towered over other children my own age by a head, and my shoulders were broader as well.

"Built like his mother," my father remarked to Rabbi Kagba as my mother hefted a large water jar and limped toward the tent. "A crooked foot doesn't even slow her down. And the boy'll be strong as an ox. Smart too, eh?"

Rabbi Kagba agreed. "It's Sarah's doing. She is a good woman. A good mother to all your sons. For a four-year-old to know his letters by sight and sound." He shook his head in awe. "The lad recites the *Shema* and *Kiddush* letter perfect. The lad will be reading *Torah* by this time next year."

All the families in the camp enjoyed my birthday feast. My father chose a woolly, black-and-tan sheepdog puppy named Beni as his gift to me. The puppy was the most aggressive in the litter, and his needle-sharp teeth grasped the hem of the new coat Mother had woven for me. Beni and I enacted a brawl, which ended with me giving him a swift kick. The pup accepted my dominance, but the new coat was already torn.

That night the puppy and I slept together on my mat. My mother repaired the tear and questioned Father about the dog. "Nehi is so young, Lamsa. How will he know what to do? How to take care of the creature?"

"You don't understand how it is out here. Every boy needs a dog. They'll grow up together, those two. Their hearts will be knit. Within a few months, you'll see. Beni will be Nehi's protector. Stand between him and an angry ewe, for instance. Or some wild animal. Beni is bred to give his life for his master, even if his master is only a boy. Later he'll serve Nehi as he learns his duties with the lambs."

My mother bit off the thread and examined the mended hole. "Almost good as new. I had intended it to be like Joseph's coat, you know? Something unique for our son. Special."

My father stooped and kissed her forehead. "Ah, Sarah, what's a little tear in the hands of a weaver? His coat . . . mended now. Not perfect. But it's right for the coat of a herdsman's son to show a little wear."

Within days Beni and I were inseparable.

With the passing months, the young dog assumed the role of protector, just as my father had predicted. Beni remained at my heels as I played with other children. Even though Beni was only a growing adolescent, he placed himself fiercely between me and all other canines. Stiff-legged, snarling, and barking, Beni let the pack know that I was his human lamb to care for, and no stranger could come near without permission.

My father had chosen the right companion for me.

My mother was comforted by the relationship between the dog and me. I could not sleep unless Beni was curled up next to me. This miracle of shepherds and their herd dogs was unlike anything Mama had ever witnessed in Jerusalem. In the city, cats kept as mousers were the only household pets.

By the next spring Beni was no longer a puppy but a lanky young dog. He flashed a white set of adult teeth and was the envy of the pack of herd dogs.

One day clouds had gathered on the high mountain peaks, a portent of an afternoon storm. A massive thundercloud towered above the crags, fiercely bright in its highest reaches while oppressively dark beneath.

A herd of roe deer, with newborn, spotted fawns, grazed near the sheep. I came to my mother and asked, "Mama, I want to take Papa his meal."

She scanned the distance between the tent and the spot where Father sat with his staff in hand, about 150 yards.

She packed the lunch basket, then stroked the dog's head. "Stay on the path," she instructed me. "Don't wander." Then, "You watch over Nehemiah, Beni." The dog wagged his tail, and we two set out.

I held my father's meal with one hand and clasped Beni's tail with the other. We walked the long way round, skirting a pasture dotted with new lambs and their mothers.

Then I noticed the fawns and let go of Beni's tail. I pointed. "Look, Beni! New baby deer! Look at the two tiny ones. Pretty little things."

The dog paused. His eyes traced my gesture across the meadow. Two dozen buff-hued does, and half again as many fawns, grazed at the rim of the forest between me and my father. The route was much shorter to cut through the herd of deer rather than go around. The dog struck out on his own, turning to look as if expecting me to follow him. I hesitated a long moment but remained on the path as my mother had commanded.

I called to my dog, "Come on! Beni, come back!"

Tail still wagging, Beni trotted toward the newborn fawns. After all, his young master had pointed to the fragile creatures. A signal to a stock dog was a command to be obeyed. Did I mean for Beni to herd them, to bring them back?

Dozens of black-tipped ears pricked toward the dog. A score of sable-ringed muzzles lifted to sniff the air.

Suddenly alarmed, one doe wheeled around. Her body became an animated wall, protecting her startled fawn.

The first threat to Beni came from a large, round-rumped doe, the mother of twins. She lowered her head and pawed the ground, warning the canine to come no closer. Oblivious and unafraid, the dog trotted on toward the herd. The doe squealed, preparing to charge. Beni had trespassed into the fawns' nursery.

Beni tucked his tail and, confused by the doe's aggressive behavior, hesitated. A brace of angry mothers encircled him. Sensing danger, the dog bristled and barked. He bared his teeth.

Two does charged, lashing out at Beni with sharp, accurately aimed hooves. Beni yelped and fell. He tried to rise but was knocked back. First one doe struck with powerful front hooves; then a second doe pounced, bringing the full weight of her body onto him. A third pounced again. The young dog was unable to escape repeated blows as he was butted and kicked from all sides.

I froze and shouted, "Papa!" My terrified cries drew Mother from the tent.

My father bellowed and swung his shepherd's staff around his head as he sprinted toward the melee of attacking deer. They scattered. With their little ones, the deer sprang into the forest, disappearing into the shadows of the deep woods.

Bloody and near death, Beni lay panting in the grass. Weeping, I stumbled to the battered body of my friend, then dropped to my knees and began to wail.

My father stooped and with a glance took in the broken body of the dog. "Nehi! Go get a blanket from your mother. Quickly. Go . . ."

Sobbing, I scrambled back up the path toward the tent. My mother met me and scooped me into her arms. "Oh, my boy! My boy!"

"Mama! They hurt Beni," I cried. "The mother deer! Papa says bring a blanket quick!"

Mother returned to the tent and snatched a blanket off a sleeping mat. Neighbors and camp children paused in their chores to shield their eyes against the sun and take in the tragedy.

"What is it?"

"Sarah? What's happened?"

"Nehi's dog got too close to the fawns."

"Stupid dog."

"Young dog. Curious. He's never seen new fawns before."

"Went out to have a sniff and . . ."

"Good thing the boy was not with him."

Rabbi Kagba approached her. "Sarah. The does were protecting their young. It could have been Nehemiah hurt. Aye. Instead, it's the dog. Be grateful."

Sarah nodded grimly and placed me in Kagba's arms. The old man soothed, "There, there, Nehi. It's finished now. We will pray. Come, Nehemiah. We will pray."

"Mama, ask the Lord! Get out the oil of God. Pray, Mama!"

I covered my face and wept bitterly. "Lord, Abba! Save my little friend. Save my Beni!"

As Mother jogged unevenly toward the scene, she guessed the matter was probably already settled. How could anything survive such an assault? She hurried down the path to where a circle of rough shepherds gathered around and offered unhelpful advice.

"Master Lamsa, sir, might as well slit his throat and end it." An elder drew his knife and offered it to my father.

He reached for it but, at the sight of Mother, held back. "A moment, Raphael. Let me check the damage to the little fellow."

"He's broken to pieces."

"Was he protecting the lad?"

"No. Just trotted off on his own, like."

"Still a pup. Curious. They don't know better at this age."

"Should have stayed with his child instead of going off to have a look at the fawns."

Father worked to staunch the bleeding of the dying dog.

Beni's fur was matted and covered in blood. He lay trembling in the trampled grass.

The men parted to let Mother into the circle.

"Beni. Oh! Poor little fellow." The dog blinked when my mother knelt beside him and stroked his head. His eyes were glazed and his breath shallow.

"Oh, Lamsa," Mother whispered. "He's suffering. Oh, what? What to do! Poor boy! Nehi is with the rabbi."

An older shepherd clucked his tongue. "Begging your pardon, sir, I never seen one this bad live. Better to end it."

"No!" my mother protested, and the men fell silent.

"Sarah, look at this." My father swept his hand over the

creature. "Broken ribs, I am certain. Don't know how many. Or if his lungs are punctured. Broken left foreleg."

"Please, Lamsa! Our boy loves him so."

The ring of onlookers did not speak. No one dared to remark on the foolishness of the master's wife.

Father was quiet for a long time. He pressed his lips together and shook his head slowly from side to side. "Sarah . . ."

"Please! We must try!" Mother begged.

My father drew a deep breath. He relented. "All right. But he'll most likely not survive the night. Here . . . the blanket. Let's carry him back to the tent."

The sunset brought on *Shabbat,* but my mother had not prepared dinner. Nor did she light the *Shabbat* candles or recite the blessings. Though the day of rest began at nightfall, Mother and Father had forgotten *Shabbat.*

Exhaustion, brought on by grief, overcame me. I burrowed into Mother's shoulder and dozed, though I was not sound asleep as they thought.

Father cleaned Beni's wounds with wine and oil. The dog was conscious and seemed to be aware but did not stir as my father moved matted fur and assessed the damage.

A smoking oil lamp, casting orange light, revealed the extent of the injuries. There were eight cuts from the sharp hooves of the deer. Starting at Beni's head, gashes covered the length of his body—right leg and shoulder, rib cage and hips.

"They're deep, but I can stitch them up. A clean break of his right foreleg." Father recited the list. "I can set the leg." He shook his head. "But I think his pelvis is broken, Sarah. Look here. When I flex his back leg . . ."

Beni yelped and raised his head in pain.

"What can you do for such a thing?" Mother asked quietly.

Father washed his hands. "If it was any other dog but this . . . well, you know what would have to be done. But for Nehemiah's sake, I'll do what I can. If he lives through the night . . . I don't know. About his hind quarters, we'll have to wait and see."

My father stood, the bit of sacking used as a towel hanging forgotten from his calloused hands as he pondered.

From outside, the familiar *Shabbat* sounds of singing drifted into the tent from the small congregation. Mother and Father exchanged a glance, realizing they had missed the sunset. In Jerusalem, the exact beginning of *Shabbat* was announced by a trumpet blast from the Temple wall. All work ceased immediately. But in the shepherds' camp, the care of the animals continued as needed without fear of God's displeasure.

Father shrugged and lit a second lamp to see by. For several hours he labored over the injured canine. The leg was set with a splint lined with fleece and wrapped with wet rawhide. The cast stiffened as the leather binding dried. Mother later said she wished I was awake to see the care my father poured into the dog, but I was too frightened to move. I remained limp and pretended to be immersed in profound slumber.

"Are you hungry, Lamsa?" Mother asked.

"Aye." Father sat back on his heels and stretched as if to signal that he had done all he could. His robes were streaked with dried blood. "I must get clean for Sabbath. Lay Nehi near Beni, so the dog can see him. Love keeps souls from flying away sometimes." My father left the tent.

Mother gazed at the dog. His breath was irregular. His golden-brown eyes followed her every move as she placed me on his sleeping mat and covered us. Beni blinked at me, his boy, thumped his tail once, sighed deeply, then slept.

Would he ever wake up? I wondered.

"Merciful Lord," Mother prayed, "why should such a thing happen? If it is in your will, O Lord of heaven and earth, spare my son this loss."

Father returned with Rabbi Kagba in tow. "Sarah, the rabbi's here, come to bring us *Shabbat* dinner."

The lamplight cast a glow on the old man's face. He carried a basket of food and a jug of wine. "*Shalom,* Sarah." The rabbi extended the food. "I knew you were too busy."

My mother accepted the gift and smiled at him. "I may never get used to the kindness in the sheep camp. Even on *Shabbat.*"

"So unlike the city, eh, Rabbi?" Father's face and hands were clean, and his hair braided at the back of his neck. He had put on a fresh tunic.

Placing a cloth on the low table, Mother laid out the meal. It was a cold feast of freshly baked bread, hummus, eggs, butter, cheeses, and a variety of dried fruit. She fetched clay cups and poured the wine. She remarked she had not realized how very hungry she was until now.

Father and the rabbi reclined as Mother kindled the candles and recited the prayers, hours late, welcoming the glory of *Shekinah* into her dwelling place.

The ritual completed, Rabbi Kagba asked, "So?"

"He might recover from the wounds," Father said. "But if his pelvis is broken . . ." He inhaled deeply. "If he isn't able to stand in the morning, then . . ."

The rabbi asked, "And if the dog does not die tonight?"

My father replied, "Tomorrow we will sacrifice Eve's lamb." He lifted his cup to his lips and drank before answering the question in my mother's eyes. "In this land where Eden once resided, among us shepherds, there is a secret for healing that is known and practiced still. The life of a lamb is sacrificed to save another life."

Mother studied Beni. I stirred and reached out to touch his muzzle. The dog labored to breathe under his injuries. His bandages showed traces of blood. Would he survive the night?

Chapter 5

When dawn crept over the mountains, I was already awake. I had picked my way out of the wool blankets atop a heap of hides. I crouched in abject misery next to Beni, beside the remaining coals of the night's fire. The fear of the threatened loss of my friend bowed my head down to my shoulders.

And yet the dog still lived, if only barely.

Every few minutes I leaned forward to watch the dog's bound and bloody rib cage for movement. My own breath caught in my throat as I observed each slight and labored inhale. With each additional breath I sighed and sat back, but only for a moment, as if the power of my desire was all that kept my dog's life within its battered frame.

Mother stirred, sat up, and caught sight of me. "Nehi? Is he . . . ?"

"Beni's still alive, Mama," I answered hesitantly, fearful that being too positive might crush my last hope.

"Well then," my mother responded, "the Almighty has answered our prayers."

"But he's still so . . . so hurt!"

"Your father has a plan," Mother said, rising and draping a blanket around my shoulders. "It is the end of lambing season. The flocks are safe. This is the day when the camp will offer a sacrifice to the Lord. Your father was up early, making the preparations. He wants Beni to be present."

"For what?"

"He called it Eve's lamb," she answered. "I don't know what it means exactly, but we will both learn soon. Here he comes now."

Father's heavy tread announced his arrival outside the tent. Taking in the scene within it, he said, "All awake? Good. It's time. Dress quickly." When Mother and I had complied, he added, "The two of you must carry Beni. Take the corners of the blanket he's on. Don't drop him. Bring him and follow me."

Mother and I labored to carry Beni carefully, without jostling him. Mother winced as her bad leg protested the awkward position and bent posture. Biting her lip, she continued anyway.

Beside a blazing fire, a short distance away from the tent, was a knot of shepherds. They and Rabbi Kagba stood above a lamb tethered to a stake. Mother and I gently deposited our charge near the fire.

Bending near me, Father said, "When Mother Eve sinned and Father Adam sinned, they brought death into the world. You know this?"

"Yes, Papa," I agreed. "You taught me this, and Rabbi Kagba talked to us about it too."

"Aye." The rabbi gestured across the landscape. "In this very place the garden of Eden once abided and the Lord dwelt here. It was on this ground the first sacrifice for man's sin was made. The footsteps of Adam and Eve trod in this very dust."

"You know about sacrifice, Nehemiah." My father used my formal name. "Then you know that the price for their sin was immediate death, except the Almighty delayed the penalty so that Adam and Eve did not die that very day." Father raised a warning forefinger. "But an immediate death was still required.

Mother Eve's pet lamb, the darling of her heart, was slain that day. From its hide was fashioned clothing to cover their shame. Its meat was offered up as a burnt offering. Its blood—the innocent blood of the lamb—was poured out on the ground. We remember this event every time our people sacrifice a lamb or a goat or a bull and offer it to the Almighty at the great Temple in Jerusalem."

I looked at my father and frowned. There was no temple here, no altar of sacrifice. What was he talking about?

The rabbi spoke. "One day an even greater sacrifice is prophesied in *Torah* by the Almighty. In the Book of Beginnings the Lord spoke the words of victory here, where we now stand. One day, in the time of Messiah, a 'once and for all' payment will be made, and then, at last, all the power of sin will be broken and death will be no more. But until then . . ." He placed his hands on the head of the lamb. "Father, accept this, our sacrifice, as an atonement for our sins. Forgive us, Lord, we pray."

Father gruffly ordered: "First for our sins. But there is healing in the fleece. Since all humans in our camp are well, we will use this fleece for Beni, companion of Nehemiah and servant to the shepherds of the flock. Now, my son, Nehemiah, lay your hands on the lamb."

I did so. I felt the quaking life beneath my fingers.

"Now say this: 'Merciful Father, please accept this life as a substitution for the life of my friend.'"

As I repeated the words, a knife I had not even noticed flashed out from Father's belt, and the lamb's body fell limply away from my touch. I recoiled in shock.

The rabbi caught the lamb's blood in a cup, held it high, and prayed quietly before slowly pouring it onto the earth where Paradise had been lost. "*Baruch atah Adonai,* may our sacrifice be pleasing and acceptable in your sight. Wipe away our sins and cleanse us from all iniquity."

Before I even found my voice again, the lamb's carcass was stripped of its hide.

"Lift Beni from the blanket," Father commanded Mother and me. "Hold him just so while I wrap him." A moment later, as Father prayed, the lambskin was wrapped about the dog's rib cage and hindquarters, and gently but firmly tied there. The dog was enveloped in a poultice of healing warmth. At its touch the dog opened his eyes, blinked, and wagged—only once, but I saw it. The tiniest hope crept into my heart and curled uneasily there next to my sorrow at the death of the lamb.

"Now carry him back inside the tent and stir up the fire," Father said.

"Will he live?" I blurted.

My father's head bobbed once in agreement. "He will live. And, with the blessing, he will do well enough. You, boy, will remember what it cost."

"I will, Papa," I promised. "I will."

Throughout the months that followed the application of the coat of Eve's lamb, I watched anxiously over Beni. With my mother's help, I carried him and helped him take wobbling steps. I slipped him extra food from my plate, and my mother, bless her, pretended not to notice.

At first he could barely hobble. I bit my lip to keep from crying over his pain, and Father shook his head. For two Sabbaths it seemed that even the application of the costly treatment would not save Beni from being a cripple, unable to follow the flock . . . or worse.

Then one morning I was awakened by a hot breath on the back of my neck. When I turned over, Beni licked my face and pawed my chest, urging me to get up. From that day forward, his recovery was swift.

To quote my father, Beni forever after had "a hitch in his step." Instead of running properly, Beni's back legs moved as one, giving him a curious, hopping sort of gait. Nevertheless, once fully healed, he was almost as swift as he had been before the injury and was more determined than ever not to leave my side.

As the seasons turned, I turned five in the summer. Then, in one night, the warmth of summer slipped away. The sheep camp awakened to autumn. Beni and I followed Father to wash at the pool and pray the morning prayers. The water in the creek was cold against my tender skin. My father's voice was crisp as he prayed. Holy syllables lingered on the air. Across from the camp, aspen leaves danced like a shower of golden coins on the trees.

Sheep were up and hard at work cropping the last inches of the grass that had carpeted the meadow.

That morning Mother cooked a dozen quail. The aroma of the campfire was more pungent, making the meat tangy with a hint of incense, as sap in the wood stopped flowing.

"Good." Father spoke between bites. "I sent the brothers ahead to clear the lower pasture of poison weeds. A week is time enough. The tableland is prepared for the flock. Today I'll move the yearlings. Tomorrow Zeke will follow with the ewes and the lambs."

"When will you be back for the rest?" Mother stirred the fire.

"A few days. A week at most."

"We'll break camp and be ready to move when you return."

I wiped my mouth with the back of my hand. "Can I go with you, Papa?"

My father shook his head. "Not this year, son. You stay and help your mother."

Though I tried to control it, I felt my lower lip quiver with disappointment. "Papa, with the women?"

Father's thick brows met in disapproval. "When you can hear and obey without tears, perhaps then you will be old enough."

Shaking off the emotion, I squared my shoulders. "It was the meat. It was too hot. Not tears."

Father tested me. "I am taking your dog with the others. He is old enough for training. You are going to stay and help your mother."

I looked at Beni. The dog's tail waved in the air as if he knew he was going on an adventure. "But Beni goes and not me?" A single tear escaped and trickled down my cheek. There was no calling it back.

Father's head nodded once. That was the way it was to be. I knew that one tear had cost me an adventure.

It was the silence of the sheep camp that awakened me. The usual bleating of the yearlings was absent as the first light of morning crept up the lavender sky and illuminated the tops of the east-facing mountains.

I snuggled deeper beneath my fleece and tried to remember why this dawn was quieter than most. I sat up as Father's journey to greener pastures with the young flock jolted my memory.

"Papa's gone," I whispered. "Beni too." Then I climbed out of my warm nest and planted my bare feet on the cold dirt floor. The blue light of dawn illuminated the tent flap. I watched the stars of the constellations fade. One glance at the mound of blankets on the large sleeping mat told me my mother was still asleep.

This was a good thing, I reasoned as I dressed. While Mother slept, and my father and brothers were gone, I would have the opportunity to be the man of the house. I decided I would begin my day with ceremonial washing and prayers, as my father had taught me. Only this morning I would do it all by myself. By the time Mother awoke, I would be back from the creek, clean and ready to eat. She would be proud of me. She would tell Father that I had behaved well and thus was worthy of making future journeys with the men and older boys.

I stepped from the shelter into the crisp air and drew my cloak tight around my chin. With a peek over my shoulder into the dim interior, I made certain Mother was still sleeping. Then I set out along the well-worn path to the boulder-strewn stream, where a pool served as a *mikvah*. My stomach growled. I would be glad when it was time for breakfast. When I inhaled, the scent of pine boughs mingled with the earthiness of the deserted yearling pasture. A remnant of the meadow grass remained, grazed to stubble, but by spring the sheep manure would nourish the soil, and grass would sprout and grow lush and thick for next year's flock.

I paused at the crest of the path and placed my hands on my hips in imitation of my father. I surveyed the wide meadow. A hawk flew above it, crying.

I thought if I cut across the pasture, the way to the stream would be quicker. I stepped from the path and hurried toward the high pines that concealed the brook. Almost to the rim of the dark forest, I heard the rush of the water and the hush of soft wind in the tree tops.

Then, as I neared the wood, a single doe crept forward from the cover. I felt myself blanch as I halted mid-stride. Six, seven, and then eight deer followed her and ambled cautiously toward me.

A vision of sharp hooves trouncing Beni made me scan for a way of escape. I felt frozen in place. I could not run. The deer were much faster than the legs of a five-year-old. I could not turn to the right or the left. A dozen from the herd now blocked my path and moved to encircle me.

The spots of the fawns were fading now. Their wide brown eyes observed me curiously. A spike-horned yearling came directly toward me, snorted, then turned away.

Within moments nearly fifty deer surrounded me, towering over me, considering me. I had never seen so many deer in the open all at once. They claimed the remainder of the meadow. I was the intruder. The sheep had taken the best of summer grazing, and I must have the smell of those who had guarded the sheep and kept the deer from foraging the tall grass.

I stood with my eyes level with the shoulder of a muscled doe.

Would she charge me, as another doe had charged and struck down my dog?

I was close enough to a weanling that I could have reached out and touched her. But I kept my arms crossed over my chest, lest the mother think I meant to attack her offspring.

Quietly, I spoke. "I only want to wash and pray. Will you let me pass?" But the circle of bodies grew tighter until I could see only legs and hoofs and strong heads for butting.

The sound of teeth tearing off blades of grass filled my ears.

I wanted my mother but fought the urge to cry. It was tears, after all, that had condemned me to stay behind and face the very animals that had nearly killed Beni.

A young buck approached and lowered his head until he was nose to nose with me. The creature could have knocked me to the ground with one quick strike. It snorted, covering me with a spray of saliva.

I wiped my face and stuck out my chin. "I'm not . . . afraid. Not afraid of you."

The creature extended its neck and offered its muzzle to me. I cautiously reached out and touched the velvet nose. The buck did not draw back or flinch. Wide eyes blinked with pleasure. I smiled as I felt all my fear melt away.

Another animal crowded in, as if eager to be touched by a human child.

"You like me." I chuckled with surprise and scratched the ear of a large doe.

It was, I thought, like the story Rabbi Kagba told of Adam in Paradise, when the first man stood in the midst of all the animals God had created. They had come to Adam to receive their names. They had come at the command of the Lord to speak with their master.

"And I like you too." I laughed aloud. "We will be friends, see? I forgive you for what you did to my dog." Solemn, brown-eyed faces were everywhere, all wanting to be touched. "Papa said you thought Beni would hurt your children." My hands went from deer to deer. "But he wouldn't hurt you. He meant no harm. He was only curious. I do forgive you, friends. But you must not hurt anyone in the camp again."

Suddenly the heads of the herd rose in one motion and turned toward the copse of trees beyond the thicket. The herd parted slightly, giving me a clear view to the wood. There, in the midst of the trees, stood the Great White Hart—master, father, and king of the deer. He had a pure white bib on his chest, with a buff mantle like a cape across his broad back. Antlers were so wide they nearly touched the trunks of two trees.

I could not count the points of his antlers. There were too many. But there, in the center, was a curious pattern. The intersection of branches formed a perfect cross.

I had heard stories of the Great White Hart as the shepherds sat around the campfire. He was real enough. He had been spotted two years earlier and had been tracked but never found.

"Aye," the shepherds had exclaimed. "He's one of those who lived in Paradise with Adam afore it was sealed up. He escaped and lives on still in this land. He kills serpents. Where he grazes, we shepherds find dead snakes that were forced out of their holes when he blows water in; then the evil creatures are trampled under his feet. They say the hart's waitin' for the Messiah to come and redeem the broken world and open up the gates of Eden. Legend has it that he carried the sign of Messiah on him, but what that sign might be, no one knows."

I had dreamed of the majestic creature. Few had ever seen him. He was the legend of the mountains where Eden had once been. He had boarded the ark in the days of Noah but returned to this place after the Flood. No human but Adam and Noah had ever come close enough to touch him.

Until now.

I stood rooted while a corridor opened in the herd as does and yearlings and young bucks stepped back to make room for the hart to pass. He stepped from concealment and, fixing his gaze on me, passed through his herd directly to me.

The hart halted and waited. His head towered over me. I squinted up at the blue sky. The hart's crown, with the cross at its center, seemed to me like the branches of a tree. Thick, strong legs could have killed me with one blow, but I was strangely calm in the presence of the powerful creature.

"I've heard of you," I blurted.

The massive head lowered until the ancient face was even with mine.

"They say . . . you are the hart Adam knew. You lived in Paradise. You are the killer of serpents, knowing the serpent that caused the fall of men. You rode in the ark and spoke with Noah. You have seen the patriarchs."

The animal touched my cheek with his muzzle and breathed softly on me. It felt like a familiar, loving gesture.

"So you are the same one they tell the stories about?" I questioned. "Oh. My name is Nehi . . . Nehemiah," I corrected. "They don't have a name for you in the story. The Great White Hart or Adam's great hart is what they call you. King of all the deer." I patted the thick, muscled neck.

In reply the buck placed his right leg forward and bowed to me. Chin on knee, the hart held the pose for a long minute, then raised up. I thought I recognized pleasure in the king's wise eyes.

"Some shepherds say you aren't real," I whispered. "But now I know."

The wind sighed through the Great Hart's antlers as if he were a tall cedar tree. Did I hear a hushed voice calling my name? Or was it just the wind?

"Nehemiah . . . cupbearer to the King."

I answered the whisper: "That's my name. Called after the cupbearer who was sent from this land to Jerusalem."

The voice spoke again, more distinctly this time: *"Nehemiah . . . the King's Cup."*

I replied cheerfully, "Yes. Yes! You know my name!"

Suddenly the hushed communication between the hart and me was interrupted by a shrill call. My mother's terrified voice rang out across the meadow. "NE-HEH-MI-AHHHH!"

The hart raised his head to look for the source of the unhappy sound.

"That's my mother. She sees you here. All of you. And she knows, as mothers know, that I am with you. And she's afraid what happened to my dog will happen to me."

The herd stirred uneasily. The king bowed once again to me and backed away several paces. Then Adam's Great Hart turned and trotted back into the forest.

The herd followed as one, after their leader. I found myself alone in the field, staring after them, with my mother's terrified cries at my back.

The nearly breathless voice of Rabbi Kagba called to me: "Nehemiah! Boy!"

Weeping with relief, my mother flung herself on me, touching arms and legs and caressing my face. "Nehi! You could have been killed! They could have trampled you!"

The rabbi's eyes scanned the rim of the forest. The tribe of deer had vanished, but a circle of hoofprints left behind in the dirt surrounded me. "He is unharmed," the rabbi admonished my mother. "Tell us, boy. What happened?"

Chapter 6

S everal days later my father returned for the rest of the sheep and heard my startling story. Light and shadows from the fire danced on the faces of my mother, father, and Rabbi Kagba as they questioned me again . . . as if Mama and the rabbi hadn't already asked me enough questions.

Father tossed a stick onto the embers. "A white buck. White, you say?"

"Yes, Papa. Like the very old one in the stories."

Father leaned in close to the rabbi. "See, the child speaks of stories. Stories he's heard from shepherds telling tall tales."

The rabbi held up his hand. "Not so fast, Lamsa. This is not like any legend I've ever heard." The old man fixed his gaze on me. "Can you describe him again? What did he look like? The Great Hart? Pure white?"

I shook my head. "No. Not white everywhere, but mostly. On his back he wears a sort of pale cape. That coat was more tan than white. But very pale."

"And his antlers?" Mother asked.

"Very large. Woven together like a crown. And this was in the center of all." Putting my index fingers together, I formed them in the shape of a cross. "Like this."

Father stroked his beard. "Such detail from a lad." His heavy brows knit together. "But you, Sarah, you did not see the animal?"

Mother said, "He was surrounded by the herd. I couldn't see him, only backs and antlers, in a circle crowded all around him."

"And you, Rabbi?"

Kagba's lower lip protruded. "Nay. There was an entire herd. Acting strange for certain. Surrounding the child and then . . ."

My mother contributed, "We began to walk slowly toward them and—"

I finished the story. "Mama started yelling, and they all got scared. The Great Hart left first and then the others."

"What happened just before your mother shouted?" the rabbi queried. "You said you heard another voice say your name?"

I gave a half smile at the recollection. "Yes. The wind through his antlers whispered, 'Cupbearer, Nehemiah' and 'the cup.'"

"Was it the hart who spoke?" Father asked.

"No. I told you. A whisper. Hardly anything at all. But I heard it."

My father and the rabbi conferred.

"Too much detail for the boy to make up," Father said. "He saw something, all right. But what can such a thing portend?"

The rabbi considered the meaning. "I have told you Messiah is alive at this very moment. He is walking among the men of Israel. The appearance of the white buck, the snake killer, Adam's Hart, means something very significant."

"How can we know the meaning?" Mother queried. "Such a large thing to be given to such a small boy."

The rabbi put his arm around my shoulders. "We will know what it means by and by. Aye. In the future everything will be revealed."

Occasionally we spoke of the Great Hart as we sat around a campfire. Three times over the next summer, when I turned six, the herdsmen found snakes that had been trampled, evidence that the buck was still near. I was comforted by the knowledge of his presence.

In the dead of the following winter, on the second night of Purim, midway through my seventh year, I stood on a rooftop in Amadiya with Rabbi Kagba. The mountain passes were choked with snow, but none had fallen for about a week. The sky was clear and crystalline, with glittering stars.

It was the middle watch of the night. Raucous laughter still emanated from the adults in the dining room below, but the rabbi had gathered up his students by offering us an astronomy lesson. We all wore fleece coats and fleece-lined boots and were enfolded within closely woven woolen cloaks.

Facing east, the rabbi splayed his bony fingers to mimic a bowl-shaped object. He held his hand aloft and invited me to locate that shape in the stars.

It took awhile, but I succeeded. "There!" I said, pointing. "Over the mountain to the east."

"Just so," Rabbi Kagba said approvingly. "Its name is Kohs, the chalice. Many other nations see a drinking cup there as well. What might it remind us of?"

"The Purim feast?" one of the older boys ventured.

"Very good!" Kagba praised. "It is written: 'As they were drinking wine on the second day, the king again asked, "Queen Esther, what is your petition? It will be given you . . . Even up to half the kingdom."[1] It was thus that the brave queen saved our people from evil Haman."

So strongly was the Purim holiday habit engrained in us that at the mention of Haman's name we all hissed and stomped our feet.

The rabbi smiled. "It was truly the cup of salvation for us that day. And Kohs always rises in the east on Purim in honor of that occasion. That's enough for tonight, boys. Go about your business quietly tomorrow morning. Your elders will thank you for it later."

That night I went to bed thinking about the cup in the heavens. I wondered if the image of the chalice was meant to remind us of other stories in Scripture. At first the only one I could recall involved Passover. There were four cups of wine drunk during the Seder feasts.

Then it came to me: there was a cup in the story of Joseph the Dreamer. And his story involved his brother Benjamin.

"Same name as my dog," I said aloud for my own amusement.

Then I fell asleep.

Almost immediately I began to dream . . .

I was in a banqueting hall. It was night, judging from the flickering torches in wall sconces around the room. A young man, clean-shaven—Egyptian, I thought, from his appearance—was clothed as a prince in brightly colored silk. The eleven others in the room were all thickly bearded, except one. Each wore the drab homespun robes of shepherds like me.

Though the Egyptian seemed to be of higher rank than anyone else present, he acted as servant. I noticed something else: all the shepherds were seated in order of their ages, from the eldest to the young man whose beard was just beginning to grow in. I sat beside him and saw the light reflecting in his eyes. I was close enough to hear his breath, yet he could not see me. I said aloud, "I'm dreaming, aren't I?" but none of them heard me or looked at the place where I was seated.

This youngest fellow came in for more attentive service from the Egyptian. In fact, he received five times as much food and drink.

When the shepherds were filled to capacity, their host poured one more cup of wine for each, and then poured one for himself, using a shining silver cup. Hoisting the cup aloft, he saluted them. "Have a safe journey to your home in Canaan," he said. "Salute your father, Jacob, for me. In fact, you, young Benjamin, carry my greeting to him."

It was then I realized what story was unfolding in my dream. The Egyptian was Joseph, whom these same men, his brothers, had sold into slavery, but they didn't recognize him.

Because of famine in their land, they had come to Egypt to buy grain.

When the meal was completed, the guests thanked their host and departed. Servants appeared to clear away the platters under the supervision of a steward.

Joseph called the steward to him and handed over the silver drinking vessel. "Tonight, go to where those men keep their provision sacks," he said. "Fill each sack with as much food as you can stuff in. Also, I want you to take the money they used to pay for the grain and divide that among their sacks as well. Finally," he said, indicating the chalice, "place my cup inside the sack belonging to the youngest brother."

The scene I was watching shifted. It was morning. I was with the brothers as they drove a file of donkeys down a road not many miles from the city. A cloud of dust swirling up behind us resolved itself into a host of Egyptian chariots in swift pursuit. Each chariot had a driver and a spearman. In the leading chariot was the steward I had noticed at the end of the banquet.

The warriors overtook the shepherds and surrounded us. The sons of Jacob surrendered without a fight. Their leader asked, "What is the trouble? What have we done?"

The steward said sternly, "Why have you repaid good with evil? You stole from my master."

All of the brothers protested.

Benjamin said, "Why say such a thing? Tell him, Reuben! Tell him, Judah."

And I said, "No! No! I know what really happened," but no one paid any attention to me.

Reuben argued, "We would never do that. We even returned the silver we found in our sacks when we came to Egypt the last time. We still don't know how it got there!"

Judah added, "Why would we steal silver or gold from your master's house? If any of us has it, he will die, and the rest of us will be your slaves."

When the sacks were opened, of course the cup was located in Benjamin's possession.

"Isn't this my master's cup?" the steward said. "This is a wicked thing you did. Take them away."

All the shepherds exclaimed and tore their clothing, but the steward was unmoved. The Hebrew brothers were escorted at spearpoint back to Joseph's palace.

Once more the view in my dream changed. I was inside the palace, watching the confrontation between Joseph and his brothers. The silver cup sat on a mahogany table in the center of the room.

Stalking around it with his hands on his hips, Joseph confronted them. "Why did you do this? Don't you know that a man like me learns things in dreams?"

Judah replied, "We have no way to prove our innocence. We are your slaves."

"No, only the one with the cup shall be my slave. The rest of you, go home in peace."

Judah approached Joseph and spoke quietly to him. In my dream I felt myself lean forward to hear better. "Even though you are the second in command to Pharaoh himself," Judah said, "I must tell you something. Do you remember when, on the other trip to Egypt, you asked us if we had a father or a brother, and we answered that we had an aged father and a younger brother?"

Joseph admitted that he recalled the conversation.

"Even though we said Benjamin was the only surviving son of his mother, and our father's favorite, and that it would kill our father to be parted from him, you insisted we bring him with us this trip . . . which we did."

Joseph listened but said nothing. Judah continued, "If we go home without Benjamin, our father will die. The shock will kill him. Now I, myself, pledged to bring Benjamin back safely. Please, I beg you. Let me stay here as your slave in place of my brother, and let him go home."

I saw Joseph trembling. His brothers may have mistaken it for anger, but I knew better.

The Prince of Egypt, unable to control himself any longer, burst out crying. "I am Joseph, your brother. Is my father still living?"

The brothers shouted in amazement, babbling questions and comments.

"Listen," Joseph said, when he could speak again. "Don't be

afraid because you sold me into slavery in Egypt. God used all of that to save our whole family from starvation. You must go home and bring my father back here with you. Bring all your families! There will be land for you in Goshen."[2]

Something like mist swirled around my vision then, until all the people were obscured. Only the silver cup, shining like a brilliant star, remained in my view, before it too faded.

Chapter 7

*O*n the frosty morning after the Purim celebration, remembering the warning, I tiptoed out of the house. Almost immediately I encountered Rabbi Kagba. He blew on his hands to warm them and greeted me.

I asked, "About the cup in the sky? I thought of another cup in Scripture. The one Joseph the Dreamer hid in Benjamin's sack. What happened to it?"

"What a penetrating question," the scholar murmured. "One I have never been asked in all these years. It is said that the cup remained with Joseph all his days, passing to his children and grandchildren, even down to the times when our fathers were slaves in Egypt."

"What happened to it then?" I demanded.

Kagba spread his hands. "No one knows. It was hidden so it would not be stolen by the Egyptians. Some say it left Egypt with Joseph's body in the time of the Deliverer and was later in the great Temple in Jerusalem. Then, still later, it was carried away from there to be saved from the Babylonian invaders." The rabbi shrugged. "Who can say? What is also known is that it is said the cup will reappear in the Day of Messiah. So, perhaps soon, eh?"

❦

The following night the rabbi and I were again on the roof of my home.

"Aren't you cold?" Kagba asked.

"Yes, but I want to know more. Once you showed me a great hart in the sky. Where is it?"

Grasping my shoulders, Kagba turned me completely around to face west. "Just there. See it? The form the Greeks call Andromeda and we call the Hart is setting behind that peak. In fact," he mused, "this is the only time of year when the Cup and the Hart can both be seen in the sky . . . and only a short while."

"Does that mean something too?"

"You are full of questions again tonight, young son of Lamsa. Yes, I think it does. You see, we didn't talk about it, but I believe the cup also represents the suffering that is required before redemption can take place. When the cup is full, it is as if the hart has laid down his life and so he departs for a season." Then more cheerfully he added, "But he will rise again, when the cup of suffering is poured out."

Chapter 8

When the Passover before my eighth birthday came, I was out in the fields at night, tending the sheep with my father. Rabbi Kagba had joined us, as he often did when the starry host was on display.

"If we were shepherds in Bethlehem," Father said, "this would be our busiest time of year. The herdsmen of Migdal Eder supply most of the lambs for the Passover pilgrims, except for families that have raised their own."

"How many lambs?" I asked.

"One for every ten people." The rabbi paused. "Half a million people in the Holy City for this holiday. Fifty thousand lambs."

I shook my head and whistled softly. A night bird answered from the rushes by the pond. "I've never seen more than five hundred in one place, and only then when we bring all the flocks together for shearing."

Rabbi Kagba squinted at the sky, judging the progress of the waxing moon, then setting in the west. "Nine days more till this year's Passover. Look where Jupiter, the Righteous King, hangs beside the moon. I saw such a sight three decades and more ago now, when I met the shepherds of Bethlehem and the child in the manger."

"What child?" I demanded.

My father shushed me. "Just listen," he corrected.

The rabbi continued, "I mentioned him before. He is more than thirty now, in his prime, and no doubt going about his work. In fact, I hear that he has caused quite a stir."

"Who?" My curiosity did not allow me to remain silent.

"The one I believe to be the Messiah," Kagba said. "The one born of the virgin, born in Bethlehem, as it is written by the prophet Micah. You remember. His name is Jesus of Nazareth, called son of Joseph. I followed the stars to worship him, those thirty-some years ago. Thirty years," he repeated. "I hope I have the strength to seek him again."

"Are there still signs in the heavens about him?" I peered at Jupiter. Sometimes I thought I saw fragments of light swirling very near the Righteous King, like moths around a flame, but I could never be certain.

"Signs still? Of course," Kagba replied. "And they are there before you. What is that bright star?"

"Spica," I replied. "Some say it's a wheat sheaf, but others see a baby—"

"Held by his virgin mother," the rabbi interrupted. "Just like the prophecy in Isaiah."

"Oh!" I responded. "More?"

"What is that outline to the west of the virgin?"

"Easy," I answered. "The lion."

"The lion of the tribe of Judah. You see, there is the beginning and the conclusion of the life of Messiah, all recorded in the stars: both his virgin birth and his destiny to reign as David's heir and the King of Judah."

"And right there," I said, pointing, "the one just below the Atonement star. The one you called the Virgin's Heart. That's the cup you showed us on Purim. Kohs, yes?"

Kagba nodded thoughtfully. "In Bethlehem we met the rabbi who was present at Jesus' circumcision. He told me a story about the baby's dedication and redemption in the Temple. Jesus is a firstborn son, after all. The rabbi told me that Mary, the baby's mother, encountered an old prophet, a true man of God. He prophesied over the child and then he said: 'And a sword will pierce your heart too.'"[1]

"Too?" Father rumbled. "Whose is the other heart to be pierced?"

Kagba said grimly, "That thought has always bothered me as well."

My attention had partly drifted away from the discussion of Jesus of Nazareth but had remained focused on the stars. "Look at where the cup is in the sky. If the virgin's heart were bleeding, it would fill the cup," I said.

Father and Rabbi Kagba exchanged a look, but neither commented on my observation.

❦

The snows melted and the rivers swelled. The foothills were carpeted with red poppies, purple lupines, and frolicking lambs.

Summer arrived, the time of moving the flocks around the meadows and pastures, and the celebration of my eighth birthday. After the shearing season was complete, my three older brothers set out with a caravan to Jerusalem. They would stay with my mother's parents on the Street of the Weavers.

In their cargo was the output of my mother's winter and spring labor over her loom: prayer shawls of the finest cloth in the most eye-catching designs. They were custom orders for the wealthy worshippers of the Holy City. One of which she was especially proud had a wavy edge, bordered with a band of azure blue. The

Hebrew letters around its fringes proclaimed the *Shema*: "Hear, O Israel: The LORD our God, the LORD is one."[2]

Limping painfully as she came out of the tent to display it in the sunlight, she remarked, "The man who ordered it has waited an entire year for it. I hope he likes it!"

Every year Mama dispatched such custom work with the caravan to Jerusalem, along with a carefully wrapped special parcel to her sister in Joppa.

"It's beautiful, Mama," I said.

Then it was the autumn again. I found it lonely and quiet around camp with my brothers and most of the other shepherds away on the caravan to Jerusalem. The intense labor of the shearing season was over, and the excitement of lambing was still months away.

The flock was slowly transitioning back toward winter life near Amadiya but had not yet arrived there. The sheep were moved a short distance every morning to fresh pasture. Every third day the encampment itself had to be uprooted and relocated. I spent as much time helping my mother pack and unpack as I did tending the sheep.

The route we traveled from the high mountain pastures back to the Sapna Valley west of Amadiya was not through pleasant scenery. There had been so much snow the previous winter that the rivers still flowed swiftly despite the lateness of the season. The frequent bends, twists, and turns of the main watercourse meant too many difficult crossings with too few men to assist.

Instead of the usual track, Father directed our herdsmen to follow a smaller tributary. Our descent from the mountains was along a series of small, gorse-choked meadows separated from each other by narrow, precipitous, rocky gorges.

It was a late afternoon between the High Holy Days and the Feast of Tabernacles. The sheep were two days' journey farther downstream. Tomorrow it would be time to reposition our camp again. Tonight, my parents and I would have supper with a handful of herders who had returned for a load of supplies to take to their fellows.

The night was chilly in the high country. I was grateful for the heavy, fleece-lined coat and fleece-lined leather boots my mother had made for me.

My chores completed for the moment, I sat on a boulder on a ledge facing the upstream bend of the canyon. Beni was beside me. Even before we heard the dog growl, I felt the animal stiffen and watched his ears prick up. The fur on the back of Beni's neck stood erect. The dog stared intently up the trail along which the flock had been driven three days before.

Snatching up my shepherd's staff, I leapt upright. Twisting side canyons led into remote and trackless wilderness, home to Armenian leopards and even wolf packs. I glanced down at my friend to make certain Beni was not going to dash off and get hurt, but the dog was plastered beside me.

What had the animal sensed?

Some dust rose over the rock wall separating this pasture from the one upstream. I studied the swirling cloud of grit. It seemed to be moving closer.

The clatter of horses' hooves announced the true nature of the disturbance. A band of riders swept into view around the bend.

As the lead horseman caught sight of our camp, he threw his right hand into the air, signaling a halt.

"Papa!" I waved and called to my father, standing at the entry to our tent. "Riders! Riders coming!"

I saw Father turn in the direction I pointed.

With cupped hands, Father called the four shepherds away from the creek and back to camp. The five men formed a protective barrier in front of the tent. "How many?" Father's voice boomed up to me.

I counted, then pantomimed two handfuls and two left over: twelve. The troop of horsemen remained motionless for a time. They clustered around the one who appeared to be their chief. When they moved forward again, it was at a measured, walking pace.

Rabbi Kagba emerged from his own tent and stood some distance apart from the other men.

The cavalcade approached the camp and drew rein on a sandy shelf across the creek. The leader halted his men again, then rode forward into the water. "*Shalom* to the camp!" he called out.

My shoulders relaxed. They were Jewish travelers. Father stepped forward. "*Shalom* to you. Who are you, with your fine mounts in this lonely place? And what do you want?"

"My name is Zimri," the captain of the troop responded. "We are going to the Holy City to serve the one who will liberate us from the Romans."

My pulse quickened at the words. A band of Jewish warriors going to serve the Messiah! Zimri's words could mean nothing else.

"We planned to reprovision in Amadiya," Zimri continued, "but we have been riding for three days and are short of food. Can we buy some from you?"

"No," my father replied curtly. "We won't sell to you. But we will welcome you to our cook fire and feed you. Turn your horses out to graze and join us. We have plenty of bread and roast meat."

There was ample food. A roasted haunch of mutton was

soon sliced and handed round to the newcomers by Mother and Hepzibah, along with stacks of unleavened bread. "Will this leave your other men short of food," Zimri questioned, "when they get back to camp?"

Father waved dismissively. "We have plenty for them."

I knew no one else was expected tonight. My father's motive for the lie must be to make the number of attendants seem larger than it really was.

"For me and my men," Zimri said, "I thank you. It's a long ride from Ecbatana."

As darkness fell, small knots of Zimri's men coalesced around our herdsmen, exchanging stories, but mostly eating in silence. Over my shoulder I toted a goatskin wine bag from which I filled their cups. One rider wiped grease from his face on a sleeve while catching me with the other hand. "Not so fast, boy," he said, draining the cup at a single swallow. "A refill before you move on. I've been thirsty all the way from Shirak."

I nodded and poured more wine. I was puzzled but kept quiet. Zimri had said the group came from Ecbatana, which was to the east over the mountains. Shirak was due north.

Another rider called out and waved a cup for me to fill, so soon I forgot my question.

"You have a fine camp, brother Lamsa," Zimri praised. "Your tent is draped with fine cloth, and your dress announces your good fortune as well."

"I am just a shepherd," Father returned. "My good fortune is my family." He nodded toward me and toward Mother, who was carrying around another platter of meat.

My mother's face showed pain. The weight of the serving tray and the uneven ground made it difficult for her to walk, yet she did not complain.

"My skillful wife has taught the weavers of Amadiya," Father continued. "Now we ship bolts of cloth to Jerusalem instead of only sending the raw wool."

"So you go to seek the Messiah?" Kagba questioned Zimri.

"Aye!" Zimri agreed. "And we won't be alone either. But I hope we get there soon enough to share in the spoils. I hear he's been catching small Roman patrols in the hills of the Galil and east of Jordan and cutting Roman throats. Soon enough of us will gather to take Tiberias and the armory there, and after that, Jerusalem herself."

Rabbi Kagba's eyes narrowed, and his face twisted into a frown. "Surely you don't mean Jesus of Nazareth? He preaches peace and offers healing and reconciliation with the Almighty. I hope to seek him myself."

"That one?" Zimri said loudly. "I've heard of him, but I wonder if he's still alive." He laughed coarsely. "If you want to find him anywhere but on a cross, you better get there soon! Preach peace to the Romans? Might as well cut his own throat, eh, boys?"

There was a round of laughter amongst all the riders in which our men shared uneasily.

"If the Romans haven't already killed him," Zimri continued, "Bar Abba will. Death to all traitors, I say. Death to all who would offer their backs to the Roman lash."

Leaning toward his guest, Father said firmly, "I will not challenge you about this, but neither will I allow you to insult my good friend, the rabbi. I don't know about such things as messiahs, but Kagba is a learned man and must be respected."

Zimri's sneer was broad, fueled by the wine he had consumed. He clapped his hand to his right thigh, where a short sword hung. "Religion and learning are all well in their place, but not when it comes to getting the Roman boot off Judea's neck! No, bar Abba has it right. And now that I think of it, I must ask you for your contribution to our cause."

"What are you talking about?" Father demanded coldly. "You have been fed. Be on your way."

Zimri shook his head. "Those who cannot or will not fight always hide behind some pretext or other while the real patriots spill their blood. You who are well off must share the load in some way."

Holding the now-empty wineskin, I witnessed Zimri stretch his left arm high above his head. It was an awkward, unnatural movement, as if the Jewish horseman were reaching toward the waxing moon that hung in the sky to the south.

Then Zimri dropped his hand abruptly, and pandemonium broke loose. All of Zimri's rebels drew their swords. The shepherds, wary men at all times, jumped up, staffs in hand, and the battle was on.

Rabbi Kagba was too old to fight and, besides, was unarmed. There were twelve bandits against Father and four shepherds.

"Grab the boy!" Zimri yelled as he slashed with his blade and Father parried with his six-foot-long staff. "Grab him! Then they'll throw down their weapons."

The greasy ruffian lunged toward me but missed when I tripped and fell backward over a heap of firewood.

"No!" Mother shouted, crashing the serving platter against the bandit's head. He warded off a second blow with his upraised arm, then struck my mother across the face, knocking her down.

"Run!" Father yelled. "Run and hide! Kagba! Help him!"

The same bandit who had felled my mother reached across the heap of sticks and seized my ankle. Then Beni, dashing in from outside the firelight, sunk his teeth into the cutthroat's wrist. The man howled and released his hold on me and dropped his sword as well. Beni kept his jaws clamped tight, even when the rebel swung around in a circle, bellowing with pain. He hammered on Beni's skull with his other fist. "Get him off me!" the bandit shrieked. "Help!"

"Run, Nehi!" Father yelled again. "Go!"

My father stabbed with the point of his staff and hit Zimri in the forehead with it, opening a gash. The bandit chief staggered backward, blood smeared across his eyes, and lashed out with his sword.

I fled.

All I could think to do was to run toward the boulder from which I had first seen the bandit troop. It was on a steep slope above the camp. Once there I would be outside the firelight and could even throw rocks down on the rebels.

As I ran, the sounds of battle continued behind me: the clatter of staff against sword, muttered oaths, sharp exclamations of pain. Over it all came shrieking and ferocious growling from the combat between the bandit and Beni.

I had just reached the base of the boulder when there was a single high-pitched yelp and the growling stopped. I almost turned back at that. How could I fly when my father, mother, and best friend were in danger?

I was climbing the rock for a better view when a hand seized the hem of my robe and dragged me downward.

"Down from there. Come here, boy!"

It was Rabbi Kagba. "No time for second thoughts. Your father and the men are giving you every chance to get away. We must not squander it. Up this canyon. All the way up. Hurry! No time to waste."

Into the darkness we ran. Beads of the sweat of fear dotted

my face and trickled into my eyes. I did not know if my mother or Beni still lived, or how much longer my father could hold out with a wooden staff against an iron sword in the hands of a much younger man.

Halfway up the canyon the footing turned to loose gravel, and I fell. My chin collided with a rock, opening a painful gash. I was dazed.

Panting, Rabbi Kagba lifted me. "Come on, Nehemiah. We can't stop yet. Listen!"

Sandaled feet scrabbled up the same path we had recently climbed, echoing from below. How many bandits were in pursuit I could not tell.

Hand in hand, the elderly rabbi and I continued upward into the night.

Part Two

Whoever dwells in the shelter of the Most High
will rest in the shadow of the Almighty. . . .
You will tread on the lion and the cobra;
you will trample the great lion and the serpent.

PSALM 91:1,13[1]

Chapter 9

Rabbi Kagba and I traveled all night, climbing steadily upward. Our path into the mountains was illuminated by moonlight. The trees cast wavering shadows on the rocky crags. I spent the hours casting fearful looks over my shoulder, until while doing so I fell over a dead branch. When I tried to catch myself, I skidded along a jagged edge, which sliced parallel grooves in both my palms.

The old man kept his eyes on the stars as if they were a map that would, in a thousand miles or so, lead us to Jerusalem. The rabbi jabbed a bony finger at the path of the constellations. "See? There is the great lion of the tribe of Judah. He rises in the east and sets in the west. Soon he will be passing over Jerusalem. A thousand miles from where we are yet we will see him even as he looks down on the Temple Mount. The one we seek may be looking up at him even now. Follow the lion in the sky, and you will find Jerusalem. You will also find Messiah . . . Jesus, son of Joseph, son of Jacob."

"I won't follow anything other than you," I protested. Why did the teacher speak as if I must find my own way, alone, to the Holy City? It could not happen! "We will go together, you and I. We will find my brothers and see the Messiah together."

Rabbi Kagba, breathless, did not reply for a long time.

He pointed to the east-west track of the stars in the heavens. "You must learn, boy. You will never be lost if you set your course by the twelve star patterns that recount the story of our redemption. From here caravans make their way to Israel and Jerusalem."

I trudged in thought for several paces, then asked, "Must we still journey by night, Rabbi? I'm so tired."

"Yes. Thirty years ago I journeyed from my homeland, by night. I followed the tale of redemption recorded in the stars. And my companions and I found the newborn King of Israel in Bethlehem. The House of Bread, its name means. Surely by now Jesus is acclaimed in Jerusalem. In his thirties. A fine, strong man. I pray we find him well and soon to sit upon David's throne."

We halted beside a stream just as daybreak lit up the eastern sky. I used the momentary rest and the growing light to pick splinters out of my ravaged hands.

The horror of the battle in the sheep camp was miles behind us but very near and real in my mind. Had my mother and father survived? Were the bandits still combing the hills in search of any shepherds who might have escaped? There was more money in slaves than in sheep.

My teacher's voice cracked as he spoke. "'As the deer pants for water' . . . I understand the meaning of that thirst better now." He was clearly suffering the strain of the climb.

As he rested on a fallen log, beams of light shot through the trees, illuminating the rabbi's ashen face. We had not had water in many hours. There was a limpid pool nearby. I plucked a large, green frond and fashioned a cup. Scooping it full of clear water, I carried it to the scholar. The rabbi drank slowly.

I threw myself on the ground beside the pool and sucked up the water greedily, then returned to face Rabbi Kagba.

"What has happened to my father? To my mother?" I finally had worked up the courage to ask the unthinkable.

"Your father is a warrior," Rabbi Kagba said. "It is written, 'You will tread on the lion and the cobra; you will trample the great lion and the serpent.'[1] Any snakes, crawling or human, foolish enough to battle your father will soon learn their mistake. Don't let your heart be troubled, Nehemiah. Lamsa has killed bears and lions. He has rescued a lamb from the jaws of a leopard. Pity the man who seeks to overthrow your father."

"Then may we not turn back now?" I urged. "Return to camp?"

His grizzled head wagged. "Jerusalem! Lamsa instructed me to take you to find your brothers and see King Jesus. I will not turn back. But I may not be able to go forward if we don't sleep awhile."

The rabbi pointed to the form of a fallen tree. Away from the trail we followed, and not visible until I circled it, the downhill side of the log was propped up by a rock. The soil beneath had washed away, leaving a hollow large enough to shelter us. The outstretched, overhanging bark was shaped like the feathers of an enormous wing.

"'Whoever dwells in the shelter of the Most High,'" the rabbi quoted, "'will rest in the shadow of the Almighty.'[2] See here, boy: the Lord has prepared a nest for us. We can rest here out of sight of any who might be looking for us."

My stomach growled and I rubbed it. "Sir, I'm hungry. Will the Lord give us breakfast too?"

"Aye, count on it," the rabbi affirmed, scanning the forest floor. "It is written, 'Call on me in the day of trouble; I will deliver you.'[3] Nehi, my boy, the Lord provides for all his children. Look there, at the base of the cedar: a crop of mushrooms. Big ones, some as big as my hand. Go on, boy. Pick as many as you can eat. Wash them there in the pool. Two of that size is enough to fill me up. When we set out again, we'll take a sack full with us."

I plucked the thick, meaty caps and rinsed them in the clean water. The rabbi made the blessing for the bread, and then we two made a meal. *They are very good,* I thought as I munched, *and filling too.*

A wave of exhaustion swept over me. With the rabbi already in the shelter of the fallen tree and snoring softly, I crept in beside him. In moments I was also fast asleep.

When I awoke, I did not immediately recognize where I was or remember how I came to be there. The wounds in my hands stung, and my chin and jaw ached. Dirt sifted down the back of my neck, and a sharp rock pressed into my ribs. I wanted to move, to stretch, but was overcome with a sense of dread.

Then recollection flooded me: The riders in camp. The attack. The escape into the darkness. The endless struggling uphill into blackness. The ominous sounds of pursuit. The collapse into the shelter beneath the fallen tree and the over-powering need to sleep away the dangers of daytime.

What about my mother and father and Beni? Were they alive, or had all been killed? I refused to believe any of them were dead, even though I had seen how desperate the fight was. I shook away the gloomy thoughts. Surely my father was seeking for me . . . or was it only the murderer Zimri who followed us?

How I longed for the security of our camp! For Father's steady, confidence; for Mother's quiet, peaceful strength; for Beni's exuberant defense. Anguish bit off chunks of my hope. How much had been stolen from me in less than a day!

Lying very still, I listened. A bird chirped across the canyon. Rabbi Kagba's breathing was rasping but steady.

A swirl of air brought the scent of pine. We must have climbed very high indeed to be so near an evergreen forest.

I squinted at the light lancing down outside the shelter. A flat, dark green, knife-shaped leaf, sticking upright in the soft amber-hued soil, cast almost no shadow. *So, it's near noon,* I thought. *The rabbi said we must remain in hiding until nightfall; then we can emerge and decide our next move.*

A towering white thundercloud loomed up above the opposite peak. It spread out across the gorge, obscuring the light for a minute before retreating again.

I reached over my head and patted the reddish-brown roof formed by the fallen yew tree. It must have been a giant before some storm brought it down. Its trunk was at least eight feet across. When the rabbi and I discovered the hollow on the downslope side, I had seen that the log stretched some sixty feet along the hillside.

How long until it was night again? Was there still a reason to remain hidden, or were we fleeing from shadows without substance?

A pair of finches, fighting over a sprig of red berries, fluttered to the ground in front of me. They chattered and argued, tugging against each other until a plump gray-and-rust-colored thrush swooped in and settled the dispute by seizing the twig and flying off with it.

I looked over my shoulder at the rabbi. Still sleeping. I wondered if I should emerge and seek the water I was craving, or imitate Kagba and try to sleep more.

Outside the overhang, a ledge of decomposed granite formed a bench just before the hillside dropped away into the canyon.

A lizard, blue throat pouch pumping rhythmically, stretched his legs in the sunshine.

I envied him and wondered again, *What danger could there be on this pleasant-seeming day?* Imitating the lizard, I half emerged from hiding. It was good to feel the sun on the back of my neck and stiff shoulders.

Across the chasm the thunderclouds built again, threatening an afternoon storm. A pair of stones clicked together somewhere below our perch. That slight sound was followed by the sifting of sand and the crunch of gravel hurtling into the abyss.

A voice called out, "We're still on their trail, Captain. Two sets of tracks—one small, one larger—came up this way."

Despite the warm sun, the gruff words that replied sent a chill down my spine. Zimri's unmistakable voice echoed up the passage: "Good. They can't be far ahead. Let's catch them before it comes on to rain so we can get off this cursed mountain."

Someone posed a question I could not overhear, but Zimri's answer was clear enough: "We'll kill the old man and sell the boy. That way we get something out of this mess."

My instinct was to burrow instantly back into shelter and pull dirt over my head, but I had to know what we were facing. I bellied-crawled to the lip of the ledge, my face and body sheltered from view by a clump of wild pistachio shrubs, and peered over.

Three switchbacks below, about two hundred feet of elevation and a half mile of traversing the hillside, was a single file of eight horsemen and a riderless ninth animal led by a rope. So my father and our servants had accounted for four of the raiders. My spirits rose with that observation, even though it left unanswered my parents' fate. I also noted with grim satisfaction that Zimri's forehead was bandaged, and another bandit had one arm in a sling.

It would take them no more than twenty minutes to climb the rest of the distance to the ridgeline and the fallen yew tree. When the rebels reached there and saw that the footprints stopped, they would scour the area.

Should I rouse the rabbi now? Could the two of us flee ahead of the horsemen to another hiding place?

I felt a sprinkle of water on my head. Wind from the thundercloud spattered me with raindrops. Would the rain come soon enough and hard enough to wipe out our tracks?

Rabbi Kagba was still asleep! His breath was hoarse and his color not good. Even if I could rouse him, could the elderly man move swiftly enough to escape?

Back out onto the ledge I found the choice no longer existed. After the rain squall passed, the trackers were coming on faster now.

Hope and pray and hide were the sole options that remained.

I scrunched as far back beneath the overhang as I could. I resolved to make the bandits dig us out. I would not go easily into slavery or let them kill my friend.

Outside the shelter, storm clouds spilled over the brink of the peaks and tumbled down, misting the gorge with vapor. Above me thunder boomed and rolled, bouncing off the walls of the ravine.

A solid sheet of rain swept toward me, like a gray curtain blotting out sight and sound.

Time passed. A flash of lightning briefly illuminated the underbelly of the storm before the day was shattered by a crash so immense that the ground jumped under my stomach, and I with it. I held my breath.

Rain—soaking, glorious rain—turned soil into mud and erased footprints while forming puddles in every crack and crevice. Maybe the storm was ferocious enough that the riders turned back to seek safety at a lower elevation.

A horse snorted and called. Another answered, sounding nervous amid the clashing peals of thunder and slashing rain. When Zimri spoke again, his voice came from right above my head. The raiders had drawn up alongside the fallen yew tree!

"Well?" Zimri demanded.

"It's not good, Captain," the tracker responded. "Washed out. Their tracks are gone. Nothing since that last switchback."

I felt like cheering until I heard Zimri say, "Maybe they went to ground right around here. We should search."

I lifted my hand to the tree trunk, as if trying to push them away, ward them off.

A centipede, perhaps driven to seek protection from the storm, skittered over my hand. Yet my gasp of alarm and Kagba's tortured breathing were both covered by the stamp of impatient horses.

Another bolt of lightning slammed into a tree across the canyon, making it explode. The thunderclap that followed terrified the horses. I heard several riders shouting, "Hold up!" and "Stupid beast!"

"Captain," the tracker said, "we didn't meet them coming back down, and there's no place to hide around here. It's more likely they went to ground up ahead, where there might be caves to crawl into, not here on this unprotected stretch."

Without wanting to sound cowardly, the man was suggesting it was not wise for men on horseback to remain outlined on the highest part of the ridgeline in a lightning storm.

"All right," Zimri grudgingly agreed. "We'll push on."

When the hoofbeats moved off in the distance, I breathed a sigh of relief. Wiping my forehead, I checked my friend. The good rabbi was still fast asleep.

❧

Throughout the afternoon Rabbi Kagba slept while I kept watch. We remained in the shelter. I did not think that if the raiders turned back along the trail they would stop and search the yew tree. Still, I would not give them any chance to catch me unawares, or leave any sign that might give us away.

The thunder and lightning moved off toward the east, but the rain continued to fall, almost without letup.

When there was no more than an hour of gray daylight remaining, a trickle of water managed to thread its way through a crevice to drip into Rabbi Kagba's ear. The scholar groaned, rolled over, and awoke. Rubbing his eyes and coughing softly, he asked, "Nehemiah? Have I been asleep long?"

I smiled. "Nearly the entire day, Rabbi. It's almost sunset again. The storm has lasted all afternoon."

"Ah?" Kagba stared out at the drizzling rain. "So it was good we had cover here, even if there was no threat."

I explained how our hiding place had served a greater purpose than just shelter from the weather.

Rabbi Kagba looked distressed as he listened, then laughed. "Truly it is written, 'He will take pity on the weak and the needy and save the needy from death.'[4] And perhaps it should be added, 'He also pities the ignorant and insensible!'"

"Do you think we could go out now?" I asked. "Since they went up the trail past us, couldn't we turn back toward Father's camp?"

Though I did not speak it, I was anxious about my father and mother.

Aware of what was really being asked, Kagba said kindly, "We should not attempt to go down the dangerous slope in this weather. Besides, as soft as the ground is now, we might not hear riders approaching. No, it's best not to chance it. We should remain here tonight. Tomorrow we'll go out, if the way is clear. I have an idea that should serve us well. Have we anything to eat?"

"I saw some nuts . . . pistachios, I think . . . growing in the bushes near the ledge. I could crawl out and gather some."

"Excellent!" the rabbi praised. "Only wait until after sundown, when it should be completely safe."

When I returned from my expedition, I emptied a half pound of nuts from a makeshift pouch formed in my robe. I had also gathered a double handful of red berries such as the birds fought over. "What about these?" I asked.

The rabbi praised me again. "Here we have shelter and provision both. These are yew berries. The leaves and the seeds are poison." He paused to pat the tree trunk like greeting an old friend. "But the fruit is sweet and can be eaten. Well done, Nehemiah. It seems the Almighty has provided both food and drink for us! As it is written, 'Stay awake and you will have food to spare,'[5] and again, 'Come, all you who are thirsty, come to the waters.'[6] Eat and drink and rest again, boy. Tomorrow we must journey."

Chapter 10

*T*he second morning after we took refuge beneath the yew tree, dawn's curtain lifted on a day that was overcast and chilly. The threat of rain was not great, and the air was sparkling clear. A covey of quail chirping and pecking in the brush could be heard from across the canyon. A hawk screaming above the highest peak to the east made himself known, though a mile and more away. If a group of men, especially a troop of horsemen, was anywhere near, the rabbi and I would hear them at a great distance.

"Now we'll go back to Papa's camp," I said.

"I've been giving that much thought," the rabbi replied. He pointed to the saddle between two peaks to the southeast. "There is a village just over that pass. If we make for that location, there should be no risk at all of encountering Zimri and his men. There are easier routes, so no one will think to look for us there."

Sticking out my lower lip, I also narrowed his eyes. "But my papa and mama will be worried about me," I said stubbornly.

"True enough," Kagba agreed, "but once at the village we can send word to them. Remember, your father instructed me to keep you safe, and I must do what I think he would want."

I nodded slowly. I did not like the plan but I accepted it.

Picking at the tattoo of scabs on my face, I asked, "How long will it take us?"

"No more than two more days if we leave soon. We'll have to shelter on the mountain tonight but tomorrow we should easily reach our goal. Gather more nuts and berries, and we'll eat them on the way."

Descending the first fifty yards into the ravine from the ridgeline was scary. The hillside was steep, and Kagba would not let us use the trail, in order to avoid leaving tracks. We deliberately crossed rocky ground, sliding at times and catching hold of scrub brush to slow ourselves. I gritted my teeth as each precarious handhold dug into the lacerated flesh of my palms.

The creek at the bottom of the gorge was full of the runoff of the storm. We quenched our thirst, then crossed the stream by jumping from boulder to boulder.

It was the hike up the other face that gave us the most difficulty. Even though I located a game trail for us to follow, the slope was precipitously steep. Despite rest and nourishment, Rabbi Kagba was barely capable of the ascent. After the first hundred yards he could manage no more than ten paces at a time without stopping to rest and breathe.

I seized the dried, gnarled branch of a juniper, already bent at one end to form a handle. This I gave to Kagba to use as a walking stick.

"Thank you, my boy," Kagba wheezed. "And give me a handful of those juniper berries. I will inhale their scent. It helps clear the lungs."

Despite the use of the cane and the aid of the juniper aroma, Kagba grew slower and slower until he was barely creeping. It was clear we would not reach the summit of the pass before nightfall, despite our best efforts.

Even worse, we remained exposed to the view of anyone using the switchbacks on the other hillside. Once more I missed having Beni's alert watchfulness of sight, sound, and smell. How I longed for him to be able to give me warning.

It was on another of our frequent halts that I heard it: the unmistakable sounds of a horse snorting and harness jingling. I eyed the top of the ridge we had left and the hillside on which we now stood. It was not good. We would be fully in view from the trail. There was not even brush enough to crouch behind.

"Rabbi!" I said urgently. "Riders! Riders coming. We have to hide!"

"Eh? What?" The scholar returned between gasps for air.

I doubted if Kagba even heard the warning over the sounds of his own labored breathing. Without trying to explain, I grasped the rabbi's hand and tugged him up the slope.

From my sudden burst of speed the rabbi caught the urgency and did what he could to move faster.

A series of rocky ledges terraced the hill like giant steps. They provided no cover, but at their top was a larger clump of junipers. If we could reach that foliage, we might be safe.

After I leapt easily atop a stone block, I then had to haul up my friend. Kagba dropped the cane, which clattered down the slope. No time to retrieve it!

Shooting a glance over my shoulder, I caught the glint of sunlight reflecting off something on the trail across the canyon. We had only moments before we were spotted!

The next rank of boulders was even taller than before. I would have trouble climbing it and much more difficulty hoisting my friend. What to do?

A rocky outcropping resembling squared stones protruded from the rest, making an overhang above the shelf of slate.

Could we possibly squeeze into the narrow space, like rabbits hiding from a fox?

Then I spotted it. Right in front of the overhang there was a gap in the ledge, a crevasse that plunged into the mountain. I peered over the edge. It was a drop about the height of a man, but was wide enough to admit us . . . and there was no choice.

"Rabbi, follow me!" Lying flat on my stomach, I pivoted so my legs hung over the lip of the chasm, then pushed myself into the void.

I landed, sprawling, but picked myself up immediately. "Hurry!" I urged. "I'll help you."

Guiding Rabbi Kagba's toes onto tiny ledges in the rock, I eased the scholar downward until both of us were concealed behind the rock wall. We stood panting with fright and exertion. His words fractured by coughing, Kagba said, "Thank . . . you."

In the expanse of stone at the back of our landing was another small opening. It could not be seen or even suspected from the outside. Only by falling into the crevice, or climbing down inside it as we had, could the entry be discovered.

Once through the arch the cave increased in height until there was room for Kagba to stand upright. The passage stretched upward into darkness, reaching toward the heart of the mountain.

Even when the danger of discovery had passed, it was clear we would not be going farther that night. I foraged for evergreen branches, using pine needles and a thin layer of dried leaves to make a bed for the old man to lie upon.

The rabbi gratefully spread his cloak and stretched out. He was waxy and ashen in the dim light. His cracked lips were parted as he slept, and his breathing labored.

I sat in the shadows in the mouth of the cave and scanned the terrain beyond. No sign of our pursuers. Had Zimri and his men given up their quest for a slave to sell? Had they set out for Jerusalem and the rebellion?

A heaviness settled over me, like nothing I had ever felt. I was homesick. Scared. Filled with dread at the nearness of our enemies. Had my mother and father been killed? What had become of the shepherds we had left behind? What good were shepherd staffs against sword blades?

The old man stirred. His voice trembled as he spoke. "I . . . I must have dozed off. A pleasant dream. You and I set out for Jerusalem to see the great King." He paused.

"It will be dark soon," I said. "Are you cold, Rabbi? Shall I build a fire tonight?"

The rabbi continued as if I had not spoken. "And when we entered the great Temple, there were your mother and your father. And yes, even your dog."

"My mother and father?"

"Yes," the rabbi wheezed.

"Alive?"

"Oh yes. There among thousands who came to greet Jesus. Son of Joseph. Son of Jacob. And you . . . in my dream you were carrying something . . . a gift for the King."

"Shall I search for something for us to eat?"

"Asparagus. I saw some growing beside the path. Ah, this land was truly Eden."

I nodded, but remembered that if this had been Eden, death had still entered here. The old man seemed very near to Paradise. "I'll go find something for us to eat, then. You rest."

The rabbi's arm raised slightly in agreement and then fell back on the bed. "I'm not going anywhere."

I found a plot of wild asparagus and filled my tunic with big, thick stalks. Nearby, a blackberry vine was loaded with ripe berries. A few mushroom caps rounded off the harvest. I discovered a clutch of eight partridge eggs in a thicket. I had seen hungry herders puncture holes in the shells and suck out the raw yolk, but I much preferred eggs as my mother cooked them.

I took only four of the eggs, leaving the others in the nest. Raw or cooked, such nourishment would help strengthen the rabbi.

Clouds like great fortresses heaped upon the heights. There would soon be another thunderstorm. Laden with the bounty of the mountain, I hurried back to the shelter.

Rabbi Kagba was propped up but shivering. I displayed the harvest.

"A man could live here forever . . . if a man could live forever." Kagba smiled. "I don't fancy eating my eggs raw as some do."

"You're shivering. I'll build a fire and dry out the air and . . . we can cook them."

Kagba lay back and stared at the gloomy ceiling as I labored to build a fire on the floor of the cave. As sparks cast by the rabbi's flint and steel caught amid leaves and pinecones, I breathed the flames to life and fed it with sticks and dry foliage.

"My father said a man must know how to make a . . ." My words trailed away as I raised my eyes to the ceiling and I gasped. The walls of the cavern, suddenly illuminated, were alive with painted splendor. Shadows danced upon primitive paintings.

"Well done, Nehemiah." The rabbi seemed cheered as he stretched his hands to the blaze. He chuckled at the visions all around us.

"What are these?" I looked into painted stars and spotted the constellations of the Cup and the Virgin.

Kagba was delighted, but not surprised. "A Jew has been here before us. Look there. The story of Joseph, son of Jacob, in his coat of many colors. Aye. There is the boy, Joseph, in his splendid coat. The coat, a gift of honor from his father. And Joseph dreams . . . the sun and the moon and stars bow down to him. He tells his brothers they will one day bow to him. And there, the coat torn to shreds and Joseph is sold by his jealous brothers . . . Joseph's hands bound as he is led away to Egypt by slave traders. In prison with the baker and Pharaoh's cupbearer."

Every inch of the interior was painted with the biblical account of Joseph's life. And there, in the last frames, was Joseph's silver cup buried in the grain sack of his brother Benjamin to trap him. And, finally, Joseph weeping over his reunion with his brothers.

"Who did such a thing?" I turned round and round in place, examining the panels in awe.

"One who knew the story well, I think," Rabbi Kagba whispered.

"But why? Why paint the story of Joseph here?"

The old rabbi considered. "Here in a cave for hundreds of years? Someone lived here, plainly. Someone who had reason—"

"But who? Why?"

"Whoever he was, he knew the story of the Prince of Egypt. Perhaps he was on the run. As we are, eh? I would think one who was trying to escape the captivity of Babylon. Everything means . . . something." Kagba closed his eyes and smiled slightly. For the first time in days, as warmth radiated in the space, some color returned to his gray-green complexion.

As the old man slept, I searched for stones to use in the cook fire. In the corner of the cavern was piled a heap of rocks. I sorted through them, looking for a flat rock to heat and cook on.

I examined stones and discarded them. At last I found the perfect rock for cooking. When I tugged at it, several stones tumbled down. The top of a clay amphorae protruded from the opening left there.

"Rabbi!"

The old man had dozed off again. His breath was steady and even.

I tore at the heap, revealing four sealed storage jugs. Each was about two spans high.

Should I open them? What if something terrible was in them? I had heard of shepherds stumbling across burial caves and making grizzly discoveries.

Human bones?

Pagan gods?

Some terrible curse written on a parchment?

I decided to wait until the rabbi awakened.

Heating the flat stone red-hot in the coals, I then cracked the eggs and fried them. I waved eggs and berries and warm asparagus on a broad leaf beneath the nose of my teacher.

"Rabbi? Wake up. I have dinner for you."

His eyelids fluttered open. "Well." The rabbi inhaled deeply and struggled to sit. "Well, now. My boy. Look at this. A feast."

"It will make you strong."

He accepted the leaf plate. "How did you manage this, Nehemiah? Fried eggs." He prayed the blessing without waiting for an answer.

"Amen." I jerked my thumb toward the rubble heap and the four containers. "I found the stone over there . . . see? On top of the clay jars."

The rabbi plopped a whole egg into his mouth and turned

his head to follow my gesture. "What!" he exclaimed around his food. "What are those, boy?"

"Under a heap of stones. I was looking for a cooking stone. I didn't mean to uncover them, but you see, there they are."

The rabbi swallowed and waved a stalk of asparagus in the air. "What have you found?"

Weighed with remorse, I sat back on my heels. "I'll put everything back, sir. I was only looking for a flat rock, you see, and . . . I can put it all back as it was. I . . . was afraid."

Kagba's eyes gleamed. "No. A Jew like ourselves lived here for a very long time. He would not live in a place of desecration. Eat. Such good food. You are a fine cook. Finish your meal, and we will see what treasure our friend left for us."

Chapter 11

A flash of lightning illuminated the world outside the cave in monochrome shades. Thunder followed, opening the heavens with a torrent of rain. Water sluiced off the rocky ledges and streamed down the embankment, but the cavern remained dry. The previous occupant had chosen his home well.

The fire burned low. The rabbi reached out from his bed and touched each clay jar as if they were old friends. "Something very good, I think. I heard of a man . . . ah, well. No use speculating until we know, eh? We need more light, I think."

I heaped dry wood onto the embers and stood back as the flames caught hold and blazed up. The branches crackled. The old man's skin took on the color of parchment. He made an attempt to stand but winced and gave it up. "You'll have to be the one, Nehemiah."

I licked my lips and picked at the red wax that sealed lid to base. The wax was brittle and broke in pieces with the digging of my fingers. Within minutes the first lid was free.

I hovered over it, with my hands encircling the neck of the jar. Waiting for the rabbi's instruction, I glanced up to see an almost childlike eagerness on the face of the sage.

"All right, then," the old man whispered hoarsely. "Open it."

I nodded once and pried it open. It made a popping noise

as air trapped for centuries rushed out. The sweet aroma of lavender scented the space, overpowering the wood smoke. I sat back. The rabbi must be first to see.

The old man leaned forward. "Tilt the opening toward the light, boy. I cannot make it out. "

I obeyed. A soft sigh of pleasure escaped the rabbi's lips. He smiled as he reached in and took hold of the contents, pulling out a scroll wound in supple sheepskin and tied with strips of leather.

On the exterior of the scroll were Hebrew letters spelling out the name of the author.

The rabbi extended it, face up, toward me. "You must read it."

I squinted in the light. The ink was distinct, undimmed by centuries. "'Within is the SCROLL OF BARUCH BEN NERIAH, SCRIBE OF THE PROPHET JEREMIAH. Written in his own hand. Various writings of Jeremiah about the exile.'"

"So." Rabbi Kagba cradled it like an infant. "As I rest and recover here, the good Lord has given us something to read and study. You know of the scribe Baruch. Companion to the prophet."

I exhaled with relief that my teacher had been correct. The jars were not full of evil, frightening things, as I had feared. "He helped Jeremiah hide the Temple treasures. I am happy there were not bones inside."

"Only the flesh and bones of history." Rabbi Kagba mopped his brow. "What was, what is, and what will be." The rabbi swept a hand over the Joseph murals. "There is a legend concerning a treasure that Baruch carried away. Hidden until the day when the Messiah will come to Jerusalem." He frowned. "Well then. Open the others. Hurry!"

The second container held the complete scroll of the prophet

Jeremiah and the book of Nehemiah, as well as a number of short documents containing an inventory of Temple treasures.

The old man scanned them quickly, running his finger down the list. "Ahhhh. Here it is! As I thought it might be."

He laid the list aside. The third jar held a tightly rolled copy of the five books of Moses—all protected in the exact same manner as the first scroll.

The last jar remained to be opened. I plucked at the red wax seal and pried the lid off, welcoming the *whoosh* of ancient air. I peered in. This time there was no scroll, but a fleece-wrapped package.

"Rabbi Kagba. It's not like the others," I said, some nervousness returning.

"Fetch it out, boy. My hand is too large."

Reaching in elbow-deep, I grasped the prize and brought it into the light. Beneath thick wrapping, with smooth leather on the outside and fleece on the inside, I felt something the size and shape of a cup. Three strands of knotted leather bound the hide to it. On the exterior of the skin the label read, BEHOLD THE SILVER CUP OF JOSEPH, SON OF JACOB, PRINCE OF EGYPT.

A message inscribed on sheepskin fluttered to the floor at my feet.

The rabbi picked it up, read it, and passed it to me. "Nehemiah. This was written to you, I think."

The comment startled and confused me. Written to me? How could that be? What did he mean? At the rabbi's urging I read the letter aloud.

"INSTRUCTION—
CUPBEARER GUIDED BY THE HAND

OF THE ALMIGHTY,
FEAR NOT,
YOU OF CHILD'S HEART WHO DRAWS FORTH
THE CUP OF JOSEPH'S SUFFERING.
TAKE BENJAMIN'S COINS FOR PASSAGE
AND BEAR JOSEPH'S CUP HOME TO JERUSALEM.
THE CUP OF SUFFERING,
JOSEPH'S INHERITANCE
FOR THE ONE WHO IS TRUE KING OF ISRAEL.
HIS NAME IS SALVATION,
WONDERFUL,
COUNSELOR,
SON AND HEIR
OF HOLY PROMISES,
AS FORETOLD WITHIN THESE WRITINGS.
AS JOSEPH'S LIFE A PROPHECY PORTRAYED,
THE SUFFERING
SAVIOR OF ISRAEL'S CHILDREN,
SO THE LORD HIMSELF,
CONCEIVED BY THE HOLY SPIRIT,
BORN OF A VIRGIN,
WILL BE BORN AS A BABE
AND SUFFER FOR OUR SAKES,
THE TRUE REDEEMER OF ISRAEL.
CUPBEARER TO THE KING,
GO FORTH TO HIM WITHOUT TREMBLING.
FOR THE SAKE OF HIS BROTHERS
MESSIAH
MUST DRINK THIS CUP.
HE WILL PARTAKE OF SUFFERING
AS JOSEPH

SAVED HIS BROTHERS,
WHO SOLD HIM AS A SLAVE.
THEREFORE WATCH AND WAIT HERE
FOR A SERVANT CLOTHED IN WHITE RAIMENT
WHOM THE LORD WILL SEND TO GUIDE YOU
THROUGH THE MOUNTAINS
AND LEAVE YOU WHERE THE PLAINS BEGIN.
IT IS WRITTEN 'WHAT MAN INTENDS FOR EVIL,
THE LORD INTENDS FOR GOOD.'

The rabbi whispered in awe, "The cup. From the Book of Beginnings. It was for you these instructions are given."

"Not me. I'm just Nehemiah, son of Lamsa and Sarah."

Rabbi Kagba wagged an admonishing finger. "But named for the cupbearer of the King who rebuilt the walls of Jerusalem."

"But not me, sir."

"You drew it forth. You hold the silver cup of Joseph the Revealer of Secrets, dreamer of dreams. The cup Benjamin carried away in his grain sack . . . could it be? The cup Baruch the Scribe spirited off to hide during the exile! Nehemiah, break the strings. Open it!"

Urged by the rabbi to haste, I tore at the leather, finally slipping it off the package. Joseph's cup, black with tarnish, tumbled out onto the rabbi's bed.

We stared at it a long moment without speaking, neither of us moving to touch it.

It seemed unremarkable—the size and shape of a *Kiddush* cup, blackened inside and out. Time and tarnish had concealed any beauty of Joseph's ancient chalice. It seemed not only ordinary but common and ugly. It was not even worthy of a thief to steal such a thing.

I began to rub the tarnish with my cloak, much as I had learned to clean dishes for my mother without being told to do so.

The rabbi stopped me. "No. Leave it tarnished, boy. It is a disguise. Concealment and protection. It appears a thing that no thief will value. Unpolished. Black and worthless in the eyes of men. But when you see him, Messiah, Jesus of Nazareth, then you must clean the cup and present it to him."

"You must come too! You'll know what to do, Rabbi. I will carry it, but you must—"

The old man wagged his head wearily. "No, my boy, I cannot. This task has been given to you. I will stay here awhile."

"Zimri and his men . . . what if they find you?"

"Listen, now. Don't interrupt. I will rest here in the cave. Look about. You will gather food for me. Bring firewood. There is water in the pool just there. When I recover, I will return home. I will find your parents, if they live, and tell them the task the Almighty has given to you."

"But how can I go without you?" My voice quaked with panic. "Jerusalem?"

"Our footsteps were guided to this place, and we were hidden from the eyes of our enemies. It was you who moved the stones and found the scrolls and the ancient treasure." The old man blinked at the fire.

I waited, knowing that some important thought had struck the rabbi. "What is it, sir?"

"The note said . . . in Benjamin's sack there was the cup and also money. Twenty pieces of silver. The price for which Joseph's brothers sold him into slavery. Aye. The instructions speak of coin for your passage to Jerusalem. Draw out the silver that is there for your journey."

Reaching deep a second time, I found the heavy money pouch in the bottom of the jar and held it up triumphantly. "Look!"

"No need to count it. It is said Joseph's brothers sold him for twenty pieces of silver. And Joseph put the same amount of silver into Benjamin's sack and sent him on his way. Money is nothing. But the cup you hold is the sign of God's love and mankind's redemption."

"The real treasure is . . . this?" I frowned at the black, remarkably unremarkable thing. Hard to believe it had any value.

"The cup . . . but not just any cup. Nehemiah, you will wait here with me. Wisdom now will visit you in dreams. It is written: At the proper time the Lord will send a servant clothed in white to guide you to safety through the mountain passes."

"But how long, Rabbi? What if he doesn't come?"

"He will come." The rabbi closed his eyes with a contented exhale. "Aye. This was all seen and known long afore you were born. He will come."

"And after he leads me out of the mountains? And I am left alone at the plains? What then? How will I get safely to Jerusalem? I am a boy. Zimri will catch me and sell me if he can. The route is full of men like him. How can I know who is safe?"

The rabbi considered the question. "I know of a place. You will come to a caravansary along the great caravan road. Take one coin to the master of the inn. Tell him you were sent ahead to prepare a place for your family. He will give you a chamber. You must stay and watch all those guests who enter. There will be many rough sorts, indeed, happy to steal a boy and sell him. So watch the travelers until you see Jews who gather for morning prayers and rest on the *Shabbat* Day. While they are adorned with phylacteries and prayer shawls, approach them with one silver coin. Tell them you are separated from your family. That your brothers are in Jerusalem and your brothers will pay them if they deliver you safely to Jerusalem, to your family. Do you hear me, boy? Obey my every instruction."

I drank in the words. "And you will find my mother and father? And tell them everything?"

"Aye. If they are alive."

"And if they are . . . dead?" I could not conceive of such an outcome. Whatever manly courage I had gained at being divinely appointed to an important task threatened to evaporate.

The rabbi continued, "Then you alone will find your brothers. And your mother's parents on the Street of Weavers. But most important, remember: you are Nehemiah . . . cupbearer. Before all else, you must first seek and find Jesus of Nazareth. He is son of Mary, and Joseph is his foster father. Bring this, Joseph's cup, only to Jesus."

"When? How?"

"When you see Jesus enter Jerusalem, proclaimed as King. Then allow no one to take this from your hands but Jesus. No one but you is anointed to present the cup to the King. Reveal the cup's identity to no one. Speak of its discovery to no man or woman along the road, lest they slay you and steal the treasure. Let everyone you meet believe the cup is a black, worthless thing, the last possession of a lost boy who seeks his brothers in Jerusalem."

Chapter 12

As Rabbi Kagba pored over the manuscripts that had been freed from the clay storage jars, I set to work foraging for supplies. I hauled an improvised broom behind me with which to brush away my tracks as I walked.

From time to time I heard the insistent whine of horses across the canyons or above our hiding place. Was Zimri still on the prowl in search of a valuable slave?

I felt the nearness of the enemy. I lived as though my enemy were right around every bend in the trail.

The mountains were thick with wild crops sown by some ancient unknown hand. Apricot trees grew from craggy outcroppings. Mushrooms the size of fired clay platters provided the main meat of our meals. I toasted these over smoky coals, infusing them with flavor. A lifetime of helping my mother dry the wild fruits and vegetables had given me the skill and knowledge to preserve food. I prepared a packet of supplies for my travels and packaged the rest for the rabbi's journey home.

Daily Rabbi Kagba grew stronger. Perhaps he would be ready to travel at the same time I set out for Jerusalem. The old man made certain my soul was well fed for the journey as well. For ten days and nights the rabbi read aloud the prophecies about the Messiah from the scrolls of the prophets. He told again the story of what he had witnessed in Bethlehem: the stories of shepherds, of angels, of the infant king pursued by the brutal soldiers of the usurper Herod.

"The babe is grown up now, boy! How I long to speak with him of heavenly things come down to earth!"

At night I lay my head on the pillow and gazed up into the flickering shadows, half expecting a white-robed character to step from the paintings and call me to come away.

But each night I slept a dreamless sleep and awakened as dawn crept through the entrance to our shelter.

On the eleventh day a great storm swept over the peaks and howled at the mouth of the cave. Water dripped into the pool inside the cavern. The rabbi slept deeply in spite of the crash of lightning against the boulders above us.

I crept toward the portal to see the fury of the gale. Rain fell slantways. A jagged bolt fractured the blackness as it blasted a gnarled pine tree. The ground shook. Bark and limbs exploded and burned. Not even the torrent of rain quenched the embers.

Gradually the downpour slackened, and the wind was tamed.

Silence was broken only by water dripping from the trees. In the east, the full moon rose, outlining thunderheads in silver. The clouds seemed like the mountains of a distant world.

Chin in hand, I lay for a long time at the mouth of the cave, expecting God to walk up the hill and call my name. At last I could not keep my eyes open. I rose and tossed a few more sticks onto the coals and stretched out my hands to warm myself. Then I staggered back to bed and lay down.

Perhaps the servant of the Lord was not coming after all. The letter had been written hundreds of years before. Maybe the Almighty had forgotten. Maybe he had even forgotten where he had put Joseph's cup, as very old people sometimes forgot things.

Ah well, what was one more day in this place? The rabbi was growing stronger, was he not?

I yawned and closed my eyes. The warmth of the fire flowed over me like a blanket pulled up around my chin. I remembered my mother tucking me in. Soft fleece and soft words. I smiled, almost feeling her nearness. Sleep came over me.

The fire had burned low when I heard the wind whisper my name: *"Nehemiah. Cupbearer to the King."*

I replied to the rabbi without opening my eyes. "Yes, sir? Do you need something?"

The rabbi did not reply. While I waited, I dozed and again heard my name distinctly. *"Nehemiah. Get up."*

Now I rose and went to the rabbi's side. "Yes, sir. What is it you need?"

Rabbi Kagba turned over and blinked up at me in confusion. "What is it, boy?"

"Did you call me, sir?"

"No. What is it?"

"There was a fierce thunderstorm. I watched until I was too tired. When I lay down, you called to me," I explained.

The old man said, "Not I."

"But I heard your voice."

The rabbi put a finger to his lips. "Shhhhh. Go lie down. And if you hear the voice again, answer in this way: 'Here I am, Lord.'"

I returned to my mat and waited, all sense of drowsiness lost in expectation. Water dripped into the pool. The embers crackled and hissed. Hours passed, but now there was no call. I drifted back to sleep at last.

"Nehemiah . . ." The voice was deep and resonant, as though it came from a deep well. *"Nehemiah! Cupbearer to the King."*

"Yes, yes, that's my name." I recalled the rabbi's instruction. "Here I am, Lord."

The voice replied, *"Nehemiah, get up. Put on your cloak and sandals. Take up your provisions and the cup. It is a long journey. My servant stands outside the portal. He waits for you."*

I glanced toward the entrance.

Someone . . . or something . . . glowed white in the moonlight.

I stammered, "T-tell him I . . . am coming."

I gathered my things without waking the rabbi. I heard movement—the crunch of gravel and a treading underfoot of fallen leaves. My own voice seemed like the voice of a stranger. "Yes, I'm coming!"

For a moment I stood above the sleeping form of the old man. Would I ever see the rabbi again?

Rabbi Kagba opened his eyes. "So, Nehemiah, the one you have been waiting for? He has come, as the Lord said he would?"

The luminescent being passed before the portal.

"Yes. He's there," I confirmed. "Yes, look. See how he moves! White like a candle."

The old man sat up and nodded. "Hurry. And the Lord be with you!"

I turned away as my teacher spoke the benediction at my back. I hesitated as the hope of a holy destiny became a reality. Stepping forward out of the warmth of cave, I croaked, "It is me. Nehemiah."

Something like a sigh replied. Suddenly the familiar, beautiful face of the Great White Hart peered at me.

"You!" I exclaimed.

The thick neck bowed deeply, presenting to my view the sign of the cross at the center of the antlers.

Stretching out my hand, I touched the crown of my old friend. "You! Clothed in white! Who better to lead me? Adam's beloved hart!"

The hart knelt in the mud and, with a turn of his head, indicated that I should climb onto his back. Grasping the thick base of the antlers, I mounted, swinging my leg over the withers and settling in.

The creature swayed and rose to his full height.

I clung tightly to the antlers. "All right, I'm ready!"

Facing west, the hart took a few paces. And then, as if he had wings, he leapt up the embankment and entered the dark, trackless forest.

Fireflies danced in the brush as if to light the way for us. The rhythmic chirp of crickets accompanied the song of nightingales and hoot owls.

The hart's warm back and rocking motion lulled me to a pleasant drowsiness. Hovering on the border of slumber, my head jerked up. What if I fell to the ground? What if I dropped the sack containing the treasure?

A myriad of stars shone through the branches of the trees, in imitation of the dancing fireflies. I adjusted the shoulder sling and held tightly to the fleece bag containing Joseph's cup.

Even if I fell and the beast continued on without me, I hoped I would not lose the treasure.

As if sensing the unsteady seating of his passenger, the hart halted on a stony precipice overlooking the plain. A vast valley spread out beneath us. Reflected moonlight on the waters turned the rivers of Eden into silver ribbons.

I unfastened my belt, then wrapped it around my waist and

secured it to the rack of antlers. Once I was safely tied on, the great animal set out through the forest again.

There was little sound to accompany the swift movement of the hart. His hooves seemed to barely touch the ground. Only an occasional cracking of twigs was heard. The hart's steady breath rose in a vapor from flared nostrils as he flew onward.

Near sleep, I squinted toward a bright gleam on the far side of the mountain slope. Fire and smoke meant humans were near. Humans meant danger to me and my mount.

Were these the same men who had hunted me for the bounty of a slave? And how much would the magical hide of a white hart fetch in the court of some potentate of the East? I guessed that every piece of the mythical beast would fetch a high price in the dark arts marketplaces, where sorcerers and court magicians searched for ingredients for potions.

I stroked the hart's thick neck. "Did Adam teach you how to carry a man on your back? Did you fly with him over the mountains of Paradise?"

The hart snorted and effortlessly leapt over a fallen tree.

Hours passed. My head bobbed forward. I began to slip. The hart turned his muzzle and nudged me upright onto his back.

At last I could not keep my eyes open any longer. My head fell forward, and my fingers released the strap of the sack containing Joseph's cup. The hart evidently did not notice the clank of the precious cargo as it tumbled out of the bag and onto the ground.

It would be many hours before I realized I had dropped the treasure somewhere on the trail.

Chapter 13

Morning dawned, lighting treetops like a stand of verdant candles. I burrowed deeper into the warmth of the hart as we lay side by side in the sage. The steady drumming of the hart's heart pounded in my ear. I opened my eyes to see that I was in the center of the hart's harem. Does and yearlings dotted the gentle slope of the hillside where they slept at night. How many were there in the herd? Perhaps as many as fifty, I guessed. Their tan hides concealed them from the eyes of any human or other predator traveling the narrow track below.

As if on cue, the clumsy clopping of a troop of horses echoed from the trail, disturbing the peace. Yet the does did not stir from their hiding places. I tried to sit up, but my protector gently placed his chin over me in warning: Stay down! Keep quiet!

A gruff human voice spoke. "I think it's time we push on."

Another answered, "You were stupid, Gomer. We could have had the woman, too, if you hadn't let her do herself in."

"Not my fault, Zimri! I turn my back, and she's off the cliff."

"Do you know what she was worth?"

I gasped as I recognized Zimri's gruff chiding.

My fingers gripped the strap of the pack containing the cup. I pulled the bag against my chest and discovered it was limp, without shape, empty. I moaned softly, "Gone!"

The bandits' conversation fell silent.

Zimri demanded, "What was that?"

"I don't know . . . sounded like . . . like . . ."

"Sounded human. Like a groan." The bandit chief pulled up his mount. "You sure we got them all? None escaped?"

"Sure. You seen as good as we did."

Where had the cup gone? I slid my hand into the pouch and searched. My mind reeled in disbelief as I buried my face into the sack in horror.

The precious cargo must have fallen to the ground during last night's journey!

I fought the urge to stand and run back along the trail we had traveled. The warm golden eye of Adam's hart observed me with a kind of comprehension.

Below the resting herd Zimri shouted, "Hey! Who's up there?"

As if by command, a covey of more than a hundred quail erupted from the dense undergrowth above the trail. They flew across the path of the bandits, drawing their attention away from the herd, away from me and the white hart.

I resisted the need to cry out in anguish, but silently screamed, "Oh God! The Cup of Joseph is gone!"

Zimri commanded, "All right, then. Let's get along. The pilgrims will be like those quail, flocking on the pilgrim road. All headed to Jerusalem. Easy prey."

The riders moved on.

Magpies chattered in the trees. Tears escaped my eyes and coursed down my cheeks. I turned the bag inside out. "It's gone. Gone." I moaned again.

One by one the herd rose and shook sand from their coats. The hart studied me with what seemed to be curiosity. The animal did not rise, as if awaiting some signal from me.

"You see?" I held the bag beneath the hart's nose. "See here? I lost it! Somewhere along the road last night, it fell out. I don't even know how we came to be here. I don't know where we are. Don't know where to look." Once more I buried my face in the empty sack. "I don't even know . . . when it could have happened!"

Gripping the fleece container, I jumped to my feet. My guardian remained curled on the soft earth, his legs tucked beneath him.

"What am I supposed to do now? It was given to me to carry! I was the cupbearer to the King. Now look—one night out and . . . just look!" I tore at the bushes around me and turned useless circles. "Gone. What am I supposed to do? Cupbearer to the King. I could not even care for it for a single night! Gone. How can I ever find it?"

The hart gave a deep groan, then slowly unfolded himself and rose to his full height. He nudged me with his muzzle, nearly knocking me to the ground with his suppressed power.

"What?" I sniffed. "What?"

The hart faced the forest and the wild half trail over which we had journeyed last night. He ambled toward it, gazed back at me, then strode very deliberately toward the broken brush.

I shook my head, hands hanging limply at my sides. "Crazy. What are you doing? What? It's . . . gone! That's all."

Still the hart walked on calmly. Where the brush parted, the beast turned and lowered his head. He looked a question at me.

Slinging the empty bag around my neck, I said, "All right. Hopeless. But show me the way back. Show me if you can, so I can look for the rest of my life."

The search was tedious on foot, exhausting and dispiriting. My legs ached. My sandal rubbed a blister on my heel. Sweat dripping from my forehead hurt my eyes.

"It's the hart's fault, God. It is his fault the Cup of Joseph is lost!" I muttered blame in the desperate breath of a half prayer as I retraced the route from the long night ride.

Hours passed. The hart, his legs strung taut like the strings of hunters' bows, could have leapt over me and vanished in a breath. Instead, he trailed patiently behind as if waiting for something.

Waiting for what? I wondered. *Why does he stay with me? I am cupbearer to the King, and I have lost the cup!*

I scoured the bushes and the ground for the treasure but was uncertain this was the path we had taken. Here and there a broken twig or branch gave sign that something big . . . and ancient and wise . . . had passed this way.

Black and ugly under ages of tarnish, the divinely appointed cup could be buried in the sand. It could look like a stone. It could hang like a fallen pinecone caught in a gorse bush. Safety, yes, for who would notice such a thing? But its disguise could also make it impossible for me to spot and recover.

What if it was buried in sand?

What if the black shape was concealed in a shadow?

The trail wound up and up. The hart's brow was almost against my back, urging me onward.

At last we came to the bank of a river that ran deep and swift from the recent rains. Impossible to cross, nor did I remember crossing it in the night. Where were we? Where was the cup, hidden for long ages only to be lost by a foolish boy?

I sank down on a stump, buried my face in my hands, and groaned. Then I shouted at the hart, "Did you carry me across this water last night? I don't remember! I don't remember crossing!

What if I lost it there? What if the water's swallowed it? Oh, I am lost! Lost! How will I ever show my face at home? How can I say to my brothers I have lost this thing I was meant to carry to the King?"

The beast stepped forward, wading up to his knees in the torrent. Pausing, he glanced over his shoulder at me. Sunlight glinted in his golden eyes.

"Then take me back if you can." I leapt to my feet. "Carry me if you will!" Plunging into the icy water, I plastered my face against the side of the hart. The animal dipped low and positioned his antlers like a ladder for me to grasp and climb.

Scrambling up onto the hart's neck, I slid over the withers and onto his back. And the search continued.

We moved at a slow but steady pace, retracing the path from the night before. I clung to the base of the antlers and leaned over the hart's right shoulder. I squinted, searching the ground.

For seven hours we followed a thin, shallow tributary of the river. Gaudy butterflies with wings as broad as my hand fluttered beside me. Lizards scrambled up boulders. Squirrels bustled out of the great hart's way. Startled flocks of partridge and quail rose in clouds.

The cup was nowhere to be seen.

In the late afternoon I noticed something large and ominous skulking just out of sight. I caught sight of coarse gray hide that appeared for an instant, then vanished in the brush.

I was suddenly aware of movement behind us: a wolf. Perhaps there was more than one stalking the lone buck, waiting for nightfall. The hart must have known we were being pursued, but he moved on steadily without sign of alarm.

How many miles had we retraced because of my carelessness? The sun began to sink low on the western horizon.

Little gray owls with white-ringed eyes perched on the branch of an ancient oak tree. A thick patch of wild wheat grew on a gentle slope near the brook.

At last the buck paused. He knelt low, and I slid onto the ground.

"Are you tired, old man?" I asked. "I haven't seen you take even a single sip of water. Nor graze neither. I bet you're hungry and thirsty. If you say so, we'll stop here."

Was the wolf watching us? I peered over my shoulder as I stooped by the water to drink from the pristine stream. I cupped my hand to scoop up the cool liquid. Raising my palm to my lips, I let out a cry. There, before my eyes in a patch of wheat, was Joseph's cup. It stood upright beside a flat stone as if it had been carefully placed there for a thirsty traveler to use in drawing water.

I laughed and snatched it up, then held it aloft for the hart to see. "Look. Look what I found! Look where it was, all along!" The hart calmly grazed as I filled the cup and drained it, then filled it again and poured the water over my hands and head.

The hart was likewise thirsty from our journey. He bowed his head and drank deeply.

I sighed, kissed the cup, and said aloud the Scripture the rabbi had taught me when I first met the hart so many years before: "'As the hart pants for streams of water, so my soul pants for you, my God.'"[1]

I held the treasure to my cheek and closed my eyes, as though embracing a brother. "Of course you would be found on a journey amongst the grain. I should have known."

Sitting back on my heels, I slipped the cup into its sack and then slung the strap over my neck.

I was in the shadow of the hart. For the first time I noticed jagged scars on the animal's legs and shoulders. Evidence of fierce battles both ancient and recent etched the hide like tributaries flowing to a river. A pattern of teeth marks crisscrossed the hart's throat and shoulder.

"Wolf!" I said aloud.

Heads of dry grain hissed in the wind. The hair on the back of my neck prickled with fear of an unseen threat. But what?

Perhaps sensing danger at the same instant, the hart's head jerked up. His nostrils flared, searching the air, and golden eyes fixed on a distant point. Ears twitching, he turned this way and that to locate a sound.

"What?" I whispered.

A low growl answered.

A massive wolf crouched a few yards away. Yellow eyes gleamed, and saliva dripped from its jowls.

On the opposite side of the stream a second snarl replied.

The hart seemed to grow even larger as his muscles hardened in anticipation of combat. He snorted and tossed his head. Instantly, he placed himself as a wall of protection between me and the ravenous wolf pack.

Clasping the cup, I dashed to the oak tree. The little owls screeched and fluttered away. Tearing at the bark, I clambered up the trunk and into the limbs. At the same instant two wolves leapt, snarling and barking, onto the back of the hart.

Suddenly four more dashed from the cover, tearing at his flanks and legs. Drops of blood splattered his white coat.

"Run!" I shouted to the hart, but the great buck did not run. He held his ground. Bucking fiercely, he tossed the attackers off. They crashed into rocks and tree trunks. Stunned and confused, they scrambled to their feet and circled unsteadily.

Then the buck turned on them. He attacked, striking with sharp hooves and powerful legs. Bellowing with rage, he swung his antlers right and left. Impaling the leader, he lifted and tossed its body hard against a boulder. The wolf whined, raised its head once, then collapsed. It did not get up.

Now the pack wove their approach warily. The hart backed his rump against the tree. Using the tree as protection for his hindquarters, he lowered his head and positioned his antlers at a deadly angle. He was directly beneath me.

A brash young wolf darted in, attempting to sink its fangs into the hart's leg. One hard kick to the head sent the creature sprawling into a heap. It did not rise.

Now the enemy band pulled back and skulked at the edge of the clearing. The hart did not move away. For just an instant he lifted his head as if to signal me that this was our chance to escape.

I climbed down until I was in range of the hart's broad back. Holding to a branch, I lowered myself until my toe touched the hart's shoulder. The buck snorted impatiently.

Three of the wolf pack crouched in order to attack.

What if I missed the mark? What if I fell to the ground and was pounced on?

My fingers were slipping. It was now or never.

The bark cut into my palm, reopening the recent wounds.

"Oh, Lord!" I cried. Releasing my grip, I fell heavily, slipping to the right of the hart's broad back. Lunging, I grasped the antlers and pulled myself onto the deer, finding my balance.

In a flash the hart leapt into the air. Soaring over wolves and fallen timbers, he tore through the woods. I shouted with exhilaration as we outran the baying pack. The hart jumped the brook easily and bolted up a steep embankment, leaving the pursuers in the dust.

We ran for miles, the hart never tiring. The howling of the pack fell away. After a time we were alone in the wood. The wind rushed in my ears and the voice whispered, *"Take this cup! Nehemiah! Cupbearer to the King . . ."*

The enemy was defeated, far behind us, yet still the hart and I galloped on.

The hart's pace slowed to a measured, steady tread, but the travel continued a very long time. Finally the great buck entered a narrow passage between an overhanging pair of thorn bushes.

We emerged from the tunnel in a meadow enclosed on all sides by a thicket of acacias so closely planted their branches were interwoven to form a spiked fence.

The hart's herd already rested in the clearing. An outer ring of bucks, hail and strong, protected an inner ring of older animals. In the very center of the two circles were the does and fawns.

The buck carried me into the heart of the herd and stopped. Gratefully, I slid from the beast's back to the soft grass. As the buck moved away to graze on tender shoots, I recognized I also was extremely hungry.

The herd watched me for a moment, then accepted my presence.

Turning out the contents of my pack produced plenty to eat. I brushed the remaining dirt from a wild carrot and took a bite. Selecting from the other items collected, I cracked, shelled, and enjoyed a handful of nuts, then tried an onion.

An inquisitive fawn approached. Stretching a velvety nose close to my hand, the young deer sniffed the onion, then sneezed and backed up a pace. I coaxed it to return by offering a chunk of carrot, which the fawn accepted, while I ate two apricots and enough berries to stain my hands dark red.

When the feast concluded, I was thirsty. Once again, the hart showed the way. At the far end of the enclosure, beneath the boughs of fragrant myrtle trees, a spring of clear water bubbled up to fill a rock-lined pool. The antlered head bent as the hart drank, then the buck sidestepped out of the way, allowing me to approach with Joseph's cup.

The sweetness of myrtle blossoms surrounded me as I dipped the cup into the pool. "The scent of Eden," Rabbi Kagba called the oil of myrtle. "It's why myrtle is one of the things we wave to celebrate Tabernacles. It takes us back to a time of innocence, a time Messiah will first embody and then restore."

It had to be Tabernacles by now. The attack on Father's camp had been between the Day of Atonement and the start of this, the next feast. We shepherds spent much of our lives dwelling in tents like the children of Israel in the wilderness. But here I was, on the Feast of Tabernacles, sheltered in a booth made by the hand of the Almighty from the very outgrowth of Eden. It was on such a night that all devout Jews invited the exalted wanderers—the patriarchs and the prophets who had gone before—to join us for the feast.

I filled the cup to the brim, swallowed a mouthful of cool water, then drained it. Back on the dense matting of springy grass, I was satisfied. Now exhausted, I curled up with the cup under my arm and fell asleep . . .

Almost immediately I heard someone call my name.

"Nehemiah?"

The sound alerted me but caused me no anxiety. "Who's there?"

"My name is Zaphenath Paneah," a pleasant, youthful voice announced.

"I don't know anyone by that name," I returned. "Not a Hebrew name. Sounds Syrian?"

"Farther south."

"Egyptian?"

"Bravo," the voice applauded. "You guessed it."

"Where are you? I can't see you. Is this a dream?"

"Perhaps. I am a Dreamer of Dreams myself."

"That's what Rabbi Kagba called Joseph the Patriarch."

"A brilliant man, your rabbi. A scholar and a good teacher. The two are not always the same. So, I am Zaphenath Paneah, which means Revealer of Secrets . . . but I was born Joseph, son of Jacob, the son of Isaac, the son of Abraham. Abraham," he repeated. "My great-grandfather."

"I dreamed about you before, only I couldn't talk with you. So this *is* a dream!"

"Again, perhaps. Or perhaps I was sent to you, cupbearer to the King, to reveal secrets to you and to answer your questions. You do have questions, don't you?"

"About the cup? Of course! Many! And why can't I see you?"

A slender, dark-haired, clean-shaven male form wavered slightly, then snapped into focus. "Better?" Joseph asked. "Now, a few questions for you. First, do you know why I hid my cup in Benjamin's grain sack?"

"The rabbi says it was a test. You wanted to see if your other brothers would leave Benjamin to save themselves, or if they were truly sorry for having sold you into slavery. Had their hearts been changed?"

"And they passed the test," Joseph agreed. "Why is my cup now in your possession?"

"Rabbi Kagba says I am to take it to the Messiah. He believes a man named Jesus of Nazareth is the Anointed One, and he wants me to deliver your cup to him."

"Why?"

I was puzzled by the query. "Because he told me to."

"You misunderstand me," Joseph the Dreamer corrected. "Why should Messiah receive it?"

I thought for a moment. "I don't know. To honor him?"

"Truly, but there is more. Do you remember how I was freed from prison in Egypt?"

"When Pharaoh's cupbearer remembered how you could explain dreams and brought you to Pharaoh."

"And the cup came to me in gratitude from both Pharaoh and the cupbearer. But it is more than that. It is the symbol of my redemption. It represents the faithfulness of the Almighty in redeeming my life from the pit . . ."

"Yes."

"From slavery . . . from false accusations . . . from imprisonment . . ."

"All those," I acknowledged. "Yes, yes, and yes."

"And since Pharaoh made me the authority in Egypt, second only to himself, the cup came to represent how I was honored. Now pay attention."

"I'm ready for you to go on." Somewhere nearby a deer snorted and moved in the darkness. How much of this was only a dream?

Joseph resumed his tale. "When famine came to all the land, I was able to save my family because I was then in a position to help them, you see? I was able to redeem them from death, just as I had been redeemed from death myself."

"So the cup is important?" I offered.

"Exactly. It is first a cup of suffering, because of what I went through in order to receive it. Next, it is the cup of redemption. And it is also the cup of God's faithfulness."

"Explain that bit."

"All the way back when my brothers tossed me into the pit and then sold me, God knew that many years later I would be able to save my family. And I am a shadow."

I frowned. "I was right. You are a dream."

Joseph continued as if I had not interrupted. "I was a shadow of things to come. I was betrayed by my brothers because of envy. Sold for pieces of silver. Carried away in chains. Falsely accused. But I rose from there to save my entire family. From before I was thrown into the pit, God already knew what the end result would be. Remember this: The Almighty is never taken by surprise. And his plans always succeed. No matter how desperate a situation may appear, he is working constantly for your welfare."

I summed up: "This is what Rabbi Kagba said: 'What man means for evil, God means for good.'"[2]

"Well done, cupbearer," Joseph praised. "Your rabbi will be proud. Just remember what I have said. Think on it as you go to meet Messiah, because he is the final revealer of secrets." Joseph's form began to shimmer like a reflection in a pond when tiny ripples mar the surface.

"Wait!" I asked. "Don't go. I have many more questions."

"Don't worry, cupbearer," Joseph the Dreamer replied as he faded from view. "You will see me again. We have many miles to travel and many secrets to unfold before you reach the goal of your journey. Sleep, Nehemiah. Sleep."

Chapter 14

*I*t had been a day since I had last drunk water, and my throat and mouth were parched. I knew the hart was also thirsty, yet he did not slow his pace or stop to rest.

He carried me through a narrow canyon of rich red sandstone. Its course ran north and south. Stone buttresses were worn smooth as glass from the water of an ancient river. Though the path was something men would not follow for fear of becoming lost, the hart seemed familiar with this secret route.

The sun had risen hours ago in the east, but I could not see it, and the wadi floor remained in deep shadow. As the sun climbed higher, daylight dripped slowly down from the top of the wall like a waterfall. Etched into the stone I saw a pattern shaped like a cup, tipped as if to pour out golden liquid onto me.

At high noon the sun appeared briefly as it reached its zenith. For a few minutes it beamed directly down on us. Then, as suddenly as it had appeared, it vanished over the western rim of the canyon. Among the shadows on the east wall thorn bushes grew, and I saw a shape something like a crown.

There were no other footprints in the fine white sand of the dry bed—only the hart's. I thought perhaps this course had held Eden's pure head waters. And when the hand of the Lord had lifted Paradise into the sky beyond the reach of mortal men, the spring had also been lifted.

I looked up, certain now that the sky was not the sky at all. Heaven's cobalt blue stream flowed above me. If only I could mount up on wings like an eagle, I would drink from those heavenly waters and never thirst again.

Removing Joseph's blackened cup from its pouch, I held it up to the sky river and cried, "Please, fill this cup, Lord. Let me drink. I am thirsty!" My voice echoed and the walls resounded with my complaint.

The hart did not pause but continued on as darkness descended and the river above me became dark and sprinkled with stars. I fell asleep as Orion stepped across the gulf . . .

When I opened my eyes, it was nearly dawn. We had emerged from the canyon, and the hart knelt beside a spring of fresh water. I stepped from his back and dipped the cup into the cold, bubbling liquid. I drank deeply and sat beside where he lay. We watched together as dawn pushed back the darkness from a valley far below us.

Again, I slept.

It was dawn when I roused. Not yet fully awake, I said in a drowsy voice, "Mama. I've been having the strangest dream. Mama?"

My eyes and my awareness both snapped open at once. Instead of being in the shepherding tent or in my bed in Amadiya, I was on a hard slab of rock. The pillow under my head was the leather and oilcloth-wrapped parcel containing the Cup of Joseph. Tucked against my right side was the leather pouch containing the silver coins. Pulled up around my ears was the fur-trimmed woolen cloak.

If so much of what I thought was a dream was in fact real, was it possible the rest of the memory was also true?

The white hart stood at the edge of a precipice, gazing into the distance. When I raised up, the hart turned toward me. The beast raised his muzzle and swung it toward the land spread out below our perch, summoning me to join him.

In the morning haze it was at first difficult for me to distinguish what I was seeing. Gradually, as the sun warmed the valley, a veil of mist cleared. The light increased, revealing a sizable town no more than a handful of miles away from the bottom of the slope. The unknown city was a pendant glistening golden, strung from a thread of highway that ran east and west, disappearing from view in both directions.

"Is that where I'm supposed to go?" I asked.

The antlered crown dipped briefly in acknowledgment.

I had a sudden chill of realization. "You have brought me over the mountains, but this is where you're leaving me." I tried to picture traipsing into a caravansary beside the majestic hart while stupefied onlookers marveled and pointed, but I could not. Such a picture had more air of unreality than to be standing here, having this conversation with the creature.

I shrugged my clothes into order and secured the cloak around my shoulders, taking care to have both cup and coin purse safely fastened but out of view. "Thank you," I said to the hart. "Am I right to think that we have both been given orders to carry out?"

Once more the glorious corona of antlers bobbed in acknowledgment.

"Then please carry a message for me: Thank the one who sent you to me. Will I see you again?"

This time there was no answering response.

"Then, may Almighty bless you," I said and began the descent toward the village.

Halfway down the gentle incline, I turned to look back. The Great White Hart, nose raised into the west as if both scenting danger and pointing the way, stood outlined against an azure sky.

When I reached the bottom of the slope, I looked again. This time the rock ledge was bare. Scan as I might the expanse of dark green brush and brown earth, I spotted no white form moving against the backdrop.

Chapter 15

*B*efore I could enter the city, I had to cross an arched bridge over a small river. The structure, built of squared stone shaped to form slender, graceful pillars, looked ancient and much more attractive than the squalid, flat-roofed buildings I had glimpsed of the town.

Halfway across the span I met a man leading a donkey who waddled beneath the weight of stuffed saddlebags. "Please, sir," I said politely, and with some fear of meeting a stranger. "Can you tell me the name of this place?"

The portly man paused in gnawing a pomegranate to ask suspiciously, "How can you not know that, boy? Where are your parents? Aren't you very young to be wandering alone so early?"

"I was sent ahead to make arrangements for my family to follow," I said in a matter-of-fact tone. "I am Nehemiah bar Lamsa, but I will ask someone else if it's too much bother."

The man revealed a gap-toothed grin. "My pardon, son of Lamsa. I know your father, and your mother's workmanship in cloth. I am the traveling peddler, Obed of Zakho." Over his shoulder he jerked a thumb stained red with juice. "From which I am just leaving. May I offer directions?"

"The caravansary?"

"There are two, and right you are to ask. The one on this

side is owned by a pig of a Parthian. He overcharges, cooks with pork fat, and his beds all have fleas. What you want is the inn on the far side of town. Its proprietor is my brother, Asa. Mention your father to him and say that you met me, and he will take good care of you."

"And how will I find . . ."

Obed waved his hand and tugged the donkey into forward motion. "You can't miss it. Straight through town, just past the synagogue. *Shalom*, Nehemiah bar Lamsa. Remember me to your parents."

I passed the rival caravansary without stopping. The acrid stench of a muddy swine pen warned me away. There was a brace of pigs corralled right outside the innkeeper's home, alongside a dozen camels.

The town of Zakho was waking up by the time I reached its center. A pair of Jewish men, fringes of their prayer shawls flapping and phylacteries bouncing in their haste, hurried toward morning prayers. A half-dozen Parthian stonecutters passed by. I recognized their floppy, Parthian headgear and the hammers and quarrying tools they carried.

At the synagogue the late arrivals were pushing in to join the *minyan*. Past the building's ornately carved entry stood a wooden stockade. The main double gate for beasts of burden was still barred, but a smaller portal in one panel offered entry for me. I hammered on the door, and it was opened by an elderly porter. "What is your business, young sir?" the servant said.

"I am to arrange a room for my parents, Lamsa and Sarah of Amadiya," I said. "I was told to ask for Asa. Is he here?"

"Indeed he is. I'll take you to him."

While the peddler Obed had named his brother, he had failed to mention that it was his *twin* brother. Identical to Obed in face, stout build, and medium height, Asa's head was bald and almost spherical. Since Obed had been wearing a turban, I wondered if the similarity was exact.

I repeated my requirements.

"Welcome to Zakho, boy," Asa said. "Welcome to the Jerusalem of the North."

"Sir?"

"Don't you know your people's history, boy? When King Shalmanezer carried away Israel into exile, this became our home. Seven hundred years ago that was, but we remain here still. Or don't they teach you that in Amadiya?"

"I'm a shepherd, sir, and I've never traveled, that is, until now." I drew myself up even straighter. "I am told I should offer you one silver coin for half a week's lodging, bread, and suppers. Within that time my parents and I will join a caravan bound for Jerusalem."

The terms were agreeable and, after handing over a silver shekel, I was shown to a room on the second floor of an adjoining building. The lower floor did not contain rooms but rather open stalls filled with straw for animals. It was also shelter for people too poor to afford better accommodations.

The room was small but clean and serviceable. Once inside I sat down to think. I was overwhelmed with loneliness. I had always been surrounded with those who cared about me: Father, Mother, older brothers, Beni, the good rabbi, the other shepherds, my mother's weavers who treated me like an extra nephew. Now I was completely alone. With the immediate danger over and time to reflect on what I had lost, I felt crushed and ready to cry. I wanted to run home to Amadiya and beg for help.

Three things stopped me: the idea of finding my brothers in Jerusalem as soon as possible, the commission I had been assigned by Rabbi Kagba to take the Cup of Joseph to the Messiah, and the mystery of the White Hart.

I lifted my chin. "I will take a bath and wash my clothes," I said aloud. "I will have a good meal. Then I will be ready to locate a caravan and go to Jerusalem."

I wasted no time setting out to locate a caravan bound for the Holy City. The afternoon of my arrival in Zakho, I made my way around the compound, hunting a suitable group. I did not forget to secure the sack of coins and the bundle containing the cup to my waist under my clothing before leaving my room.

There were two bands of travelers within the fences of Asa's caravansary. The first group I approached looked weary and their clothing travel-worn, as if they had come a long distance. Even the camels appeared gaunt, their eyes hollow and staring and their humps shrunken.

The caravan leader, a man named Eram, was a perfect match for his charges. His face was as scored with the crevices of age and rough living as the canyons back of Amadiya.

"My family and I want to go to Jerusalem," I said. "We can pay."

The travel master tilted his head and tugged thoughtfully on an earlobe lengthened by several decades of such abuse. "And I would love to take you," the man replied. "But we are returning from there, heading east and not west." He shook his head glumly. "It was not a profitable trip."

"But you were there? In Jerusalem? Can you tell me about it?"

Eram shrugged. "News is cheap and gossip free. But later. Right now I must see which of these spavined beasts will live to cross the mountains and which I must sell here. Go see Jehu over there. He is heading west." Eram indicated a younger man with a pointed beard who leaned against a heap of bolts of silk.

"Jerusalem?" Jehu said, stroking his beard. "How many are you, boy? And can you keep up? I have a load of fine cloth, spice, and amber I am eager to sell in the markets in Damascus and Caesarea before I go on to Jerusalem."

This was beginning to sound promising. The animals looked healthy and the fittings well cared for. Eagerness to arrive was also in my thoughts. "How long does the passage last? Two Sabbaths?" I guessed.

Jehu roared with laughter, calling to a drover, "Did you hear that? Boy, do you see wings on these animals? Two Sabbaths? The best crossing we've ever made is forty-five days. And we are the fastest. What do you say? Will you join up with us?"

I was taken back. Rabbi Kagba had not told me the length of the journey. A month and more before arriving, and then I still had to locate my brothers?

"I . . . I'll have to think about it," I said. "And you stop for Sabbath, of course."

Hooking his thumbs in a wide silk sash tied around his middle, Jehu burst into another gale of laughter. "We are not religious pilgrims, boy. This trip is all about profit! Stop for Sabbath? Weren't you the one who was just in a great hurry?"

"I have to think," I repeated, and I retreated to my chamber.

Chapter 16

*T*he following morning I went to Sabbath service at the synagogue with Asa and Eram. Jehu did not attend. His caravan was preparing to leave Zakho and would not wait for the end of Sabbath to depart.

I sat in the women's gallery beside Asa's wife. The reading was from the Book of Beginnings: "Now the Lord had said to Abram, 'Get thee out of thy country . . . unto a land that I will shew thee.'"[1]

I was curiously pleased at the scripture. It made me feel that I was doing the right thing in embarking on the trip to Jerusalem. This was further confirmed for me when the rabbi, offering his commentary on the passage, mentioned that Abram had passed through Zakho on his way from Haran to Canaan. "Then as now," the rabbi said, "we were a resting place for travelers."

Eram, shuffling his feet with some show of embarrassment, was called up to read the Scripture portion that followed. It was from the prophet Isaiah: "Lift up your eyes on high, and behold, who hath created these things, that bringeth out their host by number: he calleth them all by names by the greatness of his might."[2]

It was just like Rabbi Kagba said: The Almighty not only created the starry host, but he had a name for each of them and each name meant something. The recollection made me wonder about the scholar's fate. It caused a catch in my throat and a sniff of homesickness until I caught Asa's wife watching me. Then I straightened my back and squared my shoulders.

Eram concluded with, "They that wait upon the LORD shall renew their strength; they shall mount up with wings as eagles; they shall run, and not be weary; and they shall walk, and not faint."[3] Then Eram rolled up the scroll, handed it back to the attendant, returned to his place, and resumed tugging at his ear.

It was still another confirmation for my pilgrimage. Jerusalem might be far away to the south and west, but the promise I heard was that I would be strong enough to make the journey.

It was time to tell Jehu my decision: I would be going with the caravan to Judea, even if they were not properly devout Jews.

❧

When I returned to the corral area of the caravansary, I found it more than half empty. Calling to the aged porter, I asked, "Where is Jehu?"

Brandishing a wooden pitchfork in a wrinkled, age-spotted hand, the servant replied, "Gone! Gone to Jerusalem."

"So soon?"

"I tried to tell him it was bad fortune to flaunt the Almighty so, but he went anyway." The old man made it sound like a personal affront as well as an impiety.

"Did they have other provisions to get?" I inquired. "Somewhere else to stop nearby?"

The porter was already shaking his shaggy locks before the question was completed, "Over the hills and gone," he said, indicating the road. The highway was devoid of travelers as far to the west as I could see.

"Could I catch them? How far to the next stopping place?"

"Boy!" the servant said sternly. "They will make twenty miles before they stop again. Farther and faster than you could manage on foot. Twenty miles," he repeated, then added, "if they make it that far."

"What do you mean?"

"Bandits," the porter said gruffly. "Left on a Sabbath and made too much show of wealth. Bragging about his load of silk and how much it was worth. Word of it got all around Zakho."

"Do you really think they're in danger?"

Grudgingly the porter admitted, "Jehu took some thought about it. Signed on three more men to go along as guards." Dropping a leather water bottle at the end of a braided horsehair rope into the well, he added, "Though what good one of them may do, I'm sure I don't know. Had his arm in a sling. What good'll that do in a fight? But they insisted: 'Sign us all or none,' their leader said."

After offering to tote the skin to water a pen of donkeys, I asked, "How long will I have to wait? I want to get on the road soon."

"Who can say?" the porter said, laying his arm across my shoulders. "Tomorrow or next week? Who can say?"

It was not the answer I hoped to hear.

I was back in the Zakho synagogue for the evening *Havdalah* service. By this rite Sabbath ended and the new week inaugurated. I tasted the wine and savored the aroma as the box of spices was passed around. The sharp sweetness of cinnamon, cloves, and myrtle pepper mingled with the penetrating tang of laurel and the exotic allure of orange peel.

Making sure I used all five of my senses, just as my mother taught me, I admired the entwined flames of the braided candle. Extending my hands, I sensed its warmth while I listened to the blessing:

"Blessed art thou, God, our Lord, King of the Universe,
    who distinguishes
    holiness from the everyday,
    light from dark,
    Israel from the nations,
    the seventh day from the six work days.
    Blessed art thou, God,
    who distinguishes holiness from the everyday."

When the candle was extinguished in the last of the wine, the end of the *Havdalah* service brought Sabbath to a close. Some of the men dipped a fingertip in the wine and touched their eyelids with it for good luck. Neither Rabbi Kagba nor my father had ever followed that custom, so neither did I.

Outside the synagogue a pair of torches lighted the entry. There was no illumination between the religious building and the caravansary, but the latter was only a few paces away.

I had only stepped into the darkness when I heard shouts of alarm and hoofbeats approaching at high speed. From the direction of the bridge came a horseman at full gallop.

The mounted man was upon me almost before I had time to react. I looked up and saw a black-cloaked figure on a black steed bearing down on me. Flinging myself out of the way, I had only a second to spare as the rider thundered past.

Flashing hooves dug sharply into the soil exactly where I had been standing.

But the nearness of sudden death was not what made me quake with alarm.

In the momentary glimpse of the mounted man's face provided by the torches, I recognized Zimri! Had the bandit chief also noticed me?

The assassin hurtled through Zakho without pausing and dashed away into the countryside beyond. There was no sign I had been spotted, no signal that the rebel was returning.

Yet still I could not stop myself from also bolting into flight. Ignoring calls from Asa, asking what was wrong, I sprinted across the stable yard. Up the stairs I charged, taking the steps two at a time.

There was no authority in Zakho to whom I could report, no one I trusted with my complete story, nothing to be done.

All of my anxiety centered on the cup! Unreasonably, I was suddenly fearful for its safety.

Inside my room I tore the covers off the bed and gasped with alarm. It wasn't there! The Cup of Joseph was not at the head of the bed. I rummaged through the fleece and coverlet, hoping I had tossed the sacred object aside without meaning to do so.

Down on my knees I went, handling and squeezing each bit of fabric. It was then that I saw it: a dark bundle, partly unrolled, lying between the wall and the bed frame at the head of the bed.

I snatched it up, feeling the comforting solid form within the folds. Even then I was not fully reassured until I unwrapped it completely and cradled the black, nondescript chalice in my arms.

The parcel had merely tumbled off the pallet, probably when I slammed the door on my way to the synagogue. I vowed to never leave it behind again.

The vision of Zimri galloping past slammed again into my thoughts. The bandit was still out there, somewhere. He had not been after me this time, but if we met again I would certainly be in danger.

I could not stay in Zakho any longer. The need to connect with a safe caravan and leave this part of the world behind was stronger than ever. I prayed earnestly for the remainder of my stay in Zakho to be brief. I wanted to travel with the right companions in a caravan to Jerusalem, but mostly I felt an urgent need to get the journey underway.

I bolted the door securely. Reknotting the fabric, I patted the sacking around the cup into a more comfortable shape. Using it for a pillow, I fell asleep.

Chapter 17

*I*t wasn't even dawn when the bawling of camels and the shouting of drovers woke me. A new caravan had arrived at the caravansary.

Standing on the balcony, I studied the new arrivals. I counted forty beasts of burden, a good number for safe traveling. I saw family groups come in together and be assigned quarters beneath my room.

The man who strode about giving orders to everyone must be the master. He was of medium height and build, with sturdy shoulders and muscular forearms. The fringes of his prayer shawl proclaimed him to be an observant Jew. In fact, all the men in this caravan appeared to be respectable Jews.

Emerging from the inn, Asa greeted the newly arrived chief by shouting across the yard: "Hosea! Welcome! We looked for you these three days past."

"Had a new baby born on the crossing between here and Ecbatana," the leader called back. Hooking a thumb over his shoulder, he gestured toward a baby camel lurching unsteadily beside her mother. "Had to stay over a day, and that put us too late to get here before Sabbath. But here we are. Food ready?"

"Fresh bread, butter, and dates. Come inside and eat."

"I will, soon as I see all the families properly disposed and the animals fed."

"Sir," I called down to Asa, "might I join you for breakfast? I'd like to speak with the caravan master."

"Hosea?" Asa returned. Then, guessing at my purpose, he added, "You could not do better than him, lad. Come down and welcome."

※

Hosea was even more muscular up close than he had seemed from a distance. The caravan captain had a puckered scar on his brawny right forearm. He was gruff but not unkind when he spoke to me. "What's this about joining the caravan?" he asked. "Where are your parents, boy? Is it true they sent you to make arrangements?" Hosea lowered his chin and looked down a long, crooked nose. "The truth, now, mind."

"Yes, sir," I agreed. "I am supposed to go to my grandfather's shop in Jerusalem, in the Street of the Weavers. My brothers are already there. My parents will be joining me later." It wasn't really a lie so much as a hopeful utterance, I told myself.

Asa, seated beside me on a wooden bench next to a smoldering fire, turned, and looked at me. "Why the story, then? About you being sent here to set things up?"

"My good friend, Rabbi Kagba, said I should tell people that my parents were coming soon. He said then no one would take advantage of me. He said when I found observant Jews I could trust them and then I could explain."

I still did not make reference to the cup, nor to the special mission that had been assigned to me. I had told enough of the tale to get me to Jerusalem. The rest was no one's business.

"When I heard that you keep Sabbath," I added to Hosea, "I was sure God had sent the right caravan for me."

Hosea laughed, exchanging a glance with the innkeeper. "So I'm an answer to prayer, am I? There's few would make that claim about me."

"I can pay." I explained the bargain the rabbi had insisted was fair. "You will be paid the rest when we reach the Holy City."

Hosea waved away the reference to pay. "I believe you, lad. That's not the issue. I cannot take you, alone as you are. Someone must be willing to be responsible for you. See that you're fed. Doctored, if needed. Assign you your duties. On my caravans everyone works if they want to eat."

"I'm a good worker," I maintained stoutly, looking to Asa to back me up.

The caravansary owner nodded.

"All right, let me locate the family I think will serve your need. If they agree, then I'll take you on. Mind, now," he said sternly. The bench legs squealed on the wooden floor as he stood and pushed away from the table. "It's no easy task you've set for yourself. We walk from sunup to sunset, six days a week, and then tend the animals before we rest ourselves. And there's no turning back. This time of year it'll take six Sabbaths with the blessing of the Name . . . eight if we're unlucky. You still want to sign on?"

I nodded vigorously.

Hosea expressed his approval. "You will be able to help this family, I think. They are making this journey because of some healer they heard of. Jesus, I think his name is. One son is going blind, and the other son's wife is barren." The caravan master shook his head. "It's a long journey. I hope they find what they're looking for."

Hosea returned with an older man and his wife and two children younger than me. "This is Raheb and his good wife, Reena. They are traveling west with their sons and daughters-in-law, and these, their two grandchildren."

"Pleased to meet you, Nehemiah," said Raheb, a pleasant-seeming man, nearing sixty, broad of build and face. "Here are Beryl"—he tapped a small girl of about four on the shoulder—"and Michael." He lightly thumped the head of a boy a year or two younger than me. "These two require a lot of looking after," Raheb said. "And they're a bit small for their chores. But you look strong. Shepherd, I hear? Would you help them in exchange for your meals?"

"Gladly, sir," I agreed.

"Then it's settled," Hosea offered. "We leave day after tomorrow at daybreak. You can start helping by watering the camels today."

By the time we were a few days' journey out of Zakho, I had learned a great deal more about Raheb's family. They were loving, pious, close-knit, and diligent. Raheb was a hard worker, his advice sought as frequently as his muscular strength, and he made both available in a cheerful, modest way. Reena was a good cook, caring and unflustered by life amid dirt and sweaty camels, never shirking her labor but always finding time to hug Beryl or tell Michael a story.

They were both a comfort and a grief to me. My guardians represented a place of plenty and safety after all my running and hiding . . . and also a constant reminder of how much I missed my own parents.

I learned more about my temporary family than just their

character. I came to understand their motives as well, much to my surprise.

Going on pilgrimage to the Holy City was something all pious Jews aspired to accomplish. *Torah* enjoined three pilgrim festivals each year: Tabernacles, Passover, and the Festival of Weeks that culminated in Pentecost. Among devout Jews living far from Jerusalem, it was a custom to pay a substitute to appear at the Temple. This allowed distant believers to participate in the sacrifices by proxy in those years in which they could not travel. Ever since my mother moved to Amadiya when she married Father, my Jerusalem grandparents had performed those ceremonies for us.

This year I would be going myself.

But the circumstances that took Raheb and his children to Jerusalem involved more than fulfilling a religious obligation. Raheb's son, Tobit, father of my friends Michael and Beryl, had an eye disease that was robbing him of his sight. His eyes watered constantly and were often glued shut in the morning when he awoke. He was so sensitive to the glare of the desert sun that he kept a headscarf wrapped about his face by day, peering out at the world through narrow slits.

Raheb's other son, Yacov, was wed six years earlier, but he and Dinah had no children. She was barren. She doted on her niece and nephew, but a lurking sadness never fully left her face.

What shocked me was learning the cause of their deciding to make *aliyah* this year: the presence of Jesus of Nazareth.

Stories were swapped around a community campfire. It seemed that everyone had an opinion about the rabbi from Galilee. "I heard once there was a crowd so great it was impossible to get near him," one traveler reported. "So four companions tore off the roof of the house where Jesus was and lowered their crippled friend down to him. This Jesus told him to get up and walk . . . and he did."

"That's all?" a scoffer challenged. "No magic words? No special prayers?"

"No, but he did say the man's sins were forgiven."

Mutters of "Blasphemy!" and "Who does he think he is?" swirled around the leaping flames.

"Perhaps he's a madman, deluded," another remarked.

The original reporter continued, "Jesus asked them if it was harder to forgive sins or to heal a paralyzed man. He said making the man walk was the proof he could forgive sin too."

I did not know what to make of that tale. How could I understand a man who claimed to be able to forgive sins? Didn't that authority belong to God alone? Wasn't Messiah supposed to be a leader who would be like Moses? Or like Joshua? A man who would free us Jews from the power of Rome and restore David's kingdom?

My doubts were echoed by the next speaker. "He's a charlatan! Mark my words: he's just another swindler, claiming to be a messiah . . . right up until he and all his followers get themselves crucified. We don't need a healer, or a smooth-talking liar, or a philosopher! We need a strong military leader. We need another Judah Maccabee."

There were murmurs of agreement at these words. We were hoping to arrive in Jerusalem by Hanukkah, celebrating the rededication of the Temple after the famous Judah the Hammer defeated our foes two hundred years earlier.

Tobit stepped forward into the firelight. Since it was night, his eyes were unbound, but they were red and inflamed all around them. He squinted painfully in the flaring brilliance and wiped away tears that coursed down his cheeks. "I have heard he gave sight to a man born blind. Born . . . blind! No one has ever heard of such a thing. Perhaps it isn't true. But if it is, if he will touch me and keep me from losing my sight, I will follow him, warrior or not."

"I heard," Hosea rumbled, "that he even raised the dead."

"Now you've gone too far," someone sneered. "Is he supposed to be Elijah or Elisha?"

Hosea said, "I have a cousin in the synagogue in Capernaum. He's the one who told me the cantor's daughter was dead and Jesus brought her back to life." Then, speaking very carefully and deliberately, the caravan leader pronounced each of these words: "Or are you calling *me* a liar?"

The one who issued the objection retreated immediately. "Spoke hastily . . . please forgive me . . . some misunderstanding."

When we went to bed that night, I found the Cup of Joseph to be more uncomfortable than usual as my pillow. How would I know whether Jesus was worthy to receive it or not? If he was not who Rabbi Kagba hoped, what would I do with it? Why was I carrying it across a thousand-mile journey away from home, if it turned out to be all wrong?

Then I thought about Tobit's eyes and Dinah's weary sadness. "Almighty, for all their sakes, make the stories be true," I prayed. "And let me know the truth without mistake." I remembered the White Hart and my vision of Joseph the Dreamer. I was sent to Jerusalem for a purpose. The cup had come to me, out of all those who had carried it or who might have found it over the centuries. I was the one appointed for this reason, even if I did not yet understand it.

Chapter 18

We journeyed across the Land between the Rivers—Mesopotamia, as the Greek-speakers called it. Despite the promise of abundant water in its name, the area was in the grip of a prolonged drought. Dry, dusty plains stretched for miles, punctuated by all-too-rare clumps of trees and occasional muddy pools. Wells, some of them dug back in the days of Father Abraham, still furnished the life blood of the trade routes.

Hosea urged us to use our water sparingly. "I plan each day's journey to take us from watering hole to watering hole," he lectured the group. "But there are no guarantees. A sandstorm or a greedy caravan that gets there first . . . either of these can upset the plan. If we are forced to go a second or a third day on just what we can carry, then so be it, we will."

"And what happens if it's four days?" someone asked.

"Then those who have not been careful will either beg or begin to die," Hosea said.

The very next morning we rehearsed Hosea's warning. Raheb made certain every waterskin for our group was completely filled before we left the well. It was my duty to haul the bulging, dripping bags out of the water source. Tobit and Yacov saw to it that they were secured to the packsaddles of the camels.

During the very first week of our journey, we experienced the truth of Hosea's words.

Before dawn the camels began bawling as if jackals ran amid their lines. Raheb and Yacov dashed about with drawn swords but found nothing.

Just as they returned to the remains of the previous night's campfire, the tremor struck. The earth rolled and pitched beneath my feet. A tent collapsed on Reena and her daughters-in-law, but they were not hurt.

We sorted ourselves out and resumed our travel.

When it was almost evening, we arrived at a place Hosea called Beth Mah-buwah, the House of the Spring. What we expected to find was a sheltered spot with water seeping out of a rock face. Our leader said the spring filled a pool to overflowing.

Instead, we found the cliffside fractured, the spring dried up, and the pool split, drained and empty.

"The earthquake," Hosea muttered. "In ages past one tremor broke the rock and started the fountain. Now another has closed it again."

"Could another reopen it?" Raheb asked.

"Not soon enough to help us," the caravan leader responded. "Nor would you want to be close by when it did." He gestured to a heap of boulders that had fallen from the top of the precipice. "That would have crushed anyone too close. Still, we camp here tonight anyway," he ordered. "Well away from the cliff, in case the earth is still not comfortable. Use your water carefully. With the blessing, we should reach another well by tomorrow night . . . but we cannot know until we reach it."

On the next day's march Raheb's family was at the front of the caravan. Michael trotted along beside me. My new young companion kept up a constant chatter about whatever popped into his head: what he named each of the goats we herded, what he would see in Jerusalem, the earthquakes he had felt when home in Ecbatana . . . and water. Often he talked about water.

"My father has been on caravan before," he said. "They weren't careful with water like we are. Once they got lost and went a week without finding a well. Two men were driven crazy, Papa says."

Michael's list of the horrors of being without water increased my own anxiety. I was relieved when we reached the edge of the barren tableland and spotted a cluster of trees near its base. I saw bronze sunlight glinting off a pool. The oasis was anchored in place by a large hawthorn tree, but palms and junipers were dotted around it too.

"We're there, and the water is there." I shaded my eyes against the glare. Then renewed worry struck me. "But another caravan is already there," I said, noticing human forms in the grove.

Raheb, leading a camel, arrived alongside me. "It's all right, Nehi. This is the best water for a week, Hosea says. There'll be plenty. Besides, I don't even see any animals."

He was right. As we descended the slope and drew nearer to the camping place, there were no camels, no horses, no donkeys anywhere in sight. I saw people resting against the trunks of trees or reclining beside the water, but no beasts of burden.

Suddenly Raheb stopped me. "Nehemiah," he said tersely, "stay here with Michael. Reena," he called to his wife, "go no farther. Keep together. Yacov, stay with them."

"Grandfather," Michael said, "why are we stopping? There's the water. Why can't we—"

Raheb sounded angry when he repeated, "Stay here!"

Raheb, Hosea, and a party of men, spread out in a line like scouts approaching enemy territory, moved cautiously toward the grove. They advanced among the nodding palms, swords or spears in hand. Hosea called them together for a brief conference, then they trudged back up the hill toward us.

Raheb reported to our family, "Bandit attack. That's why there are no animals."

Reena whispered a question I could not hear, but Raheb answered by saying, "All of them. None escaped. You stay here. We'll get done as quickly as we can."

Raheb told me to stay with the children, but I had been struck by a burning question. "I'm a shepherd's son," I said. "I've seen dead men, and I've seen bandits. Please let me come."

There were fifteen bodies scattered among the trees. All were men. All had been stripped of their clothing.

The caravan had defended itself, but bodies tangled in blankets near campfire ashes told the tale: they had been attacked while they slept. Their guards had failed them.

Or betrayed them.

I found Jehu locked in the embrace of death with his assailant. He had plunged a knife into the heart of his opponent even as a curved dagger slashed his throat.

The dagger had been wielded by the bandit I saw on the trail with his arm in a sling when the rabbi and I were hiding. *One of Zimri's men.*

I trembled. I had almost joined Jehu's company. I would have been in the camp when Zimri's men attacked.

Wielding shovels or using our hands, we buried the bodies well away from the oasis. We dug a trench beneath a sandy knoll, loaded it with the dead, then collapsed the overhanging brow of earth onto them.

Then we brought our caravan into camp.

There was little conversation that night. We realized that crossing the desert exposed us to many dangers besides being short of water. I was glad the Almighty had led me to Hosea and Raheb. I prayed fervently that as we kept the Sabbath, so the Almighty would keep us.

It was four Sabbaths before the start of Hanukkah—four more weeks until our caravan would arrive in Jerusalem. Miles from any town, we kept Sabbath night in camp and worshipped during the following day.

When the service was held, Raheb was called up to read the words of the prophet Malachi. It was a grim passage, I thought, about how the priests stole from God and defiled their worship with theft and trickery. Raheb read God's accusation to the wicked priests: "A son honors his father, and a servant his master. If then I am a father, where is my honor? And if I am a master, where is my fear? says the LORD of hosts to you, O priests, who despise my name."[1]

After the service the assembly scattered to their individual camps. A traveler named Saul of Hebron, passing in the opposite direction, had shared a meal and the worship service with the caravan. He trudged alongside us.

"Things must have been bad in Malachi's day," Saul said, "but they have not gotten any better since. High Priest Caiaphas lords it over the people, because he is backed up by Governor Pilate. His priests cheat the people when they change money for Temple coin. They charge outrageous prices for sacrificial lambs. It is a rotten business, stinking to heaven. No one stands up to them." Then he brightened. "No one except one man . . . Jesus of Nazareth."

My wandering attention refocused at the sound of that name.

"I've heard of him," Raheb said, "but he's supposed to be a man of peace. Meek, they say, and kind."

"Not on this occasion," Saul argued. "Some time ago it was. I saw it! Made a whip and scattered the moneychangers left and right. He may be the very king of peace for all I know, but at the time of which I speak, he was a Prince of Righteousness! Consumed with righteous anger for the One God, whom he called Father."

"A madman, then," Raheb responded.

Saul shrugged. "A brave and righteous madman. No one else challenges the high priest . . ."

"And lives," Raheb concluded drily. "He can't last long, can he? Not after challenging the Levites and the hypocrite merchants right in their lair."

"Perhaps not, but I'd pay good money to see him do it again," Saul concluded. "So would you, I wager. Not since the Maccabees did anyone stand up to the corrupt priests like this Jesus."

That night I worried as I tried to fall asleep. What would I do with the cup if Jesus was arrested . . . or even killed . . . before I met him? How could I complete my mission?

I wrestled so with these concerns that I was relieved when a voice I recognized as belonging to Joseph the Dreamer called to me . . .

"Nehemiah? Will you go on a journey with me?"

"Yes, please," I responded.

There was a crashing noise followed by billows of air. It was like when a tent's guy ropes are released and the shelter collapses with a rush. Just like that, night collapsed to become day. I no longer slept on a sandy trailside. Instead, I stood next to Joseph on a rocky ridge hemmed in on both sides by deep valleys. Above it loomed another rocky outcropping.

Built on the point of the lower ridge was a citadel. In front of the fortress a conference was taking place. A rank of tired-looking warriors with notched swords and tattered bowstrings faced a man dressed as a priest but wearing a circlet of gold atop his head.

"The one speaking is Abram, my great-grandfather," Joseph said, indicating the leader of the warriors. "Facing him is Melchizedek, the king of Salem, where we are now. As to the rest, just listen."

"We pursued the Elamites as far as Damascus," Abram said, "the ones who kidnapped my nephew, Lot, and his family." Abram paused to rub his hands up and down his blood-stained robe. "We attacked the enemy camp by night and routed them. When they fled, we chased them. We rescued Lot and all my kin and all his possessions. We also took spoils of war from the enemy. Now we have returned from the fight, but before we go home, I ordered that we turn aside here. You, Melchizedek, are king. You are also priest of the Most High God. Since we serve the same God and he has helped me, I am here to offer him thanks."

"You have done well, Abram," the priest said. "And wanting to honor God also does you credit. But you are tired. You have traveled and fought, so here is refreshment for you." Snapping his fingers, Melchizedek summoned a row of servants bearing trays of bread and jugs of wine. Moving down the row of Abram and his allies, Melchizedek broke the loaves and handed some to each man. Then he poured wine into a silver cup and carried it down the row of parched combatants for each to drink from. As the king offered the wine, he touched the foreheads of Abram and his men. Melchizedek spoke words for every warrior pronounced too softly for me to overhear. A blessing spoken over each man?

I stared at the cup. It was polished silver that gleamed in the sun. "That looks just like your cup," I said to Joseph. "Except shiny and new-looking."

"That's because it is my cup . . . before it was mine. Listen."

When each man had received the bread and the wine, Melchizedek spoke loudly again. "Abram, you are blessed by God Most High, Possessor and Maker of Heaven and Earth. And blessed, praised, and glorified be God Most High, who has given your enemies into your hands."

Now it was Abram's turn to summon a column of servants. Each bore a pack on his back. At Abram's command the attendants unrolled the bundles at Melchizedek's feet. The contents displayed contained gold coins, jeweled necklaces, bracelets and rings, gold and silver plates. "For the service of the Most High," Abram said. "A tenth of all the spoils, for a thank offering."

Melchizedek nodded gravely. Walking directly toward Abram he extended the silver cup from which the king of Salem had dispensed the wine and his blessing. "For you. A memorial of this day. Whenever you eat bread and drink wine from this cup, you will remember that you honored the Most High and that he has blessed you."

The two groups of men parted. While Joseph and I watched them go, the Dreamer said, "So here is a true and honorable priest of the Almighty. And what does his name mean, Nehemiah?"

"King of Righteousness."

The Dreamer concurred. "And since he is the Master of

Salem, which means 'peace,' he is also the Prince of Peace. Do you know where Salem is located?"

"Salem is . . . the same as Jerusalem!" I realized. "And so that rocky cliff," I said, turning and pointing, "that's where the Temple is now."

"No moneychangers or corrupt priests here today," Joseph said. "But here were more shadows of things to come. Now let me take you home."

The Dreamer swirled the edge of his robe around my shoulders. Daytime and Salem disappeared. A cup of jewel-like stars spilled across the night sky from the constellation called the Cup.

Chapter 19

A herd of goats traveled with our caravan, providing fresh milk for the youngest of our pilgrims. Extra milk, curdled in goatskin bags, became cheese. The animals also furnished a supply of fresh meat we would not otherwise have enjoyed.

Part of the work assigned me by Hosea was to move the small flock along parallel to the plodding camels. The duty was not hard. The shaggy goats naturally followed their four-footed leader, a rangy wether wearing a bell around his neck. All I had to do was prod those that lagged behind and keep track of any injuries they suffered. Raheb praised me for noticing when a ewe scratched her udder on a thorn bush, or if a young animal turned up lame from a stone caught in the cleats of his hoof. Keeping a flock healthy was something I had learned at my father's side and through the skill of my mother. Doctoring with olive oil, in which mint, lavender flowers, and sulfur had been steeped answered for most of their hurts.

At the beginning of our journey, Raheb, or one of his sons, assisted me with the flock. I was proud when, after a week of travel, my guardian recognized I was an experienced herdsman and left the goats in my care.

Michael often walked with me, but only for part of each

day. He was too small to keep up without running, so wore out quickly. Still, I was glad for the company.

He told me stories about living in Ecbatana, within sight of the tombs of Queen Esther and Mordecai. I responded with tales of facing down wolves and leopards in the canyons of my home. (I may have exaggerated slightly.)

One afternoon, as the shadows were drawing in, Michael's uncle Yacov brought us the word that we would be stopping for the night in another hour or so. Bending toward his nephew, he offered, "I'll carry you back with me now, Michael."

"Please," my friend replied, "let me stay with Nehi. I'm not a bit tired. Let me stay till we bring in the flock."

Standing erect, Yacov appeared to judge the distance to the procession of the caravan: about a quarter of a mile. The camels trudged along the flat plain while my herd, and others like it, grazed amid the brush that fringed a serpentine line of small hills. Squinting at the horizon, he agreed to let Michael remain with me. "But as soon as the sun touches those peaks," Yacov said, stretching one hand toward the west, "bring the flock up quickly. I don't want you out here after dark."

"We will," I said.

The dark orange disk of the solar coin was merely a handsbreadth over the peaks when I counted the flock one final time in preparation for bringing them down the slope. "Nine, ten, eleven," I recited, before stopping in consternation. Beginning again brought me to the same conclusion. "We're missing one."

"It's Beulah," Michael remarked with assurance.

He was right. The ewe he named had been more trouble than any of the rest, sometimes butting me in the back out of sheer contrariness. She often found the most awkward, brush-choked gullies in which to wander. Beulah seemed to take delight in hiding her scraggly brown-and-white blotched hide amid matching shrubs and rubble.

"She can't have gone far," I reasoned. "I'll start the leader back toward camp, and the rest will follow. You go with them, to keep them moving, while I go find her."

"I'd rather stay with you," Michael said.

I judged the heavens. Half the sun was below the distant rocky ridge, but the clear sky was still full of light. The flock was grazing contently amongst the scrawny hawthorns, wild olive shrubs, sickle grass, and yellow bedstraw. "All right. We'll make it quick."

I was certain Beulah was no farther than the sharp spine of a limestone outcrop fifty paces away. As I trudged up the incline, I prayed she had not tumbled down the other side into a ravine.

The Cup of Joseph, tied in its covering around my waist and slung behind my back, clunked against my shepherd's staff as it swung with each stride. When I reached the jagged array of boulders forming the backbone of the knoll, I clambered atop it in order to see better. The other side of the ridge did fall sharply into a narrow defile . . . and Beulah was nowhere in sight.

Panting from the climb, Michael joined me at the summit.

"I can't see her," I said. "Let's go back to the others."

"We can't leave her out here," he objected. "Something will get her for sure."

Over our heads a vast flock of cranes, flying south to their winter home, swept past. They soared above us, a living river in the sky, like a stream of clouds flowing downwind.

"Her own fault," I argued.

"There's still plenty of light. Look, there's a path."

It was generous to call it a path. A game trail, no wider than one of my feet, snaked downward by way of a long, slanting plunge into the gulley below.

"Bet there's a pool of water." Michael sniffed. "Don't you smell it? Bet that's what she's after."

I considered what my friend said. The air wafting upward from the shadowed gorge was noticeably cooler and moister feeling than that of the exposed hillside. Tracing the descent of the narrow track with my eyes, I spotted a brown-and-white form darting around a curve. "You're right. There she goes."

With that we also plunged headlong down into the canyon. At each bend in the trail I spotted Beulah for an instant, just before she disappeared again behind a screen of brush or a dusty limestone cornice.

When we reached the bottom, the goat was still bouncing ahead of us toward a goal only she knew. The floor of the gorge was filled with deep sand that made harder walking than the rock-strewn slope had been. It was barely wide enough for two horses or donkeys to pass side by side.

There was no water in the ravine, but we were definitely heading in an upstream direction. The dry creek bed wandered into the heart of the mountain. Side branches appeared along the way. Beulah darted left or right as her mood took her. There was no longer any main channel. All the ravines looked alike: constricted and choked with grit, mere threads of gravel flanked by sheer stone precipices.

I was angry at the goat and determined to catch her. I would tie the sash from my robe around her neck and drag her back to camp. I was sure that soon she would dash into a dead-end canyon, and then her game and this chase would be over.

Soon stretched into a very long time. The pale blue light reaching into the depth of the gully changed to azure, then cobalt, and then to purple. The lateness of the hour had just penetrated my thinking when I turned a final corner to come face-to-face with a blank rock wall . . . and no Beulah.

"Where did she go?" Michael wondered aloud. "Even a goat can't climb that," he said, gesturing toward the cliff. "She disappeared."

Thinking of an explanation, I suggested, "At that place where the last two canyons came together? We thought she followed the left, but she must have ducked into the other way." I saw Michael shiver. The night was growing cold, but with our cloaks and fleece-lined leather boots, his shaking must be from fear too. "Enough," I decided. "It's late. We're late. And we've wasted enough time on one stupid goat. Let's go back."

"But, Nehi, . . . which way is back?" he queried.

"It's easy," I said with assurance. "It's this way." After three steps I looked at my feet and stopped.

"What's the matter?"

"No footprints," I mumbled. "We didn't come this way after all." Facing about, I added, "Silly mistake. Here we go. Follow me."

Three dead ends and five wrong turns later, I admitted we were lost.

"If I could just see the stars," I lamented. "But down here in the bottom of this ravine I can barely see any bit of sky." Michael's bottom lip trembled, and I feared he might cry. "Don't worry," I reassured him. "All we have to do is climb out of here—it doesn't matter where—and as soon as I can see the stars, I can get us home."

My friend sniffed and wiped his nose with the sleeve of his robe. "Is that the truth? Or are you just making up another story?"

"Truth," I insisted. "My teacher, Rabbi Kagba, taught me."

The canyon walls were so sheer that finding an incline we could ascend was not easy. Two more box canyons provided no outlet. As it grew still darker, I began to fear we would have to spend the night in the gully.

"What's that noise?" Michael asked, then answered his own question. "Hoofs. I hear hoofbeats. They're coming to find us! Over here!" he called.

"Wait!" I said urgently, catching him right before he ran toward the sound of riders. "Wait! No one in our caravan has a horse. Camels and donkeys don't sound like that."

"But it doesn't matter," he protested. "They will help us."

I was not so sure. "Just keep quiet. Remember when we found the caravan that had been attacked by bandits?"

Michael's voice squeaked. "And murdered?" Now he looked like he wanted to run the other direction.

"They won't turn into this draw," I explained. "Get behind me. Crouch down and keep still till we see who it is. They won't see us if we stay below this ledge."

The clopping beat of horses being slowly ridden in file echoed off the canyon walls. I did not have to see them before scooting as far back into the shelter as I could. I recognized Zimri's voice. Clamping my hand over Michael's mouth, I hissed, "It's them— the bandits! Don't move!"

He gave a trembling nod, and I released his mouth but kept a hand on his shoulder.

Leading a troop of six riders, Zimri was in advance. The chief murderer did most of the talking, plotting an attack on a group of pilgrims heading west. He spoke of how they would launch the assault when the camp was asleep and the fires burning low. He talked of knifing the men in their bedrolls and carrying away the women and children as slaves.

I realized with a shudder he was speaking of our caravan. Biting my lip, I squeezed Michael's arm. We were almost safe. Half of the riders were already past our position.

Michael tapped me in the back of the head, then on my cheek. Was the boy trying to give away our position? Angrily, I shrugged away his touch. A moment later he tapped harder, drumming my face with his fingertips.

Pivoting away from the annoying slapping turned my face to the rock wall . . . and brought me eye-to-eye with a horned viper no more than three feet from my nose. The snake's tongue darted in and out, testing the air. He must have emerged from his den for a night's hunting.

Horned vipers are deadly poison.

The broad, fat, arrow-shaped head lifted from the stone shelf and swung slowly back and forth, as if deciding what to do about me. The serpent was three feet long. Father taught me they could strike more than half of their body length. I was safe for the moment . . . and then the snake slithered another foot forward.

The last rider in the line of bandits clucked to his mount. Lagging behind the others, he trotted to catch up. The snake heard the change in the rhythm and turned his ugly, evil snout toward the noise.

I waited, holding my breath, as the horsemen retreated down the canyon.

When the snake again fixed his unblinking gaze on me, I could not wait any longer. Seizing Michael, I lunged away from the rocks. We tumbled together onto the sand as the viper struck at empty space where my chin had been a moment before.

Now our line of travel had been decided for us: we scrambled quickly in the opposite direction taken by the bandits. By following the hoofprints in the sand, I knew we would emerge from the ravines eventually.

And, soon enough, we did.

"But we're still lost," Michael whimpered.

"Not for long," I corrected, inhaling the expanse of the heavens the same way I enjoyed breathing the open air. "Look," I urged my friend, "there's where the sun set. That star is the jewel on the forehead of Ophiuchus, the Snake Handler."

"Snake handler?" Michael repeated nervously.

"It's all right," I reassured him. "He's winning. I'll tell you that story some other time. But look, there's Mizar in the handle of the Plow. Halfway between Mizar and the jewel is our camp."

"How do you know?" Michael sniffed suspiciously.

I shrugged. "I just know. Besides, can't you smell the smoke of the cookfires? It's coming from that same direction. Hold my hand. We'll be there in less than an hour."

We spotted the dots of the campfires in only a few minutes and arrived safely well before my allotted time was up.

When we told of our near encounter with the bandits, and what we overheard, Michael's mother hugged him fiercely and gave me angry looks, but Hosea thanked me. The caravan captain ordered the guards to be doubled. Then he brought me more praises, together with my supper. I understood that I was not going to be punished for my foolishness.

Yacov brought in the flock of goats. Not one was missing. Even Beulah had somehow rejoined them, wagging and bleating like the picture of innocence.

Two Sabbaths later the mood around the caravan's cookfires was upbeat. So far the trip had been unusually easy, free from bad weather, bandits, and illness. There had been the normal difficulties of life on the trail: animals that pulled free of their pickets and wandered off in the night, straps that broke, dumping supplies and trade goods into the dirt, but nothing major.

"Tomorrow we reach the river," Hosea announced to a circle of families, traders, and drovers. "And the Almighty permitting, we will cross it."

"The Euphrates," I whispered to Michael. "It's the border between the Parthians and the Romans."

"Since Sabbath begins at sunset tomorrow," Hosea continued, "we will rest the night, the Sabbath day, and perhaps one day more. We reached here three days ahead of the best crossing I ever made, and we need to resupply and do mending. An extra day will do us good."

I slept next to the remains of the fire, beside Michael. Reena and her granddaughter, Beryl, snuggled together just beyond Michael. Raheb was snoring close to me. Sons Tobit and Yacov and their wives rested in a pair of canvas shelters one rank farther back.

Raheb's snoring awakened me. I blinked up at the panorama of stars, trying to recall what Rabbi Kagba had taught me about the sky this time of year. To the south the pale orange dot hovering above my big toe was Mars, what the rabbi had called Ma'Adim, the Adam.

I examined the starry pattern surrounding Mars. An owl hooted in some rushes off in a dry wash while I pondered. The constellation in which Mars hung was the Sign of the Two Fish. Some said its name linked the two kingdoms of the Jews: Israel and Judah.

But Rabbi Kagba, while agreeing with that position, also taught something more. He said the image of the fishes, their tails connected by a ribbon, was also a reference to the Jews and the Gentiles. The rabbi quoted the words of the Almighty about his anointed Messiah, as recorded by the prophet Isaiah: "It is too light a thing that you should be my servant to raise up the tribes of Jacob . . . I will make you as a light to the nations, that my salvation may reach to the end of the earth."[1]

Another owl called from the opposite side of the camp. An errant swirling breath of wind tugged a handful of sparks from the dying fire and tossed them aloft to glimmer beside Mars.

The bandit assault came from both sides of the camp at once. A dozen men, faces wrapped in scarves up to their eyes, wearing dark robes and brandishing short swords, charged in. They attacked in silence from the pitch-black surroundings before bursting into the pale light of the glowing embers.

I shouted and, in so doing, saved Raheb's life. A bandit slashed downward at Raheb's head but missed when my protector rolled out of the way. Jumping to his feet, Raheb parried a second blow with a stick of firewood.

Others in the camp were not so fortunate. Cries of pain echoed in the night.

Then the air was split by a trumpet blast. Hosea, an antelope horn to his lips, sounded the alarm. "Bandits! Up! Up and fight!" the caravan master shouted.

Now the night rang with the sound of blows given and received. Across the fire from me, Reena gathered Michael and Beryl to her.

Tobit and Yacov flanked their father, engaging the lone assailant with their swords, while their father hammered away at him with the chunk of wood. The bandit gave ground before their combined onslaught. The echoing alarm and the speed with which surprise had been lost disconcerted the attackers.

They were outnumbered by the men of the caravan by three or four to one.

A pair of camels, their ties slashed by the marauders, blundered into the scene. They trampled directly across the fire, scattering it and plunging the battle into even greater darkness.

Driven apart from Raheb and his sons by the animals, the bandit seized the moment to escape, but not empty-handed. Knocking Reena down with his shoulder, he grabbed Beryl and began to carry her away with him while the child kicked and screamed.

I launched myself at the kidnapper, tackling him around the knees and bringing the man down. Beryl rolled free and ran back to the protection of her grandfather.

The bandit raised his blade over my head. I winced and cried out, flinging up my arm to ward off the blow. Raheb's improvised wooden club pinwheeled across the intervening space, smashing into the attacker's head and his sword at the same moment, and felling him.

"Away! Get to the horses!" one of the bandits shouted.

In the next instant the assailants disappeared into the countryside, their black robes allowing the night to swallow them up. "Don't follow!" Hosea bellowed, then repeated himself to Tobit and his brother, who wanted to continue the battle. "I say, don't follow! Give them no chance to pick you off in the night. Stir up the fires. Post guards. Tend your wounded."

Of all of us in Raheb's camp only he had sustained any injury, and it was a slight cut on his arm. Our attacker, nose driven back into his skull, was dead.

Beryl, in the arms of her mother, was still whimpering with fright, but quieter now. All Raheb's family gathered around me. "Boy, I am in debt to you for two lives tonight," Raheb said. "For my own and for my granddaughter's. Command me. Anything of mine is yours."

The souk outside the walls of Damascus was a sprawling city in its own right. Camel-traders attempted to outshout grain merchants. Dealers in silk or spice or silver necklaces competed with each other for the attention of passersby from every corner of the Roman Empire and beyond. Next to Antioch, Damascus was the most important city in the Roman province of Coele-Syria, whose borders included the Jewish homeland of Judea.

Hosea spat noisily when he shared that fact with me. The idea that from an outpost of pagan Assyrians, a pagan Imperial Legate held authority over the Jewish Holy City was worse than distasteful to pious Jews. Then he shrugged. "Of course the Romans have great disdain for all things not Roman, not just Jewish. The present appointee, one Lucius Aelius Lamia, has never been to Syria, much less Jerusalem. They say he never leaves Rome."

Damascus existed at the juncture of the highway called Via Maris, which connected the lands of the East to the Sea of Middle Earth, and the King's Road, leading to the spices of Arabia. The mingling of Syrian dialects with the tongues of Cypriots, Armenians, Nabateans, and Ethiopians was overwhelming to the ear. A form of Greek was used as the trade language, but the sons of Abraham with whom we dealt spoke Aramaic and Hebrew as well.

Equally confusing to the senses were the sights and smells of the place. I stood in one spot, revolving slowly and gawking. "If Damascus were the ark after the Flood, Noah just opened the gates," I marveled. "Look at all the strange creatures."

"And pickpockets," Raheb observed wryly. "Don't forget them. Keep your coins and your wits about you, or someone will make off with them both."

At that instant a cry of "Stop! Stop, thief!" resounded from the direction of a dealer in dried fruit, proving Raheb's point. Few of the other tradesmen even bothered looking up. Most resumed their patter as soon as the disturbance faded into the distance.

I hitched the parcel containing the cup around so that it rode at the front of my waist.

The Roman authorities had little concern for either commerce or crime outside the walls. Inside Damascus, it was another story. Tramping squads of Roman soldiers scowled at everyone they met, as if daring us to resist their might.

"Damascus has a kind of independence," Raheb told me. "It is the northern-most city of those ten states called the Decapolis. The emperor likes the tax money he collects from here, so Rome's boot is lighter on its throat."

The emperor had even made an effort to show the regard Rome had for the local deity. An earlier temple to the god of the Assyrians, a storm god named Ba'al Hadad, had been dramatically expanded with Roman arches and columns. The structure was then rededicated under what the emperor said was Hadad's Roman name: Jupiter. Of course the statue dedicated to the worship of Caesar himself was larger and grander than Jupiter's.

"Rome is happy to appease the religious sensitivity of conquered people," Raheb observed with heavy sarcasm. "High Priest Caiaphas would probably let them do the same in Jerusalem if he thought he could get away with it."

Outside the pagan temple, merchants sold clay models of a squatting, bearded figure wearing a conical cap and bull's horns and holding a lightning bolt. It made the Assyrian god look like an angry dwarf. "Unless that's supposed to be Caesar," Hosea muttered under his breath.

I was relieved when we got back to our own circle of camels and tents and away from the clamor. I felt guilty somehow, as if carrying the Cup of Joseph into such an unholy place had further tarnished it.

I said as much to Raheb around the supper fire that night . . . leaving out the part about the cup, of course.

"Just remember," he warned me. "The Almighty cares for the Gentiles too. Didn't he send the prophet Jonah to warn Nineveh to repent? It was, by all accounts, an even more wicked city than Damascus."

Seated with our group and several other families for a supper of fragrant saffron rice and mouth-watering minced lamb, Hosea asked, "Does anyone have a story to share? About Damascus, I mean."

To the surprise of everyone, including myself, I waved my hand. "My teacher, Rabbi Kagba, told me a story of Damascus."

Bushy eyebrows raised, Hosea gestured for me to proceed.

"It was thirty-three years ago, he said. My rabbi, who studied the ancient writing, learned Messiah was about to be born in Judea. My teacher came through here on his way to Jerusalem."

I stopped, suddenly shy at the way the entire group, adults and children both, were silently, attentively listening.

"Is that all?" Michael said. "That's not a story."

I resumed. "It was here . . . in Damascus . . . that the rabbi met all the other scholars who were seeking the newborn king. Rabbi Kagba told me they all saw the sign of his birth in the sky while they were still on their journeys, before they met in Damascus."

Everyone glanced upward into the heavens. The blazing torches of the souk blotted out all the stars, except for a triangle of bright beacons hovering in the southwest . . . in the direction of Jerusalem.

"But at Jerusalem they found King Herod ruling still."

Hosea and Raheb both made sounds of derision at the mention of the Butcher King.

"After escaping Herod, they were guided by the star to a house in Bethlehem where they found him . . . the infant child."

I paused again.

"His name? Tell us his name, boy?"

"Jesus of Nazareth."

A profound silence existed over the group. No spoons clinked against bowls, no one spoke for the space of ten heartbeats, and then pandemonium broke loose.

"You mean the Healer," Raheb said.

"The Teacher? The Prophet?" Hosea added.

"The one we are going to seek?" Raheb continued. "You've known this all along and never spoke of it until now?"

"I . . . the rabbi sent me to find him too," I said. "But I wasn't sure if I should speak of it or not. Rabbi Kagba had heard that old Herod killed the boy babies of Bethlehem, trying to murder a challenger to his throne. The rabbi says Herod even killed his own sons."

Hosea nodded in agreement.

"That's why Jesus grew up in secret," I said. "But for three years my teacher has been hearing of the miracles and the wisdom of this Jesus." I waited again for the babbling to cease. "My teacher sent me to learn if the stories are true. To see for myself if Messiah has come."

"It is a question written very much on all of our hearts," Hosea acknowledged. "By the Feast of Dedication, we will know."

Chapter 20

*O*ur caravan camped beside a creek flowing down from Mount Hermon. Even though it would still take two more weeks to reach Jerusalem, I felt great excitement on this Sabbath. On the day after tomorrow we would enter the northern reaches of the Promised Land.

I was especially eager to set foot in Eretz-Israel. Soon I would see my grandparents and my brothers.

"From Dan to Beersheba, our land stretches," Hosea said when he announced our location. "Of course, King David ruled much farther north than this. And his son, Solomon, farther still. Now the country is all broken into little patches for this Herod or that Herod . . . but the land is still the land. It will all come right when Messiah comes to rule as King."

The *Havdalah* service had already concluded. Now a mixed group of northbound and southbound travelers swapped gossip by firelight. While the men talked politics, I visited with a pair of ten-year-old twin boys named Jachin and Sorek, who sometimes completed each other's sentences.

"We're going to Damascus," Jachin said.

Sorek concluded, "To see our uncle."

Hugging the pack containing the cup, I asked, "And you come from Jerusalem?"

"Near there," Jachin said. "Bethlehem."

"The place where the Temple lambs are raised," his brother explained.

Hearing the name of the village brought Rabbi Kagba's tale to my mind. "Isn't that where the prophet named Jesus was born?"

"Him? Naw, he's from . . ."

"Nazareth."

"But we saw him once," Jachin added. "Last year, at Tabernacles, I think."

"And you heard him speak?" I persisted.

"Sure," Jachin said. "But we didn't understand what he meant."

Sorek offered, "He said if anyone was thirsty they should come to him and drink. But he didn't have any water with him, not even a cup."

"And what did the grown-ups say to that?" I asked.

"Some of them think he's crazy," Jachin said.

"Some people say he's a prophet, and some say he's King Messiah," Sorek added.

Then Jachin concluded, "But the Pharisees and the priests don't think that. Not at all."

The air was very still that night as I slept . . .

The fronds of the date palms lining the road hung limp in the flickering firelight. The sky revolved overhead.

Eventually the easily recognized form of the Lion of Judah spun into view directly above me, accompanied by one of the seven lights. Awakened by no cause I could identify, I studied the stars. I thought the extra spark of light was Shabbatai but wasn't entirely certain. If the wandering star was in fact the Lord of the Sabbath, there was a close conversation going on between it and the star in the lion's paw called Regulus, the Little King.

"It was on just such a night that David studied the stars," a familiar voice commented. "Like tonight, Shabbatai was in the form of the Lion in those days too. But David's thoughts were on other things."

Even without asking the identity of the speaker, I said, "Hello, Joseph. So you have a story for me about King David?"

"You're already in it," the Dreamer corrected. "Look."

It was true. Without any noise or sense of motion, the caravan camp had vanished. The night sky was identical, including the presence of the Lord of the Sabbath, but now I lay on a hillside in front of a cave. The hilltop was fortified by a stone wall. Looming over the very crown of the knoll was a massive terebinth tree. In the distance the lights of a small village twinkled.

"Where are we?"

"This place is called Adullam," Joseph said. "Over there, those lights you see are Bethlehem."

"But why are we here?"

Joseph gestured for silence and pointed to a ledge a dozen feet away beside the tree trunk. Four men stood there, conversing by the light of a single torch. They were dressed as warriors, with swords by their sides and round shields slung across their backs. Three of the men wore conical metal helmets. The fourth was bareheaded and his hair, like his beard, was red.

The red-haired man spoke. "That's my home there," he said to the other men as he gestured toward the twinkling lights of Bethlehem. "I tended my father's sheep from the time I was eight or nine years old."

A fellow shepherd! I felt an instant connection to the speaker. A shepherd boy, grown into a warrior-king.

"I sometimes led the flock to pasture below this very spot," David continued. "Up here is a good place to watch over them. In those days there were lions in these hills. Bears too sometimes."

The description of the danger caused me to shiver and look over my shoulder. I wished Beni was nearby. I could always rely on the dog for warning.

"Back then, when I was kept many nights away from home," David said, "I looked at the lights, just as now, and dreamed of being back in Bethlehem. Do you know what I missed then? A drink of water from the well by the gate. It still seems to me that no water quenches my thirst like that water does." David shrugged. "The Philistines garrisoned there are worse than any lions or bears. Not only can they not be driven away as easily, but their presence in my home town feels evil to me."

The shepherd king's tired face showed longing, I thought.

David added, "I wish someone would get me a drink from that well!" Then he turned his back on the sight and entered the mouth of the cave.

David's three comrades exchanged looks and nods, but their captain did not witness the sign of agreement. From a stack of weapons beneath the terebinth, each of the three men selected a stout, oak-handled spear mounted with a forged, dagger-shaped blade.

One of the men raised his head and scanned the night, causing me to do the same. "Four hours till dawn," he said.

"Time enough," another agreed, and the three set off down the slope at a jogging pace. "Quiet and speed, yes?"

"Grab hold of my cloak," Joseph instructed me. "Unless you want to try running to keep up with them."

What followed this instruction happened with a rush. With no sense of fear, I found myself soaring over the Judean hills like a hawk on an updraft. Joseph and I spiraled toward the outline of the Lion of Judah, then downward again toward Bethlehem's glow.

"Watch!" Joseph urged.

Though very little time seemed to have passed, David's warrior companions were already on the outskirts of the City of David. Hidden in a creek bed, they waited until a pair of Philistine guards had passed, then burst out of concealment. As quickly as the sentries turned, they were stunned by blows from the spear shafts.

The three Jewish soldiers moved as a single shadow under the eaves of a cottage. Waiting until another sentry moved away, the three flitted across the intervening space toward a gated opening at the far side of the city wall.

I marveled at their bravery. By the light of a single watch fire I counted ten sleeping Philistines. Then I ticked off twenty similar watch fires before losing count. Two hundred of the enemy against three!

"There is the well," Joseph said.

A wooden frame held a leather waterskin balanced above a stone-encircled shaft. The well was near the city gate, but the area around was completely void of shelter or concealment.

Standing beside them in the darkness, I heard David's men converse. They were at the last building before the naked expanse of the village square. There were no guards in sight.

"I'll get the water," the leader of the three instructed, "while you keep watch."

When the loop of rope holding one end of the lever was released, the goatskin bag plunged into the well with a muffled splash. The trio of Jewish warriors froze for an instant at the sound. When no alarm followed, the leader hoisted the bulging container aloft.

Grasping the sack with one hand, he slashed the supporting rope with his sword. "That'll give them a surprise come morning," he said.

The men were halfway back across the open space toward where I stood when warning shouts rang out. "Captain! Two sentries down! Spies in the camp! Sound the alarm!"

A guard in a watchtower over the gate heard the cry and hammered on a shield with his sword. The clanging ripped apart the quiet of the night. Soon the alarm was raised in every corner of Bethlehem.

At the city gate the Jewish captain paused with the waterskin in hand. "Go on," one of his friends urged. "We'll make it hard for them to follow. Just don't spill it!"

Within moments a score of Philistines converged on the gate. The first rank was skewered on Jewish spears, making the others hesitate. Side by side, the pair of David's soldiers fought within the narrow confines of the gate where they could not be outflanked.

Swords rang against shields, and men cried out with pain. A heap of fallen Philistines clogged the portal and had to be dragged aside before fresh troops could continue the battle.

The Jewish soldiers agreed it was time to leave. I also urged them to go, but they could not hear me. "Let's go before they send a company around the outside of the wall behind us."

With final thrusts and slashes, the pair melted into the darkness and sprinted into the brush. Within seconds, it seemed to me, they overtook their leader toting the water bag.

"Back to the cave," Joseph warned. "Hang on."

After a swooping flight that would have done credit to a bat, we were back beneath the terebinth. David's men were already there. David stood beside them, examining the blood oozing from a dozen superficial wounds and calling for them to be attended and their injuries bandaged.

"Where is your cup, lord?" the leader of the trio requested.

Darting into the cave, David's servant emerged with a silver chalice.

"Yours?" I asked.

"And yours, cupbearer," Joseph confirmed.

Holding the cup at arm's length, David allowed his men to raise the waterskin and fill the gleaming container until it overflowed. Drips of water from David's well splashed my feet.

The shepherd king regarded the brimming chalice for a long time. At last he shook his head. Having the men step back a pace, David lifted the cup toward the now-graying sky. "To you, O Lord, I lift this cup." Then, as he poured it out on the ground at the base of the terebinth, he said, "Be it far from me, O Lord, to drink this. Is it not the same as the blood of these men, who went at risk of their very lives? May I ever be worthy of how you have blessed me with friends of such courage, loyalty, and sacrifice."

"See," Joseph instructed me, "where the water pools on the ground and mingles with the blood of David's warriors? Remember: even a cup of water may be a valuable offering. Remember: obtaining a drink of living water may be free and still be costly at the same time. Now wake up, Nehemiah."

"Wake up? I'm not asleep," I protested.

But it was Raheb who shook my arm and repeated the command. A yellow sun hung over the eastern hills. "Are you going to sleep all day?" my protector teased. "Let's get going. Only one more Sabbath till Jerusalem."

My first view of Jerusalem was exactly as my mother had described it to me in countless bedtime stories: "When you see it from afar, you think it's a snow-covered mountain, set with gold. Closer up, you'll see that people from everywhere in the world gather to see the Temple of the Almighty."

Then she added, "We have a reputation. No other people have a God so near and so attentive to their needs.

"If the wind is calm, the smoke of the sacrifices is a thick, black column, propping up the sky. And when the breeze carries it toward you, your mouth will water from the smell of roasting meat and spices. And oh, the music and the babble of voices. You could carry me all over the world, blindfolded, and put me down in Jerusalem, and I would know my home without looking!"

The sights and the sounds and the aroma: it was all true.

I also recalled how Mother frowned sometimes and admitted, "It isn't all wonderful there, Nehi. It is crowded. Some parts are very dirty, and you must be watchful for pickpockets and thieves." Brightening, she concluded, "But it's wonderful to be there, just the same. The Temple, the Temple! There is no other like it in all the world. And your grandparents will be so proud when they meet you. So very proud!"

Now that the moment of meeting was fast approaching, I hoped her words remained true. I was nervous about the news I carried but intensely eager to see them and my brothers.

It was late afternoon on the first day of Hanukkah when I parted from the caravan at the Damascus Gate. Hosea's charges had arrived at an inn outside the northern wall of the city. Raheb and his family were going to accompany me to the Street of the Weavers before saying good-bye.

However, just inside the battlements, patrolled by Roman sentries, we met a crowd of people flowing toward the Temple Mount. "Hold on, friend," Raheb said, accosting a passerby. "Is it time for the evening sacrifice? Is that why everyone is rushing?"

Squinting at the winter sun obscured by clouds, the man shook his head. "It's the rabbi from Nazareth," he explained. "He's teaching and healing up there on the mount. Everyone is going to watch and listen. Some say he may be arrested . . . or will flee. This may be our last chance to see him." Pulling free, the man dashed away with the multitude.

Gathering in a doorway out of the press of the throng, Raheb said, "You hear? He's there now—Jesus! Tobit, your eyes! We should go at once so we don't miss him." To me, he added, "Nehemiah? You'll come with us. Yes? You want to see Jesus too? We'll take you to the shop afterward."

I wanted to see Jesus . . . but I wanted my own family more.

"Just go," I offered. "I know my way from here. Mama taught me. It's this way," I said, pointing. "Two turns and the Street of the Weavers is right there. I can't miss it."

Raheb looked doubtful. "I don't think . . ."

"Please," I insisted. "I want you to. And I will see you again, I promise." Looking pointedly at the scarf wound around Tobit's head, shielding his damaged eyes, I concluded, "You must not miss Jesus."

After that, our good-byes were brief. Michael hugged me, said he'd never forget me. Raheb and his sons told me I had been a great blessing to them on the trail. Raheb renewed his vow that even after paying my debt to the caravan, he still owed me far more than he could repay for rescuing his granddaughter.

All the time their eyes returned to the Temple Mount. The air rang with the clatter of sandals going to see the Healer.

"Go on!" I said again.

And they were gone.

I made my way up the crowded Street of the Weavers. Every caravansary and inn and private house was bursting with travelers who had come for the holiday. I was lucky. I knew I had a place to stay. I imagined knocking on the door of my grandparents' shop and meeting them for the first time. What a celebration there would be!

A sudden breeze coursed through the narrow lane like icy water in a river. Snowflakes swirled like downy feathers around me.

The faces of travelers turned up in wonder as they trudged through the unusual weather. Hands extended, palm up, to catch the flakes. Children tasted frozen water for the first time. It was a sort of miraculous sign to many who believed that any unusual storm or event in nature was sent by God as a message from heaven. What was the Lord saying on this snowy afternoon in Jerusalem? To religious Jews, pure white covering Jerusalem was the Lord's promise that Israel's sins, though as scarlet, would soon be made as white as snow. What else could it mean?

Not all considered the weather a blessing, however. Few beggars were in sight; the storm had driven them underground. I spotted Herodian and Roman soldiers scattered among Jewish travelers. Many had come to the Street of the Weavers to shop for heavy winter cloaks. My fleece boots and sheepskin coat protected me from the chill. I was dressed as the son of a shepherd would dress in winter. It was fortunate that when I had fled I was clothed in the proper gear of a cold mountain autumn. Even so, my nose and ears were cold.

I pitied the ragged street urchins in tattered clothes who made their living as torch bearers and who lived in the quarries beneath the Temple Mount. A half-dozen boys about my age clustered around a feeble scrap wood fire burning on the street in a metal pot. The boys were known as link boys or Jerusalem Sparrows, a poor and too plentiful flock. As pilgrims passed the boys called out, offering to serve as city guides. It was not yet dark enough for travelers to need torches, so business was bad for them. The Sparrows kept one another warm by huddling close.

I thought about the Messiah I had come to find, the king named Jesus whom Rabbi Kagba had knelt before. Was Jesus in Jerusalem too? Did he raise his face to the sky and smile as snowflakes clung to his beard? Rabbi Kagba had seen him as a baby during this same season when snow had fallen on Bethlehem and the Hanukkah lights had blazed in the Temple. I knew every detail of the story, including the horrific slaughter of Bethlehem's babies by Herod.

Thirty-three years had passed since the birthday of the Son of David. Not much had changed. The Romans were still here. The Herodian guard patrolled the crowds of Jerusalem. Where was this man called Jesus who would drink from Joseph's cup and lead our people to freedom? Rabbi Kagba had taught me that when Jesus was crowned, there would be no more suffering or poverty.

I searched faces, but no one looked kingly to me. The poor were everywhere. Clearly King Jesus was not yet on his throne.

Snow crunched beneath my feet. I tucked my chin deeper into my coat as my anticipation grew. I felt as if I knew this lane well. My mother's stories of her home had prepared me for the noise and the bustle of Hanukkah pilgrim crowds. Merchants were removing woolen cloth, heavy wool cloaks, and finished prayer shawls from the fronts of shops. I knew from my mother that I would find my grandparents' business was the best and the busiest, always crowded and prosperous. I imagined her here as a little girl, and my longing for her became almost unbearable. I refused to let myself cry. I was too big for that. I had been through too much to give in now. Only a few minutes more and my grandmother would wrap her arms around me. *Did she look like Mama?* I wondered.

Mama had mentioned the smells of the city. But today the white blanket of snow hid the sheep dung and garbage littering the pavement and filled cracks and crevasses until rough-hewn stones were smooth. Along with the scent of damp wool cloaks, the fresh, familiar tang of snowfall reminded me of winter in my mountain home.

In the midst of the holiday crowds, the pristine meadows and pine trees of my homeland seemed another world away. I wondered about my mother and father. For the first time I considered how I would tell my brothers and my grandparents about the bandit attack and my adventures as I traveled to Jerusalem. I would not be able to report as to the fate of my mother and father. Would my brothers think I was a coward for running away? Would they believe me if I told them about Joseph's cup, the Great White Hart, and my thousand-mile trek to find the Messiah? I hoped they would not be angry that I had not returned to the camp to find out if my parents were alive.

Even so, I was energized by the excitement of seeing my brothers again and meeting my grandparents for the first time.

"Fourth shop from the high end of the Weavers," I recited, navigating the final steps carefully so as not to slip on paving stones.

The light in the sky grew dim. I looked to the top of the street and counted down. "One . . . two . . . three . . . four!"

I gasped and halted in my tracks. The little shop of Boaz the Weaver was gutted from fire. A white carpet of new-fallen snow in front of the charred door had no footprints.

I had traveled one thousand miles! It could not be that I had come so far for nothing!

I counted doors from the head of the street again. "One, two, three!" Tears brimmed over. I wiped them away with the back of my hand.

Plucking at the sleeve of a heavily cloaked woman, I cried, "I am looking for the shop of Boaz the Weaver! Do you know—"

"Burned down." She jerked her thumb toward the shell. "'Twas the finest weaver on the street. Some say 'twas no accident."

"But . . . are they all dead?"

She mumbled on. "Murder, if it was set deliberate. One perished in the disaster."

"One dead! Who?"

Her tone was matter-of-fact. Old news. Grief over and done with. "It was a visiting grandson what died. Roof fell in on him."

One of my brothers, dead! I stared in horror at the fallen beams and scorched stone. "Which? What was his name?"

"Lord above, I couldn't say. Big family it was. So many of them."

"Where are the others?"

The woman stared at me with sudden interest. "And who are you?"

"When did it happen?" I had imagined the reunion with such joy.

"Autumn. Around Tabernacles. But . . . who are you that it matters?"

Tears streaked my cheeks. No holding them back. "I'm Nehemiah. Youngest son of Lamsa and of Sarah, who used to weave here in her father's shop. I'm grandson of Boaz the Weaver whose shop this was. My three brothers were here . . . It was . . . You speak of my brother and the fire! Dead in the fire! But which brother? Do you know the name?" Images of my older brothers at our parting so long ago flooded my memory. Who could imagine that we would never see one another again?

She considered me in stunned silence. "You! Here? Son of Sarah! And herself married a herdsman from Babylon. Herself gone so long and so far away. Don't know which grandson it was that died. There are more than a few grandsons. You know that well enough. It's a big clan. Where is your mother, boy?"

I could not take my eyes from the rubble. "I . . . I don't know," I whispered. "My grandfather Boaz. My grand-mother . . . Mama lived here. I know the stories. Fourth door from the top of the Street of Weavers. I came to find them. My family. My brothers. Please! Can you help me?"

"They've gone away, I heard, to live near your mother's sister."

"But where?"

She clucked her tongue. "You poor child. Where's your mother? Your father? I imagine they aren't far from you, eh? Well, it'll be hard news for them."

"My mother has many sisters. Where are my grandparents? My grandfather? Boaz the Weaver? Please tell me if you know."

"Sorry. Can't say. Don't know. Not sure. Gone to the sea-shore, I heard. Lost everything. Some reason for the bad fortune, no doubt. Punishment doesn't come without a reason. So. You never know."

Anger against her welled up in me. How could she say such a thing? Accuse so unjustly? What had my father and mother done wrong to deserve an attack by bandits? What had I done wrong to lose my family and my pleasant life? "You are wrong! And it's wrong to say such a thing!"

She raised her head indignantly and sniffed the wind. "I see you are an insolent, prideful boy. Pride. Reason enough for the House of Boaz to burn down over his head. Tell your mother and father when they come. Go to the elders at the Temple. Your grandfather's prayer shawls . . . famous, as you know. Your family was very proud of that, I am sure." She sniffed. "Someone among the priests will no doubt have the details of where they've gone. Where to find them." She brushed her hands on her skirt, indicating our conversation was over. "You should learn to respect your elders, or worse than this will come upon you. Even so . . . I am sorry for your bad fortune, boy." She scurried off, leaving me alone in the middle of the darkening street.

Chapter 21

*T*he gloom of twilight settled over the Street of the Weavers. I sank onto a cold, blackly charred beam in the ruins of my grandfather's shop and wept. Months of longing and hope for reunion with my family were turned to ashes beneath my feet. I felt the presence of death in this place where my brother died. Which brother? Who among the three was no longer living? In my imagination I lived the deaths of each. I tried to picture my world without them.

I touched Joseph's cup, wrapped in the bag beneath my cloak. Oh, the suffering of all who had drunk from this cup! I closed my eyes a long moment. When I opened them again, I saw the city in a new way. The world around me had a sharpness of detail I had never seen before. Death had brought a new clarity to life. Beyond the shattered walls of my grandfather's shop, crowds thinned and businesses were shuttered.

As it darkened, Hanukkah candles appeared in the windows of homes and businesses. The warm glow and companionship of the orphan Sparrows' fire beckoned me. Several boys lit their torches and hailed travelers, leading them away from the Street of the Weavers. I climbed out of the destruction of my life and made my way down the steps to the watch fire.

Four Sparrows remained, warming hands and backsides

when I approached the blaze. Their torches were yet unlit, propped against a wall. Potential customers seemed fewer than ever. I hesitated just beyond the ring of light. Surly young faces lifted. Eyes narrowed with suspicion. They stared at me, hating me for the warmth of my fleece coat and mountain boots.

The leader, a gaunt boy of about eleven, considered me. "You want a torch, or what?"

A red-haired boy about my age rubbed his hands together. "He don't want a torch. He's been up the street there, visiting ghosts."

Two dark-haired boys, whom I guessed to be brothers, exchanged a glance. "Ghosts?"

Their red-haired companion nodded. "He's been up in the ruins of the weaver Boaz. Ain't you, kid?"

I nodded.

The leader tilted his head and took a step toward me. "You're not from around here. Not with such a coat and warm boots. Where are you from?"

I answered, "From the land where Eden used to be. Paradise . . . north of Babylon. The great mountains beyond the two rivers."

"I am Timothy," said the leader. "That is Red. On account of his hair. And these brothers are Obed and Jesse. Their father was a religious sort before the Romans killed him."

"I am called Nehi. Nehemiah. But Nehi to all who know me."

"Why are you here?" the brothers asked in unison.

"My family." The words caught in my throat.

Red asked, "What was you doing in the ruins of the weaver's shop?"

I could barely speak. "My mother grew up there. It belonged to my grandfather and his father on back for generations."

Timothy raised his chin. "So, are you related to Boaz?"

Red echoed the question. "Your mother? She the daughter of old Boaz and his wife?"

I nodded. "Boaz. My grandfather. I came all this way to find them."

Red snorted. "Well, you come here for nothing. They've been gone awhile. I seen the fire. Never seen anything burn so hot or fast. There was a young man died in it too. Burned up. Horrible thing. Screaming for help. No help for it. A grandson. What relation of yours?"

"Please. Do you know the name of the boy who was killed?"

The four Sparrows exchanged looks, but none had an answer. "Sorry."

"I had three brothers," I replied hoarsely. "Now I have two. But I don't know which one died."

This revelation brought silence to us all. I held my palm over the fire, then drew it back quickly. Too close to the heat. I imagined . . .

The leader cleared his throat. "Your grandparents were good to us boys, always. She, the lady, brought us fresh bread sometimes. Not crumbs or scraps, but real hot, steamy, fresh bread."

"She was good to us," the brothers agreed.

Red added, "I suppose we should return the favor. What are your plans, Nehi?"

"I don't have any plans now." I glanced toward the ruins. "There is what is left of my plans."

The leader puckered his brow. "Nice coat and boots. You'll be warm enough."

"I am grateful to the Eternal. Grateful for . . ." Though I was grateful for my warm clothes, the grief I felt made gratitude for anything else difficult.

Red asked, "Where will you sleep tonight?"

I shrugged. "Don't know."

Timothy instructed, "Stay with us, then. We are going to the Temple Courts tonight. They'll be lighting the giant Menorah and giving out bread to everyone after the service."

"We share what we get, see?" Red said. "If I get a crust, but you get a whole loaf, we share equal. Get it?"

One of the brothers spoke. "And you can sleep with us Sparrows in the quarry afterward. It's the least we can do, seeing how your grandmother fed us. We have charcoal fires there to warm us, and we divide the bread among ourselves."

Red put his arm around my shoulder. "Come on, then. You've come to the right place."

I could not speak to thank them. The lump in my throat made it hard to swallow. I had gone from being alone and friendless to being taken in and cared for by the orphan boys whom my grandmother had cared for.

It was because of free bread that I missed meeting Jesus of Nazareth that very night. The brothers, unlit torches in hand, wanted to immediately find fares to guide.

Red and Timothy argued against it: "If you come too late, the loaves will be all gone. Every beggar in Jerusalem will be on the steps below the Royal Porch."

As the brothers scampered away in the gathering gloom, Jesse retorted over his shoulder, "We heard there's a band of pilgrims coming in from Bethany tonight. We'll earn enough pennies to buy our own bread!"

When I questioned Red about it, he replied there was no reason not to have both bread and pennies, so he and Tim and

I set out. At the far south end of the Temple Mount, a group of Pharisees distributed barley loaves. It was a *mitzvah* to provide for the needy, and the Pharisees made a great show of it. An assembly of the ultra-pious fraternity, in sumptuous robes and broad phylacteries, gathered on the steps between two passageways. They looked on from some distance away as their servants tended wicker baskets of round, hard bread. When each container was emptied, a trumpet blew to signal that another full vessel had been uncovered.

As we waited in a line of beggars, Tim remarked in a low voice, "The bread doesn't taste worse because they blow their trumpets over it."

"The Pharisees always salt their gifts that way," Red added with a grin.

I was warm enough in my cloak and boots, but my friends stomped their feet and clapped their hands as we waited in the cold. The file of waiting supplicants snaked back and forth across the steps. It moved forward very slowly.

As we neared the front of the line, someone hurriedly approached the largest Pharisee. The man's sandals clattered on the steps in his haste. "He's there now," I heard the man say. "Solomon's Colonnade."

Three of the Pharisees gathered in conference. It was then I overheard them mention the name Jesus.

"Jesus of Nazareth?" I repeated.

"Has to be," Tim said. "Look at how agitated the fat Pharisee is."

"Jesus is here? Now?"

"Other side of the mount," my friend said. "You want to see him?"

I nodded eagerly.

"Come on, then." Darting around the three people ahead of us in the queue, Red snatched up two loaves of bread and shouted a thank-you while Tim secured one more.

"This way," Red urged. "In here."

There were two tunnels in the south face of the Temple Mount, called the Huldah Gate in honor of the prophetess. These passages led beneath the Royal Porch. Sloping steeply upward, they opened onto the Temple plaza at the south end of the Court of the Gentiles.

We emerged from corridors choked with the smoke and soot of flickering torches to be blasted by cold air. Snow had begun to sweep across the expansive courtyard. The plaza was brightly lit by four towering menorahs. Shining in the lamplight, swirling showers of snow formed lazy spirals. Leaning back, I looked up. The descending pillars of icy crystals reached into the sky like ghostly fluted columns.

"But where is he?" I said with frustration.

"This way," Tim urged, and we sprinted on. We hugged our loaves of bread as we ran. I kept one hand on Joseph's cup.

From a distance I heard the Levite choirs singing hymns of praise and thanksgiving. I saw a crowd of people jammed between the shuttered booths of the moneychangers and the columned portico lining the eastern rim of the court.

"There." Red pointed. "He'll be in the middle of that mob."

"Wait," Tim warned, laying his hand on my arm to stop my headlong charge. "Temple guards."

A dozen green-uniformed and helmeted sentries marched with purpose toward the assembly. Reaching the back of the throng, they roughly thrust the onlookers aside.

"What? What's happening?" I demanded, tugging against Tim's restraint.

"You know the high priest doesn't like this Jesus," Tim said.

"Looks like they're going to arrest him for sure," Red added.

"Arrest the Messiah? Why?"

Yanking me around in front of him, Tim demanded, "What do you know about it? You said you just got here."

"Yes, but I . . . I have to see him."

I was too late.

Fearful of the scowling guards, the crowd dispersed.

Red gestured to the pair of brother Sparrows who edged toward them. "What's happened?" he asked as they drew near.

"Jesus, the rabbi from Galilee," one brother said. "He was with the folks from Bethany. They hired us to link for them."

"The priests was going to arrest him," the other sibling explained.

"Or kill him. Said he was a blasphemer. We was standing near him."

"That's how we helped. We saw the guards and snuffed out our torches . . . and Jesus slipped away."

"Away," I repeated in distress. I could not locate my family, and now I had let my mission slip away as well. "Where's he gone?"

"Why does it matter?" Red asked. "He's escaped."

I started to explain, then stopped as I spotted the embroidered hem of a prayer shawl flapping in the breeze. That bright blue band with the scalloped rim embroidered with white letters of the *Shema* was my mother's workmanship. There could not be two shawls that much alike.

Pulling free of Tim's hand, I approached the young man wearing the shawl and tugged at his arm. "Sir," I said, "that tallith. Did you get it at the shop of Boaz?"

The tall, aristocratic-looking man smiled. "In fact I did. Why do you ask?"

"Because I am their grandson. I am Nehemiah. Called Nehi. I just came here from beyond the two rivers to find them." It was too difficult to explain, and I waved my hand in frustration.

"By your accent I knew you are from the East," the man said.

"My mother, Sarah, is their daughter. I didn't know their shop had burned. Do you know . . . can you tell me . . . where my family has gone?"

Again the smile. "It so happens, I can. My shawl . . . your mother's work, yes? Her skill sought after and well known. I ordered it a year and a half ago and received delivery only weeks before the fire. So, Joppa. On the seacoast. Staying near relatives. Does that help?"

"Yes. My aunt, Mother's older sister, lives there. Her husband, Adonijah, is an exporter of woolen cloth."

"I know Adonijah, the fabric exporter. Your aunt and uncle live near the custom house at the quay."

"One more thing, sir. They say one of my brothers . . . perished in the fire. Do you know . . . I mean, I don't even know which . . ."

Sorrow clouded the cheerful face. "I heard someone had been lost, but no, I'm sorry. I don't know his name." He gazed at me intently. "Nehemiah, do you have a place to stay, boy?"

Looking back at the row of raggedly dressed Sparrows, an elbow peeking out of a rent in a cloak here and a knee showing through a hole there, I knew I could not desert them. "Yes," I said. "I am with friends."

"Very well, then. Should you need me, my name is Joseph of Arimathea . . . the Younger. The Sparrows are clever. They can find my home if you need me. And since it's too cold for many fares tonight, boys, here." Joseph shook a leather bag of coins over each upturned palm, dispensing pennies, then met my eyes again. "Joppa," he said again. "You'll find them."

He turned to go. The snow was falling harder now, obscuring the flames of the menorahs.

"One more thing, please," I pleaded. "Rabbi Jesus. Do you know where he's gone?"

"After tonight," Joseph said, casting an angry glance toward a knot of priests pushing beggars out of the way in their haste to escape the cold, "I believe he would be wise to leave Jerusalem. What his destination might be . . ." He sighed and we parted.

Timothy rubbed his cheek as he considered the departing merchant. The prayer shawl billowed in the breeze like the lifted wings of a soaring bird. "So, Joseph of Arimathea knows your family. I'm impressed. He is a rich man. You are well connected. Why would you choose to stay with us rather than in his mansion?"

I shrugged. "You said you would share the bread with me. I've been looking forward to it all night."

"Well then. Come on." Red clapped me on the back. "Bread and pennies, see? And a nice warm cavern to go home to."

I felt safe in the company of the link boys. Their torches lit the way for us as we made our way down the slick paths to the caverns beneath the Temple Mount.

Red locked arms with mine. We held one another steady. He explained the working of the Sparrows' charity as we descended into the vast shelter. Solomon's quarry was reserved for the orphan sons of Jerusalem.

By decree of the ruling seventy of the Sanhedrin, Solomon's former stone quarry was a shelter for torch-bearing Sparrows

from the ages of about five to twelve. In recent years, after bul-
lying and abuse had increased among the population, married
couples who were servants of righteous families took turns living
in the cavern as custodians. These were called shepherds. The
shepherds' tent was erected inside at the center of the quarry.
Outside the tent flap a fire blazed in a rock-lined pit like the
hub of a wheel. From the center, smaller camp fires spread like
spokes. The number of Sparrows varied. This month Red told
me there were just under two hundred boys. These were orga-
nized and grouped by age. The youngest and most vulnerable
children slept nearest the main fire and the overseers' tent. *They
were like the lambs in my father's lambing caves*, I thought, as we
neared the entrance of the shelter.

We approached a row of latrines outside and stopped to use
them.

Timothy explained, "It's not so bad. We all contribute our
wages. Work crews of boys haul water and wash clothing. The
older boys cook and help distribute bread. Torches are donated by
the Temple charity. That fellow you met, Joseph of Arimathea,
is a big contributor."

I involuntarily touched Joseph's cup tied at my waist. I
pondered the fact that, just like Joseph of old and his coat
of many colors, I had met a man named Joseph who now
wore my mother's finest prayer shawl. *Did it mean something?* I
wondered.

"Our fares are set by law," Red continued. "Nobody dares
cheat us these days. We get paid when we carry our torches.
Whoever don't pay gets hauled up before the judges and whipped."

Timothy coughed into his hand. "It's better now than when
I first came. In the spring, when the days get longer, we don't
have so much business. The farmers come, and lots of boys get

hired to work outside the city. Lucky ones get apprenticed in trades."

Red pantomimed a hammer blow. "I'd like to be a blacksmith. Work by a forge. Never be cold again. That's what I'd like. But . . . it's not so bad."

Timothy plucked my sleeve. "Except we have no one . . . not like a family. Not like somebody like you. A shepherd's son. What a coat. And such boots."

Red agreed. "If you was on your own, going to Joppa, there's some in the pass who would kill you for such a coat and boots. But not here. They can't hurt you here."

Again my thoughts went to the danger of travel and the offer of Joseph of Arimathea to help me. Perhaps I should speak with him again.

The Sparrows' cavern was dimly lit by the fires. Smoke curled lazily upward and drifted like mist against the blackened stone ceiling. Groups of Sparrows made their nests in fresh straw.

I followed my new friends to the shepherds' tent, where we placed our bread into heaping baskets for distribution.

Timothy said over his shoulder, "You know what I heard about Jesus? The one you're so keen to meet? He fed five thousand people with five loaves of bread and two fish."

Red shook his head in disbelief. "We sure could use someone like him here in Jerusalem."

"Aye," Timothy agreed. "But no wonder the priests hate him so. If even half the rumors are true about Jesus, he makes them and all their fine charity look small, don't he?"

Red argued, "Don't know why he doesn't just call down fire from heaven, if he's the Messiah like they say. He healed a blind beggar named Peniel, who begged his whole life at Nicanor

Gate. If he can give Peniel eyes, why can't he make bread grow from trees?"

I asked, "Why don't you follow him and see for yourself?"

The boys exchanged an uneasy look. Timothy explained, "You know what would happen if we left our place to follow Jesus?"

Red blurted, "They'd throw us out, just like they did to poor Peniel after he could see. The elders chased him out of Jerusalem. Told him to never come back to synagogue! Threatened his parents. He was disowned. If us Sparrows went out the gates even one time to meet Jesus? When we came back, our places would be gone. There'd be some other boy carrying my torch."

"It ain't worth it."

"No. Ain't worth it," Red echoed. Dozens of fellow link boys hailed my friends as we passed. This was a sort of family. They were brothers, united by suffering and loneliness. They were bonded, just as the shepherds' families who watched my father's flocks were bonded to one another. I realized this was the one haven of safety for orphans in the vast and dangerous city. For a Sparrow to lose his place beside the fires of Solomon's quarry was to lose everything.

We washed in a common trough and then made our way to the circle of twenty-five boys, where Timothy and Red introduced me all around. Then we heaped up clean straw to make our beds.

My stomach growled. "How much longer?"

Red raised a finger. "The last of the brothers will be returning soon. We count them all. Timothy is captain of our circle. He will count and report. We don't eat until we're all in the roost, so to speak. Not one is left out."

Minutes ticked past, and stragglers arrived at the cave one

by one. They snuffed out their torches and picked their way through their companions settling into their home group.

It was late, and baskets of bread had yet to be divided and distributed. I was exhausted from grief and disappointment. Hunger gnawed at my belly and kept me awake. I fixed my gaze on the shepherds' tent, waiting for an adult to emerge and take charge.

"When?" I asked again.

Timothy shrugged, counted the boys in our circle, then stood. "Wait here," he instructed. He made his way toward the bread baskets outside the overseers' tent. Waiting in a line of other captains, he seemed confident and undisturbed by hunger pains. At last an elderly couple emerged. The white-haired man raised his hands and blessed the meal, then took charge of distributing a half loaf for each Sparrow to our captains.

Red said, "If all your family is dead, maybe you can come here. Come live with us all. Become a Sparrow."

I gave a half smile and thanked him for the invitation.

From here and there in the cave I heard the sound of coughing. It was hard to imagine being sick without my mother to tend me. I tried to imagine living the lonely life of a boy in Solomon's quarry. A hush of anticipation fell over the cavern.

My eyes stung with tears as I took my bread from Timothy. What if all my family was dead? Or what if I couldn't find them? I remembered my mother's cooking in the sheep camp. Meat roasting over the fire. Sometimes trout. Fresh bread slathered with butter. Vegetables. Nuts and dried fruit. Rich cheese.

I held the crust of bread in my hands and tried to be thankful. How I longed for Mama's gentle voice and sweet prayers for me as she lit the *Shabbat* candles.

Timothy sat down cross-legged beside me. "What are you

staring at? This isn't bread Jesus conjured up. Looking at it won't make it grow bigger." He tore at his morsel. "Eat!"

I nodded and raised the scrap of supper to my mouth. It was tasteless and stale. The generosity of the Temple charity was somehow tarnished by the lack of quality of the bread. But when a boy was starving, he would not complain.

I studied Red as he picked off small mouthfuls and seemed to savor each bite. Behind, in the ring of younger boys, some- one began to cough with the force of a barking dog.

Timothy paused but did not raise his eyes. After a while he replied, "It's the season when so many boys get sick. The sick- ness carries many away." Then he leaned close to me. "Nehi, get away from here. Quickly. Tomorrow. Go see the man who wears your mother's prayer shawl. Beg a favor of him. An escort to Joppa. Find your family if you can. Leave this place."

Chapter 22

*T*he day was cold, the air clear and biting. Blackened snow, fouled with soot and grit and churned into slush underfoot, was heaped in corners and alleyways. Only the parapets surrounding the roofs and the tops of walls enclosing terraces and gardens still boasted coats of pure white.

Red, Timothy, and I stood outside the gates of the manor belonging to Joseph of Arimathea, the Younger. It was set just inside the wall of the Holy City, on a hill atop Jerusalem's far southwestern border. The home was modest in comparison to the palace of High Priest Caiaphas, or that of another Pharisee named Nicodemus, both of whose dwellings we had passed in coming from the caverns. Yet those grand homes were near enough to be called neighbors. The finely fitted amber sandstone of this wall and the ornate scrollwork of this gate proclaimed the wealth of the family within.

I was at my destination, but now I hesitated. My fingers touched the knob of a bell pull that hung beside the gate. I flinched away from the chilly brass and stopped.

"Go on," Timothy urged. Guessing at the cause of my reluctance, he added, "He said you could call on him for help."

I offered a crooked grin. "That was kind of him." Sweeping

one hand across my shepherd's garb, I continued, "But this is daylight. Do I look like I belong inside these walls?"

"So he gives us each another penny and tells us to go away," Red said pragmatically. "Go on, ring it. If you don't, I will."

Plucking up my courage, I gave the rope a tug. We heard no corresponding signal from within.

"Harder!" Timothy ordered.

This time a melodious jangling sounded inside the enclosed courtyard, followed immediately by the rhythm of swiftly tapping feet. We heard the sliding swish of a bolt being withdrawn. The portal was opened by a pleasant-faced woman older than my mother, but of the same size and build, and about the age I guessed my grandmother to be.

"Bless me," she said, running her eyes over the three of us, then fixing her gaze on me. "However did you get here so soon? And where have you left Abel?"

"Ma'am?" I said. "Is this the home of Joseph the Younger?"

"Of Arimathea the Younger," Timothy corrected.

"Aren't you the link boys I sent Abel to summon?"

I was baffled and then grateful when Timothy responded as our leader. With a bow he indicated Red and himself. "We have the honor to be Jerusalem Sparrows. At your service. But we don't know of any summons, nor were we sent here by anyone named Abel."

"Then why have you come?" she asked, bending forward. Her brow furrowed, but it displayed the same good-natured lines as her smiling mouth. Suddenly her expression cleared, and she put her knuckles on her hips. "Wait! What did you say your names were?"

"I'm Timothy, this is Red, and the one we guided here . . .

the one who is seeking admittance . . . is Nehemiah of Amadiya."

She laughed then, a peal of laughter that rivaled the chimes of the bell pull.

The youthful form of Joseph of Arimathea, again wearing my mother's unique handiwork, emerged from the home's entry across the courtyard. "Hadassah? Have they come? I want to send for—" As his eyes lighted on me, he stopped.

Grasping my shoulders, Hadassah pulled me in front of her, facing the young master. "I believe you wanted to locate Nehemiah, grandson of Boaz the Weaver?" she said.

The housekeeper ushered us into the receiving room of the home, where I encountered still more surprises: Raheb and his son Tobit, from the caravan, were also there!

"So now our party is complete, I think," Joseph said. "But perhaps explanations are called for."

The mystery was soon unraveled. Joseph said, "I did not realize you had traveled with my friends. Otherwise I would have insisted that you come home with me. You see, my father is partners in business with Raheb here, and the two of them with Lazarus of Bethany."

I was listening to the explanation, but I could not stop staring at Tobit's face. There were no bandages, and his eyes were not watering or red or puffy.

"They were in the group from Bethany I met on the Temple Mount," Joseph continued. "And they have been staying in the Bethany home where Jesus of Nazareth has also been residing. I think Tobit may want to add something."

Both Tobit and his father wore wide grins.

"Healed me!" Tobit responded. "I knelt beside Jesus. He

dabbed my eyes with mud, then told me to go and wash. Now I can see perfectly!"

"And Dinah, my boy Yacov's wife," Raheb added cheerfully, "says she believes she will be barren no longer. Says when she touched the fringe of the rabbi's tallith she felt something change, knows it."

I had missed my own encounter with Jesus of Nazareth. "That is truly amazing, wonderful news," I said. Then I asked Joseph, "But you sent for me, sir?"

He smiled. "I thought about it all the way home from the service. It is not an easy or a safe road for a boy to travel to Joppa alone. I have a load of exports I'm taking to a ship waiting there. You can go with me. Two more days, and then on your way."

Two days, and Jesus no farther away than a home in Bethany? "You are very kind. Thank you." I could see Jesus, complete my mission, and then locate my family in Joppa. I said as much to the group.

Raheb shook his head. "They've gone. The teacher and his band of students."

"Gone where? Gone far?"

"Far enough, I suppose," Raheb explained. "The other end of the country. Up to Perea, they said. Complete wrong direction from Joppa altogether."

Once more I found myself part of a caravan, but it was a far cry from tramping through the brush, herding goats. Joseph of Arimathea rode a fine, prancing sorrel horse at the head of a file of ten camels loaded with trade goods. This was a wealthy commercial venture, carrying the wines of Bethany for shipment abroad. Wicker baskets strapped to the flanks of the camels each contained amphorae of the latest vintage.

There were no straggling drovers coaxing lame animals, nor any lost children to be accounted for. The journey from Jerusalem to the sea coast would be completed in two days, rather than the weeks I had spent on the trail from Zakho. Instead of walking, I was mounted on a cooperative red-haired donkey named Esau. The bindings securing the fleece pad on which I rode were silk. Though still dressed in my thick coat and shepherd's boots, I felt like a prince.

We were accompanied by Terah, Joseph's steward. All the camel drovers were armed with short swords. Counting myself, we made a party of thirteen. As one of the main highways in Judea, the road from Jerusalem to Joppa was patrolled by Roman legionaries, a party of whom overtook us in quick march. The Roman officer, a centurion on a black horse, saluted Joseph as he rode by.

After we passed a village identified for me by Joseph as Emmaus, we entered a narrow, rock-walled canyon. The track descended rapidly from the heights of Jerusalem.

"This is the same route Joshua followed when he routed the Amorites," Joseph observed. "And the same course Judah Maccabee came up when he launched the great battle near Emmaus and freed our land from the Greeks."

I was surprised when, a mile later, the road climbed back out of the gorge, crossing the summit of a row of hills to its south.

Once atop the ridge, we paused to let the animals rest. Joseph handed me a bottle of water flavored with lemon juice and a sesame seed cake dripping with honey and scented with cinnamon.

We rested beside a shining bronze plaque affixed to a stone

pylon. Even though I had never been on this road before, I did not need to see the newly placed mile marker to know we were on a recently completed Roman road. The perfectly smooth, level, cobblestone surface, bordered on both sides by curbing, attested to the efforts of the Empire.

"Say what you like about the Romans," Joseph confided in me, "but they are superior engineers. The two greatest needs of this land are aqueducts for water and better roads. The Romans surveyed this." He swept his hand over the ravine from which we had emerged. "For a thousand years and more, the road to Jerusalem has gone up that canyon, following every bend of the stream bed. This new route saves three miles of the journey and is much more pleasant."

The wind out of the west had a surprising saltiness about it. A distant line of dark blue, bisecting the world from north to south, confirmed that I really did scent the ocean.

We camped for the night eighteen miles from Jerusalem. The hill on which we stopped was the last elevation above the coastal lowlands. The Plain of Sharon spread out before us—a tattered blanket sporting patches of brown earth, yellow stubbled fields, and gray rock outcroppings.

The sun was still high in the west. Joseph saw my questioning look and answered my unspoken query. "There is good water here—and some grazing. Better than we would find on the lower slopes. Tomorrow will be an easy half day's journey."

Within moments a pavilion was set up for Joseph, which he invited me to share. A fire was kindled, and a haunch of mutton soon roasted on a spit. South of our chosen camping place was a solitary knoll crowned with the tumbled stones of a ruined fortress.

"Gezer," Joseph said. "Built by the Canaanites long ages ago, then captured by the Philistines and the Egyptians in turn. Later it was fortified by King Solomon."

"But no one lives there now?" I asked.

"Owls and badgers and foxes. Why?"

"I thought I saw someone moving among the boulders at its summit."

Shading his eyes against the sunset, Joseph studied the remains of Gezer. "A wild goat, perhaps?" He shrugged. "Tell me again the story your rabbi told you, the one about seeking the infant Jesus."

Even Rabbi Kagba seldom drilled me as did Joseph of Arimathea on that occasion. He wanted to know every detail, making me rack my brain for barely remembered bits of the tale. Between bites of roast meat and chunks of fresh bread, I tried to keep pace with Joseph's insatiable appetite for more about Jesus of Nazareth.

"All within the Sign of the Two Fish: Jupiter, the Righteous King, and Saturn, the Lord of the Sabbath . . . coming together and moving apart and coming together again, three times in a year and a half." I waved my dinner knife toward the horizon. Jupiter, together with Mars and the moon, danced between the signs of the Bull and the Twin Brothers.

"The Sign of the Two Fish means our nation," Joseph said eagerly. Lifting his chin into the breeze, he murmured wistfully, "Could it be true? Could Messiah come in our lifetime? Could the cup of prophecy be filled and ready to be drained?"

At his words I touched again Joseph's cup at my waist and remembered more of what my teacher had said. "'And a sword will pierce your heart too,'" I quoted from memory.

"Eh? What's that?"

I recounted what Rabbi Kagba had told me about the prophecy over Jesus' mother at his dedication in the Temple. "The rabbi did not like the sound of those words."

Joseph shook his head slowly. "Neither do I. There is much I do not understand. In one place Holy Scripture says Messiah will 'proclaim freedom for the captives and release from darkness for the prisoners.'[1] Like releasing us from the grip of Rome," he added in an aside to me. "But in another place doesn't it say, 'He was pierced for our transgressions, he was crushed for our iniquities'?[2] How can they both be true? I've heard Jesus teach. I've seen his miracles. I want to believe in him, but something holds me back."

The discussion was interrupted by a shout from the shadowed highway: "*Shalom* to the camp."

Drawing a short sword, Joseph's steward leapt to his feet and took a stance between his master and the unknown intruder. The ten guards drew their weapons and formed a protective circle about the camp.

"Easy," said a hooded, cloaked figure, advancing to the edge of the firelight. "I'm alone. No threat to you."

Terah and the guards relaxed slightly at those words, but I did not. I remembered how Zimri's band of outlaws had sought shelter at my father's camp before attacking us.

"Can I come to the warmth?" the stranger inquired.

This man was bulkier than Zimri's sinewy form, and his voice was gruffer. I let the tension leave my shoulders.

"Come in and welcome," Joseph invited.

The newcomer squatted between Joseph and me, extending broad, calloused palms toward its warmth. His face bristled with a coarse, wiry beard. The heavy ridges of his eyebrows made his eyes into deep holes above a crooked, flattened nose.

"Is it safe to travel alone so late, even on this highway?" Terah asked.

The lone man shrugged. "Perhaps not." With those words he stretched, lifting his left hand high above his head.

It was the same signal Zimri had given to launch the bandit attack on my father's camp! "Joseph!" I said with alarm, but too late.

The robber's right hand darted into the fold of his robe. A knife flashed in the firelight before he seized me with one arm. He yanked me to my feet and pressed the blade to my throat.

Joseph's guards sprang forward. The bandit barked at them, "Get back or he dies! I am bar Abba, and you know I mean what I say."

Bar Abba! The notorious murderer who slaughtered and stole while pretending to be a freedom fighter. This was the assassin Zimri had said he was going to Judea to join.

"Hold!" Joseph shouted to his men. Then to my attacker: "What do you want?"

A ring of cloaked men appeared from the darkness at bar Abba's sign. There were as many of them as Joseph's entourage.

"Want?" Bar Abba smirked. "I want your men to throw down their weapons. And then I want your camels and your shipment."

As the tip of his dagger jabbed my neck, Joseph ordered his men to drop their swords, and they complied.

I recognized Zimri even before he spoke. "Didn't I tell you this would work?" he said to bar Abba as he strode forward. "For some reason they value the life of this shepherd's cur." Approaching me, he threatened, "You are so much trouble. I will enjoy slitting your throat."

"No, you won't," bar Abba corrected. "He makes a valuable hostage. Remember who is chief here. All right, quickly now."

Struggling in bar Abba's grasp, I shouted at Zimri, "What about my mother? What about my father?"

Zimri sneered and shook his head, drawing his thumb across his neck.

A dull, hollow ache swelled up in my chest, threatening to choke me. I no longer cared whether I lived or died. I let my hands be tied behind my back. A rope leash around my throat was handed to Zimri.

I watched without seeing while Joseph and Terah were stripped of their fine clothes and valuables. After being forced to repack the camels, Joseph's attendants were trussed up like chickens in the marketplace and piled in a heap.

It was when all but three of bar Abba's men had sheathed their weapons and grasped the lead ropes of the camels that I heard the shout from the black hillside: "Now!"

Suddenly, beside each of the robbers appeared a pair of Roman soldiers, their javelins prepared to skewer all of bar Abba's men. The legionaries looked to a muscled, russet-haired centurion for their orders.

A tug on the rope jerked me off my feet, and the tip of Zimri's knife dug into my ear.

"Call off your men or he dies!" Zimri snarled.

The centurion shrugged. "Go ahead. He's nothing to me. The only difference to you is, if you kill him, I will kill you here and now . . . crucify you where you stand. But if you don't, you might actually live to have a trial. Doesn't matter to me. Your choice."

The pressure of the knife in my ear increased for a moment. My heart beat wildly.

Then Zimri tossed down his blade. A pair of Roman soldiers pinioned his arms to his sides.

Desperate to escape, bar Abba flung himself at the centurion. His upraised sword swept toward the officer, who parried it with his own. Their blades rang together. Bar Abba jabbed at the Roman with a knife in his other hand.

The assassin was larger and stronger, bull-like in his fighting. The centurion was cool and quicker in his movements.

Lowering his shoulder, bar Abba attempted to butt the centurion out of the way and did succeed in knocking the Roman down. As the bandit chief tried to flee, the officer caught him by the ankle and brought him sprawling to the ground.

Immediately the officer planted one knee against bar Abba's back, but the bandit whipped around, slashing with his dagger. The knife edge skittered off a metal bracelet on the Roman's wrist.

Then the Roman drove his clenched fist into bar Abba's chin, following through on the blow by letting the point of his elbow crash against the robber's cheekbone.

Bar Abba sagged, and the fight was over.

Once order was restored, Joseph of Arimathea confronted the Roman. "Marcus Longinus. How could you risk the life of this boy like that?"

"Would it have been better to let that scum carry him away to be killed later or sold as a slave? No, I know his kind, cowards who will do anything to save their own hides. You'll see. Bar Abba and Zimri will race to see which one can sell the other out faster." Then to me he said, "But I am sorry, son. I would not want you harmed for anything."

Resuming his discussion with Joseph, the centurion explained, "I've been after bar Abba for three years. We received word that his band was hiding in the ruins of Gezer. When we saw your camp, we expected they would attack you."

"So you staked us out like a goat to draw in a lion!" Joseph protested.

"A little gratitude, if you please," Marcus Longinus corrected. "It is bar Abba's practice to leave no living witnesses to his robberies. What would have happened if we had not been here at all?"

To that question, Joseph had no response.

As the sun rose, the troop of Roman soldiers and their prisoners set out toward Jerusalem while we returned to our trek to Joppa. All I could think was that I was alive . . . but now I knew my parents to be dead.

Chapter 23

As we approached Joppa, the highway skirted olive groves and stands of pomegranate trees. Still lower on the downward slope were vineyards, their gnarled trunks standing in the wintry chill like upright walking sticks. Savagely pruned until only a single pair of branches was left upon each vine, the barren rows looked the way I felt inside.

Joppa was built on a promontory extending out into the sea. Waves crashed around the western base of its hundred-foot-tall summit, dotted with houses. I was fascinated by my first view of the Great Sea. I had heard of it, but nothing in Rabbi Kagba's teaching or my parents' descriptions prepared me for how vast it seemed. Nor was its appearance comforting. It appeared to me a trackless wilderness where drowning could be expected at any moment.

Approaching Joppa as we did from the southeast, the morning light shone directly on the city, but its appearance was not improved by it. The town was built entirely of gray rock. I saw no color, nor even any whitewash, to relieve the dullness. Flat-roofed boxes were what passed for homes. They varied in size alone but not in shape.

Perhaps it was the weariness in my own soul that drained any interest in Joppa from me. I wanted my mother and father. I wanted my home. I wanted things to be as they had been before this ordeal began, only now never could be again.

Joseph of Arimathea tried to engage me in conversation by recounting bits of Joppa's history. "This is where King Hiram of Tyre landed the cedar beams from Lebanon used to build our Temple. And you remember it was from Joppa that the prophet Jonah tried to flee from the Almighty." He gazed into my staring, uncaring eyes and abruptly began prattling. "Jonah," he repeated awkwardly. "No harbor, though. Rowed out to the ships. Out there." Vaguely, he gestured toward a row of vessels bobbing at anchor, then shut his mouth and kept it closed.

My grandparents, I learned, lodged with a man called Simon the Tanner. While tanning was a despised, smelly trade, it was also lucrative. Simon's home was among the largest dwellings in Joppa. Simon was kin to Nicodemus the Pharisee and well known to Joseph.

These and other such random thoughts bobbed in my head like the vessels on the waves. I had never met my mother's parents before. I wondered if they would be pleased to see me, or hate me because I was alive and my mother was not. I was certain my brothers would blame me. How could they not, when I halfway blamed myself?

When Joseph's caravan arrived in the street outside Simon's home, he asked me to wait with Terah while he entered to alert the household. It was, he said, so we would not catch them by surprise, because we were arriving earlier than expected.

His small deception was meant to be an act of kindness, but it did not fool me. I knew he wanted to deliver the news about the death of their daughter before he introduced me to my grandparents.

Moments passed. An older couple emerged from the gate. The woman was short and plump. The man, not much taller, but slimmer. Both had pale, drawn faces. The woman tottered slightly, clutching the man's arm for support.

"Boaz, Rebekah," Joseph said, "this is your grandson, Nehemiah. Nehi, here are your—"

Dropping to her knees, my grandmother extended her arms toward me. In her face she looked so much like my mother!

Bursting away from Terah's hand on my shoulder, I ran to her and fell into her arms. She pressed me to her, letting me bury my face in her neck, both of us weeping. We rocked back and forth, she and I, clinging to each other for comfort.

She was perfumed with the aromas of baking: flour and spices. But there was also a faint hint of jasmine and lavender and rose . . . just like my mother.

My grandfather stood awkwardly beside us both, stiffly patting first one head and then the other. "Come in, come in," he kept urging, as if grief would be less if hidden from daylight.

My grandmother and I shuddered as one, and we both sniffed. Drawing back slightly, she held me at arm's length and peered into my eyes. "Dear, sweet child. I see your mother. I see my Sarah."

Once inside the house we sat on a bench with me between my grandparents. Each of them held one of my hands. My grandmother patted my hand over and over again.

"Where are my brothers?" I said. "When can I see them?"

"They've gone . . . left for Amadiya . . . before word came that you were in Jerusalem."

"But how can I . . . ? I've got to see them," I said with desperation. "I have to tell them . . . you know."

Gently, my grandfather said, "I've already sent a messenger

after them. He's well mounted and riding fast. He will catch them and turn them around. Don't worry."

"And which . . . who . . . ?" I asked and stopped, fearing to bring more sorrow into this grief-stricken gathering.

"What is it, my boy?" Grandfather asked.

Joseph came to my aid. "We heard that one of your grandsons—one of Nehi's brothers—was killed in the fire. But we did not learn the name."

"Oh," Grandmother said abruptly.

I saw the hurt of the recollection hit her like a slap to the face, and my own heart was pierced again. "I'm sorry. I'm so sorry," I said, uncaring whether I made sense or not.

"Terrible! Terrible!" Grandmother murmured. "It was the drunken brother of a cloth merchant. A guest. He started the fire. Not one of my grandchildren. But a horrible end for anyone."

How could I feel crushed and lifted both at the same time? Not one of my brothers, but both of my parents? Good news, bad news. Relief and groans coming heartbeats apart?

"We are rebuilding the shop," my grandfather confirmed. "It will be complete by Passover. But what with the crowds and all . . . well, we won't try to move back until after the holiday."

For a long time we did not notice Joseph, standing self-consciously beside the door. "I should go," he said. "I am going with my cargo as far as Alexandria. If tide and wind cooperate, I will return in two Sabbaths. With your permission, I will look in on Nehemiah again then."

For a time, immediately after his departure, I barely noticed that Joseph of Arimathea had gone. I was so grateful to be with my grandparents . . . to feel their love and know the security of being in their home . . . that I wanted no more adventures! For so long I had been on the run, or in hiding, or facing bandits, or living by my wits, that I was ready to be a child again, though I would not have admitted it if asked.

My grandmother's embrace and the gruff kindliness of my grandfather kept my days free of sorrow or fear. When I woke in the room next to my grandparents, it took me a moment to recognize where I was, and then I took comfort in my grandfather's snores. By the sound of his rasping breath, I received proof that I was physically safe.

With that reassurance, I next prayed earnestly to return to sleep as quickly as possible, before my thoughts overwhelmed me. My brothers had still not returned, and the deep-rooted guilt I felt at having fled from Zimri remained unresolved.

And then there was the matter of my mission and the Cup of Joseph. Opinion was divided, it seemed, about Jesus of Nazareth. Was he a healer, a miracle worker, a prophet sent by the Almighty—or a charlatan, a deceiver, a traitor, or a collaborator?

How was it possible for the Messiah, the Anointed One, the long-awaited prophet promised through Moses and all the others, to be unrecognized as who he truly was? Was it Jesus who was flawed . . . or men who were blind?

Perhaps we could have resolved these questions by going to Jerusalem, but my grandparents refused to take me.

Shortly after my arrival in Joppa, word came that a plague was strangling the Holy City.

"The choking sickness," Grandfather called it. "All who can afford to are fleeing the city. Thanks be to the Almighty that we came away before it struck. The fire, you see, was a blessing in disguise."

"But the poor beggars," Grandmother lamented. "Things

like these always hit the homeless the hardest. Those who cannot escape—who have no money for warm clothing and good food—are the first to die."

I thought of my friends: Red, Timothy, and the others, and wondered how they were. The caves beneath the city might remain above freezing, but they could not be called either truly warm or entirely dry. I myself had seen how the Sparrows struggled to obtain enough to eat.

"Can't we go help them?" I asked. "Do something for them? They helped me."

Grandfather would not even consider it.

Grandmother said, "It's good that you want to help, Nehi, but your grandfather is right. We cannot risk returning there. Not now."

There soon came a day when my nighttime worries and frets crept into the daylight hours. The comforting *thump* and *swish* of shuttle and frame as my grandmother worked her loom no longer reassured me. Instead, the sight of her laboring over the skeins of blue and white thread reminded me how very much I missed my mother and my home in Amadiya.

Grandmother noticed when I leaned against the door frame, gnawing on my lower lip and frowning. When my grandfather emerged from his makeshift counting office, I heard her whispering to him but could not make out what was said.

"Nehemiah," Grandfather said, clapping his hand on my shoulder, "let's go down to the waterfront. There's a shipping agent there I want to visit. Besides, there are some famous sights in Joppa that visitors come especially to see. You might like it."

I was grateful for the diversion.

"Even without a proper harbor," Grandfather explained, "Joppa is a famous seaport. Greeks and Persians and our people all come here to visit."

I had not seen anything especially noteworthy in Joppa, so I was curious what would draw attention from many different races.

A series of rocky ledges that formed one bit of Joppa's shoreline marched in ranks out into the salt water until disappearing beneath it. Some distance offshore they reemerged as dangerous reefs, barely breaking the surface, poised to tear the bellies out of unsuspecting ships.

Only one rock reared much higher than the waves. From the place I stood it appeared about the size and shape of the oak cabinet in my mother's workshop in Amadiya—the one in which she kept the finest thread for the most elaborate, custom-ordered prayer shawls.

I remarked on this to Grandfather, but he assured me it was really much larger. "About the size of the shed where we keep the chickens."

This did not sound much more impressive to me. I must have appeared skeptical that anyone cared about so insignificant a chunk of rock.

"Doesn't look like much," Grandfather agreed, "but that's Andromeda's Rock. It's the place where she was chained; later she was rescued by Perseus."

Now I recognized the tale, as repeated to me by Rabbi Kagba. "I know about this," I said. "My teacher showed me the star patterns from the story."

According to ancient legend, Andromeda's mother had angered the Greek gods by her prideful boasting. They sent a sea monster to destroy their cities. The attacks would only stop if she sacrificed her daughter, Andromeda, to the monster. The legend had a happy ending when a hero named Perseus, riding Pegasus, the flying horse, killed the monster and rescued Andromeda.

I nodded. "She, her mother, Perseus, the horse, and even the monster are all named in the heavens, at least by the Greeks. And the other people who live in our country—the Parthians who used to be Persians—say their race was founded by Perseus and Andromeda."

Grandfather looked unhappy. "You know this story very well already."

"But I like seeing the place where they say it happened. Is it true?"

Grandfather brightened at my expression of interest. He inclined his head and offered with a grin, "Perhaps an enterprising Greek merchant opened an inn here and needed to attract travelers."

"Didn't the prophet Jonah leave from here when he tried to flee from the Almighty?" I inquired. "Joseph told me that."

"And in Jonah's story the Almighty made a great fish swallow Jonah, not to kill him, but to save him," Grandfather mused. "That's kind of like a sea monster, isn't it?"

Now my thoughts were racing. "Who lived here before the Greeks or us Jews?"

"The Philistines. They worshipped a god named Dagon. He was supposed to be half man and half fish."

"Now that'd be a monster," I said, picturing the image. "What about the people Jonah was supposed to preach to? What did they worship?"

"The wicked old city of Nineveh?" Grandfather pondered aloud. "I think they worshipped Dagon too."

"So when Jonah came alive out of the great fish and preached, they saw how much greater our God was than theirs. Even sea monsters obey the Almighty."

Grandfather wiped his forehead. "Have you thought about training to become a rabbi, Nehemiah?"

"Rabbi Kagba says I could be a scholar, like him," I reported honestly.

"He may be right there," Grandfather agreed. "I wonder what your mentor would think about what Jesus of Nazareth said about Jonah."

"Jesus? He talked about Jonah?"

Grandfather shrugged. "So says a Pharisee customer of mine. He doubts Jesus is really the Messiah, so he asked the man from Galilee to give him a sign. 'What sign will you perform, so I might believe in you?' he says he asked."

After all I had heard about lame men being made to walk and blind men to see and even dead children raised to life, it seemed to me like a very rude question. However, I inquired, "And what did Jesus say?"

Stroking his full, white beard, Grandfather stared at Andromeda's Rock and returned, "Supposedly all he said was, 'No sign will be given to it except the sign of the prophet Jonah.'"[1]

"The sign of Jonah? What does that mean?"

Grandfather spread his hands wide. "I have no idea. Neither did the Pharisee, though he likes to be thought very learned. 'A runaway prophet?' the Pharisee said. 'A disobedient man?'" Grandfather chuckled at remembering the exasperated Pharisee, and when he chuckled, he wheezed and then coughed. "I said, 'Doesn't this Jesus preach repentance, just like Jonah?' And he said, 'But that's not a sign! All prophets do that!'"

"What about being swallowed by the great fish?" I ventured, wide-eyed at the thought.

Grandfather was seized with a paroxysm of laughter and coughing. "That's just what the Pharisee said! Said he'd like to see Jesus manage that one!"

"Three days in the fish," I pondered aloud. "Buried at the bottom of the sea. Like being dead and then coming back to life. That truly would be a sign."

"Eh? What's that you say?"

"Nothing, Grandfather. Just thinking aloud."

Chapter 24

*T*he news from Jerusalem did not improve. True to my grand-parents' premonitions, the plague of the choking sickness fell hardest on the beggars of the Holy City. Word had come to Joppa from Grandfather's business acquaintances that nearly all the Sparrows were stricken with the illness and many had died.

No one but God kept account of Sparrows, it seemed. No one knew any of the names, living or dead. Had my friends survived?

The Pharisee who brought the news said it was a sign of God's judgment on sin. "Just like cripples and those who con-tract leprosy," he said. "This disease is proof that God strikes evildoers and lawbreakers. No one among the truly pious is in jeopardy."

I felt myself staring at the man. He was speaking of my friends as if they deserved this affliction! But I knew those the Pharisee thought pious, by which he meant the wealthy, had fled from disease or locked themselves behind high walls and barred gates until the plague snuffed itself out, together with the life of the last victim.

"I have heard," my grandfather said, "that Lazarus of Bethany, widely regarded as a righteous man, has taken on him-self the role of caregiver to the beggars, especially the link-bearer children."

The Pharisee sniffed. "I'm sure he means well—a charitable act. But he's misguided. Those orphan beggars? Pickpockets and thieves, every one. No doubt they deserve this punishment."

I struggled with anger at his fat, pompous, arrogant face! The Pharisee must have seen the burning hostility in my eyes because when he glanced at me, he swiftly turned away.

My grandmother had also noticed my distress. She came and stood beside me. A calming spirit, like that I had always known from my mother, enveloped me.

My grandfather, his eyes narrowed and his voice polite but cold, explained, "My daughter and her husband—this grandson's parents—were attacked by bandits and are likely dead. You should be more careful in what you say about orphans."

I clung to my grandmother and sobbed as the weight of Grandfather's words fell across me. So he, too, believed my mother and father were dead!

"Didn't mean . . . ," the Pharisee fumbled. "Your family aren't beggars," he finished awkwardly. Lifting the weight of several chins, the Pharisee nodded curtly to a waiting servant, who had stood silent with downcast eyes. The Pharisee completed his transaction for a dozen expensive prayer shawls and left.

"Listen, Nehemiah," my grandfather said, "I'm sorry you had to endure that preening Pharisee. I didn't mean to upset you. We will not lose hope. Not you or me or your grandmother. The plague in Jerusalem is a terrible thing. Even your rabbi Jesus seems to have fled from it."

❧

A single clay lamp burned in the hall outside my bedroom. Flickering light tossed fragments of shadows against the walls. The tiny flame labored to push back the darkness. It exhaled a ribbon of sooty smoke that streaked the plaster and pooled over-head like an upside-down puddle of oily water.

Every night my grandmother lit the lamp—to comfort me, she said.

Every morning she scrubbed at the wall and climbed on a chair to clean the ceiling.

I sat cross-legged on the floor, my back to the entry. The meager illumination fell over my shoulder onto Joseph's cup. The lambskin wrapping lay across my lap.

Idly, I scratched the blackened surface of the cup but could not raise an answering gleam. There was not even so much shine as what reflected from my fingernails. Unlike the wall and the ceiling soiled with smoke, the tarnished surface of the cup refused to be cleaned.

The obstinate stain matched my own gloomy outlook.

Did everyone I loved die? Were my parents dead? And Rabbi Kagba? Were my friends in Jerusalem all gone? Was I a curse and a danger to my grandparents?

What if this unattractive object was not really Joseph's cup at all? What if everything I had experienced had been for nothing? What if everything I had believed had proven untrue—worse than false, treacherous?

Yet, as I reviewed what Rabbi Kagba had taught me, I could not extinguish the remaining glimmer of hope. He had spoken confidence into my life. Like the diminutive glow of the oil lamp, part of me still worked at pushing back bleak despair. I had dreamed of Joseph the Dreamer. Together we had wit-nessed Father Abraham and the king-priest Melchizedek, and King David and his mighty men.

Dreams, I argued with myself. *Only dreams and no substance in which to place any trust.*

And Adam's Hart? There was the something I could not explain away. I had ridden the White Hart.

Together with the cup I held in my hands—tarnished and unlovely but real and significant—the memory of the hart confirmed everything my mentor had prophesied over me: I would see Messiah. I would be cupbearer to the King.

"Your thoughts can be hopeful and gloomy by turns," remarked a familiar voice.

"I was just thinking about you," I replied to Joseph the Dreamer, who stood in the corner of my room. "And yes, you're right. But the path is so uncertain. The weight of grief and suffering seems all out of proportion to the fragment of hope."

Joseph nodded. His expression was sympathetic and not at all disapproving or disappointed in me. He said, "When I was in the pit, pleading with my brothers for my life, do you think I was cheerful?"

I shook my head. Though Joseph was used by the Almighty for great purposes, his life was no less difficult because he believed in his destiny.

"When I was in prison, for something I did not do," he offered, "I dreamed of home. I dreamed of my father, of my brother, Benjamin, of my mother, Rachel, who had died long years before. I missed her a lot."

This was painful for me to hear. Even knowing that in *olam haba*, the world to come, all was put right, I was still sorry on Joseph's behalf.

"And when I awoke amid happy thoughts of home and being loved, only to find myself on the wet, stinking floor of the prison in Egypt, do you think I did not grieve for what I had lost?"

I shook my head. "It must have been a torment."

"Every day!" Joseph confirmed. "And each day I had to

draw on the tiny bit of hope given me by the faith of my father and grandfather." Joseph flicked his fingers toward the lamp outside my door. Pinprick sparks shimmered upward, as when my mother tossed spice into the Sabbath flames for a sweet savor.

"Hope," Joseph said earnestly, "is no less real because it seems small amid the darkness. Faith is no less yours to claim because you struggle against doubt."

Below me my grandparents had a dinner celebration with a few close friends, but none were my age. I heard their banter, but no one present was interested in talking with me.

As soon as I was excused from supper, I came to the rooftop. The location carried my thoughts back to an earlier year—that Purim when Rabbi Kagba opened the skies and showed me the heavenly cup and the celestial hart. Bundled again in my shepherd's coat and boots, I peered into a cloudy sky for some glimpse of my old starry friends. Misty banners, torn from the fabric of the storm, carried news of the tempest toward Jerusalem but did not linger in Joppa.

Waves crashed against Andromeda's Rock. Long swells swept in from the northwest, to land with hollow, jarring thuds on Joppa's promontory. I wondered if they came from Cyprus, or perhaps as far away as the Pillars of Hercules.

The wind howled in my ears, screeching pipes to the drumbeat of the breakers. These were lonely, disquieting sounds on a lonely, unpeaceful night.

Still no word of my brothers. No news about my teacher either.

I was safe, I was loved, I was cared for, yet I was restless.

Several houses up the street I glimpsed a man striding pur-
posefully along as he passed beneath a blazing torch. He was
alone and completely wrapped in a long cloak, with a hood over
his head. The wind threatened to turn his robes into sails and
spin him off east, like the clouds.

Like a ship quartering into the gale to avoid being flung on
the rocks, he had to lean into the blast. *Why would anyone be out
on such a bitter night?* I wondered. I rubbed wind-plucked tears
from my eyes and watched.

Two houses away he stopped. Peering back the way he had
come, he counted entries, as if uncertain of his destination. When
his tabulation ceased, he was pointing at Grandfather's gate!

Beneath my gaze he pulled the bell rope, but no one
answered. Between the tumult of the storm and the merry-
making, I doubted if anyone would. "They can't hear you," I
shouted. "Are you seeking Boaz the Weaver?"

A familiar face lifted toward me. Joseph of Arimathea corrected, "Yes, I am, Nehemiah. But I'm also seeking you!"

"Wait! I'll be right down!"

Moments later Joseph warmed himself in front of the fire
amid a crowd of attentive onlookers. He answered my grandmother's question about why he was out on such a fearful
night. "And well you might ask. I barely got off my ship from
Alexandria before the storm hit. They were so anxious to sail off
toward a safer harbor that they almost threw me overboard. Just
like Jonah, eh?" He smiled. "My steward was expecting me and
met me. Just in from Jerusalem, he has received some startling
news. My business partner, Lazarus of Bethany . . . ?"

"Friend of Jesus of Nazareth," Grandfather remarked. "Yes?"

"Caring for the Jerusalem Sparrows, he took sick with the
strangling sickness."

"And Jesus healed him?" Grandmother asked.

"No . . . he died," Joseph corrected.

I was stunned and shocked. My heart sank.

A rotund spice merchant laughed mockingly. "That's a prophet from Galilee for you. Couldn't even save his own friend!"

"No," Joseph continued slowly. "But Jesus brought Lazarus back from the dead."

After a stunned silence, a tumult of queries equal in volume and confusion to the storm outside barraged Joseph.

"What d'ya mean?"

"Then he wasn't really dead!"

"But he's real, I tell you!"

"Four days in the tomb," Joseph said. "Really and truly dead, and Jesus called him out of the grave . . . so they say."

"That'll light a fire under High Priest Caiaphas. The whole country will want to see Jesus and Lazarus both!"

Joseph ignored the mocking banter and addressed my grandfather. "Has any word come directly regarding Nehemiah's parents?"

Grandfather shook his head. "We've still had no *real* word about them . . . good or bad," he emphasized with a look at me. "Only what the bandit Zimri implied." He paused. "Then again, he is a bandit and not to be trusted and cruel by choice."

A spark of hope, like the pinprick sparks that had shimmered upward when Joseph gestured toward the lamp, ignited in my heart. Could the bandit have lied? Might my parents still be alive somewhere? And searching for me?

"Then," Joseph said, "here is a request: I would like to take Nehemiah on as an apprentice in my export business, if he agrees. I want him to accompany me to the Holy City when

I leave tomorrow. Of course, his parents may not give their consent when they return, but until then, you can approve his employment, if you will."

Turning, Grandfather put his hands on his hips. With raised eyebrows he looked a question at me.

I nodded eagerly. "Yes, please!" I confirmed.

And so it was settled.

Chapter 25

Our journey to the home of David ben Lazarus in Bethany was briefly interrupted outside the Holy City. Joseph reined his horse and dismounted near a stone wall outside Jerusalem.

Two men stacked carefully hewn limestone blocks to form a waist-high barricade. The wall surrounded a newly planted garden. Inside the enclosure was a border of fragrant juniper shrubs. The place was busy with workmen. Boys about my age mixed mortar. Older boys worked as hod carriers, assisting the masons.

At the sight of Joseph, I noticed heads lean together and anxious whispers pass between the laborers. Whatever this building site was, Joseph clearly had authority over it. He pushed aside a wooden gate as I slid from my donkey and hesitated.

"Come on, then," he instructed. I tied our mounts to the limb of a tree.

The gate opened onto a winding gravel path that was a beehive of activity. Another boy, wielding a branch of a juniper as a broom, swept the curving track clear of dust. A man wearing the apron of a stone mason edged the path with more stacked stone. Joseph greeted the mason, then asked, "Where is Hyram?"

The stone-setter indicated a grass-covered knoll at the back of the property. Between the fence and the small hill were beds of lavender. When the weather warmed, the lavender would perfume the air with rich sweetness.

The trail skirted a pair of ancient olive trees, so gnarled and massive at their bases that the garden must have been constructed around them. The path ended against a rocky knoll. The flank of the hillside in front of me was faced with flat stones. At the center of the wall's base was a square hole, slightly shorter than me, leading inward.

A man emerged from the opening. He wore his mason's apron with one corner turned up, designating him the overseer of the work. "*Shalom,* Master Joseph," he said.

"*Shalom,* Master Hyram," Joseph returned. "You've made good progress."

"I think you'll be pleased with the tomb." Hyram tugged his forelock.

"I think my father will be pleased too. I am eager to have it done before the Passover holiday."

I felt a pang of renewed guilt. According to our beliefs, it was a very necessary mark of respect for children to see their parents honorably interred. Joseph was paying great homage to his father with this gift.

I, on the other hand, had run away. My father and mother, if dead as I feared, may have remained unburied except for the kindness of strangers. I squinted with the pain of regret.

Though I did not speak, Joseph noticed my distress and somehow understood its cause. "We will not give up hope, boy," he whispered to me. Then, to divert me, he asked, "Would you like to see inside? I have no torch, but I think there's enough light."

I nodded.

A massive stone disk, taller than me, stood on edge in a

channel cut for the purpose. It rested against the outer wall of the tomb and was wedged there by a block beneath it.

I eyed it suspiciously. "Safe?"

Joseph nodded. "But once the wedge is removed, the covering rolls into place, sealing the entry."

The master mason explained proudly, "When shut, it will take at least four men to roll it back up the slope. Sir, would you like to inspect the work?"

Joseph nodded, then motioned for me to go first. "Go ahead. Go in."

The opening was so small that even I had to duck to enter. Joseph followed me. The mason remained outside.

Inside, the floor was lower than the entry, so I stood upright. I was surrounded by hewn stone walls bearing the fresh marks of hammers and chisels.

There was no carving or other adornment in the tomb, but the corners were all perfectly square. Every angle was completely uniform. The floor, walls, and ceiling were smooth and level. It had cost a lot of labor and expense.

On three sides of the chamber were low benches cut out of the very rock. Each was the length of a man lying down and about twice his width. Because the tomb was brand-new, there were no bone boxes or niches cut in the walls, as would be true when multiple generations of Joseph's family had been buried there. It was a rich man's tomb, different from the primitive burial caves of my homeland.

"It's almost like a little house, you know? When no one's in it." I paused. "I mean, nobody dead."

Joseph touched the cool wall. "Yes. I suppose. I like to think of this place as where my family will gather to await the resurrection at the last day. We are not Sadducees, who expect no resurrection. No, my father and I expect to be reunited, even if parted for a time. Of course," he added thoughtfully, "if what Jesus did for Lazarus is true, then perhaps all of what we know about death will change."

There seemed nothing left to see or say, especially since my mother and father were again strongly, forcefully in my mind.

The mason lowered his face and smiled in at us. "Is it to your liking, sir?"

Joseph gave a short laugh. "I am in no hurry to move in, but I am sure it will be a comfortable place to wait for the resurrection."

The mason stepped aside as we emerged. "I was hoping you would be pleased with our progress."

Joseph touched his money belt. "A bonus if you're finished before Passover. I'll return before *Shabbat* to pay the workers for their labor up to now."

I squared my shoulders and attempted to match the stride of Joseph as we returned up the gravel path to our mounts. I felt the eyes of the boys take me in furtively, then look away. Perhaps they imagined I was the son of the wealthy merchant.

"Come along." Joseph untied the reins and gave me a boost onto my donkey. "The day is passing, and I want to reach Bethany before sunset."

❧

It was dusk when we passed the Mount of Olives and reached the hamlet of Bethany, a couple miles east of Jerusalem. The villa of Lazarus was set below a hill crowned with a fig orchard, in the midst of a vineyard.

I shuddered at the thought of all that had taken place here over the last weeks. I hoped I would have a chance to meet and speak to a real, live dead man. I wondered what he would look like and imagined it all somewhat fearfully, but with excitement.

The vines had been thoroughly pruned. Twisted stalks, crusted with gray bark, looked like roots protruding out of the red earth. But even amid winter's desolation, rebirth was apparent. Beginning where each branch grew nearest the trunk of the parent vine, pairs of tiny, dark green leaves fluttered.

"Banners of returning life," Joseph said to himself. Then he turned and spoke to me over his shoulder as we rode. "What do you know about vineyards?"

I shrugged. "My folks are shepherds. Papa drinks wine, which comes from vineyards. That's it."

Joseph gave a laugh. "The wines of Lazarus are drunk by emperors and kings as far away as Brittania. It comes from here. As hard as it is to believe right now, in six months these hillsides will be completely shadowed by lush growth. The branches will be bent with the weight of the clusters. And the laborers of David ben Lazarus will harvest them so he can work his magic. From dead sticks to the taste of new wine in three quarters of a year."

"So kings drink it. Lazarus makes good wine, then?" I said.

"The best! He says it takes the vines nine months to give birth, but the children of his vineyard will travel far and wide."

"I bet my papa said *Kiddush* on *Shabbat*. Your friend's wine poured into cups in Amadiya," I said, thinking of home and Joseph's cup at the same time.

Joseph nodded vigorously. "Shared in Rome and Alexandria." Then in a more thoughtful tone he added, "It's strange. Every year before this the wine is what I wanted to talk about—how many barrels, how much to charge, where it would be shipped. My family is proud to be his partner. But this year? I want to hear from him his own story about what happened. Was he really dead? What was it like? Who is this Jesus?"

These were the very questions in my head.

From the vineyard a cheerful voice joined our conversation. "Yes, Master Lazarus was truly dead. I can vouch for that. But still, those are all very good questions! Very good, indeed."

A young man, perhaps as old as twenty but thin-bearded, fresh-faced, and smiling, emerged from the shadows beside the fence enclosing the vineyard. "*Shalom,* sir. The master and his sisters are not at home. They've all gone off to follow Jesus. Leaving the vineyard in the care of Samson, the steward. But who knows when they'll be back? The Herodians would like Lazarus dead permanently."

Joseph stopped his horse and pivoted the animal to face the stranger. "I can understand that. But . . . who are you, and how do you know so much?"

"My name is Peniel. I've seen you here before, sir. I am also one blessed with the vision of Jesus." He touched his eyes. "I serve as a messenger from Lazarus to his servants."

I knew the name of Peniel. He was one of those whom Jesus had miraculously healed of blindness.

Joseph nodded. "Ah. Yes, I remember now. Peniel, the beggar of Nicanor Gate. The man born blind, they say."

I blurted out, "The one Jesus gave eyes. I heard about you from one of the Sparrows."

He bowed elaborately. "That's me. They'd love to put my eyes out again, I fear. So I stick to the back roads and mind my own business. One thing you learn as a beggar, silence is a virtue. You learn more if you act dumb or invisible." Grinning still more widely, Peniel stroked the nose of Joseph's horse. "Now I'm learning to be a scribe. I love a good story. So, you are here seeking Lazarus?" He snapped his fingers in recollection. "Master Joseph . . ."

"Joseph of Arimathea, the Younger . . ."

As we dismounted and entered the Lazarus home, Peniel explained, "The Temple rulers—high priest and others—they want to kill Jesus . . . Lazarus too. They already tried. So the master and our band have gone away from Jerusalem."

"Gone?" My voice and Joseph's chimed as two octaves of the same note.

"Don't worry," Peniel reassured us. "I was sent back to meet those Lazarus said might be coming. I can guide you to them. That's my job . . . that and learning your stories." Then, addressing me, Peniel asked, "And you are a servant to Joseph?"

"Apprentice," Joseph corrected, giving a lift to my pride. "Nehemiah bar Lamsa. From Amadiya near Gan Eden."

"You have an unusual accent." Peniel eyed me with pleased curiosity. "We won't travel until tomorrow. There's a fire and a kettle of stew and fresh bread. What do you say? Will you stay up late and tell me your tale? I'll tell you stories of Jesus if you will tell me how you happened to come from Paradise to Jerusalem. If I can share a ride on your donkey, we can reach the village where Jesus is within a day."

Part Three

Jesus told them, "You are going to have the light
   just a little while longer.
Walk while you have the light, before darkness
   overtakes you.
Whoever walks in the dark does not know
   where they are going.
Believe in the light while you have the light,
   so that you may become children of light."

JOHN 12:35–36[1]

Chapter 26

*I*t was after dark when we arrived at the village where Jesus and his followers were staying. Campfires of pilgrims dotted the hillside outside the walls.

Peniel, whose eyesight was keen even in the darkness, led the way toward the gate of the inn. "Jerusalem is only a day's walk from here. But somehow the people know. They've heard Jesus is here, so they camp here. Build their fires by the road in hopes he'll show himself."

Joseph replied quietly, "And my friend Lazarus?"

Peniel answered, "Yes. Yes. They all want to see Lazarus. To speak with him about where he was. What he saw, you know? Yes. Everyone wants to see Lazarus."

Joseph was silent for a few paces, and I guessed that, like everyone else, he was anxious to see his old business partner and learn the truth. "Lazarus. Good man. The Herodians want Lazarus dead . . ."

Peniel lifted a brow. "Dead again, you mean."

"Dead is dead. And as much as they want to kill Jesus, they want Lazarus dead . . . permanently. Jesus and his disciples mustn't come to Jerusalem for Passover."

In the distance the lights of Jerusalem gleamed through the haze of smoke like a new constellation in the mist.

Peniel raised his fist to knock on the gate of the inn. "Master Joseph, is that why you've traveled so far to find the Lord? To warn him of danger? Why you've come by night? You could have given me the message. I would have delivered it to him. So, what's your story, if you don't mind my asking? I do love a good story."

I could hear a smile in Peniel's voice.

Joseph cleared his throat. "I am no different from everyone else."

"Except you're very rich." Peniel laughed and banged on the gate. "Not that money means anything to Jesus. But money will open these gates. Just watch."

The watchman growled, "Gates are closed for the night. Go beg a place beside a pilgrim's fire."

Peniel replied confidently as he held silver coins up to the peephole, "It's Peniel. A friend of the master. Go ask the big fisherman."

"They're all gathered 'round in there," the gruff voice answered. "Your master is teaching. Mustn't be disturbed, Peter says."

"A denarius for the one who opens the gate. Two more for the innkeeper who provides a place to sleep and bread."

"How many of you?" hissed the sentry.

"Two men. One boy. Go on. Peter the fisherman will tell you. Say to him, Peniel is waiting outside the gate."

The port slammed shut. Minutes passed before the bolt of the gate slid back and the hinges groaned.

"Hurry," instructed the gatekeeper. "There's a mob would like to break in here. Beggars and sick among them."

When Joseph and Peniel had walked through the entrance, the gatekeeper tugged me by my coat, as if I weren't moving fast enough for his liking. Then he slammed and locked the gate behind us. His hand whipped out to snap up the coin in Peniel's fingers before scuttling away into the shadows.

Peniel shook his head, then set off through the dark courtyard of the caravansary. "I guarantee he wouldn't have bothered to fetch Peter if there hadn't been a coin in it for him."

Joseph remarked quietly, "How much would it take for the sentry to open the gates to the Temple Guards?"

We moved to the watch fire and warmed ourselves. A large, bearded man stepped from the portico. I spotted a dagger tucked into his belt.

"It's Peter," Peniel mumbled. "Not happy."

Peter gripped the weapon with one hand as he challenged, "Peniel. So, you're back at last. With news from Jerusalem, I hope. And who are your friends?"

"*Shalom,* Peter," Peniel greeted him. "This is Joseph of Arimathea. The younger Joseph. A merchant and friend of Master Lazarus. He was on a journey when all unfolded with Lazarus . . . Missed it all."

"And? Why sneak in here by cover of night? Business couldn't wait?" Peter was clearly irritated.

Joseph extended his hand. "I am a friend of Master Lazarus, as your companion explained. A partner in wine exporting. If you speak with Lazarus, he will vouch for me. I am here to warn your master—"

Peter's chin rose in defiance. "You think he doesn't know? That we don't know? This could have waited till morning, Peniel." He shifted his gaze to Joseph. "Look, money will buy people like you a lot of things, but Jesus doesn't care if you're rich or poor, see? He treats everyone the same. Money won't buy an audience with the Lord. He's teaching. Pharisees sitting there among us. He's giving it to them straight, and they don't much like it." He turned his surly gaze on me. "And what are you here for, boy?"

I stammered. "I . . . I am . . . My name is Nehemiah. Cupbearer."

Peter waved his hand dismissively. "So what?"

Fumbling for the precious cup at my waist, I held it up. "I . . . you see, sir . . . I brought this . . . a gift for . . ."

Peter squinted at the ancient vessel, then snorted with disdain. "If Joseph of Arimathea's silver won't buy you an audience to see Jesus, why do you think this dirty old cup will open the door?"

"But . . . I came so far! It's Joseph's cup," I pleaded.

Peter shook his shaggy head. "Peniel! Are you crazy? What were you thinking? You want me to interrupt the Lord for this?" Lifting his chin, he scoffed, "So, Joseph of Arimathea, some of us can't be bribed. Your journey is for nothing. Now we are all warned: Caiaphas wants to kill Jesus. And kill Lazarus. Big surprise. You can go now." Then, "Let your friends out the way they came, Peniel." Peter spun on his heel and reentered the building.

I thought that except for Roman soldiers or bandits, Peter was one of the rudest fellows I had ever met. We stood together, silently staring after him. My heart sank. Though Peter ridiculed the gift, surely Jesus would recognize the Cup of Joseph the Great when he saw it. Silently vowing I would never again show the cup to any man but Jesus, I replaced it in its bag.

Peniel's good humor was undiminished. "Sorry. Sorry. He's not a bad sort, really. Just unpleasant when he doesn't get his sleep. He's been standing watch with his sword drawn . . . just in case. I should have known, eh?"

"Perhaps Lazarus?" Joseph asked. "He will be glad to see me."

Peniel held up a finger to his temple and laughed. "Without fear! Lazarus slept like a dead man, but now that he is awake, he is always happy to see old friends."

Peniel hurried into the inn, leaving Joseph and me stretching our hands to the fire. Only a few minutes passed before our guide came out on the portico and, with a wave of his hand, called us to enter. As we approached, he put his finger to his lips and nodded. I followed Joseph and Peniel into the inn's large dining room, where travelers were fed. The space was packed with people. Rich and poor sat together on the floor in front of Jesus. Some listened with wondrous expressions on their upturned faces. Others among the crowd glared at him with resentment. Firelight flickered behind the teacher as he taught them. All were hushed as the clear, pleasant voice of the one I had been searching for filled the room.

"There was a rich man, who used to wear purple and fine linen, and every day he ate and drank and spent his wealth extravagantly for his own pleasure. And there was a poor man named Lazarus, who was laid down at that rich man's door . . ."

All eyes then turned to a fellow sitting near Jesus.

Joseph whispered, "That is Lazarus. There."

Excitement tickled my stomach like a feather. It was like the first time I met the Great White Hart in the forest or heard a new story from Rabbi Kagba. I would have laughed for the joy of being so close to Jesus. Perhaps he heard my happy thoughts.

Jesus locked his kind brown eyes on my face and met my smile with a nod. He had gained everyone's attention by speaking of the man he had raised from the dead.

Jesus continued his story. "Poor Lazarus lay there at the rich man's door. He was afflicted with boils. He longed to fill his stomach with crumbs that fell from the rich man's tray. Dogs came and licked the poor man's boils."

I saw those who were wealthy stir uneasily. Jesus was a wonderful storyteller. I was fascinated instantly.

"Now it happened that the poor man died, and the angels carried him into Abraham's bosom. Then the rich man died and was buried. And while the rich man was tormented in Sheol, he lifted up his eyes from a distance and saw Abraham, with Lazarus in his welcoming embrace. And the rich man called in a loud voice . . ." Jesus cupped his hands and shouted, "'O my father! Abraham! Have mercy on me and send Lazarus to dip his finger in water and wet my tongue, for I am tormented in this flame!'"

I shuddered at the vision of it.

"Abraham said to him, 'My son, remember you received your pleasures when you were living, and Lazarus his hardships. And look—now he is comfortable and happy here, and you are suffering. Besides all these things, a great gulf is fixed between us and you. So those who wish to cross over from here to you cannot, neither from there cross over to us.'"

I studied the rich men in the hall. Their faces were not happy. Here and there among the best dressed I spotted fear in their eyes.

"The tormented man cried to Abraham, 'If that is so, O my Father, I beseech you! Send Lazarus to my father's house, for I have five brothers! Let Lazarus go and testify to them, so they may not also come to this place of torment!'"

There was a hush in the room. Everyone knew that the real Lazarus had indeed returned from death to testify.

But Jesus continued with the story. "Abraham said to the tormented man, 'They have Moses and the Prophets. Let your brothers hear them!' But the rich man called out to Abraham, 'No! My father Abraham! But only if a man from the dead goes to them, they will repent!' Abraham replied, 'If they will not hear Moses and the prophets, neither will they believe, even if a man should return from the dead!'"[1]

Silence descended upon the room as Jesus finished the lesson. The rich men were mostly Pharisees who had come from Jerusalem to challenge Jesus and see Lazarus with their own eyes. Now they stared at Lazarus and contemplated the purpose of Jesus' story.

The death and resurrection of Lazarus was proof of the absolute truth of Jesus' story. Even though a man had returned from death to bear witness of eternal life, the leaders of Israel refused to believe the five books of Moses and they rejected Lazarus, the living, breathing evidence of Jesus' identity!

I considered the combined years of the elders of Israel who sat in the room. Surely their ages, if added together, would equal the years since Moses had parted the Red Sea. Yet they rejected the prophecies of the five books of Moses and were searching for reasons to reject Jesus. I was only a boy, and I believed that Jesus was our Messiah! Hadn't my own rabbi told me his name and the prophecies of his coming? So why was Jesus so feared and hated? I remembered also that Joseph of old, dreamer of dreams, had been hated by his brothers and yet had saved them all. Hatred of a righteous one was not rational. Surely what men intended for evil, God meant for good.

I slipped my hand into the pouch and touched the cold silver of Joseph's cup. I was sure that Jesus of Nazareth was the long-awaited Messiah, Son of David, the King of Israel! The books of Moses, all the prophets, and now Lazarus returned from the dead, all bore witness.

I glanced up at Joseph of Arimathea for his response to the teaching. He was, after all, a very rich man. His lips were tight, his face pale. A ripple of outrage swept through the wealthy in the congregation. Poor men grinned smugly, suddenly proud of their poverty. The crowd between us and Jesus was densely packed with knots of men arguing the point of the message. I saw Jesus slip out, surrounded by his disciples. Peter glowered over his shoulder.

Joseph clasped my hand and stepped back in the shadows into a small anteroom stacked with dishes, lest he be recognized by his friends from Jerusalem. Peniel followed us. Through the parted curtain I watched as some began to leave. They cast menacing glances at Lazarus as he followed Jesus.

Peniel inclined his head and said in a matter-of-fact tone to Joseph, "So. That's Jesus. He has a way of tossing the cat among the pigeons, as the saying goes. He's offended every rich man in the room, eh? And you. You're richer than most of them put together. What do you think?"

"My friend Lazarus of Bethany is also a wealthy man. He was rich when he died. Rich when Jesus called him from the grave. This parable is flawed, I fear. So, what do you think?" he asked Peniel. "Will wealth cast a man into hell?"

Peniel laughed. "I was a poor, blind man who begged at the Nicanor Gate. I can close my eyes and recognize the bitter voices of many in this room. I tell you, after I was healed, they hated me and cast me out because I was blind and now I see. Jesus gave me eyes to see. But a dark heart is much harder to heal. My heart recognized the Lord before I ever saw light." He put his hand on my shoulder. "Nehemiah? What do you think, boy?"

I hesitated and tried to imagine what Rabbi Kagba would say. "I think . . . the parable isn't flawed. What he said here tonight is true."

Peniel nodded as a great man in luxurious purple robes swept past. I opened the curtain just wide enough for him to see me. His lip was curled in disdain. He looked down his nose at me and chuffed away.

Joseph frowned. "What's Jesus want? That we give away our wealth? Live like paupers?"

"Not the point. You missed the point," Peniel replied calmly. "Lazarus was wealthy, yet he gave of his wealth and ultimately risked his life to help the poor children of Jerusalem. Lazarus lived among the beggars—became one of them—while these . . . others . . . slammed their gates and stayed comfortably in their warm houses. They did not raise a finger to help. These fellows worship wealth and success. They have the prophecies about Jesus and reject them. Now even when they have proof that Jesus is the one we have waited for, they reject the prophecies and reject the testimony of Lazarus, a man who has returned from the dead. Nothing will convince them. That's the point of the story. Not about going to hell because you have money. No. It's about rejecting truth. Jesus is truth. My restored vision will not convince them. Look at their backs as they go. These are not men who will be embraced by our Father Abraham."

That night all the wealth and position of my master were unable to purchase a room in the crowded caravansary. One night's lodging cost as much as a week's would have cost. Friends and enemies of Jesus all slept in bedchambers beneath the same roof.

There was not one bed remaining in the establishment. Jesus and his disciples took up an entire wing.

Joseph again asked Peniel, "I have traveled a long way to

meet Jesus, and so has the lad. Please, go tell my friend Lazarus I'm here."

Peniel hurried to the sleeping quarters of Jesus and his band. When he returned, he shrugged cheerfully. "Peter is on guard duty tonight. If it was James or John . . . maybe. But the followers of Jesus are not men to be trifled with. As the Lord sleeps, they draw their swords and post themselves as guards across every entrance lest an assassin creep in and . . ." He drew his finger slowly across his throat. "These are dangerous times. Your friend Lazarus paid for tonight's lodging for all of us. Most everyone's asleep now. Sorry." He yawned. "As for me, my quarters are in the stable with the rest of the boys. Sorry. You'll have to wait till morning."

My master slept on a cot in a tent, hastily pitched on the roof of the inn. I saw the glint of moonlight on the blade of his sword as he unsheathed it. I was given a thick fleece on the floor as my bedroll. Lying down just inside the tent flap, I could see the stars. I longed for my mother and father and our mountain home. The story in the constellations was the same no matter where I lay my head.

I wondered what Rabbi Kagba must have felt the night before he learned of old Herod's plots and warned the parents of the newborn King of Israel to flee from Bethlehem to Egypt. More than three decades after that time, constellations still shone brightly in heaven, telling the story of the Messiah and the great battle for mankind's redemption. On earth, the son of Herod the Butcher King had taken his father's place and still sought to destroy the Redeemer.

I studied the starry cup of salvation, which hung between the Virgin and the Lion of Judah. The Atonement star, the one Rabbi Kagba referred to as the Heart of the Virgin, was poised directly above the outline of the cup. Keeping pace with their passage across the heavens was the distinctive outline of the Lion of Judah.

My fingers closed around the cup, and I quietly whispered the portion of Jeremiah that had been read on the day of my circumcision.

"The word of the LORD came to me saying,
   'Before I formed you in the womb
   I knew you, before you were born I set you apart!'
   'Ah, Sovereign LORD,' I said, 'I am only a child!'
   But the LORD said to me, 'Do not say, "I am only a child." You must go to everyone I send you to and say whatever I command you. Do not be afraid of them, for I am with you and will rescue you!'"[2]

I was unafraid as I fixed my gaze upon heaven's goblet. I was certain that my journey and my role as cupbearer had been preordained like the path of the stars, long before my life on earth had begun. I did not fear the assassins of Herod Antipas, who were surely lurking very near. I was unafraid of the Pharisees, who envied the love of the people for Jesus, or the Romans, who feared his power and plotted his destruction. God's plan was written in the books of Moses and inscribed above me in the stars. My name, Nehemiah, cupbearer to the King of kings, and Joseph's name were woven into the story too.

An owl hooted from a tree in the courtyard. Pilgrim fires beyond the walls of the inn burned to embers. The whole world was waiting for the dawn when the rightful owner of Joseph's cup would be crowned as Israel's true King!

I closed my eyes at last. "I am not afraid, heavenly Father,"

I prayed as I drifted toward sleep. "I know that my King Jesus rests beneath this very roof. Nothing can turn back your purpose. What men intend for evil, you intend for good . . . to save the lives of many. And I am nearly at the end of my journey."

All the world was asleep. A cool breeze stirred the fabric of the tent. Even in my slumber the sounds were familiar. I dreamed of my father's sheep lying in the moonlight of our high mountain pastures. The smoke of pine and wood from the pilgrim fires blended with the familiar song of a nightingale on the rooftop. Was I in a village in Eretz-Israel? Or in my distant homeland? I could not tell. I felt comforted with the sense that my mother was asleep near me. She sighed and turned over on her bed. In the distance I saw the strong silhouette of my father standing watch over his flocks.

The wind carried his voice across the miles. "Nehi?"

"Here I am, Papa," I whispered.

"Where are you?"

"Here. On the rooftop of an inn near Jerusalem, Papa. Apprenticed to a rich merchant." My answer confused me. Was I not at home? "I'm dreaming," I said aloud.

"You are Nehemiah," noted a voice that was not my father's.

"Cupbearer to the King," I replied. I touched the ancient cup and opened my eyes.

The dream dissolved, and every detail of my journey flooded into my consciousness.

Someone was walking on the rooftop pavilion. My master did not awaken. Parting the flap, I saw a man standing on the parapet. With stars above him and watch fires below, he seemed almost suspended between heaven and earth. He looked out across the hills and valleys toward Jerusalem. In an instant I recognized him.

"It's him. It's Jesus," I whispered, clasping the cup and crawling out from the warmth of my nest.

He turned his head slightly as I emerged. I knew he heard me. It was cold, and my feet were bare. Shoeless feet seemed proper, somehow. I remembered the instruction of God to Moses when he approached the burning bush: "Take off your sandals, for the place where you are standing is holy ground."[3]

I approached slowly, holding the cup in both hands as an offering. I halted an arm's length from his back. The moonlight cast his shadow over me. There were no clouds in the sky, yet the breeze carried the fresh scent of rain.

"Sir?"

"Nehemiah." There was a pleasant smile in his voice when he said my name. I was not surprised that he knew me. I thought he probably knew everything. "You are a long way from home."

"Yes, sir. From the mountains of Gan Eden, I came to find you. To bring you this . . . this gift."

My reply seemed to satisfy him. "Well then, Nehemiah. Just where you are meant to be." He turned then and smiled down at me with my outstretched hands and upturned face. His eyes seemed sad as he studied the gift for a long moment: the cup, Joseph's cup, tarnished and neglected, waiting to be filled. "And how is my old friend, your teacher, Rabbi Kagba?"

"Alive when last I saw him. He wanted to come to you himself but sent me with this instead."

He nodded, pressed his lips together, and touched the rim with his index finger. "In his place you will bear the cup into Jerusalem as I enter the city, Nehemiah."

"Please, Lord. Will you take it from me now? It's been a

terrible burden. I almost lost it once. I dropped it in the woods with the Great Hart. And you see, I didn't polish it. No one knows what it is. Who it belonged to. I was afraid of thieves, so I left it as we found it. Not even a thief wants an old tarnished cup. They couldn't recognize it as it is."

"But you, Nehemiah, you know what it means."

"Yes, sir. The rabbi told me. And Joseph, son of Jacob, the Prince of Egypt himself, appeared to me in dreams. He told me it means something that your earthly father's name is also Joseph, son of Jacob. And that you are called Son of Joseph."

Jesus smiled. "Everything means something."

I blurted, "Now I'm so close and I'm afraid I'll lose it. Afraid I'll fail you."

"No chance of that." He placed his hand upon my head. "You'll have to carry the cup for me until it's time for me to drink from it. You'll travel with us now. A boy among the other boys, Nehi."

I felt relieved. The burden was lifted. I had found Jesus. Or rather, I had searched and searched until at last Jesus had found me on the rooftop. I knew I would be safe with him. Joseph's cup would be safe beneath his protection. "I am your servant, Lord."

"There's work to be done before Passover. It's the duty of the cupbearer to polish the cup. I'll need it shined up, inside and out, for our Passover supper together in Jerusalem. Hidden beneath the tarnish of the ages, you'll find the pattern of the cup is quite beautiful."

I was suddenly very tired. I drew the cup against my heart. "I was dreaming of my mother and father. Of my home."

Jesus bent down until his eyes looked deeply into my eyes. "They are well, Nehemiah. You will see them when the time is right."

I inhaled and exhaled deeply as the grief of months vanished with his assurance. Peace flooded my heart. I had no doubt then that I'd see them again . . . somehow, somewhere. If Jesus could heal the suffering Tobit and the blind Peniel and bring the dead Lazarus back to life, surely he could accomplish the goal of reuniting me with my parents. My memory of the throat-slashing motion of Zimri that had announced to me their death now faded in the light of the clear truth in Jesus' simple words. "Thank you, Lord."

"Now, go to sleep. And tell no one about our conversation. Tomorrow you will join the boys who follow our camp."

"How will I know when to give you the cup?"

"You'll know. Very soon."

He kissed my brow, and I returned to the warmth of my fleece bedroll. My head barely touched the pillow, and I was fast asleep.

Chapter 27

Morning came late and gloomy. A bank of dark thunderheads, low on the eastern horizon, blocked the sunrise.

I opened my eyes as someone quietly recited morning prayers inside the tent. I recognized my mother's weaving in the prayer shawl wrapped around the man, but the voice was not familiar to me.

"Blessed is he who spoke and the universe came into being. Blessed is he who keeps the whole world going."

Was I home in the shepherd camp of Amadiya? On the road? In Joppa? Jerusalem?

I sat up slowly, and my hand fell upon the cup. I remembered then. The inn. Jesus. Lazarus. Peter. Peniel, the cheerful scribe.

"Blessed is he who does what he says. Blessed is he who decrees and finishes." It was not my father but Joseph of Arimathea who recited the blessing upon the day. "Blessed is he who has mercy upon the earth. Blessed is he who has mercy upon creation. Blessed is he who gives a good reward to those who fear him."

My conversation with Jesus on the rooftop last night returned to my memory in a flash, as a dream returns to mind when one is fully awake. I stared at the cup and wondered if I had truly met Jesus here, or if the meeting was only a dream.

"Blessed is he who lives and endures forever. Blessed is he who rescues and redeems us. Blessed is his name!"

Rubbing my eyes, I stared at Joseph. He was a good man, searching for the truth like everyone else.

"Blessed are you, Lord our God, King of the universe and our merciful heavenly Father, who is praised by your people and glorified by the tongues of your pious servants. We praise you through the songs of David, your servant, O Lord our God, with praises and songs. We glorify you and declare your Name and your rule, O God; your great Name glorified forever and ever. Blessed are you, Lord, the King who is to be praised."

I offered my small "Amen" at the end of my benefactor's prayers.

"*Shalom,* Nehemiah." Joseph removed his prayer shawl.

"Good morning." I stood and yawned. I smelled baking bread, and my stomach growled.

"You're hungry." Joseph folded the prayer shawl I had watched my mother fashion so very long ago. "Throw on your cloak. Let's go."

I washed, dressed, and laced my sandals, then followed Joseph down the steep outside steps. As my foot touched the pavement, I heard the loud bang of the barn door and the angry shouts of a dozen boys. A brawl tumbled out of the stable into the courtyard. Like a pack of puppies, the tribe seemed divided into two factions.

Two boys about my age grappled and fell, then rolled on the ground. Punches punctuated the cheers and jeers.

"Get him, Avel!"

"Slaughter him, Davin!"

"Don't let him get away with that!"

"Shut his lying mouth!"

"In the gut. Hit him in the belly!"

"That's it. That's it!"

Pious heads popped out of windows to observe. Pharisees, prayer shawls billowing like the wings of gulls, swooped into the melee.

Then I spotted Jesus, framed in a doorway. He observed the battle for only an instant, then waded into it. Grasping both combatants by the backs of their tunics, he separated them. Still they swung. Jesus held them out of reach of one another as they flailed, then finally gave up. They scowled at one another across the gulf of his arm's reach.

The crowd grew thick—Pharisees, servants of Pharisees, and the men and women of Jesus' band. They looked on in silence.

"Avel." Jesus looked at the bloody face of the fair-haired boy in his right hand. "What's this?"

Avel wiped his nose with the back of his sleeve. "This . . . this cur—"

Jesus shook Avel a little. Avel fell silent. Jesus addressed the boy in his left hand. "All right, then. What's your name?"

A gruff, ragged servant of one of the Pharisees replied defiantly, "He's my boy. Davin is his name. We are in service to Hamid, a Pharisee of Jerusalem and a member of the council."

Davin spat, "And your boy Avel swung first."

Avel shouted, "He was calling you names, Master! Said you are a fraud. Said it was all tricks what you do!"

Davin wriggled and kicked at Avel. "It's true. My father and my master say you're nothing but a troublemaker! Say you're nothing. Nothing! Going to turn the world upside down and get everybody crucified!"

Davin's father raised his chin and stepped forward. "All true. Now I'll thank you to put my boy down."

Jesus effortlessly swung the boy into his father's reach. Then he set Avel to the side. "Go on, Avel. That's enough."

The father placed his son behind him and drew himself up to challenge Jesus. His hands clenched and unclenched. For a moment I thought he would strike Jesus.

Peter rushed between them and faced off with the father. "Get back! You . . . you and that devil's spawn of yours! You're nothing but scum! Pawns of Israel's oppressors."

I spotted Avel's bloody face scowling out from among Jesus' disciples. A woman took his arm, guided him to the side, and dabbed his nose. The crowd of onlookers became a divided mob.

The opposition shouted and cursed Jesus as a pretender and a blasphemer.

Jesus' followers defended their teacher vehemently.

"Jesus can fight for himself, all right!"

"Lord, call down hell fire on them! Burn them up—like Elijah!"

Jesus' eyes flashed angrily, and I thought for a moment he might summon bolts of lightning and brimstone from the sky. Instead, he raised his hand and addressed his people. "That's enough! Be still. You don't know what you are saying!"

Instantly both factions fell silent. Jesus searched the faces of the opposition, fixing his gaze on one opulently dressed Pharisee.

Joseph muttered, "That's Hamid."

Jesus summoned the ruler. "Come here, Hamid. Take your servant and your servant's son. The place to settle this debate is not here. Not now."

The ruler snapped his finger and called his servants as if they were dogs. He warned Jesus, "The time is coming. You are right about that. It will be settled."

The confrontation broke up. Those who had come to discredit Jesus grumbled as they returned to the business of saying morning prayers and preparing to travel to Jerusalem.

Joseph and I hung back as Jesus stooped in front of Avel and the woman tending his nose.

"Well, Avel. You'll have two black eyes, I think." Jesus looked up at the woman. "A cold compress, eh, Mother?"

I knew her name from the stories Rabbi Kagba had told me. Mary. She was beautiful. Her brown eyes with flecks of gold had smile lines at the corners. Hair and eye color was so much like her son.

Mary nodded. "Not broken. Not this time, eh, Avel?"

"No. I'm sorry." The boy cast his blue eyes downward, then hung his head. "I . . . I just couldn't help it. He was so . . . so . . ."

I was surprised that Jesus did not reach out and staunch the flow of blood or heal the bruised eyes. Jesus said quietly, "Pray for the boy you think is your enemy, Avel. Perhaps he will one day learn the truth for himself and become your brother."

"I could have shut his mouth."

Mary murmured, "Poor boy. Yes, Avel, pray for him. He doesn't speak his own words, but only repeats what he has been taught."

Jesus patted Avel on the back. "No more of this, Avel. It solved nothing, as you see."

Avel's friends circled around him. Jesus' disciples joined them.

Jesus said, "Things that cause people to sin are sure to come, but woe to the person from whom they come. It would be better for him to be thrown into the sea with a millstone around his neck than to cause one of these little ones to sin."[1]

Peter growled, "I'll pray for them. Pray them right into

hell where they belong. I look forward to the day when we bury these . . . hypocrites! I'll never forgive them for such arrogant disrespect for you, Lord. Who knows what other sins they hide?"

Jesus did not acknowledge Peter but continued speaking as if he had not heard his words. "Watch yourselves. If your brother sins, rebuke him and if he repents, forgive him. If he sins against you seven times in a day and seven times comes back to you and says, 'I repent,' forgive him."[2]

The apostles said to the Lord, "Increase our faith!"

Jesus held up his thumb and forefinger, demonstrating how a small fragment of faith could accomplish mighty deeds . . . such as forgiveness. "If you have faith as small as a mustard seed, you can say to this mulberry tree, 'Be uprooted and planted in the sea,' and it will obey you."[3]

At that instant, Joseph placed his hand on my shoulder. "There's Lazarus." He inclined his head toward the man I had seen near Jesus the night before. He stood behind Jesus' mother and spoke to Avel over her shoulder. In the morning light Lazarus looked to be about the same age as Jesus. He glanced up at Joseph, then came to where we stood at the foot of the stairs.

"My old friend." Lazarus clapped my master on his back. "I'm glad you've come."

"I returned to Joppa and heard all the news," Joseph said, making the same gesture of companionship. "I came straight away to find you . . . to see. The news was all . . . about you. Is it true?"

Lazarus replied with a single nod. "Yes. If it had not been for Jesus, you would have returned home and found my place at the table empty and my cup poured out."

For a moment Joseph's eyes brimmed with emotion. He did

not remove his hand from Lazarus's shoulder. "Well. Well then. We have both been on far journeys, it seems. One for business and the other for . . . for . . . ," he stammered.

"For the business of the Kingdom of God." Lazarus lifted his chin slightly. His brow furrowed. "It is more beautiful than we could ever have imagined . . ."

"The parable that Jesus told last night . . . It seems this is a far land in which every man will want to dwell. I must speak with him. I have a question that only he will be able to answer. If it is possible."

"Yes. Yes. I know he'll want to speak with you. Tonight is *Shabbat*. Then after that?"

Joseph cleared his throat. "I've got to return to Jerusalem before *Shabbat*. Some business to take care of. But then I'll come back." He added, "My apprentice, Nehemiah, I'd like him to stay here among Jesus' followers until I return."

Lazarus agreed with a laugh. "Nehemiah. Well then, you can stay among our boys. There are a dozen or so who travel with us. They all have duties in the camp. You may have noticed Avel, whose desire is to be a bodyguard." He laughed. "We will put you to work."

And so it was that Joseph delayed his conversation with Jesus. He would return first to Jerusalem to inspect the completion of the family tomb, since Passover was rapidly approaching. If the work was done, he would pay the wages of the men who labored there.

"Please, Master Joseph," I asked, "while you're there, can you go by my grandparents' shop? I'd like to know if it's really getting rebuilt."

Joseph agreed to check on the work in the Street of the Weavers, then left me in the care of his friend Lazarus.

So it was that I took my place among Avel and his two brothers, Ha-or Tov and Emet. Ha-or Tov was twelve, had curly, red hair and pale skin, and was the eldest of the three. Avel was ten and a cheerful boy. Emet was six, fair-haired like Avel, and had somber brown eyes. A wild sparrow perched on his shoulder, flitted to his head, and then to his hand. He fed the bird bread crumbs and called him *Yediyd*, which means "friend."

It was the bird and his endearing actions that made me laugh for almost the first time since the night my father's camp was attacked. There was a story in the bird—a tiny sparrow crushed by the hands of evil, but then healed by Yeshua and now a gift of great joy to a poor boy, Avel said, nodding at his little brother.

The brothers had once been counted among the orphan boys of Jerusalem, living in the caverns beneath the city as Sparrows until they were adopted by an old shepherd of Bethlehem named Zadok.

Zadok had the look of a man who had been mauled by a lion. I had grown up with men who were scarred and battered in the battle to protect the flocks from wild beasts. He was missing one eye, wore a patch over the socket, and his face was creased with an old wound.

That morning he fed the livestock, which were a part of Jesus' band of followers. Mary, the mother of Jesus, spoke to the old man cheerfully as he passed. She and a number of other women served the disciples breakfast. It seemed to me that perhaps Mary was related to Zadok in some way. There was a familiar family bond between them.

The children of the camp ate separately from the adults. I was seated between Avel and Emet. Between bites of bread and eggs, the brothers poured out the story of Zadok.

Avel wore his black eyes like badges of honor. He shrugged.

"Look at my old father there. That patch. A spear hit him in the face, and that's where he lost his eye. Jesus could give him two eyes, but he don't want it. He says his face is a reminder of what the Herods did to his sons, and he is proud of his wounds."

Emet added, "Zadok's a fighter too. So I guess it's right we're his sons."

The old man had spent his life watching over the flocks at Bethlehem. He had a wife and three small sons when Jesus was born in a lambing cave. He had seen angels appear in the sky and had been among the first to hold the infant King of Israel. Mary, Joseph, and the baby had stayed in Zadok's house. When the Magi arrived to pay homage, it was at the home of Zadok where they found Jesus.

I had heard some of the story from Rabbi Kagba. The foreigners had warned Mary and Joseph to flee from Herod. Then the soldiers had come. I was familiar with that much of the tale.

Avel filled in the rest. "Zadok fought the Herodian guards like they were wolves. But he was struck down, and his boys were slaughtered by the soldiers of Herod the Great. So Zadok lost his sons and his eye in the fight. He carried a deep scar across his face and in his heart until Jesus returned to Bethlehem many years later."

Ha-or Tov added, "We three were lost sheep, see? Homeless. No family. Then Jesus healed us—my eyes."

"My broken heart," Avel added.

"My ears, my mouth," Emet said.

Ha-or Tov picked up the story. "And then Jesus brought us to the house of Zadok in Bethlehem and entreated Zadok to accept us as true sons."

So it was that Avel, Emet, and Ha-or Tov had filled the places and hearts of the family that had been lost.

Now old Zadok and his boys were among the circle of about a hundred close followers who had left every worldly possession to be with Jesus.

Breakfast nearly finished, Emet rested his chin in his hand and tilted his head slightly like a puppy waiting to be fed. "All right, then. Now you know everything about us. We know nothing about you. Except that you talk funny. You're not from around here, for sure. What's your story?"

I thought of the hart. The cup. My great journey. The purpose of my life and the meaning of my name. Surely they would not believe me. I summed up everything: "I am also the son of a shepherd. His name is Lamsa. And my mother, Sarah, is a weaver of prayer shawls in the land where Eden once was on earth. Very far from here."

The little bird flitted from Emet's shoulder to Avel's right index finger when he pointed at me. "There's got to be more to it than that."

I stuck out my finger, and the sparrow hopped onto my hand. I laughed and then spoke the horrible words as if they were nothing. "I was separated from my family when bandits attacked our camp. My grandparents are in Joppa, and I am an apprentice to Joseph of Arimathea."

"A very rich fellow." Ha-or Tov narrowed his eyes. "So why did he leave you here?"

The question was so straightforward I could not think of any answer but the truth. I passed the sparrow back to Avel, who kissed it on the beak, then handed it to Emet.

"My true master—Joseph of great reputation—has given me a task. I'm to polish his family's old *Kiddush* cup for Passover. I'll bring it to Jerusalem."

Emet asked, "That's it?"

I replied, "That's it."

Avel's head bobbed thoughtfully. "Have you got it? The cup, I mean?"

I reached into the pouch and produced the tarnished vessel. Holding it out to my new friends, I said, "That's it. Clean it. That's my task."

The three were unimpressed. Avel shrugged. "Joseph is so rich he could buy all the *Kiddush* cups in Jerusalem. Brand-new. Gold, even. But he's got to have this old thing, eh?"

"It goes way back." I rubbed it with the fabric of my tunic. "Tradition."

Avel agreed. "Well then. Good luck, Nehemiah. That's all I have to say. Fellows like your master think tradition is everything. If Joseph wants an old beat-up cup for Passover, I guess you're stuck with it. It'll take you all the way till Passover to get it shined, I think."

Ha-or Tov stuck out his lower lip. "Suppose it's just all that color. Black. You scrub and scrub and . . . nothing."

I turned the thing over in my hand, hoping for even a glimmer of light, but the tarnish of ages was thick and unforgiving of my task. From across the courtyard I heard Mary laughing with two other women and a small girl. I remembered what my rabbi had taught me: for his safety, the birth of the King of Israel, Messiah, Redeemer, was hidden from all the world in a stable. But above the earth the stars of the heavens proclaimed his coming.

"One day, in God's timing, the curtain will be pulled back and the glory of the Holy of Holies will shine forth."

I frowned at the dark cup in my hand and knew that the dark layer would somehow be stripped away to reveal its secret.

Chapter 28

Mary and other women labored in preparation for the *Shabbat* celebration, which would begin at sunset. Only a handful of Pharisees remained at the inn. The rest had returned to Jerusalem. The gates of the caravansary were closed and locked, preventing crowds from mobbing the place where Jesus stayed.

Within the earshot of everyone Jesus took his place in the portico and told stories no one had ever heard before.

In the courtyard of the inn was a large mulberry tree. Climbing up, cup in hand, I shared a thick lower branch with the sparrow, Yediyd. As I drank in Jesus' tales, I rubbed at the blackened silver with a soft scrap of fleece. I worked until my fingers ached. My efforts to polish Joseph's cup seemed hopeless. Only a slight gleam of silver shone through at the rim and on a raised, rounded shape on the side. Perhaps a cluster of grapes? I wondered. I wished now I had begun to shine it long before.

Others in the camp labored so they could rest with the Master during *Shabbat*. I would not complete my task before *Shabbat* began at sunset, when I would be forced to lay it aside. And when I resumed? Perhaps I would not even have it cleaned before Passover!

Could I have come so far and suffered so much, only to

end my journey in abject failure? The cup was so unworthy of presenting to anyone, let alone the Messiah. Hopping up to a smaller branch near my head, Yediyd bobbed and flicked his tail, sensing my anxiety.

Jesus unfolded a lesson that seemed directed at me. "Suppose one of you had a servant plowing, or looking after the sheep."

My head rose at the mention of shepherd's work. I was familiar with the nature of a herdsman's labor. There was never a day of rest for a shepherd. The task of caring for the flock was endless.

Jesus continued, "Would you say to the servant when you came in from the field, 'Come along now and sit down to eat?' Would you not rather say, 'Prepare my supper, get yourself ready, and wait on me while I eat and drink. After that, you may eat and drink'? Would you thank the servant because he did what he was told to do?"

How many times had my family eaten a *Shabbat* meal prepared by hireling shepherds around the watch fire? And when my father and brothers had finished their *Shabbat* meals, they took their turn watching the flocks. Only then did the hireling shepherds eat.

I scrubbed at the stubborn tarnish and pictured the scene Jesus described. It seemed to me he glanced at me in the tree. Yediyd bowed and preened. "So you also, when you have done everything you were told to do, should say, 'We are unworthy servants; we have only done our duty.'"

Jesus' words confirmed I had not done my duty until my assignment was complete. Only I did not know how to accomplish the task given me.

A barrage of questions erupted from the disciples as I clambered down from the mulberry tree. Bypassing them, I hastened over to where Mary laid out and smoothed the wrinkles from prayer shawls that had recently been cleaned.

Some of the knotted corners were tangled and messy. Unhurriedly, Mary prized out the snarls so the fringes hung properly. She was chatting pleasantly with Martha, the sister of Lazarus.

Noticing me looking on, Martha observed, "Mary is the best at untying knots there is. No one else has the patience or the skill."

I held the cup out to Jesus' mother, confident she did not know what it was, but that perhaps she could tell me how to make it bright and suitable to present.

"Nehemiah?" A smile lit the crinkled lines of her face. She turned her brown-gold eyes on me. Stepping around the corner of the building, she wiped the flour from her hands on a blue-and-white apron. "So you are here at last, cupbearer."

Suddenly my words were not my own. "Hail, Mary . . . highly favored of the Most High. Favored among all women!"

She answered, "Blessed be the one who sent you. I have been looking for you. Not at all as I expected."

I thought she was speaking of my rabbi. "My teacher, Rabbi Kagba, whom you knew from early days, sends his greetings to the mother of the Lord. He told me you are a gracious and righteous woman, and that you would help me."

She smiled again. "Ah. The student of Rabbi Kagba, among the Magi from beyond the two rivers."

"He sent me in his place. Told me to bring your son this final gift from distant kings who knelt to him and recognized him first among all men, except for us shepherds."

She took the cup from me and peered into the dark well of it. Her pleasant eyes grew sad, and I thought for a moment she must have seen something terrible and tragic in it.

Mary whispered, "Your burden is a very old one, Nehemiah. To know something wonderful . . . that what men intend for evil, God intends for good. Yes. A sword to pierce a mother's heart. To know and yet never to speak of it."

"Joseph's cup. The ancient son of Jacob, who saved all his people after his brothers meant him evil."

"Only a few would recognize the glory of this cup."

"Unless I clean it, it won't be worthy." I showed her my chapped fingers.

Once again I became just a boy, and she became a woman of practical household knowledge.

She instructed, "You'll never get it clean only by scrubbing. The tarnish is too deep."

"Then how?"

"Come with me."

First, Mary immersed the cup in a pot of boiling water and left it there. She led me to a stack of baggage that traveled with the camp. Rummaging through wooden boxes, she produced a plain container crusted with white powder. "Natron," she said. "From the shore of the Dead Sea."

I knew it well. Natron was a common substance carried for trade among the caravans that crossed my father's lands. It was a form of salt, a preservative. First found at the springs of Wadi al Natron in Egypt, the ancients used the mineral to embalm royalty. It was a chief ingredient in the preservation of fresh fish. Mixed with olive oil, it made a fine soap.

With a long metal spoon, Mary fished out the vessel and wrapped it in a towel. The cup seemed unchanged to me, yet she assured me the boiling water had loosened the grime. Then she measured out a small amount of the pale mineral and mixed it with olive oil and lemon juice. Placing the substance in a wooden bowl, she instructed, "Rub this on when the metal cools a bit. With time and effort the cup will reveal what lies beneath the crust of ages."

❦

Jesus, Lazarus, and the other disciples left the caravansary in the afternoon to teach and to heal among the multitude of pilgrims who gathered outside the gates. My new friends, Peniel the scribe, Ha-or Tov, Avel, Emet, and the old shepherd, Zadok, accompanied them. Even the little sparrow, Yediyd, chirped once, ruffled his feathers, then flitted away and swooped over the wall of the inn to pursue them.

Only the women remained behind to prepare for our *Shabbat* supper. I wanted to fly away with all my heart. But the morning lessons of Jesus about a servant sticking to his task kept me rooted beside the mulberry tree.

Mary examined my progress on the cup and frowned. "Perhaps it's more than tarnish. It seems . . . yes . . . as though it may have been in a fire. Scorched. Smoke." She presented me with a second batch of cleanser. "You'll conquer it. You wouldn't have been given the task if it was impossible."

With the second application the black crust began to transfer from the cup to the fleece cloth. I held it up to the light. The faint image of a cluster of grapes and leaves on a vine had begun to emerge. I shared the joy of my progress with Mary. She held the object tenderly, in both hands, as if it were a bird with a broken wing. With a tone of awe she remarked, "Look here. Scorch marks. Yes. You can see the scar. The silver passed through the fire. *Tish b'Av* . . . It must have been."

"*Tish b'Av?*"

She traced the outline of the vines as though she had seen them

267

before. "You know of it, Nehemiah. The day the Babylonians destroyed Solomon's Temple." She kissed the chalice. "Joseph's cup had a place of honor in Solomon's Temple. And then, when Jerusalem burned, the cup and all the other treasures disappeared."

I answered, knowing the story well. "Our people were exiled and made slaves. And when the captivity ended, many Jews returned with Nehemiah. But my father's family never returned to Eretz-Israel."

Mary touched my forehead. "Until now, this moment. Until you returned, bringing it with you, Nehemiah, cupbearer to the King. Blessed be God forever." She pressed it into my hands and returned to her preparation.

The caravansary was filled with the delicious aromas of cooking food. Fresh bread. Lamb roasting in a deep pit. Everything was ready when Jesus and the company returned.

But still the cup was not finished as the sun sank lower to the horizon. My friends gushed about the events and miracles of the day.

Avel grimaced. "There were ten of them. Lepers!"

Emet pantomimed missing limbs and shuffling gaits.

Ha-or Tov held his nose and said, "We smelled them coming!"

Yediyd the sparrow riding his shoulder, Avel exclaimed, "And then . . . all ten! Jesus says to them, 'Go show yourselves to the priests.' Ten of them at once. And they left and all were healed as they went! But only one bothered to come back and say thank you."[1]

Peniel inquired of me, "So, how was your day?"

I replaced the cup in its pouch. "Quiet."

The boys were still yammering as they went to wash.

Mary sought me out and asked to examine the result of my labor.

"Half done," I mumbled, trying not to think of all I had missed in that glorious day.

"Come with me." She brought me to a clay pot in the stable. "Water and new wine," she said, removing the lid and dropping the paste-covered cup into the liquid. "This will be our last work until *Shabbat* ends. Now we rest and let God finish what he began."

"If you say so." I felt like a failure.

She stooped until her face was inches from mine. "Truly, Nehemiah. It is *Shabbat*. You have not failed. Only . . . rest and rejoice now. Great things await us as you bring the Cup of Joseph back to Jerusalem, and it is revealed at last."

Our *Shabbat* supper was served in the open courtyard of the inn. Low tables were spread with heaping platters for our feast and crowned with wildflowers gathered from green velvet hills.

The departing sun, shimmering like molten silver, set the sky on fire as it dropped into the western horizon. Even in my homeland I had never seen such colors in a sundown. Clouds like the orange and red banners of an angelic army unfurled above our heads. I thought of the two angels I was taught accompany every Jew to Sabbath supper.

Jesus wrapped himself in his prayer shawl and sang *"Shalom Aleichem,"* welcoming the Sabbath. "Peace upon you, O ministering angels, angels of the Exalted One—from the King who reigns over kings, the Holy One, blessed is he." His voice was a clear, bright baritone, rivaling that of the finest cantor, and seemed to color the air around us. "May your coming be for peace, O angels of peace, angels of the Exalted One—from the King who reigns over kings, the Holy One, blessed is he."

I wondered if Jesus had commanded the beauty of this evening into existence just for the joy of those whom he loved. I had not seen such glory before. Nor have I seen any sunset like it since.

"Bless me for peace, O angels of peace, angels of the Exalted One—from the King who reigns over kings."

We sang the next lines with him. "The Holy One, blessed is he. May your departure be to peace, O angels of peace, angels of the Exalted One, from the King who reigns over kings, the Holy One, blessed is he."

The voices of men, women, and children were charged with expectation as we sang, "May your departure be to peace, O angels of peace. He will charge his angels for you, to protect you in all your ways . . . your going and returning, from this time and forever more."[2]

Natural light faded to lavender and bright pink; then Mary lit the candles at the table of her son and his favored disciples. She stood above where he was seated. As she gazed down at him, her eyes contained the same deep sorrow I had seen when she looked into Joseph's cup for the first time. She briefly patted his shoulder. It was a gesture of pride and encouragement. But there was something else. I heard a whisper in my heart and knew that this was the last ordinary *Shabbat* mother and son would share together. I think that good woman sensed the end of all things familiar as well.

Jesus placed his hand over Mary's finger, raised his face to her, and sang *"Lecha Dodi"*:

> "Wake up, wake up, for your light has come!
> Rise up and shine; awaken, awaken, utter a song.
> The glory of the Lord is revealed on you.
> Why are you downcast? Why are you disconsolate?

In you will my peoples afflicted find shelter
as the city is built upon its hilltop."

We all joined in the song as holiness descended and filled the place.

"O Sanctuary of the King, royal City—
arise and depart from the unheaval.
Too long have you dwelt in the valley of weeping.
He will have compassion upon you."

The voices of Jesus and Mary blended in perfect harmony as they must have over a lifetime of Sabbaths.

"Shake off the dust—arise!
Don your splendid clothes, my people.
Through the son of Jesse, the Bethlehemite,
draw near to my soul, redeem it!"

Lazarus sat at his right hand, John at his left. Others, including Peter and Zadok, shared the head table. A handful of Pharisees was among the guests, but mostly it was a family gathering.

Martha and the other Mary, the two sisters of Lazarus, sang the blessing at my table. But I missed my mother. I longed to see my father's face. I remembered the wonderful discussions of *Torah* that seasoned every morsel of my family's *Shabbat* meals.

And then stars winked on above our heads. The music and prayers turned to questions.

A Pharisee seated opposite Peter lifted his hand and asked Jesus, "Rabbi! Rabbi? When will the Kingdom of God come? We all look for it, as the song says."

Jesus answered, "The Kingdom of God does not come with observation, nor will they say, 'Here it is,' or 'There it is.' Because the Kingdom of God is within you."[3]

Everyone understood the question, and I think there was a little disappointment at the answer. Everyone, including me, longed for the moment when the King, the Son of David, would accept the crown of David, son of Jesse. When would he take his rightful place in Jerusalem and establish the kingdom of righteousness on earth forever?

Jesus did not expand on his answer until the meal was ended and the last song was sung. The strangers and doubters among us drank their last cup of wine, recited their prayers with perfect memorization, and toddled off to bed.

The embers of the fire burned low, and one by one the candles burned out. The other boys went to sleep in the stable. Though I was tired, I took my place behind the mulberry tree and listened as Jesus spoke to a few disciples who remained.

"The time is coming when you will long to see one of the days you have spent with the Son of Man, but you will not see it. People will tell you, 'There he is!' or, 'Here he is!' Do not go running off after them. For the Son of Man in his day will be like the lightning, which flashes and lights up the sky from one end to the other.

"But first I must suffer many things and be rejected by this generation. Just as it was in the days of Noah, so also it will be in the days of the Son of Man." He swept his hand over the remains of our feast. "People were eating and drinking, marrying and being given in marriage, up to the day Noah entered the ark. Then the Flood came and destroyed them all.

"It was the same in the days of Lot. People were eating and drinking, buying and selling, planting and building. But the day Lot left Sodom, fire and sulfur rained down from heaven and destroyed them all.

"It will be just like this on the day the Son of Man is revealed. On that day no one who is on the housetop, with possessions inside, should go down to get them. Likewise, no one in the field should go back for anything. Remember Lot's wife! Whoever tries to keep their life will lose it, and whoever loses their life will preserve it. I tell you, on that night two people will be in one bed; one will be taken and the other left. Two women will be grinding grain together; one will be taken and the other left."

"Where, Lord?" Peter asked.

I heard Jesus reply, "Where *tzion* is, there the eagles will gather together."[4]

I was the son of a shepherd, and I had learned the meaning of Jesus' parable from experience. Was it not the psalm my mother prayed over me every night of my life?

"He who dwells in the shelter of the Most High will rest in the shadow of the Almighty. Surely he will save you from the fowler's snare . . . He will cover you with his feathers, and under his wings you will find refuge."[5]

I had always loved the eagles of my high mountain home. Eagles mated for life and tenderly fed, protected, and raised their young together. The behavior of eagles marked the seasons for us shepherds. In the spring, Mama and I had observed as eagles spread their wings over giant nests and protected their vulnerable chicks. In the summer they taught the fledglings to fly by carrying them on their wings. In the autumn, sensing the onset of fierce winter storms, the great eagles gathered and circled in the heavens before they took their young and flew away to a safe haven. Those of us who were shepherds on earth knew the significance of eagles gathering in the heavens. When we saw this sign, it was time to move the flock to safety.

Some may say that night they heard Jesus use the Hebrew word *ah-tzam*, which means "body."

"Where the body is, the eagles will be gathered."

But my ears, long accustomed to the ancient Hebrew pronunciation still used in my mountains, heard him utter the word *tzion*.

On that *Shabbat* night beneath the stars, Jesus told us that, when the time was right, we would recognize the signs, and he would gather his flock from Zion into a refuge where they would be safe from storms that were coming upon the earth.

These were my thoughts when I finally could not hold my eyes open. *Shabbat* rest overcame my ability to take in even one more word. I fell asleep with my back against the trunk of the mulberry tree.

Chapter 29

All day I sensed the profound holiness of this Sabbath and did not want it to end.

Outside, the clouds broke briefly. Three stars hung in the sky as the *Havdalah* service began, separating Sabbath holiness from the six ordinary days of the week. It was the end of the seventh day. I had marked my journey across the vast wilderness by counting Sabbath rests.

Havdalah means "separation." That evening we could not have known that Jesus would soon be separate from us. Jesus' friend, Lazarus, was given the honor of leading us in the ritual.

Everyone knew that Lazarus, the owner of sacred vineyards, had died and been called back to life by Jesus. Lazarus had experienced separation from this world and knew from experience that after death comes life. He poured *Havdalah* wine made from grapes of his own vineyard.

Lazarus lifted the cup to recite the first blessing of the *Havdalah*. "*Baruch atah Adonai.* Blessed are you, Lord, our God, King of the universe, who creates the fruit of the vine."

I answered with the guests, "Amen."

Every Jew could recite by heart this blessing. These very words had been spoken by Melchizedek to Abraham.

Isaac, Jacob, Joseph, and Moses had recited the ancient

blessing from the beginning of our nation. King David had blessed the waters of Bethlehem as he offered the cup to the Lord. "Blessed are you, who made all things exist by your word. By whose will all things come to be."

On this night, seeing Lazarus and Jesus together, *Havdalah* took on new meaning.

Jesus, by his word, had turned water into wine. He had called forth from the grave a man who had been dead four days. I was only a child, yet as I watched, I understood. Lazarus spoke, and I knew that Jesus was the fulfillment of everything proclaimed in the first blessing and those blessings yet to come.

The second *Havdalah* blessing was recited over the fragrant spices. It was Mary, the beautiful sister of Lazarus, who came forward to present the spice box to Jesus.

Rabbi Kagba had taught me that the spices represent a compensation for mankind's loss of the *Shekinah* spirit. My rabbi, along with other wise men from the East, had offered *Havdalah* spices to the infant King of Israel.

Shekinah had departed from the Temple, but Jesus was the embodiment of all *Shekinah*'s glory and peace.

Jesus thanked Mary for her gift, then opened the spice box. Intense fragrance swirled into the room. He breathed it in, then passed the box, first to his mother.

Lazarus proclaimed, "Blessed are you, Lord, our God, King of the universe, who creates . . ."

Jesus' mother inhaled deeply of the scent. Perhaps the memory of the first box of spices given to her baby boy made her smile. She passed the spice box on to Lazarus. He closed his eyes, breathed in, and nodded. His brow furrowed. I wondered if he recalled the smell of the burial spices that had covered his body when he came out of his tomb?

The reality of seeing Lazarus alive filled me with awe. I considered, for the first time, that perhaps Jesus would raise my parents from death. I would ask him when I presented him with Joseph's cup. All things would be made new now that the King was coming to Jerusalem!

The third blessing was recited over a candle with three wicks. Jesus lit the candle from a few remaining embers. It was unlawful to kindle a fire during Sabbath, so this ritual marked the end of the day of rest.

I was not mistaken. Lazarus looked directly at Jesus when he proclaimed these words: "Blessed are you, Lord, our God, sovereign of the universe, who creates the light."

Three wicks, but one flame—impossible to distinguish one from another. The candle was passed from hand to hand, finally coming to me. I was the last to hold the light.

With a nod, Lazarus signaled me to bring the candle forward to the head table. Lazarus took it from me, and I resumed my seat.

We raised our cups and sipped the last wine of Sabbath, leaving a few drops in the bottom.

Then Jesus, the Light of the World, poured blood-red wine from his cup onto a plate. Jesus' face and the light of the three-wick candle were reflected in the wine.

He took the light from Lazarus and held it high as we all spoke the final blessing together. "*Baruch atah Adonai, Eloheinu, melekh ha'olam* . . . Blessed are you, who separates sacred from secular; between light and darkness; between Israel and the nations; between the seventh day and the six days of labor."

Then Jesus slowly lowered the flame toward the wine he had poured out. He hesitated and then, with a sigh, dipped the wicks into the wine and extinguished the flame. In that instant his reflection vanished, along with the light. "Amen," he said quietly, dipping his finger and touching wine to eyelids, mouth, heart, and the back of his neck.

In my heart I heard the word *separation*. I sensed the end of something . . . and the beginning of something. But what? I imitated the actions of Jesus. Dipping my finger into the drops of wine that remained, I anointed myself. Though my family had not followed this custom of anointing with wine, I felt somehow that everything Jesus did meant something.

Surely Jesus would be crowned during Passover. He would establish his kingdom and take over the palace in Jerusalem. Perhaps, when Jesus drank the last drops of wine from Joseph's cup, there would be no more simple Sabbath meals shared with us common folk.

We sang a psalm at the end of the service, then all began to laugh with joy.

Everyone laughed except Jesus. What was the sorrow I glimpsed in his eyes?

Zadok called to me along with his sons. He clapped me on the back and presented us each with a toy wooden sword he had made. The blades were engraved with the Hebrew word *Chazak*, which means "courage."

As the grown men talked, the women cleared the tables. I crossed swords with Avel, Emet, and Ha-or Tov. My thoughts, however, were on Joseph's cup, which had been soaking for days. I could hardly restrain myself from running to Mary and asking her to fetch it for me. But I played like a boy with my companions and pretended to be thinking of nothing else.

At last Yediyd flew from its perch and settled on Emet's shoulder. Emet found crumbs to feed it, and I hurried to find the Lord's mother. She cleared dishes from the table with the other women.

"Do you think it's finished?" I asked, tucking my sword in my belt.

She knew instantly what I meant. "The cup! It has begun, at least. While we rested, the new wine was at work. And you've been thinking about it today. Waiting for the day to end? Come on, then. Let's have a look."

I followed her to the wine jar containing the precious chalice. Using a long spoon, she fished it out of the concoction. The paste had nearly dissolved. Wine dripped from the metal.

Mary examined it. "Ahhh, a stubborn case. But this will give you a start." At first it seemed unchanged; then Mary picked at the rim with her finger and a dark strip peeled off, revealing bright silver beneath. Finely engraved grape leaves shone beneath. Mary wrapped the cup in a towel and gave it to me. "It is worthy. Yes. Beneath centuries of neglect, tarnish, and soot there is something so beautiful . . . Look! Nehemiah, you'll have to be diligent. For his Passover supper in Jerusalem. The tarnish will yield to you, if you don't give up."

Sabbath officially ended, but Jesus continued teaching into the night. I held the cup in my hands and rubbed and rubbed as Jesus spoke. Layers of grime began to wear away under my patient labor. The beauty of the silver slowly shone through.

It was late when Joseph of Arimathea arrived at our lodging. He had left Jerusalem the moment Sabbath ended, in the company of several Pharisees who were his friends. They had ridden hard through the rain to reach the village where we stayed. Joseph and the others were soaking wet but did not stop to change. I spotted Joseph when he slipped into the dining hall.

Joseph stood, dripping, at Lazarus's back while his two companions moved to sit beside the once-dead man.

Avel frowned at the cup and complimented my labor. "Well, it's something, isn't it?"

"Maybe by Passover." I scrubbed harder.

Avel leaned in closer and whispered, "That's Rabbi Gamaliel, who came in with your master. A member of the council of seventy. And Nicodemus, his nephew, with him. Must be important if they rode all this way through the storm. Gamaliel and Nicodemus are good friends of Lazarus. They come often to hear the Lord teach. Zadok says they're good men."

In the distance thunder boomed and rain sluiced off the eaves. The storm drummed on the rooftop.

By candlelight, Jesus told us one last story.

"Two men went up to the temple to pray, one a Pharisee and the other a tax collector. The Pharisee stood by himself and prayed, 'God, I thank you that I am not like the rest of men, extortioners, grafters, adulterers, or even like this tax collector. I fast twice a week; I give tithes on everything I earn!'"

I saw the shadows on Joseph's face. His eyes narrowed as he pictured the scene. His expression was set like flint as he listened. I did not know why he lingered in the back while his friends had taken their places with Lazarus.

"But the tax collector, standing afar off, would not so much as raise his eyes to heaven but beat his chest, saying, 'Oh God, be merciful to me, a sinner!'"

Jesus looked across the heads of the crowd and seemed to speak directly to Joseph. "I say to you that this man returned to his house more righteous than the Pharisee. For everyone who exalts himself will be humbled, and everyone who humbles himself will be exalted."[1]

There was a stirring among the rich exalted men in the crowd that night. I heard them muttering as they made their way to their bedchambers. Only Joseph, Gamaliel, and Nicodemus remained behind with Lazarus, Zadok, Peniel, and the twelve of Jesus' closest disciples.

A few of us boys stayed in the room. I tucked the cup into its pouch and moved forward with my friends, wanting to show Jesus my progress.

Peter and James rebuked us. "Go on to the stable with you! The master is tired."

But Jesus heard them and called us to him. He placed his hands on our heads and blessed us.

I will never forget what happened after that. Jesus put his hand on my shoulder and said, "The Kingdom of heaven is for those who are like these boys. I say to you, he who will not receive the Kingdom of God like a little boy will never enter into it."[2]

I tried to think what he meant by that. What set boys apart from the men who towered over us? Yediyd perched on Emet's head. He reached up to scratch Yediyd's feathery belly. Avel drew himself erect and grinned at a sour-faced disciple. Ha-or Tov, who clasped a wooden sword, raised it high, saluted, and bowed. And I reached into the pouch and held the half-clean cup up to show its renewed gleam to the rightful owner.

"By Passover," I promised.

Jesus smiled. "Boys. The happy stewards of God's Kingdom."

Then Joseph cleared his throat and asked Jesus, "Good Teacher, what must I do to inherit everlasting life?"

Jesus leveled his eyes on Joseph's face and smiled. "Why do you call me good? There is no one good, except One, that is God. You know the commandments: 'Do not commit adultery,'

'Do not murder,' 'Do not steal,' 'Do not bear false witness,' 'Honor your father and your mother.'"

Joseph's face seemed so eager as he answered, "All these things I have done from my boyhood." He looked at me, and I knew by his reply that he was trying to tell Jesus that he was indeed trusting God like a little child.

Jesus lowered his chin and moved his hand from my shoulder to that of Joseph. "You lack one thing."

"What is it, Lord?"

"Go. Sell everything you have and give it to the poor and you will have treasure in heaven. Then come, follow me."

The light in Joseph's face dissolved into sorrow because, as everyone knew, Joseph was very rich.

When Jesus saw his sorrow, he said quietly, "How difficult it is for those who have wealth to enter into the Kingdom of God! It is easier for a rope . . . *khav-la* . . . to go through the eye of a needle than for a rich man to enter the Kingdom of God."

Thunder clapped and those in the room muttered, "Who then can be saved?"

Avel, who stood apart from us a few paces, told me later he thought he heard Jesus say it was easier for a camel . . . *gam-la* . . . to go through the eye of a needle than for a rich man to enter the kingdom.

That would have meant it was impossible for any rich man to be saved! How could a camel pass through the eye of a needle?

But I was there at Jesus' right hand and I heard him speak the Aramaic word *khav-la*, "rope," distinctly. Though rope and camel sound alike, I understood, by the unchanged language of my homeland, exactly what Jesus said. As a son born to a weaver, I knew well enough that to thread a rope through the eye of a needle meant that only a single strand could fit. In my earliest childhood I sat at the feet of my mother and watched her weave a bell rope—*khav-la*—to hang around the neck of a ram. The rope began with one single thread between her fingers.

Strip away all the extra fiber and what remains is one thread. The core of a rope is a single strand. In the end, only that core thread will fit through the eye of a needle.

Jesus spoke the truth. A man is born in this life with nothing and will take nothing with him when he leaves. Rich or poor, it is only that thread of faith in God at the core of a human soul that will pass through the gates of eternity.

Jesus answered, "Those things which are impossible with men are possible to God."

The metaphor made perfect sense to me.

Simon Peter shook his shaggy head and waved a brawny hand to encompass threadbare clothing and worn sandals. "Look! We have left everything and followed you!"

Jesus answered, "Truly I say to you that there is no man who leaves houses or parents, or brothers or sisters, or wife, or children for the sake of the Kingdom of God, who will not receive many times more at this time, and in the world to come, life everlasting."[3]

These words seemed to please the disciples. Visions of wealth and government positions made them smile. I saw their expressions light up, and I knew why, even though I was a boy.

It was after this that Joseph, Gamaliel, and Nicodemus drew Lazarus and Jesus and his closest followers aside and explained why they had come that very night through the rain.

"You must not go to Jerusalem," Nicodemus said. "There is a plot that reaches from the palace of Herod into the heart of the Sanhedrin. Herod and the high priest are now the best of friends. It is the common hatred of you that has given them common cause."

Jesus thanked them for coming and wished them good night. I remained by the fire, polishing the cup. Did he not see me there?

Lightning flashed through the windows. Thunder shook the house.

When the room was empty, Jesus said to his twelve closest friends, "We are going up to Jerusalem, and everything that is written by the prophets about the Son of Man will be fulfilled. I will be delivered over to the Gentiles. They will mock me and spit in my face. They will scourge me and curse me and kill me. On the third day I will rise again."[4]

I found a quiet place to be alone in the stable. Removing the cup from its covering, I admired the pattern that had begun to emerge. It had been so black and dingy—seemingly disreputable—so how could it be so valuable? How could something so shabby be the heir to so much history and prophecy? Why wasn't it shined up and in a palace somewhere before we found it? How could it be that so much meaning was contained within something so obscure?

Thunder boomed and echoed hollowly, rolling around the hills outside.

I thought I fully understood the vessel's significance. In Abraham's case, it was a symbol of worship and reverence for the Almighty. With Joseph the Dreamer, the cup represented how God's plan may permit suffering, but never suffering without purpose. For David, it was an emblem of kingship and divine appointment and recognizing that loyalty and faithfulness might bring danger and sacrifice.

But if nothing was left to be revealed, why had the cup been so tarnished? Why couldn't I polish it before now? It had possessed no form or comeliness to make it desirable. In its former state it was a very poor gift for anyone, let alone for Messiah.

While still puzzling over the chalice, I returned to our bed of straw and fell asleep . . .

🍂

"*Shalom,* Nehemiah."

"*Shalom,* Joseph. I was expecting you," I replied to the Dreamer.

"You have been thinking about the cup, yes? Here is a psalm for you: 'For in the hand of the LORD there is a cup of his wrath . . . and all the wicked of the earth drink it down to its dregs.'"[5]

I shivered. "I don't like the sound of that."

Cupping my face in his hands, Joseph said, "Have no fear, Nehemiah. Would you like to meet someone?"

"Where are we going this time?"

"We're already there. See?"

In a tiny room, no larger than the pantry in my home in Amadiya, sat an elderly man with a furrowed brow. His flowing hair and equally long beard were both snow white, like the hart's hide. *A prophet, surely,* I thought. At first I did not recognize the repeated scratching noise I heard. By the smoking light of a single oil lamp I saw a pen in the prophet's hand. He was intently inscribing line after line on a roll of parchment.

"Who is it?" I asked.

"Look over his shoulder," Joseph encouraged. "See if you can read what he's written there."

I read, "'Behold, I have taken from your hand the cup of . . . my wrath.'"[6]

"This is Isaiah," I said. "He writes of the time when God's judgment against Judah will be complete and the exiles will return to the land."

"Very good!" Joseph applauded. "The rabbi has taught you well. And answer me this: Why was the nation judged?"

"Because we were stubborn and rebellious and arrogant. Because we did not listen to the prophets who warned us not to worship other gods."

"Again, well said. And is such a judgment only leveled against nations? What does the Almighty expect of each man?"

"The same?"

"Now, Nehemiah, answer me this: How is the cup of wrath emptied? Can it just be poured out? Or must someone drink it?"

"This is a riddle and not a lesson," I objected.

Joseph smiled. "A fair objection. Look to see what Isaiah has now written."

"'He has no form or comeliness . . . that we should desire him.'[7] That's what I said about the cup," I noted. "But I still don't understand."

In response Joseph pointed at the parchment, urging me to bend closer to the scratching pen.

The prophet read aloud what his pen had recorded. "'But he was wounded for our transgressions, He was bruised for our iniquities.'"[8] Laying aside the quill Isaiah raised his face and his hands to the ceiling and groaned aloud. "Ah, but no, Lord," he said. Then, as if weights pressed on his arms, his shoulders sagged. The pen was inexorably reapplied to the scroll. The writing resumed.

A peal of thunder rattled the shutters of the prophet's chamber.

I'm sure I wore an expression of horror to match Isaiah's.

"No wonder Isaiah looks so miserable," I said. "He is writing this about the Messiah? About our coming king? But how can it be?"

Joseph's index finger remained outstretched, forcing my eyes back to the inscription.

"'The LORD has laid on Him the iniquity of us all. . . . You make His soul an offering for sin.'"[9]

"Like a drink offering," Joseph commented.

Isaiah wrote, "Because He poured out His soul unto death . . . He bore the sin of many, and made intercession for the transgressors."[10]

"Please, no more," I pleaded. "Messiah is going to die? Why? How can it be?"

Joseph spoke gently to me. "For the cup of God's wrath to be removed once and for all, it is necessary for someone to drink it. Every last drop. Every consequence of sin and rebellion from our Father Adam to the last man on earth—every debt, yours and mine—must be paid. Either we must drink it, or someone who is both willing and able to drain the cup must do it for us. Do you see?"

Thunder grumbled and muttered outside as it drifted off to the east.

"No," I protested, "I don't see and I don't want to. Please take me home. This is a bad dream. I want to wake up."

The lip of the cup had pressed a groove into my cheek. The outside of the bowl was damp with my tears.

It was not yet light. The boys of the camp slept in fresh straw. We were sprawled this way and that, like a pile of puppies. Our wooden swords were planted in the soft ground of the stable. The tiny sparrow perched on a hilt, its head beneath its wing.

Avel's arm lay across my face. Emet's feet were too close to my head. Ha-or Tov was mostly buried in our bedding. Peniel had long ago climbed into the loft and snored contentedly apart from our disheveled sleeping quarters.

Dawn was only beginning to creep up the eastern rim of the sky when Joseph came to the barn door. My eyes opened at the groaning of hinges.

"Nehemiah!" he called in a loud whisper.

I was already awake but exhausted. Long hours I had wrestled with what Jesus said about being killed and rising again. I did not know what he meant, did not like it, but was afraid to ask him to explain further. In all that I was not alone. Whispered conversations, some angry, some fearful, had circled round the disciples the way the stars pivoted overhead in a single night.

"Here I am," I replied.

"Get up, Nehemiah," Joseph urged. "Dress quickly. I've had a message. We must set out for Jerusalem at once."

Slipping out from the blanket atop the straw, I tugged my robe over my tunic. After donning my sandals, I secured the cup around my waist.

Stepping outside, I glanced at the sky. The thunderstorm had passed, leaving chilly, sparkling air in its wake. Clearly visible in the south, the constellation of the Snake Handler prepared to crush the head of the serpent. And the serpent was still poised to strike the hero's heel.

Beside the entry was a half barrel set in the ground as a watering trough. Plunging my head into the chilly water did little to make me more alert.

"Trouble?" I asked.

"Matters I must attend to," he replied. "But also, there is something waiting for you in the Holy City."

"For me?" I said doubtfully, plucking a bit of straw from my hair.

Joseph did not explain but turned to greet Lazarus as he strode across the courtyard.

No one slept well after Jesus made his strange, ominous prophecy. Lazarus bore a pained expression.

"Nehi?" I heard Avel's voice call from inside the stable.

"Make your good-byes," Joseph instructed. "We're leaving right away."

"You're leaving?" Ha-or Tov asked.

I shielded my eyes as sunlight beamed over the rooftop. "Master Joseph says something is waiting for me."

My trio of friends gathered around me.

Peniel joined us.

"It must be something good," Peniel observed.

We stood in sleepy silence, hugging ourselves awake. We were not trying, yet could not help overhearing the conversation between Joseph and his friend Lazarus.

"I have many sources," Joseph said. "In both palaces—Herod's and Lord Caiaphas's. I even know a few of the servants in the governor's household. Whatever they are plotting, I'll find it out. I'll be able to warn you before you come to Jerusalem."

"We will come," Lazarus responded. "You don't know him as I do. He'll not draw back. His face is set like flint on Jerusalem. This is why he came. And as for me, I'll never be afraid of death again."

Birds in the mulberry tree awakened, and the air resounded with chatter. There was a hint of sage and lavender on a gentle breeze.

Behind us Jesus called out, "*Shalom*, Joseph. Lazarus . . . and my boys."

I stepped into view so Joseph would know I was ready to leave and also because I wanted to speak to Jesus before we departed.

"Rabbi," Joseph said, "I have something I want to give you." Summoning me to his side, Joseph sent me to get the dark blue cloth pouch embroidered with David's harp and the Lion of Judah.

When I retrieved it from Joseph's saddlebag and presented it to him, he looked at me with a question in his eyes.

I nodded my approval.

Opening it, Joseph withdrew the specially ordered prayer shawl my mother had made. "I want you to have this," Joseph said, presenting it to Jesus. "It was woven by Nehemiah's mother for me. But the boy agrees . . . we want you to have it."

Jesus accepted the prayer shawl. "In time for morning prayers. Also in time for Passover." He seemed pleased. Putting it around his shoulders, he embraced Joseph and thanked him. "It is beautiful." He directed his praise to me. "I am a carpenter by trade, but I know fine workmanship in cloth. Your mother is an artist."

"She is . . ." I took some comfort that Jesus spoke of her as if she was still among the living. Of course, he could not know everything because I had not given him all the details. Then, I thought, perhaps Jesus did know about the battle and the bandits. After all, he knew that I would be there, bringing Joseph's cup. "Yes," I concluded. "My mother is the best weaver in the world, some say."

Jesus ran his fingers along the hem of the cloth. "Yes. Of course she is."

"And," I blurted, "I'm almost done polishing the cup. I worked all night off and on. I'm afraid that, if we are leaving, something might happen to it. Please, sir, I want you to take the cup." I stepped forward and tugged the bundle to the front of my waist. "Before anything . . . before you go to Jerusalem."

Jesus shook his head. "No. You are the cupbearer, are you not?"

Emet shoved my wooden sword into my hand. "And other things. The other Nehemiah slept with a sword, they say."

Jesus nodded. "So he did. Cupbearer. Builder. Soldier. So I have a special assignment for you. Before Passover I will come to Jerusalem."

An excitement stirred in me at his words. The King was coming! Maybe he had not meant what he said last night about being tortured and killed. Maybe the one he referred to was not himself?

I asked, "When will you come, Lord?"

"You will know when I approach." The flock of birds rose from the mulberry tree and flew as one toward the sunrise. Jesus put his hand on my head. "Cupbearer, you will meet me there. Bring the cup to me then as you were instructed. Yes? There is only one right time to give it to me."

Chapter 30

On the way back to the Holy City, I made one attempt to ask my master, Joseph, what could possibly be waiting for me. Rousing himself from a deep reverie, he offered a wry smile. "I'm sorry, Nehemiah. I am thinking about a great many things right now. I will not let Lazarus or Jesus be assassinated when they come to Jerusalem. But right now I have to ponder who I can trust . . . and who I can't." Giving a cautionary gesture, he concluded, "You won't be disappointed. I promise."

With that, I reined my donkey to a halt until Joseph's horse was half a dozen paces in advance. Then I resumed following. I made no further attempt to unravel the mystery before the heights of the Temple loomed ahead.

After the storm the sky was fiercely blue, the air severely clean. A pale yellow sun still struggled to warm the landscape, but that day there was no wind competing against it.

We traveled the main highway running north to the Galil. Every half mile or so another converging stream of humanity poured in alongside us. Rivulets of tramping pilgrims coalesced into a river going to David's City. The Passover pilgrimage was already fully in motion. Those who had come from farthest away were the earliest en route—pious travelers from all corners of the world, seeking the Temple of the Almighty.

With the increased number of visitors and the lack of wind, the pillar of sable smoke from the sacrifices was twice as thick as I had seen it before. It towered far up into the heavens.

The sight reminded me of my mother's description of her home. It made me miss my mother and father worse than ever. It was so wrong for me to be here without them.

We approached the city by way of Damascus Gate, the same direction by which I had arrived with the caravan.

Dismounting, we left our animals in the care of a groom. As we passed through the gate, we were scrutinized by a hard-eyed Roman decurion. The Imperial officer had his full contingent of ten troopers lining the sides of the gate. Each was in armor and carried shield, short sword, and javelin.

"Taking no chances with rebels," Joseph muttered to me.

We stood on the main thoroughfare of the city. I thought we would follow it toward Joseph's home, but instead we took the first turning. We veered into the commercial district, the same part of the city as the burned-out remains of my grandparents' shop.

My stomach turned over, and I felt queasy. Did we have to go this way? It was an all-too painful reminder of my lost childhood, my missing family. I knew my grandparents weren't coming back to the Holy City until after Passover. There was nothing for me there now except sorrow.

"Come along," Joseph urged, seemingly oblivious to my distress. *But he's a good man, caring for his friends' safety,* I reminded myself. *I must not be too selfish about my own feelings.*

The Street of the Spice Merchants was one short row of shops before the Dried Fruit sellers, and then the Potters' stalls. Following that area were the Cloth Dyers. The Street of the Weavers was just beyond.

In the distance a dog barked. It was not an angry sound nor a fearful one, but a joyful noise of recognition. Instantly I was carried in my deepest longing to the last time I had seen Beni, my best friend: on the night of Zimri's attack. On the night when everything in my life changed, already some seven months in the past, a lifetime ago.

And then I saw him . . . or, rather, he saw me.

Bounding toward me in his singular stiff, plunging lope was Beni's woolly, black-and-tan mottled form. I had only a moment to shoot a bewildered, wondering look at Joseph and catch a glimpse of his smile in return before Beni bowled into me at full speed. Knocking me over, the herd dog planted his forefeet on my chest and licked my face. I bubbled with laughter, pushed him away, then pulled him back again.

For Beni to have made the journey all the way from Amadiya to Jerusalem could only mean—

I jumped up.

My mother, the hem of her robe lifted to her ankles so she could manage her limping run without tripping, dashed toward me, calling out my name. Coming up the street behind her were my father and brothers and Rabbi Kagba.

Mother swept me into an embrace, held me by my shoulders to look into my eyes, then crushed me to her again. All the while Beni danced on his hind legs around the scene, while passersby gawked.

"How? What?" I questioned, lifting my gaze to my father.

He knew exactly what I was asking. "We won the fight. But we had some injuries. Me"—he pointed to his head—"and Beni must have two of the hardest heads in Gan Eden. By the time we set out to follow, you were over the mountain."

Rabbi Kagba arrived, slightly out of breath and puffing.

"Nehemiah, how you have grown. I met your father searching for you and told him the direction you had taken. When we reached Zakho, your caravan had already left."

"And then," Father added, "an early snow closed the passes for a time and made us later still. But now, here we all are."

Mother on one side, Father on the other, and Beni, smiling in the way only herd dogs can grin, we entered the Street of the Weavers. Instead of the depressing ash heap I had seen before, a new shop rose in its place. The walls were up, the roof was on, and the hammering and sawing suggested the interior finish was progressing. A workman fitted the sliding panels on the street front that would open to display the wares to potential customers.

"We rented a house across the street," Mother explained. "It's small, barely big enough for us all, so your grandparents won't come up from Joppa until the new shop is complete. After Passover."

My teacher plucked at my elbow. He thumped his thumb against the bundle containing the cup. "Have you seen him?"

"Yes," I said. "And he is everything you told me . . . and more. He is coming here for Passover. I am to complete my mission then."

Joseph of Arimathea, who had not wanted to interrupt our reunion, spoke at last. "And I find I must order another prayer shawl. Nehemiah is right about Jesus of Nazareth. No man ever spoke like he does, or does the things he can do. I gave him the first shawl. He has promised to wear it at Passover."

Every day potential customers came to the place where our shop was being rebuilt. They asked the workers, "Where is it? The place where the world-famous prayer shawls once were sold?"

I heard the workmen answer, "Burned to the ground. Gutted. Being rebuilt, as you can see. But nothing to buy here now."

And the people went away disappointed.

There was nothing to be done. The work always took a little longer than one expected, the foreman explained to my father. So we were told we must be patient.

One morning, from the balcony of the rented house, Mama peered across the street as the workmen set the shutters of the new weaver's shop in place. "Oh! I can see it now. As it was . . ."

I was at the opposite window, playing with Beni. Papa was at the table going over papers with my three brothers. We all looked up to listen because Mama's voice was so soft we knew she was not speaking to us.

Wistful, remembering the glory of the old shop, she said, "I was too lame to go play with the other girls . . . not as lame as I am now. But I had such joy. I used to sit there in the window as a girl and weave and sing the songs of the loom, while the pilgrims came to listen on all the holidays."

Papa's face appeared pained. "Sarah, the new shop may be done before Passover."

She clucked her tongue, knowing it was impossible. "My loom is a thousand miles away. My father and mother are weaving for sailors in Joppa. My sisters are selling prayer shawls from their houses. And I have nothing to offer. Our prayer shawls . . . all the world once came here. Now even the sign is gone, and the shop is vacant for the first time since the days of the Maccabees. One hundred and sixty years of the forefathers of Boaz the Weaver. And it will not be ready when the pilgrims come."

My elder brothers exchanged looks with Papa.

He sighed. "Well, Sarah, you never know. There's always next year. And maybe a miracle. It could happen."

"We'll be back in our mountains . . . Gan Eden, among the flocks next year." She turned away from the window.

Beni left me and sidled over to my father to be petted.

For a minute, Papa's lower lip protruded slightly, as it did when he was in deep thought. Then he dismissed her melancholy, all business now. "I am sending these three sons to Joppa today to carry samples of raw wool, fabric, and a letter to the exporter. They must stay with your parents."

Mama limped to her chair and sat down. "Of course. My parents will welcome them. But will the boys come back in time for Passover? Or will our table in this house of exile be empty except for us few?"

Mama loved to cook for large crowds. Passover in the shepherds' camps back home had always been packed with joyful celebration. The thought that my brothers would also be absent made the holiday seem bleak and lonely.

Ezra asked me, "May I take your dog, Nehemiah? I'm training him, and we're getting on well. No fields around here to work him. Do you mind?"

Beni smiled and wagged at me eagerly, as if to ask permission. The city was not fun for him. Nothing much for a dog to learn here. Only Jerusalem's cats to chase and neighbors who complained about barking.

"All right, then." I felt left out. My brothers were going, and I must stay. There was still Joseph's cup, which I polished every day as I awaited the arrival of Jesus.

And so it was settled.

My brothers and my dog set out for Joppa that very morning. In the afternoon I wandered over to the shop and watched carpenters sand the cabinets.

A new, unfinished sign was laid out on the woodcarver's

bench. The carver carefully fashioned letters on the plank. Only one Hebrew word was so far engraved on the signboard: *BEIT*, which means "house."

I asked the woodcarver, "Will it be ready to hang before Passover?"

He laughed at my question and did not look at me as he lightly tapped the chisel to begin the next letter.

So it seemed that Mama was right. Nothing would be ready by Passover. The pilgrims would come, hoping to buy the most beautiful prayer shawls in the world to worship and pray and then as a shroud in which they would be buried. This year they would take away nothing. As their fathers and grandfathers had come generations before, they would come to the fourth shop from the head of the Street of the Weavers, but they would find an empty shell.

It was less than two weeks until Passover. I watched from the window of our rented house as the lanes of the city became glutted. The stalls of Jerusalem overflowed with goods. Drovers leading donkeys loaded with merchandise navigated through the crowds. Early pilgrims packed the narrow lanes and shopped for souvenirs. Fresh bedding and newly washed clothes hung like multicolored flags from the upper balconies of every shop and dwelling along the Street of the Weavers.

Across the street, stone masons and carpenters put finishing touches on the lower story of our rebuilt shop. Cabinets and shelves and countertops were fitted. Upstairs our residence was being painted. Papa had promised to pay the artist that very day.

Mama's leg was swollen and painful. She leaned against my

father's arm as we entered the building to inspect the work. The smell of clean sawdust and chiseled limestone hung in the new interior.

Mama ran her hands over the smoothly sanded countertop. "Beautiful. I can see a bolt of fine fabric laid out here. And, over there, stacks of prayer shawls on the shelves. Oh! My mother and father will be so pleased, Lamsa."

"Close your eyes." Papa led her to the opposite corner of the room, where something big was covered by a tarp. He pulled the covering away, revealing a brand-new loom. "Now look!"

The frame of the loom was painted with grapevines—like the heavenly loom she had once dreamed about in the wilderness of our mountains.

Mama gasped and clapped her hands together, then stroked the wood as though it were a harp. "Oh my! My! To work on such an instrument! But who will play this?"

Papa kissed her cheek. "My love, you know it is for you. We'll stay here in Jerusalem for a time. Rabbi Kagba says the new King of Righteousness will reign here. We will stay in Jerusalem. The great city of blessing. I have given instructions to our eldest son. With the help of my steward, he will return and tend the flocks. He is the heir and will rule the flocks in my place. I'll return from time to time to oversee his work. But now I am at an age where I want to return. Jerusalem must be our home and the home of Nehemiah now that Messiah will reign."

Mama wiped tears away. "My dream, Lamsa. My prayer— that Nehemiah could attend Yeshiva here in the city. We'll attend his *bar mitzvah* on the very mountain where Abraham offered his son Isaac to the Lord. There's time enough to prepare for our future. Now, this year in Jerusalem . . . and always!

How can I tell you what I feel?" When she leaned heavily on the countertop, I knew her leg was in great pain.

Perhaps my father had also seen how difficult it would be for her to journey back to our homeland. I wondered if that was perhaps a part of the reason for his decision.

The master builder swept his hand toward the steps leading to the upper story. "Sir, the main room upstairs is completed. A few weeks only and the bedchambers . . . ready to furnish. But now? The large upper room is ready—a beautiful room, as you commissioned, sir. The artist just completing the wall mural of Paradise, the garden of Eden from whence you come." He laughed. "A place I would like to dine, if I may say so."

Mama brightened. "Passover *seder*? Here? Jerusalem. Our first meal. Now that will be Paradise."

The builder bowed to her. "As you hoped. The upper room is indeed ready for the first supper, madam."

Papa replied, "As we prayed it would be."

The builder strode proudly to the stairway. "This way."

Mama eyed the steep steps with consternation. Her leg was not up to the climb. She bit her lip and hung back. "Lamsa, dearest, you go. And, Nehi, go up with him."

The builder, not comprehending the severity of Mama's pain, urged, "But the mural, madam. Ah, to see it is to drink the pure waters of Eden!"

She answered, "I'll wait here. Bask in the glory of our beautiful weaver's shop . . . imagine the shelves stocked with our handiwork. And, most of all, enjoy my new loom."

Papa and I followed the builder up the steps. There was no handrail, and the stairwell was narrow. We emerged into a room immersed in color and the scent of fresh paint and linseed oil.

The artist, a thin, paint-spattered old man, was cleaning his brushes when we entered. He glanced up and smiled at me with a mouth only half full of teeth. "This is the boy?" he asked my father. "The boy who rode the Great Hart and came from afar to Jerusalem?"

"Yes. Nehemiah, my son."

"Well then." He chuckled. "Well. Well."

The painting of Eden covered the west wall. Sunlight from the east streamed through the window and splashed the scene of ferns and trees and flowers in bloom beside a flowing brook.

I gasped. In the midst of the forest stood the Great White Hart. Steady amber eyes seemed almost alive. He gazed at me serenely. A deep wound over his heart oozed blood, to show his sorrow for the loss of Eden. Now, at the end of my journey, the great protector and companion who had carried me through so much danger was portrayed before me as if I was seeing him as he was.

And Joseph's cup was at his feet. Yes! Joseph's cup! I recognized the pattern of the engraving without question. The silver chalice stood on a boulder beside a brook so real I could almost taste the water. Grapevines curled around it, and clusters of grapes gleamed in the sunlight. But it was not wine that filled the cup. Water from the eternal spring and blood from the wound in the Great Hart's heart mingled together and filled the vessel to its brim.

"But how?" I looked up at my father.

The contractor said, "The view of the Temple Mount through the arched window is spectacular. I haven't seen a view so beautiful even in the palaces of the rich men."

Papa put a hand on my head. He gestured at the painting and then through the window at the Temple. "From the land of

Eden to Solomon's Temple Mount. It's been a long journey, eh, Nehemiah?" Clearly, Papa was pleased with the artist's vision. "The garden, as it must have been on our mountain, before all was lost. And now, here—in Jerusalem—all will be restored."

Papa fished for silver coins with which to pay the artist. A few small drops of red paint marred the new wood planks of the floor. The old man apologized and stooped to clean away the paint.

"Leave it," Papa insisted. "As if the blood of suffering flowed from your brush, all of creation groans as we wait in hope for the Redeemer. A few drops on the floor. A foretaste of all the feasts we will celebrate in this place. A reminder that the cup of sorrow will be followed by the cup of great joy! And we will begin our celebration of new life this Passover."

Chapter 31

My family and Rabbi Kagba worshipped together within the walls of the great Temple. Choirs and musicians and the prayers were almost drowned out by the clamor of buying and selling in the stalls of the merchants and moneychangers.

I scanned the faces of beggars and boys, hoping to find my Sparrow friends, who had taken me in on my first terrible night in Jerusalem. I did not find them among the throng.

I spent the week working to polish Joseph's cup. At last it was no longer a cup. As each layer of tarnish was removed, the intricate pattern of vine and leaf and cluster of grapes was revealed. It had become Joseph's silver chalice. Beneath my polishing cloth, the ancient gift was worthy of the coming King.

I showed it first to Rabbi Kagba. Tears misted his eyes. "Good job, my boy. Good job. At last I will see him with my own eyes. His hands will encircle this silver. The wine will reflect his face. And he will pour himself out with the wine as the *Havdalah* blessings are spoken."

There were rumors that Jesus had come as far as Bethany, that he slept beneath the roof of Lazarus and would enter Jerusalem soon. We did not know if this was true.

Joseph of Arimathea stopped by to tell us that the chief priest had met with Herod Antipas to discuss what steps must be taken if Jesus and Lazarus entered Jerusalem. The increased patrols of Roman soldiers and Herodian guards were evident. City officials were on edge. Rebellion and riots were a possibility.

Sabbath arrived. Though we could have walked to the Temple to celebrate, Mama's leg was worse than ever. We worshipped quietly at home. Rabbi Kagba led us in the same prayers I had heard on the lips of Jesus only a week earlier.

That night, when three stars shone in the sky, Sabbath ended. I asked the rabbi when he thought Jesus would come.

"Soon," the old man said. "As the Passover moon grows, the heavens once again give signs of his coming glory to us."

As everyone slept, I pocketed the chalice and tiptoed across the street to the new building. I climbed the stairs to the upper room. The aromas of paint and blooming night flowers mingled. I sat on the floor in front of Eden. In the darkness it seemed more than a painting. I felt I could have stepped into that perfect world. I might have dipped the cup into the brook and raised it to my lips.

The wound on the hart's breast seemed the color of wine. "Ah, we have traveled so far," I whispered. "So many wounds. So much heartache. And now, Jesus the King is coming! He will drink from this cup, and all things will be made new."

Over my shoulder, the moon rose in the east over the Temple Mount. I held the chalice up, toward the starry constellation of the cup, for the Lord of heaven to see it was clean and ready. "Here it is, my heavenly Father. I have done all you asked. I will give it to your King when he comes. Now, please, Lord, bless my family. Heal my mother's leg. Increase my father's work. His flocks and herds. The travels of my brothers back to Gan Eden. And . . . show me! Show me what I must do to serve your kingdom."

I crossed the street and went to bed, feeling certain that Jesus was very near to me. The tarnish of obscurity was washed away. The revelation was at hand. Somewhere, perhaps as close as Bethany, Jesus was also gazing at the stars and watching the Passover moon grow more full every night.

I closed my eyes and blessed the one from above who made the moon and the stars. And I blessed the one who had left heaven's glory to come down to earth to live among us. Jesus was his name. Certainly his eyes now looked up toward heaven from earth as if he were a man like all the rest of us. But he was not just any man.

I longed for the moment when Jesus would take this cup from my hand, lift it and bless it, and drink deeply from it. I fell asleep with this vision before my eyes.

Morning of the first day dawned. For the first time since I received it, I felt at ease leaving the chalice beneath the roof of my father, mother, and Rabbi Kagba.

At breakfast I said, "Papa, when I arrived, the shop and the house were in ruins. It was cold and snowy, and I was alone. Four link boys who live in the caverns beneath the Temple—they're called Red, Timothy, and two brothers, Obed and Jesse—gave me shelter and bread." I looked at Mama. "They told me my grandmother had fed them before the fire. Before she went away to Joppa."

Rabbi Kagba said, "A good and righteous woman. Repaid for her kindness when you were taken in."

"Oh, my dear boy. What shall we do?"

Papa reached for silver coins. "Some offering to help them during Passover?"

I shook my head. "I don't know if they're alive. The sickness took so many."

Papa replied, "And if they are alive, we'll repay them."

"Not money, Papa. They work very hard. I was thinking, maybe with our new building . . ."

Mama asked, "What?"

I looked through the window and imagined Passover next year when the weaver's shop was open for business and the shelves were filled. "I thought about it a lot in the night. When Jesus comes and is our King, the Temple will truly be a house of prayer as it was in the early days. Everyone in the world will come. Everyone will buy a prayer shawl from us. Mama, you will need help weaving. I thought that maybe, if the Sparrows are still alive, you could teach them to weave."

My suggestion was like a lamp, lighting every face around the table. Mama clapped her hands. "Oh yes! Yes! Glorious plan!"

"Ap-prent-ices." The rabbi drew the word out, pronouncing every syllable as if they were holy. "Fine! Fine!"

Papa studied me. "Lots of space. We'll have the builders add a room on the rooftop so your friends can sleep close to the stars."

Mama added, "As I did when I was a girl, dreaming of a bridegroom. Your father. Though I didn't know it was him I was longing to meet!"

"You'll have to find your friends," Papa said. "You know where the Sparrows live?"

And so it was settled. Leaving the cup wrapped beneath my pillow and sheathing my wooden sword, I set out to find the Sparrows.

As the sun beat down on Jerusalem, I passed the head of the Street of the Butchers. A butcher cleaned and carved chunks of meat from a slaughtered ox. Children hauled guts and fat to soap makers, hides to the tanners. The smallest children fanned away flies.

It was in the muck of the Shambles that I found the first of my four Sparrows.

"Hey! Hey, Nehemiah! Nehemiah!"

I turned on my heel and peered down the lane where every shop displayed haunches of sheep or goats and plucked chickens for sale.

"Nehemiah!" A boy's voice called to me once more, and I spotted the wild red hair of Red. His arms waved broadly. His face was beaming. He wore an apron, but it did little to protect his clothing from his task.

I raised my wooden sword and laughed. "Courage, Red!" I shouted.

He jogged to me and swept his hand over his filthy apron. "Still fighting the battle."

"You look like you've been in the thick of it," I teased.

"I've been hired to haul guts away to the knacker. Soap making. There's a need for every bit of an animal, you know. You learn things here. Even things you don't want to know."

"Well, brother, you're still alive," I said.

"So are we all." Red told me what I wanted to know. "Me, Obed, Jesse, Timothy."

"You made it through the sickness."

"Aye. Thanks to Lazarus . . . the famous Lazarus. You heard all about that, I suppose?"

"I met him."

"Well then. Lazarus spooned broth down my throat and Jesse's too, before he died. He'll remember me. Timothy and Obed never did get sick. But it swept through the Sparrows' camp. Almost as soon as you were gone, it started. Hey, did you find your family? I see somebody's rebuilding your grandfather's shop."

"All of them. Grandparents in Joppa. The rest—Mother, Father, my brothers—here in Jerusalem. And my family says . . . well, they wonder if the four of you would like to learn weaving."

By way of reply, Red removed his apron and flung it away. Leaving a wheelbarrow overflowing with entrails in the middle of the street, he took my arm. "Don't look back. It will do something to you, I promise. I'll never eat meat again. Not that I ever did. Enough of this. The boys are all at work. Not linking. But temporary like, for the holidays. So much work with all the pilgrims. Every crook in the city needs errand boys. Work like dogs, and they pay us like slaves."

Cheerful now, Red led me to the sheep pens where Timothy was hard at work scrubbing Passover lambs. Obed and Jesse shoveled manure.

Our reunion was joyful. The news that they were wanted as weaver apprentices was met with astonished jubilation. To become an apprentice was, after all, the goal of every Sparrow.

"I'll tell you the whole truth, Nehemiah," Timothy confided. "I know your father is a herdsman and all . . . no offense. But working here in the stock pens, I've grown to hate sheep."

Obed and Jesse agreed. "Me too."

Red confirmed, "And I hate everything that is inside a sheep."

"A torch for me, any day," said Timothy.

"And a loaf of bread," agreed Red.

"Me too," said the brothers, again in unison.

Red sprang the news. "But here's good news: Nehemiah's family is looking for apprentices. Weavers. Wool . . . not sheep, boys!"

Jesse's eyes widened. "How many apprentices? One? Two?"

"Four," I replied.

Red answered for all. "As much as we may hate sheep, I don't have anything against wool. Such as it is, off the sheep."

I clapped them on their backs. "It's settled, then. But my mother won't let you into the house if you don't wash."

They washed in a public fountain.

As we headed toward home, Timothy asked, "So, did you meet Jesus?"

"Yes. He even spoke to me," I told them. "And he's coming to Jerusalem."

Timothy twisted his mouth and jerked his thumb toward the Street of the Butchers. "See that carcass? That's what the rulers have planned for Jesus and his disciples if they enter Jerusalem at Passover."

Red concurred, "I heard the high priest's servant talking about it. They'll kill him. One way or another. They want him dead and gone."

The brothers piped, "Lazarus . . . dead too."

"Yes, Lazarus. Almost Lazarus as much as Jesus."

Red said, "The Sadducees don't believe in the afterlife. Lazarus turned their cart of steamy religious guts right over! They don't like hearing there's a heaven and a hell."

Timothy stopped as a squad of Roman soldiers marched by. "Especially not hell, I bet. Well, Romans—there's the proof it isn't getting better. Proof Jesus ought to keep his head down. The whole city is buzzing with rumors."

Jesus was all the talk of the city, it seemed.

As we walked through the crowds, I listened to the litany of the boys who had died and those who had lived by the miracle of Master Lazarus's kindness and that of his sister Mary and her servant, Tavita. The story of every painful swallow, hacking cough, and delirious nightmare was retold to me by my Sparrow brothers.

Once again I heard about the slow, horrible death of Lazarus as they had seen it.

The tears of his sisters.

Mourning for the passing of a good man.

Jesus coming too late.

Lazarus's rotting, putrid body in the tomb!

The voice of Jesus commanding death to retreat!

The stone rolled back and a smell far worse than bad meat left in the gut wagons of Butcher Street!

The presence of death seemed so close in my friends' eyewitness accounts that I could see it all. We passed the path that led to the Sparrows' cavern, but I hardly registered where I was.

Then we halted at the turning. Red paused in his narrative and glanced up at the sky. The report of Jesus commanding the shroud-wrapped body out of the tomb was only half told.

All four of my companions made puzzled-boy faces at one another. Suddenly a great noise like a flock of geese rose up from the east from outside the city walls.

"What's that?"

"Huh?"

"People. Lots of them."

"Listen! Cheering?"

I peered at the bright morning sky. An enormous flock of

birds darkened the sun as they flew toward the Mount of Olives. Gasping, I remembered the mulberry tree at the inn. I heard again in my mind the promise of Jesus as the birds had erupted suddenly from the tree. *"You will know when I am coming."*

At that instant two hundred Sparrow boys of the stone quarry gave a shout in unison. They tore up the paths, emerging from their dark poverty. "He is coming! Jesus is coming!"

Rags and blankets fluttered like flags in their grimy hands. They pushed and swarmed around us. I was caught up in the rush through the lanes.

"Come on! Hurry!"

"He's coming now!"

"Riding on a donkey!"

I did not question the truth that Jesus was approaching. We banged on doors and sounded the news.

Striving to outdo each other, we hammered on each portal, shouting the tidings, "Come and see! He is coming! Jesus is coming!" then raced to the next.

Colorful robes and blankets were snatched from the parapets of balconies to be waved in welcome as the common folk of Jerusalem joined in the rush to honor him.

This was the first day of the week. No work had been done on the Sabbath. No laundry had been washed. No shops had been open. No merchandise had been bought or sold. No fires were lit; no food purchased, until today. So the whole city was jammed with everyone making good all the things they had failed to do before the Sabbath rest and overflowing with pilgrims who had come for the Passover, now only days away. The city was ababble with voices speaking every tongue imaginable, shouting, laughing, singing, as if a competition had been decreed!

And into this glorious, riotous tumult, Jesus arrived!

The cry of "He is here" resounded from the city walls like the crashing of giant waves. Concentric circles of joy splashed every street and penetrated every shadow. Storefronts and houses were left unlocked and empty. We poured through the lanes and surged past startled Roman soldiers and growling Herodian guards.

Red and Timothy locked arms to keep from being trampled. "Stay close!"

Jesse and Obed linked to me. "Careful—stay on your feet!"

"Stay on your feet! Don't wanta get crushed!"

We burst into the light outside the walls.

"Blessed is he . . . ," shouted the crowds across the valley to the east.

" . . . who comes in the name of the Lord!" we bellowed back.

"Son of . . ."

"David!"

"Hosanna to the King!"

"Hosanna in the highest!"

Now the human flood was a river rushing on the road to meet the King. *Had it been like this when King David had danced for joy before the holy ark as it entered Jerusalem?* I wondered. Rabbi Kagba had taught me that when the ark containing the *Torah*, the very Word of Almighty God, arrived in Jerusalem, there was a mighty celebration.

Had it been like this on that occasion? Or was this greater still?

Palm branches stripped from trees were raised to welcome the Son of David.

All the poor of Jerusalem had light on their faces that day. It was well past sunrise, but it seemed that, all around me, every countenance shone with the blaze of dawn.

Here and there a Levite priest scowled or a scribe ducked into a doorway and slammed it forcefully to show his disapproval.

But not the people of the Land.

"He is . . ."

" . . . on the Mount of Olives!"

The faces of Pharisees displayed shocked anger and, I thought, fear of what was coming.

Who could resist such a force as Jesus?

We were carried down the road in the flood.

Just outside the eastern wall two tides met—heaping torrents of cheering, shouting people. The noise and the spectacle rivaled any ocean breakers I had seen at Joppa's shore. We who flowed out of the Holy City crashed into the current arriving from the Bethany road.

Red and Jesse snapped up palm fronds and waved them furiously. Red handed me one, and I shook it as if to make it seen back in Amadiya. "Look! There!"

"The Lord our Banner!" men shouted.

Down came the shirts and the tunics plucked from the wash lines. They fluttered to the ground with the colors of a thousand autumn leaves. They and a myriad of cloaks were spread on the ground before Jesus as the little donkey climbed the road to the Eastern Gate.

"Look! He comes!"

"Hosanna in the highest!"

"Hosanna to Jesus our King!"

As they came closer, we five scrambled up the embankment onto a boulder. From this vantage point I recognized Lazarus and the twelve disciples. Their faces beamed with pride and delight. And behind them was the old shepherd, Zadok, with Peniel,

Avel, Emet, and Ha-or Tov! Jesus' mother was surrounded by women who sang the song of David:

> "Give praise to the LORD, proclaim his name;
> make known among the nations what he has done.
> Sing to him, sing praise to him; tell of all his wonderful
>   acts."[1]

I waved my palm branch and shouted and laughed as he approached.

"Blessed is he who comes in the name of the Lord!"

The silver chalice left beneath my pillow came to mind as the crush of humanity parted for him. I could not turn back to fetch it! Oh, why had I not carried it with me as I had done every other day?

"I know those boys in the procession," I shouted to the Sparrows over the tumult. "Look there—it's Peniel! And Emet, with the little bird riding on his shoulder. And that one there is Avel . . . and Ha-or Tov, with the red hair! Their father is old Zadok!"

"Praise to the Lord!"

The song of the women was joined by the multitude. I roared the lyrics off-key, but it didn't matter. Every phrase was broken by gales of laughter as we sang.

> "He remembers his covenant forever,
> the promise he made, for a thousand generations,
> the covenant he made with Abraham,
> the oath he swore to Isaac.
> He confirmed it to Jacob as a decree,
> to Israel as an everlasting covenant."[2]

As the procession neared us, Jesus spotted me on the rock. He locked me in his gaze for a long moment. His eyes were filled with sadness.

How could he be sad at such a moment? The sight shook something deep within me. Was it because I had not brought Joseph's chalice to him?

I cupped my hands around my mouth and called, "I have your *Kiddush* cup, Lord! Don't worry. It's ready for you, all polished up! I'll bring it!"

I thought Jesus heard me. Was that a nod of acceptance? He turned his face to the walls and yawning gate. Then the moment was past.

The crowd closed on the road behind him, and Red jumped from the boulder.

Timothy studied me with new respect. "Hey, Nehemiah, I think he was looking at you. I mean, he seemed like he was staring right at you."

My smile faded at the haunting impression of sorrow. I answered quietly, "Yes. I think so too."

"Hurry up! Come on, boys. He's going into the city!" The flood of humanity swept toward the gates.

I locked arms with the Sparrows. We shouldered our palm branches like soldiers marching to war and followed the triumphal procession through the Eastern Gate and into Jerusalem.

"Who is he?" someone asked.

"It's Jesus, the prophet from Nazareth in Galilee," came the reply.

A litany of miracles followed.

"He fed five thousand with a few loaves of bread!"

"Free bread?"

"I was there in the field! Best bread I ever tasted."

"It was like Moses and the manna!"

"He turned water into wine at a wedding in Cana. Such wine—like nothing you ever drank!"

"We'll never be hungry or thirsty again with such a man as our King."

"I was deaf, but now I can hear!"

"I was blind, but Jesus gave me sight!"

"He brought a dead girl back to life in Capernaum. I know her mother, and the story's true!"

"Whoever heard of such a thing?"

"And surely you've heard of Lazarus?"

"He healed a paralyzed man who begged beside the well of my city for years."

"I've seen it. Lepers . . . completely restored!"

"I was lame and now . . . look. I can walk!"

The question on the mind of every man, woman, and child in the crowd that day was, "What can Jesus do for me?"

We clung to one another and fought to remain standing in the irresistible surge of seekers. I wondered how I could bring the chalice to Jesus with such a multitude surrounding him. Then my longing turned to my mother. If Jesus had opened the ears of the deaf and given sight to the blind, surely he could heal my mother's lameness.

We burst through the city gates and someone shouted, "This way! The prophet Jesus has entered the Temple!"

"Come on!"

"Let's see what miracle he'll do now!"

There was no chance for me to turn to the right or the left. No way I could go home and fetch the chalice or give my mother and father the news that the great Healer was at hand.

My friends and I were caught up, swept toward the Temple Mount in a relentless, dangerous current.

Lining the streets were Roman soldiers and Herodian guards. Their swords were drawn and ready as a warning that no rebellion would be tolerated. Faces were grim, mouths tight, and eyes fierce as they observed us. I thought, *They must also be fearful of what might happen.* If Jesus could feed his army with only a handful of bread, and heal their wounds, and even raise the dead, what chance did the armies of Rome have to oppose him?

A young man spit and taunted a Roman officer at the turning in the street. "Go back to your barracks and lock the door. Now you're going to see something!"

The soldier raised his short sword and growled, "I'll show you something, Jew!"

"Kill us, and he'll raise us up alive again. You can't fight that!"

The soldier's lips pressed tightly as he appeared to consider the miracles Jesus had performed over the last three years.

I saw terror in the eyes of our oppressors as we swept past them. We were two hundred thousand strong that day, and the soldiers were only a few thousand. And no matter how many of us or how few of them, I was convinced Jesus by his power *alone* could defeat every enemy!

I felt my wooden sword press against my leg. The inscription declared COURAGE. How brave I felt that day. The swords of mighty conquerors were nothing compared to the power of Jesus and the fierce love of the common folk who roared for him to be their king!

Red raised his fist and, in the fierce, breaking voice of a boy, proclaimed the thoughts of every Jewish man in the mob. "Hey, you Roman swine! If you kill us, Jesus will bring us back to life.

He will feed us and clothe us, and we will fight you again until you're all killed!"

We were still together when we reached the Temple Mount. Flocks of priests and Pharisees with scowling faces and crossed arms stood back indignantly as the throng swarmed into the courtyard crammed with booths of merchants and moneychangers.

The roaring of the human horde grew suddenly quiet. Instantly the pushing and shoving became still.

"There he is!"

"Look! It's him! Jesus!"

"He's talking to the overseer of the merchants!"

"What's he saying?"

"His face! Look how angry!"

"He's angry! Look at Jesus!"

I saw at once that something was wrong. A hush of expectance fell over us. Timothy and Red climbed onto the base of a column, then helped me and Jesse and Obed up.

A semicircle of Pharisees confronted Jesus. His disciples glared back at the Temple authorities. The moneychangers who converted secular currency into Temple shekels cursed and shouted at Jesus, "Who do you think you are?"

"What right do you have to tell us . . ."

"This is the way we've always done it!"

Those packed around me buzzed, "Those crooks! Jesus must have told them to get honest scales for a change!"

"What's Jesus saying?"

"What's going on?"

"Quiet!"

"Everybody shut up!"

"I can't hear what he's saying!"

Clinging to the pillar, we boys heard every angry word. And then, suddenly, Jesus picked up a moneychanger's table. He held it over his head and sent it crashing to the pavement. Coins flew everywhere!

Jesus roared in a voice that resounded in all the Temple courts, "It is written, 'My house shall be called a house of prayer,' but you have made it a 'den of thieves'!"[3]

People cheered as Jesus ripped into the merchants, over-turning their tables, opening the cages of the doves, and driving the crooks out.

I laughed and drew my wooden sword. "Courage! Look— he's wrecking the place. Look what Jesus is doing!"

A cloud of doves rose up. The air was filled with the flutter of their wings. Once again the vision of the birds rising from the mulberry tree came to my mind. The flock was free! Jesus had told me I would know when he was coming!

Well, he had arrived. The smashing and crashing of stalls and benches flying through the air was a certain sign of his zeal. Like a prophet of old, he was cleaning the scum from the pure waters of righteousness!

The mob surged forward, scrambling for loose coins. Startled guards, terrified that this was the beginning of a dreaded riot, retreated with the moneychangers.

"Come on!" Timothy leapt from the column.

Red shouted, "Let's go, boys . . . come on! Let's get something!"

I hesitated for a moment, then thought of my mother. I remembered the cup beneath my pillow. "I've got to go back, boys . . . to get my mother!"

I did not know if they heard me. They vanished into the crowd. I scanned the crush for a way out. As everyone moved forward, I jumped into a clear space, clambered onto a portico, and began to run the opposite direction.

Jesus was taking possession of the Temple Mount. I imagined Romans locking the gates and shutting everyone in . . . or out. I had to find a way to bring my mother to Jesus so she could join the multitude of those who would be healed!

I sprinted toward a broad gate that led to the causeway and the ritual baths. Traffic through that gate was thin, and I had a chance to escape.

Behind me the chanting of the people increased:

"Hosanna to the King!"

"Hail Jesus, Messiah!"

"Hosanna to the Son of David!"

When I emerged into the city, the flight of doves circled above my head. I laughed out loud and sprinted for home.

Chapter 32

At my back, the voices of thousands acclaimed the arrival of Messiah. The Temple courts resounded like a giant coliseum filled with spectators, and still more pilgrims came.

I ran down the sloping street, pushing through the human tide that flowed inexorably up to enter the gates in hopes of seeing Jesus. Stretcher bearers carried the sick and the lame through the crush.

Panic seized me. What if my mother could not reach Jesus? Suppose I came too late and the way into the Temple was blocked? And what if the crowd gathered around him was too large for us to make it through?

Breathless, I came to the turning leading to the narrow Street of Weavers. The lane ahead was deserted.

"Mama!" I shouted. "Papa! Rabbi Kagba! Come—come quickly!"

Tools lay scattered in front of the new shop where the workers had dropped them. The door of the rented house was wide open.

"Papa, where are you? We must take Mama to the Temple! Jesus—it's him! He's here!" I flung myself into the house and stood panting as I scanned the empty room. "Mama!"

I dashed up the stairs, knowing they had gone without me.

Had I passed them in the crowds as I had hurried down to fetch them?

Disappointment turned to hope. What if they were already there? I stood at the top of the stairs for a long moment, then scrambled back to the ground floor and out onto the street.

All was silent except for a single blind boy, about my age, tapping the paving stones with his stick. He groped vacant air. His path was like a jagged crack in a clay cup—going nowhere. "Who's there?" the blind boy called. "Is someone there?"

I was still and silent, not wanting to be asked for help. I had to get away. Had to get back.

"I know you're there. I hear your breathing. Please, answer me."

I replied with an inward groan, "I'm Nehemiah. I've come back to find my mother. And my father and the rabbi too. To take them to Jesus, the Messiah, so my mother's lameness will be healed."

The boy cried, "Yes, the Healer! Oh, please, please, boy! They've all gone. Everyone gone but me. I can't find my way. They all ran past me, and now I'm lost. Please, take me to him!"

Impatience and panic gripped me. "Where do you live? Where is your family?" I stared up toward the Temple walls. A squad of soldiers tramped by at the head of the street.

"I live with the Sparrows in the cavern. I can't carry a torch, but they let me stay because my brother is there. They've gone, and I am lost. Please, Nehemiah, have pity on a poor, blind beggar. Lead me to Jesus, that I may be healed. Oh! What it will mean to me to see the color of the sky!" He leaned heavily against his stick. His free arm was stretched out as far as he could reach, the hand palm up like a beggar. His feet were pointed in the wrong direction. "If you don't lead me to Jesus, I'll never

322

be healed. I have heard of him all these months. Though I have tried to find him, I always arrive too late. If you don't help me, guide me, I will be lost in darkness forever!"

I shook myself awake. I wondered if a blind boy could run. "Yes. Yes. Of course, I will. My family has already gone." I gazed at the boy's blue marbled eyes. "What is your name?"

"Hallelujah is my name."

From the Temple Mount I heard the crowds cheering for Jesus: "Hallelujah!"

"It's a good name! A great name for this day." Grasping his hand, I placed it on my shoulder. "Come on then, Hallelujah. We'll be the very last to enter the gates, I'm sure. Everyone is already there. I pray the gates are still open. I bet my mother is with Jesus even now. Even now he is healing the blind and the lame. She is among those who will dance today! And you will be among those who see."

And so, the blind Hallelujah gripping my shoulder, I turned back, forgetting to bring the chalice. Our progress was slow as every uneven flagstone caught the toe of the blind boy's sandal. We picked our way carefully up the steep street, coming at last to the broad steps.

He tested the ground with his stick, tapping, tapping as we walked.

I wanted to cry, "Hurry," but instead made myself speak his name in encouragement again and again:

"Hallelujah! Jesus is in Jerusalem!

"Hallelujah, Jesus will see you. And you will see his face today!

"Hallelujah, don't be afraid.

"Hallelujah! Jesus will heal you if only you have faith in him.

"Hallelujah! We will not be too late."

At last we came to the entrance of the Temple. The crowd seemed impenetrable. Ahead of us, as Jesus healed someone, we heard the repeated shouts of "Hallelujah! Blessed is the Son of David!"

A multitude blocked our way in through the gate. "Come on," I urged. "Hold tight. Hallelujah! We'll hug the wall and inch our way through the gate."

Slowly, our faces against the rough stone, we slid past the mob and emerged in the sunlight of the outer court.

Another loud shout of acclamation swept over us, echoing against the walls and pillars. I aimed for a column, thinking I could climb up and have a look. Using the boy's stick, I pried a path through the pilgrims and came to the base of a pillar at last.

"Here—put your hands on the column. Don't let go. I'll climb up and have a look." His unseeing eyes gazed upward as I clambered onto the base and searched the human sea.

"Hallelujah! There he is!" I cried. Jesus, wearing the prayer shawl my mother had made, sat at the top of the steps of the treasury where the offerings for the poor were given. He was surrounded by perhaps two hundred sick and lame and blind, who all waited their turn to be touched and healed. I spotted my mother in the very front of the supplicants. A circle of hundreds of observers fanned out, filling every space in the court.

Jesus placed his hands over the ears of a deaf-mute girl and, raising his eyes to heaven, proclaimed that her ears be opened and her tongue loosed.

With a cry of joy, the girl began to speak: "Mama! Oh, Mama! I can hear! I can hear!"

The cheers of the people drowned out the girl's voice. Her mother fell at the feet of Jesus and wept for joy.

"Hallelujah!"

"Praise God!"

"Blessed is our Messiah, who comes in the name of the Lord!"

I spotted the scowling Herodians mingling with sour-faced priests in the back of the porch.

"What happened?" Hallelujah grasped my leg.

I answered, "He is healing people! One after another."

He pleaded, "I must go to him. Please, find a way!"

But the crowd between the column and Jesus was so dense I could not see any way through.

And then I spotted Red and Timothy and the brothers standing on the base of a column near Jesus. I shouted, "Red!"

I saw him look up as he heard my voice. His head turned as he searched for me.

"Here! On the pillar! Red!"

He saw me, and his face broke into a broad grin. He waved and nudged Timothy, Jesse, and Obed. I saw his lips form the words, "There's Nehemiah."

Others turned to glance at me. I waved broadly and cupped my hands around my mouth. "I've got Hallelujah!" I called.

We were all participants in a great drama unfolding before our eyes.

"I . . . NEED . . . HELP!" I shouted.

Then I reached down and grasped the fabric of Hallelujah's ragged tunic. "Come on!" I commanded as, with all my strength, I pulled and hefted him up beside me.

"Hold on!" I positioned his arms, then indicated to Red and the boys the situation. How to get one blind boy through the human sea and near enough for Jesus to touch and heal?

My friends grasped the situation instantly. Timothy panto-mimed a boat sailing over the sea.

"Yes!" I agreed.

Red shouted to the crowd, "People, help us! We must pass our friend Hallelujah over your heads. He is blind and must be healed this very day!"

Hands reached out to receive the blind boy. Hallelujah fell into their arms, sailed over the human sea, bobbed like a little ship headed toward the far shore, where Jesus waited to receive him. Jesus stood and waded down among the sick to take him.

My mother sat on the steps at Jesus' feet. Taking Hallelujah onto his shoulder, Jesus smiled and waved at me. Then he placed his hand on my mother's head and spoke quietly to her. She grasped the fringe of the prayer shawl that she had made so many months before.

Jesus swung Hallelujah down to the ground beside him, then spoke to my mother once more.

I saw her lips move. "Yes! Yes! Thank you, Lord!"

What had happened? Something was instantly changed. She wiped away tears and tested her lame leg. Then she took one step and another, climbing the stairs with ease.

The crowd roared, "Hallelujah!"

Jesus' lips were curved in a smile as he pointed toward me.

I saw her look up. She squinted, trying to find me, and nodded slowly. She laughed as she spotted me hanging from the pillar like a monkey.

"Nehemiah!" she cried and then turned to descend the steps without fear. "That's my boy!" That's when I knew for certain something miraculous had transpired. Her gait was strong and steady. There was no trace of pain in her expression.

And then, Jesus, Son of David, took the face of the blind Sparrow in his hands. His eyes searched the eyes of the boy, and then he kissed each eye with the tenderness of a father saying good night to his son.

I did not hear the words Jesus spoke to the boy, but in an instant, the eyes of Hallelujah were opened, and the people went wild with joy.

A strong man grasped me, and I found myself being passed from hand to hand above the heads of the people. My mother embraced me when I reached the steps. "Oh, Nehemiah! My leg is healed! Oh, look what he has done!"

From every corner of the Temple Mount children were passed hand over hand until a chorus surrounded Jesus. Timothy, Red, Jesse, and Obed joined Ha-or Tov, Avel, and Emet. My friends embraced me. A hundred other children joined us as Jesus touched and healed everyone who had come to the steps.

"Hosanna to the Son of David!"

"Hallelujah! Sing praises to our King!"

"Blessed is he who comes in the name of the Lord!"

There was no silencing the crowd.

Moments later the chief priests and teachers of the law, with the Temple guards around them, elbowed their way to the platform where Jesus stood.

Caiaphas, the chief priest, raised his arms, demanding silence. The people obeyed and a hush fell over us, not because anyone was afraid, but rather because we did not know how anyone could object to the miracles happening before our eyes.

Caiaphas's face was hard and cruel as he challenged Jesus, "Do you hear what these children are saying?"

Jesus' voice was clear and pleasant as he replied, "Yes. I hear them. And have you never read, 'From the lips of children and infants you have ordained praise'?"[1]

The captain of the guard stepped forward and demanded, "All right, the show is over. Break it up and go back to your places. By order of the Sanhedrin, the Temple gates will be closed until morning."

Jesus was surrounded by his disciples and escorted out before I had a chance to thank him.

Papa and Rabbi Kagba found us. My mother walked from the Temple that day without a limp and without pain for the first time. Red, Timothy, Jesse, Obed, and Hallelujah came home with us to the Street of the Weavers.

Over dinner my mother asked Hallelujah, now that he could see, if he might like to become a weaver of prayer shawls. And that is how there came to be five apprentices.

It was Rabbi Kagba who brought the chatter of excitement back to reality that evening.

"When I was a young man and saw the signs in the heavens that foretold the birth of a King in Israel, I came here from afar with other men who had also read the signs. What we found at the news of the newborn King was not joy among the rulers of this city and this nation, but envy and murder in their hearts. Can we believe that anything has changed?"

My father leaned forward and searched Kagba's face for an answer. "You're right. Of course, you're right. Jesus gave every miraculous sign today—from the healing of my Sarah and giving sight to this boy, Hallelujah—but it wasn't enough for the high priest or the Herodians."

The rabbi answered, "They will try to kill him, just as they did when he was a baby."

Mama gasped, "Oh no! Please say it can't be!"

Rabbi Kagba replied, "Even though Jesus has done all these miraculous signs in their presence, they still will not believe in him. This fulfills the word of the prophet Isaiah, 'Who has believed our message and to whom has the arm of the LORD been revealed?'[2] For this reason they won't believe because, as Isaiah says elsewhere, 'He has blinded their eyes and hardened their hearts, so they can neither see with their eyes, nor understand with their hearts, nor turn—and I would heal them.'"[3]

I asked, "Please tell me why. What does it mean? Every good thing that happened today, and every day with Jesus!"

The rabbi addressed me patiently. "Isaiah saw Jesus' glory and spoke about him. Even now, I have heard that many among the leaders believe in Jesus. But, because of the Pharisees, they won't admit their faith, for fear they'll be put out of the synagogue."

"Like they did with Peniel, who was born blind," I said.

Mama added, "They love the praise of men more than praise from God."

"True," agreed the rabbi. "So true."

My father, a man of action, asked, "What can we do? How can we help him?"

It was Timothy who came up with the answer. "Jesus needs spies who can tell him what they are planning."

Red had an idea. "Link boys? Us Sparrows are nothing but poor beggars in the eyes of the rich rulers."

"They think we don't have ears to hear their plots," Jesse agreed.

Hallelujah added, "They talk in front of me about important matters as if I am made of stone. I might have been blind, but I still had ears."

Obed agreed. "When we carry the torches and lead them through the city, they continue discussing whatever the council discussed in privacy."

My father snapped his fingers. "Of course! You boys! You can do it. Information—this is the way we can help protect Jesus."

After supper, I went out with the five Sparrows, hopefully to carry torches for exalted rulers who traveled the city after dark.

We waited on a corner just outside the Chamber of Hewn Stone, where the religious rulers met to discuss the matter of Jesus and his followers. Lamps burned within. Their meeting continued for long hours.

By and by the door opened and light pooled on the pavement. A solitary figure slipped out. For a moment, I thought I recognized him as one of the twelve close friends of Jesus, the disciple called Judas Iscariot.

A voice from within the hall addressed him. "You should at least think about it . . . as a patriot, eh? We know you are a patriot above all. Remember what was said tonight. It is better for one man to perish for the sake of our entire nation."

"I will," the man answered. "Yes, I promise I will . . . at least think about it."

I hoped that the fellow would hire us to link for him so we could learn more, but he deliberately turned away from the light of our torches and vanished into the shadows.

We had heard that Jesus and his band had returned to stay at the home of Lazarus in Bethany. I decided it was impossible that one of Jesus' closest friends would be here tonight, so I put Judas Iscariot out of my thoughts.

Timothy hissed to Red and Hallelujah, "You two, follow him! See where he goes. Report back to Nehemiah's house."

They sprinted into the darkness in pursuit.

Minutes passed. Suddenly the great doors gaped wide, illuminating the square with light as pompous men and their servants and scribes flooded out.

"Here they come." Timothy clutched his torch and thrust one into my hand. "A link, sirs?"

I followed his script. "A link?"

"A torch to light your way home?"

Two pompous, red-faced men hailed us. And three others called for Jesse and Obed. We had struck gold!

Timothy whispered eagerly, "We've got Caiaphas and his father-in-law, Annas! High priest. Hold your torch high and forward. He likes the shadows pushed back."

The two men barely acknowledged us. They spoke to one another as though we had no brains or ears to hear them and no voices to repeat what they said.

Caiaphas declared, "Herod Antipas is as eager as we are." Then he commanded us, "Guide us to the palace of Herod Antipas."

Annas said, "This is getting us nowhere. Look how the whole world has gone after Jesus."

Caiaphas snorted. "They'll be a rabble. Murder us in our beds if we don't put a stop to them."

I held my torch high in imitation of Timothy. He knew the route to the palace by heart. He glanced at me and raised his eyebrows as the conversation of our customers spilled out a treasure of information.

Caiaphas tugged his beard. "It was Lazarus. The last straw. There will be no stopping Jesus unless Lazarus is dead. They all come to see Lazarus!"

"As much as Jesus, I think."

"Our assassins have failed. Time and again. No one can get near him."

"I say we start with Lazarus. Silence him and all the glory fades. Then we discredit Jesus. Say it was all a great hoax."

"Gamaliel and Nicodemus oppose us."

"We question Jesus in matters of the law, and he manages to outsmart us every time. A clever fellow."

"He turns every point back on us—a verbal sword in the heart."

"A real sword would put an end to his clever talk."

"We can't get anyone near enough. He is surrounded by bodyguards. Fanatics. His disciples would die for him."

"Die *with* him, you mean."

"We'll have to arrest him by night. When the people are asleep and unaware."

"A trial. With judges in attendance whom we know will vote with us."

"We can bribe witnesses. We will see to it that those in the council who favor Jesus are delayed . . . distracted . . . prevented . . . from attending our next meeting."

I glanced over my shoulder to see Caiaphas smile. "And then there's the traitor in Jesus' own camp."

"We can't be sure of him."

"I think we can. He will turn. He is disillusioned already. Not well liked by the others, I hear. I tell you, he will do whatever we tell him."

Timothy nudged me as we reached the steps of Herod's estate.

Silently I put out my hand to receive our payment. The coins dropped in my palm. Neither of the rulers looked at our faces. They continued to talk over us as they pulled the bellrope.

Annas declared, "Lazarus is a problem. He must die and remain a dead man."

"Herod can see to that. His court is filled with assassins."

The gates swung open for the conspirators. We stood rooted with our torches high as the two gained entry, and the portal slammed shut.

Timothy and I pivoted on our heels and jogged to the next street. "Don't say anything," Timothy warned. "Every shadow hides an informant."

And so we hurried home to the Weavers' Street. One by one the others returned. We gathered in the lower room with my parents and Rabbi Kagba, and each of us gave our report of the murderous treachery that grew more fierce as the hours passed.

That night I heard Rabbi Kagba's footsteps pacing on the rooftop above the little room where I slept with five Sparrows. From north to south and back again the old man tramped. I knew he was worried about what was coming. So was I. I remembered the stories of the old man who had once been young.

Thirty-three years before, Rabbi Kagba had lain awake beneath the stars of Jerusalem with a dozen other great men from the East. The worry of imminent doom had raced through his mind and made him rise and pace and wonder what was to be done.

The slaughter of all the baby boys in Bethlehem and the escape of only one to Egypt had taught him something. The nightmare of murder had not been mere imagination to be brushed away with the morning light. Though the death of only one was the goal, the lives of many might be lost in the battle. It was indeed possible that men could accomplish evil so profound that the human heart could hardly comprehend it.

In Ramah, the cry of Rachel weeping for her children resounded even now. Jesus, sole survivor of the wrath of demon kings and princes, had grown up to become the Redeemer they hated and feared. He had returned to banish them from their dark thrones. The murderous creatures that ruled the hearts of rulers now made plans to finish what the soldiers of Herod the Great Butcher King had begun. "Jesus must die," they hissed. "And all those who follow him."

A vision of massacre played in my mind.

The moon shone through our window, bathing the sleeping Sparrows in silver monochrome.

I sat up as Rabbi Kagba descended the stairs and called softly to my father from the landing, "Lamsa! Wake up, Lamsa."

I heard the padding of my father's bare feet toward the rabbi. "You too?" he asked. "I can't get it out of my mind either. What shall we do, Rabbi?"

"I'm certain tomorrow they'll kill Lazarus to prove Jesus is a charlatan. That's their plan, Lamsa."

"Yes," Papa agreed. "I am sure of it. Murder, perhaps on the road tomorrow."

I sat up and untangled myself from the blankets. Standing, I carefully picked my way through the heap of legs and arms and slack-jawed faces.

Poking my head out the door, I croaked, "Papa? Rabbi Kagba? I'm awake too. Dreaming, but awake. A nightmare, really. We should go. Bethany. Go right now, I mean. Tonight. Ride to the house of Lazarus in Bethany. Warn Lazarus he should not return to Jerusalem in the morning."

Kagba studied me from the shadows for a long moment.

"Yes, Nehemiah, my thoughts exactly. What do you say, Lamsa? I think your boy has summed it up."

My father clasped my arm. "There's treachery in the camp, I think. Red and Hallelujah followed their man as far as the city gates. The Eastern Gate. The road to Bethany. Nehi, would you recognize the fellow if you saw him again? I mean, if he is one of the disciples of Jesus?"

"It was dark, Papa. I think so. But I can't say for sure."

Kagba interrupted. "The point is Lazarus. A good man. They will kill him first. His life, returned from the land of the dead, is a cause for them. They want Lazarus back in his tomb to stay. I say we ride to Bethany tonight. And Nehemiah must come with us."

Papa nodded. "The moon is almost full. The road will be illuminated. All right, then. Dress quickly. If we leave now, we'll be in Bethany before sunrise."

Chapter 33

As the Sparrows slept, I dressed quickly. My father saddled the horses below in the courtyard. I removed Joseph's cup from beneath my pillow and held it in the light. Gleaming silver seemed to glow from within.

For a moment I considered carrying it with me to Bethany, then thought better of it. Hadn't Jesus told me I must carry the cup for him until he was ready to take it from me in Jerusalem?

I held the cup close to my cheek, remembering the righteous men who had drunk from it. With a kiss I rolled it in its protective fleece, then returned the bundle to its hiding place beneath my pillow.

Mama's sleepy voice called to me from her bedchamber. "Nehemiah?"

I stood in the doorway of her room. "Yes, Mama."

"From the beginning I knew God had some special task for your life."

"Yes, Mama."

"And so you are in God's hands. You are the light in my life. Please—after what you boys saw tonight—be careful of wolves in the flock."

Wolves. Did she mean the man I had seen leave the council who looked so much like Judas? "Yes, Mama, I will. I don't think the fellow is a follower of Jesus. I'm almost sure. None of those men could betray him."

"But if it was, he will be desperate to keep his betrayal a secret."

"Don't worry."

"I'll try. I'll keep praying," she answered quietly.

Papa saddled his big bay and Kagba's strong mule for the journey. My father climbed onto his saddle, then reached down, grasped my arm, and swung me onto the bay's back. I hugged his back, grateful for his warmth. "All right, then," Papa said. "Angels go with us, and angels stay with those who remain behind."

The *clip clop* of hooves was the only sound as we rode through the deserted streets of the city.

Pilgrim fires winked on the slopes of the Mount of Olives. It was as though the stars had fallen to earth. The moon hung low in the west and cast our long shadows before us.

We did not speak as we rode. Our thoughts had turned from the elation of yesterday to the dangers of the coming day and tomorrow. We were united in our focus on two goals. First, to warn Jesus and Lazarus of the threat we had heard from the lips of the high priest himself. The second was somehow more troubling to me: to be certain that the informant I had seen at the door of the council was not a member of Jesus' inner circle.

The sky had only begun to lighten as we rode through the vineyards of Lazarus. A single light shone from the wall above the gatehouse of his estate.

Crickets chirped. A night bird sang from the brush. I smelled wildflowers and the scent of my father's leather jerkin. How could our desperate mission seem so peaceful?

As if he heard my thoughts, Rabbi Kagba said in a hoarse voice, "I have longed to see him as a man. To speak with him and kneel before him. But once again I come to warn him of danger. More than thirty years. The stars are the same."

Papa said, "As if no time has passed, eh?"

"Perhaps no time has passed. God's ancient promises exist outside of time."

My father said, "It seems there is always a battle between good and evil. Will it ever end?"

"The devil has a long memory, Lamsa. He remembers the perfection of Eden. He caused the fall of man and the curse of death upon what was a perfect world. On that day, God promised that a Savior would come and crush the head of the serpent."

"But doesn't it also say the serpent will strike the Savior's heel?" Papa replied. "A wound to our Redeemer. What does that mean?"

The rabbi motioned to the constellation of Ophiuchus. The stars depicted a fierce battle between a man and a serpent. "Look there in the sky! The outcome is certain. The stars are unchanged; God's promise is unchanged. Satan has feared this hour, and we are alive to see it. We are witnesses to the coming of our Redeemer. The serpent's head will be crushed, but our Savior will be wounded. Yes. Yes. We cannot be surprised. Not a fatal wound, but a wound all the same. The Devil does not believe what God has declared in his Word and etched in the stars, eh? Working in the lives of evil men, the Dark Prince of this world believes that the wound he inflicts on our Savior will be fatal. But it is written: in the end, the innocence of Eden will be restored. The outcome is certain, so we must do good and never fear."

The gates of Lazarus's estate loomed above us. Papa rang the bell.

An aged gatekeeper called down, "Who are you, and what do you want?"

Papa stood in the stirrups. "Please summon your master, Lazarus. My name is Lamsa. I come from beyond the two rivers where Eden once existed. And my son, who is known by Jesus, is with me—Nehemiah, cupbearer to the King. And here is Rabbi Kagba, one of the Magi who first paid homage to Jesus and then warned his mother and father of the danger of Herod's plots when Jesus was only a baby. We have come to bring news and warning once again."

The servant mumbled, "Daylight in an hour. Still early. Though the house is already stirring." He left his post, taking the lantern with him.

Long minutes passed. I felt the chill of the early morning.

After a time, the gates groaned open. A woman's voice welcomed us. "Come in, come in! Hurry!"

By the light of the gatekeeper's lamp, I recognized Mary, the beautiful sister of Lazarus. Her clear brown eyes smiled up at me. She was wrapped in a warm shawl. Her oval face was framed by thick, dark, wavy hair. Her teeth were straight and white.

The aroma of baking bread made my stomach growl.

"Welcome, Nehemiah. Are you hungry?"

"Yes, ma'am."

"Breakfast's almost ready." She reached up to help me slide off the horse. "And welcome, Lamsa and Rabbi Kagba. The Lord told us to prepare a meal for you—that you would be coming to break bread with us this morning."

I bowed deeply to Mary in unison with my father and Kagba.

The rabbi spoke first. "I'm glad he expected us."

Papa added, "We rode from Jerusalem with urgent news for your brother."

"Yes. *Shalom* and welcome." She took my hand. "Come along. They're waiting for you to join them at the table."

Nothing surprised me anymore. If Jesus had foretold our arrival, surely he knew why we had come.

We entered an inner courtyard, open to the sky. Lazarus's sister Mary asked us to wait there for a moment, saying she would return to fetch us soon.

Seated on a stone bench beneath a fig tree was a pair of clean-shaven strangers. By their expensive clothing, they were wealthy men. They surveyed us. One whispered to the other, who shook his head.

Beside me, I felt my father stiffen. He made no move to speak to the foreigners, nor did they greet us.

Rabbi Kagba murmured, "Greeks. Here to see Jesus?" He shrugged. "Who knows how far his fame has spread."

On the opposite side of the terrace was a scalloped, two-tiered fountain. Rabbi Kagba and my father used the waters to wash the dust of travel from hands and faces. I needed it to scrub away the sleep.

In a couple of minutes Mary came back. She was accompanied by a servant, who carried a tray of food to the other visitors. Mary ushered us into a large dining room. Beneath a wall mural depicting a waterfall dropping into a verdant valley sat Jesus. Surrounding him were his closest disciples and a number of others, including Lazarus and the shepherd Zadok. About twenty in all. The meal of hot bread and dried dates and figs was already in progress, accompanied with quiet conversation. I spotted the man named Judas Iscariot, seated between Andrew and John. Grabbing my father's hand, I squeezed it and received a reassuring press in return. This fellow Judas looked very, very like the man I had seen at the council, but still I could not be sure.

My attention was diverted by another drama enacted immediately after we entered the chamber. Rabbi Kagba's body trembled, and his eyes brimmed with tears.

Jesus rose and strode quickly to him. Seizing my teacher's arms with both hands, Jesus said, "Welcome. Welcome, my friend."

Dropping to his knees, Kagba said, "My Lord, I hoped . . . I have waited . . . thirty years and more I have cherished . . ."

Instead of lifting Kagba immediately, Jesus knelt alongside him. "And now you're here," he returned, smiling. "Thirty years is a long time to hope without seeing. Please, come and join us. And you are Lamsa of Amadiya," Jesus said, greeting my father while assisting Kagba in rising. "Welcome. You must be proud of your son. Welcome, cupbearer."

Jesus indicated places immediately to his right, beside Zadok. With some jostling, the others moved aside.

"Judas," Jesus remarked.

Breaking off a conversation with Andrew, Judas looked up. I stared at him. For a fleeting instant there was something furtive in his expression . . . or had I just imagined it?

"Yes, Lord?"

"We have not taken the offering for the poor to the Temple. Would you see to that right away? If you've finished eating, that is."

"Of course."

"For the Sparrows," Jesus added, patting me on the shoulder. "This time, all for the Sparrows."

Judas frowned. I saw his jaw clench as if he were about to protest, but he ducked his chin, nodded curtly, and strode from the room.

Zadok was a big man. When he stood to make room for us,

his head of bristling white hair seemed to almost touch the ceiling while his brawny shoulders were wider than the table. An ancient scar running from an eye patch down across his cheek showed where someone had tried to split his head in two. But it was his remaining eye, intense and searching, that held me captive, as it did Rabbi Kagba.

"I know you!" Kagba said.

"As well you should, Kagba of Tarsus," Zadok rumbled. "It was to my house you came. You and the others. Your gift. Myrrh, wasn't it? Strange choice, that. Burial spice for a newborn."

All the other discussion ceased. Everyone knew an important reunion was taking place.

Zadok explained, "You know the tale. When the Master here was naught but a babe, learned men came to worship him: Perroz. Gaspar. Melchior and Balthasar from Ecbatana. And Kagba here. They brought gifts and a warning."

"It was Melchior who dreamed it," Kagba said, emotion making his voice catch in his throat. "We warned Joseph to take Mary and the baby and flee into Egypt—to our people in Alexandria. But we—" He stopped abruptly, then seized Zadok's wrists. "Your wounds! We never dreamed Herod would . . . could be . . . was so . . ."

"Ruthless?" Zadok supplied. "Aye."

Both men sighed heavily.

Zadok's shoulders shuddered. He swallowed a deep breath, as if attempting to rid himself of painful memories. "Slaughtered the babies, did the Butcher King. My babies among them." He indicated his ravaged features. "I tried but failed."

"We did not know." Kagba pleaded for forgiveness.

"You brought the warning," Zadok returned. "In those days, no one was safe . . . just like now."

Those words signaled an eruption of many voices in confirmation.

"He's right!"

"Another Herod—the same demons!"

"Worse, even. Roman soldiers make no pretense of caring about Jews."

"It is even worse than you know," my father contributed. "Listen to my son."

Silence fell again as I retold the tale of how the Sparrows carried out their spying missions and what we had overheard passing between the high priest and his father-in-law. "And I heard someone . . . offered money to betray Jesus."

"One of us?" Simon Peter bellowed. "Name him! Point him out!"

"No, I . . . it was dark. I can't," I concluded.

Lumbering to his feet, Peter said, "You must leave here, Lord. You and Lazarus. You must go today."

Several of the disciples jumped up, waving their arms and repeating Peter's words.

"Simon," Jesus said sternly, "sit down. Sit down, all of you." When the uproar had subsided again, he continued. "Listen." Clapping our host on the back, Jesus taught, "A man, just like friend Lazarus here, planted a vineyard. He rented it to some sharecroppers and went away. At harvest time the owner sent a servant to receive his share of the crop. But the tenants beat the servant and drove him away empty-handed.

"A second messenger was treated the same way. A third they clubbed almost to death and threw him out. So the vineyard owner said, 'What shall I do to get what belongs to me? I'll send my son. They will respect him.'"

The silence of anticipation made me feel as if the very walls leaned inward to listen. The painted spray of the waterfall, so real and lively a moment earlier, appeared frozen in midair.

Jesus continued, "When the tenants saw the son arrive, they plotted together. 'This is the heir,' they said. 'We'll kill him and take the vineyard for our own.' And they did."

"Ah, no!" Zadok groaned.

"What will the vineyard owner do now?" Jesus asked. "Won't he come and execute those thieves and murderers and give the vineyard to others to tend and enjoy?"[1]

"But, Lord—" Peter protested.

"Haven't you read," Jesus said, interrupting the rising protests, "where is it written about the cornerstone, Rabbi?"

Kagba licked his lips as if his mouth had difficulty working. "The Psalms. One hundred eighteen."

Indicating approval, Jesus quoted, "'The stone the builders rejected has become the cornerstone; the Lord has done this, and it is marvelous in our eyes.'[2] Now I agree that Lazarus must flee. He must leave here today. But I . . ." Jesus' jaw tightened. The lines of his face took on the appearance of chiseled stone. "I must and I will attend Passover . . . in Jerusalem . . . this year. Do you understand?"

There was no further debate. At last it was Zadok who responded, "Lord, we do not understand, but we obey."

Dawn broke. I was reunited with Zadok's sons Ha-or Tov, Avel, and Emet while the grown men discussed the dangers of Jerusalem.

Avel leapt onto an upturned barrel, waved his wooden sword, and growled, "Oh, that I was a grown-up! They wouldn't get past me."

Emet piped up. "David was a boy when he killed Goliath."

Ha-or Tov agreed. "But Goliath was right there. Out in the open. Standing in a field. The assassins of Herod Antipas lurk in the shadows. You heard what Nehemiah said."

"So where will Lazarus hide, do you think?" Emet asked.

I answered, "They aren't telling. And they shouldn't tell."

Zadok appeared at the stable door and crooked his gnarled finger. "You've done good, Nehemiah. Now the sisters of Master Lazarus have asked to speak with you. Details. You know these women. They want to hear it over again in case you left out a word or two."

I followed the old man into Lazarus's house. The servants busied themselves with preparation for the journey of their master.

I heard them discuss who would go with him and who would remain behind.

I felt the cold eyes of Judas on me as I passed. I was still troubled by the similarity between Judas and the man I had seen outside the Chamber of Hewn Stone. Though I could not say Judas was the man who whispered treason, there was something in his manner that made me glance at him, then look away swiftly lest he see suspicion in my face.

I climbed the stairs to the chamber of Master Lazarus to give my report once again to his sisters. I stood in the partially open doorway as Martha selected tattered clothes for their brother to wear in order to hide his wealth from possible bandits along the way, and Mary packed his traveling garments in a leather bag.

Lazarus sat at his desk and sorted which documents he would take and which he would leave behind.

"Today, they said?" Martha worried. "Kill you today?"

Lazarus nodded. "But you mustn't be afraid, sister. Never

again. Though they may kill the body, I have seen with my own eyes what glory awaits us all."

Mary held a cloak up to the light. "This one, I think. And you can purchase more when you arrive."

Martha's brow furrowed. "If you arrive . . ."

Mary scolded, "The strongest servants travel with him. They have fine new swords and know how to use them. Our brother will be safe. Why else would we receive such news and—" She glanced up and saw me there. "Nehemiah. Come in. Come in."

Lazarus motioned for me to sit beside him. "It's no accident you heard what you heard. Tell my sisters so they will know everything."

"Yes, sir." I repeated the events. "So we carried torches for Caiaphas and Annas, you see. I think they are as afraid of Master Lazarus as they are of Jesus."

Mary stooped and brought her face very close to mine. "A plot to take his life."

I answered truthfully. "Today they have set everything in motion. We guided the priests to the palace of Herod Antipas, but they made their plans along the way. They spoke over our heads as if we were stones. They said they would see to it that your brother would be killed this very day."

Mary stood and spread her hands. "Yes. So you must not delay, brother. You ride out this morning, or they kill you today."

Martha added, "And no one must know where you've gone, or when you're coming home."

Lazarus nodded deeply and placed a hand on my head in blessing. "Thanks be to God for your sharp ears, boy."

I replied, "The Sparrows of Jerusalem love you, sir. For what you did for them when they were dying. All of them wish you well, and they would have done the same to warn you. I know they pray for your safe escape."

Lazarus snapped up the satchel and carried it down to where horses and two strong, ebony-skinned men waited for him.

The courtyard was suddenly crowded with men, women, and children—followers of Jesus and servants of the great household. I spotted my father and Kagba near the gates. I knew my father was not pleased that Lazarus was riding out in broad daylight and that so many knew he was going. How long would it be before the Herodian assassins were on his trail?

Lazarus embraced his sisters.

Jesus stepped from the house into the light. "I have prayed that you will be safe, my friend," Jesus said. "There is much for you to accomplish."

Lazarus implored him, "Come with me, Lord! I beg you. Ride with me to safety. The Greeks have offered you refuge in their own land. Then, when the day is right, you can return."

Jesus clasped his friend's hand, then stepped back as Lazarus and his companions mounted up. "It's time for the Son of Man to be glorified. You are a planter, so you already know this: unless a kernel of wheat falls to the ground and dies, it remains only a single seed. But if it dies, it becomes a great harvest. 'Anyone who loves his life will lose it, while anyone who hates his life in this world will keep it for eternal life.' As hard as it is, my servants must follow me, and my father will honor the one who serves me."

Lazarus cried, "I'm leaving only because you command it. I beg you to come with me!"

"What would you have me say?" Jesus asked. "'Father, save me from this hour?' What's about to happen is the very reason I came. So I say, 'Father, glorify your name.'"

Then a voice like thunder came from heaven: "I have glorified it and will glorify it again."

All of us who gathered there heard it. Many said it had thundered, but I knew we had just heard heaven speak.

Jesus looked up at Lazarus and said, "Those of you who heard the words know the truth. It's time for judgment on this world. It's time for the prince of darkness to be driven out. You can depend on this: when I'm lifted up, I'll draw all men to me."

Behind me I heard murmuring. Turning, I saw a man I did not recognize speak to Judas. "What's he mean?"

Judas challenged Jesus, "We've heard from the law that Messiah will remain forever, so how can you say, 'The Son of Man must be lifted up'?"

The stranger asked, "Who is this 'Son of Man'?"

Lazarus saluted and rode out.

Then Jesus said, "While you still have light, walk in it. The man who walks in the dark does not know where he's going. Put your trust in the light while you have it, so that you may become sons of the light."[3]

"Bah," I heard Judas's companion mutter. "He speaks in riddles."

On the road, Lazarus spurred his mount into a gentle lope as he rode through his vineyards. The gates were closed.

When we turned back to where Jesus had been standing, he was gone.

Chapter 34

My father, Rabbi Kagba, and I rode out from Bethany shortly after the departure of Lazarus. I glanced over my shoulder to see Ha-or Tov, Avel, and Emet raise their wooden swords in a salute: "Courage!"

We approached the boundary of Lazarus's vineyards.

Kagba sighed. "We have done what we could do. I hope it is enough."

I asked, "Where do you think Master Lazarus has gone?"

My father replied, "If it were me, I would ride east. Twenty miles from Bethany to cross the Jordan. Twenty more and he'll make Medeba, in the kingdom of Nabatea. He'll be safe there. Another day's ride to Petra. Neither Herod nor Pilate have authority there."

I said quietly, "Papa, I wish Jesus had gone away with Lazarus. Or maybe gone to a ship and sailed away with the men from Greece."

Kagba interjected, "I must search the Scriptures. I have not read that, as a grown man, Messiah would flee from those who seek his life. He will defeat his enemies, not run from them. Since he and his family stayed in Egypt until the death of Herod, the prophecy, 'Out of Egypt I called my son' has been fulfilled.[1] But now the hour has come. Jesus will turn and fight the brood of vipers."

My father added, "If Jesus showed he was afraid of them, who would believe he was the one we have been waiting for? He must come to Jerusalem for Passover. The whole city expects Jesus to claim the throne of his father David and claim his rightful place as true King of Israel."

Kagba looked very weary. "There will be many who'll die for him. The Romans will not let go of their dominion over the Holy City without a fight."

My father said, "And that's why Caiaphas declared that Jesus will die for many."

I asked, "Papa, do you think Jesus and his disciples will come again to the Temple? Today?"

"Yes," Papa said. "He will come. And today his enemies are waiting and prepared for him. It will be a day of conflict."

I leaned my face against Papa's back and let the gentle motion of the horse lull me near sleep. Even as I rested, my mind replayed every nuance of the high priest's malicious plot. I thought of Joseph's cup and considered with amazement that Joseph, like Jesus, had been hated and falsely accused. I whispered the promise Joseph the Dreamer had spoken: "What men intend for evil, God intends for good."

The morning sun rose behind us and warmed my back. Mid-morning we reached the summit of the Mount of Olives. Thousands of pilgrims had pitched their tents on the slopes surrounding the city. It seemed as though all of Israel was stretched out before us.

When we arrived home in Jerusalem, the Sparrows were already out among the people. They gathered facts and rumors we could use to help protect Jesus.

My mother prepared a wonderful meal. We ate together and told her everything that had happened in Bethany.

"Do you think Jesus will come back to Jerusalem today?" Mama danced as she carried a plate of chicken to us. "I want to thank him. There was no chance to thank him properly for what he's done for me. Look!" She strode across the room and back. Spreading her arms wide, she declared, "See? Never before! Never in my life!"

"He'll come. Yes," Papa said, but there was no joy in his voice, only admiration. "A man of great courage."

"And resolve," my teacher concurred.

Papa broke the bread and spoke the blessing. "David against Goliath. Yes, Jesus is coming back. He will celebrate Passover here in Jerusalem."

I finished lunch and bounded up the stairs. Taking the cup from its hiding place, I examined it in daylight once more. Had I missed anything?

The sun flashed on the silver-etched vines. For an instant I saw the face of Jesus among the vineyard looking back at me. And then I saw him as a little boy holding up the cup of blessing. He had the saddest eyes, yet the kindest eyes I had ever seen.

I saw the little boy pour out the wine of the *Havdalah*, saying farewell to Sabbath. Like a mirror, the wine held his reflection. He lowered the candle to the wine. Three wicks but one holy flame. He paused as light filled the surface, and then he extinguished the flame. His face vanished from the vines in the blink of an eye, and the cup seemed to be just a cup again.

I held cool metal to my cheek and closed my eyes. "He poured himself out," I said, but I did not yet know what it meant. "Father, I never asked before now . . . but if I ask, will you show me? What did Joseph see when he looked into this cup?" I asked quietly, knowing that I had at last come to the end of my task. Soon the chalice would be passed to its rightful owner.

I peered into the bowl, hoping for an answer. I gasped at what appeared.

In the sunlight I saw clearly one streak of bronze-colored tarnish inside the cup, below the rim. How had I missed it? The image seemed like a crown of woven thorns. Had it been there yesterday? It seemed as though the discoloration was a part of the metal.

Dread set in as I attempted to rub it away. No matter how hard I scrubbed, the circle of thorns did not fade.

Wind stirred. I heard a child's voice whisper. Was it my own voice? Or the voice of the boy? As I gazed at the tarnish, the child spoke the prophecy the Lord had spoken when Adam sinned and the innocence of Eden was lost: "Cursed is the ground because of you. . . . It will produce thorns . . ."[2]

Suddenly I knew, like Joseph the Dreamer, I was seeing a vision of what was, what is, and what was to come.

One after another, a new, more horrible stain appeared, then disappeared inside the chalice—each image more terrible than the last:

The hand of a traitor filled with silver coins.

A lash tore the flesh of a bloody back!

Spikes pierced a man's hands and feet.

Three Roman crosses stood on a hill.

Lightning flashed.

The earth quaked!

Cries of suffering erupted as Joseph's cup seethed and roiled in a blood-red sea of evil unlike anything the human mind could comprehend.

I flung the cup away and fell to the floor. Darkness in broad daylight swirled around me. Was I dreaming? I begged to awaken.

And then, peace.

I don't know how long I slept.

I opened my eyes and saw a mother weeping, her head turned in agony to the sky, as she embraced the dead body of her innocent child! She beat her breast and would not be comforted.

I asked, "Who is she?"

I heard a voice reply, "She is Eve, weeping for her children."

Last of all, I saw the gaping mouth of an empty tomb.

It was set in a place I recognized—the newly cut tomb of Joseph of Arimathea!

Then the vision vanished.

I remembered again Jesus pouring out the wine for *Havdalah*. I had seen his face shining in the liquid as the flame of the candle was extinguished. I understood. Jesus was the light. He was the candle. His blood was the wine of blessing and redemption. He was the promised Redeemer who would call us forth from the tomb. Jesus would open wide the gates of Eden for us to return home.

I groped for the chalice and drew it to me as I curled up on the floor. Opening my eyes, I saw reflected sunlight on the silver where the cross had been. The inside of the cup was spotless—clean and untarnished.

I lay there for a time, trying to take it all in. At last, I sat up and cradled the chalice in my hands. One last time I examined it. "Clean. Worthy of the Lamb of God who takes away the sin of the world."

I stood and wrapped it in the fleece, then replaced it under my pillow.

Outside my window I heard the voice of Red call to me, "Nehemiah! Are you up there? Wake up! Jesus has returned. He's teaching at the Temple. Hurry!"

The instant I stepped onto the street, Red clapped me on the back and sprinted away. I followed, as over his shoulder he grinned with excitement. "Hurry up! We can't tell your mother or she won't let you come. There's going to be trouble, I think!"

"What's happened?" Close on his heels, I got the story in shouted bits and pieces as we dodged through the throng.

"Big crowd. Jesus teaching. Priests and Pharisees come along and . . . it's like a contest of riddles. Them asking questions I don't understand, and him answering with answers I don't understand. But I think he's winning. Some of the men in the crowd cheered when Jesus called the Pharisees 'blind fools'! Can't you run faster? It's really good. They're boiling over. Want him arrested! His disciples are looking like they'll fight, and about ten thousand common folk will join in if they try to take Jesus away!"

I laughed, not knowing why. There was nothing funny about such news, but I did not want to miss the riot if the confrontation came to blows. "Hurry, then!" I shouted as we dashed through the souk.

Shoppers turned away from haggling and followed after us.

Crossing the causeway, we ran up the steps and entered the Temple. Red was a master at weaving through a packed crowd.

I half suspected he may have been a skilled thief to supplement his income, but today he had only one goal: to get close enough to witness the battle of wits between the teachers of the law and Jesus of Nazareth.

On the treasury steps, the enemies of Jesus gathered around him in a half circle like a pack of wolves. What may have begun as a quiet attempt to discredit him had exploded into red-faced shouts of outrage:

"Jesus! Blasphemer!"

"Who do you think you are?"

"Are you more righteous than us?"

"How dare you accuse us before the people!"

Red led me to the other boys, about the third rank back from the bottom step. Together we snaked through and inched our way onto the stairs. Through the press of spectators and accusers I saw Jesus, unperturbed, as he answered their rage.

" . . . You give a tenth of your income, but you don't do the things that really matter . . . like justice, mercy and faithfulness. You should have practiced those without neglecting the other. You blind guides! You strain out a gnat but swallow a camel."[3]

A man I had seen with the high priest shouted, "You ignorant, Galilean fraud! You law breaker! Blasphemer! You heal on the Sabbath and call your violation mercy!"

Jesus answered, "Woe to you, teachers of the law and Pharisees, you hypocrites! You clean the outside of the cup, but inside it is full of greed and self-indulgence. Blind Pharisee! First clean the inside of the cup, and then the outside also will be clean!"[4]

The people cheered and laughed at Jesus' words.

The uproar increased among the Temple officials. "Are you calling us unclean?"

Jesus bore into them. "Shame on you, teachers of the law!

Pharisees! You are like whitewashed tombs, which look beautiful on the outside but on the inside are full of dead men's bones and everything unclean. You look good to people on the outside, but inside you're packed with hypocrisy and wickedness!"[5]

Another shout of approval from the people.

Red nudged me hard. "Aren't you glad you didn't miss this?"

"Not for anything." But my heart pounded. My eyes were wide as I saw Temple guards and Herodian soldiers standing ready to draw their swords and slaughter anyone who made a wrong move.

Jesus did not draw back. "Judgment is coming on you, hypocrites! You build elaborate tombs to honor the prophets and you decorate the graves of the righteous. And you say, 'If we had lived in the days of our forefathers, we wouldn't have joined in, when they shed the blood of the prophets.' But the truth is this: you're the offspring of those who murdered the prophets! Fill up the cup, then, with the measure of your forefathers' sin! You snakes! You brood of vipers! How will you escape being condemned to hell? Therefore, I am sending you prophets and wise men and teachers. Some of them you'll crucify. Others you'll flog in your synagogues and pursue from town to town." Fixing his eyes on Caiaphas, he continued, "And so on your heads will come all the righteous blood shed on earth. Every bit, from the blood of righteous Abel to the blood of Zechariah. The same Zechariah whom you murdered between the Temple and the altar. Listen to me: all this will come upon this generation!"[6]

At a signal of the high priest, the soldiers drew their weapons. The people grew quiet and nervous. Many in the back left the scene.

"You are a lying prophet." Caiaphas shook his fist in Jesus' face. "Destruction will come upon you, not us. All the evil of the ages be heaped upon your soul, and not upon the people!"

Jesus shook his head slowly. Sadness filled his eyes. "O Jerusalem! Jerusalem! You who kill the prophets and stone those sent to you. How many times I wanted to gather your children together like a hen gathers her chicks under her wings. But you weren't willing. Look . . ." Jesus' gaze wandered over the magnificent buildings of the Temple Mount.

The eyes of the throng followed, even the high priest's.

"See," Jesus continued, "your house is left to you desolate." Jesus then parted the crowd. "I tell you, you won't see me again until you say, 'Blessed is he who comes in the name of the Lord.'"[7]

The outrage at his proclamation was so fierce and incoherent I could no longer hear what anyone said. I expected the soldiers would rush in and arrest him on the spot.

Instead, Jesus walked through the people and out of the Temple grounds. His disciples came behind him. Scowling, Peter, James, and John walked backward with their hands on their swords.

Avel spotted me and the Sparrows and called, "Come on, boys! Follow us!"

I wormed my way out of the crush with Timothy, Jesse, Obed, Red, and Hallelujah. We left the Temple with the band of Jesus' followers.

Judas pleaded with him, "But this is the Great Temple! Say the word, and the people will fight for you to be their King!"

I heard Jesus answer sadly, "Do you see all these great buildings? I'm telling you the truth—not one stone here will be left on another. They'll all be thrown down."[8]

Jesus was silent as we left the city through the Eastern Gate. His followers continued to chatter and cheer themselves about the battle of wits that had just taken place. They congratulated each other for being on the right side. After all, hadn't Jesus spoken the harsh truth in a way that no one had ever dared speak before?

There was an arrogant jubilation among the men as they discussed in detail the shocked expressions on the faces of the opposition and their escalating rage.

Peter blustered, "But you notice, they were afraid to fight us! They didn't use their swords, did they? Afraid of what the people would do."

"A victory," James asserted. "They'll back down, you'll see."

Thomas shook his head. "I'm not so sure. But the priests and Pharisees were on the defensive. That much is certain."

With a sideways glance, I saw Judas scowling. He of all the men did not approve of the outcome. "We should've fought them," he said. "I think we missed our chance today. That's all."

It was a short distance to the Mount of Olives. Jesus went to a quiet garden, spread his cloak, and sat down. It had been a long day.

"Lord," Matthew asked, "you say the stones of the Temple will be thrown down. When? And what will be the sign of your return? And what signs will there be for the end of this age?"

I joined the Sparrows as we climbed onto the low branches of an ancient olive tree.

Others in the group gathered around Jesus with an eagerness to hear what he had to say about the end of Jerusalem. Would he call down fire from heaven? Maybe tomorrow? Or before the end of Passover?

Jesus kept his gaze fixed on Jerusalem as he spoke. "Make sure no one fools you. Many will come using my name, claiming, 'I'm the Messiah.' They'll deceive many. You'll hear of wars and rumors of wars, but see to it you aren't alarmed. These things will happen, but that still won't be the end, not yet. Nation will rise against nation and kingdom against kingdom. There will be famines and earthquakes all over the world. But these are just the beginning of birth pangs—the labor pains of the end of the world."

Red nudged me and whispered, "Sounds to me like he's saying the end of the world is a long ways off."

Jesus now turned his eyes on his followers. "You must know this too: you'll be handed over to be persecuted and put to death. And you'll be hated everywhere because of me. When persecution comes, many will turn away from the faith. They will even betray and hate one another."

Near the back of the circle I watched Judas stand and walk away. He went to a boulder and looked out across the valley at the Temple.

Jesus briefly glanced at him as he spoke. "Many false prophets will come on the scene and will deceive many people. Wickedness will grow so big that even love will turn cold."

Then Jesus looked right at us boys as we perched in the tree. "But he who stands firm to the end will be saved. And this good news will be preached to the whole world. There will be witnesses in all nations . . . and then . . . *and then*," he emphasized, "the end will come."[9]

Avel stroked the sparrow on Emet's shoulder, then smiled up at me. "He's talking to us, boys."

I nodded.

Jesus continued, "There'll be great tribulation, unlike anything ever, from the beginning of the world until now, and never to be equaled again."

My stomach churned as he described the terrible days that will come before the end of the world.

"The sun will be darkened and the moon will not give its light; the stars will fall from the sky, and the heavenly bodies will be shaken. At that time the sign of the Son of Man will appear in the sky, and all the nations of the earth will mourn. They'll see the Son of Man coming on the clouds of the sky, with great power and glory. And he will send his angels with a loud trumpet call, and they will gather his elect from the four winds, from one end of the heavens to the other . . . when you see these things, you know that it is near. Right at the door.

"I tell you, the generation that sees these things will not pass away until all these things have happened. Heaven and earth will pass away, but my words will never pass away.

"No one knows about that day or hour, not even the angels of heaven, nor the Son, but only the Father. As it was in the days of Noah, so it will be at the coming of the Son of Man. Before the Flood, people were eating and drinking and marrying up to the day Noah entered the ark. And they didn't know what would happen until the Flood came and took them all away. That's how it will be at the coming of the Son of Man. Two men will be in the field. One will be taken and the other left behind. Two women will be grinding with a hand mill. One will be taken and the other left. So pay attention! Keep watch! You don't know what day your Lord will come . . ."[10]

Jesus spoke to us for a long time about his final return to Jerusalem and the end of the world.

The sun sank low in the western horizon as his teaching finally came to an end, and the last of our questions were answered. I knew he was not only speaking to us that day, but to those who would come after us. There were some among us who listened with disappointment.

"When the Son of Man comes in his glory, and all the angels

with him, he will sit on his glorious throne. All the nations will be gathered before him, and he will separate the people one from another as a shepherd separates the sheep from the goats. He will put the sheep on his right and the goats on his left. Then the King will say to those on his right, 'Come, you who are blessed by my Father; take your inheritance, the kingdom prepared for you since the creation of the world. For I was hungry, and you gave me something to eat. I was thirsty, and you gave me something to drink. I was a stranger, and you invited me in. I needed clothes, and you clothed me. I was sick and you looked after me. I was in prison and you came to visit me.'

"Then the righteous will ask, 'When did we do these things for you?'

"And the King will reply, 'I tell you the truth: whatever you did for one of the least of these brothers and sisters of mine, you did for me.'"[11]

The sun was setting, but I felt he spoke to me. "Even if all you have to give in my name is a cup of cold water, you will not lose your reward."

He finished teaching us and said quietly, "As you know, the Passover is in two days. And the Son of Man will be handed over to be crucified."[12]

Some among the women began to weep quietly. Other disciples argued with him. The one named Judas turned his head and narrowed his eyes as he studied Jesus. It was right then that I was sure it had been Judas whom we had seen outside the door of the Chamber of Hewn Stone.

Jesus and Judas locked eyes with a hard look. I knew there was no event to come that would surprise the Lord. The Cup of Joseph, which I had believed contained such hope, had taken on a new and tragic meaning.

A heaviness hung over us all as Jesus departed for Bethany with his disciples.

I returned to Jerusalem with the Sparrows to await my final instructions from the Lord.

Chapter 35

In the morning I awakened to my mother's voice outside in front of the new shop. She was singing to the rhythm of her loom shuttle:

> "He is mighty.
> He is mighty!
> May he soon rebuild his house.
> Speedily, speedily,
> and in our days!"

I sat up from my bed.

Hallelujah was already at the window. "Listen to our new mother sing!" Hallelujah said with awe in his tone. "Look! Look!"

Red rubbed his face. "Hallelujah, what's happening?"

I did not wait for Hallelujah's reply. I rushed to the window, and the other boys crammed in around me. A crowd of people twenty deep was in front of the new shop. There was my mother, singing and weaving, as the brand-new sign was being hung above the door by a workman on a ladder.

> "He is distinguished;
> he is great.

He is exalted!
May he come soon
and rebuild his house.
Speedily, speedily,
and in our days, soon!
God, rebuild.
God, rebuild.
God, rebuild your house, soon!"

For a moment the early-morning sun glinted on the red and gold gilded letters of the sign.

"What's it say?" asked Timothy, who could not read.

Red demanded, "Does anybody know what it says?

The brothers chimed in, "*BEIT*. 'House.' I can't read the rest."

"The first word is *house*," I agreed.

Hallelujah shook his head in wonder. "What colors are those? Somebody tell me the names of the colors on the sign."

"Hallelujah, look! Red is the color, just like the color of Red's hair."

"And gold is the color like the sun."

Hallelujah breathed a long sign of approval. "Ahh . . ."

Timothy asked me, "But what's the sign say, Nehemiah? You can read. Tell us!"

I was lost for a moment in the words of the song as my mother sang. The crowd grew larger as her voice drew them. "Rebuild! Rebuild."

I answered, "The letters in gold on the new sign spell *BEIT TALLITOT*. 'House of Prayer Shawls.'"

Someone in the crowd called, "House of Prayer. But where are the shawls?"

Another cried, "I have come all the way from Cyprus and

was told by my brother to bring him one like our grandfather bought from this shop. But where are they?"

As Mama's song came to an end, my father stepped forward, smiling. He raised his hands high to silence the questions. "The House of Prayer Shawls is once again open! Look! The most beautiful *tallitot* in the world will be on the shelves and available this afternoon."

All heads turned to scan the Street of the Weavers. At the bottom of the lane, I spotted my three brothers with a string of a dozen donkeys loaded with baskets. Ezra was in the lead. Beni panted at his heels.

I shouted, "Ezra! Beni!"

My dog barked and ran ahead. Ezra waved. "We've got them!" he shouted. "Father sent us to Joppa and to the house of every relative to collect them. Look—we've brought them!"

A cheer went up from all the people. We boys rushed from the rented house to swarm around my brothers to help unload the cargo and carry prayer shawls, *Shabbat* tablecloths, and scarves to fill the shelves.

"Sometimes miracles happen," Papa said as Mama embraced him. He instructed my elder brothers to wash and eat and then return to help stock the shop for what would surely be a rush of customers.

My mother clasped Papa's hand and bounded up the stairs of our new home.

At Ezra's command, Beni lay obediently outside on the threshold like a sentinel.

I followed Mama and Papa upstairs.

"The Lord has rebuilt," Mama whispered. They stood before the painting my father had commissioned for our large room above the shop. "The flowers. The Great White Hart. The colors in the water. Perfection, Lamsa. As it must have been . . . our mountains as they were when Eden was still there."

While Jerusalem boiled with religious and political turmoil, Mama spent the day furnishing the room as my brothers worked organizing the inventory downstairs. Papa told her the upper room must be ready for Rabbi Kagba to preside over our first supper, which would be the Feast of Unleavened Bread and the beginning of Passover.

Papa and Rabbi Kagba gathered the young Sparrows, who had never experienced a proper Passover meal.

"There is no leaven in this house . . . nothing to clean out," Rabbi Kagba taught. "Leaven represents sin in the heart of men. Like a spot of yeast goes through all the dough, a little bit of sin will spread through a man's heart. That's why for the Feast of Unleavened Bread we sweep our houses and clean out every crumb. In the same way we sweep our lives clean of every crumb of sin." The old man leveled his gaze on us. Red blushed as he asked, "Boys? Have you any sin in your life? Confess it now and sweep clean your inner house. Make your heart ready for the coming of the Lord. For he truly is coming!"

Red blurted eagerly, "Oh, Rabbi, I can tell you! I am crammed full of leaven and that's a fact. Stale bread, that's me. Feed me to the birds! I'm so full of yeast and sin like no boy you ever met. My fare has been stolen bread and apples and such at least once a week from the souk. If I counted the dried apricots I have crammed in my pockets. There's never, never enough to eat and so . . ."

Rabbi Kagba put a hand on Red's arm. "And so, your heart you have swept clean. You will never steal so much as a single apricot again. And now, my boys, we begin new life in a brand-new house."

Papa concurred. "So, boys, that is why we have not broken bread in our new house before now. No crumbs of leavened bread. We have reserved sharing our first supper in the upper room for this Passover . . . the Feast of Unleavened Bread."

As workmen carried furniture up the steps, I sat on the window ledge and watched. Mama stood before the painting with her arms crossed, head tilted, and chin slightly raised like a little girl in awe. She studied every detail, each brushstroke and color of Eden. Leaning very close, she gazed into the hart's amber eyes and asked me, "Is this what he looks like up close, Nehi?"

"Yes," I replied. "When I look at him, it's like seeing an old friend. Mama, he is waiting for Messiah to redeem the world, just as we are."

Mama hung red curtains she had woven around the window, framing the glory of the Temple Mount. A long table of polished, striped acacia wood was the centerpiece. She had been weaving the fabric for red and gold cushions for many weeks. Now the pillows were covered, and I helped her carry them upstairs.

"When Jesus is King," she said with satisfaction, "my dream is that he may one day eat supper with his disciples right here in our upper room. I would cook for him and, with strong, steady legs, climb these stairs and place the steaming platters in front of him."

I did not tell her the sorrows I had seen in my vision, or what Jesus had said about being crucified. I think she would not have believed me anyway. Who could imagine such a thing coming true? She would have said my vision was only a bad dream brought on by exhaustion. She would have said that Jesus was just telling another parable. Perhaps he only meant to teach us something important.

But I was certain of what I had seen, and I couldn't guess what the lesson of such a parable could be.

Mama gathered us boys, and calling the Sparrows her sons, we went to the potter's shop together. After what seemed like hours, she selected and purchased new dishes, matching clay cups, serving platters and trays, painted with vines and clusters of grapes. Red, Timothy, Jesse, Obed, Hallelujah, and I helped carry the crockery home in a cheerful procession. The boys had eaten from broken shards of pottery, but never from unbroken plates.

Red declared he would feel like he was the richest boy in the world if only he could ever eat one meal from such finery.

My mother gazed at him with amazement. "Well, it's all for you! This Passover! Such a meal we will share here!"

So the room was ready for our first supper.

The Day of Preparation dawned. The Sparrows and I rose early and went with Papa and Rabbi Kagba to select a lamb. I never liked this part of the Passover tradition. The choosing of an innocent, perfect lamb for sacrifice always seemed a sad thing to me. Even in our mountains, where lambs from my father's flocks were plentiful.

In Jerusalem the stock pens were crowded with tens of thousands of lambs born and raised in Bethlehem. They were set aside for the very purpose of dying as sin offerings.

Papa knew what was good and best and better among the pens of milling sheep. He examined them all and finally picked an animal from the lambs that had not yet been washed. It was his intention that the Sparrows would learn to wash it and brush it, using the day to prepare it for slaughter. By the end of that time, the boys would be attached to it.

In this way they would learn the hard lesson that the sin

of all men required the atoning death of a gentle and beautiful creature that knew nothing of sin. It was a hard lesson to learn. I knew that firsthand. I recalled vividly the sadness and shock I'd experienced when the innocent lamb had died in my dog Beni's place. It was far different in my mountains, when we lived our days with the sheep, than simply purchasing a chunk of meat in the city marketplace.

While Papa taught the Sparrows something about the care and feeding of lambs, Rabbi Kagba and I set out together to draw water from the well to wash it.

Hand-over-hand I helped pull up the bucket and pour it into the ceremonial jar. Rabbi Kagba balanced it on his shoulder, and we headed back toward home.

We had just turned the corner of our street when I spotted Peter and James walking toward us.

I waved. "*Shalom!* Peter! James!"

"Look!" Peter's brooding face broke into a smile. "It's Nehemiah and the rabbi."

"*Shalom,*" Rabbi Kagba greeted them. "Is everything well with your master?"

"Aye." Peter nodded. "Jesus sent us to find you—that is, I think he meant you. He told us to come to the city. He said a man carrying water would meet us and . . . we're to follow you."

My teacher's eyes misted with emotion. "The first supper . . . ah, yes. So it will be as I dreamed it would be. Come along, then. Follow us."

My father knelt in the dirt as we approached. The boys stroked the baby lamb and spoke kindly to it as boys often speak gentle words to small, dumb creatures. The lamb was sitting across Red's lap. It laid its head against his shoulder and closed its eyes.

Papa stood as Peter and James approached. "*Shalom,* brothers. Is your master well?"

"He is well and sends his greetings."

"Jesus is coming into Jerusalem for Passover?" my father asked. "In spite of everything?"

"He is," James replied. "With the twelve of us."

Peter added, "The teacher asks if the room is ready so he can eat Passover with his disciples?"

My father's face lit with understanding. "I have just the place for your master. The upper room in my new house. Everything new and ready—no meal ever before eaten there. Please, if you will do me the honor. I'm unworthy that Jesus should enter under my roof, but if the Lord will only come and bring his disciples here to my new house, you'll see. New dishes and cups. Please, yes, the table is ready. The room is prepared. If Jesus will eat the first supper here beneath the roof of my house, then my house and my family will be blessed forever. "

"He told us you would say that." James's eyes were somber, not like a man looking forward to a celebration. "Yes. Jesus will come to your house for dinner this evening."

My thoughts flew to Joseph's silver chalice. Not only would I present it to Jesus tonight, he would take his first drink from it in the upper room of my home!

Peter said to me, "And he told me, 'Nehemiah will have the cup ready.' I don't know what cup he means, boy, but I suppose he knows . . . and you know, Nehemiah?"

I nodded but did not speak. Peter's gruff voice and wild looks somehow always caused me to lose my voice.

My father embraced James. "You can't imagine the joy! After my wife was healed—she would walk a thousand miles to fix a meal for Jesus. It's her dream to feed him. Well, that's a woman for you. And her prayer! She mentioned it again only this morning." He mimicked my mother's voice, "If only I could cook a meal for Jesus!"

Peter said, "I heard she's a good cook."

Papa exclaimed, "Such a cook she is! But I promise if she never cooked another meal, she wants only to cook supper for Jesus. Could there be such an honor? Serving Jesus his Passover supper as he prepares to enter into his kingdom?"

"Why am I surprised?" Peter asked. "So, it's settled. I suppose it was always settled. We just didn't know the details—upper room of the weaver's shop. Thank you very much. Tell your wife thanks as well. And now Jesus has sent us fishermen to select a lamb. I'm not very good at it. I get attached to the little things before I carry them home."

Papa put a hand on Peter's arm. "No, please. I am a shepherd and the son of a shepherd. This morning I selected the best lamb of the flock from Bethlehem. My boys are washing its fleece right now. What an honor it would be if Jesus and his close friends would accept the lamb I had intended to be offered for my family. If Jesus would accept the sacrifice from my hands for his good and the good of his friends, even though I'm not worthy for him to enter under my roof, then I'll be doubly blessed!"

The arrangement pleased everyone and sent my mother spinning with joy. Jesus the Lord, her Healer and Redeemer, was coming to bless her upper room by breaking bread there.

A steady stream of pilgrims flooded the shop to purchase prayer shawls as Mama prepared the supper for our special guests.

My three elder brothers manned the counters for two hours

and then the shop was closed as preparation for Jesus' arrival continued.

It was mid-afternoon when Mama brought me in to the back room. Everything smelled of clean woolen fabric, fresh paint, and newly sanded wood. The shelves were stocked with fabrics made famous by the weavers of my family. I felt proud.

Mama opened the chest and, with a wave of her hand, motioned for me to come and see. "Nehemiah, these are the very best prayer shawls and *kittels* I ever made on my loom. Ever in my life. Sometimes something extraordinary happens, you know. When you pray or sing or create or just live, and God pours his love through us into something. So every year from our far mountains, from the place where Eden once was, I sent something special I had made to my sister for safekeeping. That is why these were saved from the fire that took everything. God saved them for this night, you see. These were never offered for sale. How could I sell such things? But I thought I saved them for special occasions in our own family. Like your *bar mitzvah*, or your wedding someday. Everything here. Ready for the most holy moments in our lives. Or one day, when perhaps I might have a grandchild of my own. And here . . ." She held up a man-sized *kittel*, the white robe worn by a bridegroom for his wedding. Later the robe he wore at his wedding would become the garment a man wore for his burial.

But that night, I knew Mama thought only of the wedding feast of the Messiah, not his death and burial. "So, Nehemiah, what do you think? For Jesus, the bridegroom of Israel?"

The light glistened white as snow on the fabric. The detail on the border was like a grapevine and clusters of grapes. "He will like that one, yes. I think so, Mama."

I tried not to think of the use of the *kittel* as burial clothes.

It seemed too ominous, considering what Jesus had said about his death.

"Yes, Mama. I remember how you sang when you made this one. And this too." I wondered if she had something special for me.

She retrieved a smaller white *kittel* and held it up for me to see. "I made this one for your *bar mitzvah*. Also grapevines. See? And *Kiddush* cups all around. I did not know what was about to happen. I just thought it was right for my son, Nehemiah, named after the cupbearer. You see? You should wear it tonight, I think."

I accepted it, excited, fearful I might make some mistake, and thankful I had lived to see this day. Did she see the nervousness in my eyes?

I focused on the exquisite prayer shawls. Running my fingers over the fabric, I traced the blue thread of the fringes. I remembered my mother patiently knotting one strand after another by the lamplight in our camp.

Removing the stack, she laid them out on a bench. "And all of these—they're the special ones. I want you to take them upstairs and put one at the seat of each of the disciples . . . and one for Jesus, as our gift."

I knew that Joseph of Arimathea had given Jesus one of the special prayer shawls Mama had made, and Jesus wore it often. But my mother's heart was so eager to give something extra. Her face beamed like a hopeful little girl's as she asked me to help her choose. I embraced her, telling her there never was a woman like her, so talented and so kind.

Together, we selected the most beautiful *tallith* for Jesus to wear. It was the one she had named "Joseph's Coat of Many Colors."

"Of course," I said, certain the Holy Spirit had guided my mother's hands in the weaving and her heart in the naming.

The twelve shawls selected for the disciples were all different but of equal beauty and intricacy. But there was one gift that troubled me deeply—the twelfth *tallith* meant for Judas Iscariot.

I carried the precious gifts to the upper room and laid them at each of the seats. I only prayed that I was wrong about Judas . . . that somehow he would prove to be a true friend of the Lord.

She came up to inspect the room. As she stood before the painting of Eden, her eyes welled. "Eden. Like this house must be reborn. Beauty for ashes. Out of the ashes of my childhood, now the Lord has blessed me with this honor. Yes. Beauty for ashes in every life. My son as the cupbearer. My house rebuilt. Jesus coming here tonight for the first supper. I am blessed to have prepared it for him. What more could any woman ask?" She kissed my forehead. "I'm proud of you, Nehemiah. You have come a long way and suffered much to come to this night. Now go and wash and put on your wedding garment. The bridegroom of Israel is on his way."

While I washed and changed into my new clothes, Mama took her place at the loom again and began to sing at the window. I smoothed the fabric of my *kittel* and studied my reflection in the bronze mirror. I looked very grown-up.

The sun was almost down when I carried Joseph's silver chalice from the rented house, through the shop, and up the stairs of our restored home. The lamps and candles were already lit. *Matza* bread, wine from the vineyard of Lazarus, and all the ritual elements of the Passover meal were in place.

As the service progressed, Mama would carry the steaming platters of the feast to serve the guests.

Only the cup had yet to be placed in Jesus' hands, and all would be fulfilled.

I was alone in the upper room. The sense of holiness was heavy, a tangible weight of anticipation in the atmosphere. Through the window the buildings of the Temple were bathed in golden sunlight.

With a glance toward the painting of the great wounded hart, I unwrapped the chalice and held it up to the light. The golden light of Jerusalem reflected in the polished silver.

I was ready for my task as cupbearer to the King!

My teacher had taught me the meaning of every blessing that would be recited over the wine in Joseph's cup. This night, Jesus would bless and drink the four traditional cups offered at Passover from the chalice. Each cup of wine represented God's plan of redemption for Israel and for all of mankind through the Messiah.

Suddenly my mother burst into song with the rhythm of her loom. I knew then that Jesus and his disciples had turned the corner and were coming up the street!

Peering out the window, I saw sunlight glint on the lettering of the sign above the door and read the words HOUSE OF PRAYER.

My mother sang as the loom boomed like a drum:

> "He is pure,
> he is unique,
> he is powerful,
> he is wise,
> he is King."

In my white robe, I stood at attention behind Jesus' seat, Joseph's chalice in my hands. My heart pounded with excitement as I heard the door open.

My mother continued with great joy:

> "He is awesome,
> he is Redeemer!
> He is righteous!"

I tried to remember all the rituals of the Passover cup I had been taught. I stammered as I rehearsed what I had learned about the chalice of the Messiah. Would I be worthy when the moment came? Would I remember to say and do what I was supposed to do?

Mama's lilting voice added:

> "Take this cup,
> the cup of sanctification.
> Take this cup.
> I will bring you out of bondage.
> Take this cup.
> I will deliver you.
> Take this cup.
> I have redeemed you!"

Tears streamed down my cheeks as I realized the moment I had longed for was at last upon me. The ancient silver chalice, which had held so much suffering and pain, was polished like new inside and out. Jesus would soon stretch out his hands to take the cup, drink from it, and then offer it back for all to drink who came to his table.

Everything fled from my mind as I heard the bell above the door, and Jesus entered the House of Prayer.

Mama announced his arrival in song.

"He is the Omnipotent God!
Rebuild! God, rebuild your house soon!"

I heard Jesus greet my family downstairs: "*Shalom! Shalom! Thank you for taking me in. Well done, good and faithful friends.*"

And then . . . I heard his footsteps on the stairs!

My mother sang,

> "He is holy.
> He is compassionate.
> He is all righteous!
> Oh, God,
> rebuild your house soon!"

Chapter 36

Twas only nine that evening as I sat on the stairs leading to the upper room where Jesus ate with his disciples. Judas, the betrayer, stood and stumbled out, almost tripping over me as he fled from the light into the darkness.

After the door slammed, I heard Jesus speak the words we later learned by heart.

Some believe he was addressing his followers, but I am certain Jesus spoke the first words directly to his Father.

The eyes of the Son raised heavenward and fixed on a throne, a holy altar, on mighty, outstretched hands that had governed galaxies and worlds, and ordained kingdoms and the lives of men and angels. "Blessed are you, O Lord, King of the universe who created this fruit of the vine I offer to you."

Jesus reached higher, stretching upward, until the chalice penetrated heaven. "Take this cup." He spoke with tenderness to his loving Father.

All time stood still in that moment. There was no time, no day or night, only eternity. The walls and ceiling of the chamber dissolved, and suddenly I saw the faces of all who had lived before and multitudes who would live in years to come. They gathered with us around the table, waiting eagerly to drink from the silver cup Jesus offered.

All who called on the Name of Jesus were brought together in that moment, in that place forever and ever.

Jesus offered the cup to all. "Drink from it, all of you. This is my blood of the covenant, which is poured out for many for the forgiveness of sins. I tell you, I will not drink from this fruit of the vine until that day when I drink it anew with you in my Father's kingdom."[1]

The chalice floated from hand to hand, and the precious contents were shared by all—first by Jesus' closest friends and then passed along.

I reached eagerly for it and looked deeply into the red wine. Again I saw my own reflection in the mirror of liquid. I was no longer a boy, but a man grown strong and courageous. I raised the cup to my lips and whispered, "Amen." I tasted the wine, closed my eyes, and smiled.

I found myself watching the flocks on a distant mountain illuminated by a golden light. The Great White Hart stood beside me. Eden restored. Not of this earth, I knew.

Not of this time.

I passed the chalice to another. I did not know who took it from my hand.

I heard Jesus' mother begin to sing,

> "I love the LORD, for he heard my voice;
> he heard my cry for mercy.
> Because he turned his ear to me,
> I will call on him as long as I live."[2]

All of us lining the stairs and those who supped in the room below joined in Mary's song.

"For you, LORD, have delivered me from death,
my eyes from tears,
my feet from stumbling,
that I may walk before the LORD
in the land of the living.

What shall I return to the LORD
for all his goodness to me?
I will lift up the cup of salvation
and call upon the name of the LORD."[3]

When all in the house had tasted from it, the empty cup returned to me. I held it close to my heart as if embracing an old friend. We had traveled many miles together to this holy moment and to this room where past and future became one eternal present.

Was I still to be cupbearer to the King? I peered over the top step. Tears misted my eyes as Jesus stood and wrapped himself in his seamless robe. He held me gently in his gaze for a long moment and nodded.

I wrapped the cup in my cloak.

"Come," he said, "follow me. The moment is at hand. We will go now to the Mount of Olives and pray."

Thus the first part of my journey came to an end.

But, in truth, it was only the beginning.

Notes

Part One
1. Psalm 42:1, adapted from NIV

Chapter 1
1. Psalm 42:1, adapted from NIV
2. See Matthew 24:27.

Chapter 2
1. Psalm 23:1–2 ESV
2. Psalm 23:3 ESV
3. Psalm 23:4 ESV

Chapter 3
1. Numbers 24:17 ESV
2. Isaiah 7:14 ESV

Chapter 6
1. Esther 7:2
2. Read the story in Genesis chapters 37 and 39 through 45.

Chapter 8
1. Luke 2:35, adapted from NIV
2. Deuteronomy 6:4

Part Two
1. Psalm 91:1, 13

Chapter 9
1. Psalm 91:13
2. Psalm 91:1
3. Psalm 50:15
4. Psalm 72:13
5. Proverbs 20:13
6. Isaiah 55:1

NOTES

Chapter 13
1. Psalm 42:1, adapted from NIV
2. See Genesis 50:20.

Chapter 16
1. Genesis 12:1 KJV
2. Isaiah 40:26 KJV
3. Isaiah 40:31 KJV

Chapter 18
1. Malachi 1:6, adapted from ESV

Chapter 19
1. Isaiah 49:6 ESV

Chapter 22
1. Isaiah 61:1
2. Isaiah 53:5

Chapter 23
1. Matthew 12:39 ESV

Part Three
1. John 12:35–36

Chapter 26
1. Luke 16:19–31, adapted from multiple versions
2. Jeremiah 1:4–8, adapted from NIV
3. Exodus 3:5

Chapter 27
1. Matthew 18:6–7, adapted from multiple versions
2. See Matthew 18:21–22.
3. Luke 17:6

Chapter 28
1. See Luke 17:11–19.
2. See Psalm 91:11.
3. Luke 17:20–21, adapted from NIV and NKJV
4. Luke 17:22–36, adapted from NIV
5. Psalm 91:3–4, adapted from NIV

Chapter 29
1. Luke 18:9–14, adapted from NIV and NKJV
2. See Luke 18:16–17.
3. Luke 18:18–30, adapted from NKJV
4. Luke 18:31–33, adapted from NIV
5. Psalm 75:8, adapted from NIV and NKJV
6. Isaiah 51:22 ESV

7. Isaiah 53:2 NKJV
8. Isaiah 53:5 NKJV
9. Isaiah 53:6, 10 NKJV
10. Isaiah 53:12 NKJV

Chapter 31

1. Psalm 105:1–2
2. Psalm 105:8–10
3. Matthew 21:13 NKJV

Chapter 32

1. Matthew 21:16, adapted from NIV
2. Isaiah 53:1
3. John 12:40

Chapter 33

1. Read the story in Matthew 21:33–44.
2. Psalm 118:22–23, as quoted by Jesus in Matthew 21:42
3. Read the story in John 12:25–36.

Chapter 34

1. See the prophecy in Hosea 11:1.
2. Genesis 3:17–18
3. Matthew 23:23–24, adapted from NIV
4. Matthew 23:25–26, adapted from NIV
5. Matthew 23:27–28, adapted from NIV
6. Matthew 23:29–36, adapted from NIV
7. Matthew 23:37–39, adapted from NIV
8. Matthew 24:2, adapted from NIV
9. Read the story in Matthew 24:3–14.
10. Matthew 24:29–31, 33–43, adapted from NIV
11. Matthew 25:31–40, adapted from NIV
12. Matthew 26:1–2, adapted from NIV

Chapter 36

1. Matthew 26:27–29
2. Psalm 116:1–2
3. Psalm 116:8–9, 12–13

Authors' Note

*J*esus clearly believed in the power of stories. He told parables—stories—to stretch the minds and transform the hearts of his listeners. We, too, believe in the life-changing power of stories, and that's why we're passionate about writing fiction.

In every work of our fiction, there is truth, based on research, and there is imagination, based on our minds and perspectives. We weren't here on this earth as Jesus walked among the people, but through the verses of Scripture and our imagination, we have portrayed to the best of our ability what he might have said and the way in which he might have said it. *Take This Cup* is how we imagine the events might have happened for young Nehemiah and his family, for Joseph of Arimathea, for the Sparrows of Jerusalem, for the boy Hallelujah, and for all the other characters in this story whose lives, bodies, and hearts were transformed by Jesus. It also traces the path of the legend of the Holy Grail and how we imagine the cup might have passed through the hands of ordinary people, such as Nehemiah, changing their hearts and life paths.

There are many legends about Joseph of Arimathea, the wealthy Jewish man who asked for permission to bury Jesus' body properly after his death. It is said he used the Holy Grail— the cup that Jesus used during the Last Supper—to collect Jesus' blood while he was being crucified. Then, afterward, it is said that Joseph traveled to England, bringing the cup with him. Which of the legends are true, and which are just stories? None of us is likely to know until we enter the realm of heaven, where the desires of our hearts will be met and our questions answered.

But can lives, bodies, and hearts truly be transformed today while we are here on earth? With Jesus, *anything* is possible! Through *Take This Cup,* may the Messiah come alive to you . . . in more brilliance than ever before.

Bodie & Brock Thoene

About the Authors

B ODIE and BROCK THOENE (pronounced *Tay-nee)* have written over sixty-five works of historical fiction. That these best sellers have sold more than thirty-five million copies and won eight ECPA Gold Medallion Awards affirms what millions of readers have already discovered—that the Thoenes are not only master stylists but experts at capturing readers' minds and hearts.

In their timeless classic series about Israel (The Zion Chronicles, The Zion Covenant, The Zion Legacy, The Zion Diaries), the Thoenes' love for both story and research shines. With The Shiloh Legacy and *Shiloh Autumn* (poignant portrayals of the American Depression), The Galway Chronicles (dramatic stories of the 1840s famine in Ireland), and the Legends of the West (gripping tales of adventure and danger in a land without law), the Thoenes have made their mark in modern history. In the A.D. Chronicles, they stepped seamlessly into the world of Jerusalem and Rome, in the days when Yeshua walked the earth. Now, in the Jerusalem Chronicles, the Thoenes continue that journey through the most crucial events in the life of Yeshua on earth.

Bodie, who has degrees in journalism and communications, began her writing career as a teen journalist for her local newspaper. Eventually her byline appeared in prestigious periodicals such as *US News and World Report,* the *American West,* and the *Saturday Evening Post.* She also worked for John Wayne's Batjac Productions and ABC Circle Films as a writer and researcher. John Wayne described her as "a writer with talent that captures the people and the times!"

Brock has often been described by Bodie as "an essential half of this writing team." With degrees in both history and education, Brock has, in his role of researcher and story-line consultant, added the vital dimension of historical accuracy. Due to such careful research, the Zion Covenant and Zion Chronicles series are recognized by the American Library Association, as well as Zionist libraries around the world, as classic historical novels and are used to teach history in college classrooms.

Bodie and Brock have four grown children—Rachel, Jake, Luke, and Ellie—and eight grandchildren. Their children are carrying on the Thoene family talent as the next generation of writers, and Luke produces the Thoene audiobooks. Bodie and Brock divide their time between Hawaii, London, and Nevada.

www.thoenebooks.com
www.familyaudiolibrary.com

Thoene Family Classics™

THOENE FAMILY CLASSIC HISTORICALS
by Bodie and Brock Thoene

Gold Medallion Winners*

The Zion Covenant
*Vienna Prelude**
Prague Counterpoint
Munich Signature
Jerusalem Interlude
Danzig Passage
*Warsaw Requiem**
London Refrain
Paris Encore
Dunkirk Crescendo

The Zion Chronicles
*The Gates of Zion**
A Daughter of Zion
The Return to Zion
A Light in Zion
*The Key to Zion**

The Shiloh Legacy
*In My Father's House**
A Thousand Shall Fall
Say to This Mountain
Shiloh Autumn

The Galway Chronicles
*Only the River Runs Free**
Of Men and of Angels
*Ashes of Remembrance**
All Rivers to the Sea

The Zion Legacy
Jerusalem Vigil
Thunder from Jerusalem

Jerusalem's Heart
Jerusalem Scrolls
Stones of Jerusalem
Jerusalem's Hope

A.D. Chronicles
First Light
Second Touch
Third Watch
Fourth Dawn
Fifth Seal
Sixth Covenant
Seventh Day
Eighth Shepherd
Ninth Witness
Tenth Stone
Eleventh Guest
Twelfth Prophecy

Zion Diaries
The Gathering Storm
Against the Wind

Jerusalem Chronicles
When Jesus Wept
Take This Cup

THOENE FAMILY CLASSIC ROMANCE
by Bodie Thoene

Love Finds You in Lahaina, Hawaii

THOENE FAMILY CLASSIC AMERICAN LEGENDS
Legends of the West
by Brock and Bodie Thoene

Legends of the West
Volume One
Sequoia Scout
The Year of the Grizzly
Shooting Star

Legends of the West
Volume Two
Gold Rush Prodigal
Delta Passage
Hangtown Lawman

Legends of the West
Volume Three
Hope Valley War
The Legend of Storey County
Cumberland Crossing

Legends of the West
Volume Four
The Man from Shadow Ridge
Cannons of the Comstock
Riders of the Silver Rim

Legends of Valor
by Jake Thoene and Luke Thoene

Sons of Valor
Brothers of Valor
Fathers of Valor

THOENE FAMILY CLASSIC CONTEMPORARY
by Bodie, Brock, and Luke Thoene

Icon

THOENE CLASSIC CONTEMPORARY
by Bodie and Brock Thoene

Beyond the Farthest Star

THOENE CLASSIC NONFICTION
by Bodie and Brock Thoene

Little Books of Why
Why a Manger?
Why a Shepherd?
Why a Star?
Why a Crown?
Writer-to-Writer

THOENE FAMILY CLASSIC SUSPENSE
by Jake Thoene

Chapter 16 Series
Shaiton's Fire
Firefly Blue
Fuel the Fire

THOENE FAMILY CLASSICS FOR KIDS
Sherlock Holmes &
The Baker Street Detectives
by Jake Thoene and Luke Thoene

The Mystery of the Yellow Hands
The Giant Rat of Sumatra
The Jeweled Peacock of Persia
The Thundering Underground

The Last Chance Detectives
by Jake Thoene and Luke Thoene

Mystery Lights of Navajo Mesa
Legend of the Desert Bigfoot

by Rachel Thoene

The Vase of Many Colors

THOENE FAMILY CLASSIC AUDIOBOOKS

Available from

www.thoenebooks.com

or

www.familyaudiolibrary.com

To Allan and Euan,
who set the ball rolling.

Not my accent – I didn't lose that so much as wipe it off my shoe, as soon as I started to live in England – but rather my own temperament, the prototypically Scottish part of my character that was chippy, aggressive, mean, morbid and, despite my best endeavours, persistently deist. I was, and always would be, a lousy escapee from the unnatural history museum . . .

Philip Kerr, 'The Unnatural History Museum'

INTRODUCTION

Whenever I'm on tour, I'm always on the lookout for local music and bands I haven't heard of. On my first trip to New Zealand, I was sitting watching TV in my Auckland hotel room and liked the snippets of music I heard on an advert for the latest album by the Mutton Birds. I didn't know the Mutton Birds, but they seemed to be popular in New Zealand. At tour's end, I found myself with an hour to kill at the airport and some spare currency. I bought the album at a CD booth, and listened to it back in Edinburgh. There are plenty of great songs on *Rain, Steam and Speed*, but one – 'The Falls' – really got to me. It was slow and haunting and mythic. The lyrics were all about invention: how we invent the world by means of our insatiable curiosity. I loved the song's refrain – 'There must be a story behind all that . . .'

There must be a story.

I was still recovering from jet lag when the French TV crew hit town. They were in Edinburgh to make a documentary about the Scottish parliament, and wanted to talk to a few of the doubters. I never did find out how they got my name, but it's true that I was sceptical about the costings, the site chosen for the building, and the need for another layer of bureaucracy. (I'm more sanguine these days.) I'd agreed to meet them at the recently opened Museum of Scotland on Chambers Street. There was a spot on the lower ground floor that would provide the perfect backdrop to our conversation. As we walked into the building, a member of staff sauntered over. He'd recognised me, and had something he wanted to say.

'You should take a look at the little dolls, Mr Rankin.'

I asked him which little dolls he meant. He winked, and told me to take the lift to the fourth floor. Plenty of people over the years have come up to me with their excited notions of plots for my next book. I've found precious few of them to be helpful or viable, but I was intrigued by these 'little dolls'. . . which is how I made the acquaintance of the Arthur's Seat coffins. They're tucked away at the back of the fourth floor, in a section dedicated to religious belief and the afterlife. As soon as I saw them, I knew they would make a great story, especially as no one had come up with an incontrovertible interpretation of their meaning. In other words, there was a story to tell about them. Maybe fiction could provide a sense of closure which so far had been lacking from their history.

There must be a story behind all that . . .

My books have always been attempts to explain aspects of Scotland to both outsiders and natives. I like using 'hidden' stories – Mary King's Close (*Mortal Causes*), cannibalism (*Set in Darkness*) – as my starting points. There are things you can say in fiction which can't always be contained by history books. It's true also that I take real-life unsolved crimes (such as the Bible John murders in *Black & Blue*) and extrapolate from them to say something about the world we've made for ourselves. Maybe that's why I became so intrigued, soon after my experience with the Arthur's Seat coffins, by the story of Emmanuel Caillet, a young Frenchman whose body had been found on a Scottish mountainside. No one could explain why he'd come so far from home in order to kill himself, or even *why* he would kill himself. One theory – no wilder than many of the others – had it that he was involved in an Internet role-playing game, and that this had led to his murder. The perils we face when going online have been well documented, of course. Cyberspace is the perfect haunt of creeps, charlatans and hunters. It's a place full of shape-shifters.

Moreover, it's a place beyond Rebus's ken.

I knew that by using role-playing as the basis for a plot, I would be taking Rebus into new territory, to a place where he would feel utterly lost. In other words, it was a way of allowing Siobhan to show her mettle. This would be *her* case, an opportunity for her to prove she's as capable a detective as her mentor, but with a different set of skills. Meantime, I would give Rebus a quest of his own, but with physical clues – the dolls – rather than hi-tech ones.

The Falls is as much Siobhan's book as Rebus's. They share pretty well equal 'screen time', and are together only infrequently. Perhaps the point I was trying to make is that Siobhan doesn't need Rebus any more. She's happy to work with him, but as equals. I also promote Gill Templer (apart from Rebus, the only character to have survived from book one of the series), and retire 'Farmer' Watson.

Rebus himself seems to feel that the tectonic plates are shifting, that younger officers are moving into positions of responsibility while he remains a dinosaur. He can share his worries with Bobby Hogan, a colleague from the 'old school', but not with Morris Gerald Cafferty. I decided that Cafferty, criminal Edinburgh's Mr Big, would be sidelined in *The Falls*. In past books, he had proven to be a useful foil: someone Rebus felt close to, but not in a good way. Cafferty tempts and teases Rebus, helps him out where no help is wished for. The two men are too alike not to have some respect for each other; but at any moment one of them is quite capable of destroying the other also. Cafferty could have been useful to me in *The Falls*, but I left him out as a favour to a mentor of mine, Allan Massie. Allan was writer-in-residence for a time at Edinburgh University, and helped me with my early short stories. He also introduced me to Euan Cameron, an editor in London who would eventually publish *Knots & Crosses*. I acknowledged my debt to both in the dedication page to *The Falls*, and alluded to another 'series' writer, Anthony Powell, when I stated that Allan and Euan had 'set the ball rolling'.

So why is Cafferty missing? Well, in a newspaper review of one of my previous Rebus novels, Allan Massie had stated a dislike of Cafferty – this Cafferty-less book is the result.

You see, sometimes I do listen to my critics.

May 2005

1

'You think I killed her, don't you?'

He sat well forward on the sofa, head slumped in towards his chest. His hair was lank, long-fringed. Both knees worked like pistons, the heels of his grubby trainers never meeting the floor.

'You on anything, David?' Rebus asked.

The young man looked up. His eyes were bloodshot, dark-rimmed. A lean, angular face, bristles on the unshaved chin. His name was David Costello. Not Dave or Davy: David, he'd made that clear. Names, labels, classification: all very important. The media had varied its descriptions of him. He was 'the boyfriend', 'the tragic boyfriend', 'the missing student's boyfriend'. He was 'David Costello, 22' or 'fellow student David Costello, in his early twenties'. He 'shared a flat with Ms Balfour' or was 'a frequent visitor' to the 'disappearance riddle flat'.

Nor was the flat just a flat. It was 'the flat in Edinburgh's fashionable New Town', the 'quarter-million flat owned by Ms Balfour's parents'. John and Jacqueline Balfour were 'the numbed family', 'the shocked banker and his wife'. Their daughter was 'Philippa, 20, a student of art history at the University of Edinburgh'. She was 'pretty', 'vivacious', 'carefree', 'full of life'.

And now she was missing.

Detective Inspector John Rebus shifted position, from in front of the marble fireplace to slightly to one side of it. David Costello's eyes followed the move.

'The doctor gave me some pills,' he said, finally answering the question.

'Did you take them?' Rebus asked.

The young man shook his head slowly, eyes still on Rebus.

'Don't blame you,' Rebus said, sliding his hands into his pockets. 'Knock you out for a few hours, but they don't change anything.'

It was two days since Philippa – known to friends and family as 'Flip' – had gone missing. Two days wasn't long, but her disappearance was out of character. Friends had called the flat at around seven in the evening to confirm that Flip would be meeting up with them within the hour at a bar on the South Side. It was one of those small, trendy places which had sprung up around the university, catering to an economic boom and the need for dim lighting and overpriced flavoured vodkas. Rebus knew this because he'd walked past it a couple of times on his way to and from his place of work. There was an old-fashioned pub practically next door, with vodka mixers at a pound-fifty. No trendy chairs though, and serving staff who knew their way around a brawl but not a cocktail list.

Seven, seven-fifteen, she probably left the flat. Tina, Trist, Camille and Albie were already on their second round of drinks. Rebus had consulted the files to confirm those names. Trist was short for Tristram, and Albie was Albert. Trist was with Tina; Albie was with Camille. Flip should have been with David, but David, she explained on the phone, wouldn't be joining them.

'Another bust-up,' she'd said, not sounding too concerned.

She'd set the flat's alarm before leaving. That was another first for Rebus – student digs with an alarm. And she'd done the mortise lock as well as the Yale, leaving the flat secure. Down a single flight of stairs and out into the warm night air. A steep hill separated her from Princes Street. Another climb from there would take her to the Old Town, the South Side. No way she'd be walking. But records from her home telephone and mobile had failed to find a match for any taxi firm in the city. So if she'd taken one, she'd hailed it on the street.

If she'd got as far as hailing one.

'I didn't, you know,' David Costello said.

'Didn't what, sir?'

'Didn't kill her.'

'Nobody's saying you did.'

'No?' He looked up again, directly into Rebus's eyes.

'No,' Rebus assured him, that being his job after all.

'The search warrant . . .' Costello began.

'It's standard, any case of this kind,' Rebus explained. It was, too: suspicious disappearance, you checked all the places the person might be. You went by the book: all the paperwork signed, clearance given. You searched the boyfriend's flat. Rebus could have added: *we do it because nine times out of ten, it's someone the victim knows*. Not a stranger, plucking prey from the night. It was your loved ones who killed you: spouse, lover, son or daughter. It was your uncle, your closest friend, the one person you trusted. They'd been cheating on you, or you'd cheated them. You knew something, you had something. They were jealous, spurned, needed money.

If Flip Balfour was dead, her body would turn up soon; if she was alive and didn't want to be found, then the job would be more difficult. Her parents had appeared on TV, pleading with her to make contact. Police were at the family home, intercepting calls in case any ransom demand should arrive. Police were wandering through David Costello's flat on the Canongate, hoping to turn up something. And police were here – in Flip Balfour's flat. They were 'babysitting' David Costello – stopping the media from getting too close. This was what the young man had been told, and it was partly true.

Flip's flat had been searched the previous day. Costello had keys, even to the alarm system. The phone call to Costello's own flat had come at ten p.m.: Trist, asking if he'd heard from Flip, only she'd been on her way to Shapiro's and hadn't turned up.

'She's not with you, is she?'

'I'm the last person she'd come to,' Costello had complained.

'Heard you'd fallen out. What is it this time?' Trist's voice had been slurred, ever-so-slightly amused. Costello hadn't answered him. He'd cut the call and tried Flip's mobile, got her answering service, left a message asking her to phone him. Police had listened to the recording, concentrating on nuance, trying to read falseness into each word or phrase. Trist had phoned Costello again at midnight. The group had been to Flip's flat: no one home. They'd been ringing round, but none of her friends seemed to know anything. They waited until Costello himself arrived at the flat, unlocking it. No sign of Flip inside.

In their minds, she was already a Missing Person, what police called a 'MisPer', but they'd waited till next morning before calling Flip's mother at the family home in East Lothian. Mrs Balfour had wasted no time, dialling 999 immediately. After receiving what she felt was short shrift from the police switchboard, she'd called her husband at his London office. John Balfour was the senior partner in a private bank, and if the Chief Constable of Lothian and Borders Police wasn't a client, someone certainly was: within an hour, officers were on the case – orders from the Big House, meaning Force HQ in Fettes Avenue.

David Costello had unlocked the flat for the two CID men. Within, they found no signs of a disturbance, no clues as to Philippa Balfour's whereabouts, fate, or state of mind. It was a tidy flat: stripped floors, fresh paint on the walls. (The decorator was being interviewed, too.) The drawing room was large, with twin windows rising from floor level. There were two bedrooms, one turned into a study. The designer kitchen was smaller than the pine-panelled bathroom. There was a lot of David Costello's stuff in the bedroom. Someone had piled his clothes on a chair, then placed some books and CDs on top, crowning the structure with a wash-bag.

When asked, Costello could only assume it was Flip's work. His words: 'We'd had a falling-out. This was probably her way of dealing with it.' Yes, they'd had arguments before, but no, she'd never piled up all his stuff, not that he could remember.

John Balfour had travelled to Scotland by private jet – loaned him by an understanding client – and was at the New Town flat almost before the police.

'Well?' had been his first question. Costello himself offered an answer: 'I'm sorry.'

Much had been read into those words by CID officers, discussing the case in private. An argument with your girlfriend turns nasty; next you know, she's dead; you hide the body but, confronted by her father, innate breeding takes over and you blurt out a semi-confession.

I'm sorry.

So many ways to read those two short words. Sorry we argued; sorry you've been troubled; sorry this has happened; sorry I didn't look after her; sorry for what I've done . . .

And now David Costello's parents were in town, too. They'd taken two rooms at one of the best hotels. They lived on the outskirts of Dublin. The father, Thomas, was described as 'independently wealthy', while the mother, Theresa, worked as an interior designer.

Two rooms: there'd been some discussion back at St Leonard's as to why they'd need two rooms. But then, when David was their only son, why did they bother to live in an eight-bedroom house?

There'd been even more discussion about what St Leonard's was doing in a New Town case. The nearest cop shop to the flat was Gayfield Square, but additional officers had been drafted in from Leith, St Leonard's and Torphichen.

'Someone's been pulling strings,' was the universal view. 'Drop everything, some posh bit's done a runner.'

Privately, Rebus didn't disagree.

'Do you want anything?' he said now. 'Tea? Coffee?'

Costello shook his head.

'Mind if I . . . ?'

Costello looked at him, seeming not to understand. Then realisation dawned. 'Go ahead,' he said. 'The kitchen's . . .' He started to gesture.

'I know where it is, thanks,' Rebus said. He closed the door after him and stood for a moment in the hallway, glad to be out of the stifling drawing room. His temples throbbed and the nerves behind his eyes felt stretched. There were sounds coming from the study. Rebus stuck his head round the door.

'I'm putting the kettle on.'

'Good idea.' Detective Constable Siobhan Clarke didn't take her eyes from the computer screen.

'Anything?'

'Tea, please.'

'I meant—'

'Nothing yet. Letters to friends, some of her essays. I've got about a thousand e-mails to go through. Her password would help.'

'Mr Costello says she never told him.'

Clarke cleared her throat.

'What does that mean?' Rebus asked.

'It means my throat's tickly,' Clarke said. 'Just milk in mine, thanks.'

Rebus left her and went into the kitchen, filled the kettle and searched for mugs and tea-bags.

'When can I go home?'

Rebus turned to where Costello was standing in the hall.

'Might be better if you didn't,' Rebus told him. 'Reporters and cameras . . . they'll keep on at you, phoning day and night.'

'I'll take the phone off the hook.'

'Be like being a prisoner.' Rebus watched the young man shrug. He said something Rebus didn't catch.

'Sorry?'

'I can't stay here,' Costello repeated.

'Why not?'

'I don't know . . . it's just . . .' He shrugged again, ran his hands through his hair, pulling it back from his forehead. 'Flip should be here. It's almost too much. I keep remembering that the last time we were here together, we were having a row.'

6

'What was it about?'

Costello laughed hollowly. 'I can't even remember.'

'This was the day she disappeared?'

'The afternoon, yes. I stormed out.'

'You argue a lot then?' Rebus tried to make the question sound casual.

Costello just stood there, staring into space, head shaking slowly. Rebus turned away, separated two Darjeeling teabags and dropped them into the mugs. Was Costello unravelling? Was Siobhan Clarke listening from behind the study door? They were babysitting Costello, yes, part of a team running three eight-hour shifts, but they'd brought him here for another reason, too. Ostensibly, he was on hand to explain names that occurred in Philippa Balfour's correspondence. But Rebus had wanted him there because just maybe it was the scene of the crime. And just maybe David Costello had something to hide. The betting at St Leonard's was even money; you could get two-to-one at Torphichen, while Gayfield had him odds-on favourite.

'Your parents said you could move into their hotel,' Rebus said. He turned to face Costello. 'They've booked two rooms, so one's probably going spare.'

Costello didn't take the bait. He watched the detective for a few seconds more, then turned away, putting his head around the study door.

'Have you found what you're looking for?' he asked.

'It could take some time, David,' Siobhan said. 'Best just to let us get on with it.'

'You won't find any answers in there.' He meant the computer screen. When she didn't answer, he straightened a little and angled his head. 'You're some sort of expert, are you?'

'It's something that has to be done.' Her voice was quiet, as though she didn't want it to carry beyond the room.

He seemed about to add something, but thought better of it, and stalked back towards the drawing room instead. Rebus took Clarke's tea through.

'Now that's class,' she said, examining the tea-bag floating in the mug.

'Wasn't sure how strong you'd want it,' Rebus explained. 'What did you think?'

She considered for a moment. 'Seems genuine enough.'

'Maybe you're just a sucker for a pretty face.'

She snorted, fished the tea-bag out and tipped it into the waste-bin. 'Maybe,' she said. 'So what's *your* thinking?'

'Press conference tomorrow,' Rebus reminded her. 'Reckon we can persuade Mr Costello to make a public appeal?'

Two detectives from Gayfield Square had the evening shift. Rebus headed home and started to fill a bath. He felt like a long soak, and squeezed some washing-up liquid under the hot tap, remembering it was something his parents had done for him when he was a kid. You came in muddy from the football pitch, and it was a hot bath with washing-up liquid. It wasn't that the family couldn't afford bubble-bath: 'It's just washing liquid at a posh price,' his mother had said.

Philippa Balfour's bathroom had boasted over a dozen different 'balms', 'bathing lotions' and 'foaming oils'. Rebus did his own stock-take: razor, shaving cream, toothpaste and a single toothbrush, plus a bar of soap. In the medicine cabinet: sticking plasters, paracetamol and a packet of condoms. He looked in the packet – one left. The sell-by was the previous summer. When he closed the cabinet, he met the gaze of his reflection. Grey-faced, hair streaked grey, too. Jowly, even when he stuck out his chin. Tried smiling, saw teeth which had missed their last two appointments. His dentist was threatening to strike him from his list.

'Get in line, pal,' Rebus muttered, turning away from the mirror before undressing.

The retirement party for Detective Chief Superintendent 'Farmer' Watson had commenced at six. It was actually the third or fourth party of its kind, but was to be the last – and the only official gathering. The Police Club on Leith Walk had been decked out with streamers, balloons and a huge banner which read FROM UNDER ARREST TO A WELL-DESERVED REST. Someone had dumped a bale of straw on the dance-floor, completing the farmyard scene with an inflatable pig and sheep. The bar was doing roaring business when Rebus arrived. He'd passed a trio of departing Big House brass on his way in. Checked his watch: six-forty. They'd given the retiring DCS forty minutes of their valuable time.

There'd been a presentation earlier in the day at St Leonard's. Rebus had missed it; he'd been babysitting at the time. But he'd heard about the speech made by Assistant Chief Constable Colin Carswell. Several officers from the Farmer's previous postings – some now retired themselves – were on hand to say a few words. They'd stuck around for the evening's proceedings, and looked to have been drinking the afternoon away: ties discarded or hanging limply askew, faces shiny with alcoholic heat. One man was singing, his voice battling the music from the ceiling-mounted loud-speakers.

'What can I get you, John?' the Farmer said, leaving his table to join Rebus at the bar.

'Maybe a small whisky, sir.'

'Half-bottle of malt over here when you've a minute!' the Farmer roared at the barman, who was busy topping up pints of lager. The Farmer's eyes narrowed as he focused on Rebus. 'Did you see those buggers from the Big House?'

'Passed them as I came in.'

'Bloody orange juices all round, then a quick handshake before home.' The Farmer was concentrating on not slurring his words, overcompensating as a result. 'Never really understood the phrase "biscuit-ersed" before, but that's what those lot were: biscuit-ersed to a man!'

Rebus smiled, told the barman to make it an Ardbeg.

'A bloody double, mind,' the Farmer ordered.

'Been enjoying a drink yourself, sir?' Rebus asked.

The Farmer blew out his cheeks. 'Few old pals came to see me off.' He nodded in the direction of the table. Rebus looked, too. He saw a posse of drunks. Beyond them stood tables spread with a buffet: sandwiches, sausage rolls, crisps and peanuts. He saw faces he knew from all the Lothian and Borders Divisional HQs. Macari, Allder, Shug Davidson, Roy Frazer. Bill Pryde was in conversation with Bobby Hogan. Grant Hood was standing next to a couple of Crime Squad officers called Claverhouse and Ormiston, and trying not to look as though he was sucking up to them. George 'Hi-Ho' Silvers was finding that DC Phyllida Hawes and DS Ellen Wylie weren't about to fall for his chat-up lines. Jane Barbour from the Big House was exchanging gossip with Siobhan Clarke, who'd at one time been attached to Barbour's Sex Offences Unit.

'If anyone knew about this,' Rebus said, 'the bad guys would have a field day. Who's left to mind the store?'

The Farmer laughed. 'It's a skeleton crew at St Leonard's, all right.'

'Good turn-out. Wonder if I'd get as many at mine.'

'More, I'd bet.' The Farmer leaned close. 'The brass would all be there for a start, just to make sure they weren't dreaming.'

It was Rebus's turn to smile. He lifted his glass, toasted his boss. They both savoured their drinks, then the Farmer smacked his lips.

'How long d'you think?' he asked.

Rebus shrugged. 'I've not got my thirty yet.'

'Can't be long though, can it?'

'I'm not counting.' But he was lying: most weeks he thought about it. 'Thirty' meant thirty years of service. That was when your pension hit the max. It was what a lot of officers lived for: retirement in their fifties and a cottage by the sea.

'Here's a story I don't often tell,' the Farmer said. 'My first week on the force, they had me working the front desk, graveyard shift. This young lad – not even in his teens – comes in, walks straight up to the desk. "I've broke my wee sister," he says.' The Farmer's eyes were staring into space. 'I can see him now, the way he looked, the exact words . . .

"I've broke my wee sister." I hadn't a clue what he meant. Turned out he'd pushed her down the stairs, killed her.' He paused, took another gulp of whisky. 'My first week on the force. Know what my sergeant said? "It can only get better." ' He forced a smile. 'I've never been sure he was right . . .' Suddenly his arms went into the air, the smile broadening into a grin. 'Here she is! Here she is! Just when I thought I was being stood up.'

His embrace almost swamped DCI Gill Templer. The Farmer planted a kiss on her cheek. 'You're not the floor-show by any chance?' he asked. Then he mimed a slap to his forehead. 'Sexist language – are you going to report me?'

'I'll let it go this time,' Gill said, 'in exchange for a drink.'

'My shout,' Rebus said. 'What'll you have?'

'Long vodka.'

Bobby Hogan was yelling for the Farmer to go settle an argument.

'Duty calls,' the Farmer said by way of an apology, before heading unsteadily across the floor.

'His party piece?' Gill guessed.

Rebus shrugged. The Farmer's speciality was naming all the books of the Bible. His record was just under a minute; no way would it be challenged tonight.

'Long vodka,' Rebus told the barman. He raised his whisky glass. 'And a couple more of these.' He saw Gill's look. 'One's for the Farmer,' he explained.

'Of course.' She was smiling, but the smile didn't reach her eyes.

'Fixed a date for your own bash?' Rebus asked.

'Which one is that?'

'I just thought, first female DCS in Scotland . . . got to be worth a night out, hasn't it?'

'I drank a Babycham when I heard.' She watched the barman dribble angostura into her glass. 'How's the Balfour case?'

Rebus looked at her. 'Is this my new Chief Super asking?'

'John . . .'

Funny how that single word could say so much. Rebus

wasn't sure he caught all the nuances, but he caught enough.

John, don't push this.

John, I know there's a history between us, but that's long dead.

Gill Templer had worked her arse off to get where she was now, but she was also under the microscope – plenty of people would want her to fail, including some she probably counted as friends.

Rebus just nodded and paid for the drinks, tipping one of the whiskies into the other glass.

'Saving him from himself,' he said, nodding towards the Farmer, who was already on to the New Testament.

'Always the willing martyr,' Gill said.

A cheer went up as the Farmer's recitation finished. Someone said it was a new record, but Rebus knew it wasn't. It was just another gesture, another version of the gold watch or mantel-clock. The malt tasted of seaweed and peat, but Rebus knew that whenever he drank Ardbeg from now on, he'd think of a small boy walking through the doors of a police station . . .

Siobhan Clarke was making her way across the room.

'Congratulations,' she said.

The two women shook hands.

'Thanks, Siobhan,' Gill said. 'Maybe it'll be you one day.'

'Why not?' Siobhan agreed. 'Glass ceiling's what truncheons are for.' She punched her fist into the air above her head.

'Need a drink, Siobhan?' Rebus asked.

The two women shared a look. 'About all they're good for,' Siobhan said with a wink. Rebus left the pair of them laughing.

The karaoke started at nine. Rebus went to the toilets and felt the sweat cooling on his back. His tie was already off and in his pocket. His jacket was slung over one of the chairs near the bar. Personnel at the party changed as some headed off, either to prepare for the night shift or because their mobile or pager had news for them. Others arrived, having been home to change out of work clothes. A female officer from the St Leonard's comms room had turned up in a short skirt, the first time Rebus had seen her legs. A rowdy quartet from one of the Farmer's postings in West Lothian arrived bearing photos of the Farmer from a quarter-century before. They'd slipped a few doctored prints into the mix, grafting the Farmer's head on to beefcake bodies, some of them in positions which went several leagues beyond compromising.

Rebus washed his hands, splashing some of the water on to his face and the back of his neck. Then of course there was only an electric hand-drier, so he had to use his handkerchief as a towel. Which was when Bobby Hogan walked in.

'See you're bottling it too,' Hogan said, making for the urinals.

'Ever heard me sing, Bobby?'

'We should do a duet: "There's a Hole in My Bucket".'

'We'd be about the only buggers who knew it.'

Hogan chuckled. 'Remember when it was us that were the young turks?'

'Long dead,' Rebus said, half to himself. Hogan thought he'd misheard, but Rebus just shook his head.

'So who's next for the golden cheery-bye?' Hogan asked, ready to head out again.

'Not me,' Rebus stated.

'No?'

Rebus was wiping at his neck again. 'I can't retire, Bobby. It would kill me.'

Hogan snorted. 'Same here. But then the job's killing me too.' The two men studied one another, then Hogan winked and yanked open the door. They walked back out into the heat and noise, Hogan opening his arms wide to greet an old friend. One of the Farmer's cronies pushed a glass towards Rebus.

'Ardbeg, right?'

Rebus nodded, sucked at where some had spilled on to the

back of his hand, then, picturing a small boy with news to impart, raised the glass and downed it.

He took the set of keys from his pocket and unlocked the main door of the tenement block. The keys were shiny new, cut just that day. His shoulder rubbed against the wall as he headed for the stairs, and he kept a tight grip on the banister as he climbed. The second and third shiny keys unlocked the door to Philippa Balfour's flat.

There was no one inside, and the alarm hadn't been set. He switched on the lights. The loose rug underfoot seemed to want to wrap itself around his ankles, and he had to fight his way loose, holding on to the wall. The rooms were just as he'd left them, except that the computer was now missing from its desk, having been transferred to the station, where Siobhan was certain someone from Balfour's Internet service provider could help bypass the password.

In the bedroom, someone had removed the neat pile of David Costello's clothes from the chair. Rebus presumed the culprit to be Costello himself. He wouldn't have done so without permission – nothing left the flat unless okayed by the bosses. Forensics would have checked the clothes first, maybe taken samples from them. Already there were rumours of belt-tightening. A case like this, the cost could spiral skywards like smoke.

In the kitchen, Rebus poured himself a big glass of water and went through to sit in the drawing room, pretty much where David Costello had sat. A little of the water dribbled down his chin. The paintings on the walls – framed abstracts – were playing tricks, moving with him as he moved his eyes. He bent down to place the empty glass on the floor, and ended up on his hands and knees. Some bastard had spiked the drinks, only explanation. He turned and sat down, closed his eyes for a moment. MisPers: sometimes you worried in vain; they either turned up, or didn't want to be found. So many of them ... photos and descriptions were always passing through the office, the faces slightly out of focus as though they were in the process of becoming ghosts. He blinked open his eyes and raised them to the ceiling, with its ornate cornicing. Big flats, the New Town had, but Rebus preferred it where he lived: more shops, not quite so smug . . .

The Ardbeg, it had to've been spiked. He probably wouldn't drink it again. It would come with its own ghost. He wondered what had happened to the boy: had it been accident or design? The boy would be a parent himself these days, maybe even a grandparent. Did he still dream about the sister he'd killed? Did he remember the young, nervous uniform standing behind the reception desk? Rebus ran his hands over the floor. It was bare wood, sanded and sealed. They hadn't taken the boards up, not yet. He felt for a gap between two planks and dug his nails in, but couldn't get any purchase. Somehow he knocked the glass and it started rolling, the noise filling the room. Rebus watched it until it stopped in the doorway, progress blocked by a pair of feet.

'What in the hell's going on?'

Rebus stood up. The man in front of him was in his mid-forties, hands in the pockets of a three-quarter-length black woollen overcoat. The man opened his stance a little, filling the doorway.

'Who are you?' Rebus asked.

The man slid a hand from his pocket, angled it towards his ear. He was holding a mobile phone. 'I'm calling the police,' he said.

'I'm a police officer.' Rebus reached into his own pocket, brought out his warrant card. 'DI Rebus.'

The man studied the card and handed it back. 'I'm John Balfour,' he said, his voice losing a little of its edge. Rebus nodded; he'd already figured as much.

'Sorry if I . . .' Rebus didn't finish the sentence. As he put the warrant card away, his left knee unlocked for a second.

'You've been drinking,' Balfour said.

'Sorry, yes. Retirement do. Not on duty or anything, if that's what you mean.'

'Then might I ask what you're doing in my daughter's flat?'

'You might,' Rebus agreed. He looked around. 'Just wanted to . . . well, I suppose I . . .' But he couldn't find the words.

'Will you leave, please?'

Rebus bowed his head a little. 'Of course.' Balfour moved so that Rebus could pass him without any contact. Rebus stopped in the hallway, half turned, ready with a further apology, but Philippa Balfour's father had walked over to the drawing-room window and was staring out at the night, hands gripping the shutters at either side.

He walked downstairs quietly, halfway sober now, closed the main door after him, not looking back, not looking up at the first-floor window. The streets were deserted, pavements glistening from an earlier downpour, street light reflected in them. Rebus's shoes were the only noise to be heard as he started the climb back up the slope: Queen Street, George Street, Princes Street, and then North Bridge. People were heading home from pubs, seeking taxis and lost friends. Rebus took a left at the Tron Kirk and headed down the Canongate. A patrol car was parked kerbside, two bodies inside: one awake, the other asleep. They were detective constables from Gayfield, and had either drawn the short straw or were disliked by their boss: no other way to explain this thankless night-shift. Rebus was just another passer-by to the one who was awake. He had a newspaper folded in front of him, angled towards what light there was. When Rebus thumped the roof of the patrol car, the paper flew, landing on the head of the sleeper, who jerked awake and clawed at the smothering sheets.

As the passenger-side window was wound down, Rebus leaned on the sill. 'Your one o'clock alarm call, gentlemen.'

'I nearly shat myself,' the passenger said, trying to gather up his newspaper. His name was Pat Connolly, and he'd spent his first few years in CID waging a campaign against the nickname 'Paddy'. His colleague was Tommy Daniels, who seemed at ease – as he did in all things – with his own nickname of 'Distant'. Tommy to Tom-Tom to Distant Drums to Distant was the logic behind the name, but it also said much about the young man's character. Having been so rudely awakened from sleep, upon seeing and recognising Rebus all he'd done was roll his eyes.

'Could've fetched us a coffee,' Connolly was complaining.

'Could have,' Rebus agreed. 'Or maybe a dictionary.' He glanced towards the newspaper crossword. Less than a quarter of the grid had been filled in, while the puzzle itself was ringed by doodles and unsolved anagrams. 'Quiet night?'

'Apart from foreigners asking directions,' Connolly said. Rebus smiled and looked up and down the street. This was the heart of tourist Edinburgh. A hotel up by the traffic lights, a knitwear shop across the road. Fancy gifts and shortbread and whisky decanters. A kiltmaker's only fifty yards away. John Knox's house, hunched against its neighbours, half hidden in scowling shadow. At one time, the Old Town had been all there was of Edinburgh: a narrow spine running from the Castle to Holyrood, steep vennels leading off like crooked ribs. Then, as the place became ever more crowded and insanitary, the New Town had been built, its Georgian elegance a calculated snub to the Old Town and those who couldn't afford to move. Rebus found it interesting that while Philippa Balfour had chosen the New Town, David Costello had elected to live in the heart of the Old.

'Is he home?' he said now.

'Would we be here if he wasn't?' Connolly's eyes were on his partner, who was pouring tomato soup from a thermos. Distant sniffed the liquid hesitantly, then took a quick gulp. 'Actually, you could be the very man we want.'

Rebus looked at him. 'Oh aye?'

'Settle an argument. Deacon Blue, *Wages Day* – first album or second?'

Rebus smiled. 'It *has* been a quiet night.' Then, after a moment's reflection: 'Second.'

'Ten notes you owe me,' Connolly told Distant.

'Mind if I ask one?' Rebus had crouched down, felt his knees crack with the effort.

'Fire away,' Connolly said.

'What do you do if you need a pee?'

Connolly smiled. 'If Distant's asleep, I just use his thermos.'

The mouthful of soup almost exploded from Distant's nostrils. Rebus straightened up, feeling the blood pound in his ears: weather warning, force-ten hangover on its way.

'You going in?' Connolly asked. Rebus looked at the tenement again.

'Thinking about it.'

'We'd have to make a note.'

Rebus nodded. 'I know.'

'Just come from the Farmer's leaving do?'

Rebus turned towards the car. 'What's your point?'

'Well, you've had a drink, haven't you? Might not be the best time for a house call . . . sir.'

'You're probably right . . . Paddy,' Rebus said, making for the door.

'Remember what you asked me?'

Rebus had accepted a black coffee from David Costello. Popped two paracetamol from their foil shroud and washed them down. Middle of the night, but Costello hadn't been asleep. Black T-shirt, black jeans, bare feet. He'd made an off-licence run at some point: the bag was lying on the floor, the half-bottle of Bell's sitting not far from it, top missing but only a couple of decent measures down. Not a drinker then, Rebus surmised. It was a non-drinker's idea of how you handled a crisis – you drank whisky, but had to buy some first, and no point lashing out on a whole bottle. A couple of drinks would do you.

The living room was small, the flat itself reached from a turreted stairwell, winding ever upwards, the stone steps worn concave. Tiny windows. They'd planned this building in a century where heat was a luxury. The smaller the windows, the less heat you lost.

The living room was separated from the kitchen only by a step and what looked like partition walls. An open doorway, double-width. Signs that Costello liked to cook: pots and pans hanging from butcher's hooks. The living area was all books and CDs. Rebus had trawled the latter: John Martyn, Nick Drake, Joni Mitchell. Laid-back but cerebral. The books looked like stuff from Costello's English Literature course.

Costello was seated on a red futon; Rebus had chosen one of two straight-backed wooden chairs. They looked like the stuff he saw on Causewayside, placed outside shops for which the description 'antique' encompassed school desks from the sixties and green filing cabinets salvaged from office refits.

Costello ran his hand through his hair, didn't say anything.

'You asked if I thought you did it,' Rebus said, answering his own question.

'Did what?'

'Killed Flip. I think that's how you phrased it: "You think I killed her, don't you?" '

Costello nodded. 'It's so obvious, isn't it? We'd fallen out. I accept that you have to regard me as a suspect.'

'David, right now you're the *only* suspect.'

'You really think something's happened to her?'

'What do you think?'

Costello shook his head. 'I've done nothing but rack my brains since this all started.'

They sat in silence for a few moments.

'What are you doing here?' Costello asked suddenly.

'As I said, it's on my way home. You like the Old Town?'

'Yes.'

'Bit different from the New. You didn't want to move nearer Flip?'

'What are you trying to say?'

Rebus shrugged. 'Maybe it says something about the pair of you, the parts of town you prefer.'

Costello laughed drily. 'You Scots can be so reductive.'

'How's that?'

'Old Town versus New, Catholic/Protestant, east coast/ west . . . Things can be a mite more complicated than that.'

'Attraction of opposites, that's all I was getting at.' There was another silence between them. Rebus scanned the room.

'Didn't make a mess then?'

'Who?'

'The search party.'

'Could have been worse.'

Rebus took a sip of coffee, pretended to savour it. 'You wouldn't have left the body here though, would you? I mean, only perverts do that sort of thing.' Costello looked at him. 'Sorry, I'm being . . . I mean, it's just theoretical. I'm not trying to say anything. But the forensics, they weren't looking for a body. They deal in things you and me can't even see. Flecks of blood, fibres, a single hair.' Rebus shook his head slowly. 'Juries eat that stuff up. The old idea of policing, it's going out the window.' He put down the gloss-black mug, reached into a pocket for his cigarette packet. 'Mind if I . . . ?'

Costello hesitated. 'Actually, I'll take one from you if that's all right.'

'Be my guest.' Rebus took one out of the packet, lit it, then tossed both packet and lighter to the younger man. 'Roll yourself a joint if you like,' he added. 'I mean, if that's your thing.'

'It's not.'

'Student life must be a bit different these days.'

Costello exhaled, studying the cigarette as if it was something alien to him. 'I'd assume it is,' he said.

Rebus smiled. Just two grown-ups having a smoke and a chat. The wee sma' hours and all that. A time for honesty, the outside world asleep, no one eavesdropping. He got up and walked over to the bookshelves. 'How did you and Flip meet?' he asked, picking a book at random and flipping through it.

'Dinner party. We clicked straight away. Next morning, after breakfast, we took a walk through Warriston Cemetery. That was when I first felt that I loved her . . . I mean, that it wasn't just going to be a one-night stand.'

'You like films?' Rebus said. He was noticing that one shelf seemed to be all books about movies.

Costello looked over towards him. 'I'd like to try writing a script some day.'

'Good for you.' Rebus had opened another book. It seemed to be a sequence of poems about Alfred Hitchcock. 'You didn't go to the hotel?' he asked after a pause.

'No.'

'But you've seen your parents?'

'Yes.' Costello took another draw, sucking the life from the cigarette. He realised he'd no ashtray and looked around for something suitable: candle-holders, one for Rebus and one for him. Turning from the bookshelves, Rebus's foot brushed something: a metal toy soldier, no more than an inch high. He stooped to pick it up. The musket had been snapped off, the head twisted over to one side. He didn't think he was responsible. Rebus placed it quietly on a shelf before sitting down again.

'Did they cancel the other room then?' he asked.

'They sleep in separate rooms, Inspector.' Costello looked up from where he'd been tidying the tip of the cigarette against the rim of the makeshift ashtray. 'Not a crime, is it?'

'I'm not best placed to judge. My wife left me more years ago than I can remember.'

'I'll bet you *do* remember.'

Rebus smiled again. 'Guilty.'

Costello rested his head against the back of the futon, stifled a yawn.

'I should go,' Rebus said.

'Finish your coffee at least.'

Rebus had already finished it, but nodded anyway, not about to leave unless pushed out. 'Maybe she'll turn up. People do things sometimes, don't they? Take a notion to head for the hills.'

'Flip was hardly the hill-heading type.'

'But she could have had a mind to take off somewhere.'

Costello shook his head. 'She knew they were waiting for her in the bar. She wouldn't have forgotten that.'

'No? Say she'd just met someone else . . . you know, an impulse thing, like in that advert.'

'Someone else?'

'It's possible, isn't it?'

Costello's eyes darkened. 'I don't know. It was one of the things I thought about – whether she'd met someone else.'

'You dismissed it?'

'Yes.'

'Why?'

'Because something like that, she'd have told me. That's the way Flip is: doesn't matter if it's a grand's worth of designer dress or a Concorde flight courtesy of her parents, she can't keep it to herself.'

'Likes attention?'

'Don't we all, from time to time?'

'She wouldn't pull a stunt, would she, just to get us all looking for her?'

'Fake her own disappearance?' Costello shook his head, then stifled another yawn. 'Maybe I should get some sleep.'

'What time's the press conference?'

'Early afternoon. Something to do with catching the main news bulletins.'

Rebus nodded. 'Don't be nervous out there, just be yourself.'

Costello stubbed out his cigarette. 'Who else could I be?' He made to hand the packet and lighter back to Rebus.

'Keep them. Never know when you might feel the need.' He got to his feet. The blood was beating in his skull now, despite the paracetamol. *That's the way Flip is:* Costello had spoken of her in the present tense – a casual remark, or something more calculated? Costello stood up too, now, and he was smiling, though without much humour.

'You never did answer that question, did you?' he said.

'I'm keeping an open mind, Mr Costello.'

'Are you now?' Costello slipped his hands into his pockets. 'Will I see you at the press conference?'

'Could be.'

'And will you be on the lookout for slips of the tongue?

22

Something like your forensic bods?' Costello's eyes narrowed. 'I may be the only suspect, but I'm not stupid.'

'Then you'll appreciate we're on the same side . . . unless you know differently?'

'Why did you come here tonight? You're not on duty, are you?'

Rebus took a step closer. 'Know what they used to think, Mr Costello? They thought murder victims kept an imprint of their killer on their eyeballs – last thing they ever saw. Some killers, they gouged out the eyes after death.'

'But we're not so naïve these days, Inspector, are we? You can't hope to know someone, to get the measure of them, just from eye contact.' Costello leaned in towards Rebus, his eyes widening slightly. 'Take a good long look, because the exhibit's about to close.'

Rebus met the gaze, returned it. Costello was the first to blink, breaking the spell. Then he turned away and told Rebus to leave. As Rebus made for the door, Costello called out to him. He was wiping the cigarette packet with a handkerchief. He did the same with the lighter, then tossed both items towards Rebus. They fell at his feet.

'I think your need's probably greater than mine.'

Rebus stooped to pick them up. 'Why the handkerchief?'

'Can't be too careful,' Costello said. 'Evidence can turn up in the strangest places.'

Rebus straightened, decided against saying anything. At the door, Costello called out goodnight to him. Rebus was halfway down the stairwell before he returned the sentiment. He was thinking about the way Costello had wiped both lighter and packet. All the years he'd been on the force, he'd never seen a suspect do anything like that. It had meant Costello was expecting to be set up.

Or, perhaps, that was what it was intended to look like. But it had shown Rebus a side of the young man that was cool and calculating. It showed someone who was capable of thinking ahead . . .

2

It was one of those cool, crepuscular days that could have belonged to any of at least three Scottish seasons; a sky like slate roofing and a wind that Rebus's father would have called 'snell'. His father had told a story once – many times actually – about walking into a grocer's in Lochgelly one freezing winter's morning. The grocer had been standing by the electric fire. Rebus's father had pointed to the cold cabinet and asked, 'Is that your Ayrshire bacon?' to which the grocer had replied, 'No, it's my hands I'm heating.' He'd sworn it was a true story, and Rebus – maybe seven or eight years old – had believed him at the time. But now it seemed an old chestnut of a joke, something he'd heard elsewhere and twisted to his own use.

'Not often I see you smiling,' his *barista* said as she made him a double *latte*. Those were her words: *barista, latte*. The first time she'd described her job, she'd pronounced it 'barrister', which had led a confused Rebus to ask if she was moonlighting. She worked from a converted police-box at the corner of the Meadows, and Rebus stopped there most mornings on his way to work. 'Milky coffee' was his order, which she always corrected to '*latte*'. Then he'd add 'double shot'. He didn't need to – she knew the order by heart – but he liked the feel of the words.

'Smiling's not illegal, is it?' he said now, as she spooned froth on to the coffee.

'You'd know better than me.'

'And your boss would know better than either of us.' Rebus paid up, punted the change into the marge tub left for tips, and headed for St Leonard's. He didn't think she knew he was a cop: *you'd know better than me* . . . it had been said casually, no meaning behind it other than to continue their banter. In turn, he'd made his remark about her boss because the owner of the chain of kiosks had once been a solicitor. But she hadn't seemed to understand.

At St Leonard's, Rebus stayed in his car, enjoying a last cigarette with his drink. A couple of vans sat at the station's back door, waiting for anyone who was being taken to court. Rebus had given evidence in a case a few days ago. He kept meaning to find out what the result had been. When the station door opened, he expected to see the custody line, but it was Siobhan Clarke. She saw his car and smiled, shaking her head at the inevitability of the scene. As she came forwards, Rebus lowered the window.

'The condemned man ate a hearty breakfast,' she said.

'And a good morning to you too.'

'Boss wants to see you.'

'He sent the right sniffer dog.'

Siobhan didn't say anything, just smiled to herself as Rebus got out of the car. They were halfway across the car park before he heard the words: 'It's not a "he" any more.' He stopped in his tracks.

'I'd forgotten,' he admitted.

'How's the hangover, by the way? Anything else you might have managed to forget?'

As she opened the door for him, he had the sudden image of a gamekeeper opening a trap.

The Farmer's photos and coffee machine had gone, and there were some Good Luck cards on top of the filing cabinet, but otherwise the room was just as before, down to the paperwork in the in-tray and the solitary potted cactus on the windowsill. Gill Templer looked uncomfortable in the Farmer's chair, his daily bulk having moulded it in ways which would never fit her slimmer proportions.

'Sit down, John.' Then, when he was halfway on to the seat: 'And tell me what last night was all about.' Elbows on the desk, she placed the tips of her fingers together. It was something the Farmer had often done when trying to hide irritation or impatience. She'd either picked it up from him, or it was a perk of her new seniority.

'Last night?'

'Philippa Balfour's flat. Her father found you there.' She looked up. 'Apparently you'd been drinking.'

'Hadn't we all?'

'Not as much as some.' Her eyes moved down again to the sheet of paper on her desk. 'Mr Balfour's wondering what you were up to. Frankly, I'm more than a little curious myself.'

'I was on my way home . . .'

'Leith Walk to Marchmont? Via the New Town? Sounds like you got bad directions.'

Rebus realised that he was still holding his beaker of coffee. He placed it on the floor, taking his time. 'It's just something I do,' he said at last. 'When things are quiet, I like to go back.'

'Why?'

'In case anything's been missed.'

She seemed to consider this. 'I'm not sure that's the whole story.'

He shrugged, said nothing. Her eyes were on the sheet again.

'And then you decided to pay Ms Balfour's boyfriend a call. How wise was that?'

'That really was on the way home. I stopped to talk to Connolly and Daniels. Mr Costello's light was on; I thought I'd make sure he was all right.'

'The caring copper.' She paused. 'That's presumably why Mr Costello felt it necessary to mention your visit to his solicitor?'

'I don't know why he did that.' Rebus shifted a little on the hard chair; disguised it by reaching for his coffee.

'His lawyer's talking about "harassment". We might have to pull the surveillance.' Her eyes were fixed on him.

'Look, Gill,' he said, 'you and me, we've known each other for donkey's. It's no secret how I work. I'm sure DCS Watson quoted scripture on the subject.'

'That was then, John.'

'Meaning what?'

'How much did you have to drink last night?'

'More than I should have, but it wasn't my fault.' He watched as Gill raised an eyebrow. 'I'm positive someone slipped me a Mickey Finn.'

'I want you to see a doctor.'

'Christ Almighty . . .'

'Your drinking, your diet, your general health . . . I want you to take a medical, and whatever the doctor says is necessary, I want you to abide by it.'

'Alfalfa and carrot juice?'

'You'll see a doctor, John.' It was a statement. Rebus just snorted and drained his coffee, then held up the beaker.

'Half-fat milk.'

She almost smiled. 'It's a start, I suppose.'

'Look, Gill . . .' He got up, tipped the beaker into the otherwise pristine waste-bin. 'My drinking's not a problem. It doesn't interfere with my work.'

'It did last night.'

He shook his head, but her face had hardened. Finally she took a deep breath. 'Just before you left the club . . . you remember that?'

'Sure.' He hadn't sat down; was standing in front of her desk, hands by his sides.

'You remember what you said to me?' His face told her all she needed to know. 'You wanted me to go home with you.'

'I'm sorry.' He was trying to remember, but nothing was coming. He couldn't remember leaving the club at all . . .

'On you go, John. I'll make that appointment for you.'

He turned, pulled open the door. He was halfway out when she called him back.

'I lied,' she said with a smile. 'You didn't say anything. Going to wish me well in the new job?'

Rebus tried for a sneer but couldn't quite manage one. Gill held her smile until he'd slammed shut the door; after he'd gone, it fell away again. Watson had given her chapter and verse all right, but nothing she hadn't already known:

Enjoys his drink a bit too much, maybe, but he's a good cop, Gill.
He just likes to pretend he can do without the rest of us . . .
Maybe that was true, as far as it went, but maybe, too, the
time was coming fast when John Rebus would have to learn
that *they* could do without *him.*

It was easy to spot the crew from the leaving do: local
chemists had probably sold out of aspirin, vitamin C and
patented hangover cures. Dehydration seemed a major
factor. Rebus had seldom seen so many bottles of Irn-Bru,
Lucozade and Coke in the grip of so many pallid hands. The
sobersides – who'd either not been to the party or who'd
stuck to soft drinks – were gloating, whistling shrilly and
slamming drawers and cupboards wherever possible. The
main incident room for the Philippa Balfour inquiry was
based at Gayfield Square – much closer to her flat – but with
so many officers involved, space was an issue, so a corner of
the CID room at St Leonard's had been set aside. Siobhan
was there now, busy at her terminal. A spare hard disk sat
on the floor, and Rebus realised that she was using Balfour's
computer. She held a telephone receiver between cheek and
shoulder, and typed as she talked.

'No luck there either,' Rebus heard her say.

He was sharing his own desk with three other officers,
and it showed. He brushed the remnants from a bag of crisps
on to the floor and deposited two empty Fanta cans in the
nearest bin. When the phone rang he picked it up, but it was
just the local evening paper trying to pull a flanker.

'Talk to Press Liaison,' Rebus told the journalist.

'Give me a break.'

Rebus was thoughtful. Liaison had been Gill Templer's
speciality. He glanced across towards Siobhan Clarke.
'Who's in charge of PL anyway?'

'DS Ellen Wylie,' the journalist said.

Rebus said thanks and cut the connection. Liaison would
have been a step up for Siobhan, especially on a high-profile
case. Ellen Wylie was a good officer based at Torphichen. As
a liaison specialist, Gill Templer would have been asked for

advice on the appointment, maybe even made the decision herself. She'd chosen Ellen Wylie. He wondered if there was anything in it.

He rose from the desk and studied the paperwork now pinned to the wall behind him. Duty rosters, faxes, lists of contact numbers and addresses. Two photos of the missing woman. One of them had been released to the press, and it was duplicated in a dozen news stories, clipped and displayed. Soon, if she wasn't found safe and well, space would be at a premium on the wall, and those news stories would be discarded. They were repetitious, inaccurate, sensationalised. Rebus lingered on one phrase: *the tragic boyfriend*. He checked his watch: five hours until the news conference.

With Gill Templer promoted, they were down a DCI at St Leonard's. Detective Inspector Bill Pryde wanted the job, and was trying to stamp his authority on the Balfour case. Rebus, newly arrived at the Gayfield Square incident room, could only stand and marvel. Pryde had smartened himself up – the suit looked brand new, the shirt laundered, the tie expensive. The black brogues were immaculately polished and, if Rebus wasn't mistaken, Pryde had been to the barber's, too. Not that there was too much to trim, but Pryde had made the effort. He'd been put in charge of assignments, which meant putting teams out on the street for the daily drudgery of doorsteppings and interviews. Neighbours were being questioned – sometimes for the second or third time – as were friends, students and university staff. Flights and ferry crossings were being checked, the official photograph faxed to train operators, bus companies and police forces outwith the Lothian and Borders area. It would be someone's job to collate information on fresh corpses throughout Scotland, while another team would focus on hospital admissions. Then there were the city's taxi and car hire firms ... It all took time and effort. These comprised the public face of the inquiry, but behind the scenes other questions would be asked of the

MisPer's immediate family and circle of friends. Rebus doubted the background checks would amount to anything, not this time round.

At last, Pryde finished giving instructions to the group of officers around him. As they melted away, he caught sight of Rebus and gave a huge wink, rubbing his hand over his forehead as he approached.

'Got to be careful,' Rebus said. 'Power corrupts, and all that.'

'Forgive me,' Pryde said, dropping his voice, 'but I'm getting a real buzz.'

'That's because you can do it, Bill. It's just taken the Big House twenty years to recognise the fact.'

Pryde nodded. 'Rumour is, you turned down DCI a while back.'

Rebus snorted. 'Rumours, Bill. Like the Fleetwood Mac album, best left unplayed.'

The room was a choreography of movement, each participant now working on his or her allotted task. Some were donning coats, picking up keys and notebooks. Others rolled their sleeves as they got comfortable at their computers or telephones. New chairs had appeared from some darkened corner of the budget. Pale blue swivel jobs: those who'd managed to grab one were on the defensive, sliding across the floor on castors rather than getting up to walk, lest someone else snatch the prized possession in the interim.

'We're done with babysitting the boyfriend,' Pryde said. 'Orders from the new boss.'

'I heard.'

'Pressure from the family,' Pryde added.

'Won't do any harm to the operation budget,' Rebus commented, straightening up. 'So is there work for me today, Bill?'

Pryde flicked through the sheets of paper on his clipboard. 'Thirty-seven phone calls from the public,' he said.

Rebus held up his hands. 'Don't look at me. Cranks and desperadoes are for the L-plates, surely?'

Pryde smiled. 'Already allocated,' he admitted, nodding

towards where two DCs, recently promoted out of uniform, were looking dismayed at the workload. Cold calls constituted the most thankless task around. Any high-profile case threw up its share of fake confessions and false leads. Some people craved attention, even if it meant becoming a suspect in a police investigation. Rebus knew of several such offenders in Edinburgh.

'Craw Shand?' he guessed.

Pryde tapped the sheet of paper. 'Three times so far, ready to admit to the murder.'

'Bring him in,' Rebus said. 'It's the only way to get rid of him.'

Pryde brought his free hand to the knot in his tie, as if checking for defects. 'Neighbours?' he suggested.

Rebus nodded. 'Neighbours it is,' he said.

He gathered together the notes from initial interviews. Other officers had been assigned the far side of the street, leaving Rebus and three others – working teams of two – to cover the flats either side of Philippa Balfour's. Thirty-five in total, three of them empty, leaving thirty-two. Sixteen addresses per team, maybe fifteen minutes at each . . . four hours total.

Rebus's partner for the day, DC Phyllida Hawes, had done the arithmetic for him as they climbed the steps of the first tenement. Actually, Rebus wasn't sure you could call them 'tenements', not down in the New Town, with its wealth of Georgian architecture, its art galleries and antique emporia. He asked Hawes for advice.

'Blocks of flats?' she suggested, raising a smile. There were one or two flats per landing, some adorned with brass nameplates, others ceramic. A few went so low as to boast just a piece of sellotaped card or paper.

'Not sure the Cockburn Association would approve,' Hawes remarked.

Three or four names listed on the bit of card: students, Rebus guessed, from backgrounds less generous than Philippa Balfour's.

The landings themselves were bright and cared for:

welcome mats and tubs of flowers. Hanging baskets had been placed over banisters. The walls looked newly painted, the stairs swept. The first stairwell went like clockwork: two flats with nobody home, cards dropped through either letterbox; fifteen minutes in each of the other flats – 'just a few back-up questions . . . see if you've thought of anything to add . . .' The householders had shaken their heads, had professed themselves still shocked. Such a quiet little street.

There was a main door flat at ground level, a much grander affair, with a black-and-white-chequered marble entrance hall, Doric columns either side. The occupier was renting it long term, worked in 'the financial sector'. Rebus saw a pattern emerging: graphic designer; training consultant; events organiser . . . and now the financial sector.

'Does no one have real jobs any more?' he asked Hawes.

'These are the real jobs,' she told him. They were back on the pavement, Rebus enjoying a cigarette. He noticed her staring at it.

'Want one?'

She shook her head. 'Three years I've managed so far.'

'Good for you.' Rebus looked up and down the street. 'If this was a net curtain kind of place, they'd be twitching right now.'

'If they had net curtains, you wouldn't be able to peer in and see what you're missing.'

Rebus held the smoke, let it billow out through his nostrils. 'See, when I was younger, there was always something rakish about the New Town. Kaftans and wacky baccy, parties and ne'er-do-wells.'

'Not much space left for them these days,' Hawes agreed. 'Where do you live?'

'Marchmont,' he told her. 'You?'

'Livingston. It was all I could afford at the time.'

'Bought mine years back, two wages coming in . . .'

She looked at him. 'No need to apologise.'

'Prices weren't as crazy back then, that's all I meant.' He was trying not to sound defensive. It was that meeting with Gill: the little joke she'd made, just to unsettle him. And the way his visit to Costello had KO'd the surveillance . . . Maybe it was time to talk to someone about the drinking . . . He flicked the stub of his cigarette on to the roadway. The surface was made of shiny rectangular stones called setts. When he'd first arrived in the city he'd made the mistake of calling them cobbles; a local had put him right.

'Next call,' he said now, 'if we're offered tea, we take it.'

Hawes nodded. She was in her late thirties or early forties, hair brown and shoulder-length. Her face was freckled and fleshed-out, as though she'd never quite lost her puppy fat. Grey trouser-suit and an emerald blouse, pinned at the neck with a silver Celtic brooch. Rebus could imagine her at a ceilidh, being spun during Strip the Willow, her face bearing the same concentration she brought to her work.

Below the main door flat, down a curving set of external steps, was the 'garden flat', so called because the garden at the back of the building came with it. At the front, the stone slabs were covered in more tubs of flowers. There were two windows, with two more at ground level – the place boasted a sub-basement. A pair of wooden doors was set into the wall opposite the entrance. They would lead into cellars beneath the pavement. Though they would have been checked before, Rebus tried opening them both, but they were locked. Hawes checked her notes.

'Grant Hood and George Silvers got there before you,' she said.

'But were the doors locked or unlocked?'

'I unlocked them,' a voice called out. They turned to see an elderly woman standing just inside the flat's front door. 'Would you like the keys?'

'Yes please, madam,' Phyllida Hawes said. When the woman had turned back into the flat, she turned to Rebus and made a T shape with the index finger of either hand. Rebus held both his thumbs up in reply.

Mrs Jardine's flat was a chintz museum, a home for china waifs and strays. The throw which covered the back of her sofa must have taken weeks to crochet. She apologised for the array of tin cans and metal pots which all but covered the floor of her conservatory – 'never seem to get round to fixing the roof'. Rebus had suggested they take their tea there: every time he turned round in the living room he feared he was about to send some ornament flying. When the rain started, however, their conversation was punctuated by drips and dollops, and the splashes from the pot nearest Rebus threatened to give him the same sort of soaking he'd have had outside.

'I didn't know the lassie,' Mrs Jardine said ruefully. 'Maybe if I got out a bit more I'd have seen her.'

Hawes was staring out of the window. 'You manage to keep your garden neat,' she said. This was an understatement: the long, narrow garden, slivers of lawn and flowerbed either side of a meandering path, was immaculate.

'My gardener,' Mrs Jardine said.

Hawes studied the notes from the previous interview, then shook her head almost imperceptibly: Silvers and Hood hadn't mentioned a gardener.

'Could we have his name, Mrs Jardine?' Rebus asked, his voice casually polite. Still, the old woman looked at him with concern. Rebus offered her a smile and one of her own drop scones. 'It's just that I might need a gardener myself,' he lied.

The last thing they did was check the cellars. An ancient hot-water tank in one, nothing but mould in the other. They waved Mrs Jardine goodbye and thanked her for her hospitality.

'All right for some,' Grant Hood said. He was waiting for them on the pavement, collar up against the rain. 'So far we've not been offered as much as the time of day.' His partner was Distant Daniels. Rebus nodded a greeting.

'What's up, Tommy? Working a double shift?'

Daniels shrugged. 'Did a swap.' He tried to suppress a yawn. Hawes was tapping her sheaf of notes.

'You,' she told Hood, 'didn't do your job.'

'Eh?'

'Mrs Jardine has a gardener,' Rebus explained.

'We'll be talking to the bin-men next,' Hood said.

'We already have,' Hawes reminded him. 'And been through the bins, too.'

The two of them looked to be squaring up. Rebus considered brokering the peace – he was St Leonard's, same as Hood: he should be sticking up for him – but lit another cigarette instead. Hood's cheeks had reddened. He was a DC, same rank as Hawes, but she had more years behind her. Sometimes you couldn't argue with experience, which wasn't stopping Hood from trying.

'This isn't helping Philippa Balfour,' Distant Daniels said at last, stopping the confab dead.

'Well said, son,' Rebus added. It was true: big inquiries could blind you to the single essential truth. You became a tiny cog in the machine, and as such you made demands in order to assure yourself of your importance. The ownership of chairs became an issue, because it was an easy argument, something that could be resolved quickly either way. Unlike the case itself, the case which was growing almost exponentially, making you seem ever smaller, until you lost sight of that single essential truth – what Rebus's mentor Lawson Geddes had called 'the SET' – which was that a person or persons needed your help. A crime had to be solved, the guilty brought to justice: it was good to be reminded sometimes.

They split up amicably in the end, Hood noting the gardener's details and promising to talk to him. After which there was nothing else to do but start climbing stairs again. They'd spent the best part of half an hour at Mrs Jardine's; already Hawes' calculations were unravelling, proving another truism: inquiries ate up time, as if the days went into fast forward and you couldn't show how the hours had been spent, were hard pressed to explain your exhaustion, knowing only the frustration of something left incomplete.

Two more no-one-homes, and then, on the first landing, the door was opened by a face Rebus recognised but couldn't place.

'It's about Philippa Balfour's disappearance,' Hawes was

explaining. 'I believe two of my colleagues spoke to you earlier. This is just by way of a follow-up.'

'Yes, of course.' The gloss-black door opened a little wider. The man looked at Rebus and smiled. 'You're having trouble placing me, but I remember you.' The smile widened. 'You always remember the virgins, don't you?'

As they were shown down the hall, the man introduced himself as Donald Devlin, and Rebus knew him. The first autopsy Rebus had ever attended as a CID officer, Devlin had done the cutting. He'd been Professor of Forensic Medicine at the university, and the city's chief pathologist at the time. Sandy Gates had been his assistant. Now, Gates was Professor of Forensic Medicine, with Dr Curt as his 'junior'. On the walls of the hallway were framed photos of Devlin receiving various prizes and awards.

'The name's not coming to me,' Devlin said, gesturing for the two officers to precede him into a cluttered drawing room.

'DI Rebus.'

'It would have been Detective Constable back then?' Devlin guessed. Rebus nodded.

'Moving out, sir?' Hawes asked, looking around her at the profusion of boxes and black bin-liners. Rebus looked too. Tottering towers of paperwork, drawers which had been wrenched from their chests and now threatened to spill mementoes across the carpet. Devlin chuckled. He was a short, portly man, probably in his mid-seventies. His grey cardigan had lost most of its shape and half its buttons, and his charcoal trousers were held up with braces. His face was puffy and red-veined, his eyes small blue dots behind a pair of metal-framed spectacles.

'In a manner of speaking, I suppose,' he said, pushing a few strands of hair back into some semblance of order across the expanse of his domed scalp. 'Let's just say that if the Grim Reaper is the *ne plus ultra* of removers, then I'm acting as his unpaid assistant.'

Rebus recalled that Devlin had always spoken like this, never settling for six words where a dozen would do, and tossing the odd spanner into the dictionary. It had been a nightmare trying to take notes while Devlin worked an autopsy.

'You're moving into a home?' Hawes guessed. The old man chuckled again.

'Not quite ready for the heave-ho yet, alas. No, all I'm doing is dispensing with a few unwanted items, making it easier for those family members who'll wish to pick over the carcass of my estate after I've shuffled off.'

'Saving them the trouble of throwing it all out?'

Devlin looked at Rebus. 'A correct and concise summary of affairs,' he noted approvingly.

Hawes had reached into a box for a leatherbound book. 'You're binning all of it?'

'By no means,' Devlin tutted. 'The volume in your hand, for example, an early edition of Donaldson's anatomical sketches, I intend to offer to the College of Surgeons.'

'You still see Professor Gates?' Rebus asked.

'Oh, Sandy and I enjoy the occasional tincture. He'll be retiring himself soon enough, I don't doubt, making way for the young. We fool ourselves that this makes life cyclical, but of course it's anything but, unless you happen to practise Buddhism.' He smiled at what he saw as this little joke.

'Just because you're a Buddhist doesn't mean you'll come back again though, does it?' Rebus said, delighting the old man further. Rebus was staring at a framed news report on the wall to the right of the fireplace: a murder conviction dated 1957. 'Your first case?' he guessed.

'Actually, yes. A young bride bludgeoned to death by her husband. They were in the city on honeymoon.'

'Must cheer the place up,' Hawes commented.

'My wife thought it macabre too,' Devlin admitted. 'After she died, I put it back up.'

'Well,' Hawes said, dropping the book back into its box and looking in vain for somewhere to sit, 'sooner we're finished, the sooner you can get back to your clear-out.'

'A pragmatist: good to see.' Devlin seemed content to let

the three of them stand there, in the middle of a large and threadbare Persian carpet, almost afraid to move for fear that a domino effect would ensue.

'Is there any order, sir?' Rebus asked. 'Or can we move a couple of boxes on to the floor?'

'Better to take our tête-à-tête into the dining room, I think.'

Rebus nodded and made to follow, his gaze drifting to an engraved invitation on the marble mantelpiece. It was from the Royal College of Surgeons, something to do with a dinner at Surgeons' Hall. 'Black/white tie and decorations' it said along the bottom. The only decorations *he* had were in a box in his hall cupboard. They went up every Christmas, if he could be bothered.

The dining room was dominated by a long wooden table and six un-upholstered, straight-backed chairs. There was a serving-hatch – what Rebus's family would have called a 'bowley-hole' – through to the kitchen, and a dark-stained sideboard spread with a dusty array of glassware and silver. The few framed pictures looked like early examples of photography: posed studio shots of Venetian boat-life, maybe scenes from Shakespeare. The tall sash window looked out on to gardens at the rear of the building. Down below, Rebus could see that Mrs Jardine's gardener had shaped her plot – either by accident or design – so that from above it resembled a question mark.

On the table lay a half-finished jigsaw: central Edinburgh photographed from above. 'Any and all help,' Devlin said, waving a hand expansively over the puzzle, 'will be most gratefully received.'

'Looks like a lot of pieces,' Rebus said.

'Just the two thousand.'

Hawes, who had at last introduced herself to Devlin, was having trouble getting comfortable on her chair. She asked how long Devlin had been retired.

'Twelve . . . no, fourteen years. Fourteen years . . .' He shook his head, marvelling at time's ability to speed up even as the heartbeat slowed.

38

Hawes looked at her notes. 'At the first interview, you said you'd been home that evening.'

'That's right.'

'And you didn't see Philippa Balfour?'

'Your information is correct thus far.'

Rebus, deciding against the chairs, leaned back, putting his weight on the windowsill, and folded his arms.

'But you knew Ms Balfour?' he asked.

'We'd exchanged pleasantries, yes.'

'She's been your neighbour for the best part of a year,' Rebus said.

'You'll recall that this is Edinburgh, DI Rebus. I've lived in this apartment nearly three decades – I moved in when my wife passed away. It takes time to get to know one's neighbours. Often, I'm afraid, they move on before one has had the opportunity.' He shrugged. 'After a while, one ceases trying.'

'That's pretty sad,' Hawes said.

'And you live where . . . ?'

'If I could just,' Rebus interrupted, 'bring us back to the matter in hand.' He'd moved off the windowsill, hands now resting on the table-top. His eyes were on the loose pieces of the jigsaw.

'Of course,' Devlin said.

'You were in all evening, and didn't hear anything untoward?'

Devlin glanced up, perhaps appreciative of Rebus's final word. 'Nothing,' he said after a pause.

'Or see anything?'

'Ditto.'

Hawes wasn't just looking uncomfortable now; she was clearly irritated by these responses. Rebus sat down across from her, trying for eye contact, but she was ready with a question of her own.

'Have you ever had a falling-out with Ms Balfour, sir?'

'What is there to fall out about?'

'Nothing now,' Hawes stated coldly.

Devlin gave her a look and turned towards Rebus. 'I see you're interested in the table, Inspector.'

Rebus realised that he'd been running his fingers along the grain of the wood.

'It's nineteenth-century,' Devlin went on, 'crafted by a fellow anatomist.' He glanced towards Hawes, then back to Rebus again. 'There *was* something I remembered . . . probably nothing important.'

'Yes, sir?'

'A man standing outside.'

Rebus knew that Hawes was about to say something, so beat her to it. 'When was this?'

'A couple of days before she vanished, and the day before that, too.' Devlin shrugged, all too aware of the effect his words were having. Hawes had reddened; she was dying to scream out something like *when were you going to tell us?* Rebus kept his voice level.

'On the pavement outside?'

'That's right.'

'Did you get a good look at him?'

Another shrug. 'In his twenties, short dark hair . . . not cropped, just neat.'

'Not a neighbour?'

'It's always possible. I'm merely telling you what I saw. He seemed to be waiting for someone or something. I recall him checking his watch.'

'Her boyfriend maybe?'

'Oh no, I know David.'

'You do?' Rebus asked. He was still casually scanning the jigsaw.

'To talk to, yes. We met a few times in the stairwell. Nice young chap . . .'

'How was he dressed?' Hawes asked.

'Who? David?'

'The man you saw.'

Devlin seemed almost to relish the glare which accompanied her words. 'Jacket and trousers,' he said, glancing down at his cardigan. 'I can't be more specific, never having been a follower of fashion.'

Which was true: fourteen years ago, he'd worn similar cardigans under his green surgeon's smock, along with bowties which were always askew. You could never forget your first autopsy: those sights, smells and sounds which were to become familiar. The scrape of metal on bone, or the whispering of a scalpel as it parted flesh. Some pathologists carried a cruel sense of humour and would put on an especially graphic performance for any 'virgins'. But never Devlin; he'd always focused on the corpse, as if the two of them were alone in the room, that intimate final act of filleting carried out with a decorum bordering on ritual.

'Do you think,' Rebus asked, 'that if you thought about it, maybe let your mind drift back, you could come up with a fuller description?'

'I rather doubt it, but of course if you think it important . . .'

'Early days, sir. You know yourself, we can't rule anything out.'

'Of course, of course.'

Rebus was treating Devlin as a fellow professional . . . and it was working.

'We might even try to put together a photofit,' Rebus went on. 'That way, if it turns out to be a neighbour or someone anyone knows, we can eliminate him straight away.'

'Seems reasonable,' Devlin agreed.

Rebus got on his mobile to Gayfield and made an appointment for the next morning. Afterwards, he asked if Devlin would need a car.

'Should manage to find my own way. Not utterly decrepit just yet, you know.' But he got to his feet slowly, his joints seemingly stiff as he showed the two detectives out.

'Thanks again, sir,' Rebus said, shaking his hand.

Devlin just nodded, avoiding eye contact with Hawes, who wasn't about to offer him her own thanks. As they made their way up to the next landing, she muttered something Rebus didn't catch.

'Sorry?'

'I said: bloody men.' She paused. 'Present company excluded.' Rebus didn't say anything, prepared to let her get it off her chest. 'Do you suppose for one second,' she went on, 'that if it had been two female officers down there, he'd have said anything?'

'I think that would depend how he was handled.'

Hawes glared at him, seeking levity that wasn't there.

'Part of our job,' Rebus went on, 'is pretending we like everyone, pretending we're interested in everything they have to say.'

'He just—'

'Got on your nerves? Mine too. Bit pompous, but that's just his way; you can't let it show. You're right: I'm not sure he'd have told us anything. He'd dismissed it as irrelevant. But then he opened up, just to put *you* in your place.' Rebus smiled. 'Good work. It's not often I get to play "good cop" around here.'

'It wasn't just that he got on my nerves,' Hawes conceded.

'What then?'

'He gave me the creeps.'

Rebus looked at her. 'Not the same thing?'

She shook her head. 'The old-pal act he played with you, that irritated me a bit, because I wasn't part of it. But the newspaper clipping . . .'

'The one on the wall?'

She nodded. '*That* gave me the creeps.'

'He's a pathologist,' Rebus explained. 'They've thicker skins than most of us.'

She thought about this, and allowed herself a little smile.

'What?' Rebus asked.

'Oh, nothing,' she said. 'It's just that, as I was getting up to leave, I couldn't help noticing a piece of the jigsaw on the floor under the table . . .'

'Where it still sits?' Rebus guessed, smiling too now. 'With that kind of eye for detail, we'll make a detective of you yet . . .'

He pressed the next door-buzzer, and it was back to work.

The news conference took place at the Big House, with a live feed to the inquiry room at Gayfield Square. Someone was trying to clean fingerprints and smears from the TV monitor with a handkerchief, while others tilted the blinds against the afternoon's sudden burst of sunshine. With the chairs all filled, officers were sitting two and three to a desk. A few of them were taking a late lunch: sandwiches and bananas. There were mugs of tea and coffee, cans of juice. The conversation was muted. Whoever was in charge of the police camera at the Big House, they were coming in for some stick.

'Like my eight-year-old with the video-cam . . .'

'Seen *Blair Witch* a couple times too many . . .'

It was true that the camera seemed to be swooping and diving, picking out bodies at waist height, rows of feet, and the backs of chairs.

'Show's not started yet,' a wiser head counselled. It was true: the other cameras, the ones from TV, were still being set up, the invited audience – journalists clutching mobile phones to their ears – still settling. Hard to make out anything that was being said. Rebus stood at the back of the room. A bit too far from the TV, but he wasn't about to move. Bill Pryde stood next to him, clearly exhausted and just as clearly trying not to show it. His clipboard had become a comforter, and he held it close to his chest, now and then pulling back to look at it, as though fresh instructions might magically have appeared. With the blinds closed, thin beams of light pierced the room, highlighting motes of dust which would otherwise have remained invisible. Rebus was reminded of cinema trips in childhood, the sense of expectation as the projector came to life and the show began.

On the TV, the crowd was settling. Rebus knew the room

– a soulless space used for seminars and occasions such as this. One long table sat at the end, a makeshift screen behind it displaying the Lothian and Borders badge. The police video-cam swung round as a door opened and a file of bodies trooped into the room, quieting the hubbub. Rebus could hear the sudden whirr of camera motors. Flashes of illumination. Ellen Wylie first, then Gill Templer, followed by David Costello and John Balfour.

'Guilty!' someone in front of Rebus called out as the camera zoomed in on Costello's face.

The group sat down in front of a sudden array of microphones. The camera stayed with Costello, panning back a little to take in his upper body, but it was Wylie's voice that came over the loudspeaker, preceded by a nervous clearing of the throat.

'Good afternoon, ladies and gentlemen, and thank you for joining us. I'll just go over the format and some of the rules, before we get started . . .'

Siobhan was over to Rebus's left. She was sitting on a desk alongside Grant Hood. Hood was staring at the floor. Maybe he was concentrating on Wylie's voice: Rebus remembered that the pair of them had worked closely together on the Grieve case a few months before. Siobhan was watching the screen, but her gaze kept wandering elsewhere. She held a bottle of water, and her fingers were busy picking off the label.

She wanted that job, Rebus thought to himself. And now she was hurting. He willed her to turn his way, so he could offer something – a smile or shrug, or just a nod of understanding. But her eyes were back on the screen again. Wylie had finished her spiel, and it was Gill Templer's turn. She was summarising and updating the details of the case. She sounded confident, an old hand at news conferences. Rebus could hear Wylie clearing her throat again in the background. It seemed to be putting Gill off.

The camera, however, showed no interest in the two CID officers. It was there to concentrate on David Costello, and – to a far lesser extent – Philippa Balfour's father. The two men sat next to one another, and the camera moved slowly between them. Quick shots of Balfour, then back to Costello. The auto-focus was fine until the cameraman decided to zoom in or out. Then, the picture took a few seconds to clear.

'Guilty,' the voice repeated.

'Want a bet?' someone else called back.

'Let's have a bit of shush,' Bill Pryde barked. The room fell silent. Rebus gave him a round of mimed applause, but Pryde was looking at his clipboard again, then back to the screen, where David Costello was beginning to speak. He hadn't shaved, and looked to be in the same clothes as the previous night. He'd unfolded and flattened a sheet of paper against the table-top. But when he spoke, he didn't glance down at what he'd written. His eyes flitted between cameras, never sure where he should be looking. His voice was dry and thin.

'We don't know what happened to Flip, and we desperately want to know. All of us, her friends, her family . . .' he glanced towards John Balfour '. . . all those who know and love her, we need to know. Flip, if you're watching this, please get in touch with one of us. Just so we know you're . . . you've not come to any harm. We're worried sick.' His eyes were shining with the onset of tears. He stopped for a second, bowed his head, then drew himself straight again. He picked up the sheet of paper but couldn't see anything there that hadn't been said. He half turned, as if seeking guidance from the others. John Balfour put his hand out to squeeze the younger man's shoulder, then Balfour himself started speaking, his voice booming as if the microphones might somehow be defective.

'If anyone's holding my daughter, please get in touch. Flip has the number for my private mobile phone. I can be reached at any time, day or night. I'd like to talk with you, whoever you are, why ever you've done what you've done. And if anyone knows Flip's whereabouts, there'll be a number onscreen at the end of this broadcast. I just need to know Flip's alive and well. To people watching this at home, please take a second to study Flip's photograph.' A further clicking of cameras as he held up the photo. He turned slowly so every camera could capture the moment. 'Her name's Philippa Balfour and she's just twenty. She's my daughter. If you've seen her, or even just think you may have, please get in touch. Thank you.'

The reporters were ready with their questions, but David Costello was already on his feet and making for the exit.

It was Wylie's voice again: 'Not appropriate at this time . . . I'd like to thank you for your continuing support . . .' But the questions battered against her. Meantime the video-cam was back on John Balfour. He looked quite composed, hands clasped on the table in front of him, unblinking as the flash-guns threw his shadow on to the wall behind.

'No, I really don't . . .'

'Mr Costello!' the journalists were yelling. 'Could we just ask . . .?'

'DS Wylie,' another voice barked, 'can you tell us something about possible motives for the abduction?'

'We don't have any motives yet.' Wylie was sounding flustered.

'But you accept that it *is* an abduction?'

'I don't . . . no, that's not what I meant.'

The screen showed John Balfour trying to answer some-one else's question. The ranks of reporters had become a scrum.

'Then what *did* you mean, DS Wylie?'

'I just . . . I didn't say anything about . . .'

And then Ellen Wylie's voice was replaced by Gill Templer's. The voice of authority. The reporters knew her of old, just as she knew them.

'Steve,' she said, 'you know only too well that we can't speculate on details like that. If you want to make up lies just to sell a few more papers, that's your concern, but it's hardly respectful to Philippa Balfour's family and friends.'

Further questions were handled by Gill, who insisted on some calm beforehand. Although Rebus couldn't see her, he imagined Ellen Wylie would be shrinking visibly. Siobhan was moving her feet up and down, as though all of a sudden some adrenalin had kicked in. Balfour interrupted Gill to say that he'd like to respond to a couple of the points raised. He did so, calmly and effectively, and then the conference started to break up.

'A cool customer,' Pryde said, before moving off to regroup his troops. It was time to get back to the real work again.

Grant Hood approached. 'Remind me,' he said. 'Which station was giving the longest odds on the boyfriend?'

'Torphichen,' Rebus told him.

'Then that's where my money's going.' He looked to Rebus for a reaction, but didn't get one. 'Come on, sir,' he went on, 'it was written all over his face!'

Rebus thought back to his night-time meeting with Costello . . . the story of the eyeballs and how Costello had come up close. *Take a good long look . . .*

Hood was shaking his head as he made to pass Rebus. The blinds had been opened, the brief interlude of sun now ended as thick grey clouds rolled back over the city. The tape of Costello's performance would go to the psychologists. They'd be looking for a glimmer of something, a short outburst of bright illumination. He wasn't sure they'd find it. Siobhan was standing in front of him.

'Interesting, wasn't it?' she said.

'I don't think Wylie's cut out for liaison,' Rebus answered.

'She shouldn't have been there. A case like this for her first outing . . . she was as good as thrown to the lions.'

'You didn't enjoy it?' he asked slyly.

She stared at him. 'I don't like blood sports.' She made to move away, but hesitated. 'What did you think, really?'

'I thought you were right about it being interesting. Singularly interesting.'

She smiled. 'You caught that too?'

He nodded. 'Costello kept saying "we", while her father used "I".'

'As if Flip's mother didn't matter.'

Rebus was thoughtful. 'It might mean nothing more than that Mr Balfour has an inflated sense of his own importance.' He paused. 'Now wouldn't that be a first in a merchant banker? How's the computer stuff going?'

She smiled – 'computer stuff' just about summed up Rebus's knowledge of hard disks and the like. 'I got past her password.'

'Meaning?'

'Meaning I can check her most recent e-mails . . . soon as I get back to my desk.'

'No way to access the older ones?'

'Already done. Of course, there's no way of telling what's been deleted.' She was thoughtful. 'At least I don't think there is.'

'They're not stored somewhere on the . . . mainframe?'

She laughed. 'You're thinking of sixties spy films, computers taking up whole rooms.'

'Sorry.'

'Don't worry. You're doing okay for someone who thinks LOL means Loyal Orange Lodge.'

They'd moved out of the office and into the corridor. 'I'm heading back to St Leonard's. Need a lift?'

She shook her head. 'Got my car with me.'

'Fair enough.'

'It looks like we're getting hooked up to HOLMES.'

This was one piece of new technology Rebus did know something about: the Home Office Large Major Enquiry System. It was a software system that collated information and speeded up the whole process of gathering and sifting. Its application meant that Philippa Balfour's disappearance was now the priority case in the city.

'Won't it be funny if she traipses back from an unannounced shopping spree?' Rebus mused.

'It would be a relief,' Siobhan said solemnly. 'But I don't think that's going to happen, do you?'

'No,' Rebus said quietly. Then he went to find himself something to eat on the way back to base.

Back at his desk, he went through the files again, concentrating on family background. John Balfour was the third generation of a banking family. The business had started in Edinburgh's Charlotte Square in the early 1900s. Philippa's great-grandfather had handed the running of the bank to her grandfather in the 1940s, and he hadn't taken a back seat until the 1980s, when John Balfour had taken over. Almost the first thing Philippa's father had done was open a London office, concentrating his efforts there. Philippa had gone to a private school in Chelsea. The family relocated north in the late eighties after the death of John's father, Philippa changing to a school in Edinburgh. Their home, Junipers, was a baronial mansion in sixteen acres of countryside somewhere between Gullane and Haddington. Rebus wondered how Balfour's wife Jacqueline felt. Eleven bedrooms, five public rooms . . . and her husband down in London a minimum of four days each week. The Edinburgh office, still in its original premises in Charlotte Square, was run by an old friend of John Balfour's called Ranald Marr. The two had met at university in Edinburgh, heading off together to the States for their MBAs. Rebus had called Balfour a merchant banker, but Balfour's was really a small private bank geared to the needs of its client list, a wealthy elite requiring investment advice, portfolio management, and the kudos of a leatherbound Balfour's chequebook.

When Balfour himself had been interviewed, the emphasis had been on the possibility of a kidnapping for profit. Not just the family phone, but those in the Edinburgh and London offices were being monitored. Mail was being intercepted in case any ransom demand arrived that way: the fewer fingerprints they had to deal with, the better. But as yet, all they'd had were a few crank notes. Another possibility was a deal gone sour: revenge the motive. But Balfour was adamant that he had no enemies. All the same, he'd denied the team access to his bank's client base.

'These people trust me. Without that trust, the bank's finished.'

'Sir, with respect, your daughter's well-being might depend . . .'

'I'm perfectly aware of that!'

After which the interview had never lost its edge of antagonism.

The bottom line: Balfour's was conservatively estimated to be worth around a hundred and thirty million, with John Balfour's personal wealth comprising maybe five per cent of the whole. Six and a half million reasons for a professional abduction. But wouldn't a professional have made contact by now? Rebus wasn't sure.

Jacqueline Balfour had been born Jacqueline Gil-Martin, her father a diplomat and landowner, the family estate a chunk of Perthshire comprising nearly nine hundred acres. The father was dead now, and the mother had moved into a cottage on the estate. The land itself was managed by Balfour's Bank, and the main house, Laverock Lodge, had become a setting for conferences and other large gatherings. A TV drama had been filmed there apparently, though the show's title meant nothing to Rebus. Jacqueline hadn't bothered with university, busying herself instead with a variety of jobs, mainly as a personal assistant to some businessman or other. She'd been running the Laverock estate when she'd met John Balfour, on a trip to her father's bank in Edinburgh. They'd married a year later, and Philippa had been born two years after that.

Just the one child. John Balfour himself was an only child, but Jacqueline had two sisters and a brother, none of them currently living in Scotland. The brother had followed in his father's footsteps and was on a Washington posting with the Foreign Office. It struck Rebus that the Balfour dynasty was in trouble. He couldn't see Philippa rushing to join Daddy's bank, and wondered why the couple hadn't tried for a son.

None of which, in all probability, was pertinent to the inquiry. All the same, it was what Rebus enjoyed about the job: constructing a web of relationships, peering into other people's lives, wondering and questioning . . .

He turned to the notes on David Costello. Dublin-born and

educated, the family moving just south of the city to Dalkey in the early nineties. The father, Thomas Costello, didn't seem to have turned a day's work in his life, his needs supplied by a trust fund set up by his father, a land developer. David's grandfather owned several prime sites in the centre of Dublin, and made a comfortable living from them. He owned half a dozen racehorses, too, and spent all his time these days concentrating on that side of things.

David's mother, Theresa, was something else again. Her background could at best be called lower middle class, mother a nurse, father a teacher. Theresa had gone to art school but dropped out and got a job instead, providing for the family when her mother got cancer and her father fell apart. She worked behind the counter in a department store, then moved to window-dressing, and from there to interior design – for shops at first, and then for wealthy individuals. Which was how she met Thomas Costello. By the time they married, both her parents were dead. Theresa probably didn't need to work, but she worked anyway, building up her one-woman company until it had grown into a business with a turnover in the low millions and a workforce of five, not including herself. There were overseas clients, and the list was still growing. She was fifty-one now, and showing no signs of slacking, while her husband, a year her junior, remained the man about town. Press clippings from the Irish news showed him at racing events, garden parties and the like. In none of the photos did he appear with Theresa. Separate rooms in their Edinburgh hotel . . . As their son said, it was hardly a crime.

David had been late going to university, having taken a year out to travel the world. He was now in the third year of his MA degree in English Language and Literature. Rebus remembered the books in his living room: Milton, Wordsworth, Hardy . . .

'Enjoying the view, John?'

Rebus opened his eyes. 'Deep in thought, George.'

'You weren't dropping off, then?'

Rebus glared at him. 'Far from it.'

As Hi-Ho Silvers moved away, Siobhan came and rested against the side of Rebus's desk.

'So how deep in thought were you?'

'I was wondering if Rabbie Burns could have murdered one of his lovers.' She just stared at him. 'Or whether someone who reads poetry could.'

'Don't see why not. Didn't some death-camp commander listen to Mozart of an evening?'

'Now there's a cheery thought.'

'Always here to make your day that little bit brighter. Now what about doing me a favour?'

'How can I refuse?'

She handed him a sheet of paper. 'Tell me what you think that means.'

Subj: Hellbank
Date: 5/9
From: Quizmaster@PaganOmerta.com
To: Flipside1223@HXRmail.com

Did you survive Hellbank? Time running out. Stricture awaits your call.
QuiM

Rebus looked up at her. 'Going to give me a clue?'

She took back the sheet of paper. 'It's an e-mail printout. Philippa had a couple of dozen messages waiting for her, dating back to the day she went missing. All of them except this one are addressed to her other name.'

'Her other name?'

'ISPs—' she paused – 'Internet service providers will usually allow you a range of log-on names, as many as five or six.'

'Why?'

'So you can be . . . different people, I suppose. Flipside 1223 is a sort of alias. Her other e-mails all went to Flip-dot-Balfour.'

'So what does it mean?'

Siobhan expelled air. 'That's what I'm wondering. Maybe it means she had a side we don't know about. There's not a single saved message from her or to her in the name of Flipside 1223. So either she's been erasing them as she goes, or else this got to her by mistake.'

'Doesn't look like coincidence, does it, though?' Rebus said. 'Her nickname's Flip.'

Siobhan was nodding. 'Hellbank, Stricture, Pagan Omerta . . .'

'Omerta's the mafia code of silence,' Rebus stated.

'And Quizmaster,' Siobhan said. 'Signs herself or himself QuiM. Little touch of juvenile humour there.'

Rebus looked at the message again. 'Beats me, Siobhan. What do you want to do?'

'I'd like to track down whoever sent this, but that's not going to be easy. Only way I can think of is to reply.'

'Let whoever it is know that Philippa's gone missing?'

Siobhan lowered her voice. 'I was thinking more along the lines of *her* replying.'

Rebus was thoughtful. 'Think it would work? What would you say?'

'I haven't decided.' The way she folded her arms, Rebus knew she was going to do it anyway.

'Run it past DCS Templer when she gets in,' he cautioned. Siobhan nodded and made to leave, but he called her back. 'You went to uni. Tell me, did you ever mix with the likes of Philippa Balfour?'

She snorted. 'That's another world. No tutorials or lectures for them. Some of them I only ever saw in the exam hall. And you know what?'

'What?'

'The sods always passed . . .'

That evening, Gill Templer hosted a celebratory gathering at the Palm Court in the Balmoral Hotel. A tuxedoed pianist was playing in the opposite corner. A bottle of champagne sat in an ice-bucket. Bowls of nibbles had been brought to the table.

'Remember to leave space for supper,' Gill told her guests. A table in Hadrian's had been booked for eight-thirty. It had just gone half past seven, and the last arrival was coming through the door.

Slipping off her coat, Siobhan apologised. A waiter appeared and took the coat from her. Another waiter was already pouring champagne into her glass.

'Cheers,' she said, sitting down and lifting the glass. 'And congratulations.'

Gill Templer lifted her own glass and allowed herself a smile. 'I think I deserve it,' she said, to enthusiastic agreement.

Siobhan already knew two of the guests. Both were fiscals depute, and Siobhan had worked with them on several prosecutions. Harriet Brough was in her late forties, her black hair permed (and maybe even dyed, too), her figure hidden behind layers of tweed and thick cotton. Diana Metcalf was early forties, with short ash-blonde hair and sunken eyes which, rather than masking, she exaggerated with dark eye-shadow. She always wore brightly coloured clothes, which helped to heighten still further her waif-like, undernourished look.

'And this is Siobhan Clarke,' Gill was telling the last member of the party. 'A detective constable in my station.' The way she said 'my station', it was as if she'd taken on ownership of the place, which, Siobhan supposed, wasn't so far from the truth. 'Siobhan, this is Jean Burchill. Jean works at the museum.'

'Oh? Which one?'

'The Museum of Scotland,' Burchill answered. 'Have you ever been?'

'I had a meal in The Tower once,' Siobhan said.

'Not quite the same thing.' Burchill's voice trailed off.

'No, what I meant was ...' Siobhan tried to find a diplomatic way of putting it. 'I had a meal there just after it opened. The guy I was with ... well, bad experience. It put me off going back.'

'Understood,' Harriet Brough said, as though every

mishap in life could be explained by reference to the opposite sex.

'Well,' Gill said, 'it's women only tonight, so we can all relax.'

'Unless we hit a nightclub later,' Diana Metcalf said, her eyes glinting.

Gill caught Siobhan's eye. 'Did you send that e-mail?' she asked.

Jean Burchill tutted. 'No shop talk, please.'

The fiscals agreed noisily, but Siobhan nodded anyway, to let Gill know the message had gone out. Whether anyone would be fooled by it was another matter. It was why she'd been late getting here. She'd spent too long going over Philippa's e-mails, all the ones she'd sent to friends, trying to work out what sort of tone might be convincing, what words to use and how to order them. She'd gone through over a dozen drafts before deciding to keep it simple. But then some of Philippa's e-mails were like long chatty letters: what if her previous messages to Quizmaster had been the same? How would he or she react to this curt, out-of-character reply? *Problem. Need to talk to you. Flipside.* And then a telephone number, the number for Siobhan's own mobile.

'I saw the press conference on TV tonight,' Diana Metcalf said.

Jean Burchill groaned. 'What did I just say?'

Metcalf turned to her with those big, dark, wary eyes. 'This isn't shop, Jean. Everyone's talking about it.' Then she turned to Gill. 'I don't think it was the boyfriend, do you?'

Gill just shrugged.

'See?' Burchill said. 'Gill doesn't want to talk about it.'

'More likely the father,' Harriet Brough said. 'My brother was at school with him. A very cold fish.' She spoke with a confidence and authority that revealed her upbringing. She'd probably wanted to be a lawyer from nursery school on, Siobhan guessed. 'Where was the mother?' Brough now demanded of Gill.

'Couldn't face it,' Gill answered. 'We did ask her.'

'She couldn't have made a worse job than those two,' Brough stated, picking cashews out of the bowl nearest her.

Gill looked suddenly tired. Siobhan decided on a change of subject and asked Jean Burchill what she did at the museum.

'I'm a senior curator,' Burchill explained. 'My main specialism is eighteenth- and nineteenth-century.'

'Her main specialism,' Harriet Brough interrupted, 'is death.'

Burchill smiled. 'It's true I put together the exhibits on belief and—'

'What's truer,' Brough cut in, her eyes on Siobhan, 'is that she puts together old coffins and pictures of dead Victorian babies. Gives me the collywobbles whenever I happen to be on whichever floor it is.'

'The fourth,' Burchill said quietly. She was, Siobhan decided, very pretty. Small and slender, with straight brown hair hanging in a pageboy cut. Her chin was dimpled, her cheeks well defined and tinged pink, even in the discreet lighting of the Palm Court. She wore no make-up that Siobhan could see, nor did she need any. She was all muted, pastel shades: jacket and trousers which had probably been called 'taupe' in the shop; grey cashmere sweater beneath the jacket, and a russet pashmina fixed at the shoulder with a Rennie Mackintosh brooch. Late forties again. It struck Siobhan that *she* was the youngest person here by probably fifteen years.

'Jean and I were at school together,' Gill explained. 'Then we lost touch and bumped into one another just four or five years back.'

Burchill smiled at the memory.

'Wouldn't want to meet anyone I was at school with,' Harriet Brough said through a mouthful of nuts. 'Arseholes, the lot of them.'

'More champagne, ladies?' the waiter said, lifting the bottle from its ice-bucket.

'About bloody time,' Brough snapped.

Between dessert and coffee, Siobhan headed to the loo. Walking back along the corridor to the brasserie, she met Gill.

'Great minds,' Gill said with a smile.

'It was a lovely meal, Gill. Are you sure I can't . . . ?'

Gill touched her arm. 'My treat. It's not every day I have something worth celebrating.' The smile melted from her lips. 'You think your e-mail will work?' Siobhan just shrugged, and Gill nodded, accepting the assessment. 'What did you reckon to the press conference?'

'The usual jungle.'

'Sometimes it works,' Gill mused. She'd had three glasses of wine on top of the champagne, but the only sign that she wasn't stone-cold sober was a slight tilt to her head and heaviness to her eyelids.

'Can I say something?' Siobhan asked.

'We're off duty, Siobhan. Say what you like.'

'You shouldn't have given it to Ellen Wylie.'

Gill fixed her with a stare. 'It should have been you, eh?'

'That's not what I mean. But to give someone that as their first liaison job . . .'

'You'd have done it better?'

'I'm not *saying* that.'

'Then what are you saying?'

'I'm saying it was a jungle and you threw her in there without a map.'

'Careful, Siobhan.' Gill's voice had lost all its warmth. She considered for a moment, then sniffed. When she spoke, her eyes surveyed the hallway. 'Ellen Wylie's been bending my ear for months. She wanted liaison, and as soon as I could, I gave it to her. I wanted to see if she was as good as she thinks she is.' Now her eyes met Siobhan's. Their faces were close enough for Siobhan to smell the wine. 'She fell short.'

'How did that feel?'

Gill held up a finger. 'Don't push this, Siobhan. I've enough on my plate as it is.' It seemed she was about to say something more, but she merely wagged the finger and forced a smile. 'We'll talk later,' she said, sliding past

Siobhan and pushing open the door to the loos. Then she paused. 'Ellen's no longer liaison officer. I *was* thinking of asking you . . .' The door closed behind her.

'Don't do me any favours,' Siobhan said, but she said it to the same closed door. It was as if Gill had hardened overnight, the humiliation of Ellen Wylie an early show of strength. The thing was . . . Siobhan *did* want liaison, but at the same time she felt disgusted with herself, because she'd enjoyed watching the press conference. She'd enjoyed Ellen Wylie's defeat.

When Gill emerged from the toilets, Siobhan was sitting on a chair in the corridor. Gill stood over her, gazing down.

'The spectre at the feast,' she commented, turning away.

3

'I was expecting some pavement artist,' Donald Devlin said. To Rebus's eyes, he was wearing the exact same clothes as when they'd last met. The retired pathologist was seated at a desk beside a computer and the only detective at Gayfield Square who seemed to know how to use the Facemaker programme. Facemaker was a database of eyes, ears, noses and lips, consolidated by special effects which could morph the details. Rebus got an idea of how the Farmer's old colleagues had been able to graft his features on to beefcake torsos.

'Things have moved on a little,' was all Rebus said, in reply to Devlin's comment. He was drinking coffee from a local café; not up to his *barista*'s standards, but better than the stuff from the station's vending machine. He'd had a broken night, waking up sweating and shaking in his living-room chair. Bad dreams and night sweats. Whatever any doctor could tell him, he knew his heart was okay – he could feel it pumping, doing its work.

Now, the coffee was just barely stopping him from yawning. The detective at the computer had finished the draft and was printing it out.

'There's *something* ... something not quite right,' Devlin said, not for the first time. Rebus took a look. It was a face, anonymous and forgettable. 'It could almost be female,' Devlin went on. 'And I'm pretty sure *he* was not a *she.*'

'How about this?' the detective asked, clicking the mouse. Onscreen, the face developed a full, bushy beard.

'Oh, but that's absurd,' Devlin complained.

'DC Tibbet's idea of humour, Professor,' Rebus apologised.

'I *am* doing my best, you know.'

'We appreciate that, sir. Lose the beard, Tibbet.'

Tibbet lost the beard.

'You're sure it couldn't have been David Costello?' Rebus asked.

'I *know* David. It wasn't him.'

'How well do you know him?'

Devlin blinked. 'We spoke several times. Met one another on the stairs one day, and I asked him about the books he was carrying. Milton, *Paradise Lost*. We started a discussion.'

'Fascinating, sir.'

'It was, believe me. The laddie's got a brain on him.'

Rebus was thoughtful. 'Think he could kill someone, Professor?'

'Kill someone? *David?*' Devlin laughed. 'I doubt he'd find it quite cerebral enough, Inspector.' He paused. 'Is he still a suspect?'

'You know what it's like with police work, Professor. The world's guilty until proven otherwise.'

'I thought it was the other way round: innocent until proven guilty.'

'I think you're confusing us with lawyers, sir. You say you didn't really know Philippa?'

'Again, we passed on the stairs. The difference between David and her is that she never seemed to want to stop.'

'Bit stuck-up, was she?'

'I don't know that I would say that. She was, however, raised in a somewhat rarefied atmosphere, wouldn't you think?' He grew thoughtful. 'I bank with Balfour's, actually.'

'Have you met her father then?'

Devlin's eyes twinkled. 'Good Lord, no. I'm hardly one of their more important clients.'

'I meant to ask,' Rebus said. 'How's your jigsaw coming along?'

'Slowly. But then that's the inherent pleasure of the thing, isn't it?'

'I've never been one for jigsaws.'

'But you like your puzzles. I spoke to Sandy Gates last night, he was telling me all about you.'

'That must have done BT's profits a power of good.'

They shared a smile and got back to work.

At the end of an hour, Devlin decided that a previous incarnation had been closer. Thankfully, Tibbet had stored each and every version.

'Yes,' Devlin said. 'It's far from perfect, but I suppose it's satisfactory . . .' He made to rise from his chair.

'While you're here, sir . . .' Rebus was reaching into a drawer. He pulled out a fat dossier of photographs. 'Some pictures we'd like you to look at.'

'Pictures?'

'Photos of Ms Balfour's neighbours, friends from university.'

Devlin was nodding slowly, but with no show of enthusiasm. 'The process of elimination?'

'If you feel you're up to it, Professor.'

Devlin sighed. 'Perhaps some weak tea to aid concentration . . . ?'

'I think we can manage weak tea.' Rebus looked over to Tibbet, who was busy with his mouse. As Rebus got closer, he saw a face on the screen. It was a pretty good resemblance of Devlin's own, save for the addition of horns. 'DC Tibbet will fetch it,' Rebus said.

Tibbet made sure to save the image before rising from his chair . . .

By the time Rebus got back to St Leonard's, news was coming in of another thinly veiled search, this time of the lock-up on Calton Road where David Costello garaged his MG sports car. The forensic unit from Howdenhall had been in, finding nothing of apparent consequence. They already knew Flip Balfour's prints would be all over the car. No surprise either that some of her belongings – a lipstick, a pair of sunglasses – were in the glove compartment. The garage itself was clean.

'No chest freezer with a padlock on it?' Rebus guessed. 'No trapdoor leading to the torture dungeon?'

Distant Daniels shook his head. He was playing errand

boy, transferring paperwork between Gayfield and St Leonard's. 'A student with an MG,' he commented, shaking his head again.

'Never mind the car,' Rebus told him. 'That lock-up probably cost more than your flat.'

'Christ, you could be right.' The smile they shared was sour. Everyone was busy: highlights of yesterday's news conference – with Ellen Wylie's performance edited out – had been broadcast on the nightly news. Now, sightings of the missing student were being followed up, meaning lots of phone calls . . .

'DI Rebus?' Rebus turned towards the voice. 'My office.'

And it *was* her office. Already, she was making it her own. Either the bunch of flowers on the filing cabinet had freshened the air, or she'd used something out of a can. The Farmer's chair had gone, too, replaced by a more utilitarian model. Where the Farmer had often slouched, Gill sat straight-backed, as if poised to rise to her feet. She held a piece of paper out, so that Rebus had to get out of the visitor's chair to reach it.

'A place called Falls,' she said. 'Do you know it?' He shook his head slowly. 'Me neither,' she confided.

Rebus was busy reading the note. It was a telephone message. A doll had been found in Falls.

'A doll?' he said.

She nodded. 'I want you to go take a look.'

Rebus burst out laughing. 'You're having me on.' But when he looked up, her face was blank. 'Is this my punishment?'

'For what?'

'I don't know. Maybe for being drunk in front of John Balfour.'

'I'm not that petty.'

'I'm beginning to wonder.'

She stared at him. 'Go on, I'm listening.'

'Ellen Wylie.'

'What about her?'

'She didn't deserve it.'

'You're a fan of hers then?'

'She didn't deserve it.'

She cocked a hand to her ear. 'Is there an echo in here?'

'I'll keep saying it till you start listening.'

There was silence in the room as they held one another's stare. When the phone rang, Gill seemed inclined not to answer. Eventually she reached out a hand, eyes still locked on Rebus.

'Yes?' She listened for a moment. 'Yes, sir. I'll be there.' She broke eye contact to put the phone down, sighed heavily. 'I have to go,' she told Rebus. 'I've a meeting with the ACC. Just go to Falls, will you?'

'Wouldn't want to get under your feet.'

'The doll was in a coffin, John.' She sounded tired all of a sudden.

'A kids' prank,' he said.

'Maybe.'

He checked the note again. 'It says here Falls is East Lothian. Let Haddington or somewhere take it.'

'I want *you* to take it.'

'You're not serious. It's a joke, right? Like telling me I tried chatting you up? Like telling me I was to see a doctor?'

She shook her head. 'Falls isn't just in East Lothian, John. It's where the Balfours live.' She gave him time for this to sink in. 'And you'll be getting that appointment any day . . .'

He drove out of Edinburgh along the A1. Traffic was light, the sun low and bright. East Lothian to him meant golf links and rocky beaches, flat farming land and commuter towns, fiercely protective of their own identities. The area had its share of secrets – caravan parks where Glasgow criminals came to hide – but it was essentially a calm place, a destination for day-trippers, or somewhere you might detour through on the route south to England. Towns such as Haddington, Gullane and North Berwick always seemed to him reserved, prosperous enclaves, their small shops supported by local communities which looked askance at the retail-park culture of the nearby capital. Yet Edinburgh was exerting its influence: house prices in the city were forcing more people further out, while the green belt found itself eroded by housing and shopping developments. Rebus's own police station was on one of the main arteries into town from the south and east, and over the past ten years or so he'd noticed the increase of rush-hour traffic, the slow, pitiless convoy of commuters.

Falls wasn't easy to find. Trusting to instinct rather than his map-book, he managed to miss a turning and ended up in Drem. While there, he stopped long enough to buy two bags of crisps and a can of Irn-Bru, had a bit of a picnic right there in the car, his window down. He still thought he was out here to prove a point, the point being to put him in his place. And as far as his new Detective Chief Super was concerned, that place was some distant outpost called Falls. Snack finished, he found himself whistling a tune he only half remembered. Some song about living beside a waterfall. He got the feeling it was something Siobhan had taped for him, part of his education in post-seventies music. Drem was just a single main street, and that street was quiet around him. The odd passing car or lorry, but no one on the pavement. The shopkeeper had tried engaging him in conversation, but Rebus hadn't had anything to add to her remarks about the weather, and he hadn't been about to ask directions to Falls. He didn't want to look like a bloody tourist.

He got the map-book out instead. Falls barely registered as a dot. He wondered how the place had come by its name. Knowing how things went, he wouldn't be surprised to find that it had some obscure local pronunciation: Fails or Fallis, something like that. It took him only another ten minutes along winding roads, dipping and rising like a gentle roller-coaster, before he found the place. It would have taken less than ten minutes, too, had a combination of blind summits and slow-moving tractor not reduced his progress to a second-gear crawl.

Falls wasn't quite what he'd been expecting. At its centre was a short stretch of main road with houses either side.

Nice detached houses with well-tended gardens, and a row of cottages which fronted the narrow pavement. One of the cottages had a wooden sign outside with the word Pottery painted neatly on it. But towards the end of the village – more of a hamlet actually – was what looked suspiciously like a 1930s council estate, grey semis with broken fences, tricycles sitting in the middle of the road. A patch of grass separated this estate from the main road, and two kids were kicking a ball back and forth between them, with little enthusiasm. As Rebus drove past, their eyes turned to study him, as though he were some rare species.

Then, as suddenly as he'd entered the village, he was out into countryside again. He stopped by the verge. Ahead in the distance he could see what looked like a petrol station. He couldn't tell if it was still a going concern. The tractor he'd overtaken earlier came past him now, then slowed so it could make a turn into a half-ploughed field. The driver didn't pay Rebus any heed. He came to a juddering halt and eased himself from the cab. Rebus could hear a radio blaring inside.

Rebus opened his car door, slamming it shut after him. The farmhand still hadn't paid him any attention. Rebus rested his palms against the waist-high stone wall.

'Morning,' he said.

'Morning.' The man was tinkering with the machinery at the back of his tractor.

'I'm a police officer. Do you know where I could find Beverly Dodds?'

'At home probably.'

'And where's home?'

'See the cottage with the pottery sign?'

'Yes.'

'That's her.' The man's voice was neutral. He still hadn't so much as glanced in Rebus's direction, concentrating instead on the blades of his plough. He was thick-set, with black curly hair and a black beard framing a face that was all creases and curves. For a second, Rebus was reminded of cartoon drawings from the comics of his childhood, strange faces that could be viewed either way up and still make sense. 'To do with that bloody doll, is it?'

'Yes.'

'Piece of bloody nonsense, going to you lot about that.'

'You don't think it has anything to do with Ms Balfour's disappearance?'

'Course it hasn't. Kids from Meadowside, that's all it is.'

'You're probably right. Meadowside's that patch of houses, is it?' Rebus nodded back towards the village. He couldn't see the boys – they, along with Falls, were hidden around a bend – but he thought he could hear the distant thud of the football.

The farmhand nodded agreement. 'Like I said, waste of time. Still, it's yours to waste, I suppose . . . and my taxes paying for it.'

'Do you know the family?'

'Which one?'

'The Balfours.'

The farmhand nodded again. 'They own this land . . . some of it, any road.'

Rebus looked around, realising for the first time that there wasn't a single dwelling or building in sight, other than the petrol station. 'I thought they just had the house and grounds.'

Now the farmhand shook his head.

'Where is their place, by the way?'

For the first time, the man locked eyes with Rebus. Satisfied with whatever checks he'd been making, he was cleaning his hands by rubbing them down his faded denims. 'The track the other end of town,' he said. 'About a mile up that way, big gates, you can't miss them. The falls are up there too, about halfway.'

'Falls?'

'The waterfall. You'll want to see it, won't you?'

Behind the farmhand, the land rose gently. Hard to imagine any point nearby high enough for a waterfall.

'Wouldn't want to waste your tax money on sightseeing,' Rebus said with a smile.

'It's not sightseeing though, is it?'

'What is it then?'

'The scene of the bloody crime.' Exasperation had crept into the man's voice. 'Don't they tell you anything back in Edinburgh . . . ?'

A narrow lane wound uphill out of the village. Anybody passing through would probably assume, as Rebus had, that it was leading to a dead end, maybe turning into somebody's driveway. But it opened out a little eventually, and at that point Rebus pulled the Saab up on to the verge. There was a stile, as the local had explained. Rebus locked his car – city instinct, hard to resist – and climbed over, into a field where cows were grazing. They showed about as much interest in him as the farmhand had. He could smell them, hear their snorts and munching. He did his best to avoid the cow-pats as he walked towards a line of nearby trees. The trees indicated the route of the stream. This was where the waterfall could be found. It was also where, the previous morning, Beverly Dodds had found a tiny coffin, and within it a doll. When he found the waterfall from which Falls had derived its name, he laughed out loud. The water dropped a full four feet.

'Not exactly Niagara, are you?' Rebus crouched down at the foot of the waterfall. He couldn't be sure exactly where the doll had been lying, but he looked around anyway. It was a scenic spot, probably popular with the locals. A couple of beer cans and some chocolate wrappers had found their way here. He stood up and surveyed the land. Scenic and isolated: no habitations in sight. He doubted anyone had seen whoever placed the doll here, always supposing it hadn't been washed down from above. Not that there *was* much above. The burn could be traced in its meandering route down the hillside. He doubted there was anything up there except wilderness. His map didn't even show the burn, and there'd be no dwellings up there, just hills where you could walk for days without seeing another human soul. He wondered where the Balfours' house was, then found himself shaking his head. What did it matter? It wasn't dolls he was chasing out here, coffin or no coffin . . . it was wild geese.

He crouched down again, rested a hand in the water, palm up. It was cold and clear. He scooped some up, watched it trickle through his fingers.

'I wouldn't drink any,' a voice called. He looked up into the light, saw a woman emerging from the line of trees. She wore a long muslin dress over her thin frame. With the sun behind her, the outline of her figure was discernible beneath the cloth. As she came forward, she ran a hand behind her head to pull back long curly blonde hair, taking it out of her eyes. 'The farmers,' she explained. 'All the chemicals they use run off the soil and into the streams. Organo-phosphates and who knows what.' She seemed to tremble at the thought.

'I never touch the stuff,' Rebus said, drying his hand on his sleeve as he stood up. 'Are you Ms Dodds?'

'Everybody calls me Bev.' She stuck out a skeletal hand which itself was at the end of a tapering arm. Like chicken bones, Rebus thought, making sure not to squeeze too hard.

'DI Rebus,' he said. 'How did you know I was here?'

'I saw your car. I was watching from my window. When you drove up the lane, I just knew instinctively.' She bounced on her toes, pleased to have been proved right. She reminded Rebus of a teenager, but her face told a different story: laughter lines around the eyes; the skin of the cheekbones sagging. She had to be in her early fifties, albeit with the zest of someone far younger.

'You walked?'

'Oh yes,' she said, looking down at her open-toed sandals. 'I was surprised you didn't come to me first.'

'I just wanted a look around. Where exactly was it you found this doll?'

She pointed towards the fall of water. 'Right at the foot, sitting on the bank. It was completely dry.'

'Why do you say that?'

'Because I know you'll have been wondering if it floated downstream.'

Rebus didn't let on that he'd been thinking exactly this, but she seemed to sense it anyway and bounced on her toes again.

'And it was out in the open,' she went on. 'I don't think it could have been left there by accident. They'd have noticed and come back for it.'

'Ever considered a career in the police, Ms Dodds?'

She tutted. 'Please, call me Bev.' She didn't answer his question, but he could see she was pleased by it.

'I don't suppose you brought it with you?'

She shook her head, which sent her hair tumbling, so that she had to draw it back again. 'It's down in the cottage.'

He nodded. 'Lived here long, Bev?'

She smiled. 'Haven't quite got the accent yet, have I.'

'You've a way to go,' he admitted.

'I was born in Bristol, spent more years than I care to remember in London. Divorce sent me scampering, and this is where I ran out of breath.'

'How long ago was that?'

'Five, six years. They still call my home "the Swanston cottage".'

'The family who lived there before you?'

She nodded. 'Falls is that kind of place, Inspector. Why are you smiling?'

'I wasn't sure how it would be pronounced.'

She seemed to understand. 'Funny, isn't it? I mean, there's just the one little waterfall, so why "Falls"? Nobody seems to know.' She paused. 'It was a mining village.'

His forehead furrowed. 'Coal mines? Here?'

She stretched out her arm towards the north. 'A mile or so that way. Little came of it. This was back in the thirties.'

'Which was when they built Meadowside?'

She nodded.

'But there's no mining now?'

'Not for forty years. I think most of Meadowside is unemployed. That patch of scrubland, it's not the meadow in question, you know. When they built the first houses there was a proper meadow there, but then they needed more houses ... and they built right on top of it.' She shivered again, and changed the subject. 'Think you can get your car turned?'

He nodded.

'Well, take your time,' she said, beginning to move away. 'I'll head back and make some tea. See you at Wheel Cottage, Inspector.'

'Wheel,' she explained, pouring water into the teapot, for her potter's wheel.

'It began as therapy,' she went on. 'After the break-up.' She paused for a moment. 'But I found out I was actually quite good at it. I think that surprised quite a number of my old friends.' The way she said these last two words made Rebus think that these friends had no place in her new life. 'So maybe "wheel" stands for the wheel of life too,' she added, lifting the tray and leading him into what she called her 'parlour'.

It was a small, low-ceilinged room with bright patterns everywhere. There were several examples of what he took to be Beverly Dodds's work: glazed blue earthenware shaped into dishes and vases. He made sure she noticed him noticing them.

'Mostly early stuff,' she said, trying for a dismissive tone. 'I keep them for sentimental reasons.' Bangles and bracelets slid down her wrists as she pushed her hair back again.

'They're very good,' he told her. She poured the tea and handed him a robust cup and saucer of the same blue colouring. He looked around the room but couldn't see any sign of a coffin or doll.

'In my workshop,' she said, seeming to read his mind again. 'I can fetch it, if you like.'

'Please,' he said. So she got up and left the room. Rebus was feeling claustrophobic. The tea wasn't tea at all but some herbal alternative. He considered pouring it into one of the vases, but pulled out his mobile instead, intending to check for messages. The screen was blank, no signal showing. The thick stone walls perhaps; either that or Falls was in a dead zone. He'd known it happen in East Lothian. There was just the one small bookcase in the room: arts and crafts mostly, and a couple of volumes on 'Wiccan'. Rebus picked one up, started to flip through it.

'White magic,' the voice behind him said. 'A belief in the power of Nature.'

Rebus put the book back and turned towards her.

'Here we are,' she said. She was carrying the coffin as though part of some solemn procession. Rebus took a step forward and she held it at arm's length towards him. He lifted it gently from her, as he felt was expected, and at the same time a thought hurtled through his brain: *she's unhinged ... this is all her doing!* But his attention was diverted to the coffin itself. It was made of a dark wood, aged oak maybe, and held together with black nails, akin to carpet tacks. The wooden panels had been measured and sawn, the cut edges sandpapered but otherwise untreated. The whole thing was about eight inches long. It wasn't the work of a professional carpenter; even Rebus, who wouldn't know an awl from his elbow, could tell that. And then she lifted off the lid for him. Her eyes were wide and unblinking, fixed on his, awaiting his response.

'It was nailed shut,' she explained. 'I prised it open.'

Inside, the small wooden doll lay with arms flat by its sides, its face rounded but blank, dressed in scraps of muslin. It had been carved, but with little artistry, deep grooves in the surface where the chisel had done its work. Rebus tried lifting it out of its box, but his fingers were too clumsy, the space between doll and coffin sides too tight. So he turned the container upside down and the doll slid into his palm. His first thought was to compare the cloth wraparound to the various materials on show in the parlour, but there were no obvious matches.

'The cloth's quite new and clean,' she was whispering. He nodded. The coffin hadn't been outdoors long. It hadn't had time to stain or suffer damp.

'I've seen some strange things, Bev . . .' Rebus said, his voice trailing off. 'Nothing else at the scene? Nothing unusual?'

She shook her head slowly. 'I walk up that way every week. This,' touching the coffin, 'was the only thing out of place.'

'Footprints . . . ?' Rebus started, but he broke off. It was asking too much of her. But she was ready with an answer.

'None that I could see.' She tore her eyes away from the coffin and towards him again. 'I *did* look, because I knew it couldn't just have appeared out of thin air.'

'Is there anyone in the village who's keen on woodwork? Maybe a joiner . . . ?'

'Nearest joiner is Haddington. Offhand, I don't know anyone who's . . . I mean, who in their right mind would do something like *this*?'

Rebus smiled. 'I bet you've thought about it though.'

She smiled back. 'I've thought of little else, Inspector. I mean, in general maybe I'd shrug something like this off, but with what's happened to the Balfour girl . . .'

'We don't know anything's happened,' Rebus felt bound to say.

'Surely it's connected though?'

'Doesn't mean it's not a crank.' He kept his eyes on hers as he spoke. 'In my experience, every village has its resident oddball.'

'Are you saying that I—' She broke off at the sound of a car drawing up outside. 'Oh,' she said, getting to her feet, 'that'll be the reporter.'

Rebus followed her to the window. A young man was emerging from the driver's side of a red Ford Focus. In the passenger seat, a photographer was fixing a lens on to his camera. The driver stretched and rolled his shoulders, as though at the end of a long journey.

'They were here before,' Bev was explaining. 'When the Balfour girl first went missing. Left me a card, and when this happened . . .' Rebus was following her into the narrow hall as she made for the front door.

'That wasn't the cleverest move, Ms Dodds.' Rebus was trying to keep his anger in check.

Hand on the doorhandle, she half turned towards him. 'At least *they* didn't accuse me of being a crank, Inspector.'

He wanted to say, *but they will*, but the damage was already done.

The reporter's name was Steve Holly, and he worked for the Edinburgh office of a Glasgow tabloid. He was young, early twenties, which was good: maybe he'd take a telling. If they'd sent one of the old pros out, Rebus wouldn't even have bothered trying.

Holly was short and a bit overweight, his hair gelled into a jagged line, reminding Rebus of the single strand of barbed wire you got at the top of a farmer's fence. He had a notebook and pen in one hand, and shook Rebus's with the other.

'Don't think we've met,' he said, in a way that made Rebus suspect his name was not unknown to the reporter. 'This is Tony, my glamorous assistant.' The photographer snorted. He was hefting a camera bag over one shoulder. 'What we thought, Bev, is if we take you to the waterfall, have you picking the coffin up off the ground.'

'Yes, of course.'

'Saves the hassle of setting up an interior shot,' Holly went on. 'Not that Tony would mind. But stick him in a room and he comes over all creative and arty.'

'Oh?' She looked appraisingly at the photographer. Rebus repressed a smile: the words 'creative' and 'arty' had different connotations for the reporter and Bev. But Holly was quick to pick up on it, too. 'I could send him back later, if you like. Do a nice portrait of you, maybe in your studio.'

'It's hardly a studio,' Bev countered, stroking a finger down her neck, enjoying the thought. 'Just the spare bedroom with my wheel and some drawings. I pinned white sheets to the walls to help with the light.'

'Speaking of light,' Holly broke in, staring at the sky meaningfully, 'we'd better get a move on, eh?'

'Perfect just now,' the photographer explained to Bev. 'Won't stay that way for long.'

Bev looked up too, nodding agreement, one artist to another. Rebus had to admit: Holly was good.

'Do you want to stay here, mind the fort?' he was now asking Rebus. 'We'll only be fifteen minutes.'

'I've got to get back to Edinburgh. Any chance I can have your number, Mr Holly?'

'Should have my card somewhere.' The reporter began searching his pockets, produced a wallet and from it a business card.

'Thanks,' Rebus said, taking it. 'And if I could have a quick word . . . ?'

As he led Holly a few steps away, he saw that Bev was standing close beside the photographer, asking him if her clothes were suitable. He got the feeling she missed the presence of another artist in the village. Rebus turned his back on them, the better to mask what he was about to say.

'Have you seen this doll thing?' Holly was asking. Rebus nodded. Holly wrinkled his nose. 'Reckon we're wasting our time?' His tone was matey, inviting the truth.

'Almost certainly,' Rebus said, not believing it, and knowing that once Holly saw the bizarre carving he wouldn't believe it either. 'It's a day out of the city anyway,' Rebus went on, forcing levity into his tone.

'Can't stand the countryside,' Holly admitted. 'Too far from the carbon monoxide for my liking. Surprised they sent a DI . . .'

'We have to treat each lead seriously.'

'Sure you do, I understand that. I'd still have sent a DC or DS, tops.'

'Like I say—' But Holly was turning away from him, ready to get back to work. Rebus gripped his arm. 'You know that if this *does* turn out to be evidence, we could want it kept quiet?'

Holly nodded perfunctorily and tried for an American accent. 'Get your people to speak to my people.' He released his arm and turned back to Bev and the photographer.

'Here, Bev, that what you're wearing? I just thought, nice day like this, maybe you'd be comfier in a shorter skirt . . .'

Rebus drove back up the lane, not stopping by the stile this time, keeping going, wondering what else he might find. A half-mile further along, a wide driveway surfaced with pink chippings ended abruptly in a set of tall wrought-iron gates. Rebus pulled over and got out of the car. The gates were padlocked shut. Beyond them he could see the driveway curve through a forest, the trees blocking any view of a house. There were no signs, but he knew this had to be Junipers. High stone walls either side of the gates, but eventually tapering down to a more manageable height. Rebus left his car, walked a hundred yards down the main road, then hoisted himself over the wall and into the trees.

He got the feeling that if he tried a short cut, he could end up wandering the woods for hours, so he made for the driveway and hoped that around the curve he wouldn't find another, and another after that.

Which was precisely what he did find. He wondered idly about deliveries: how did the postman get on? Probably not something that concerned a man like John Balfour. He'd walked a full five minutes before the house came into view. Its walls had aged the colour of slate, an elongated two-storey Gothic confection with turrets either end. Rebus didn't bother getting too close, couldn't even be sure there'd be anyone home. He supposed there'd be security of some kind – maybe a police officer manning the phone – but if so it was low-key. The house looked on to a spread of manicured lawn, flowerbeds either side. There was what looked like a paddock beyond the far end of the main building. No cars or garages, probably out of sight around the back. He couldn't imagine anyone actually being happy in such a dour setting. The house almost seemed to have a frown on it, a warning against gaiety and ill manners. He wondered if Philippa's mother felt like an exhibit in some locked museum. Then he caught sight of a face at an upstairs window, but as soon as he saw it, it vanished again. Some apparition maybe, but a minute later the front door was hauled open and a woman came running down the steps and on to the gravel driveway. She was heading towards him, wild hair obscuring her face. When she tripped and fell, he ran forwards to help her, but she saw him coming and got quickly to her feet, ignoring her skinned knees and the chippings still sticking to them. A cordless phone had slipped from her hand. She picked it up.

'Stay away!' she shrieked. When she pushed the hair away from her face, he saw that it was Jacqueline Balfour. As soon as the words were out, she seemed to regret them, and put up two pacifying hands. 'Look, I'm sorry. Just . . . just tell us what it is you want.'

And then he realised, realised that this stricken woman standing before him thought he was her daughter's abductor.

'Mrs Balfour,' he said, raising his own hands, palms out towards her, 'I'm a police officer.'

She had stopped crying finally, the pair of them seated on the front step, as if she were unwilling to let the house take possession of her again. She kept saying she was sorry, and Rebus kept saying he was the one who should be apologising.

'I just didn't think,' he said. 'I mean, I didn't think anyone would be home.'

Nor was she alone. A WPC had come to the door, but had been ordered firmly by Jacqueline Balfour to 'just go away'. Rebus had asked if she wanted him to go too, but she'd shaken her head.

'Is there something you've come to tell me?' she asked, handing back his dampened handkerchief. Tears: tears he'd caused. He told her to keep it, and she folded it neatly, then unfolded it and started the process again. She still hadn't seemed to notice the damage to her knees. Her skirt was tucked between them as she sat.

'No news,' he said quietly. Then, seeing all hope drain from her: 'There might be a lead down in the village.'

'The village?'

'Falls.'

'What sort of lead?'

Suddenly he wished he'd never started. 'I can't really say just now.' An old fallback and one that wouldn't work here. All she had to do was say something to her husband, and he'd be on the phone, demanding to know. And even if he didn't, or if he hid the news of the strange find from her, the media would hardly be so tactful . . .

'Did Philippa collect dolls?' Rebus asked now.

'Dolls?' She was playing with the cordless phone again, turning it in her hand.

'It's just that someone found one, down by the waterfall.'

She shook her head. 'No dolls,' she said quietly, as if feeling that somehow there should have been dolls in Philippa's life, and that their absence reflected badly on her as a mother.

'It's probably nothing,' Rebus said.

'Probably,' she agreed, filling the pause.

'Is Mr Balfour at home?'

'He'll be back later. He's in Edinburgh.' She stared at the phone. 'No one's going to call, are they? John's business friends, they've all been told to keep the line clear. Same thing with family. Keep the line clear in case *they* phone. But they won't, I know they won't.'

'You don't think she's been kidnapped, Mrs Balfour?'

She shook her head.

'What then?'

She stared at him, her eyes red-veined from crying, and shadowed underneath from lack of sleep. 'She's dead.' It came out almost in a whisper. 'You think so too, don't you?'

'It's far too early to be thinking that. I've known MisPers turn up weeks or months later.'

'Weeks or months? I can't bear the thought. I'd rather know . . . one way or the other.'

'When was the last time you saw her?'

'About ten days ago. We went shopping in Edinburgh,

just the usual places. Not really meaning to buy anything. We had a bite to eat.'

'Did she come to the house often?'

Jacqueline Balfour shook her head. 'He poisoned her.'

'Sorry?'

'David Costello. He poisoned her memories, made her think she could remember things, things which never happened. That last time we met . . . Flip kept asking about her childhood. She said it had been miserable for her, that we'd ignored her, hadn't wanted her. Utter rubbish.'

'And David Costello put these ideas in her head?'

She straightened her back, took a deep breath and released it. 'That's my belief.'

Rebus was thoughtful. 'Why would he do something like that?'

'Because of who he is.' She left the statement hanging in the air. The ringing of the phone was a sudden cacophony. She fumbled to find the right button to press.

'Hello?'

Then her face relaxed a little. 'Hello, darling, what time will you be home . . . ?'

Rebus waited till the call was finished. He was thinking of the press conference, the way John Balfour had said 'I' rather than 'we', as if his wife had no feelings, no existence . . .

'That was John,' she said. Rebus nodded.

'He's in London a lot, isn't he? Doesn't it get lonely out here?'

She looked at him. 'I do have friends, you know.'

'I wasn't suggesting otherwise. You probably go into Edinburgh a lot.'

'Once or twice a week, yes.'

'Do you see much of your husband's business partner?'

She looked at him again. 'Ranald? He and his wife are probably our best friends . . . Why do you ask?'

Rebus made show of scratching his head. 'I don't know. Just making conversation, I suppose.'

'Well don't.'

'Don't make conversation?'

'I don't like it. I feel like everyone's trying to trap me. It's like at business parties, John's always warning me not to give anything away, you never know who's fishing for some info on the bank.'

'We're not competitors here, Mrs Balfour.'

She bowed her head a little. 'Of course not. I apologise. It's just . . .'

'No need for apologies,' Rebus said, getting to his feet. 'This is your home, your rules. Wouldn't you say?'

'Well, when you put it like that . . .' She seemed to brighten a little. All the same, Rebus reckoned that whenever Jacqueline Balfour's husband was at home, it was *his* rules they played by . . .

Inside the house, he found two colleagues sitting comfortably in the lounge. The WPC introduced herself as Nicola Campbell. The other officer was CID based at Fettes HQ. His name was Eric Bain, more usually called 'Brains'. Bain was seated at a desk upon which sat a land-line telephone, notebook and pen, and a recording machine, along with a mobile phone connected to a laptop. Having established that the current caller was Mr Balfour, Bain had slid the headphones back down around his neck. He was drinking strawberry yoghurt straight from the pot, and nodded a greeting at Rebus.

'Cushy number,' Rebus said, admiring the surroundings.

'If you don't mind the crushing boredom,' Campbell admitted.

'What's the deal with the laptop?'

'It connects Brains to his nerdy friends.'

Bain wagged a finger at her. 'It's part of the TT technology: tracking and tracing.' Concentrating on the last vestiges of his snack, he didn't see Campbell mouth the word 'nerd' at Rebus.

'Which would be great,' Rebus said, 'if there was anything worth the effort.'

Bain nodded. 'Lots of sympathy calls to start with, friends

and family. Impressively low number of crackpots. Not being listed in the book probably helps.'

'Just remember,' Rebus warned, 'the person we're looking for might be a crackpot too.'

'Probably no shortage of nutters around here,' Campbell said, crossing her legs. She was seated on one of the room's three sofas, copies of *Caledonia* and *Scottish Field* spread out in front of her. There were other magazines on a table behind her sofa. Rebus got the feeling they belonged to the house, and that she'd read each and every one of them at least once.

'How do you mean?' he asked.

'Been through the village yet? Albinos in the trees picking at banjos?'

Rebus smiled. Bain looked puzzled. 'I didn't see any,' he said.

Campbell's look said it all: *that's because in some parallel world, you're up in the trees with them* . . .

'Tell me something,' Rebus said, 'at the press conference, Mr Balfour mentioned his mobile phone . . .'

'Shouldn't have done that,' Bain said, shaking his head. 'We'd asked him not to.'

'Not so easy to trace a mobile call?'

'They're more flexible than land-lines, aren't they?'

'But still traceable?'

'Up to a point. Lot of dodgy mobiles out there. We could trace one to an account, only to find it'd been nicked the previous week.'

Campbell suppressed a yawn. 'You see how it is?' she told Rebus. 'Thrill after thrill after thrill . . .'

He took his time heading back into town, aware of traffic picking up in the opposite direction. The rush hour was starting, executive cars streaming back into the countryside. He knew of people who commuted to and from Edinburgh every day now from as far afield as the Borders, Fife and Glasgow. They all said housing was to blame. A three-bedroom semi in a nice part of the city could cost £250,000 or more. For that money, you could buy a big detached place in West Lothian, or half a street in Cowdenbeath. On the other hand, Rebus had had cold callers to his flat in Marchmont. He'd had letters addressed to 'The Occupier' from desperate buyers. Because that was the other thing about Edinburgh: no matter how high the prices seemed to go, there were always buyers. In Marchmont it was often landlords, looking for something to add to their portfolio, or parents whose kids wanted a flat near the university. Rebus had lived in his tenement twenty-odd years, and had seen the area change. Fewer families and old people, more students and young, childless couples. The groups didn't seem to mix. People who'd lived in Marchmont all their lives watched their children move away, unable to afford a place nearby. Rebus didn't know anyone in his tenement now, or the ones either side of him. As far as he could tell, he was the only owner-occupier left. More worrying still, he seemed to be the oldest person there. And still the letters and offers came, and the prices kept rising.

Which was why he was moving out. Not that he'd found a place to buy yet. Maybe he'd go back into the rental market, that way he had freedom of choice: a year in a country cottage, then a year by the seaside, and a year or two above a pub . . . The flat was too big for him, he knew that. Nobody ever stayed in the spare bedrooms, and many nights he slept on the chair in the living room. A studio flat would be big enough for him; everything else was excess.

Volvos, BMWs, sporty Audis . . . they were all passing him on their way home. Rebus was wondering if he wanted to commute. From Marchmont he could walk to work. It took about fifteen minutes, the only exercise he ever got. He wouldn't fancy the drive every day between Falls and the city. The streets had been quiet when he'd been there, but he guessed tonight the narrow main road would be lined with cars.

When he started looking for a parking space in Marchmont, however, he was reminded of another reason for moving out. In the end, he left the Saab on a yellow line, and went into the nearest shop for an evening paper, milk, rolls and bacon. He'd called into the station, asked if he was needed: he wasn't. Back in his flat, he took a can of beer from the fridge and settled into his chair by the living-room window. The kitchen was more of a mess than usual: some of the hall stuff was in there while the rewiring went on. He didn't know when the electrics had last been done. He didn't think they'd been touched since he bought the place. After the rewiring, he had a painter booked to slap on some magnolia, freshen the place up. He'd been told not to make too many renovations: whoever bought the place would probably just do it all over again anyway. Rewiring and decorating: he'd stop at that. The Property Centre had said it was impossible to tell how much he'd get for the place. In Edinburgh, you put your home on the market for 'offers over', but that premium could reach thirty or forty per cent. A conservative estimate valued his Arden Street shell at £125,000 to £140,000. There was no mortgage outstanding. It was cash in the bank.

'You could retire on that,' Siobhan had told him. Well, maybe. He'd have to split it with his ex-wife, he supposed, even though he'd written her a cheque for her share of the place soon after they'd split up. And he could slip some money to Sammy, his daughter. Sammy was another reason for selling, or so he told himself. After her accident, she was finally out of the wheelchair but still used a pair of sticks. Two flights of tenement stairs were beyond her . . . not that she'd been a regular visitor even before the hit-and-run.

He didn't have many visitors, was not a good host. When his ex, Rhona, had moved out, he'd never got round to filling the gaps she'd left. Someone had once described the flat as 'a cave', and there was some truth in this. It provided a form of shelter for him, and that was about all he asked of it. The students next door were playing something semi-raucous. It sounded like bad Hawkwind from twenty years before, which probably meant it was by some fashionable new band. He looked through his own collection, came up with the tape Siobhan had made, and put it on. The Mutton

Birds: three songs from one of their albums. They came from New Zealand, somewhere like that, and one of the instruments had been recorded here in Edinburgh. That was about as much as she could tell him about them. The second song was 'The Falls'.

He sat back down again. There was a bottle on the floor: Talisker, a clean, honed taste. Glass beside it, so he poured, toasted the reflection in the window, leaned back and closed his eyes. He wasn't having this room redecorated. He'd done it himself not that long back, his old friend and ally Jack Morton helping. Jack was dead now, one of too many ghosts. Rebus wondered if he'd leave them behind when he moved. Somehow he doubted it, and deep down, he would miss them anyway.

The music was all about loss and redemption. Places changing and people with them, dreams shifting ever further beyond reach. Rebus didn't think he'd be sorry to see the back of Arden Street. It was time for a change.

4

On her way into work next morning, Siobhan thought of nothing but Quizmaster. Nobody had called her mobile, so she was thinking up another message to send him. Him or her. She knew she had to keep an open mind, but couldn't help thinking of Quizmaster as 'him'. 'Stricture', 'Hellbank' ... they seemed masculine to her. And the whole idea of some game being played by computer ... it all sounded so blokeish, sad anoraks stuck in their bedrooms. Her first message – *Problem. Need to talk to you. Flipside* – seemed not to have worked. Today, she was going to end the pretence. She would e-mail him as herself, and explain Flip's disappearance, asking him to get in touch. She'd kept the mobile phone beside her all night, waking every hour or so and checking to see that she hadn't slept through a call. But no calls came. Finally, as dawn approached, she'd got dressed and gone for a walk. Her flat was just off Broughton Street, in an area undergoing rapid gentrification: not as pricey as the New Town which it neighboured, but close to the city centre. Half her street seemed to be taken up with skips, and she knew that by mid-morning builders' vans would be struggling to find a parking space.

She broke the walk with breakfast at an early opener: beans on toast and a mug of tea so strong she feared for tannin poisoning. At the top of Calton Hill, she stopped to watch the city gearing up for another day. Down by Leith, a container ship was sitting off the coast. The Pentland Hills to the south wore their covering of low cloud like a welcoming duvet. There wasn't much traffic yet on Princes Street: buses and taxis mostly. She liked Edinburgh best at this time of day, before routine set in. The Balmoral Hotel was one of the closest landmarks. She thought back to the party Gill Templer had hosted there . . . how Gill had talked of having a lot on her plate. Siobhan wondered if she'd meant the case itself or her new promotion. Thing about the promotion was, John Rebus came with it. He was Gill's problem now rather than the Farmer's. Word in the office was, John had already got into a spot of bother: found drunk inside the MisPer's flat. In the past, people had warned Siobhan that she was growing too much like Rebus, picking up his faults as well as his strengths. She didn't think that was true.

No, that wasn't true . . .

Her walk downhill took her on to Waterloo Place. A right turn, she'd be home in five minutes. A left, and she could be at work in ten. She turned left on to North Bridge, kept walking.

St Leonard's was quiet. The CID suite had a musty smell: too many bodies each day spending too long cooped up there. She opened a couple of windows, made herself a mug of weak coffee, and sat down at her desk. When she checked, there were no messages on Flip's computer. She decided to keep the line open while she composed her new e-mail. But after only a couple of lines, a message told her she had post. It was from Quizmaster, a simple *Good morning*. She hit reply and asked, *How did you know I was here?* The response was immediate.

That's something Flipside wouldn't have to ask. Who are you?

Siobhan typed so quickly, she didn't correct her errors. *I'm a police officer, baesd in Edinburgh. We're investgating Philippa Balfour's disappearance.* She waited a full minute for his reply.

Who?

Flipside, she typed.

She never told me her real name. That's one of the rules.

The rules of the game? Siobhan typed.

Yes. Did she live in Edinburgh?

She was a student here. Can we talk? You've got my mobile number.

Again, the wait seemed interminable.

I prefer this.

Okay, Siobhan typed, *can you tell me about Hellbank?*

You'd have to play the game. Give me a name to call you.

My name's Siobhan Clarke. I'm a detective constable with Lothian and Borders Police.

I get the feeling that's your real name, Siobhan. You've broken one of the first rules. How do you pronounce it?

Siobhan could feel the blood rising to her face. *It's not a game, Quizmaster.*

But that's exactly what it is. How do you pronounce your name?

Shi-vawn.

There was a longer pause, and she was about to re-send the message when his response came.

To answer your question, Hellbank is one level of the game.

Flipside was playing a game?

Yes. Stricture is the next level.

What sort of game? Could she have got into trouble?

Later.

Siobhan stared at the word. *What do you mean?*

We'll talk later.

I need your cooperation.

Then learn patience. I could shut down right now and you'd never find me, do you accept that?

Yes. Siobhan was about ready to punch the screen.

Later.

Later, she typed.

And that was it. No further messages. He'd gone off-line, or was still there but wouldn't respond. And all she could do was wait. Or was it? She logged on to the Internet and tried all the search engines she could find, asking them for sites related to Quizmaster and PaganOmerta. She came up with dozens of Quizmasters, but got the feeling none of them was hers. PaganOmerta was a blank, though separating the words gave her hundreds of sites, almost all of them trying to sell her a new-age religion. When she tried PaganOmerta. com there was nothing there. It was an address rather than a site. She made more coffee. The rest of the shift was drifting in. A couple of people said hello, but she wasn't listening. She'd had another idea. She sat back down at her desk with the phone book and a copy of Yellow Pages, drew her notebook towards her and picked up a pen.

She tried computer retailers first, until finally someone directed her towards a comic shop on South Bridge. To Siobhan, comics meant things like the *Beano* and *Dandy*, though she'd once had a boyfriend whose obsession with *2000AD* was at least partly responsible for their break-up. But this shop was a revelation. There were thousands of titles, along with sci-fi books, T-shirts and other merchandise. At the counter, a teenage assistant was arguing the merits of John Constantine with two schoolboys. She'd no way of knowing whether Constantine was a comic character or a writer or artist. Eventually the boys noticed her standing right behind them. They stopped being excited, turned back into awkward, gangling twelve-year-olds. Maybe they weren't used to women listening in. She didn't suppose they were used to women at all.

'I heard you talking,' she said. 'Thought maybe you could help me with something.' None of the three said anything. The teenage assistant was rubbing at a patch of acne on his cheek. 'You ever play games on the Internet?'

'You mean like Dreamcast?' She looked blank. 'It's Sony,' the assistant clarified.

'I mean games where there's someone in charge, and they contact you by e-mail, set you challenges.'

'Role-playing.' One of the schoolboys nodded, looking to the others for confirmation.

'Have you ever played one?' Siobhan asked him.

'No,' he admitted. None of them had.

'There's a games shop about halfway down Leith Walk,' the assistant said. 'It's D & D but they might be able to help.'

'D & D?'

'Sword and sorcery, dungeons and dragons.'

'Does this shop have a name?' Siobhan asked.

'Gandalf's,' they chorused.

Gandalf's was a piece of narrow frontage squeezed unpromisingly between a tattoo parlour and a chip shop. Even less promisingly, its filthy window was covered with a metal grille held in place with padlocks. But when she tried the door, it opened, setting off a set of wind chimes hanging just inside. Gandalf's had obviously been something else – maybe a second-hand bookshop – and a change of use hadn't been accompanied by any sort of makeover. The shelves held an assortment of board games and playing pieces – the pieces themselves looking like unpainted toy soldiers. Posters on the walls depicted cartoon Armageddons. There were instruction books, their edges curling, and in the centre of the room four chairs and a foldaway table, on which sat a playing-board. There was no sales counter and no till. A door at the back of the shop creaked open and a man in his early fifties appeared. He had a grey beard and ponytail, and a distended stomach clad in a Grateful Dead T-shirt.

'You look official,' he said glumly.

'CID,' Siobhan said, showing him her warrant card.

'Rent's only eight weeks late,' he grumbled. As he shuffled towards the board, she saw that he was wearing leather open-toed sandals. Like their owner, they had a good few miles on them. He was studying the placement of pieces on the board. 'You move anything?' he asked suddenly.

'No.'

'You sure?'

'Sure.'

He smiled. 'Then Anthony's fucked, pardon my French.' He looked at his watch. 'They'll be here in an hour.'

'Who's they?'

'The gamers. I had to shut up shop last night before they had a chance to finish. Anthony must've been flustered, trying to finish Will off.'

Siobhan looked at the board. She couldn't see any grand design to the way the playing pieces were arranged. The beardie-weirdie tapped the cards laid out beside the board.

'These are what matters,' he said irritably.

'Oh,' Siobhan said. 'Afraid I'm no expert.'

'You wouldn't be.'

'What does that mean?'

'Nothing, I'm sure.'

But she was pretty sure she knew what he meant. This was a private club, males only, and every bit as exclusive as any other bastion.

'I don't think you can help me,' Siobhan admitted, looking around. She was resisting the urge to scratch herself. 'I'm interested in something slightly more high-tech.'

He bristled at this. 'What do you mean?'

'Role-playing by computer.'

'Interactive?' His eyes widened. She nodded and he checked his watch again, then shuffled past her to the door and locked it. She went on the defensive, but he merely shuffled past her again on his way to the far door. 'Down here,' he said, and Siobhan, feeling a bit like Alice at the mouth of the tunnel, eventually followed.

Down four or five steps, she came into a dank, windowless room, only partially lit. There were boxes piled high – more games and accessories, she guessed – plus a sink with kettle and mugs on the draining board. But on a table in one corner sat what looked like a state-of-the-art computer, its large screen as thin as a laptop's. She asked her guide what his name was.

'Gandalf,' he blithely replied.

'I meant your real name.'

'I know you did. But in here, that *is* my real name.' He sat down at the computer and started work, talking as he moved the mouse. It took her a moment to realise that the mouse was cordless.

'There are lots of games on the Net,' he was saying. 'You join a group of people to fight either against the program or against other teams. There are leagues.' He tapped the screen. 'See? This is a Doom league.' He glanced at her. 'You know what Doom is?'

'A computer game.'

He nodded. 'But here, you're working in cooperation with others and against a common foe.'

Her eyes ran down the team names. 'How anonymous is it?' she asked.

'How do you mean?'

'I mean, does each player know who his team-mate is, or who's on the opposing team?'

He stroked his beard. 'At most, they'd have a *nom de guerre*.'

Siobhan thought of Philippa, with her secret e-mail name. 'And people can have lots of names, right?'

'Oh yes,' he said. 'You can amass dozens of names. People who've spoken to you a hundred times . . . they come back under a new name, and you don't realise you already know them.'

'So they can lie about themselves?'

'If you want to call it that. This is the *virtual* world. Nothing's "real" as such. So people are free to invent virtual lives for themselves.'

'A case I'm working on, there's a game involved.'

'Which game?'

'I don't know. But it's got levels called Hellbank and Stricture. Someone called Quizmaster seems to be in charge.'

He was stroking his beard again. Since sitting at the computer, he'd donned a pair of metal-rimmed glasses. The screen was reflected in the lenses, hiding his eyes. 'I don't know it,' he said at last.

'What does it sound like to you?'

'It sounds like SIRPS: Simple Role-Play Scenario. Quizmaster sets tasks or questions, could be to one player or dozens.'

'You mean teams?'

He shrugged. 'Hard to know. What's the website?'

'I don't know.'

He looked at her. 'You don't know very much, do you?'

'No,' she admitted.

He sighed. 'How serious is the case?'

'A young woman's gone missing. She was playing the game.'

'And you don't know if the two are connected?'

'No.'

He rested his hands on his stomach. 'I'll ask around,' he said. 'See if we can track down Quizmaster for you.'

'Even if I had an idea what the game involved . . .'

He nodded, and Siobhan remembered her dialogue with Quizmaster. She'd asked about Hellbank. And his reply?

You'd have to play the game . . .

She knew that requisitioning a laptop would take time. Even then, it wouldn't be hooked up to the Net. So on her way back to the station she stopped off at one of the computer shops.

'Cheapest one we do is around nine hundred quid,' the saleswoman informed her.

Siobhan flinched. 'And how long before I could be online?'

The saleswoman shrugged. 'Depends on your server,' she said.

So Siobhan thanked her and left. She knew she could always use Philippa Balfour's computer, but she didn't want to, for all sorts of reasons. Then she had a brainwave and got on her mobile instead. 'Grant? It's Siobhan. I need a favour . . .'

DC Grant Hood had bought his laptop for the same reason he'd bought a mini-disc player, DVD and digital camera. It was *stuff*, and stuff was what you bought to impress people. Sure enough, each time he brought a new gadget into St Leonard's he was the centre of attention for five or ten minutes – or rather, the *stuff* was. But Siobhan had noticed that Grant was always keen to lend these bits of high-tech to anyone who asked. He didn't use them himself, or if he did he tired of them after a few weeks. Maybe he never got past the owner's manuals: the one with the camera had been chunkier than the apparatus itself.

So Grant had been only too happy to make a trip home,

returning with the laptop. Siobhan had already explained that she would need to use it for e-mails.

'It's up and ready,' Grant had told her.

'I'll need your e-mail address and pass name.'

'But that means you can access *my* e-mails,' he realised.

'And tell me, Grant, how many e-mails do you get a week?'

'Some,' he said, sounding defensive.

'Don't worry. I'll save them for you . . . and I promise not to peek.'

'Then there's the matter of my fee,' Grant said.

She looked at him. 'Your fee?'

'Yct to be discussed.' His face broke into a grin.

She folded her arms. 'So what is it?'

'I don't know,' he told her. 'I'll have to think . . .'

Transaction complete, she headed back to her desk. She already had a connector which would link her mobile phone to the laptop. But first she checked Philippa's computer: no messages, nothing from Quizmaster. Getting online with Grant's machine took her only a few minutes. Once there, she sent a note to Quizmaster, giving him Grant's e-mail address:

Maybe I want to play the game. Over to you. Siobhan.

Having sent the message, she left the line open. It would cost her a small fortune when her next mobile bill appeared, but she pushed that thought aside. For now, the game itself was the only lead she had. Even if she had no intention of playing, she still wanted to know more about it. She could see Grant, the other side of the room. He was talking to a couple of other officers. They kept glancing in her direction.

Let them, she thought.

Rebus was at Gayfield Square, and nothing was happening. Which was to say, the place was a flurry of activity, but all the sound and fury couldn't hope to hide a creeping sense of desperation. The ACC himself had put in an appearance and been briefed by both Gill Templer and Bill Pryde. He'd made it plain that what they needed was 'a swift conclusion'. Both

Templer and Pryde had used the phrase a little later, which was how Rebus knew.

'DI Rebus?' One of the woolly-suits was standing in front of him. 'Boss says she'd like a word.'

When he walked in, she told him to close the door. The place was cramped and smelled of other people's sweat. Space being at a premium, Gill was sharing this space with two other detectives, working in shifts.

'Maybe we should start commandeering the cells,' she said, collecting up mugs from the desk and failing to find anywhere better for them. 'Could hardly be worse than this.'

'Don't go to any trouble,' Rebus said. 'I'm not staying.'

'That's right, you're not.' She put the mugs on the floor, and almost immediately kicked one of them over. Ignoring the spill, she sat down. Rebus stayed standing, as was obligatory, there being no other chairs in the room today. 'How did you get on in Falls?'

'I came to a swift conclusion.'

She glared at him. 'Which was?'

'That it'll make a good story for the tabloids.'

Gill nodded. 'I saw something in the evening paper last night.'

'The woman who found the doll – or says she did – she's been talking.'

' "Or says she did"?'

He just shrugged.

'You think she might be behind it?'

Rebus slipped his hands into his pockets. 'Who knows?'

'Someone thinks they might. A friend of mine called Jean Burchill. I think you should talk to her.'

'Who is she?'

'She's a curator at the Museum of Scotland.'

'And she knows something about this doll?'

'She might do.' Gill paused. 'According to Jean, this is far from the first.'

Rebus admitted to his guide that he'd never been inside the museum before.

'The old museum, I used to take my daughter there when she was a kid.'

Jean Burchill tutted. 'But this is quite another thing, Inspector. It's all about who we are, our history and culture.'

'No stuffed animals and totem poles?'

She smiled. 'Not that I can think of.' They were walking through the ground floor's exhibit area, having left the huge whitewashed entrance hall behind. They stopped at a small lift, and Burchill turned to face him, her eyes running the length of his body. 'Gill's talked about you,' she said. Then the lift doors opened and she got in, Rebus following.

'Nothing but good, I hope.' He tried hard for levity. Burchill just looked at him again and smiled her little smile. Despite her age, she reminded him of a schoolgirl: that mixture of the shy and the knowing, the prim and the curious.

'Fourth floor,' she told him, and when the lift doors opened again, they walked out into a narrow corridor filled with shadows and images of death. 'The section on beliefs,' she said, her voice barely audible. 'Witchcraft and grave-robbers and burials.' A black coach waited to take its next cargo to some Victorian graveyard, while nearby sat a large iron coffin. Rebus couldn't help reaching out to touch it.

'It's a mortsafe,' she said, then, seeing his lack of comprehension: 'The families of the deceased would lock the coffin inside a mortsafe for the first six months to deter the resurrectionists.'

'Meaning body-snatchers?' Now this was a piece of history he knew. 'Like Burke and Hare? Digging up corpses and selling them to the university?'

She peered at him like a teacher with a stubborn pupil. 'Burke and Hare didn't dig up anything. That's the whole point of their story: they killed people, then sold the bodies to the anatomists.'

'Right,' Rebus said.

They passed funeral weeds, and photos of dead babies, and stopped at the furthest glass case.

'Here we are,' Burchill said. 'The Arthur's Seat coffins.'

Rebus looked. There were eight coffins in all. They were five or six inches long, well made, with nails studded into their lids. Inside the coffins were little wooden dolls, some wearing clothes. Rebus stared at a green and white check.

'Hibs fan,' he said.

'At one time they were all dressed. But the cloth perished.' She pointed to a photograph in the case. 'In eighteen thirty-six, some children playing on Arthur's Seat found the concealed mouth of a cave. Inside were seventeen little coffins, of which only these eight survive.'

'They must have got a fright.' Rebus was staring at the photograph, trying to place where on the massive slopes of the hill it might be.

'Analysis of the materials suggests they were made in the eighteen thirties.'

Rebus nodded. The information was printed on a series of cards attached to the display. Newspapers of the time suggested that the dolls were used by witches casting death spells on certain individuals. Another popular theory was that they were put there by sailors as good-luck charms prior to sea voyages.

'Sailors on Arthur's Seat,' Rebus mused. 'Now there's something you don't see every day.'

'Do I detect some homophobic connotation, Inspector?'

He shook his head. 'It's just a long way from the docks, that's all.'

She looked at him, but his face didn't betray anything.

Rebus was studying the coffins again. Were he a betting man, he'd see short odds on a connection between these objects and the one found in Falls. Whoever had made and placed the coffin by the waterfall knew about the museum exhibit, and had for some reason decided to copy it. Rebus looked around at the various sombre displays of mortality.

'You put this lot together?'

She nodded.

'Must make for a popular topic at parties.'

'You'd be surprised,' she said quietly. 'When it comes down to it, aren't we all curious about the things we fear?'

Downstairs in the old museum, they sat on a bench carved to resemble a whale's ribcage. There were fish in a water feature nearby, kids almost reaching in to touch them, but then pulling back at the last moment, giggling and squeezing their hands: that mix again of the curious and the fearful.

At the end of the great hall, a huge clock had been erected, its complex mechanism comprising models of skeletons and gargoyles. A naked carving of a woman seemed to be wrapped in barbed wire. Rebus got the feeling there might be other scenes of torture just beyond his vision.

'Our Millennium Clock,' Jean Burchill explained. She checked her watch. 'Ten minutes before it strikes again.'

'Interesting design,' Rebus said. 'A clock full of suffering.'

She looked at him. 'Not everyone notices straight away . . .'

Rebus just shrugged. 'Upstairs,' he said, 'the display said something about the dolls connecting to Burke and Hare?'

She nodded. 'A mock burial for the victims. We think they may have sold as many as seventeen bodies for dissection. It was a horrible crime. You see, a dissected body cannot rise up again on the day of the Last Judgment.'

'Not without its guts spilling out,' Rebus agreed.

She ignored him. 'Burke and Hare were arrested and tried. Hare testified against his friend, and only William Burke went to the gallows. Guess what happened to his body afterwards?'

That was an easy one. 'Dissection?' Rebus guessed.

She nodded. 'His body was taken to Old College, the same route most if not all of his victims were taken, and used by an anatomy class. This was in January eighteen twenty-nine.'

'And the coffins date from the early eighteen thirties.' Rebus was thoughtful. Hadn't someone once boasted to him about owning a souvenir made from Burke's skin? 'What happened to the body afterwards?' he asked.

Jean Burchill looked at him. 'There's a pocket-book in the museum at Surgeons' Hall.'

'Made from Burke's skin?'

She nodded again. 'I feel sorry for Burke actually. He seems to have been a genial man. An economic migrant. Poverty and chance led to his first sale. A visitor to his home died owing money. Burke knew that there was a crisis in Edinburgh, a successful medical faculty with not enough bodies to go round.'

'Were people living long lives then?'

'Far from it. But as I told you, a dissected corpse could not enter heaven. The only bodies available to medical students belonged to executed criminals. The Anatomy Act of eighteen thirty-two put an end to the need to rob graves . . .'

Her voice had died away. She seemed momentarily lost to the present as she considered Edinburgh's blood-soaked past. Rebus was there with her. Resurrectionists and wallets made of human skin . . . witchcraft and hangings. Next to the coffins on the fourth floor he'd seen a variety of witch's accoutrements: configurations of bones; shrivelled animal hearts with nails protruding.

'Some place this, eh?'

He meant Edinburgh, but she considered her surroundings. 'Ever since I was a child,' she said, 'I've felt more at peace here than anywhere else in the city. You might think my work morbid, Inspector, but fewer would be reconciled to the work *you* do.'

'Fair shout,' he agreed.

'The coffins interest me because they *are* such a mystery. In a museum, we live by the rules of identification and classification. Dates and provenance may be uncertain, but we almost always know what we're dealing with: a casket, a key, the remains of a Roman burial site.'

'But with the coffins, you can't be sure what they mean.'

She smiled. 'Exactly. That makes them frustrating for a curator.'

97

'I know the feeling,' he said. 'It's like me with a case. If it can't be solved, it nips my head.'

'You keep mulling it over . . . coming up with new theories . . .'

'Or new suspects, yes.'

Now they looked at one another. 'Maybe we've more in common than I thought,' Jean Burchill said.

'Maybe we have,' he admitted.

The clock had begun to sound, though its minute hand had yet to reach twelve. Visitors were summoned to it, the children's mouths falling open as the various mechanisms brought the garish figures to life. Bells clanged and ominous organ music started playing. The pendulum was a polished mirror. Looking at it, Rebus caught glimpses of himself, and behind him the whole museum, each spectator captured.

'Worth a closer look,' Jean Burchill told him. They got up and began to move forwards, joining the congregation. Rebus thought he recognised wooden carvings of Hitler and Stalin. They were operating a jagged-toothed saw.

'There's something else,' Jean Burchill was saying. 'There've been other dolls, other places.'

'What?' He tore his eyes away from the clock.

'Best thing is if I send you what I've got . . .'

Rebus spent the rest of that Friday waiting for his shift to end. Photos of David Costello's garage had been placed on one of the walls, joining the haphazard jigsaw there. His MG was a dark blue soft-top. The forensic boffins hadn't had permission to remove traces from the vehicle and its tyres, but that hadn't stopped them taking a good look. The car hadn't been washed of late. If it had been, they'd have been asking David Costello why. More photos of Philippa's friends and acquaintances had been gathered and shown to Professor Devlin. A couple of prints of the boyfriend had been slipped in, which had caused Devlin to complain about 'tactics beneath contempt'.

Five days since that Sunday night, five days since she'd disappeared. The more Rebus stared at the jigsaw on the wall, the less he saw. He thought again of the Millennium Clock, which was just the opposite: the more he'd looked at it, the more he'd seen – small figures suddenly picked out from the moving whole. He saw it now as a monument to the lost and forgotten. In its way, the wall display – the photos, faxes, rotas and drawings – comprised a monument too. But eventually, whatever happened, this monument would be dismantled and relegated to some box in a storeroom somewhere, its life limited to the length of the search.

He'd been here before: other times, other cases, not all of them solved to anyone's satisfaction. You tried not to care, tried to maintain objectivity, just as the training seminars told you to, but it was hard. The Farmer still remembered a young boy from his first week on the force, and Rebus had his memories, too. Which was why, at day's end, he went home, showered and changed, and sat in his chair for an hour with a glass of Laphroaig and the Rolling Stones for company: *Beggars Banquet* tonight, and more than one glass of Laphroaig actually. Carpets from the hall and bedrooms were rolled up either side of him. Mattresses and wardrobes, chests of drawers . . . the room was like a scrapyard. But there was a clear path from the door to his chair, and from his chair to the hi-fi, and that was all he needed.

After the Stones, he still had half a glass of malt to finish, so put on another album. Bob Dylan's *Desire*, and the track 'Hurricane', a tale of injustice and wrongful accusation. He knew it happened: sometimes wilfully, sometimes by accident. He'd worked cases where the evidence seemed to be pointing conclusively to an individual, only for someone else to come forward and confess. And in the past – the distant past – maybe one or two criminals had been 'fitted up', to get them off the street, or to satisfy the public's need for a conviction. There were times when you were sure you knew who the culprit was, but were never going to be able to prove it to the Procurator Fiscal's satisfaction. One or two cops down the years had crossed the line.

He toasted them, catching his reflection in the living-room

window. So he raised a toast to himself, too, then picked up the phone and called for a cab.

Destination: pubs.

In the Oxford Bar, he got talking to one of the regulars, happened to mention his trip to Falls.

'I'd never heard of it before,' he confided.

'Oh aye,' his companion stated, 'I know Falls. Isn't that where Wee Billy comes from?'

Wee Billy was another regular. A search confirmed that he wasn't in the bar as yet, but he walked in twenty minutes later, still wearing his chef's uniform from a restaurant around the corner. He wiped sweat from his eyes as he squeezed up to the bar.

'That you done?' someone asked him.

'Fag break,' he said, glancing at his watch. 'Pint of lager, please, Margaret.'

As the barmaid poured, Rebus asked for a refill and said that both drinks were on him.

'Cheers, John,' Billy said, unused to such largesse. 'How's tricks?'

'I was out at Falls yesterday. Is it right you grew up there?'

'Aye, that's right. Haven't been back in years, mind.'

'You didn't know the Balfours then?'

Billy shook his head. 'After my time. I was already in college when they moved back. Thanks, Margaret.' He lifted the pint. 'Your health, John.'

Rebus handed the cash over and raised his own pint, watching Billy demolish half the drink in three needy gulps.

'Jesus, that's better.'

'Hard shift?' Rebus guessed.

'No more so than usual. You working the Balfour case then?'

'Along with every other cop in the city.'

'What did you reckon to Falls?'

'Not big.'

Billy smiled, reached into his pocket for cigarette papers and tobacco. 'Expect it's changed a bit since I lived there.'

'Were you a Meadowside boy?'

'How did you know?' Billy lit his roll-up.

'A lucky guess.'

'Mining stock, that's me. Grandad worked all his days down the pit. Dad started off the same, but they made him redundant.'

'I grew up in a mining town myself,' Rebus said.

'Then you'll know what it's like when the pits close. Meadowside was fine until then.' Billy was staring at the optics, remembering his youth.

'The place is still there,' Rebus told him.

'Oh aye, but not the same . . . couldn't be the same. All the mums out scrubbing their steps, getting them whiter than white. Dads cutting the grass. Always popping into the other semis for a gossip or a loan of something.' He paused, ordered them up a couple of refills. 'Last I heard, Falls was all yuppies. Anything out of Meadowside's too dear for the locals to buy. Kids grow up and move away – like I did. Anyone say anything to you about the quarry?'

Rebus shook his head, content to listen.

'This was maybe two, three years back. There was talk of opening a quarry just outside the village. Plenty of jobs, all that. But suddenly this petition appeared – not that anyone on Meadowside had signed it, or been asked to sign it, come to that. Next thing, the quarry wasn't coming.'

'The yuppies?'

'Or whatever you want to call them. Plenty of clout, see. Maybe Mr Balfour had a hand in it too, for all I know. Falls . . .' He shook his head. 'It's not the place it was, John.' He finished his roll-up and stubbed it into the ashtray. Then he thought of something. 'Here, you like your music, don't you?'

'Depends what kind.'

'Lou Reed. He's coming to the Playhouse. I've two tickets going spare.'

'I'll think about it, Billy. Got time for another?' He nodded towards the dregs in Billy's glass.

The chef checked his watch again. 'Got to get back. Maybe next time, eh?'

'Next time,' Rebus agreed.

'And let me know about those tickets.'

Rebus nodded, watched Billy push his way back towards the door and out into the night. Lou Reed: there was a name from the past. 'Walk on the Wild Side', one of Rebus's all-time favourites. And a bass-line played by the same guy who wrote 'Grandad' for that *Dad's Army* actor. Sometimes there was such a thing as too much information.

'Another, John?' the barmaid asked.

He shook his head. 'I can hear the call of the wild side,' he said, pushing off from his stool and towards the door.

5

Saturday he went to the football with Siobhan. Easter Road was bathed in sunshine, the players throwing long shadows across the pitch. For a while, Rebus found himself following this shadow-play rather than the game itself: black puppet shapes, not quite human, playing something that wasn't quite football. The ground was full, as only happened with local derbies and when Glasgow came to town. Today it was Rangers. Siobhan had a season ticket. Rebus was in the seat next to her, thanks to another season-ticket holder who couldn't make it.

'Friend of yours?' Rebus asked her.

'Bumped into him once or twice in the pub after the match.'

'Nice guy?'

'Nice *family* guy.' She laughed. 'When are you going to stop trying to marry me off?'

'I was only asking,' he said with a grin. He'd noticed that TV cameras were covering the game. They would concentrate on the players, the spectators a background blur or piece of half-time filler. But it was the fans who really interested Rebus. He wondered what stories they could tell, what lives they'd led. He wasn't alone: around him other spectators seemed equally interested in the antics of the crowd rather than anything happening on the pitch. But Siobhan, knuckles white as she clenched either end of her supporter's scarf, brought the same concentration to the game as she did to police work, yelling out advice to the players, arguing each refereeing decision with fans nearby. The man on Rebus's other side was equally fevered. He was overweight, red-faced and sweating. To Rebus's eyes, he seemed on the verge of a coronary. He'd mutter to himself, the noise growing in intensity until there was a final defiant hurl of abuse, after which he'd look around, smile sheepishly, and begin the whole process again.

'Easy . . . take it easy, son,' he was now telling one of the players.

'Anything happening your end of the case?' Rebus asked Siobhan.

'Day off, John.' Her eyes never left the pitch.

'I know, I was just asking . . .'

'Easy now . . . go on, son, on you go.' The sweating man was gripping the back of the seat in front of him.

'We can have a drink after,' Siobhan said.

'Try and stop me,' Rebus told her.

'That's it, son, that's the way!' The voice growing the way a wave would. Rebus took out another cigarette. The day might be bright, but it wasn't warm. The wind was whipping in from the North Sea, the gulls overhead working hard to stay airborne.

'Go on now!' the man was yelling. '*Go on! Get right into that fat Hun bastard!*'

Then the look around, the sheepish grin. Rebus got his cigarette lit at last and offered one to the man, who shook his head.

'It relieves stress, you know, the shouting.'

'Might relieve yours, pal,' Rebus said, but anything after that was drowned out as Siobhan joined a few thousand others in rising up to scream their reasoned and objective judgement concerning some infringement Rebus – along with the referee – had missed.

Her usual pub was heaving. Even so, people were still piling in. Rebus took one look and suggested somewhere else. 'It's a five-minute walk, and it's got to be quieter.'

'Okay then,' she said, but her tone was one of disappointment. The after-match drink was a time for analysis, and she knew Rebus's abilities in this field were somewhat lacking.

'And tuck that scarf away,' he ordered. 'Never know where you'll bump into a blue-nose.'

'Not down here,' she said confidently. She was probably right. The police presence outside the stadium had been large and knowledgeable, channelling Hibs fans down Easter Road while the visitors from Glasgow were dispatched back up the hill towards the bus and railway stations. Siobhan followed Rebus as he cut through Lorne Street and came out on Leith Walk, where weary shoppers were struggling home. The pub he had in mind was an anonymous affair with bevelled windows and an oxblood carpet pocked with cigarette burns and blackened gum. Game-show applause crackled from the TV, while two old-timers carried out a swearing competition in the corner.

'You sure know how to treat a lady,' Siobhan complained.

'And would the lady like a Bacardi Breezer? Maybe a Moscow Mule.'

'Pint of lager,' Siobhan said defiantly. Rebus ordered himself a pint of Eighty with a malt on the side. As they took their seats, Siobhan told him he seemed to know every bad pub in the city.

'Thanks,' he said without a trace of irony. 'So,' he lifted his glass, 'what's the news on Philippa Balfour's computer?'

'There's a game she was playing. I don't know much about it. It's run by someone called Quizmaster. I've made contact with him.'

'And?'

'And,' she sighed, 'I'm waiting for him to get back to me. So far I've sent a dozen e-mails and no joy.'

'Any other way we can track him down?'

'Not that I know of.'

'What about the game?'

'I don't know the first thing about it,' she admitted, attacking her drink. 'Gill's beginning to think it's a dead end. She's got me interviewing students instead.'

'That's because you've been to college.'

'I know. If Gill's got a flaw, it's that she's literal-minded.'

'She speaks very highly of you,' Rebus said archly, gaining him a punch on the arm.

Siobhan's face changed as she picked up her glass again. 'She offered me the liaison post.'

'I thought she might. Are you going to take it?' He watched her shake her head. 'Because of what happened to Ellen Wylie?'

'Not really.'

'Then why?'

She shrugged. 'Not ready for it, maybe.'

'You're ready,' he stated.

'It's not real police work though, is it?'

'What it is, Siobhan, is a step up.'

She looked down at her drink. 'I know.'

'Who's doing the job meantime?'

'I think Gill is.' She paused. 'We're going to find Flip's body, aren't we?'

'Maybe.'

She looked at him. 'You think she's still alive?'

'No,' he said bleakly, 'I don't.'

That night he hit a few more bars, sticking close to home at first, then hailing a taxi outside Swany's and asking to be taken to Young Street. He made to light up but the driver asked him not to, and he noticed the No Smoking signs.

Some detective I am, he told himself. He'd spent as much time as possible away from the flat. The rewiring had come to a halt Friday at five o'clock with half the floorboards still up and runs of cable straggling everywhere. Skirting-boards had been uprooted, exposing the bare wall behind. The sparkies had left their tools – 'be safe enough here', they'd quipped, knowing his profession. They'd said they might manage Saturday morning, but they hadn't. So that was him for the weekend, stumbling over lengths of wire and every second floorboard either missing or loose. He'd eaten breakfast in a café, lunch in a pub, and was now harbouring lubricious thoughts of a haggis supper with a smoked sausage on the side. But first, the Oxford Bar.

He'd asked Siobhan what her own plans were.

'A hot bath and a good book,' she'd told him. She'd been lying. He knew this because Grant Hood had told half the station he was taking her on a date, his reward for lending her his laptop. Not that Rebus had said anything to her: if she didn't want him to know, that was fair enough. But knowing, he hadn't bothered trying to tempt her with an Indian meal or a film. Only when they were parting outside the pub on Leith Walk had it struck him that maybe this had been bad manners on his part. Two people with no apparent plans for Saturday night: wouldn't it have been natural for him to ask her out? Would she now be offended?

'Life's too short,' he told himself, paying off the taxi. Heading into the pub, seeing the familiar faces, those words stayed with him. He asked Harry the barman for the phone book.

'It's over there,' Harry answered, obliging as ever.

Rebus flipped through but couldn't find the number he wanted. Then he remembered she'd given him her business card. He found it in his pocket. Her home number had been added in pencil. He stepped back outdoors again and fired up his mobile. No wedding ring, he was sure of that . . . The phone was ringing. Saturday night, she was probably . . .

'Hello?'

'Ms Burchill? It's John Rebus here. Sorry to call you on a Saturday night.'

'That's all right. Is something the matter?'

'No, no . . . I just wondered if maybe we could meet. It was all very mysterious, what you said about there being other dolls.'

She laughed. 'You want to meet *now*?'

'Well, I was thinking maybe tomorrow. I know it's the day of rest and all, but we could maybe mix business with pleasure.' He winced as the words came out. He should have thought it all through first: what he was going to say, how he was going to say it.

'And how could we do that?' she asked, sounding amused. He could hear music in the background: something classical.

'Lunch?' he suggested.

'Where?'

Where indeed. He couldn't remember the last time he'd taken someone to lunch. He wanted somewhere impressive, somewhere . . .

'I'm guessing,' she said, 'that you like a fry-up on a Sunday.' It was almost as if she could feel his discomfort and wanted to help.

'Am I so transparent?'

'Quite the opposite. You're a flesh-and-blood Scottish male. I, on the other hand, like something simple, fresh and wholesome.'

Rebus laughed. 'The word "incompatible" springs to mind.'

'Maybe not. Where do you live?'

'Marchmont.'

'Then we'll go to Fenwick's,' she stated. 'It's perfect.'

'Great,' he said. 'Half-twelve?'

'I look forward to it. Goodnight, Inspector.'

'I hope you're not going to call me Inspector all the way through lunch.'

In the silence that followed, he thought he could hear her smiling.

'See you tomorrow, John.'

'Enjoy the rest of your . . .' But the connection was dead. He went back inside the pub and grabbed the phone book again. Fenwick's: Salisbury Place. Less than a twenty-minute walk from his flat. He must have driven past it a dozen times. It was fifty yards from Sammy's accident, fifty yards from where a killer had tried to stick a knife in him. He would make the effort tomorrow, push those memories aside.

'Same again, Harry,' he said, bouncing on his toes.

'You'll wait your turn like everyone else,' Harry growled at him. It didn't matter to Rebus; didn't bother him at all.

He was ten minutes early.

She walked in only five minutes later, so she was early too. 'Nice place,' he told her.

'Isn't it?' She was wearing a black two-piece over a grey silk blouse. A blood-red brooch sparkled just above her left breast.

'Do you live nearby?' he asked.

'Not exactly: Portobello.'

'But that's miles away! You should have said.'

'Why? I like this place.'

'You eat out a lot?' He was still trying to digest the fact that she'd come all the way into Edinburgh for lunch.

'Whenever I can. One of the perks of my PhD is that I call myself "Dr Burchill" whenever I'm making a booking.'

Rebus looked around. Only one other table was occupied: down near the front, a family party by the look of it. Two kids, six adults.

'I didn't bother booking for today. It's never too busy at lunchtime. Now, what shall we have ... ?'

He thought about a starter and a main course, but she seemed to know that really he wanted the fry-up, so that was what he ordered. She went for soup and duck. They decided to order coffee and wine at the same time.

'Very brunchy,' she said. 'Very Sunday somehow.'

He couldn't help but agree. She told him he could smoke if he liked, but he declined. There were three smokers at the family table, but the craving was still a little way off.

They talked about Gill Templer to start with, finding common ground. Her questions were canny and probing.

'Gill can be a bit driven, wouldn't you say?'

'She does what she has to.'

'The pair of you had a fling a while back, didn't you?'

His eyes widened. 'She told you that?'

'No.' Jean paused, flattened her napkin against her lap. 'But I guessed it from the way she used to speak about you.'

'Used to?'

She smiled. 'It *was* a long time ago, wasn't it?'

'Prehistoric,' he was forced to agree. 'What about you?'

'I hope I'm not prehistoric.'

He smiled. 'I meant, tell me something about yourself.'

'I was born in Elgin, parents both teachers. Went to Glasgow University. Dabbled in archaeology. Doctorate from Durham University, then post-doctoral studies abroad – the USA and Canada – looking at nineteenth-century migrants. I got a job as a curator in Vancouver, then came back here when the opportunity arose. The old museum for the best part of twelve years, and now the new one.' She shrugged. 'That's about it.'

'How do you know Gill?'

'We were at school together for a couple of years, best mates. Lost touch for a while . . .'

'You never married?'

She looked down at her plate. 'For a while, yes, in Canada. He died young.'

'I'm sorry.'

'Bill drank himself to death, not that his family would ever believe it. I think that's why I came back to Scotland.'

'Because he died?'

She shook her head. 'If I'd stayed, it would have meant participating in the myth they were busy establishing.'

Rebus thought he understood.

'You've got a daughter, haven't you?' she said suddenly, keen to change the subject.

'Samantha. She's . . . in her twenties now.'

Jean laughed. 'You don't know how old exactly though?'

He tried a smile. 'It's not that. I was going to say that she's disabled. Probably not something you want to know.'

'Oh.' She was silent for a moment, then looked up at him. 'But it's important to you, or it wouldn't have been the first thing you thought of.'

'True. Except that she's getting back on her feet again. Using one of those Zimmer frames old people use.'

'That's good,' she said.

He nodded. He didn't want to go into the whole story, but she wasn't going to ask him anyway.

'How's the soup?'

'It's good.'

They sat in silence for a minute or two, then she asked him about police work. Her questions had reverted to the kind you asked of a new acquaintance. Usually Rebus felt awkward talking about the job. He wasn't sure people were really interested. Even if they were, he knew they didn't want to hear the unexpurgated version: the suicides and autopsies; the petty grudges and black moods that led people to the cells. Domestics and stabbings, Saturday nights gone wrong, professional thugs and addicts. When he spoke, he was always afraid his voice would betray his passion for the job. He might be dubious about methods and eventual outcomes, but he still got a thrill from the work itself. Someone like Jean Burchill, he felt, could peer beneath the surface of this and watch other things swim into focus. She would realise that his enjoyment of the job was essentially voyeuristic and cowardly. He concentrated on the minutiae of other people's lives, other people's problems, to stop him examining his own frailties and failings.

'Are you planning to smoke that thing?' Jean sounded amused. Rebus looked down and saw that a cigarette had appeared in his hand. He laughed, took the packet from his pocket and slid the cigarette back in.

'I really don't mind,' Jean told him.

'Didn't realise I'd done it,' he said. Then, to hide his embarrassment: 'You were going to tell me about these other dolls.'

'After we've eaten,' she said firmly.

But after they'd eaten, she asked for the bill. They went halves on it, and found themselves outside, the afternoon sun doing its best to remove the chill from the day. 'Let's walk,' she said, sliding her arm through his.

'Where to?'

'The Meadows?' she suggested. So that was where they went.

The sun had brought people out to the tree-lined playing field. Frisbees were being thrown, while joggers and cyclists sped past. Some teenagers were lying with their T-shirts off, cans of cider beside them. Jean was painting some of the area's history for him.

'I think there was a pond here,' she said. 'There were certainly stone quarries in Bruntsfield, and Marchmont itself was a farm.'

'More like a zoo these days,' he said.

She threw him a glance. 'You work hard on your cynicism, don't you?'

'It gets rusty otherwise.'

At Jawbone Walk she decided they should cross the road and start up Marchmont Road. 'So where exactly is it you live?' she asked.

'Arden Street. Just off Warrender Park Road.'

'Not far then.'

He smiled, trying for eye contact. 'Are you angling for an invitation?'

'To be honest, yes.'

'The place is a tip.'

'I'd be disappointed if it were anything else. But my bladder says it'll settle for what's available . . .'

He was desperately tidying the living room when he heard the toilet flush. He looked around and shook his head. It was like picking up a duster after a bomb-strike: futile. So instead he went back into the kitchen and spooned coffee into two mugs. The milk in the fridge was Thursday's, but usable. She was standing in the doorway, watching him.

'Thank God I have an excuse for all the mess,' he said.

'I had my place rewired a few years back,' she commiserated. 'At the time, I was thinking of selling.' When he looked up, she saw she'd hit a chord.

'I'm putting it on the market,' he admitted.

'Any particular reason?'

Ghosts, he could have told her, but he just shrugged instead.

'A fresh start?' she guessed.

'Maybe. Do you take sugar?' He handed her the mug. She studied its milky surface.

'I don't even take milk,' she told him.

'Christ, sorry.' He tried taking the mug from her, but she resisted.

'This'll be fine,' she said. Then she laughed. 'Some detective. You just watched me drink two cups of coffee in the restaurant.'

'And never noticed,' Rebus agreed, nodding.

'Is there space to sit down in the living room? Now that we've got to know one another a little, it's time to show you the dolls.'

He cleared an area of the dining table. She placed her shoulder-bag on the floor and pulled out a folder.

'Thing is,' she said, 'I know this may sound barmy to some people. So I'm hoping you'll keep an open mind. Maybe that's why I wanted to know you a bit better . . .'

She handed over the folder and he pulled out a sheaf of press cuttings. While she spoke, he started arranging them before him on the table.

'I came across the first one when someone wrote a letter to the Museum. This was a couple of years back.' He held up the letter and she nodded. 'A Mrs Anderson in Perth. She'd heard the story of the Arthur's Seat coffins and wanted me to know that something similar had happened near Huntingtower.'

The clipping attached to the letter was from the *Courier*. 'Mysterious Find Near Local Hotel': a coffin-shaped wooden box with a scrap of cloth nearby. Found beneath some leaves in a copse when a dog had been out for its daily walk. The owner had taken the box to the hotel, thinking maybe it was some sort of toy. But no explanation had been found. The year was 1995.

'The woman, Mrs Anderson,' Jean was saying, 'was interested in local history. That's why she kept the cutting.'

'No doll?'

Jean shook her head. 'Could be some animal ran off with it.'

'Could be,' Rebus agreed. He turned to the second cutting.

It was dated 1982 and was from a Glasgow evening paper: 'Church Condemns Sick Joke Find'.

'It was Mrs Anderson herself told me about this one,' Jean explained. 'A churchyard, next to one of the gravestones. A little wooden coffin, this time with a doll inside, basically a wooden clothes-peg with a ribbon around it.'

Rebus looked at the photo printed in the paper. 'It looks cruder, balsa wood or something.'

She nodded. 'I thought it was quite a coincidence. Ever since, I've been on the lookout for more examples.'

He separated the two final cuttings. 'And finding them, I see.'

'I tour the country, giving talks on behalf of the Museum. Each time, I ask if anyone's heard of such a thing.'

'You struck lucky?'

'Twice so far. Nineteen seventy-seven in Nairn, nineteen seventy-two in Dunfermline.'

Two more mystery finds. In Nairn, the coffin had been found on the beach; in Dunfermline, in the town's glen. One with a doll in it, one without. Again, an animal or child could have made off with the contents.

'What do you make of it?' he asked.

'Shouldn't that be *my* question?' He didn't answer, sifted back through the reports. 'Could there be a link with what you found in Falls?'

'I don't know.' He looked up at her. 'Why don't we find out?'

Sunday traffic slowed them down, though most of the cars were heading back into the city after a day in the country.

'Do you think there could be more?' he asked.

'It's possible. But the local history groups, they pick up on oddities like that – and they've got long memories, too. It's a close network. People know I'm interested.' She rested her head against the passenger-side window. 'I think I'd have heard.'

As they passed the road sign welcoming them to Falls, she smiled. 'Twinned with Angoisse,' she said.

'Sorry?'

'The sign back there, Falls is twinned with some place called Angoisse. It must be in France.'

'How do you work that out?'

'Well, there was a picture of the French flag next to the name.'

'I suppose that would help.'

'But it's a French word, too: *angoisse*. It means "anguish". Imagine that: a town called anguish . . .'

There were cars parked either side of the main road, making for a bottleneck. Rebus didn't think he'd find a space, so turned into the lane and parked there. As they walked down to Bev Dodds's cottage, they passed a couple of locals washing their cars. The men were middle-aged and casually dressed – cords and V-necks – but wore the clothes like a uniform. Rebus would bet that midweek, they were seldom without a suit and tie. He thought of Wee Billy's memories: mums scrubbing their front steps. And here was the contemporary equivalent. One of the men said 'hello' and the other 'good afternoon'. Rebus nodded and knocked on Bev Dodds's door.

'I think you'll find she's taking her constitutional,' one man said.

'Shouldn't be long,' added the other.

Neither had stopped work on his car. Rebus wondered if they were in some sort of race; not that they were rushing, but there seemed an element of competition, their concentration intense.

'Looking to buy some pottery?' the first asked, as he got to work on the front grille of his BMW.

'Actually, I wanted a look at the doll,' Rebus said, sliding his hands into his pockets.

'Don't think that's likely. She's signed some sort of exclusive with one of your rivals.'

'I'm a police officer,' Rebus stated.

The Rover owner snorted at his neighbour's mistake. 'That might make a difference,' he said, laughing.

'Odd sort of thing to happen,' Rebus said conversationally.

'No shortage of those around here.'

'How do you mean?'

The BMW driver rinsed out his sponge. 'We had a spate of thefts a few months back, then someone daubed the door of the church.'

'Kids from the estate,' the Rover driver interrupted.

'Maybe,' his neighbour conceded. 'But it's funny it never happened before. Then the Balfour girl goes missing . . .'

'Do either of you know the family?'

'Seen them around,' the Rover driver conceded.

'They held a tea party two months back. Opened the house. It was for some charity, I forget which. They seemed very pleasant, John and Jacqueline.' The BMW driver glanced at his neighbour as he spoke the names. Rebus saw it as yet another element of the game their lives had become.

'What about the daughter?' Rebus asked.

'Always seemed a bit distant,' the Rover driver said hurriedly, not about to be left out. 'Hard to strike up a conversation with her.'

'She spoke to me,' his rival announced. 'We had quite a chin-wag once about her university course.'

The Rover driver glared at him. Rebus could foresee a duel: dampened chamoises at twenty paces. 'What about Ms Dodds?' he asked. 'Good neighbour, is she?'

'Bloody awful pottery,' was the only comment.

'This doll thing's probably been good for business though.'

'I don't doubt it,' the BMW owner said. 'If she has any sense, she'll capitalise on it.'

'Promotion's the life-blood of any new business,' his neighbour added. Rebus got the feeling they knew what they were talking about.

'Small concession might do wonders,' BMW man mused. 'Teas, home baking . . .' Both men had stopped working, growing thoughtful.

'I thought that was your car in the lane,' Bev Dodds said, striding towards the group.

While tea was being made, Jean asked if she could see some

of the pottery. An extension at the back of the cottage housed both the kitchen and the spare bedroom, which had become a studio. Jean praised the various bowls and plates, but Rebus could tell she didn't like them. Then, as Bev Dodds was sliding the various bangles and bracelets up her arms again, Jean praised those, too.

'I make them,' Bev Dodds said.

'Do you?' Jean sounded delighted.

Dodds put her arm out so she could take a closer look. 'Local stones. I wash them and varnish them. I think they act a little like crystals.'

'Positive energy?' Jean guessed. Rebus could no longer tell if she was genuinely interested or just faking it. 'Could I buy one, do you think?'

'Of course,' Dodds said delightedly. Her hair was windswept, cheeks red from the walk she'd just taken. She slid one of the bracelets from her wrist. 'How about this? It's one of my favourites, and just ten pounds.'

Jean paused at mention of the price, but then smiled and handed over a ten-pound note, which Dodds tucked into her pocket.

'Ms Burchill works at the museum,' Rebus said.

'Really?'

'I'm a curator.' Jean had slipped the bracelet on to her wrist.

'What a wonderful job. Whenever I'm in town, I try to make time for a visit.'

'Have you heard of the Arthur's Seat coffins?' Rebus asked.

'Steve told me about them,' Dodds said. Rebus presumed she meant Steve Holly, the reporter.

'Ms Burchill has an interest in them,' Rebus said. 'She'd like to see the doll you found.'

'Of course.' She slid open one of the drawers and brought out the coffin. Jean handled it with care, placing it on the kitchen table before examining it.

'It's quite well made,' she said. 'More like the Arthur's Seat coffins than those others.'

' "Others"?' Bev Dodds asked.

'Is it a copy of one of them?' Rebus asked, ignoring this.

'Not an exact copy, no,' Jean said. 'Different nails, and constructed slightly differently, too.'

'By someone who'd seen the museum exhibit?'

'It's possible. You can buy a postcard of the coffins in the museum shop.'

Rebus looked at Jean. 'Has anyone shown interest in the exhibit recently?'

'How would I know that?'

'Maybe a researcher or someone?'

She shook her head. 'There was a doctoral student last year . . . but she went back to Toronto.'

'Is there some connection here?' Bev Dodds asked, wide-eyed. 'Something between the museum and the abduction?'

'We don't know that anyone's been abducted,' Rebus cautioned her.

'All the same . . .'

'Ms Dodds . . . Bev . . .' Rebus fixed her with his eyes. 'It's important that this conversation stays confidential.'

When she nodded understanding, Rebus knew that within minutes of them leaving, she'd be on the phone to Steve Holly. He left his tea unfinished.

'We'd better be off.' Jean took the hint, and placed her own cup on the draining-board. 'That was lovely, thanks.'

'You're welcome. And thank you for buying the bracelet. My third sale today.'

As they walked back up the lane, two cars passed them. Day-trippers, Rebus guessed, on their way to the waterfall. And afterwards, maybe they'd stop by the pottery, asking to see the famous coffin. They'd probably buy something too . . .

'What are you thinking?' Jean asked, getting into the car and studying the bracelet, holding it up to the light.

'Nothing,' Rebus lied. He decided to drive through the village. The Rover and BMW stood drying in the late-afternoon sun. A young couple with two kids stood outside Bev Dodds's cottage. The father had a video camera in his hand. Rebus gave way to four or five cars, then continued along the road to Meadowside. Three boys – maybe including the two from his previous visit – were playing football on the grass. Rebus stopped and wound down his window, calling out to them. They looked at him, but weren't about to interrupt their game. He told Jean he'd only be a second, and got out of the car.

'Hello there,' he told the boys.

'Who are you?' The questioner was skinny, ribs protruding, and thin arms ending in bunched fists. His hair had been shorn to the scalp, and as he squinted into the light he managed to be four-feet-six of aggression and mistrust.

'I'm the police,' Rebus said.

'We haven't done nothing.'

'Congratulations.'

The boy kicked the ball hard. It thundered into the upper thigh of one of the other players, leading the third to start laughing.

'I was wondering if you knew anything about this spate of thefts I've been hearing about.'

The boy looked at him. 'Get a grip,' he said.

'With pleasure, son. What'll it be, your neck or your balls?' The boy tried for a sneer. 'Maybe you can tell me something about the church getting vandalised?'

'No,' he said.

'No?' Rebus sounded surprised. 'Okay then, last shot . . . what about this wee coffin that's been found?'

'What about it?'

'Have you seen it?'

The boy shook his head. 'Tell him to sod off, Chick,' one of his friends advised.

'Chick?' Rebus nodded, to let the boy know he was filing the information away.

'Never saw the coffin,' Chick said. 'No way I'm going to knock on *her* door.'

'Why not?'

'Because she's well fucking weird.' Chick laughed.

'Weird how?'

Chick was losing patience. Somehow he'd been duped into having a conversation. 'Weird like the rest of them.'

'They're all a bunch of tampons,' his pal said, coming to rescue him. 'Let's go, Chick.' They ran off, collecting the third boy and the ball on their way. Rebus watched for a moment, but Chick didn't look back. As he returned to the car, he saw that Jean's window was down.

'Okay,' he said, 'so I'm not the world's best at asking questions of schoolkids.'

She smiled. 'What did he mean about tampons?'

Rebus turned the ignition and glanced at her. 'He meant they're all stuck-up.' He didn't add the final word, didn't need to. Jean knew exactly what he meant . . .

Late that Sunday night, he found himself on the pavement outside Philippa Balfour's flat. He still had the set of keys in his pocket, but wasn't going inside, not after what happened last time. Someone had closed the shutters in her living room and bedroom. No light was being allowed into the flat, none at all.

It was one week since her disappearance, and a reconstruction was under way. A WPC with a passing resemblance to the missing student had been dressed in clothes similar to the ones Flip might have been wearing that evening. A recently bought Versace T-shirt was missing from Flip's wardrobe, so the WPC was wearing one just like it. She would walk out of the tenement and be photographed by the waiting newsmen. Then she'd walk briskly to the end of the street, where she'd step into a waiting taxi cab, commandeered for the purpose. She'd get out again and start climbing the hill towards the city centre. There would be photographers with her all the way, and uniformed officers stopping pedestrians and drivers, clipboards ready, questions prepared. The WPC would travel all the way to the bar on the South Side . . .

Two TV crews – BBC and Scottish – were readying to film the reconstruction. News programmes would show snippets of it.

It was an exercise, a way of showing that the police were doing *something*.

That was all.

Gill Templer, catching Rebus's eye from the other side of the street, seemed to acknowledge as much with a shrug. Then she went back to her conversation with Assistant Chief Constable Colin Carswell. The ACC seemed to have a few points he wished to get across. Rebus didn't doubt that the words 'a swift conclusion' would figure at least once. From past experience, he knew that when Gill Templer was irritated, she tended to play with a string of pearls she sometimes wore. They were around her neck now, and she had slipped a finger beneath them, running it back and forth. Rebus thought of all Bev Dodds's bracelets, and what the kid called Chick had said: *well fucking weird* . . . Books of Wiccan in her living room, only she didn't call it that, called it her 'parlour' instead. A Stones song popped into his head: 'Spider and the Fly', B-side to 'Satisfaction'. He saw Bev Dodds as a spider, her parlour a web. For some reason the image, though fanciful, stuck with him . . .

6

On Monday morning, Rebus took Jean's press cuttings in to work. Waiting for him on his desk were three messages from Steve Holly and a note in Gill Templer's handwriting, informing him of a doctor's appointment at eleven o'clock. He went to her office to plead his case, but a sheet of paper on her door stated that she would be spending the day at Gayfield Square. Rebus went back to his chair, grabbed his cigarettes and lighter, and headed for the car park. He'd just got one lit when Siobhan Clarke arrived.

'Any luck?' he asked her. Siobhan lifted the laptop she was carrying.

'Last night,' she told him.

'What happened?'

She looked at his cigarette. 'Soon as you finish that foul thing, come upstairs and I'll show you.'

The door swung shut behind her. Rebus stared at the cigarette, took one last puff, and flicked it on to the ground.

By the time he got to the CID room, Siobhan had set up the laptop. An officer called over that there was a Steve Holly on the line. Rebus shook his head. He knew damned well what Holly wanted: Bev Dodds had told him about the trip to Falls. He held up a finger, asking Siobhan to wait a second, then got on the phone to the museum.

'Jean Burchill's office, please,' he said. Then he waited.

'Hello?' It was her voice.

'Jean? John Rebus here.'

'John, I was just thinking of calling you.'

'Don't tell me: you're being hassled?'

'Well, not exactly hassled . . .'

'A reporter called Steve Holly, wanting to talk about the dolls?'

'He's been on to you too, then?'

'Best advice I can give, Jean: don't say anything. Refuse his calls, and if he does get through, tell him you've nothing to say. No matter how hard he pushes . . .'

'Understood. Did Bev Dodds blab?'

'My fault, I should've known she would.'

'I can look after myself, John, don't worry.'

They said their goodbyes and he put down the receiver, took the short walk to Siobhan's desk and read the message on the laptop's screen.

This game is not a game. It's a quest. You'll need strength and endurance, not to mention intelligence. But your prize will be great. Do you still wish to play?

'I sent back an e-mail saying I was interested, but asking how long the game would take.' Siobhan was moving her finger across the keypad. 'He told me it could take a few days, or a few weeks. So then I asked if I could start with Hellbank. He came back straight away, telling me Hellbank was the fourth level, and I'd have to play the whole thing. I said okay. At midnight, this arrived.'

There was another message on the screen. 'He's used a different address,' Siobhan said. 'God knows how many he's got.'

'Making him difficult to track down?' Rebus guessed. Then he read:

How can I be sure you are who you say you are?

'He means my e-mail address,' Siobhan explained. 'I was using Philippa's before; now I'm using Grant's.'

'What did you tell him?'

'I told him he'd have to trust me; either that or we could always meet.'

'And was he keen?'

She smiled. 'Not overly. But he did send me this.' She hit another button.

Seven fins high is king. This queen dines well before the bust.

'Is that it?'

Siobhan nodded. 'I asked if he could give me a clue. All he did was send me the message again.'

'Presumably because it *is* the clue.'

She ran a hand through her hair. 'I was up half the night. I don't suppose it means anything to you?'

He shook his head. 'You need someone who likes puzzles. Doesn't young Grant do cryptic crosswords?'

'Does he?' Siobhan looked across the room to where Grant Hood was making a phone call.

'Why don't you go and ask?'

When Hood came off the phone, Siobhan was waiting. 'How's the laptop?' he asked.

'Fine.' She handed him a sheet of paper. 'I hear you like a puzzle.'

He took the sheet, but didn't look at it. 'Saturday night?' he asked.

She nodded. 'Saturday night was fine.'

And it had been, too: a couple of drinks and then dinner at a decent, small restaurant in the New Town. They'd talked shop mostly, having not much else in common, but it was good to have a laugh, relive a few stories. He'd been quite the gentleman, walking her home afterwards. She hadn't asked him up for coffee. He'd said he'd find a cab on Broughton Street.

Now, Grant nodded back and smiled. 'Fine' was good enough for him. Then he looked at the sheet. ' "Seven fins high is king",' he read aloud. 'What's it mean?'

'I was hoping maybe you'd tell me.'

He studied the message again. 'Could be an anagram. Unlikely though: not enough vowels, it's all i's and e's. "Before the bust" – drugs bust maybe?' Siobhan just shrugged. 'Maybe it would help if you told me a bit about it,' Hood said.

Siobhan nodded. 'Over a coffee, if you like,' she said.

Back at his desk, Rebus watched them leave the room, then picked up the first of the cuttings. There was a conversation going on nearby, something about another press conference. The consensus was, if DCS Templer wanted you to front it, it meant she had the knives out. Rebus's eyes narrowed. There was a sentence he must have missed first time round. It was the 1995 clipping: Huntingtower Hotel near Perth, a dog finding the coffin and scrap of cloth. Three-quarters of the way through the story, an anonymous member of the hotel staff was quoted as saying, 'If we're not careful, Huntingtower's going to get itself a reputation.' Rebus wondered what was meant by that. He picked up the phone, thinking maybe Jean Burchill would know. But he didn't make the call, didn't want her to think he was . . . well, what exactly? He'd enjoyed yesterday, and thought she had too. He'd dropped her at her home in Portobello, but had declined the offer of coffee.

'I've taken up too much of your day as it is,' he'd said. She hadn't denied it.

'Maybe another time then,' was all she'd said.

Driving back to Marchmont, he'd felt that something had been lost between them. He'd almost called her that evening, but had switched on the TV instead, losing himself in a nature programme, unable afterwards to recall anything about it. Until he'd remembered about the reconstruction and headed out to watch it . . .

His hand was still resting on the receiver. He picked it up and got a number for the Huntingtower Hotel, asked to speak to the manager.

'I'm sorry,' the receptionist said. 'He's in a meeting at the moment. Can I take a message?'

Rebus explained who he was. 'I want to speak to someone who was working at the hotel in nineteen ninety-five.

'What's their name?'

He smiled at her mistake. 'No, I mean, anyone will do.'

'Well, I've been here since ninety-three.'

'Then you might remember the little coffin that was found.'

'Vaguely, yes.'

'Only I've got a cutting from a newspaper at the time. It says that the hotel might be getting a reputation.'

'Yes.'

125

'And why would that have been?'

'I'm not sure. Maybe it was that American tourist.'

'Which one?'

'The one who disappeared.'

He didn't say anything for a moment, and when he did it was to ask her to repeat what she'd just said.

Rebus went to the National Library annexe on Causewayside. It wasn't much more than a five-minute walk from St Leonard's. When he'd shown his ID and explained what he needed, he was taken to a desk where a microfilm reader sat. This was a large illuminated screen above two spools. The film was placed on one spool and would be wound on to the empty one. Rebus had used the machine before, back when newspapers had been stored at the main building on George IV Bridge. He'd told the staff that today's was 'a rush job'. Even so, he sat for the best part of twenty minutes before a librarian arrived with the film boxes. The *Courier* was Dundee's daily paper. Rebus's own family had taken it. He remembered that up until recently it had retained the look of a broadsheet from a previous era, with column-wide ads covering its front page. No news, no photos. The story went that when the *Titanic* sank, the headline in the *Courier* had been 'Dundee Man Lost at Sea'. Not that the paper was parochial or anything.

Rebus had the Huntingtower cutting with him, and wound the tape forward until he was four weeks shy of its appearance. There, on an inside page, was the headline 'Tourist's Disappearance a Mystery, Say Police'. The woman's name was Betty-Anne Jesperson. She was thirty-eight and married. She'd been a member of a tour party from the USA. The tour was called 'The Mystical Highlands of Scotland'. The photograph of Betty-Anne came from her passport. It showed a heavy-set woman with dark permed hair and thick-rimmed glasses. Her husband, Garry, said she was in the habit of waking early and going for a pre-breakfast walk. No one in the hotel had seen her depart. The countryside was searched, and police went into Perth town centre armed with copies of the photograph. But as Rebus wound the film forward a week, the story was cut down to half a dozen paragraphs. A further week along, and there was just a single paragraph. The story was in the process of vanishing as completely as Betty-Anne had.

According to the hotel receptionist, Garry Jesperson had made several trips back to the area in that first year, with a further month-long trip the year after. But then the last she'd heard, Garry had met someone else and moved from New Jersey to Baltimore.

Rebus copied the details into his notebook, then sat tapping at the page he'd just written on until one of the browsers cleared their throat, warning him that he'd started to make too much noise.

Back at the main desk, he put in a request for more papers: the *Dunfermline Press*, *Glasgow Herald* and *Inverness Courier*. Only the *Herald* was on microfilm, so he started with that. Nineteen eighty-two, the doll in the churchyard . . . Van Morrison had released *Beautiful Vision* early in '82. Rebus found himself humming 'Dweller on the Threshold', then stopped when he remembered where he was. Nineteen eighty-two, he'd been a detective sergeant, working cases with another DS called Jack Morton. They'd been based at Great London Road, back before the station had caught fire. When the *Herald* film arrived, he spooled it and got to work, the days and weeks a blur across his screen. All the officers above him at Great London Road, they were either dead or retired. He hadn't kept in touch with any of them. And now the Farmer was gone too. Soon, whether he liked it or not, it would be his turn. He didn't think he'd go quietly. They'd have to pull him screaming and kicking . . .

The churchyard doll had been found in May. He started at the beginning of April. Problem was, Glasgow was a big city, more crime than a place like Perth. He wasn't sure he'd know if and when he found something. And if it was a missing person, would it even make the paper? Thousands of people disappeared each year. Some of them left without being noticed: the homeless, the ones with no family or friends. This was a country where a corpse could sit in a chair by the fire until the smell alerted the neighbours.

By the time he'd searched April, he had no reported MisPers, but six deaths, two of them women. One was a stabbing after a party. A man, it was stated, was helping police with their inquiries. Rebus guessed the boyfriend. He was pretty sure that if he read on, he'd find the case coming to court. The second death was a drowning. A stretch of river Rebus had never heard of: White Cart Water, the body found by its banks on the southern border of Rosshall Park. The victim was Hazel Gibbs, aged twenty-two. Her husband had walked out, leaving her with two kids. Friends said she'd been depressed. She'd been seen out drinking the previous day, while the kids fended for themselves.

Rebus walked outside and got on his mobile, punching in the number for Bobby Hogan at Leith CID.

'Bobby, it's John. You know a bit about Glasgow, don't you?'

'A bit.'

'Ever heard of White Cart Water?'

'Can't say I have.'

'What about Rosshall Park?'

'Sorry.'

'Got any contacts out west?'

'I could make a phone call.'

'Do that, will you?' Rebus repeated the names and ended the call. He smoked a cigarette, staring across at a new pub on the opposite corner. He knew one drink wouldn't do him any harm. Then he remembered that he was supposed to be seeing the doctor. Hell, it would have to wait. He could always make another appointment. When, at cigarette's end, Hogan hadn't called back, Rebus returned to his desk and started going through the editions for May '82. When his mobile sounded, the staff and readers gave a look of collective horror. Rebus cursed and put the phone to his ear, getting up from his seat to head outside again.

'It's me,' Hogan said.

'Go ahead,' Rebus whispered, moving towards the exit.

'Rosshall Park's in Pollok, south-west of the city centre. White Cart Water runs along the top of it.'

Rebus stopped in his tracks. 'You sure?' His voice was no longer a whisper.

'It's what I'm told.'

Rebus was back at his desk. The *Herald* cutting was just below the one from the *Courier*. He eased it out, just to be sure.

'Thanks, Bobby,' he said, ending the call. People around him were making exasperated noises, but he didn't pay them any heed. 'Church Condemns Sick Joke Find': the coffin found in the churchyard. The church itself located on Potterhill Road.

In Pollok.

'I don't suppose you'd care to explain yourself,' Gill Templer said.

Rebus had driven to Gayfield Square and asked her for five minutes. They were back in the same stale office.

'That's just what I want to do,' Rebus told her. He placed a hand to his forehead. His face felt like it was burning.

'You were supposed to be attending a doctor's appointment.'

'Something came up. Christ, you're not going to believe it.'

She stabbed a finger at the tabloid newspaper open on her desk. 'Any idea how Steve Holly got hold of this?'

Rebus turned the paper so it was facing him. Holly couldn't have had much time, but he'd patched together a story which managed to mention the Arthur's Seat coffins, a 'local expert from the Museum of Scotland', the Falls coffin, and the 'persistent rumour that more coffins exist'.

'What does he mean, "more coffins"?' Gill asked.

'That's what I'm trying to tell you.' So he told her, laid the whole thing out before her. In the musty, leatherbound sets of *Dunfermline Presses* and *Inverness Couriers* he'd found exactly what he'd known and dreaded he would find. In July 1977, a scant week before the Nairn beach coffin had been found, the body of Paula Gearing had been washed ashore four miles further along the coast. Her death could not be explained, and was put down to 'misadventure'. In October 1972, three weeks before the finding of the coffin in Dunfermline Glen, a teenage girl had been reported missing. Caroline Farmer was a fourth-year student at Dunfermline High. She'd recently been jilted by a long-term boyfriend, and the best guess was that this had led her to leave home. Her family said they wouldn't rest until they'd heard from her. Rebus doubted they ever had . . .

Gill Templer listened to his story without comment. When he'd finished, she looked at the cuttings and the notes he'd taken in the library. Finally, she looked up at him.

'It's thin, John.'

Rebus jumped from his seat. He needed to be moving, but the room didn't have enough space. 'Gill, it's . . . there's something there.'

'A killer who leaves coffins near the scene?' She shook her head slowly. 'I just can't see it. You've got two bodies, no signs of foul play, and two disappearances. Doesn't exactly make a pattern.'

'Three disappearances including Philippa Balfour.'

'And there's another thing: the Falls coffin turned up less than a week after she went AWOL. No pattern again.'

'You think I'm seeing things?'

'Maybe.'

'Can I at least follow it through?'

'John . . .'

'Just one, maybe two more officers. Give us a few days to see if we can convince you.'

'We're stretched as it is.'

'Stretched doing what? We're whistling in the dark till she comes back, phones home or turns up dead. Give me two people.'

She shook her head slowly. 'You can have one. And three or four days, tops. Understood?'

Rebus nodded.

'And John? Go see the doctor, or I'm reeling you back in. Understood?'

'Understood. Who will I be working with?'

Templer was thoughtful. 'Who do you want?'

'Give me Ellen Wylie.'

She stared at him. 'Any particular reason why?'

He shrugged. 'She'll never make it as a TV presenter, but she's a good cop.'

Templer was still staring. 'Okay,' she said at last. 'Go ahead.'

'And is there any chance you can keep Steve Holly away from us?'

'I can try.' She tapped the newspaper. 'I'm assuming the "local expert" is Jean?' She waited till he'd nodded, then she sighed. 'I should have known better, bringing the two of you together ...' She started rubbing at her forehead. It was something the Farmer had done, too, whenever he got what he called his 'Rebus heads' ...

'What exactly are we looking for?' Ellen Wylie asked. She'd been summoned to St Leonard's, and didn't look thrilled at the prospect of working a two-hander with Rebus.

'The first thing,' he told her, 'is to cover our backsides, and that means checking that the MisPers never turned up.'

'Talking to the families?' she guessed, writing a note to herself on her pad.

'Right. As for the two bodies, we need to take another look at the PM results, see if there's anything the pathologists could have missed.'

'Nineteen seventy-seven and eighty-two? You think the records won't have been ditched?'

'I hope not. In any case, some of those pathologists have long memories.'

She made another note. 'I'll ask again: what are we looking for? You think there's a possibility of proving these women and the coffins are related?'

'I don't know.' But he knew what she meant: it was one

thing to believe something, quite another to be able to prove it, especially in a court of law.

'It might set my mind at rest,' he said at last.

'And all of this started with some coffins on Arthur's Seat?' He nodded, his own enthusiasm making no impact on her scepticism.

'Look,' he said, 'if I'm seeing things, you'll get your chance to tell me. But first we do a bit of digging.'

She shrugged, made a show of jotting another note on to her pad. 'Did you ask for me, or were you given me?'

'I asked.'

'And DCS Templer said okay?'

Rebus nodded again. 'Is there a problem?'

'I don't know.' She gave the question serious consideration. 'Probably not.'

'Okay,' he said. 'Then let's get started.'

It took him the best part of two hours to type up everything he had. What he wanted was a 'bible' they could work from. He had dates and page references for each of the newspaper stories, and had arranged with the library for copies to be made. Wylie meantime was busy on the phone, begging favours from police stations in Glasgow, Perth, Dunfermline and Nairn. She wanted case notes if any still existed, plus pathologists' names. Whenever she laughed, Rebus knew what had just been said to her: 'You don't ask for bloody much, do you?' Hammering away at his keyboard, he listened to her work. She knew when to be coy, when to get tough, and when to flirt. Her voice never betrayed the set features of her face as repetition made her weary.

'Thank you,' she said for the umpteenth time, dropping the receiver into its cradle. She scribbled a note on her pad, checked the time and wrote that down too. She was thorough, all right. 'A promise is one thing,' she said more than once.

'It's better than nothing.'

'As long as they come through.' Then she lifted the

handset again, took another deep breath, and made the next call.

Rebus was intrigued by the long gaps in the chronology: 1972, 1977, 1982, 1995. Five years, five years, thirteen years. And now, just maybe, another five-year gap. The fives made for a nice pattern, but it was immediately broken by that silence between '82 and '95. There were all sorts of explanations: the man, whoever he was, could have been away somewhere, maybe in prison. Who was to say the coffins had only been left dotted around Scotland? It might be worth putting out a more general search, see if any other forces had come across the phenomenon. If he'd done a stretch in prison, well, records could be checked. Thirteen years was a long one: had to be murder, most probably.

There was another possibility, of course: that he hadn't been anywhere. That he'd gone on with his spree right here, but somehow hadn't bothered with the coffins, or they hadn't ever been found. A little wooden box . . . a dog would chew it to pulp; a kid might take it home; someone might bin it, the better to be rid of the sick joke. Rebus knew that a public appeal would be one way of finding out, but he couldn't see Templer going for it. She would need convincing first.

'Nothing?' he asked as Wylie put down the phone.

'No one's answering. Maybe word's gone round about the crazy cop from Edinburgh.'

Rebus crumpled a sheet of paper and tossed it overarm towards the bin. 'I think maybe we're getting a bit stir-crazy,' he said. 'Let's take a break.'

Wylie was heading off to the baker's for a jam doughnut. Rebus decided he'd just take a walk. The streets around St Leonard's didn't offer a great deal of choice. Tenements and housing schemes, or Holyrood Road with its speeding traffic and backdrop of Salisbury Crags. Rebus decided to head into the warren of narrow passages between St Leonard's and Nicolson Street. He nipped into a newsagent's and bought a can of Irn-Bru, sipping from it as he walked. They said the stuff was perfect for hangovers, but he was using it to fend off the craving for a proper drink, a pint and a nip, somewhere smoky with the horses on TV . . . The Southsider was a possibility, but he crossed the road to avoid it. There were kids playing on the pavements, Asians mostly. School was over for the day and here they were with their energy, their imagination. He wondered if maybe his own imagination was putting in some overtime today . . . It was the final possibility: that he was seeing connections where none existed. He got out his mobile and a scrap of paper with a number on it.

When the call was answered, he asked to be put through to Jean Burchill.

'Jean?' He stopped walking. 'It's John Rebus. We might have struck gold with your little coffins.' He listened for a moment. 'I can't tell you about it right now.' He looked around. 'I'm on my way to a meeting. Are you busy tonight?' He listened again. 'That's a pity. Would you be up for a nightcap?' He brightened. 'Ten o'clock? Portobello or in town?' Another pause. 'Yes, town makes sense if you've been in a meeting. I'll drive you home after. Ten at the museum then? Okay, bye.'

He looked around. He was in Hill Square, and there was a sign on the railings nearest him. Now he knew where he was: at the back of Surgeons' Hall. The anonymous door in front of him was the entrance to something called the Sir Jules Thorn Exhibition of the History of Surgery. He checked his watch against the opening times. He had about ten minutes. What the hell, he thought, pushing the door and going inside.

He found himself in an ordinary tenement stairwell. Climbing one flight brought him to a narrow landing with two doors facing. They looked like they led to private flats, so he climbed a further flight. As he passed the museum threshold an alarm sounded, alerting a member of staff that there was a new visitor.

'Have you been here before?' she asked. He shook his head. 'Well, modern-day is upstairs, and just off to the left is the dental display . . .' He thanked her and she left him to it.

There was no one else around, no one Rebus could see. He lasted half a minute in the dentistry room. It didn't seem to him that the technology had moved so very far in a couple of centuries. The main museum display took up two floors, and was well presented. The exhibits were behind glass, well lit for the most part. He stood in front of an apothecary's shop, then moved to a full-size dummy of the physician Joseph Lister, examining his list of accomplishments, chief among them the introduction of carbolic spray and sterile catgut. A little further along, he came across the case containing the wallet made from Burke's skin. It reminded him of a small leatherbound Bible an uncle had gifted him one childhood birthday. Beside it was a plaster cast of Burke's head – the marks of the hangman's noose still visible – and one of an accomplice, John Brogan, who had helped transport the corpses. While Burke looked peaceful, hair groomed, face at rest, Brogan looked to have suffered torments, the skin pulled back from his lower jaw, skull bulbous and pink.

Next along was a portrait of the anatomist Knox, recipient of the still-warm cadavers.

'Poor Knox,' a voice behind him said. Rebus looked around. An elderly man, dressed in full evening attire – bow-tie, cummerbund and patent shoes. It took Rebus a second to place him: Professor Devlin, Flip's neighbour. Devlin shuffled forward, staring at the exhibits. 'There's been a lot of discussion about how much he knew.'

'You mean, whether he knew Burke and Hare were killers?'

Devlin nodded. 'For myself, I think there's no doubt he knew. At the time, most bodies worked on by the anatomists were cold indeed. They were brought to Edinburgh from all over Britain – some came by way of the Union Canal. The resurrectionists – body-snatchers – pickled them in whisky for transportation. It was a lucrative trade.'

'But did the whisky get drunk afterwards?'

Devlin chuckled. 'Economics would dictate that it did,' he said. 'Ironically, both Burke and Hare came to Scotland as economic migrants. Their job was to help build the Union Canal.' Rebus recalled Jean saying something similar. Devlin paused, tucked a finger into his cummerbund. 'But poor Knox . . . the man was possessed of a kind of genius. It was never proven that he was complicit in the murders. But the Church was against him, that was the problem. The human body was a temple, remember. Many of the clergy were against exploration – they saw it as desecration. They raised the rabble against Knox.'

'What happened to him?'

'He died of apoplexy, according to the literature. Hare, who had turned King's evidence, had to flee Scotland. Even then he wasn't safe. He was attacked with lime, and ended his days blind and begging on the streets of London. I believe there's a pub called the Blind Beggar somewhere in London, but whether it has any connection . . .'

'Sixteen murders,' Rebus said, 'in an area as confined as the West Port.'

'We can't imagine it happening these days, can we?'

'But these days we've got forensics, pathology . . .'

Devlin unhooked the finger from his cummerbund and wagged it before him. 'Exactly,' he said. 'And we'd have had no pathological studies at all had it not been for the resurrectionists and the likes of Messrs Burke and Hare!'

'Is that why you're here? Paying homage?'

'Perhaps,' Devlin said. Then he checked his watch. 'There's a dinner upstairs at seven. I thought I'd arrive early and spend some time amongst the exhibits.'

Rebus recalled the invitation on Devlin's mantelpiece: *black tie and decorations* . . .

'I'm sorry, Professor Devlin,' the curator called. 'It's time I was locking up.'

'That's okay, Maggie,' Devlin called back. Then, to Rebus: 'Would you like to see the rest of the place?'

Rebus thought of Ellen Wylie, probably back at her desk by now. 'I should really . . .'

'Come on, come on,' Devlin insisted. 'You can't visit Surgeons' Hall and miss out on the Black Museum . . .'

The curator had to let them through a couple of locked doors, after which they entered the main body of the building. The corridors were hushed and lined with portraits of medical men. Devlin pointed out the library, then stopped in a marble-floored circular hall, pointing upwards. 'That's where we'll be eating. Lots of Profs and Docs all dressed to the nines and feasting on rubber chicken.'

Rebus looked up. The ceiling was topped with a glass cupola. There was a circular railing on the first floor, with a doorway just visible beyond. 'What's the occasion?'

'Lord alone knows. I just bung them a cheque whenever an invite arrives.'

'Will Gates and Curt be there?'

'Probably. You know Sandy Gates has trouble turning down a square meal.'

Rebus was studying the inside of the large main doors. He'd seen them before, but only ever from the other side, while driving or walking down Nicolson Street. He didn't think he'd ever seen them open, and said as much to his guide.

'They'll be open this evening,' Devlin told him. 'Guests march in and straight up the stairs. Come on, this way.'

Along more corridors and up some steps. 'Probably won't be locked,' Devlin said, as they approached another imposing set of doors. 'The dinner guests like a stroll after their meal. Most of them end up here.' He tried the doorhandle. He was right; the door opened and they entered a large exhibition hall.

'The Black Museum,' Devlin said, gesturing with his arms.

'I've heard of it,' Rebus said. 'Never had cause to visit.'

'Off limits to the public,' Devlin explained. 'Never been sure why. The College could make itself a bit of money, open it as a tourist attraction.'

Its given name was Playfair Hall, and it wasn't, to Rebus's eye, as grisly as its nickname suggested. It seemed to consist of old surgical tools, looking more fit for a torture chamber than an operating theatre. There were lots of bones and body parts and things floating in hazy jars. A further narrow staircase took them up to a landing, where more jars awaited them.

'Pity the poor bugger whose job is keeping the formaldehyde topped up,' Devlin said, panting from the exertion.

Rebus stared at the contents of one glass cylinder. The face of an infant stared back at him, but it looked distorted somehow. Then he realised that it sat atop two distinct bodies. Siamese twins, joined at the head, parts of either face forming a singular whole. Rebus, who'd seen his fair share of horror, was held in grim fascination. But there were other exhibits to explore: further deformed foetuses. Paintings, too, mostly from the nineteenth century: soldiers with bits blown off them by cannonball or musket.

'This is my favourite,' Devlin said. Surrounded by obscene images, he had found a still point, the portrait of a young man, almost smiling for the artist. Rebus read the inscription.

' "Dr Kennet Lovell, February, eighteen twenty-nine." '

'Lovell was one of the anatomists charged with the dissection of William Burke. It's even likely that he pronounced Burke dead after the hanging. Less than a month later, he sat for this portrait.'

'He looks pretty happy with his lot,' Rebus commented.

Devlin's eyes sparkled. 'Doesn't he? Kennet was a craftsman too. He worked with wood, as did Deacon William Brodie, of whom you will have heard.'

'Gentleman by day, housebreaker by night,' Rebus acknowledged.

'And perhaps the model for Stevenson's *Jekyll and Hyde*. As a child, Stevenson had a wardrobe in his room, one of Brodie's creations . . .'

Rebus was still studying the portrait. Lovell had deep black eyes, a cleft chin and a profusion of dark locks of hair. He had no doubt that the painter would have flattered his subject, maybe shaved a few years and pounds from him. Still, Lovell was a handsome man.

'It's interesting about the Balfour girl,' Devlin said.

Startled, Rebus turned to him. The old man, his breathing regular now, had eyes only for the painting.

'What is?' Rebus asked.

'The caskets found on Arthur's Seat . . . the way the press have brought them up again.' He turned towards Rebus. 'One notion is that they represent Burke and Hare's victims . . .'

'Yes.'

'And now another casket seems to be some memorial for young Philippa.'

Rebus turned back to the portrait. 'Lovell worked with wood?'

'The table in my dining room.' Devlin smiled. 'He made that.'

'Is that why you bought it?'

'A small memento of the early years of pathology. The history of surgery, Inspector, is the history of Edinburgh.' Devlin sniffed and then sighed. 'I miss it, you know.'

'I don't think I would.'

They were walking away from the portrait. 'It was a privilege, in its way. Endlessly fascinating, what this animal exterior can contain.' Devlin slapped his own chest to make the point. Rebus didn't feel he had anything to add. To him, a body was a body was a body. By the time it was dead, whatever it was that had made it interesting had disappeared. He almost said as much, but knew he'd fail to match the old pathologist's eloquence.

Back in the main hall, Devlin turned to him. 'Look here, you really ought to come along tonight. Plenty of time to run home and change.'

'I don't think so,' Rebus said. 'It'll be all shop talk, you said as much yourself.' And besides, he could have added, he didn't own so much as a dinner jacket, never mind the rest.

'But you'd enjoy it,' Devlin persisted. 'Bearing in mind our conversation.'

'Why's that?' Rebus asked.

'The speaker is a priest of the Roman Catholic Church. He's discussing the dichotomy between body and spirit.'

'You've lost me already,' Rebus said.

Devlin just smiled at him. 'I think you pretend to be less able than you are. Probably useful to you in your chosen career.'

Rebus admitted as much with a shrug. 'This speaker,' he said. 'It's not Father Conor Leary, is it?'

Devlin's eyes widened. 'You know him? All the more reason to join us.'

Rebus was thoughtful. 'Maybe just for a drink before dinner.'

Back at St Leonard's, Ellen Wylie was not best pleased.

'Your idea of a "break" differs somewhat from mine,' she complained.

'I bumped into someone,' he said. She didn't say anything else, but he knew she was holding back. Her face remained tense and when she snatched up the receiver it was as though with malice aforethought. She wanted something more from him: a fuller apology maybe, or some words of praise. He held off for a while, then, as she attacked the telephone again, asked:

'Is it because of that press conference?'

'What?' She slammed the receiver back down.

'Ellen,' he said, 'it's not as—'

'Don't you fucking *dare* patronise me!'

He held up his hands in surrender. 'Okay, no more first names. Sorry if it sounded patronising, DS Wylie.'

She glowered at him, then suddenly her face changed, became looser. She forced a smile from somewhere and rubbed at her cheeks with her hands.

'Sorry,' she said.

'Me too.' She looked at him. 'For being out so long. I should have called it in.' He shrugged. 'But now you know my awful secret.'

'Which is?'

'To wring an apology from John Rebus, you first have to violate a telephone.'

This time she laughed. It was far from full-blooded, and

retained an edge of hysteria, but she seemed the better for it. They got back to work.

By the end of play, however, they'd achieved next to nothing. He told her not to worry, it was bound to be a rocky start. She shrugged her arms into her coat, asked if he was going for a drink.

'Previous appointment,' he told her. 'Another night though, eh?'

'Sure,' she said. But she didn't sound as if she believed it.

He drank alone: just the one before the walk to Surgeons' Hall; a Laphroaig, with the merest trickle of water to smooth its edges. He chose a pub Ellen Wylie wouldn't know, didn't like the thought of bumping into her after he'd turned her down. He'd need a few drinks in him to tell her she was wrong, that one tongue-tied press conference wasn't the end of her career. Gill Templer was down on her, no question of that, but Gill wasn't stupid enough to let it turn into a feud. Wylie was a good cop, an intelligent detective. She'd get her chance again. If Templer kept knocking her back, she herself would start to look bad.

'Another?' the barman said.

Rebus checked his watch. 'Aye, go on then.'

It suited him, this place. Small and anonymous and hidden away. There wasn't even a name outside, nothing to identify it. It was on a corner in a back street where only the knowing would find it. Two old regulars in the corner, sitting straight-backed, eyes hypnotised by the far wall. Their dialogue was sparse and guttural. The TV had its sound turned off, but the barman watched it anyway: some American courtroom drama, with lots of pacing about and walls painted grey. Now and then there was a close-up of a woman trying to seem worried. Unwilling to rely on facial expression alone, she wrung her hands as well. Rebus handed over his money and poured the remains of his first drink into its replacement, shaking the drips out. One of the old men coughed, then sniffed. His neighbour said something, and he nodded silent agreement.

'What's going on?' Rebus couldn't help asking the barman.

'Eh?'

'The film, what's happening in it?'

'Same as always,' the barman said. It was as if each day held its identical routine, right down to the drama being played out on the screen.

'How about yourself?' the barman said. 'How's your day been?' The words sounded rusty in his mouth: small talk with the customers not part of the routine.

Rebus thought of possible answers. The potential that some serial killer was on the loose, and had been since the early seventies. A missing girl almost sure to turn up dead. A single, twisted face shared by Siamese twins.

'Ach, you know,' he said at last. The barman nodded agreement, as though it was exactly the answer he'd expected.

Rebus left the bar soon after. A short walk back on to Nicolson Street and the doors of Surgeons' Hall now, as Professor Devlin had predicted, standing open. Guests were already filtering in. Rebus had no invite to show to staff, but an explanation and his warrant card seemed to do the trick. Early arrivals were standing on the first-floor landing, drinks in hand. Rebus made his way upstairs. The banqueting hall was set for dinner, waiters scurrying around making last-minute adjustments. A trestle table just inside the doorway had been covered with a white cloth and an array of glasses and bottles. The serving staff wore black waistcoats over crisp white shirts.

'Yes, sir?'

Rebus considered another whisky. The problem was, once he had three or four under his belt, he wouldn't want to stop. And if he did stop, the thumping head would be nestling in just about the time he was due to meet Jean.

'Just an orange juice, please,' he said.

'Holy Mother, now I can die a peaceful death.'

Rebus turned towards the voice, smiling. 'And why's that?' he asked.

'Because I've seen all there is to see on this glorious planet of ours. Give the man a whisky and don't be niggardly,' he ordered the barman, who stopped halfway through pouring the orange juice. The barman looked at Rebus.

'Just the juice,' he said.

'Well now,' Father Conor Leary said. 'I can smell whisky on your breath, so I know you've not gone TT on me. But for some inexplicable reason you want to stay sober . . .' He grew thoughtful. 'Is the fairer sex involved at all?'

'You're wasted as a priest,' Rebus said.

Father Leary roared with laughter. 'I'd have made a good detective, you mean? And who's to say you're wrong?' Then, to the barman: 'Do you need to ask?' The barman didn't, and was generous with the measure. Leary nodded and took the glass from him.

'*Slainte!*' he said.

'*Slainte.*' Rebus sipped the juice. Conor Leary looked almost too well. When Rebus had last spoken with him, the old priest had been ailing, medicines jostling for space with the Guinness in his fridge.

'It's been a while,' Leary stated.

'You know how it is.'

'I know you young fellows have little enough time to visit the weak and infirm. Too busy with the sins of the flesh.'

'Been a long time since my flesh saw any sins worth reporting.'

'And by God there's plenty of it.' The priest slapped Rebus's stomach.

'Maybe that's the problem,' Rebus admitted. 'You, on the other hand . . .'

'Ah, you were expecting me to wither and die? That's not the way I'd choose. Good food, good drink and damn the consequences.'

Leary wore his clerical collar beneath a grey V-neck jumper. His trousers were navy blue, the shoes polished black. It was true he'd lost some weight, but his stomach and jowls sagged, and his thin silver hair was like spun silk, the eyes sunken beneath a Roman fringe. He held his whisky glass the way a workman would grip a flask.

'We're neither of us dressed for the occasion,' he said, looking around at the array of dinner jackets.

'At least you're in uniform,' Rebus said.

'Just barely,' Leary said. 'I've retired from active service.' Then he winked. 'It happens, you know. We're allowed to down tools. But every time I put the old collar on for something like this, I envision papal emissaries leaping forward, daggers drawn, to slice it from my neck.'

Rebus smiled. 'Like leaving the Foreign Legion?'

'Indeed! Or clipping the pigtail from a retiring Sumo.'

Both men were laughing as Donald Devlin came along-side. 'Glad you felt able to join us,' he told Rebus, before taking the priest's hand. 'I think you were the deciding factor, Father,' he said, explaining about the dinner invitation.

'The offer of which still stands,' he added. 'I'm sure you'll want to hear the Father's speech.' Rebus shook his head.

'Last thing a heathen like John needs is me telling him what's good for him,' Leary said.

'Too right,' Rebus agreed. 'And I'm sure I've heard it all before anyway.' He caught Leary's eye, and in that moment they shared a memory of the long talks in the priest's kitchen, fuelled by trips to the fridge and the drinks cabinet. Conversations about Calvin and criminals, faith and the faithless. Even when Rebus agreed with Leary, he'd try to play devil's advocate, the old priest amused by his stubborn-ness. Long talks they'd had, and regularly . . . until Rebus had started finding excuses to stay away. Tonight, if Leary asked why, he knew he couldn't give a reason. Maybe it was because the priest had begun to offer him certainties, and Rebus had no time for them. They'd played this game, Leary convinced he could convert 'the heathen'.

'You've got all these questions,' he'd tell Rebus. 'Why won't you let someone supply the answers?'

'Maybe because I prefer questions to answers,' Rebus had

replied. And the priest had thrown up his hands in despair, before making another foray to the fridge.

Devlin was asking Leary about the theme of his talk. Rebus could see that Devlin had had a drink or two. He stood rosy-faced with hands in pockets, his smile contented but distant. Rebus was getting his OJ topped up when Gates and Curt appeared, the two pathologists dressed almost identically, making them seem more of a double-act than usual.

'Bloody hell,' Gates said, 'the gang's all here.' He caught the barman's attention. 'Whisky for me, and a glass of tonic water for this fairy here.'

Curt snorted. 'I'm not the only one.' He nodded towards Rebus's drink.

'Ye Gods, John, tell me there's vodka in that,' Gates boomed. Then: 'What the hell are you doing here anyway?' Gates was sweating, his shirt collar constricting his throat. His face had turned almost puce. Curt, as usual, looked completely at ease. He'd gained a couple of pounds but still looked slim, though his face was grey.

'I never see sunlight,' was the excuse he always gave when asked about his pallor. More than one woolly-suit at St Leonard's had taken to calling him Dracula.

'I wanted to catch the pair of you,' Rebus said now.

'The answer's no,' Gates said.

'You don't know what I was going to say.'

'That tone of voice was enough. You're going to ask a favour. You'll say it won't take long. You'll be wrong.'

'Just some old PM results. I need a second opinion.'

'We're rushed off our feet,' Curt said, looking apologetic.

'Whose are they?' Gates asked.

'I haven't got them yet. They're from Glasgow and Nairn. Maybe if you were to put in a request, it would push things along.'

Gates looked around the group. 'See what I mean?'

'University duties, John,' Curt said. 'More students and coursework, fewer people to do the teaching.'

'I appreciate that ...' Rebus began.

Gates lifted his cummerbund and pointed to the pager hidden there. 'Even tonight, we could get a call, another body to deal with.'

'I don't think you're winning them over,' Leary said, laughing.

Rebus fixed Gates with a hard look. 'I'm serious,' he said.

'So am I. First night off I've had in ages, and you're after one of your famous "favours".'

Rebus decided there was no point pushing it, not when Gates was in a mood. Hard day at the office maybe, but then weren't they all?

Devlin cleared his throat. 'Might I perhaps . . . ?'

Leary slapped Devlin's back. 'There you are, John. A willing victim!'

'I know I've been retired a good few years, but I don't suppose the theory and practice have changed.'

Rebus looked at him. 'Actually,' he said, 'the most recent case is nineteen eighty-two.'

'Donald was still wielding the scalpel in eighty-two,' Gates said. Devlin acknowledged this truth with a small bow.

Rebus hesitated. He wanted someone with a bit of clout, someone like Gates.

'Motion carried,' Curt said, deciding the matter for him.

Siobhan Clarke sat in her living room watching TV. She'd tried cooking herself a proper dinner, but had given up halfway through chopping the red peppers, putting everything in the fridge and pulling a ready-meal from the freezer. The empty container was on the floor in front of her. She sat on the sofa with her legs tucked under her, head resting on one arm. The laptop was on the coffee table, but she'd unhooked her mobile phone. She didn't think Quizmaster would be calling again. She lifted her notepad and stared at the clue. She'd gone through dozens of sheets of paper, working out possible anagrams and meanings. Seven fins high is king . . . and mentions of the queen and 'the bust': it sounded like something from a card game, but the compendium of card games she'd borrowed from the Central Library hadn't been any help. She was just wondering if she should read it through a final time when her phone rang.

'Hello?'

'It's Grant.'

Siobhan turned the sound down on the TV. 'What's up?'

'I think maybe I've cracked it.'

Siobhan swivelled her legs so her feet were on the floor. 'Tell me,' she said.

'I'd rather show you.'

There seemed to be a lot of background noise on the line. She stood up. 'Are you on your mobile?' she asked.

'Yes.'

'Where are you?'

'Parked right outside.'

She walked over to the window and looked out. Sure enough, his Alfa was sitting in the middle of the street. Siobhan smiled. 'Find a parking space then. My buzzer's second from the top.'

By the time she'd taken the dirty dishes through to the sink, Grant was at her intercom. She checked anyway that it was him, then pressed the button to let him into the tenement. She was standing by the open door when he hauled himself up the last few steps.

'Sorry it's so late,' he said, 'but I couldn't keep it to myself.'

'Coffee?' she asked, closing the door after him.

'Thanks. Two sugars.'

They took the coffees into the living room. 'Nice place,' he said.

'I like it.'

He sat down next to her on the sofa and placed his coffee mug on the table. Then he reached into his jacket pocket and pulled out a London A–Z.

'London?' she said.

'I went through all the kings I could think of from history, then anything else to do with the word king.' He held up the book so its back cover was showing. A map of the London Underground.

'King's Cross?' she guessed.

He nodded. 'Take a look.'

She took the book from him. He could hardly sit still in his seat.

'Seven fins high is king,' he said.

'And you think the king is King's Cross?'

He slid across the sofa, his finger tracing the light blue line which went through the station. 'Do you see?' he said.

'No,' she said grimly. 'So you'd better tell me.'

'Go one stop north of King's Cross.'

'Highbury and Islington?'

'And again.'

'Finsbury Park . . . then Seven Sisters.'

'Now backwards,' he said. He was practically bouncing on the spot.

'Don't wet yourself,' she said. Then she looked at the map again. 'Seven Sisters . . . Finsbury Park . . . Highbury and Islington . . . King's Cross.' And saw it. The exact same sequence, but abbreviated. 'Seven . . . Fins . . . High Is . . . King.' She looked at Grant. He was nodding. 'Well done you,' she added, meaning it. Grant leaned over and gave her a hug, which she squirmed out of. Then he leaped from the sofa and clapped his hands together.

'I couldn't believe it myself,' he said. 'The way it just suddenly screamed at me. It's the Victoria Line.'

She nodded, couldn't think of anything to say. It was indeed a section of London Underground's Victoria Line.

'But what does it mean?' she said at last.

He sat down again, leaning forward, elbows on knees. 'That's what we have to work out next.'

She slid across the sofa a little, making some space between them, then lifted her pad and read from it. ' "This queen dines well before the bust." ' She looked at him, but he just shrugged.

'Could the answer be in London?' she asked.

'I don't know,' he said. 'Buckingham Palace? Queen's Park Rangers?' He shrugged. 'Could be London.'

'All these Underground stops . . . what do they mean?'

'They're all on the Victoria Line,' was all he could think to say. Then they stared at one another.

'Queen Victoria,' they said in unison.

Siobhan had a London guidebook, bought for a weekend away which she'd never taken. It took her a while to find it. Meantime Grant booted up the computer and did a search on the Internet.

'Could be the name of a pub,' he suggested. 'Like in *EastEnders*.'

'Yes,' she said, busy reading. 'Or the Victoria and Albert Museum.'

'Not forgetting Victoria Station – also on the Victoria Line. There's a coach station there too. Worst cafeteria in Britain.'

'You're speaking from experience?'

'I bussed it down there a few weekends in my teens. Didn't like it.' He was scrolling down some text.

'Didn't like the bus or didn't like London?'

'Both, I suppose. "Bust" couldn't mean a drug bust, could it?'

'Maybe. Or some stock-market crash. There was one not that long back, wasn't there? Black Monday?'

He nodded.

'Still, more likely it's a statue,' she said. 'Maybe of Queen Victoria, with a restaurant in front of it.'

They worked in silence for a while after that, until Siobhan's eyes started to hurt and she got up to make more coffee.

'Two sugars,' Grant said.

'I remember.' She looked at him, hunched over the computer screen, one knee pumping away. She wanted to say something about the hug . . . warn him off somehow . . . but she knew she'd missed her chance.

Bringing the mugs back through from the kitchen, she asked if he'd found anything.

'Tourist sites,' he said. He took the mug from her with a nod of thanks.

'Why London?' she asked.

'What do you mean?' His eyes were still on the screen.

'I mean, why not somewhere closer to home?'

'Could be Quizmaster lives in London. We don't know, do we?'

'No.'

'And who's to say Flip Balfour was the only one playing the game? Something like this, my bet is there's a website somewhere – or was. Anyone wanting to join in could go there. They wouldn't all come from Scotland.'

She nodded. 'I'm just wondering ... was Flip bright enough to solve this clue?'

'Obviously, or she wouldn't have gone on to the next level.'

'But maybe this is a new game,' she said. He turned his head to look at her. 'Maybe it's just for us.'

'If we ever meet the bastard, I'll be sure to ask him.'

A further half-hour later, Grant was working his way through a list of London restaurants. 'You wouldn't believe how many Victoria Roads and Victoria Streets there are in this bloody place, and half of them have restaurants on them.'

He leaned back, straightening his spine. The energy seemed to have leached out of him.

'And that's before we start looking at pubs.' Siobhan ran her fingers through her hair, pulling it back tight from her forehead. 'It's too ...'

'What?'

'The first bit of the clue was clever. But this ... this is just looking at lists. Does he expect us to go to London, visit every chip shop and café in the hope of finding Queen Victoria's bust?'

'He can whistle if he does.' Grant's chuckle was empty of humour.

Siobhan looked at the book of card games. She'd spent a couple of hours flicking through it, and all the time looking for the wrong thing in the wrong place. She'd only just got to the library in time. Five minutes till closing. Left her car on Victoria Street and prayed she didn't get a ticket ...

'Victoria Street?' she said out loud.

'Take your pick, there are dozens of the buggers.'

'And some of them are right here,' she told him.

He looked up. 'Yes,' he said, 'they are.'

He went down to his car, brought back an Ordnance Survey atlas of East-Central Scotland, opened it at the index and ran his finger down the list.

'Victoria Gardens ... there's a Victoria Hospital in Kirkcaldy ... Victoria Street and Victoria Terrace in Edinburgh.' He looked at her. 'What do you think?'

'I think there are a couple of restaurants in Victoria Street.'

'Any statues?'

'Not on the outside.'

He checked his watch. 'They won't be open at this hour, will they?'

She shook her head. 'First thing tomorrow,' she said. 'Breakfast's on me.'

Rebus and Jean sat in the Palm Court. She was drinking a long vodka, while he nursed a ten-year-old Macallan. The waiter had brought a little glass jug of water, but Rebus hadn't disturbed it. He hadn't been inside the Balmoral Hotel in years. Back then it had been the North British. The old place had changed a bit in the interim. Not that Jean seemed interested in her surroundings, not now she'd heard Rebus's story.

'So they might all have been murdered?' she said, her face pale. The lights in the lounge had been turned low, and a pianist was playing. Rebus kept recognising snatches of tunes; he doubted Jean had taken in any of them.

'It's possible,' he admitted.

'But you're basing all of it on the dolls?'

Her eyes met his and he nodded. 'Maybe I'm reading too much into it,' he said. 'But it needs to be investigated.'

'Where on earth will you start?'

'We're waiting for the original case notes.' He paused. 'What's the matter?'

There were tears in her eyes. She sniffed and searched her

bag for a handkerchief. 'It's just the idea of it. All this time, I had those cuttings . . . Maybe if I'd given them to the police sooner . . .'

'Jean.' He took her hand. 'All you had were stories about dolls in coffins.'

'I suppose so,' she said.

'Meantime, maybe you can help.'

She hadn't found a handkerchief. Picked up her cocktail napkin and dabbed at her eyes with it. 'How?' she said.

'This whole thing goes back as far as nineteen seventy-two. I need to know who back then might have shown an interest in the Arthur's Seat exhibits. Can you do some digging for me?'

'Of course.'

He gave her hand another squeeze. 'Thanks.'

She gave a half-hearted smile and picked up her drink. The ice rattled as she finished it.

'Another?' he said.

She shook her head, looked around her. 'I get the feeling this isn't your kind of place.'

'Oh? And what is?'

'I think you feel more comfortable in small, smoky bars filled with disappointed men.'

There was a smile on her face. Rebus nodded slowly.

'You catch on quick,' he said.

Her smile faded as she looked around again. 'I was here just last week, such a happy occasion . . . It seems like a long time ago.'

'What was the occasion?'

'Gill's promotion. Do you think she's coping?'

'Gill's Gill. She'll tough it out.' He paused. 'Speaking of toughing it out, is that reporter still giving you grief?'

She managed a thin smile. 'He's persistent. Wants to know what "others" I was talking about in Bev Dodds's kitchen. That was my fault, sorry.' She seemed to have regained some composure. 'I should be getting back. I can probably find a taxi if . . .'

'I said I'd run you home.' He signalled for their waitress to bring the bill.

He'd parked the Saab on North Bridge. There was a cold wind blowing, but Jean stopped to look at the view: the Scott Monument, the Castle, and Ramsay Gardens.

'Such a beautiful city,' she said. Rebus tried to agree. He hardly saw it any more. To him, Edinburgh had become a state of mind, a juggling of criminal thoughts and baser instincts. He liked its size, its compactness. He liked its bars. But its outward show had ceased to impress him a long time ago. Jean wrapped her coat tightly around her. 'Everywhere you look, there's some story, some little piece of history.' She looked at him and he nodded agreement, but he was remembering all the suicides he'd dealt with, people who'd jumped from North Bridge maybe because they couldn't see the same city Jean did.

'I never tire of this view,' she said, turning back towards the car. He nodded again, disingenuously. To him, it wasn't a view at all. It was a crime scene waiting to happen.

When he drove off, she asked if they could have some music. He switched on the cassette-player and the car filled to bursting with Hawkwind's *In Search of Space*.

'Sorry,' he said, ejecting the tape. She found cassette boxes in the glove compartment. Hendrix, Cream and the Stones. 'Probably not your style,' he said.

She waved the Hendrix at him. 'You haven't got *Electric Ladyland* by any chance?'

Rebus looked at her and smiled.

Hendrix was the soundtrack for their drive to Portobello.

'So what made you a policeman?' she asked at one point. 'Is it such a strange career choice?'

'That doesn't answer my question.'

'True.' He glanced at her and smiled. She took the hint, nodding her understanding. Then she concentrated on the music.

Portobello was on Rebus's short-list come the move from Arden Street. It had a beach, and a main street of small local shops. At one time, it had been a fairly grand location, a place the gentry flocked to for reviving air and healthy doses of chill seawater. It wasn't quite so grand now, but the housing market dictated its rebirth. Those who couldn't afford the smart homes in the city centre were moving to 'Porty', which still had big Georgian houses, but without the premium. Jean had a house on a narrow street near the promenade. 'You own the whole thing?' he said, peering through the windscreen.

'I bought it years back. Porty wasn't so fashionable.' She hesitated. 'Do you want to come in for coffee this time?'

Their eyes met. His were questioning; hers tentative. Then their faces collapsed into smiles.

'I'd love one,' he said. Just as he was turning off the ignition, his mobile started ringing.

'I just thought you'd want to know,' Donald Devlin said. His voice trembled slightly, body likewise.

Rebus nodded. They were standing just inside the imposing front doors of Surgeons' Hall. There were people upstairs, but speaking in hushed tones. Outside, one of the grey transit vans from the mortuary was waiting, a police car standing beside it, roof-lights flashing, turning the front of the building blue every couple of seconds.

'What happened?' Rebus asked.

'Heart attack, it looks like. People were enjoying a post-prandial brandy, leaning against the railing.' Devlin pointed upwards. 'He suddenly went very pale, leaned over the rail. They thought he was going to be sick. But he just slumped, and his weight took him over.'

Rebus looked down at the marble floor. There was a smear of blood which would need cleaning. Men stood on the periphery, some outside on the lawns. They smoked and spoke of the awful shock. When Rebus looked back at Devlin, the old man seemed to be studying him, as if he were some specimen in a jar.

'Are you all right?' Devlin asked, watching as Rebus nodded. 'The two of you were pretty close, I gather.'

Rebus didn't answer. Sandy Gates walked up, mopping his

face with what looked like a napkin swiped from the dining room.

'Bloody awful,' was all he said. 'Probably have to be an autopsy, too.'

The body was being stretchered away. A blanket covered the body-bag. Rebus resisted the temptation to stop the attendants and pull the zip down. He wanted his last memories of Conor Leary to be of the lively man he'd shared that drink with.

'He'd just made a fascinating speech,' Devlin said. 'A sort of ecumenical history of the human body. Everything from the sacrament to Jack the Ripper as haruspex.'

'As what?'

'Someone who foretells the truth by looking at the entrails of animals.'

Gates belched. 'Half of it was above my head,' he said.

'And the other half you slept through, Sandy,' Devlin commented with a smile. 'He did the whole thing without notes,' he added admiringly. Then he looked up at the first-floor landing again. 'The fall of man, that was his starting point.' He rummaged in his pocket for a handkerchief.

'Here,' said Gates, handing over the napkin. Devlin blew his nose loudly.

'The fall of man, and then he fell,' Devlin said. 'Perhaps Stevenson was right.'

'What about?'

'He called Edinburgh a "precipitous city". Maybe vertigo is in the nature of the place . . .'

Rebus thought he knew what Devlin meant. Precipitous city . . . each and every one of its inhabitants falling slowly, almost imperceptibly . . .

'Bloody awful meal it was, too,' Gates was saying, as though he'd have preferred to lose Conor Leary after a veritable feast. Rebus didn't doubt Conor would have felt the same.

Outside, Dr Curt was one of the smokers. Rebus joined him.

'I tried phoning you,' Curt said, 'but you were already on your way.'

'Professor Devlin caught me.'

'He said as much. I think he sensed some bond between you and Conor.' Rebus just nodded slowly. 'He'd been pretty ill, you know,' Curt continued, in that dry voice that always sounded like dictation. 'After you'd left us this evening, he talked about you.'

Rebus cleared his throat. 'What did he say?'

'He said he sometimes thought of you as a penance.' Curt flicked ash into the air. A flash of blue lit his face for a moment. 'He was laughing as he said it.'

'He was a friend,' Rebus said. Inwardly he added, *and I let him go.* So many friendships he'd pushed away, preferring his own company, the chair by the window in the darkened room. He pretended sometimes that he was doing them all a favour. People he'd let get close to him in the past, they had a habit of getting hurt, sometimes even killed. But it wasn't that. It wasn't that. He wondered about Jean, and where it might be leading. Was he ready to share himself with someone else? Ready to let her into his secrets, his darkness? He still wasn't sure. Those conversations with Conor Leary, they'd been like confessionals. He'd probably revealed more of himself to the priest than to anyone before him: wife, daughter, lovers. And now he was gone . . . up to heaven maybe, though he'd cause havoc there, no doubt about it. He'd be in dispute with the angels, looking for Guinness and a good argument.

'You okay, John?' Curt reached out a hand and touched his shoulder.

Rebus shook his head slowly, eyes squeezed shut. Curt didn't make it out the first time, so Rebus had to repeat what he said next:

'I don't believe in heaven.'

That was the horror of it. This life was the only one you got. No redemption afterwards, no chance of wiping the slate clean and starting over.

'It's all right,' Curt was saying, clearly unused to the role of comforter, the hand which touched Rebus's arm more used to easing human organs from a gaping wound. 'You'll be all right.'

'Will I?' Rebus said. 'Then there's no justice in the world.'

'You'd know more about that than I would.'

'Oh, I know all right.' Rebus took a deep breath, let it out. There was sweat beneath his shirt, the night air chilling him. 'I'll be okay,' he said quietly.

'Of course you will.' Curt finished his cigarette and pushed it into the grass with his heel. 'Like Conor said: despite rumours to the contrary, you're on the side of the angels.' He took his hand from Rebus's arm. 'Whether you like it or not.'

Donald Devlin came bustling up. 'Should I order some taxis, do you think?'

Curt looked at him. 'What does Sandy say?'

Devlin took off his glasses, made a show of wiping them. 'Told me not to be so "bloody pragmatic".' He slipped the glasses on again.

'I've got the car,' Rebus said.

'You're okay to drive?' Devlin asked.

'It's not like I've just lost my fucking dad!' Rebus exploded. Then he started to apologise.

'An emotional time for all of us,' Devlin said, waving the apology aside. Then he took his glasses off and started polishing them again, as if the world could never reveal itself too vividly for him.

7

Tuesday at eleven a.m., Siobhan Clarke and Grant Hood started working Victoria Street. They drove up George IV Bridge, forgetting that Victoria Street was one-way. Grant cursed the No Entry sign and rejoined the crawl of traffic heading for the lights at the junction with Lawnmarket.

'Just park kerbside,' Siobhan said. He shook his head. 'Why not?'

'Traffic's hopeless as it is. No use making things worse.'

She laughed. 'Do you always play by the rules, Grant?'

He glanced at her. 'What do you mean?'

'Nothing.'

He didn't say anything, just flipped on the left-turn signal as they stopped three cars back from the lights. Siobhan couldn't help but smile. He had the boy-racer car, but it was all a front, behind which sat a polite wee laddie.

'Going out with anyone just now?' she asked as the lights changed.

He considered his answer. 'Not just at the moment,' he said at last.

'For a while there, I thought maybe you and Ellen Wylie . . .'

'We worked one bloody case together!' he objected.

'Okay, okay. It's just that the pair of you seemed to hit it off.'

'We got along.'

'That's what I mean. So where was the problem?'

His face had reddened. 'What do you mean?'

'I just wondered if the difference in rank was maybe a factor. Some men can't handle it.'

'Because she's a DS and I'm a DC?'

'Yes.'

'The answer's no. Never even thought of it.'

They'd reached the roundabout outside The Hub. The right fork led to the Castle, but they took the left.

'Where are we going?' Siobhan asked.

'I'll take a left along West Port. With any luck we'll find a space in the Grassmarket.'

'And I bet you'll put money in the meter, too.'

'Unless you want the honour.'

She snorted. 'I walk on the wild side, kid,' she said.

They found a parking bay, and Grant dropped a couple of coins into the machine, peeling back the ticket and sticking it to the inside of his windscreen.

'Half an hour long enough?' he asked.

She shrugged. 'Depends what we find.'

They walked past the Last Drop pub, named for the fact that criminals had swung from Grassmarket's scaffold at one time in the city's history. Victoria Street was a steep curve back up to George IV Bridge, lined with bars and gift shops. On the far side of the street, pubs and clubs seemed to predominate. One place doubled as a Cuban bar and restaurant.

'What do you reckon?' Siobhan asked.

'Not too many statues, I wouldn't have thought, unless there's one of Castro.'

They walked the length of the street, then doubled back. Three restaurants this side, along with a cheesemonger and a shop selling nothing but brushes and string. Pierre Victoire was the first stop. Peering through the window, Siobhan could see that it was a fairly empty space with little in the way of decoration. They went in anyway, not bothering to introduce themselves. Ten seconds later they were back on the pavement.

'One down, two to go,' Grant said. He didn't sound hopeful.

Next was a place called the Grain Store, through a doorway and up a flight of stairs. The place was being readied for lunchtime trade. There were no statues.

As they descended to the street, Siobhan repeated the clue. ' "This queen dines well before the bust." ' She shook her head slowly. 'Maybe we've got it wrong.'

'Then the only thing we can do is send another e-mail, appeal to Quizmaster for help.'

'I don't think he's the type.'

Grant shrugged. 'Next stop, can we at least have a coffee? I skipped breakfast this morning.'

Siobhan tutted. 'What would your mum say?'

'She'd say I slept in. Then I'd tell her it's because I was up half the night trying to solve this bloody puzzle.' He paused. 'And that someone had promised me breakfast would be on them . . .'

Restaurant Bleu was their final call. It promised 'world cuisine' but had a traditional feel as they walked through the door: old varnished wood, the small window doing little to illuminate the cramped interior. Siobhan looked around, but there wasn't so much as a vase of flowers.

She turned to Grant, who pointed towards a winding staircase. 'There's an upstairs.'

'Can I help?' the assistant said.

'In a minute,' Grant assured her. He followed Siobhan up the stairs. One small room led to another. As Siobhan entered this second chamber, she gave a sigh. Grant, following her, thought the worst. Then he heard her say, 'Bingo,' in the same instant as he saw the bust. It was Queen Victoria, two and a half feet high, in black marble.

'Bloody hell,' he said, grinning. 'We cracked it!'

He looked ready to hug her, but she moved away towards the bust. It sat on a low plinth, pillars either side and sandwiched by tables. Siobhan looked all around, but couldn't see anything.

'I'll tip it,' Grant said. He took hold of Victoria by her head-dress and eased her from the plinth.

'Excuse me,' a voice said behind them. 'Is something the matter?'

Siobhan slid her hand under the bust and drew out a

folded sheet of paper. She beamed at Grant, who turned towards the waitress.

'Two teas, please,' he instructed her.

'And two sugars in his,' Siobhan added.

They sat down at the nearest table. Siobhan held the note by one corner. 'Think we'd get any prints?' she asked.

'Worth a try.'

She got up and walked over to a cutlery tray in the corner, came back with a knife and fork. The waitress nearly dropped their crockery when she saw the customer attempting, as she thought, to dine on a sheet of paper.

Grant took the cups from the waitress and thanked her. Then he turned back to Siobhan. 'What does it say?'

But Siobhan looked up at the waitress. 'We found this under there,' she said, pointing to the bust. The waitress nodded. 'Any idea how it could have got there?' The waitress shook her head. She had the look of a small, frightened animal. Grant sought to reassure her.

'We're the police,' he said.

'Any chance of talking to the manager?' Siobhan added.

When the waitress had retreated, Grant repeated his earlier question.

'See for yourself,' Siobhan said, using the knife and fork to turn the sheet of paper in his direction.

B4 Scots Law sounds dear.

'Is that it?' he said.

'Your eyes are as good as mine.'

He reached up to scratch his head. 'Not much to go on, is it?'

'We didn't have much to go on last time.'

'We had more than this.'

She watched him stir sugar into his tea. 'If Quizmaster placed this clue here . . .'

'He's a local?' Grant guessed

'Either that or someone local is helping him.'

'He knows this restaurant,' Grant said, looking around. 'Not everyone who ventures in would bother coming upstairs.'

'You think he might be a regular?'

Grant shrugged. 'Look at what's nearby, on George IV Bridge. The Central Library and the National Library. Academics and bookworms are great ones for puzzles.'

'That's a good point. The Museum's not far away either.'

'And the law courts ... and the parliament ...' He smiled. 'Just for a second there I thought we might be narrowing things down.'

'Maybe we are,' she said, lifting her cup as though to make a toast. 'Here's to us anyway for solving the first clue.'

'How many more till we get to Hellbank?'

Siobhan grew thoughtful. 'That's up to Quizmaster, I suppose. He told me it was the fourth stage. I'll send an e-mail when we get back, just to let him know.' She placed the sheet of paper in an evidence bag. Grant was studying the clue again. 'First thoughts?' she asked.

'I was remembering a bit of graffiti from primary school. It was in the boys' toilets.' He wrote it down on the paper serviette.

LOLO
AQIC
I82Q
B4IP

Siobhan read it aloud and smiled. 'Be-fore I pee,' she repeated. 'You think maybe that's what B4 means?'

He shrugged. 'Could be part of an address.'

'Or a coordinate ... ?'

He looked at her. 'From a map?'

'But which one?'

'Maybe that's what the rest of the clue tells us. How's your Scots Law?'

'The exams were a while back.'

'Ditto. Is there some Latin word for "dear", maybe something to do with the law?'

'There's always the library,' she suggested. 'With a big bookshop just past it.'

He checked his watch. 'I'll go put more money in the meter,' he said.

Rebus was at his desk, five sheets of paper spread out in front of him. He'd shifted everything else on to the floor: files, memos, the lot. The office was quiet: most of the shift had headed to Gayfield Square for a briefing. They wouldn't thank him for the obstacle course he'd constructed in their absence. His computer monitor and keyboard now sat in the centre aisle between the rows of desks, just next to his multi-tiered in-tray.

And on his desk, five lives. Five victims, possibly. Caroline Farmer the youngest. Just sixteen when she'd disappeared. He'd finally got through to her mother this morning. Not an easy call to make.

'Oh my God, don't tell me there's news?' That sudden blooming of hope, wizened by his response. But he'd found out what he had to. Caroline had never come back. There had been unconfirmed sightings in the early days, when her photo was in all the papers. But nothing since.

'We moved last year,' her mother said. 'It meant emptying her bedroom . . .'

But for the quarter-century before that, Rebus surmised, Caroline's room had been waiting for her: same posters on the walls, same early-seventies teenage girl's clothes neatly folded in the chest of drawers.

'Back at the time, they seemed to think we'd done something to her,' the mother continued. 'I mean, her own *family.*'

Rebus didn't like to say: all too often it's a father or uncle or cousin.

'Then they started picking on Ronnie.'

'Caroline's boyfriend?' Rebus guessed.

'Yes. Just a laddie.'

'They'd split up, hadn't they?'

'You know what teenagers are like.' It was as though she were talking about events from a week or two back. Rebus didn't doubt that the memories stayed fresh, always ready to torment her waking hours, maybe even the sleeping ones too.

'But he was ruled out?'

'They gave up on him, yes. But he wasn't the same after that, family moved from the area. He wrote to me for a few years . . .'

'Mrs Farmer—'

'It's Ms Colquhoun now. Joe left me.'

'I'm sorry.'

'I wasn't.'

'Did it have . . . ?' He stopped. 'Sorry, none of my business.'

'He never talked much about it,' was all she said. Rebus wondered if Caroline's father had been able to let her go, in a way her mother hadn't.

'This may seem a strange question, Ms Colquhoun, but did Dunfermline Glen have any significance for Caroline?'

'I . . . I'm not sure what you mean.'

'Me neither. It's just that something's come to our attention, and we're wondering if it might tie in with your daughter's disappearance.'

'What is it?'

He didn't suppose she'd take the coffin in the Glen as good news; resorted instead to the old cliché: 'I'm not at liberty to disclose that at present.'

There was silence on the line for a few seconds. 'She liked to walk in the Glen.'

'By herself?'

'When she felt like it.' Her voice caught. 'Is it something you've found?'

'Not the way you think, Ms Colquhoun.'

'You've dug her up, haven't you?'

'Not at all.'

'What then?' she shrieked.

'I'm not at lib—'

She'd put the phone down. He stared at the mouthpiece, then did the same.

In the men's toilets he splashed water on his face. His eyes were grey and puffy. Last night, he'd left Surgeons' Hall and driven to Portobello, parking outside Jean's house. Her lights had been off. He'd got as far as opening the car door, but had stopped. What was he planning to say to her? What was it he wanted? He'd closed the door again as quietly as he could, and just sat there, engine and headlamps off, Hendrix playing quietly: 'The Burning of the Midnight Lamp'.

Back at his desk, one of the station's civvy staff had just arrived with a large cardboard document-box. Rebus lifted the top off and peered inside. The box was actually not quite half full. He pulled out the topmost folder and examined the typed label: Paula Jennifer Gearing (née Mathieson); d.o.b. – 10.4.50; d.o.d. – 6.7.77. The Nairn drowning. Rebus sat down, pulled in his chair and started to read. About twenty minutes in, as he was scribbling another note on a lined A4 pad, Ellen Wylie arrived.

'Sorry I'm late,' she said, shedding her coat.

'We must have different ideas of a start-time,' he said. Remembering what she'd said yesterday, she reddened, but when she glanced in his direction he was smiling.

'What have you got?' she asked.

'Our friends in the north came good.'

'Paula Gearing?'

Rebus nodded. 'She was twenty-seven. Married four years to a husband who worked on a North Sea oil platform. Nice bungalow on the outskirts of town. No kids. She had a part-time job in a newsagent's ... probably for company more than financial necessity.'

Wylie came over to his desk. 'Was foul play ruled out?'

Rebus tapped his notes. 'Nobody could ever explain it, according to what I've read so far. She didn't seem suicidal. Doesn't help that they've no idea whereabouts on the coast she actually entered the water.'

'Pathology report?'

'It's in here. Can you get on to Donald Devlin, see if he can spare us some time?'

'Professor Devlin?'

'He's the person I bumped into yesterday. He's agreed to

study the autopsies for us.' He didn't say anything about the actual circumstances of Devlin's involvement, how Gates and Curt had turned him down. 'His number will be on file,' Rebus said. 'He's one of Philippa Balfour's neighbours.'

'I know. Have you seen this morning's paper?'

'No.'

She fetched it from her bag, opened it to one of the inside pages. A photofit: the man Devlin had seen outside the tenement on the days preceding Philippa's disappearance.

'Could be anybody,' Rebus said.

Wylie nodded agreement. Short dark hair, straight nose, narrowed eyes and a thin line of a mouth. 'We're getting desperate, aren't we?' she said.

It was Rebus's turn to nod. Releasing the photofit to the media, especially one as clearly generalised as this, was an act of desperation. 'Get on to Devlin,' he said.

'Yes, sir.'

She took the newspaper with her, sat down at a spare desk and gave her head a little shake, as if clearing the cobwebs. Then she picked up the telephone, preparing to make the first call of another long day.

Rebus went back to his reading, but not for long. A name leaped out at him, the name of one of the police officers involved in the Nairn inquiry.

A detective inspector with the surname Watson.

The Farmer.

'Sorry to bother you, sir.'

The Farmer smiled, slapped a hand on Rebus's back. 'You don't have to call me "sir" any more, John.'

He gestured for Rebus to precede him down the hall. It was a farmhouse conversion just south of the bypass. The interior walls were painted a pale green and the furniture was fifties and sixties vintage. A wall had been knocked through so that the kitchen was separated from the living room only by a breakfast bar and dining area. The dining table gleamed. The kitchen's work surfaces were similarly clean, and the hob was spotless, not a dish or dirty pot in sight.

'Fancy a cuppa?' the Farmer asked.

'Some tea would go down.'

The Farmer chuckled. 'My coffee always scared you off, didn't it?'

'You got better at it towards the end.'

'Sit yourself down. I'll not be long.'

But Rebus made a circuit of the living room. Glass-fronted cabinets with china and ornaments behind. Framed photos of family. Rebus recognised a couple which until recently had graced the Farmer's office. The carpet had been vacuumed, the mirror and TV showed no signs of dust. Rebus walked over to the french doors and gazed out at a short expanse of garden which ended with a steep grassy bank.

'Maid been in today, has she?' he called.

The Farmer chuckled again, setting a tea-tray out on the worktop. 'I enjoy a bit of housework,' he called. 'Ever since Arlene passed away.'

Rebus turned, looked back at the framed photos. The Farmer and his wife at someone's wedding, and on some foreign beach, and with a gathering of grandchildren. The Farmer beaming, mouth always slightly open. His wife a little more reserved, maybe a foot shorter than him and half his weight. She'd died a few years back.

'Maybe it's my way of remembering her,' the Farmer said.

Rebus nodded: not letting go. He wondered if her clothes were still in the wardrobe, her jewellery in a box on the dressing table . . .

'How's Gill settling in?'

Rebus moved towards the kitchen. 'She's off to a flyer,' he said. 'Ordered me to take a medical, and got on the wrong side of Ellen Wylie.'

'I saw that news conference,' the Farmer admitted, studying the tray to make sure he'd not forgotten anything. 'Gill didn't give Ellen time to find her feet.'

'Purposely so,' Rebus added.

'Perhaps.'

'It's funny, not having you around, sir.' Rebus laid stress on the last word. The Farmer smiled.

'Thanks for that, John.' He walked over to the kettle, which was beginning to boil. 'All the same, I'm assuming this isn't a purely sentimental visit.'

'No. It's about a case you worked on in Nairn.'

'Nairn?' The Farmer raised an eyebrow. 'That's twenty-odd years ago. I went up there from West Lothian. I was based in Inverness.'

'Yes, but you went to Nairn to look into a drowning.'

The Farmer was thoughtful. 'Oh yes,' he said at last. 'What was her name?'

'Paula Gearing.'

'Gearing, that's right.' He snapped his fingers, keen not to seem forgetful. 'But it was cut and dried, wasn't it ... if you'll pardon the expression.'

'I'm not so sure, sir.' Rebus watched the Farmer pour water into the teapot.

'Well, let's take this lot through to the lounge, and you can tell me all about it.'

So Rebus told the story again: the doll in Falls, then the Arthur's Seat mystery, and the cluster of drownings and disappearances from 1972 to '95. He'd brought the cuttings with him, and the Farmer studied them intently.

'I didn't even know about the doll on Nairn beach,' he admitted. 'I was back in Inverness by then. As far as I was concerned, the Gearing death was as closed as it was ever likely to get.'

'Nobody made the connection at the time. Paula's body had been washed ashore four miles out of town. If anyone thought anything of it, they probably took it as some kind of memorial to her.' He paused. 'Gill's not convinced there's a connection.'

The Farmer nodded. 'She's thinking of how it would play in a court of law. Everything you've got here is circum-stantial.'

'I know.'

'All the same . . .' The Farmer leaned back. 'It's quite a set of circumstances.'

Rebus's shoulders relaxed. The Farmer seemed to notice, and smiled. 'Bad timing, isn't it, John? I manage to go into retirement just before you convince me that you may have stumbled upon something.'

'Maybe you could have a word with Gill, convince her likewise.'

The Farmer shook his head. 'I don't think she'd listen. She's in charge now . . . she knows fine well my usefulness is over.'

'That's a bit harsh.'

The Farmer looked at him. 'But you know it's true all the same. She's the one you have to convince, not an old man sitting in his slippers.'

'You're barely ten years older than me.'

'As I hope you'll live to find, John, your sixties are very different from your fifties. Maybe that medical wouldn't be such a bad idea, eh?'

'Even if I already know what he'll say?' Rebus lifted his cup and finished the tea.

The Farmer had picked up the Nairn clipping again. 'What do you want me to do?'

'You said the case was cut and dried. Maybe you could think about that, see if anything at the time jarred – anything at all, no matter how small or seemingly incidental.' He paused. 'I was also going to ask if you knew what had happened to the doll.'

'But now you know the doll's come as news to me.'

Rebus nodded.

'You want all five dolls, don't you?' the Farmer asked.

Rebus admitted as much. 'It might be the only way to prove they're connected.'

'Meaning whoever left that first one, back in nineteen seventy-two, also left one for Philippa Balfour?'

Rebus nodded again.

'If anyone can do it, John, you can. I've always had

confidence in your sheer pig-headedness and inability to listen to your senior officers.'

Rebus placed his cup back on its saucer. 'I'll take that as a compliment,' he said. Looking around the room again, preparing to rise and make his farewells, he was struck by something. This house was the only thing the Farmer controlled now. He brought order to it the way he'd controlled St Leonard's. And if he ever lost the will power or the ability to keep it in shape, he'd curl up his toes and die.

'This is hopeless,' Siobhan Clarke said.

They'd spent the best part of three hours in the Central Library, followed by nearly fifty quid at a bookshop, buying maps and touring guides of Scotland. Now they were in the Elephant House coffee-shop, having commandeered a table meant for six. It was right below the window at the back of the café, and Grant Hood was staring out at the view of Greyfriars Churchyard and the Castle.

Siobhan looked at him. 'Have you switched off?'

He kept his eyes on the view. 'You have to sometimes.'

'Well, thanks for your support.' It came out more huffily than she'd expected.

'Best thing you can do,' he went on, ignoring her tone. 'There are days when I get stuck with the crossword. I don't go knocking my brains out. I just put it to one side and pick it up again later. And often I find that one or two answers come to me straight away. Thing is,' now he turned towards her, 'you fix your mind on a certain track, until eventually you can't see all the alternatives.' He got up, walked over to where the café kept its newspapers, and came back with that day's *Scotsman*. 'Peter Bee,' he said, folding it so the crossword on the back page was uppermost. 'He's cryptic, but doesn't depend on anagrams the way some of the others do.'

He handed her the paper and she saw that Peter Bee was the name of the crossword's compiler.

'Twelve across,' Grant said, 'he had me looking for the

name of an old Roman weapon. But all it was in the end was an anagram.'

'Very interesting,' Siobhan said, tossing the paper on to the table, where it covered the half-dozen map-books.

'I'm just trying to explain that sometimes you have to clear your mind for a while, start again from scratch.'

She glared at him. 'Are you saying we've just wasted half the day?'

He shrugged.

'Well, thanks very much!' She pulled herself out of her chair and stomped off to the toilets. Inside, she stood leaning against the wash-bowl, staring down at its bright white surface. The sod was, she knew Grant was right. But she couldn't let go the way he could. She'd wanted to play the game, and now it had drawn her in. She wondered if Flip Balfour had become obsessed in much the same way. If she'd got stuck, would she have asked for help? Siobhan reminded herself that she had yet to ask any of Flip's friends or family about the game. No one had mentioned it in the dozens of interviews, but then why would they? Maybe to them it had just been a bit of fun, a computer game. Nothing to get worked up about . . .

Gill Templer had offered her the Press Liaison job, but only after engineering the ritual humiliation of Ellen Wylie. It would be nice to feel she'd rejected the offer out of a sense of solidarity with Wylie, but that had had nothing to do with it. Siobhan herself feared that it was more the influence of John Rebus. She'd worked beside him for several years now, coming to understand his strengths as well as his faults. And when it came down to it, like a lot of other officers she preferred the maverick approach, and wished she could be like that. But the force itself had other ideas. There could be room for only one Rebus, and meantime advancement was hers for the taking. Okay, so it would land her squarely in Gill Templer's camp: she'd follow orders, back her boss up, never take risks. And she would be safe, would continue to rise through the ranks . . . Detective Inspector, then maybe DCI by the time she was forty. She saw now that Gill had invited her to drinks and dinner that evening to show her how it was done. You cultivated the right friends, you treated them well. You were patient, and the rewards came. One lesson for Ellen Wylie, and a very different one for her.

Back out in the café, she watched as Grant Hood completed the crossword and threw the paper back down, leaning back in his seat and nonchalantly slipping his pen into his pocket. He was trying hard not to look at the table next to him, where a lone female coffee-drinker had been appraising his performance over the top of her paperback book.

Siobhan started forwards. 'Thought you'd already done that one?' she said, nodding towards the *Scotsman*.

'Easier the second time,' he answered in a voice which, had it been any more of an undertone, would have leapt up and broken into the chorus of 'Teenage Kicks'. 'Why are you grinning like that?'

The woman had gone back to her book. It was something by Muriel Spark. 'I was just remembering an old song,' Siobhan said.

Grant looked at her, but she wasn't about to enlighten him, so he reached a hand out and touched the crossword. 'Know what a homonym is?'

'No, but it sounds rude.'

'It's when a word sounds like another word. Crosswords use them all the time. There's even one in today's, and second time around it got me thinking.'

'Thinking what?'

'About our latest clue. "Sounds dear": we were thinking of "dear" meaning expensive or cherished, right?'

Siobhan nodded.

'But it could be a homonym, signalled by "sounds".'

'I'm not following.' But she'd tucked one leg beneath her and leaned forward, interested.

'It could be telling us that the word we want isn't d-e-a-r but d-e-e-r.'

She frowned. 'So we end up with "B4 Scots Law deer"? Is it just me, or does that actually make less sense than before?'

He shrugged, turned his attention to the window again. 'If you say so.'

She slapped at his leg. 'Don't be like that.'

'You think you're the only one who can take a moody?'

'I'm sorry.'

He looked at her. She was smiling again. 'That's better,' he said. 'Now ... wasn't there some story about how Holyrood got its name? One of the ancient kings shooting arrows at a deer?'

'Search me.'

'Excuse me.' The voice came from the table next to them. 'I couldn't help overhearing.' The woman put her book down on the table. 'It was David the First, back in the twelfth century.'

'Was it now?' Siobhan said.

The woman ignored her tone. 'He was out hunting when a stag pinned him to the ground. He reached for its antlers only to find that it had vanished and in its place he was holding a cross. Holy rood means holy cross. David saw it as a sign and built the abbey of Holyrood.'

'Thank you,' Grant Hood said. The woman bowed her head and went back to her book. 'Nice to see an educated person,' he added, for Siobhan's benefit. She narrowed her eyes and wrinkled her nose at him. 'So it might have something to do with the Palace of Holyrood.'

'One of the rooms could be called B4,' Siobhan said. 'Like a school classroom.'

He saw that she wasn't being serious. 'There could be part of Scots Law relating to Holyrood – it would make another royal connection, like Victoria.'

Siobhan unfolded her arms. 'Could be,' she conceded.

'So all we have to do is find ourselves a friendly lawyer.'

'Would someone from the Procurator Fiscal's office do?' Siobhan asked. 'If so, I might know just the person ...'

The Sheriff Court was in a new building on Chambers Street, just across from the museum complex. Grant dashed back down to Grassmarket to feed coins to the meter, despite

Siobhan's protestation that it'd have been cheaper getting a fine slapped on him. She went on ahead and asked around the court until she'd located Harriet Brough. The lawyer was wearing yet another tweed two-piece with grey stockings and flat black shoes. Shapely ankles though, Siobhan couldn't help noticing.

'My dear girl, this is splendid,' Brough said, taking Siobhan's hand and working her arm as if it were a waterpump. 'Simply splendid.' Siobhan noted that the elder woman's make-up served merely to heighten her wrinkles and the folds of skin, and gave her face a garish pall.

'I hope I'm not disturbing you,' Siobhan began.

'Not in the slightest.' They were in the court's main entrance hall, busy with ushers and lawyers, security staff and worried-looking families. Elsewhere in the building, guilt and innocence were being judged, sentences handed down. 'Are you here for a trial?'

'No, I just had a question and I wondered if you might be able to help.'

'I'd be delighted to.'

'It's a note I've found. It might relate to a case, but it seems to be in some sort of code.'

The lawyer's eyes widened. 'How exciting,' she gasped. 'Let's just grab somewhere to sit and then you can tell me all about it.'

They found a free bench and sat down. Brough read the note through its polythene jacket. Siobhan watched as she mouthed the words silently, her brow creasing.

'I'm sorry,' she said at last. 'Maybe the context would help.'

'It's a missing person inquiry,' Siobhan explained. 'We think she may have been taking part in a game.'

'And you need to solve this to reach the next stage? How very curious.'

Grant Hood arrived, breathing heavily. Siobhan introduced him to Harriet Brough.

'Anything?' he asked. Siobhan just shook her head. He

looked towards the lawyer. 'B4 doesn't mean anything in Scots Law? Some paragraph or sub-section?'

'My dear boy,' Brough laughed, 'there could be several hundred examples, though they'd more likely be 4B rather than B4. We use numerals first, as a general rule.'

Hood nodded. 'So it would be "paragraph 4, sub-section b"?'

'Exactly.'

'The first clue,' Siobhan added, 'had a royal connection. The answer was Victoria. We're wondering if this one might have something to do with Holyrood.' She explained her reasoning, and Brough took another look at the note.

'Well, the pair of you are cleverer than I am,' she conceded. 'Maybe my lawyer's mind is too literal.' She made to hand the note to Siobhan, but then snatched it back again. 'I wonder if the phrase "Scots Law" is there to put you off the scent.'

'How do you mean?' Siobhan asked.

'It's just that if the clue is meant to be wilfully obscure, then whoever wrote it might have been thinking laterally.'

Siobhan looked to Hood, who merely shrugged. Brough was pointing to the note.

'Something I learned from my hill-walking days,' she said, 'is that "law" is the Scots word for a hill . . .'

Rebus was on the phone to the manager of the Hunting-tower Hotel.

'So it might be in storage?' he asked.

'I'm not sure,' the manager said.

'Could you take a look? Maybe ask around, see if anyone knows?'

'It could have been thrown out during a refit.'

'That's the sort of positive attitude I thrive on, Mr Ballantine.'

'Maybe the person who found it . . .'

'He says he handed it in.' Rebus had already called the *Courier* and spoken with the reporter who'd covered the case. The reporter had been curious, and Rebus had admitted that another coffin had turned up in Edinburgh, while stressing that any connection was 'the longest shot in history'. Last thing he wanted was the media sniffing around. The reporter had given him the name of the man whose dog had found the coffin. A couple of calls later, Rebus had traced the man, only to be told that he'd left the coffin at Huntingtower and had thought no more about it.

'Well,' the manager was saying now, 'I won't make any promises . . .'

'Let me know as soon as you find it,' Rebus said, repeating his name and phone number. 'It's a matter of urgency, Mr Ballantine.'

'I'll do what I can,' the manager said with a sigh.

Rebus broke the connection and looked across to the other desk, where Ellen Wylie was seated with Donald Devlin. Devlin was dressed in another old cardigan, this time with most of its buttons intact. Between the pair of them, they were trying to track down the autopsy notes from the Glasgow drowning. By the look on Wylie's face they were having little luck. Devlin, whose chair was side by side with hers, kept leaning in towards her as she spoke on the phone. He might just have been trying to catch what was being said, but Rebus could see Wylie didn't like it. She kept trying to move her chair surreptitiously, angling her body so she presented a lot of shoulder and back to the pathologist. So far, she'd avoided eye contact with Rebus.

He made a note to himself about Huntingtower, then got back on the phone. The Glasgow coffin was more awkward. The reporter who'd covered the story had moved on. Nobody at the news desk could remember anything about it. Rebus eventually got a number for the church manse and spoke to a Reverend Martine.

'Have you any idea what happened to the coffin?' Rebus asked.

'I think the journalist took it,' Reverend Martine said.

So Rebus thanked him and got back to the newspaper, where he was able eventually to speak to the editor, who wanted to hear Rebus's own story. So he explained about the 'Edinburgh coffin' and how he was working for the Department of Long Shots.

'This Edinburgh coffin, where was it found exactly?'

'Near the Castle,' Rebus said blithely. He could almost see the editor writing a note to himself, maybe thinking of following the story up.

After another minute or so, Rebus was transferred to personnel, where he was given a forwarding address for the journalist, whose name was Jenny Gabriel. It was a London address.

'She went to work for one of the broadsheets,' the personnel manager stated. 'It was what Jenny always wanted.'

So Rebus went out and bought coffee, cakes and four newspapers: *The Times*, *Telegraph*, *Guardian* and *Independent*. He went through each, studying the by-lines, but didn't find Jenny Gabriel's name. Undaunted, he called each paper and asked for her by name. At the third attempt, the switchboard asked him to hold. He glanced across to where Devlin was dropping cake crumbs on to Wylie's desk.

'Transferring you now.'

The sweetest words Rebus had heard all day. Then the call was picked up.

'News desk.'

'Jenny Gabriel, please,' Rebus said.

'Speaking.'

And it was time for the spiel again.

'My God,' the reporter said at last, 'that was twenty years ago!'

'Just about,' Rebus agreed. 'I don't suppose you still have the doll?'

'No, I don't.' Rebus felt his heart sink a little. 'When I moved south, I gave it to a friend. He'd always been fascinated by it.'

'Any chance you could put me in touch with him?'

'Hang on, I'll get his number ...' There was a pause. Rebus spent the time working loose the mechanism of his ballpoint pen. He realised he had only the vaguest idea how such a pen worked. Spring, casing, refill . . . he could take it to pieces, put it back together again, and be none the wiser.

'He's in Edinburgh actually,' Jenny Gabriel said. Then she gave him a number. The friend's name was Dominic Mann.

'Many thanks,' Rebus said, cutting the call. Dominic Mann wasn't home, but his answering machine gave Rebus a mobile number to try. The call was picked up.

'Hello?'

'Is that Dominic Mann . . . ?' And Rebus was off again. This time getting the result he wanted. Mann still owned the coffin, and could drop it into St Leonard's later on in the day.

'I'd really appreciate that,' Rebus said. 'Funny thing to hold on to all these years . . . ?'

'I was planning to use it in one of my installations.'

'Installations?'

'I'm an artist. At least, I was. These days I run a gallery.'

'You still paint?'

'Infrequently. Just as well I didn't end up using it. It might have been wrapped in paint and bandages and sold to some collector.'

Rebus thanked the artist and put down the phone. Devlin had finished his cake. Wylie had put hers to one side, and the old man was eyeing it now. The Nairn coffin was easier: two calls got Rebus the result he wanted. He was told by a reporter that he'd do some digging, and was called back with the number of someone in Nairn, who then did some digging of their own and found the coffin stored in a neighbour's shed.

'You want me to post it to you?'

'Yes, please,' Rebus said. 'Next-day delivery.' He'd thought of sending a car, but didn't think the budget would stretch. There'd been memos flying on the subject.

'What about the postage?'

'Enclose your details and I'll see you get a refund.'

The caller thought about this. 'Seems all right, I suppose. Just have to trust you, won't I?'

'If you can't trust the police, who can you trust?'

He put down the phone and looked across to Wylie's desk again. 'Anything?' he asked.

'Getting there,' she said, her voice tired and irritated. Devlin got up, crumbs tumbling from his lap, and asked where the 'facilities' were. Rebus pointed him in the right direction. Devlin started to leave, but paused in front of Rebus.

'I can't tell you how much I'm enjoying this.'

'Glad someone's happy, Professor.'

Devlin prodded Rebus's jacket lapel with a finger. 'I think *you're* in your element.' He beamed, and shuffled out of the room. Rebus walked across to Wylie's desk.

'Better eat that cake, if you don't want him drooling.'

She considered this, then broke the cake in two and stuffed half into her mouth.

'I got a result on the dolls,' he told her. 'Two traced, with another possible.'

She took a gulp of coffee, washing down the sugary sponge. 'Doing better than us then.' She studied the remaining half of the cake, then dropped it into the bin. 'No offence,' she said.

'Professor Devlin will be gutted.'

'That's what I'm hoping.'

'He's here to help, remember?'

She stared at him. 'He smells.'

'Does he?'

'You've not noticed?'

'Can't say I have.'

She looked at him as though this comment said much about him. Then her shoulders fell. 'Why did you ask for me? I'm useless. All those reporters and TV viewers saw it. Everybody knows it. Have you got a thing about cripples or what?'

'My daughter's a cripple,' he said quietly.

Her face reddened. 'Christ, I didn't mean . . .'

'But to answer your question, the only person around here who seems to have a problem with Ellen Wylie is Ellen Wylie herself.'

Her hand had gone to her face, as if trying to force the blood back down. 'Tell that to Gill Templer,' she said at last.

'Gill ballsed things up. It's not the end of the world.' His phone was ringing. He started backing towards his desk. 'Okay?' he said. When she nodded, he turned away and answered the call. It was Huntingtower. They'd found the coffin in a cellar used for lost property. A couple of decades' worth of umbrellas and pairs of spectacles, hats and coats and cameras.

'Amazing, the stuff down there,' Mr Ballantine said. But all Rebus was interested in was the coffin.

'Can you post it next-day delivery? I'll see you get a refund . . .'

By the time Devlin came back in, Rebus was on the trail of the Dunfermline coffin, but this time he hit a wall. Nobody – local press, police – seemed to know what had happened to it. Rebus got a couple of promises that questions would be asked, but he didn't hold out much hope. Nearly thirty years had passed; unlikely it would turn up. At the other desk, Devlin was clapping his hands silently as Wylie finished another call. She looked across to Rebus.

'Post-mortem report on Hazel Gibbs is on its way,' she said. Rebus held her gaze for a few moments, then nodded slowly and smiled. His phone went again. This time it was Siobhan.

'I'm going to talk to David Costello,' she said. 'If you're not doing anything.'

'I thought you'd paired up with Grant?'

'DCS Templer has snared him for a couple of hours.'

'Has she now? Maybe she's offering him your liaison job.'

'I refuse to let you wind me up. Now, are you coming or not . . . ?'

Costello was in his flat. When he opened the door to them, he looked startled. Siobhan assured him that it wasn't bad news. He didn't seem to believe her.

'Can we come in, David?' Rebus asked. Costello looked at him for the first time, then nodded slowly. To Rebus's eyes, he was wearing the same clothes as on his last visit, and the living room didn't seem to have been tidied in the interim. The young man was growing a beard, too, but seemed self-conscious, rubbing his fingertips against its grain.

'Is there any news at all?' he asked, slumping on to the futon, while Rebus and Siobhan stayed standing.

'Bits and pieces,' Rebus said.

'But you can't go into details?' Costello kept shifting, trying to get comfortable.

'Actually, David,' Siobhan said, 'the details – some of them at least – are the reason we're here.' She handed him a sheet of paper.

'What's this?' he asked.

'It's the first clue from a game. A game we think Flip was playing.'

Costello sat forward, looked at the message again. 'What sort of game?'

'Something she found on the Internet. It's run by someone called Quizmaster. Solving each clue takes the player to a new level. Flip was working on a level called Hellbank. Maybe she'd solved it, we don't know.'

'Flip?' Costello sounded sceptical.

'You've never heard of it?'

He shook his head. 'She didn't say a word.' He looked across towards Rebus, but Rebus had picked up a poetry book.

'Was she interested in games at all?' Siobhan asked.

Costello shrugged. 'Dinner-party stuff. You know: charades and the like. Maybe Trivial Pursuit or Taboo.'

'But not fantasy games? Role-playing?'

He shook his head slowly.

'Nothing on the Internet?'

He rubbed at his bristles again. 'This is news to me.' He looked from Siobhan to Rebus and back again. 'You're *sure* this was Flip?'

'We're pretty sure,' Siobhan stated.

'And you think it has something to do with her disappearance?'

Siobhan just shrugged, and glanced in Rebus's direction, wondering if he had anything to add. But Rebus was busy with his own thoughts. He was remembering what Flip Balfour's mother had said about Costello, about how he'd turned Flip against her family. And when Rebus had asked why, she'd said: *Because of who he is.*

'Interesting poem, this,' he said, waving the book. It was more of a pamphlet really, pink cover with a line-drawing illustration. Then he recited a couple of lines:

' "You do not die for being bad, you die
For being available." '

Rebus closed the book, put it down. 'I'd never thought of it like that before,' he said, 'but it's true.' He paused to light a cigarette. 'Do you remember when we talked, David?' He inhaled, then thought to offer the packet to Costello, who shook his head. The half-bottle of whisky was empty, as were half a dozen cans of lager. Rebus could see them on the floor near the kitchen, along with mugs, plates and forks, the wrappings from takeaway food. He hadn't taken Costello for a drinker; maybe he'd have to revise that opinion. 'I asked you if Flip might have met someone, and you said something about how she'd have told you. You said she couldn't keep things to herself.'

Costello was nodding.

'And yet here's this game she was playing. Not an easy game either, lots of puzzles and word-play. She might have needed help.'

'She didn't get it from me.'

'And she never mentioned the Internet, or anyone called Quizmaster?'

He shook his head. 'Who is he anyway, this Quizmaster?'

'We don't know,' Siobhan admitted. She'd walked over to the bookshelf.

'But he should come forward, surely?'

'We'd like him to.' Siobhan lifted the toy soldier from the shelf. 'This is a gaming piece, isn't it?'

Costello turned his head to look. 'Is it?'

'You don't play?'

182

'I'm not even sure where it came from.'

'Been in the wars though,' Siobhan said, studying the broken musket.

Rebus looked over to where Costello's own computer – a laptop – sat ready and waiting. There were textbooks on the worktop next to it, and on the floor underneath a printer. 'I take it you're on the Internet yourself, David?' he asked.

'Isn't everybody?'

Siobhan forced a smile, put the toy soldier back. 'DI Rebus here is still wrestling with electric typewriters.'

Rebus saw what she was doing: trying to soften Costello up, using Rebus as the comedy prop.

'To me,' he said, 'the Internet is what the Milan goalie tries to defend.'

This got a smile from Costello. *Because of who he is* . . . But who was David Costello really? Rebus was beginning to wonder.

'If Flip kept this from you, David,' Siobhan was saying now, 'might there be other things she kept secret?'

Costello nodded again. He was still shifting on the futon, as if he'd never again be at rest. 'Maybe I didn't know her at all,' he conceded. He studied the clue again. 'What does it mean, do you know?'

'Siobhan worked it out,' Rebus admitted. 'But all it did was lead her to a second clue.'

Siobhan handed over the copy of the second note. 'It makes less sense than the first,' Costello said. 'I really can't believe it of Flip. It's not her sort of thing at all.' He made to hand the note back.

'What about her other friends?' Siobhan asked. 'Do any of them like games, puzzles?'

Costello's eyes fixed on her. 'You think one of them could . . . ?'

'All I'm wondering is whether Flip might have gone to anyone else for help.'

Costello was thoughtful. 'No one,' he said at last. 'No one I can think of.' Siobhan took the second note from him.

'What about this one?' he asked. 'Do you know what it means?'

She looked at the clue for maybe the fortieth time. 'No,' she admitted. 'Not yet.'

Afterwards, Siobhan drove Rebus back to St Leonard's. They were silent for the first few minutes. Traffic was bad. The evening rush hour seemed to start earlier with each passing week.

'What do you think?' Siobhan asked.

'I think we'd have been quicker walking.'

It was pretty much the response she'd expected. 'Your dolls in boxes, there's a playful quality to them, isn't there?'

'Bloody queer game, if you ask me.'

'Every bit as queer as running a quiz over the Internet.'

Rebus nodded, but didn't say anything.

'I don't want to be the one seeing a connection here,' Siobhan added.

'My department?' Rebus guessed. 'The potential's there though, isn't it?'

It was Siobhan's turn to nod. '*If* all the dolls link up.'

'Give us time,' Rebus said. 'Meanwhile, a bit of background on Mr Costello might be in order.'

'He seemed genuine enough to me. That look on his face when he answered the door, he was terrified something had happened. Besides, background check's already been done, hasn't it?'

'Doesn't mean we didn't miss anything. If I remember rightly, Hi-Ho Silvers was given the job, and that bugger's so lazy he thinks sloth's an Olympic sport.' He half turned towards her. 'What about you?'

'I try to at least *look* like I'm doing something.'

'I mean what are you going to do now?'

'I think I'm going to head home. Call it a day.'

'Better be careful, DCS Templer likes her officers to put in a full eight hours.'

'In that case she owes me . . . and you too, I shouldn't wonder. When was the last time you only worked an eight-hour shift?'

'September, nineteen eighty-six,' Rebus said, raising a smile.

'How's the flat coming on?'

'Rewiring's all but finished. The painters are moving in now.'

'Found somewhere to buy?'

He shook his head. 'It's bugging you, isn't it?'

'If you want to sell up, that's your decision.'

He gave her a sour look. 'You know what I mean.'

'Quizmaster?' She considered her answer. 'I could almost enjoy it . . .'

'If?'

'If I didn't get the sense that he's enjoying it too.'

'By manipulating you?'

Siobhan nodded. 'And if he's doing it to me, he did it to Philippa Balfour too.'

'You keep assuming it's a "he",' Rebus said.

'For convenience only.' There was the sound of a mobile. 'Mine,' Siobhan said, as Rebus reached into his own pocket. Her phone was attached to its own little charger beside the car stereo. Siobhan pressed a button, and an inbuilt microphone and speaker did the rest.

'Hands-free,' Rebus said, impressed.

'Hello?' Siobhan called out.

'Is that DC Clarke?'

She recognised the voice. 'Mr Costello? What can I do for you?'

'I was just thinking . . . what you were saying about games and stuff?'

'Yes?'

'Well, I do know someone who's into all that. Rather, Flip knows someone.'

'What's their name?'

Siobhan glanced towards Rebus, but he already had his notepad and pen ready.

David Costello said the name, but his voice broke up halfway through. 'Sorry,' Siobhan said. 'Could you give me that again?'

This time they both caught the name loud and clear: 'Ranald Marr.' Siobhan frowned, mouthing the name silently. Rebus nodded. He knew exactly who Ranald Marr was: John Balfour's business partner, the man who ran Balfour's Bank in Edinburgh.

The office was quiet. Officers had either clocked off, or were in meetings at Gayfield Square. There'd be shoe-leather patrols out there too, but scaled down now. There was almost no one left to interview. Another day without any sighting of Philippa, and no word from her, no sign that she was still alive. Credit cards and bank balance untouched, friends and family uncontacted. Nothing. Word around the station was, Bill Pryde had thrown a wobbly, sent his clipboard sailing across the open-plan office so that staff had to duck to avoid it. John Balfour had been putting the pressure on, giving media interviews critical of the lack of progress. The Chief Constable had asked for a status report from the ACC, which meant the ACC was on *everyone's* back. In the absence of any new leads, they were interviewing people for the second or third time. Everyone was jittery, frayed. Rebus tried calling Bill Pryde at Gayfield, but couldn't get through. He then placed a call to the Big House and asked to speak to Claverhouse or Ormiston in Crime Squad, Number 2 Branch. Claverhouse picked up.

'It's Rebus here. I need a favour.'

'And what makes you think I'd be daft enough to oblige?'

'Are your questions always this tough?'

'Bugger off back under your rock, Rebus.'

'Nothing I'd like better, but your mum's adopted it, says it loves her more than you ever did.' It was the only way to deal with Claverhouse: sarcasm at twelve paces.

'She's right, I'm a mean bastard at heart, which brings me back to my first question.'

'The tough one? Let's put it this way then: sooner you help me, sooner I can hit the pub and drink myself unconscious.'

'Christ, man, why didn't you say? Fire away.'

Rebus smiled into the receiver. 'I need an in.'

'Who with?'

'The *gardai* in Dublin.'

'Whatever for?'

'Philippa Balfour's boyfriend. I want a background check.'

'I put a tenner on him at two-to-one.'

'Best reason I can think of for helping me out.'

Claverhouse was thoughtful. 'Give me fifteen minutes. Don't move from that number.'

'I'll be here.'

Rebus put the phone down and sat back in his chair. Then he noticed something across the room. It was the Farmer's old chair. Gill must have turfed it out only for someone to claim it. Rebus wheeled it over to his own desk, made himself comfortable. He thought about what he'd said to Claverhouse: *sooner I can hit the pub and drink myself unconscious*. It had been part of the routine, but a large chunk of him wanted it anyway, wanted that hazy oblivion that only drink could provide. Oblivion: the name of one of Brian Auger's bands, Oblivion Express. He had their first album somewhere, *A Better Land*. A bit too jazzy for his taste. When the phone rang, he picked it up, but it was still ringing: his mobile. He fished it from his pocket, put it to his ear.

'Hello?'

'John?'

'Hello, Jean. I was meaning to call you.'

'Is this an all right time?'

'Sure. Has that journo been hassling you?' His desk phone started ringing: Claverhouse probably. Rebus got up from the Farmer's chair, walked across the office and out of the door.

'Nothing I can't handle,' Jean was saying. 'I've been doing a bit of digging, as you asked. I'm afraid I haven't found very much.'

'Never mind.'

'Well, it's taken me all day . . .'

'I'll have a look at it tomorrow, if that's all right with you.'

'Tomorrow would be fine.'

'Unless you're free tonight . . . ?'

'Oh.' She paused. 'I promised a friend I'd go see her. She's just had a baby.'

'That's nice.'

'I'm sorry.'

'Don't be. We'll meet tomorrow. Are you okay to come to the station?'

'Yes.'

They agreed a time and Rebus went back into the CID room, ending the call. He got the feeling she was pleased with him, pleased that he'd asked to meet this evening. It was what she'd been hoping for, some hint that he was still interested, that it wasn't just work for him.

Or he could be reading too much into it.

Back at his desk, he called Claverhouse.

'I'm a disappointed man,' Claverhouse said.

'I told you I wouldn't leave my desk, and I stuck to my word.'

'Then how come you didn't pick up the phone?'

'Someone caught me on my mobile.'

'Someone who means more to you than I do? Now I really am hurt.'

'It was my bookie. I owe him two hundred notes.'

Claverhouse was silent for a moment. 'This cheers me immensely,' he said. 'Right, the person you want to speak to is Declan Macmanus.'

Rebus frowned. 'Wasn't that Elvis Costello's real name?'

'Well, he obviously passed it on to someone in need.' Claverhouse gave Rebus the number in Dublin, including the international code. 'Not that I suppose the cheap bastards at St Leonard's will let you make an international call.'

'Forms will have to be filled in,' Rebus agreed. 'Thanks for your help, Claverhouse.'

'Are you going for that drink now?'

'I think I better had. Don't want to be conscious when my bookie finds me.'

'You have a point. Here's to bad horses and good whisky.'

'And vice versa,' Rebus rejoined, ending the call. Claverhouse was right: the main phones at St Leonard's were blocked for international calls, but Rebus had the feeling the Chief Super's phone would be okay. Only problem was, Gill had locked her door. Rebus thought for a second, then remembered that the Farmer had kept a spare key for emergencies. He crouched down at Gill's office door and peeled back the corner of carpet next to the jamb. Bingo: the Yale was still there. He inserted it into the lock and was inside her office, door closed after him.

He looked at her new chair but decided to stay standing, resting against the edge of her desk. He couldn't help thinking of the Three Bears: who's been sitting in my chair? And who's been making calls from my phone?

His call was answered after half a dozen rings. 'Can I speak to . . .' he suddenly realised that he didn't have a rank for Macmanus . . . 'to Declan Macmanus, please.'

'Who shall I say is calling?' The woman's voice had that seductive Irish lilt. Rebus imagined raven hair and a full body.

'Detective Inspector John Rebus, Lothian and Borders Police in Scotland.'

'Hold, please.'

While he held, the full body had become a pint of slow-poured Guinness, the beer seemingly shaped to fit its glass.

'DI Rebus?' The voice was crisp, no-nonsense.

'DI Claverhouse at the Scottish Crime Squad gave me your number.'

'That was generous of him.'

'Sometimes he just can't help himself.'

'And what can I do for you?'

'I don't know if you've heard about this case we've got, a MisPer called Philippa Balfour.'

'The banker's daughter? It's been all over the papers here.'

'Because of the connection with David Costello?'

'The Costellos are well known, Inspector, part of the Dublin social fabric, you might say.'

'You'd know better than me, which is the reason I'm calling.'

'Ah, is it now?'

'I want to know a bit more about the family.' Rebus started doodling on a sheet of paper. 'I'm sure they're blemish-free, but it would put my mind at rest if I had some evidence of that.'

'As to "blemish-free", I'm not sure I can give that guarantee.'

'Oh?'

'Every family has its dirty laundry, does it not?'

'I suppose so.'

'Maybe I could send you the Costellos' laundry list. How would that be?'

'That would be fine.'

'Do you happen to have a fax number there?'

Rebus recited it. 'You'll need the international code,' he warned.

'I think I can manage that. How confidential would this information remain?'

'As confidential as I can make it.'

'I suppose I'll have to take your word then. Are you a rugby man, Inspector?'

Rebus got the feeling he should answer yes. 'Only as a spectator.'

'I like to come to Edinburgh for the Six Nations. Maybe we'll meet for a drink next time.'

'I'd like that. Let me give you a couple of numbers.' This time he recited his office number and his mobile.

'I'll be sure to look you up.'

'You do that. I owe you a large malt.'

'I'll hold you to it.' There was a pause. 'You're not really a rugby man at all, are you?'

'No,' Rebus admitted. There was laughter on the line.

'But you're honest, and that's a start. Goodbye, Inspector.'

Rebus put the phone down. It struck him that he still

didn't know Macmanus's rank, or anything much about him at all. When he looked down at the doodles covering the sheet of paper in front of him, he found he'd drawn half a dozen coffins. He waited twenty minutes for Macmanus to get back to him, but the fax machine was playing dead.

He hit the Maltings first, and followed it up with the Royal Oak, before making for Swany's. Just the one drink in each pub, starting with a pint of Guinness. It had been a while since he'd tried the stuff; it was good but filling. He knew he couldn't do too many, so switched to IPA and finally a Laphroaig with the merest drizzle of water. Then it was a taxi to the Oxford Bar, where he demolished the last corned beef and beetroot roll on the shelf and followed it with a main course of a Scotch egg. He was back on the IPA, needed something to wash down the food. A few of the regulars were in. The back room had been taken over by a party of students, and no one in the front bar was saying much, as if the sounds of enjoyment from upstairs were somehow blasphemous. Harry was behind the bar, and clearly relishing the prospect of the revellers' departure. When someone was dispatched to fetch another round, Harry kept up a steady stream of comments along the lines of 'you'll be heading off soon ... going to a club ... the night's young ...' The young man, his face so shiny it might have been polished, just grinned inanely, taking none of it in. Harry shook his head in disgust. When the drinker headed off, tray laden with slopping pints, one of the regulars informed Harry that he was losing his touch. The stream of profanities which followed seemed, to everyone present, evidence to the contrary.

Rebus had come here in a vain attempt to flush all those little coffins out of his mind. He kept imagining them, seeing them as the work of one man, one killer ... and wondering if there were any more of them, lying rotting on barren hillsides perhaps, or tucked away in crevasses, or turned into macabre ornaments in their finders' garden sheds ... Arthur's Seat and Falls and Jean's four coffins. He saw a continuity there, and it filled him with dread. I want to be cremated, he thought, or maybe strung up in a tree the way Aborigines do it. Anything but the strict confines of a box . . . anything but that.

When the door opened, everyone turned to examine the new arrival. Rebus straightened his back, trying not to show surprise. It was Gill Templer. She saw him immediately and smiled, unbuttoning her coat and taking off her scarf.

'Thought I might find you here,' she said. 'I tried phoning, but got your machine.'

'What can I get you?'

'Gin and tonic.'

Harry had heard the order and was already reaching for a glass. 'Ice and lemon?' he asked.

'Please.'

Rebus noticed that the other drinkers had shifted a little, giving Rebus and Gill as much privacy as the cramped front bar would allow. He paid for the drink and watched Gill gulp at it.

'I needed that,' she said.

Rebus lifted his own glass and toasted her. '*Slainte*.' Then he took a sip. Gill was smiling.

'Sorry,' she said, 'rude of me to just hammer it like that.'

'Rough day?'

'I've had better.'

'So what brings you here?'

'A couple of things. As usual, you haven't been bothering to keep me up to date with any progress.'

'There's not much to report.'

'It's a dead end then?'

'I didn't say that. I just need a few more days.' He lifted his glass again.

'Then there's the small matter of your doctor's appointment.'

'Yes, I know. I'll get round to it, promise.' He nodded towards the pint. 'This is my first tonight, by the way.'

'Aye, that'll be right,' Harry muttered, busying himself drying glasses.

Gill smiled, but her eyes were on Rebus. 'How are things with Jean?'

Rebus shrugged. 'Fine. She's concentrating on the historical side.'

'Do you like her?'

Now Rebus looked at Gill. 'Does the matchmaker service come free?'

'I was just wondering.'

'And you came all this way to ask?'

'Jean's been hurt before by an alcoholic, it's how her husband went.'

'She told me. Don't worry on that score.'

She looked down at her drink. 'How's it working out with Ellen Wylie?'

'I've no complaints.'

'Has she said anything about me?'

'Not really.' Rebus had finished his drink, waved his glass to signal as much. Harry put down the tea-cloth and started pouring. Rebus felt awkward. He didn't like Gill being here like this, dropping in and catching him off-guard. He didn't like that the regulars were listening to every word. Gill seemed to sense his discomfort.

'Would you rather we did this at the office?'

He shrugged again. 'How about you?' he asked. 'Enjoying the new job?'

'I think I'll manage.'

'I'd put money on it.' He pointed to her glass, offered a refill. Gill shook her head. 'I should be going. This was just a quick one before home.'

'Same here.' Rebus made a show of checking his watch. 'I've got the car outside . . . ?'

Rebus shook his head. 'I like to walk, keeps me fit.'

Behind the bar, Harry snorted. Gill wrapped the scarf back around her neck.

'Maybe see you tomorrow then,' she said.

'You know where my office is.'

She studied her surroundings – walls the colour of a used cigarette-filter, dusty prints of Robert Burns – and began to nod. 'Yes,' she said, 'I do.' Then she gave a little wave which seemed to take in the whole bar, and was gone.

'Your boss?' Harry guessed. Rebus nodded. 'Swap you,' the barman said. The regulars started laughing. Another student appeared from the back room, the list of required drinks scribbled on the back of an envelope.

'Three IPA,' Harry began to recite, 'two lager tops, a gin, lime and soda, two Becks and a dry white wine.'

The student looked at the note, then nodded in amazement. Harry winked at his audience.

'Might be students, but they're not the only smart bastards round here.'

Siobhan sat in her living room, staring at the message on the laptop's screen. It was in response to an e-mail she'd sent to Quizmaster, informing him that she was now working on the second clue.

I forgot to tell you, from now on you're against the clock. In twenty-four hours' time, the next clue becomes void.

Siobhan got to work on the keyboard: *I think we should meet. I have some questions.* She hit 'send', then waited. His reply was prompt.

The game will answer your questions.

She hit more keys: *Did Flip have anyone helping her? Is anyone else playing the game?*

She waited for several minutes. Nothing. She was in the kitchen, pouring another half-glass of Chilean red, when she heard the laptop telling her she had a message. Wine splashed on to the back of her hand as she dashed back through.

Hello, Siobhan.

She stared at the screen. The sender's address was a series of numbers. Before she could reply, the computer told her she had another message.

Are you there? Your light's on.

She froze, the screen seeming to shimmer. He was *here*! Right outside! She walked quickly to the window. Down below, a car was parked, headlights still on.

Grant Hood's Alfa.

He waved up at her. Cursing, she ran to the front door, down the stairs and out of the tenement.

'Is that your idea of a joke?' she hissed.

Hood, easing himself from the driver's seat, seemed stunned by her reaction.

'I just had Quizmaster online,' she explained. 'I thought you were him.' She paused, narrowed her eyes. 'Just exactly how did you do that?'

Hood held up his mobile phone. 'It's a WAP,' he explained sheepishly. 'Just got it today. Sends e-mails, the lot.'

She snatched it from him and studied it. 'Jesus, Grant.'

'I'm sorry,' he said. 'I just wanted to . . .'

She handed back the phone, knowing damned well what he'd wanted: to show off his latest gadget.

'What are you doing here anyway?' she asked.

'I think I've cracked it.'

She stared at him. 'Again?' He shrugged. 'How come you always wait till late at night?'

'Maybe that's when I do my best thinking.' He glanced up at the tenement. 'So are you going to invite me in, or do we go on giving the neighbours a free show?'

She looked around. It was true that heads were silhouetted at a couple of windows. 'Come on then,' she said.

Upstairs, the first thing she did was check the laptop, but Quizmaster hadn't replied.

'I think you scared him off,' Hood said, reading the onscreen dialogue.

Siobhan fell on to the sofa and picked up her glass. 'So what have you got for us tonight, Einstein?'

'Ah, that famous Edinburgh hospitality,' Hood said, eyeing the glass.

'You're driving.'

'One glass can't hurt.'

Siobhan got up again, uttering a slight groan of protest, and headed for the kitchen. Hood reached into the bag he'd brought with him and started pulling out maps and guidebooks.

'What have you got there?' Siobhan asked, handing him a tumbler and starting to pour. She sat down, drained her own glass, refilled it, and placed what was left of the bottle on the floor.

'You're sure I'm not disturbing you?' He was teasing her – or trying to. But she wasn't in the mood.

'Just tell me what you've got.'

'Well . . . if you're absolutely sure I'm not . . .' Her glare brought him up short. He stared down at the maps. 'I got thinking about what that lawyer said.'

'Harriet?' Siobhan frowned. 'She said hills are sometimes called laws.'

Hood nodded. ' "Scots Law",' he recited. 'Meaning maybe we're looking for a word that means the same thing law does in Scots.'

'Which would be . . . ?'

Hood unfolded a sheet of paper and started to read aloud. 'Hill, heights, bank, brae, ben, fell, tor . . .' He turned the sheet towards her. 'The thesaurus is full of them.'

She took the paper from him and started reading the list for herself. 'We went through all the maps,' she complained.

'But we didn't know what we were looking for. Some of the guides have hills and mountains indexed at the back. For the rest, we check grid reference B4 on each page.'

'Looking for what exactly?'

'Deer Hill, Stag's Brae, Doe Bank . . .'

Siobhan nodded. 'You're assuming "sounds dear" means "d-e-e-r"?'

Hood took a sip of wine. 'I'm assuming a lot. But it's better than nothing.'

'And it couldn't wait till morning?'

'Not when Quizmaster suddenly decides we're against the clock.' Hood picked up the first map-book and flicked to the index.

Siobhan studied him over the top of her glass. Yes, she was thinking, but you didn't know there was a time element until you got here. She was also still shaken by the way he'd e-mailed her by phone. She wondered just how mobile

Quizmaster was. She'd given him her name, and the city where she worked. These days, how hard would it be for him to get an address? Five minutes on the Net would probably do it.

Hood didn't seem to notice that she was still staring at him. *Maybe he's closer than you think, girl,* Siobhan thought to herself.

After half an hour, she put on some music, a Mogwai EP, about as laid back as the band ever got. She asked Hood if he wanted coffee. He was sitting on the floor, back against the sofa, legs stretched out. He had spread an Ordnance Survey map across his thighs and was studying one of the squares. He looked up at her and blinked, as though the lighting in the room was new to him.

'Cheers,' he said.

When she came back with the mugs, she told him about Ranald Marr. The look on his face changed to a scowl.

'Keeping it a secret, were you?'

'I thought it could wait till morning.' Her answer didn't seem to satisfy him, and he took his coffee from her with only a grunt of thanks. Siobhan could feel her anger rising again. This was *her* place, *her* home. What was he doing here anyway? Work was for the office, not her living room. How come he didn't phone and tell her to go to *his* place? The more she thought about it, the more she realised that she really didn't know Grant at all. She'd worked with him before; they'd been to parties, gone out drinking and for that one meal. She didn't think he'd ever had a girlfriend. At St Leonard's a few of the CID called him Go-Go Gadget, a reference to some TV cartoon. He was both a useful officer and a figure of amusement at the same time.

He wasn't like her. He was nothing like her at all. And yet here she was sharing her free time with him. Here she was letting him turn that free time into yet more work.

She picked up another of the map books, *Handy Road Atlas Scotland*. The first page, square B4 was the Isle of Man. This really annoyed her for some reason: the Isle of Man wasn't even *in* Scotland! The next page, B4 was in the Yorkshire Dales.

'Bloody hell,' she said out loud.

'What is it?'

'This map, it's like Bonnie Prince Charlie won the war.' She flipped to the next page, where B4 was the Mull of Kintyre, but the page after that her eyes fixed on the words 'Loch Fell'. She studied the square more closely: the M74 motorway and the town of Moffat. She knew Moffat: a picture-postcard place with at least one good hotel, where she'd stopped once for lunch. At the top of square B4 she saw a small triangle, indicating a peak. The peak was called Hart Fell. It was eight hundred and eight metres high. She looked at Hood.

'A hart's a kind of deer, isn't it?'

He got up off the floor, came and sat next to her. 'Harts and hinds,' he said. 'The hart is the male.'

'Why not a stag?'

'Harts are older, I think.' He studied the map, his shoulder touching Siobhan's arm. She tried not to flinch, but it was hard work. 'Christ,' he said, 'it's the middle of nowhere.'

'Maybe it's coincidence,' she suggested.

He nodded, but she could see he was convinced. 'Square B4,' he said. 'A fell is another name for a law. A hart is a kind of deer . . .' He looked at her and shook his head. 'No coincidence.'

Siobhan switched her TV on and pressed for Teletext.

'What are you doing?' Hood asked.

'Checking the weather for tomorrow. No way I'm climbing Hart Fell in a gale.'

Rebus had dropped into St Leonard's, gathered together the notes on the four cases: Glasgow, Dunfermline, Perth and Nairn.

'All right, sir?' one of the uniforms had asked.

'Why shouldn't I be?'

He'd had a few drinks, so what? Didn't make him incapable. The taxi was waiting for him outside. Five minutes later, he was climbing the stairs to his flat. Another five after that, he was smoking a cigarette, drinking tea, and opening the first file. He sat in his chair by the window, his little oasis in the midst of chaos. He could hear a siren in the distance; sounded like an ambulance, hurtling along Melville Drive. He had photos of the four victims, culled from newspapers. They smiled at him in black and white. The snatch of poetry came back to him, and he knew all four shared the same characteristic.

They'd died because they'd been available.

He started pinning the photos to a large corkboard. He had a postcard, too, bought from the museum shop: three of the Arthur's Seat coffins in close-up, surrounded by darkness. He turned the postcard over and read: 'Carved wooden figures, with fabric clothing, in miniature coffins of pine, from a group found in a rocky niche on the north-eastern slopes of Arthur's Seat, in June 1836.' It struck him that the police of the time had probably been involved, which meant there might be paperwork somewhere. Then again, just how organised had the force been back then? He doubted there'd been anything like the modern CID. Probably they'd resorted to examining victims' eyeballs, looking for images of the murderer. Not too far removed from the witchcraft which was one theory behind the dolls. Had witches ever plied their trade on Arthur's Seat? These days, he suspected they'd get some sort of Enterprise Initiative.

He got up and put some music on. Dr John, *The Night Tripper*. Then back to the table, a fresh cigarette lit from the stub of the old. The smoke stung his eyes, and he squeezed them shut. When he opened them again, his vision was slow to focus. It was as if the photos of the four women were lying behind a layer of muslin. He blinked a couple of times, shook his head, trying to stave off weariness.

When he awoke a couple of hours later, he was still seated at the table, head resting on his arms. The photos were still there, too, restless faces which had invaded his dreams.

'I wish I could help,' he told them, getting up to go to the kitchen. He returned with a mug of tea, which he took over to the chair by the window. Here he was, getting through another night. So how come he didn't feel like celebrating?

8

Rebus and Jean Burchill were walking on Arthur's Seat. It was a bright morning, but there was a cold breeze blowing. Some people said Arthur's Seat looked like a lion about to spring. But to Rebus's mind it more resembled an elephant or mammoth, with a great bulbous head, a dip towards the neck, and an expanse of torso.

'It started life as a volcano,' Jean was explaining, 'same as Castle Rock. Later on there were farms and quarries, plus chapels.'

'People used to come here for sanctuary, didn't they?' Rebus said, keen to show off what knowledge he had.

She nodded. 'Debtors were banished here until they'd got their affairs in order. A lot of people think it's named after King Arthur.'

'You mean it isn't?'

She shook her head. 'More likely it's Gaelic: *Ard-na-Said*, "Height of the Sorrows".'

'That's a cheery name.'

She smiled. 'The park's full of them: Pulpit Rock, Powderhouse Corner.' She looked at him. 'Or how about Murder Acre and Hangman's Crag?'

'Where are they?'

'Near Duddingston Loch and the Innocent Railway.'

'Now that was named because they used horses instead of trains, right?'

She smiled again. 'Could be. There are other theories.' She pointed towards the loch. 'Samson's Ribs,' she said. 'The Romans had a fort there.' She gave him a sly glance. 'Maybe you didn't think they got this far north?'

He shrugged. 'History's never been my strong point. Do we know where the coffins were found?'

'The records from the time are vague. "The north-east range of Arthur's Seat" is how the *Scotsman* put it. A small opening in a secluded outcrop.' She shrugged. 'I've wandered all over and never found the spot. The other thing the *Scotsman* said was that the coffins were in two tiers, eight in each, and with a third tier just begun.'

'Like whoever did it had more to add?'

She held her jacket around her; Rebus got the feeling it wasn't just the wind making her shiver. He was thinking of the Innocent Railway. These days it was a walkway and cycle path. About a month back, someone had been mugged there. He didn't suppose the story would do much to cheer up his companion. He could tell her about suicides, too, and syringes left by the side of the road. Although they were walking the same path, he knew they were in different places.

'I'm afraid history's about all I have to offer,' she said suddenly. 'I've asked around, but no one seems to remember anyone showing particular interest in the coffins, except for the occasional student or tourist. They were kept in a private collection for a time, then handed over to the Society of Antiquaries, who gave them to the Museum.' She shrugged. 'I've not been very helpful, have I?'

'A case like this, Jean, everything's useful. If it doesn't rule something in, it can help rule other things out.'

'I get the feeling you've made that speech before.'

It was his turn to smile. 'Maybe I have; doesn't mean I don't mean it. Are you free later on today?'

'Why?' She was playing with her new bracelet, the one she'd bought from Bev Dodds.

'I'm taking our twentieth-century coffins to an expert. A bit of history might come in useful.' He paused, looked out over Edinburgh. 'Jesus, it's a beautiful city, isn't it?'

She studied him. 'Are you saying that because you think I want to hear it?'

'What?'

'The other night, when I stopped on North Bridge, I got the feeling you weren't impressed by the view.'

'I look, but I don't always see. I'm seeing now.' They were on the hill's west face, so not even half the city was spread below them. Climbing higher, Rebus knew he'd have a three-hundred-and-sixty-degree view. But this was enough to be going on with: the spires and chimney-pots, crow-foot gables, with the Pentland Hills to the south and the Firth of Forth to the north, the Fife coastline visible beyond.

'Maybe you are at that,' she said. And, smiling, she leaned forward, going up on her toes so she could peck his cheek. 'Best just to get that out of the way,' she said quietly. Rebus nodded, couldn't think of anything to say, until she shivered again and said she was getting cold.

'There's a café behind St Leonard's,' Rebus told her. 'And I'm buying. Not out of altruism, you understand, but because I've a huge favour to ask.'

She burst out laughing, slapped her hand to her mouth and started apologising.

'What did I say?' he asked.

'It's just that Gill told me this would happen. She said if I stuck close to you, I'd have to be prepared for "the big favour".'

'Did she now?'

'And she was right, wasn't she?'

'Not entirely. It's a *huge* favour I'm asking for, not just a big one . . .'

Siobhan was wearing a vest, polo neck and pure wool V-neck jumper. She had an old pair of thick cords on, tucked at the ankles into two pairs of socks. She'd given her old hiking boots a bit of a polish, and they seemed fine. She hadn't worn the Barbour in years, but couldn't think of a better chance to use it. Additionally, she was wearing a bobble-hat, and carrying a pack containing an umbrella, her mobile, a bottle of water and a flask of sweetened tea.

'Sure you've got enough gear?' Hood laughed. He was wearing jeans and trainers. His yellow cagoule looked brand new. He angled his face to the sun, so that the rays reflected off his sunglasses. They'd parked the car in a lay-by. There was a fence to climb, and after that a gently sloping field which then angled abruptly. The steep gradient was barren, except for occasional whin-bushes and rocks.

'What do you reckon?' Hood asked. 'An hour to the top?'

Siobhan slipped the backpack over her shoulders. 'With a bit of luck.'

Sheep watched them as they climbed the fence. There was a strand of barbed wire running along it, marked with tufts of grey wool. Hood gave Siobhan a foot up, then leaped over, using his hand on the fence-post for purchase.

'Not a bad day for it,' he said, as they started to climb. 'Reckon Flip would have done this on her ownio?'

'I don't know,' Siobhan conceded.

'I wouldn't have said she was the type. She'd have taken one look at this climb and got back into her Golf GTi.'

'Except she didn't have a car.'

'Good point. So how would she have got out here in the first place?'

Which was another good point: they really were in the middle of nowhere, with towns few and far between and only the odd cottage or farm giving signs of habitation. They were only forty miles from Edinburgh, but the city seemed already a distant memory. Siobhan guessed that few buses came this route. If Flip had come here, she'd have needed help.

'Maybe a taxi,' she said.

'Not the sort of fare you'd forget.'

'No.' Yet despite a public appeal, and plenty of photos of Flip in the papers, no taxi driver had come forward. 'Maybe a friend then, someone we haven't traced yet.'

'Could be.' But Hood sounded sceptical. She noticed that he was already breathing hard. A couple of minutes later, he'd shed the cagoule and folded it, tucking it beneath his arm.

'Don't know how you can wear that lot,' he complained.

She pulled the bobble-hat from her head and unzipped the Barbour.

'Is that better?' she said.

He just shrugged.

Eventually, on the steeper climb, they were reduced to scrabbling with their hands while their feet sought purchase, the stony soil crumbling and sliding away beneath them. Siobhan stopped to rest, sitting down with her knees up, heels digging in. She took a swig of water.

'Is that you wabbit already?' Hood said, ten or so feet above her. She offered him the bottle, but he shook his head and started climbing again. She could see sweat shining in his hair.

'It's not a race, Grant,' she called out. He didn't reply. After another half-minute, she turned round and followed him. He was moving away from her. So much for team work, she thought. He was like a lot of men she'd known: driven, and yet probably unable to put the reasons into words. It was more in the way of an instinct, a basic need, going beyond the rational.

The climb was levelling off a little. Hood stood up, hands on his hips, admiring the view as he rested. Siobhan watched as he bent his head and tried to spit, but his saliva was too viscous. It hung in a strand from his mouth, refusing to drop. He got a handkerchief from his pocket and wiped it away. Catching up with him, she handed him the bottle.

'Here,' she said. He looked like he might refuse, but eventually took a mouthful. 'It's clouding over.' Siobhan was interested in the sky rather than the view. The clouds were thick and blackening. Funny how the weather could change so suddenly in Scotland. The temperature must have dropped three or four degrees, perhaps more. 'Maybe a shower,' she said. Hood just nodded, handing back the bottle.

She looked at her watch and saw that they'd been climbing for twenty minutes. That meant they were maybe fifteen from the car, reckoning the descent quicker than the climb. Peering upwards, she guessed they had another fifteen or twenty minutes to go. Hood expelled breath noisily.

'You okay?' she asked.

'Good exercise,' he said hoarsely. Then he began climbing again. There were damp patches on the back of his dark blue sweatshirt. Any minute now he'd probably take it off, and be clad only in a T-shirt as the weather turned. Sure enough, he paused to pull the sweatshirt over his head.

'It's getting cold,' she warned him.

'But I'm not.' He tied the arms of the sweatshirt around his waist.

'At least put your cagoule back on.'

'I'll bake.'

'No you won't.'

He seemed ready to argue, then changed his mind. Siobhan had already zipped up her Barbour again. The countryside around them was growing less visible, either low cloud or mist. Or maybe showers blowing in.

Five minutes on, the rain began. Drizzle at first, and then a smattering of big drops. Siobhan put her hat back on, and watched Grant pull his hood up. It was getting windy, too, gusts cutting across them. Grant lost his footing and went down on one knee, cursing. For the next few dozen steps he was limping, clutching at his leg with one hand.

'Do you want to wait?' she asked, knowing what his answer would be: silence.

The rain grew heavier, but in the distance the sky was already clearing. It wouldn't last long. All the same, Siobhan's legs were soaked, her trousers sticking to her. Grant's trainers were making squelching sounds. He had switched to auto-pilot, his eyes staring, nothing at all on his mind except reaching the summit, whatever it took.

As they clambered up the last steep incline, the land levelled off. They'd reached the summit. The rain was easing. Twenty feet away stood a cairn. Siobhan knew that sometimes hill-walkers added a rock or stone each time they ended a climb. Maybe that was how this cairn had come into being.

'What, no restaurant?' Grant said, crouching down to get his breath back. The rain had stopped, a shaft of sunshine splitting the clouds and bathing the hills around in an eerie yellow glow. He was shivering, but the rain had been pouring off his cagoule and on to his sweatshirt, soaking it. No use putting it on now. His denims had changed colour to a darker, dampened blue.

'Hot tea, if you want it,' Siobhan said. He nodded and she poured him a cup. He sipped at it, studying the cairn.

'Are we scared what we'll find?' he said.

'Maybe we won't find anything.'

He conceded as much with a nod. 'Go look,' he told her. So she screwed the top back on the flask and approached the cairn, walked round it. Just a pile of stones and pebbles. 'There's nothing here,' she said. She got down on her haunches to take a closer look.

'There must be.' Grant rose to his feet, walked towards her. 'There's got to be.'

'Well, whatever it is, it's well hidden.'

He touched a foot to the cairn, then gave a push, toppling it. Dropped to his knees, running his hands through the debris. His face was screwed up, teeth bared. Soon the pile of stones was completely flattened. Siobhan had lost interest in it, was looking around for other possibilities, seeing none. Grant thrust a hand into his cagoule pocket, pulling out the two plastic evidence bags he'd brought. She watched him stuff them under the largest rock, then begin building the cairn again. It didn't get very high before it started to fall down.

'Leave it, Grant,' Siobhan said.

'Useless piece of shit!' he cried out. She couldn't be sure who or what his words were aimed at.

'Grant,' she said quietly. 'Weather's closing in again. Let's head back.'

He seemed reluctant to go. He sat on the ground, legs stretched out, arms behind him to support himself.

'We got it wrong,' he said, almost in tears. Siobhan was looking at him, knowing she needed to coax him back down the hill. He was wet and cold and losing it. She crouched in front of him.

'I need you to be strong, Grant,' she said, her hands on his knees. 'You go to pieces on me, and that's it finished. We're a team, remember?'

'A team,' he echoed. Siobhan was nodding.

'So let's act like a team and get our arses off this hill.'

He was staring at her hands. He reached out with his own, wrapping them around hers. She started to rise, pulling him with her. 'Come on, Grant.' They were both up on their feet now, and his eyes weren't moving from her.

'Remember what you said?' he asked. 'When we were trying to get parked near Victoria Street?'

'What?'

'You asked why I always had to play by the rules . . .'

'Grant . . .' She tried for a look that was sympathetic rather than pitying. 'Let's not spoil it,' she said quietly, trying to slide her hands out from his grip.

'Spoil what?' he asked hollowly.

'We're a team,' she repeated.

'That's it?'

He was staring at her as she nodded. She kept nodding and he slowly released her hands. Siobhan turned to move away, start the descent. She hadn't gone five paces when Grant flew past her, bounding down the slope like a man possessed. He lost his footing once or twice but bounced straight back up again.

'Tell me those aren't hailstones!' he called out at one point. But they were: stinging Siobhan's face as she tried to catch up. Then Grant caught his cagoule on the barbed wire as he hurdled the fence, ripping its seam. He was swearing and red-faced as he helped Siobhan over. They got into the car and just sat there for a full minute, getting their breath back. The windscreen started steaming up, so Siobhan slid her window down. The hail had stopped. The sun was coming out again.

'Bloody Scottish weather,' Grant spat. 'Is it any wonder we've a chip on our shoulder?'

'Have we? I hadn't noticed.'

He snorted, but smiled too. Siobhan looked at him, hoping it was going to be all right between them. The way he was acting, it was as if nothing had happened up there on the summit. She took off her Barbour and tossed it into the back. Grant slipped the cagoule over his head. There was steam rising from his T-shirt. From beneath the seat, Siobhan retrieved the laptop and plugged her mobile into it, booting the machine up. The mobile's signal was weak, but it would do.

'Tell him he's a bastard,' Grant said.

'I'm sure he'd be thrilled to hear it.' Siobhan started typing a message, Grant leaning over to watch.

Just been up Hart Fell. No sign of next clue. Did I get it wrong?

She pressed 'send' and waited, pouring herself a cup of tea. Grant was trying to prise his denims away from his skin. 'Soon as we get moving, I'll put the heater on.' She nodded, offered him some more tea, which he took. 'What time's the meeting with the banker?'

She checked her watch. 'We've a couple of hours. Time enough to go home and get changed.'

Grant looked at the screen. 'He's not there, is he?'

Siobhan shrugged, and Grant turned the Alfa's ignition. They drove in silence, the weather clearing ahead of them. It soon became clear that the rain had been localised. By Innerleithen, the road was bone dry.

'I wonder if we should have taken the A701,' Grant mused. 'Might have made for a shorter climb, the west side of the hill.'

'Doesn't matter now,' Siobhan said. She could see that in his mind he was still on Hart Fell. The laptop suddenly announced that there was post. She clicked, but it was an invitation to visit a porn site. 'That's not the first of those I've had,' she informed Grant. 'Makes me wonder what you got up to with your computer.'

'They pick names at random,' he said, his neck reddening.

'I think they have some kind of system that tells them when you're online.'

'I'll believe you,' she said.

'It's true!' His voice was rising.

'Okay, okay. I really do believe you.'

'I'd *never* do that, Siobhan.'

She nodded, but kept quiet. They had reached the outskirts of Edinburgh when the next message was announced. This time it was Quizmaster. Grant pulled up on to the verge and stopped the car.

'What's he saying?'

'Take a look.' Siobhan angled the laptop towards him. They were a team, after all . . .

Hart Fell is all I needed. You didn't need to climb it.

'Bastard,' Grant hissed.

Siobhan typed her response. *Did Flip know that?* There was nothing for a couple of minutes, then: *You're two moves away from Hellbank. Clue follows in approximately ten minutes. You have twenty-four hours to solve it. Do you wish to continue the game?*

Siobhan looked at Grant. 'Tell him yes,' he said.

'Not yet.' When he looked at her, she held his gaze. 'I think maybe he needs us as much as we need him.'

'Can we risk that?'

But she was already typing: *Need to know – did Flip have help? Who else was playing?*

His response was immediate: *Last time of asking. Do you wish to continue?*

'We don't want to lose him,' Grant warned.

'He *knew* I'd climb that hill. Probably the way he knew Flip wouldn't.' Siobhan chewed her bottom lip. 'I think we can push him a bit further.'

'We're two clues away from Hellbank. That's as far as Flip got.'

Siobhan nodded slowly, then began to type: *Continue to next level, but please, just tell me if Flip had anyone helping her.*

Grant sat back and sucked in his breath. Nothing came back. Siobhan checked her watch. 'He said ten minutes.'

'You like to gamble, don't you?'

'What's life without a bit of risk?'

'A much pleasanter, less stressful experience.'

She looked at him. 'This from the boy racer.'

He wiped the windscreen clear of condensation. 'If Flip didn't need to climb Hart Fell, I wonder if she needed to do any travelling at all. I mean, could she have solved the puzzle from her bedroom?'

'Meaning?'

'Meaning she wouldn't have gone anywhere that would have got her into trouble.'

Siobhan nodded. 'Maybe the next clue will tell us.'

'If there is a next clue.'

'You gotta have faith,' she sang.

'That's just what faith is to me: a song by George Michael.'

The laptop told them there was a message. Grant leaned over again to read it.

A corny beginning where the mason's dream ended.

While they were still taking it in, another message arrived: *I don't think Flipside had any help. Is anyone helping you, Siobhan?*

She typed 'No' and pressed 'send'.

'Why don't you want him to know?' Grant asked.

'Because he might change the rules, or even take the huff. He says Flip was on her own, I want him to think the same about me.' She glanced at him. 'Is that a problem?'

Grant thought for a moment, then shook his head. 'So what does the latest clue mean?'

'I haven't the faintest. I don't suppose you're a Mason?'

He shook his head again. 'Never quite got round to joining. Any idea where we might find one?'

Siobhan smiled. 'In the Lothian and Borders Police? I don't think we'll have too much trouble . . .'

The coffins had turned up at St Leonard's, as had the autopsy notes. There was just the one small problem: the Falls coffin was now in the possession of Steve Holly. Bev

Dodds had given it to him so it could be photographed. Rebus decided he'd have to visit Holly's office. He grabbed his jacket and walked across to the desk opposite, where Ellen Wylie was looking bored as Donald Devlin pored over the contents of a slim manila file.

'I have to go out,' he explained.

'Lucky you. Need any company?'

'Look after Professor Devlin. I won't be long.'

Devlin looked up. 'And where are your peregrinations taking you?'

'There's a reporter I need to talk to.'

'Ah, our much-derided fourth estate.'

The way Devlin talked, it was getting on Rebus's nerves. And he wasn't alone, if Wylie's look was anything to go by. She always sat with her chair as far from the Professor as possible, on opposite sides of the desk if she could manage it.

'I'll be as quick as I can,' he tried to reassure her, but as he walked away he knew her eyes were following him all the way to the door.

Another thing about Devlin: he was almost too keen. Being useful again had taken years off him. He relished the autopsy reports, reciting passages aloud, and whenever Rebus was busy or trying to concentrate, you could be sure Devlin had some question to ask. Not for the first time, Rebus cursed Gates and Curt. Wylie herself had summed it up by way of a question to Rebus: 'Remind me,' she'd asked, 'is he helping us or are we helping him? I mean, if I'd wanted to be a care assistant, I'd have applied to an old folk's home . . .'

In his car, Rebus tried not to count the number of pubs he passed on his route into town.

The Glasgow tabloid had its office on the top floor of a Queen Street conversion a few doors along from the BBC. Rebus chanced his luck, parked on a single yellow line outside. The main door was wedged open, so he climbed the three flights and pulled open a glass-panelled door leading to a cramped reception area where a woman working a switchboard smiled at him as she answered the latest call.

'I'm afraid he's out for the day. Do you have his mobile number?' Her short blonde hair was tucked behind both ears. She wore a black headset consisting of earpiece and microphone. 'Thank you,' she said, terminating the call, only to press a button to take another. She didn't look at Rebus, but held up a finger telling him he hadn't been forgotten. He looked around for somewhere to sit, but there were no chairs, just an exhausted-looking cheese plant in a pot it was fast outgrowing.

'I'm afraid he's out for the day,' she told the new caller. 'Do you have his mobile number?' She gave this number, then terminated the call.

'Sorry about that,' she told Rebus.

'That's okay. I'm here to see Steve Holly, but I have the feeling I know what you're going to say.'

'He's out for the day, I'm afraid.'

Rebus nodded.

'Do you have his—'

'I do, yes.'

'Was he expecting you?'

'I don't know. I'm here to pick up the doll, if he's finished with it.'

'Ooh, that thing.' She made a show of shivering. 'He left it on my chair this morning. Steve's idea of a laugh.'

'The hours must fly.'

She smiled again, enjoying this little conspiracy against her colleague. 'I think it's in his cubicle.'

Rebus nodded. 'Photos all done?'

'Oh, yes.'

'Then maybe I could . . . ?' He pointed a thumb towards where he guessed Holly's cubicle might be.

'Don't see why not.' The switchboard was sounding again.

'I'll leave you to it then,' Rebus said, turning round as if he knew exactly where he was going.

It was easy enough. There were only four 'cubicles': desks separated by free-standing partition walls. No one was working in any of them. The small coffin was sitting next to

Holly's keyboard, a couple of test Polaroids lying on top. Rebus congratulated himself: this was best-case-scenario stuff. If Holly had been here, there'd have been questions to parry, maybe a bit of grief. He took the opportunity to give the work-space a once-over. Phone numbers and news clippings pinned to the walls, a two-inch-high Scooby Doo stuck to the top of the monitor. A Simpsons desk calendar, covered with doodles, on a page three weeks out of date. A memo recorder, its battery compartment open and empty. There was a newspaper headline taped to the side of the monitor: 'Super Cally Go Ballistic, Celtic Are Atrocious'. Rebus had a little smile: it was a modern classic, referred to a football match. Maybe Holly was a Rangers fan, maybe he just appreciated a joke. As he was about to leave, he noticed Jean's name and phone number on the wall near the desk. He tore it down and pocketed it, then saw other numbers beneath . . . his own, plus Gill Templer's. Beneath these were other names: Bill Pryde, Siobhan Clarke, Ellen Wylie. The reporter had home numbers for Templer and Clarke. Rebus couldn't know if Holly had copies, but he decided to take the lot with him.

Outside, he tried Siobhan's mobile, but got a recording saying his call couldn't be connected. There was a ticket on his car, no sign of the warden. They were known around town as 'Blue Meanies' because of their uniform. Rebus, probably the only person who'd seen *Yellow Submarine* in the cinema without benefit of drugs, appreciated the name, but cursed the ticket anyway, stuffing it in his glove compartment. He smoked a cigarette on the crawl back to St Leonard's. So many of the streets now, you couldn't go the way you wanted. Unable to take a left on to Princes Street, and with traffic stalled at Waverley Bridge due to roadworks, he ended up taking The Mound, turning off down Market Street. He had Janis Joplin on the stereo, 'Buried Alive in the Blues'. Had to be better than a living death on Edinburgh's roads.

Back at the office, Ellen Wylie looked like she could sing some blues of her own.

'Fancy a little trip?' Rebus asked.

She perked up. 'Where?'

'Professor Devlin, you're invited too.'

'Sounds most intriguing.' He wasn't wearing a cardigan today, but a V-neck jumper, sagging beneath the arms but too short at the back. 'Would this be some sort of mystery tour?'

'Not exactly. We're visiting a funeral parlour.'

Wylie stared at him. 'You've got to be joking.'

But Rebus shook his head, pointing towards the coffins arranged on his desk. 'If you want an expert opinion,' he said, 'you need to ask an expert.'

'Self-evidently,' Devlin agreed.

The undertaker's was a short walk from St Leonard's. Last time Rebus had been in a funeral parlour was when his father had died. He'd walked forward, touched the old man's forehead, the way his father had taught him when his mother had died: *if you touch them, Johnny, you'll never need fear the dead.* Somewhere in the city, Conor Leary was settling into his own box. Death and taxes: shared by everyone. But Rebus had known some criminals who'd never paid a bawbee's tax in their life. It didn't matter: when the time was right, their box was still waiting.

Jean Burchill was already there. She rose from the chair in the reception area, as if glad of some company. The mood was sombre, despite the sprays of fresh-cut flowers. Idly, Rebus wondered if they got a discount from whoever did their wreaths. The walls were wood-panelled, and there was a faint smell of furniture polish. The brass doorhandles gleamed. Underfoot, the floor was tiled with marble, black and white squares like a chessboard. Rebus made the introductions. While shaking Jean's hand, Devlin asked, 'And what is it exactly that you curate?'

'Nineteenth-century,' she explained. 'Belief systems, social concerns . . .'

'Ms Burchill is helping us form a historical perspective,' Rebus said.

'I'm not sure I understand.' Devlin looked to her for help.

'I put together the display of the Arthur's Seat coffins.'

Devlin's eyebrows shot up. 'Oh, but how fascinating! And there may be some correlation with the current spate?'

'I'm not sure you could call it a "spate",' Ellen Wylie argued. 'Five coffins over a thirty-year period.'

Devlin seemed taken aback. Perhaps he wasn't often pulled up for his vocabulary. He gave Wylie a look, then turned to Rebus. 'But *is* there some historical connection?'

'We don't know. That's what we're here to find out.'

The inner door opened and a man appeared. He was in his fifties, dressed in dark suit, crisp white shirt, and grey shimmering tie. His hair was short and silver, his face long and pale.

'Mr Hodges?' Rebus asked. The man acknowledged as much with a bow. Rebus shook his hand. 'We spoke on the phone. I'm Detective Inspector Rebus.' Rebus introduced the others.

'It was,' Mr Hodges said in a near-whisper, 'one of the more remarkable requests I've received. However, Mr Patullo is waiting for you in my office. Would you care for any tea?'

Rebus assured him they'd be fine, and asked if Hodges would lead the way.

'As I explained on the phone, Inspector, these days the majority of coffins are made along what could be described as an assembly-line process. Mr Patullo is that rare woodworker who will still produce a casket to order. We've been using his services for years, certainly for as long as I've been with the firm.' The hall they trooped along was wood-panelled like the reception area, but with no exterior lighting. Hodges opened a door and ushered them inside. The office was spacious, completely lacking in clutter. Rebus didn't know what he'd expected: displays of bereavement cards, brochures for coffins maybe. But the only clue that this office belonged to an undertaker was the very lack of any outward clues. It went beyond discretion. The clients who came in here didn't want reminding of the visit's purpose, and Rebus didn't suppose it made the undertaker's job any easier if people were bursting into tears every two minutes.

'I'll leave you alone,' Hodges said, closing the door. He'd arranged enough seats for them, but Patullo was standing beside the opaque window. He carried a flat tweed cap, the brim of which he worried between the fingers of both hands. The fingers themselves were gnarled, the skin like parchment. Rebus reckoned Patullo had to be in his mid-seventies. He still had a good head of thick silver hair, and his eyes were clear, if wary. But he held himself with a stoop, and his hand trembled when Rebus made to shake it.

'Mr Patullo,' he said, 'I really appreciate you agreeing to meet us.'

Patullo shrugged, and Rebus made one more round of introductions before telling everyone to sit down. He had the coffins in a carrier bag, and brought them out now, laying them on the unblemished surface of Mr Hodges's desk. There were four of them – Perth, Nairn, Glasgow, plus the more recent one from Falls.

'I'd like you to take a look, please,' Rebus said, 'and tell us what you see.'

'I see some wee coffins.' Patullo's voice was hoarse.

'I meant in terms of craftsmanship.'

Patullo reached into his pocket for his glasses, then got up and stood in front of the display.

'Pick them up if you like,' Rebus said. Patullo did so, examining the lids and the dolls, peering closely at the nails.

'Carpet tacks and small wood nails,' he commented. 'The joints are a bit rough, but working to this scale . . .'

'What?'

'Well, you wouldn't expect to see anything as detailed as a dovetail.' He went back to his examination. 'You want to know if a coffin-maker made these?' Rebus nodded. 'I don't think so. There's a bit of skill here, but not that much. The proportions are wrong, the shape's too much of a diamond.' He turned each coffin over to examine its underside. 'See the pencil marks here where he made his outline?' Rebus nodded. 'He measured up, then he cut with a saw. Didn't do any planing, just some sandpaper.' He looked at Rebus over the top of his glasses. 'You want to know if they're all by the same hand?'

Again, Rebus nodded.

'This one's a bit cruder,' Patullo said, holding up the Glasgow coffin. 'Different wood, too. The rest are pine, this is balsa. But the joints are the same, as are the measurements.'

'So you think it's the same person?'

'As long as my life didn't depend on it.' Patullo picked up another coffin. 'Now this one, the proportions are different. Joints aren't so tidy. Either a rushed job, or my guess would be it's by someone else.'

Rebus looked at the coffin. It was the one from Falls.

'So we've got two different people responsible?' Wylie said. When Patullo nodded, she blew air from her mouth and rolled her eyes. Two culprits made for twice the work, and halved the chance of getting a result.

'A copycat?' Rebus guessed.

'I wouldn't know,' Patullo admitted.

'Which brings us to . . .' Jean Burchill dipped a hand into her shoulder-bag, produced a box, which she opened. Inside, wrapped in tissue, was one of the Arthur's Seat coffins. Rebus had asked her to bring it, and she made eye contact with him now, letting him know what she'd already told him in the café: that she was putting her job on the line. If it was discovered that she'd sneaked an artefact out of the Museum, or if anything happened to it . . . she'd be dismissed on the spot. Rebus nodded his head, letting her know he understood. She got up and placed the coffin on the desk.

'It's rather delicate,' she told Patullo. Devlin, too, had risen to his feet, and Wylie wanted a better look also.

'My goodness,' Devlin gasped, 'is that what I think it is?'

Jean just nodded. Patullo didn't pick the coffin up, but bent down so his eyes were close to the level of the desk.

'What we're wondering,' Rebus said, 'is whether you

think the coffins you've just looked at could be modelled on this.'

Patullo rubbed his cheek. 'This is a much more basic design. Still well made, but the sides are a lot straighter. It's not the casket shape we'd recognise today. The lid has been decorated with iron studs.' He rubbed his cheek again, then straightened up, gripping the edge of the desk for support. 'They're not copies of it. That's about as much as I can tell you.'

'I've never seen one outside the Museum,' Devlin said, shuffling forward so he could take Patullo's place. He beamed at Jean Burchill. 'You know, I have a theory as to who made them.'

Jean raised an eyebrow. 'Who?'

Devlin turned his attention to Rebus. 'You remember that portrait I showed you? Dr Kennet Lovell?' When Rebus nodded, Devlin turned back to Jean. 'He was the anatomist who carried out Burke's autopsy. Afterwards, I think he carried a weight of guilt over the whole affair.'

Jean was interested. 'Had he been buying corpses from Burke?'

Devlin shook his head. 'There's no historical indication that such was the case. But like many an anatomist of the day, he probably bought his share of bodies without asking too many questions as to provenance. The thing is,' Devlin licked his lips, 'our Dr Lovell was also interested in carpentry.'

'Professor Devlin,' Rebus told Jean, 'owns a table he made.'

'Lovell was a good man,' Devlin was saying, 'and a good Christian.'

'He left them to commemorate the dead?' Jean asked.

Devlin shrugged, glanced around. 'I've no evidence, of course . . .' His voice tailed off, as though he realised his animation maybe looked foolish.

'It's an interesting theory,' Jean conceded, but Devlin only shrugged again, as though realising he was being patronised.

'Like I say, it's well enough made,' Patullo commented.

'There are other theories,' Jean said. 'Maybe witches or sailors made the Arthur's Seat coffins.'

Patullo nodded. 'Sailors used to be good woodworkers. In some cases it was a necessity, for others it passed a long voyage.'

'Well,' Rebus said, 'thanks again for your time, Mr Patullo. Can we get someone to drive you home?'

'I'll be fine.'

They said their goodbyes, and Rebus directed his party to the Metropole café, where they ordered coffees and squeezed into one of the booths.

'One step forward, two steps back,' Wylie said.

'How do you reckon?' Rebus asked.

'If there's no connection between the other coffins and the one at Falls, we're chasing a wild goose.'

'I don't see that,' Jean Burchill interrupted. 'I mean, maybe I'm speaking out of turn here, but it seems to me whoever left that coffin at Falls had to get the idea from somewhere.'

'Agreed,' Wylie said, 'but it's far more likely they got it from a trip to the Museum, wouldn't you say?'

Rebus was looking at Wylie. 'You're saying we should ditch the four previous cases?'

'I'm saying their only relevance here is if they connect to the Falls coffin, always supposing *it* has anything to do with the Balfour disappearance. And we can't even be sure of *that*.' Rebus started to say something, but she hadn't finished. 'If we go to DCS Templer with this – as we should – she'll say the same thing I'm saying now. We're getting further and further away from the Balfour case.' She raised her cup to her lips and sipped.

Rebus turned to Devlin, who was sitting next to him. 'What do you think, Professor?'

'I'm forced to agree, reluctant though I am to be cast back into the darkness of an old man's retirement.'

'There was nothing in the autopsy notes?'

'Nothing as yet. It looks very much as if both women were

alive when they went into the water. Both bodies sustained some injuries, but that's not so unusual. The river would have rocks in it, so that the victim may have hit her head when falling. As to the victim in Nairn, the tides and sealife can do terrible things to a body, especially one that's been in the water for some time. I'm sorry I can't be more helpful.'

'Everything's useful,' Jean Burchill said. 'If it doesn't rule something in, it can help rule other things out.'

She looked to Rebus, hoping he might smile at hearing his own words paraphrased, but his mind was elsewhere. He was worried Wylie was right. Four coffins left by the same person, one by someone completely different, no connection between the two. The problem was, he felt there *was* a connection. But it wasn't something he could make someone like Wylie comprehend. There were times when instinct had to take over, no matter what the protocol. Rebus felt this was one of those times, but doubted Wylie would go along with it.

And he couldn't blame her for that.

'Maybe if you could give the notes a final look,' he asked Devlin.

'Gladly,' the old man said, bowing his head.

'And talk to the pathologists from either case. Sometimes they remember things . . .'

'Absolutely.'

Rebus turned his attention to Ellen Wylie. 'Maybe you should make your report to DCS Templer. Tell her what we've done. I'm sure there's work for you on the main investigation.'

She straightened her back. 'Meaning you're not giving up?'

Rebus gave a tired smile. 'I'm close to. Just a couple more days.'

'To do what exactly?'

'Convince myself it's a dead end.'

The way Jean looked at him across the table, he knew she wanted to offer him something, some form of comfort: a squeeze of the hand maybe, or a few well-intentioned words.

He was glad there were other people present, making the gesture impossible. Otherwise he might have blurted something out, something about comfort being the last thing he needed.

Unless comfort and oblivion were the same thing.

Daytime drinking was special. In a bar, time ceased to exist, and with it the outside world. For as long as you stayed in the pub, you felt immortal and ageless. And when you stumbled back out from twilight into raging daylight, people all around you going about their afternoon's business, the world had a new shine to it. After all, people had been doing the same damned thing for centuries: plugging the holes in their consciousness with alcohol. But today . . . today Rebus was just having the two drinks. He knew he could walk out after two. To stay for three or four would mean staying either until closing time or until he keeled over. But two . . . two was a manageable number. He smiled at that word: number, with its possible other meaning – that which made you numb. Comfortably numb, as Pink Floyd would say.

Vodka and fresh orange: not his first choice, but it didn't leave a smell. He could walk back into St Leonard's and no one would know. It was just that the world would seem a little softer to him. When his mobile sounded, he thought of ignoring it, but its trilling was disturbing the other drinkers, so he pushed the button.

'Hello?'

'Let me guess,' the voice said. It was Siobhan.

'In case you're wondering, I'm not in a pub.' Which was the cue for the young guy at the bandit to hit a big win, the coins disgorging noisily.

'You were saying?'

'I'm meeting someone.'

'Do these excuses get any better?'

'What do you want anyway?'

'I need to pick a Mason's brain.'

He misheard. 'You need to pick "Amazing Grace"?'

222

'A *Mason*. You know, funny handshakes, trousers rolled up.'

'Can't help. I failed the audition.'

'But you must know a few?'

He thought about it. 'What's all this about anyway?'

So she told him the latest clue.

'Let me think,' he said. 'How about the Farmer?'

'Is he one?'

'Going by his handshake.'

'Do you think he'd mind me calling him?'

'Quite the opposite.' There was a pause. 'Now you're going to ask if I know his home number, and as it happens you're in luck.' He took out his notebook, recited the number.

'Thanks, John.'

'How's it going anyway?'

'Okay.'

Rebus detected a slight reticence. 'Everything all right with Grant?'

'Fine, yes.'

Rebus raised his eyes to the gantry. 'He's there with you, isn't he?'

'That's right.'

'Message received. We'll talk later. Oh, hang on.'

'What?'

'You ever had anything to do with someone called Steve Holly?'

'Who is he?'

'A local hack.'

'Oh, him. I think we might have talked once or twice.'

'He ever call you at home?'

'Don't be daft. That's one number I keep close to my chest.'

'Funny, he has it pinned to the wall in his office.' She didn't say anything. 'No idea how he could have come by it?'

'I suppose there are ways. I'm not giving him tip-offs or anything, if that's what you're implying.'

'The only thing I'm implying, Siobhan, is that he needs watching. He's as smooth as a fresh-laid turd and gives off the same smell.'

'Charming. I've got to go.'

'Yes, me too.' Rebus cut the call and drained his second drink. Right, that was that then, time to call it a day. Except there was another race coming up on TV, and he had his eye on the chestnut, Long Day's Journey. Maybe one more wouldn't do any harm . . . Then his phone rang again, and, cursing, he pushed his way outdoors, squinting into the sudden light.

'Yes?' he snapped.

'That was a bit naughty.'

'Who's this?'

'Steve Holly. We met at Bev's house.'

'Funny, I was just talking about you.'

'Only, I'm glad we met that day, or I might not have been able to place you from Margot's description.' Margot: the blonde receptionist with the earpiece. Not enough of a conspirator to resist grassing Rebus up . . .

'What do you mean?'

'Come on, Rebus. The coffin.'

'I heard you'd finished with it.'

'Is it evidence then?'

'No, I was just returning it to Ms Dodds.'

'I'll bet. Something's going on here.'

'Bright boy. That "something" is a police investigation. In fact, I'm up to my eyes in it right now, so if you wouldn't mind . . .'

'Bev said something about all these other coffins . . .'

'Did she? Maybe she misheard.'

'I don't think so.' Holly waited, but Rebus wasn't saying anything. 'Fine,' the journalist said into the silence. 'We'll talk later.' *We'll talk later*, the very words Rebus had used to Siobhan. For a split second, he wondered if Holly had been listening in. But it wasn't possible. As the phone went dead, two things struck Rebus. One was that Holly hadn't mentioned the phone numbers missing from his wall, so probably hadn't noticed them yet. The other was that he'd just called Rebus on his mobile, meaning he knew the number. Normally, Rebus gave out his pager rather than his mobile. He wondered which he had given to Bev Dodds . . .

Balfour's Bank wasn't much like a bank at all. For a start, it was sited on Charlotte Square, one of the most elegant parts of the New Town. Shoppers queued grimly for non-existent buses outside, but inside was very different: thick carpets, an imposing staircase, and a huge chandelier, walls recently given a coat of startling white. There were no cashiers, no queues. Transactions were dealt with by three members of staff seated at their own desks, far apart so that discretion was assured. The staff were young and well dressed. Other customers sat in comfortable chairs, selecting newspapers and magazines from the coffee table as they waited to be ushered into one of the private rooms. The atmosphere was rarefied: this was a place where money wasn't so much respected as worshipped. It reminded Siobhan of a temple.

'What did he say?' Grant Hood asked.

She slipped her mobile back into her pocket. 'He thinks we should talk to the Farmer.'

'Is that his number?' Grant nodded towards Siobhan's notebook.

'Yes.' She'd placed the letter F beside the number: F for Farmer. It made the various addresses and phone numbers in her notebook harder to identify, should the book fall into the wrong hands. She was annoyed that a journalist she barely knew should have access to her home number. Not that he'd called her there, but all the same . . .

'Reckon anyone here has an overdraft?' Grant asked.

'The staff might. Not so sure about their clients.'

A middle-aged woman had come from behind one of the doors, closing it softly behind her. She made no noise at all as she walked towards them.

'Mr Marr will see you now.'

They'd expected to be led back to the door, but instead the woman headed for the staircase. Her brisk pace kept her four or five steps ahead of them: no chance for conversation. At the end of the first-floor hall she knocked on a double set of doors and waited.

'Enter!' At which command she pushed open both the doors, gesturing for the two detectives to walk past her and into the room.

It was huge, with three floor-to-ceiling windows, covered by pale linen roller-blinds. There was a polished oak committee-table, laid with pens, notepads and water-jugs. It took up only a third of the available space. There was a seating area – sofa and chair, with a TV nearby showing stock-market fluctuations. Ranald Marr himself was standing behind his desk, a huge antique expanse of walnut. Marr, too, was burnished, his tan looking as though it had its roots in the Caribbean rather than a Nicolson Street sunbed. He was tall, his salt-and-pepper hair immaculately barbered. His suit was a double-breasted pinstripe, almost certainly bespoke. He deigned to come forward to greet them.

'Ranald Marr,' he said unnecessarily. Then, to the woman: 'Thank you, Camille.'

She closed the doors after her, and Marr gestured towards the sofa. The two detectives made themselves comfortable while Marr settled into the matching leather chair. He crossed one leg over the other.

'Any news?' he asked, his face turning solicitous.

'Inquiries are progressing, sir,' Grant Hood informed him. Siobhan tried not to look askance at her colleague: *inquiries are progressing* . . . she wondered which TV show Grant had picked that up from.

'The reason we're here, Mr Marr,' Siobhan said, 'is because it looks like Philippa was involved in some sort of role-playing game.'

'Really?' Marr looked puzzled. 'But what's that got to do with me?'

'Well, sir,' Grant said, 'it's just that we've heard you like to play those sorts of games, too.'

' "Those sorts of . . ."?' Marr clapped his hands together.

'Oh, I know what you mean now. My soldiers.' He frowned. 'Is that what Flip was involved in? She never showed any interest . . .'

'This is a game where clues are given and the player has to solve each one to reach a different level.'

'Not the same thing at all.' Marr slapped his knees and rose to his feet. 'Come on,' he said, 'I'll show you.' He went to his desk and took a key from a drawer. 'This way,' he said brusquely, opening the door to the hallway. He led them back to the top of the staircase, but climbed a narrower stairwell to the second storey. 'Along here.' As he walked, Siobhan noticed a slight limp. He disguised it well, but it was there. Probably he should have been using a stick, but she doubted his vanity would allow it. She caught wafts of eau-de-Cologne. No wedding ring on show. When he made to slip the key into a lock, she saw that his wristwatch was a complicated affair with a leather strap to match his tan.

He opened the door and preceded them inside. The window had been covered with a black sheet, and he switched on the overhead lights. The room was half the size of his office, much of the space taken up with something at table height. It was a model, maybe eighteen feet long by ten wide: green rolling hills, a blue strip of river. There were trees and ruined dwellings, and, covering much of the board, two armies. Several hundred soldiers, divided into regiments. The pieces themselves were less than an inch high, but the detail on each was painstaking.

'I painted most of them myself. Tried to keep them all that little bit different, give them a personality.'

'You re-enact battles?' Grant said, picking up a cannon. Marr didn't look happy at this transgression. He nodded, lifting the piece delicately from Grant with forefinger and thumb.

'That's what I do. War-gaming, you could call it.' He placed the piece back on the board.

'I went paintballing once,' Grant told him. 'Ever done that?'

Marr allowed the officer a thin smile. 'We took the bank

staff once. I can't say I was keen: too much mess. But John enjoyed himself. He's always threatening a return fixture.'

'John being Mr Balfour?' Siobhan guessed.

There was a shelf stacked with books: some on modelling, some about the battles themselves. Other shelves contained clear plastic boxes within which rested armies, waiting for their chance at victory.

'Do you ever change the outcome?' Siobhan asked.

'That's part of the strategy,' Marr explained. 'You figure out where the defeated side went wrong, and you try to alter history.' There was a new passion in his voice. Siobhan walked over to where a seamstress's dummy had been kitted out in uniform. There were other uniforms – some better preserved than others – mounted behind glass on the walls. No weapons of any kind, just the clothes the soldiers would have worn.

'The Crimea,' Marr said, pointing to one of the framed jackets.

Grant Hood interrupted with a question. 'Do you play against other people?'

'Sometimes.'

'They come here?'

'Never here, no. I have a much larger layout in the garage at my house.'

'Then why do you need a set-up here?'

Marr smiled. 'I find that it relaxes me, helps me think. And I *do* get the occasional break from the desk.' He broke off. 'You think it a childish hobby?'

'Not at all,' Siobhan said, only half truthfully. There was a certain 'toys for the boys' feel to it, and she could see the years dropping from Grant as he studied the little model armies. 'Ever play any other way?' she asked.

'How do you mean?'

She shrugged, as if the question had been a casual inquiry merely, keeping the conversation going. 'I don't know,' she said. 'Maybe moves sent by post. I've heard of chess players doing that. Or how about the Internet?'

Grant glanced at her, seeing her gist immediately.

'I know of some Internet sites,' Marr said. 'You get one of those camera thingies.'

'Web cams?' Grant offered.

'That's it. Then you can play across continents.'

'But you've never done that?'

'I'm not the most technically gifted of people.'

Siobhan turned her attention back to the bookcase. 'Ever heard of a character called Gandalf?'

'Which one?' She just looked at him. 'I mean, I know at least two. The wizard in *Lord of the Rings*, and the rather odd chap who runs the games shop on Leith Walk.'

'You've been to his shop then?'

'I've bought a few pieces from him down the years. But I mostly buy mail order.'

'And over the Internet?'

Marr nodded. 'Once or twice, yes. Look, who was it exactly who told you about this?'

'About you liking to play games?' Grant asked.

'Yes.'

'It's taken you a while to ask,' Siobhan commented.

He glowered at her. 'Well, I'm asking now.'

'I'm afraid we're not at liberty to say.'

Marr didn't like that, but refrained from making a comment. 'Am I right in thinking,' he said instead, 'that whatever game it was Flip was playing, it was nothing like this?'

Siobhan shook her head. 'Nothing at all like it, sir.'

Marr looked relieved. 'Everything all right, sir?' Grant asked.

'Everything's fine. It's just . . . it's proving such a terrible strain on all of us.'

'I'm sure that's true,' Siobhan said. Then, with a last expansive look around: 'Well, thank you for letting us see your toys, Mr Marr. We'd better let you get back to work now . . .' But having half turned away, she stopped again. 'I'm sure I've seen soldiers like these somewhere before,' she said, as if thinking aloud. 'Maybe in David Costello's flat?'

'I think I *did* give David one piece,' Marr said. 'Was it him who . . . ?' He broke off, smiled and shook his head. 'I forgot: you won't be at liberty to say.'

'Quite so, sir,' Hood told him.

As they left the building, Grant started to chuckle. 'He didn't like it when you called them "toys".'

'I know, that's why I said it.'

'Don't bother trying to open an account, I can see you being blackballed.'

She smiled. 'He knows about the Internet, Grant. And playing those sorts of games, he's probably got an analytical mind.'

'Quizmaster?'

She wrinkled her nose. 'I'm not sure. I mean, why would he do it? What's in it for him?'

Grant shrugged. 'Maybe nothing much . . . apart from control of Balfour's Bank.'

'Yes, there's always that,' Siobhan said. She was thinking about the playing piece in David Costello's flat. A little gift from Ranald Marr . . . only Costello had said he'd no idea where it had come from, with its broken musket and the soldier's head twisted round. Then he'd called her and told her about Marr's little hobby . . .

'Meantime,' Grant was saying, 'we're no closer to solving the clue.'

He broke her train of thought. She turned towards him. 'Just promise me one thing, Grant.'

'What's that?'

'Promise you're not going to turn up outside my flat at midnight.'

'No can do,' Grant said, smiling. 'We're against the clock, remember.'

She looked at him again, remembering the way he'd been on top of Hart Fell, the way he'd gripped her hands. Right now, he looked like he was enjoying himself – the chase, the challenge – just a little too much.

'Promise,' she said again.

'Okay,' he said. 'I promise.'

Then he turned and gave her a wink.

Back at the station, Siobhan sat in a toilet cubicle and studied the hand which she'd brought up level with her eyes. The hand carried a slight tremble. It was curious how you could be quivering inside, yet manage not to show it. But she knew her body had other ways of manifesting outward signs: the rashes she sometimes got; the outbreaks of acne on her chin and neck; the eczema she sometimes suffered from on the thumb and forefinger of her left hand.

She was trembling now because she was having trouble focusing on what was important. It was important to do the job well; important, too, not to piss off Gill Templer. She didn't think her own hide was toughened the way Rebus's was. The case was important, and maybe Quizmaster was too. It rankled that she couldn't know for sure. She knew one thing: that the game was in danger of becoming an obsession. She kept trying to put herself in Flip Balfour's shoes, to think along the same lines. She couldn't be sure how well she was doing. Then there was Grant, who was looking more and more of a liability. Yet she couldn't have come this far without him, so maybe it was important that she stay close to him. She couldn't even be sure that Quizmaster was male. She had a gut feeling, but it was dangerous to depend on those: she'd seen Rebus screw up more than once on the strength of a gut feeling for someone's guilt or innocence.

She still wondered about the liaison job, and whether she'd burned her bridges there. Gill had succeeded only by becoming more like the male officers around her, people like ACC Carswell. She probably thought she'd played the system, but Siobhan suspected that it was the system which had played *her*, moulding her, changing her, making sure she would fit in. It meant putting up barriers, keeping your distance. It meant teaching people lessons, people like Ellen Wylie.

She heard the door to the Ladies' creak open. A moment later, there was a soft tapping on her cubicle door.

'Siobhan? That you in there?'

She recognised the voice: Dilys Gemmill, one of the WPCs. 'What's up, Dilys?' she called.

'That drink tonight, wondered if you were still on.'

It was a regular thing: four or five WPCs, plus Siobhan. A bar with loud music, plenty of gossip to go with the Moscow Mules. Siobhan an honorary member: the only non-uniform ever invited.

'I don't think I can manage it, Dilys.'

'Come on, girl . . .'

'Next time for definite, okay?'

'It's your funeral,' Gemmill said, moving away.

'I hope not,' Siobhan muttered to herself, getting up to unlock the door.

Rebus stood across the road from the church. He'd been home to change, but now that he was here he couldn't make himself go in. A taxi drew up and Dr Curt stepped out. As he stopped to button his jacket, he saw Rebus. It was a small, local church, just as Leary had wanted. He'd said as much to Rebus several times during the course of their conversations.

'Quick, clean and simple,' he'd stated. 'It's the only way I'll have it.'

The church might have been small, but the congregation looked large. The Archbishop, who'd attended the Scots College in Rome with Leary, would be leading the service, and what looked like dozens of priests and officiates had filed into the church already. 'Clean' it might be, but Rebus doubted the event would turn out either 'quick' or 'simple' . . .

Curt was crossing the street. Rebus flicked the remains of his cigarette on to the roadway and slid his hands into his pockets. He noticed some ash clinging to his sleeve, but didn't bother brushing it away.

'Nice day for it,' Curt commented, studying a sky which thick cloud had turned a bruised-looking grey. It felt claustrophobic, even outdoors. When Rebus brushed a hand across the back of his head he could feel the follicles coated with sweat. On afternoons like this, Edinburgh felt like imprisonment, a city of walls.

Curt was tugging at one of his shirt sleeves, making sure it came an inch below the jacket, exposing a hallmarked silver cuff-link. His suit was dark blue, the shirt white, his tie plain black. His black brogues had been given a polish. Always immaculately dressed. Rebus knew his own suit, though the best, the most formal he possessed, was shabby by comparison. He'd had it six, seven years, had sucked his gut in to get the trousers fastened. Hadn't even bothered trying to button the jacket. Austin Reed he'd got it from; maybe it was time for another visit. He got few invites these days to weddings and christenings, but funerals were another matter. Colleagues, drinkers he knew . . . they were falling off the perch. Only three weeks back, he'd been to the crematorium, a woolly-suit from St Leonard's who'd died less than a year after retiring. The white shirt and black tie had gone back on to the hanger afterwards. He'd checked the shirt collar this afternoon, before putting the shirt back on.

'Shall we go in then?' Curt said.

Rebus nodded. 'You go ahead.'

'What's wrong?'

Rebus shook his head. 'Nothing. I'm just not sure . . .' He took his hands from his pockets, busied himself with another cigarette. Offered one to Curt, who nodded and took it.

'Not sure of what?' the pathologist asked, as Rebus lit the cigarette for him. Rebus waited until he had his own one lit. A couple of puffs and then a loud exhaling of smoke.

'I want to remember him the way he was to me,' he said. 'If I go in there, it'll be speeches and other people's memories. It won't be the Conor I knew.'

'The pair of you were pretty close at one time,' Curt agreed. 'I didn't really know him that well.'

'Is Gates coming?' Rebus asked.

Curt shook his head. 'Prior commitment.'

'Did the pair of you do the autopsy?'

'It was a brain haemorrhage.'

More mourners were arriving, some on foot, others by

car. Another taxi drew up, and Donald Devlin got out. Rebus thought he spotted a grey cardigan beneath the suit jacket. Devlin took the church steps at a brisk pace and disappeared inside.

'Was he able to help you?' Curt asked.

'Who?'

Curt nodded towards the departing taxi. 'The old-timer.'

'Not really. He gave it his best shot though.'

'Then he did as much as Gates or I could have.'

'I suppose so.' Rebus was thinking of Devlin, picturing him at the desk, poring over details, Ellen Wylie keeping her distance. 'He was married, wasn't he?' he asked.

Curt nodded again. 'Widower. Why do you ask?'

'No reason, really.'

Curt looked at his watch. 'I think I'd better go in.' He stamped the cigarette out on the pavement. 'Are you coming?'

'I don't think so.'

'What about the cemetery?'

'I think I'll give that a miss too.' Rebus looked up at the clouds. 'What the Americans would call a rain-check.'

Curt nodded. 'I'll see you later then.'

'Next time there's a homicide,' Rebus confirmed. Then he turned and walked away. His head was filling with images of the mortuary, the post-mortem examination. The wooden blocks they laid the deceased's head on. The little channels on the table which drained away the body fluids. The instruments and specimen jars ... He thought of the jars he'd seen in the Black Museum, the way horror had mixed with fascination. One day, maybe not too far away, he knew it would be him on that table, maybe Curt and Gates preparing their day's routine. That was what he would be to them: part of the routine, just as another routine was being played out in the church behind him. He hoped some of it would be in Latin: Leary had been a great fan of the Latin mass, would recite whole passages to Rebus, knowing he couldn't understand.

'Surely in your day they taught Latin?' he'd asked one time.

'Maybe at the posh school,' Rebus had replied. 'Where I went, it was woodwork and metalwork.'

'Turning out workers for the religion of heavy industry?' And Leary had chuckled, the sound booming from deep within his chest. Those sounds were what Rebus would remember: the clucking of his tongue whenever he felt Rebus had said anything wantonly idiotic; the exaggerated groan whenever he rose to fetch more Guinness from the fridge.

'Ah, Conor,' Rebus said now, bowing his head so no passers-by would see the tears forming.

Siobhan was on the phone to the Farmer.

'It's good to hear from you, Siobhan.'

'Actually, I'm after a favour, sir. Sorry to disturb your peace and quiet.'

'There's such a thing as too much peace and quiet, you know.' The Farmer laughed, so she would assume he was joking, but she detected something behind his words.

'It's important to stay active.' She almost winced: it sounded like something from an agony column.

'That's what they say all right.' He laughed again: it sounded even more forced this time. 'Which new hobby are you suggesting?'

'I don't know.' Siobhan squirmed in her chair. This wasn't quite the conversation she'd expected. Grant Hood was sitting the other side of the desk. He'd borrowed John Rebus's chair, which looked like the one from the Farmer's old office. 'Maybe golf?'

Now Grant frowned, wondering what the hell she was talking about.

'I've always said golf spoils a good walk,' the Farmer said.

'Well, walking's good for you.'

'Is it? Thanks for reminding me.' The Farmer definitely sounded tetchy; she didn't know quite why or how she'd hit a nerve.

'About this favour . . . ?' she began.

'Yes, better ask it quick, before I get my jogging shoes on.'

'It's sort of a clue to a puzzle.'

'You mean a crossword?'

'No, sir. It's something we're working on. Philippa Balfour was trying to solve all these clues, so we're doing the same.'

'And how can I help?' He'd calmed a little; sounded interested.

'Well, sir, the clue goes: "a corny beginning where the mason's dream ended". We're wondering if it might be "mason" as in "Masonic Lodge".'

'And someone told you I'm a Mason?'

'Yes.'

The Farmer was quiet for a moment. 'Let me get a pen,' he said at last. Then he had her repeat the clue while he wrote it down. 'Capital M on Mason?'

'No, sir. Does that make a difference?'

'I'm not sure. Usually I'd expect a capital.'

'So it could be a stonemason or something instead?'

'Hang on, I'm not saying you're wrong. I just need to think about it. Can you give me half an hour or so?'

'Of course.'

'Are you at St Leonard's?'

'Yes, sir.'

'Siobhan, you don't need to call me "sir" any more.'

'Understood . . . sir.' She smiled. 'Sorry, can't help it.'

The Farmer seemed to brighten a little. 'Well, I'll call you back after I've given this some thought. No nearer to finding out what happened to her?'

'We're all working flat out, sir.'

'I'm sure you are. How's Gill coping?'

'In her element, I think.'

'She could go all the way, Siobhan, mark my words. There's a lot you could learn from Gill Templer.'

'Yes, sir. I'll speak to you later.'

'Bye, Siobhan.'

She put the phone down. 'He's going to mull it over,' she told Grant.

'Great, and meantime the clock's ticking.'

'Okay then, clever-clogs, let's hear *your* great idea.'

He looked at her as if measuring the challenge, then held up a finger. 'One, it reads to me almost like a story-line. Maybe from Shakespeare or somewhere.' A second finger. 'Two, does it mean "corny" as in old-fashioned, or is it maybe to do with where corn comes from?'

'You mean where corn was first grown?'

He shrugged. 'Or how it starts off life as a seed: ever heard the expression "sowing the corn of an idea"?'

She shook her head. He held up another finger.

'Three, say it's mason as in stonemason. Could it be a gravestone? That's where all our dreams end, after all. Maybe it's a carving of a corn-stalk.' He bunched the raised fingers into a fist. 'That's what I've got so far.'

'If it's a gravestone, we need to know which cemetery.' Siobhan picked up the scrap of paper on which she'd written the clue. 'There's nothing here, no map reference or page number . . .'

Grant nodded. 'It's a different kind of clue.' He seemed to spot something else. 'Could "a corny beginning" actually be "acorny", as in like an acorn?'

Siobhan frowned. 'Where would that get us?'

'An oak tree . . . maybe oak leaves. A cemetery with "acorn" or "oak" in its name?'

She puffed out her cheeks. 'And where would this cemetery be, or do we have to check every town and city in Scotland?'

'I don't know,' Grant conceded, rubbing at his temples. Siobhan let the clue drop back on to the desk.

'Are they getting harder?' she asked. 'Or is it that my brain's packing in?'

'Maybe we just need a break,' Grant said, trying to get comfortable in the chair. 'We could even call it a day.'

Siobhan glanced up at the clock. It was true: they'd put in about ten hours already. The whole morning had been spent on a wasted trip south. She could feel her limbs aching from the climb. A long hot soak with some bath salts and a glass of Chardonnay . . . It was tempting. But she knew that when she woke up tomorrow, there'd be scant time left before the clue was void, always supposing Quizmaster stuck to his rules. The problem was, the only way to know whether he would or not was to fail to solve the clue in time. It wasn't the sort of risk she wanted to take.

The trip to Balfour's Bank . . . she wondered if that had been a waste of time too. Ranald Marr and his little soldiers . . . the tip-off coming from David Costello . . . the broken playing piece in Costello's flat. She wondered if Costello had been trying to tell her something about Marr. She couldn't think what. Skulking at the back of her mind was the possibility that this whole exercise was a waste of time, that Quizmaster really was playing with them, that the game had nothing to do with Flip's disappearance . . . Maybe that drink with the girls wasn't such a bad idea . . . When her phone went, she snatched at it.

'DC Clarke, CID,' she recited into the mouthpiece.

'DC Clarke, it's the front desk. Got someone down here wants a word.'

'Who is it?'

'A Mr Gandalf.' The speaker's voice dropped. 'Weird-looking bugger, like he got sunstroke in the Summer of Love and hasn't been right since . . .'

Siobhan went downstairs. Gandalf was holding a dark brown fedora, stroking the multicoloured feather attached to its headband. He wore a brown leather waistcoat over the same Grateful Dead T-shirt he'd worn in his shop. The pale blue cords had seen better days, as had the sand-shoes on his feet.

'Hi there,' Siobhan said.

His eyes widened as though he didn't quite recognise her.

'It's Siobhan Clarke,' she said, holding out her hand. 'We met at your shop.'

'Yes, yes,' he mumbled. He stared at her hand but didn't seem inclined to shake it, so Siobhan lowered her arm.

'What brings you here, Gandalf?'

'I said I'd see what I could find about Quizmaster.'

'That's right,' she said. 'Would you like to come upstairs? I could probably rustle us up a cup of coffee.'

He stared at the door she'd just come through, and slowly shook his head. 'Don't like police stations,' he said gravely. 'They give off a bad vibe.'

'I'm sure they do,' Siobhan agreed. 'You'd rather talk outside?' She looked out at the street. Still rush hour, the traffic nose to tail.

'There's a shop round the corner, run by some people I know . . .'

'Good vibes?' Siobhan guessed.

'Excellent,' Gandalf said, his voice animated for the first time.

'Won't it be shut?'

He shook his head. 'They're still open. I checked.'

'All right then, just give me a minute.' Siobhan walked over to the desk, where a shirtsleeved officer was watching from behind a glass shield. 'Can you buzz upstairs to DC Hood, tell him I'll be back in ten?'

The officer nodded.

'Come on then,' Siobhan told Gandalf. 'What's the shop called anyway?'

'Out of the Nomad's Tent.'

Siobhan knew the place. It was more warehouse than shop, and sold gorgeous carpets and crafts. She'd splashed out there once on a kilim, because the rug she'd coveted was out of her price range. A lot of the stuff came from India and Iran. As they walked in, Gandalf waved a greeting to the proprietor, who waved back and returned to some paperwork.

'Good vibes,' Gandalf said with a smile, and Siobhan couldn't help but smile back.

'Not sure my overdraft would agree,' she said.

'It's only money,' Gandalf told her, as though imparting some great wisdom.

She shrugged, keen to get down to business. 'So, what can you tell me about Quizmaster?'

'Not a great deal, except that he may have other names.'

'Such as?'

'Questor, Quizling, Myster, Spellbinder, OmniSent ... How many do you want?'

'What does it all mean?'

'These are names used by people who've set challenges on the Internet.'

'Games that are happening right now?'

He reached out his hand to touch a rug hanging from the nearest wall. 'You could study this pattern for years,' he said, 'and still not wholly understand it.'

Siobhan repeated her question and he seemed to come to himself.

'No, they're old games. Some involving logic puzzles, numerology ... others where you took on a role, like knight or apprentice wizard.' He glanced towards her. 'We're talking about the virtual world. Quizmaster could have *virtually* any number of names at his disposal.'

'And no way of tracing him?'

Gandalf shrugged. 'Maybe if you asked the CIA or the FBI ...'

'I'll bear that in mind.'

He shifted slightly in what was almost a squirm. 'I did learn one other thing.'

'What?'

He took a sheet of paper from the back pocket of his cords, handed it to Siobhan, who unfolded it. A news cutting from three years before. It concerned a student who had disappeared from his home in Germany. A body had been found on a remote hillside in the north of Scotland. It had been lying there many weeks, even months, disturbed only by the local wildlife. Identification had proven difficult, the corpse reduced to skin and bone. Until the parents of the German student had widened their search. They became convinced the body on the hillside was that of their son, Jürgen. A revolver had been found twenty feet from the corpse. A single bullet had pierced the young man's skull. The police had it down as suicide, explained away the location of the firearm by saying a sheep or some other animal could have moved it. Plausible, Siobhan had to concede. But the parents still weren't convinced that their son hadn't been murdered. The gun wasn't his, and couldn't be traced. The bigger question was: how had he ended up in the Scottish Highlands? No one seemed to know. Then Siobhan frowned, had to read the story's final paragraph again:

Jürgen was keen on role-playing games, and spent many hours surfing the Internet. His parents think it possible that their student son became involved in some game which had tragic consequences.

Siobhan held up the clipping. 'Is this all there is?'

He nodded. 'Just the one story.'

'Where did you get it?'

'From someone I know.' He held out his hand. 'He'd like it back.'

'Why?'

'Because he's writing a book about the perils of the e-universe. Incidentally, he'd like to interview you some time, too.'

'Maybe later.' Siobhan folded the clipping but made no attempt to hand it back. 'I need to keep this, Gandalf. Your friend can have it when I'm finished with it.'

Gandalf looked disappointed in her, as though she'd failed to keep her side of some bargain.

'I promise he can have it back when I'm finished.'

'Couldn't we just photocopy it?'

Siobhan sighed. An hour from now, she hoped she'd be in that bathtub, maybe with a gin and tonic replacing the wine. 'All right,' she said. 'Come back to the station and . . .'

'They'll have a copier here.' He was pointing towards the corner where the proprietor sat.

'Okay, you win.'

Gandalf brightened at this, as though those three little words were the sweetest ones he knew.

Back at the station, having left Gandalf at Out of the Nomad's Tent, Siobhan found Grant Hood scrunching another sheet of paper into a ball and failing to hit the waste-paper bin with it.

'What's up?' she asked.

'I got wondering about anagrams.'

'And?'

'Well, if the town of Banchory didn't have that "h", it would be an anagram of "a corny b".'

Siobhan burst out laughing, slapping her hand to her mouth when she saw Grant's look.

'No,' he said, 'go ahead and laugh.'

'God, I'm sorry, Grant. I think I'm nearing a state of mild hysteria.'

'Should we try e-mailing Quizmaster, tell him we're stuck?'

'Maybe nearer the deadline.' Looking over his shoulder at the remaining sheet of paper, Siobhan saw that he was working on anagrams for 'mason's dream'.

'Call it a day?' he suggested.

'Maybe.'

He caught her tone of voice. 'You've got something?'

'Gandalf,' she said, handing over the news story. She watched him read, noticing that his lips moved slightly. She wondered if he'd always done it . . .

'Interesting,' he said at last. 'Do we follow it up?'

'I think we have to, don't you?'

He shook his head. 'Hand it over to the inquiry. We've got our work cut out with this bloody clue.'

'Hand it over . . . ?' She was aghast. 'This is *ours*, Grant. What if it turns out to be vital?'

'Christ, Siobhan, listen to yourself. It's an *inquiry*, lots of people all chipping in. It doesn't belong to us. You can't be selfish with something like this.'

'I just don't want someone else stealing our thunder.'

'Even if it means finding Flip Balfour alive?'

She paused, screwed up her face. 'Don't be stupid.'

'This all comes from John Rebus, doesn't it?'

Colour rose to her cheeks. 'What does?'

'Wanting to keep it all to yourself, like the whole investigation's down to you and you alone.'

'Bollocks.'

'You know it yourself; I can see it just by looking at you.'

'I don't believe I'm hearing this.'

He stood up to face her. They were no more than a foot apart, the office empty. 'You know it,' he repeated quietly.

'Look, all I was trying to say . . .'

'. . . was that you don't want to share, and if that doesn't sound like Rebus, I don't know what does.'

'You know your trouble?'

'I get the feeling I'm about to find out.'

'You're too chicken, always playing by the rule-book.'

'You're a cop, not a private detective.'

'And you're chicken. Blinkers on and toeing the line.'

'Chickens don't wear blinkers,' he spat back.

'They must, because *you* do!' she exploded.

'That's right,' he said, seeming to calm a little, head bobbing. 'That's right: I always play by the rules, don't I?'

'Look, all I meant was—'

He grabbed her arms, pulled her to him, his mouth seeking hers. Siobhan's body went rigid, then her face twisted away. The grip he had on her arms, she couldn't move them. She'd backed up against the desk, stuck there.

'A good close working partnership,' a voice boomed from the doorway. 'That's what I like to see.'

Grant's grip on her fell away as Rebus walked into the room.

'Don't mind me,' he continued. 'Just because I don't indulge in these new-fangled methods of policing doesn't mean I don't approve.'

'We were just . . .' Grant's voice died. Siobhan had walked round the desk and was lowering herself shakily into her chair. Rebus approached.

'Finished with this?' He meant the Farmer's chair. Grant nodded and Rebus wheeled it back towards his own desk. He noticed that on Ellen Wylie's desk, the autopsy reports were tied back up with string: conclusions reached, and of no further use. 'Did the Farmer get you a result?' he asked.

'Hasn't called back,' Siobhan said, trying to control her voice. 'I was just about to phone him.'

'But you mistook Grant's tonsils for the receiver, eh?'

'Sir,' she said, keeping her voice level, though her heart was pounding, 'I wouldn't want you to get the wrong impression about what happened here . . .'

Rebus held up a hand. 'Nothing to do with me, Siobhan. You're dead right. Let's say no more about it.'

'I think something needs to be said.' Her voice had risen. She glanced over towards where Grant was standing, body turned away from her, head twisted so his eyes were not quite on her.

But she knew he was pleading. Mr Boy-Tekky-Racer! Mr Nerdy-Well with his gadgets and flash car!

Better make that a bottle of gin, a whole crateful of gin. And sod the bath.

'Oh?' Rebus was asking, genuinely curious now.

I could finish your career right here, Grant. 'It's nothing,' she said finally. Rebus stared at her, but she kept her eyes fixed on the paperwork before her.

'Anything happening your end, Grant?' he asked blithely, settling into his chair.

'What?' Colour bloomed in Grant's cheeks.

'The latest clue: anywhere near solving it?'

'Not really, sir.' Grant was standing by one of the other desks, gripping its edge.

'How about you?' Siobhan asked, shifting in her seat.

'Me?' Rebus tapped a pen against his knuckles. 'I think today I've managed to achieve the square root of bugger all.' He threw the pen down. 'Which is why I'm buying.'

'Already had a couple of drinks?' Siobhan asked.

Rebus's eyes narrowed. 'A few. They put a friend of mine into the ground. Tonight, I was planning a private wake. If either of you would likc to join me, that would be fine.'

'I need to go home,' Siobhan said.

'I don't . . .'

'Come on, Grant. It'll be good for you.'

Grant looked in Siobhan's direction, seeking guidance, or maybe permission. 'I suppose I might manage the one,' he conceded.

'Good lad,' Rebus told him. 'One drink it is.'

Having nursed his pint while Rebus downed two double whiskies and two beers, Grant was dismayed to find another half poured into his glass as soon as there was room for it.

'I have to drive home,' he warned.

'Bloody hell, Grant,' Rebus complained, 'that's about all I've heard from you.'

'Sorry.'

'And apologies make up the rest. I can't see there's any need to apologise for snogging Siobhan.'

'I don't know how it happened.'

'Don't try to analyse it.'

'I think the case just got . . .' He broke off at the sound of a dull electronic bleeping. 'Yours or mine?' he asked, already reaching into his jacket. But it was Rebus's mobile. He angled his head to let Grant know he was taking it outside.

'Hello?' Cool twilight, taxis looking for trade. A woman nearly tripped over a cracked paving slab. A young man, shaven head and nose-ring, helped her retrieve the oranges which had tumbled from her shopping bag. A small act of kindness . . . but Rebus watched until the youth moved away, just in case.

'John? It's Jean. Are you working?'

'Surveillance,' Rebus told her.

'Oh dear, do you want me to . . . ?'

'It's okay, Jean. I was joking. I'm just out having a drink.'

'How was the funeral?'

'I didn't go. I mean, I *did* go, but I couldn't face it.'

'And now you're drinking?'

'Don't start with the help-line stuff.'

She laughed. 'I wasn't going to. It's just that I'm sitting here with a bottle of wine and the TV . . .'

'And?'

'And some company would be nice.'

Rebus knew he was in no state to drive; not much of a state for anything, if it came to it. 'I don't know, Jean. You've not seen me after a drink.'

'What, you turn into Mr Hyde?' She laughed again. 'I had that with my husband. I doubt you could show me anything new.' Her voice strained for levity, but there was an edge to it. Maybe she was nervous about asking him: no one liked a rejection. Or maybe there was more to it . . .

'I suppose I could take a taxi.' He studied himself: still in the funeral suit, the tie removed and top two buttons of the shirt undone. 'Maybe I should go home and change.'

'If you like.'

He looked across the street. The woman with the shopping was waiting at the bus stop now. She kept glancing into her bag as if checking everything was there. City life: mistrust part of the armour you wore; no such thing as a simple good deed.

'I'll see you soon,' he said.

Back in the pub, Grant was standing next to his empty pint glass. As Rebus came forwards, he raised his hands in a show of surrender.

'Got to go.'

'Yes, me too,' Rebus said.

Grant looked somehow disappointed, as though he'd wanted Rebus to go on drinking, getting drunker. Rebus looked at the empty glass, wondering if the barman had been persuaded to ditch its contents.

'You all right to drive?' Rebus asked.

'I'm fine.'

'Good.' Rebus slapped Grant's shoulder. 'In that case, you can give me a lift to Portobello . . .'

Siobhan had spent the past hour trying to clear her head of anything and everything to do with the case. It wasn't working. The bath hadn't worked; the gin was refusing to kick in. The music on her hi-fi – Mutton Birds, *Envy of Angels* – wasn't cocooning her the way it usually did. The latest clue was ricocheting around her skull. And every thirty seconds or so . . . here it came again! . . . she watched a replay of Grant pinning her arms, while John Rebus – of all people! – watched from the doorway. She wondered what would have happened if he hadn't announced his presence. She wondered how long he'd been there, and whether he'd heard any of their argument.

She leaped back up from the sofa and started pacing the room again, glass in hand. No, no, no . . . as if repeating the word could make everything go away, never have happened. Because *that* was the problem. You couldn't unmake something.

'Stupid bitch,' she said aloud in a sing-song voice, repeating the phrase until the words lost their meaning.

Stupidbitchstupidbitch . . .

No no no no no no . . .

The mason's dream . . .

Flip Balfour . . . Gandalf . . . Ranald Marr . . .

Grant Hood.

Stupidbitchstupidbitch . . .

She was over by the window when the track ended. In the momentary silence, she heard a car turning into the end of her street, and instinct told her who it was. She ran to the lamp and stamped down on the floor-switch, plunging the room into darkness. There was a light on in her hallway, but she doubted it could be seen from outside. She was afraid to move, afraid she would cast a telltale shadow. The car had stopped. The next track was playing. She reached down for the remote and used it to turn off the CD player. Now she could hear the car idling. Her heart was pounding.

Then the door buzzer, telling her someone was outside and wanting in. She waited, didn't move. Her fingers were so tight around the glass that they began to cramp. She changed hands. The buzzer again.

No no no no . . .

Just leave it, Grant. Get in the Alfa and go home. Tomorrow we can start pretending it never happened.

Bzzzz bzzzz zzzz . . .

She began to hum softly to herself, a tune she was making up. Not even a tune really; just sounds to compete with the buzzer and the blood singing in her ears.

She heard a car door close, relaxed a little. Nearly dropped the glass when her phone started ringing.

She could see it by the light of the streetlamp. It was lying on the floor by the sofa. Six rings and the answering machine would kick in. Two . . . three . . . four . . .

Maybe the Farmer!

'Hello?' She slumped on to the sofa, phone to her ear.

'Siobhan? It's Grant.'

'Where are you?'

'I've just been ringing your doorbell.'

'Mustn't be working. What can I do for you?'

'Letting me in would be a start.'

'I'm tired, Grant. Just going to bed.'

'Five minutes, Siobhan.'

'I don't think so.'

'Oh.' The silence was like a third party, some huge, humourless friend only one of them had invited.

'Just go home, eh? I'll see you in the morning.'

'That might be too late for the Quizmaster.'

'Oh, you're here to talk about work?' She slid her free hand up her body, tucking it beneath the arm holding the phone.

'Not exactly,' he admitted.

'No, I didn't think so. Look, Grant, let's call it a moment of madness, eh? I think I can live with that.'

'That's what you think it was?'

'Don't you?'

'What are you scared of, Siobhan?'

'How do you mean?' Her voice hardening.

A short silence before he relented, telling her: 'Nothing. I didn't mean anything. Sorry.'

'I'll see you in the office then.'

'Right.'

'Get a good night's sleep. We'll crack the clue tomorrow.'

'If you say so.'

'I do. Goodnight, Grant.'

''Night, Shiv.'

She ended the call, didn't even take the time to tell him she hated 'Shiv': girls at school had used it. One of her boyfriends at college had liked it, too. He told her it was slang for a knife. Siobhan: even the teachers at her school in England had had trouble with her name. 'See-Oban' they'd pronounce it, and she would have to correct them.

Night, Shiv . . .

Stupidbitch . . .

She heard his car move off, watched the play of headlights across her ceiling and far wall. She sat there in the dark, finishing her drink without tasting it. When her phone rang again, she swore out loud.

'Look,' she roared into the mouthpiece, 'just let it go, okay?'

'Well . . . if you say so.' It was the Farmer's voice.

'Oh, hell, sir, I'm sorry.'

'Expecting another call?'

'No, I . . . maybe another time.'

'Fair enough. I've been doing some ringing round. There are people who know the Craft far better than I do, I thought maybe they could shed some light.'

His tone told her what she needed to know. 'No joy?'

'Not as such. But a couple of folk have still to get back to me. Nobody home, so I left messages. *Nil desperandum*: that's what they say, isn't it?'

Her smile was bleak. 'Some of them probably do, yes.' Hopeless optimists, for example.

'So you can expect another call tomorrow. What time's the cut-off?'

'Late morning.'

'Then I'll make some follow-up calls first thing.'

'Thank you, sir.'

'It's nice to feel useful again.' He paused. 'Things getting you down, Siobhan?'

'I'll cope.'

'I'd put money on it. Speak to you tomorrow.'

'Goodnight, sir.'

She put the phone down. Her drink was finished. *This all comes from John Rebus, doesn't it?* Grant's words to her during their argument. Now here she was with an empty glass in her hand, sitting in the dark, staring out the window.

'I'm not like him at all,' she said out loud, then she picked up the phone again and called his number. Got his answering machine. She knew she could try his mobile. Maybe he was out on the bevvy; almost certainly he was out on the bevvy. She could meet up with him, explore the city's late openers, each dimly lit howff protection against the dark.

But he'd want to talk about Grant, about the clinch he thought he'd found them in. It would be there between them, no matter what the conversation.

She thought about it for a minute, then called his mobile anyway, but it was switched off. Another answering service; another message not left. Last-chance saloon was his pager, but she was winding down now. A mug of tea . . . she'd take it to bed with her. She switched the kettle on, looked for the tea-bags. The box was empty. All she had were some little sachets of herbal stuff: camomile. She wondered if the petrol station at Canonmills would be open . . . maybe the chip shop on Broughton Street. Yes, that was it . . . she could see the answer to her problems! She slipped her shoes and coat on, made sure she had keys and money. When she went out, she checked that the door had locked behind her. Down the stairs and out into the night, searching for the one ally she could depend on, no matter what.

Chocolate.

9

It had just gone seven-thirty when the phone woke her up. She staggered from bed, padded through to the living room. She had one hand on her forehead; the other reached for the handset.

'Hello?'

'Good morning, Siobhan. Didn't wake you, did I?'

'No, I was just making breakfast.' She blinked a few times, then stretched her face, trying to get her eyes open. The Farmer sounded like he'd been up for hours.

'Well, I don't want to keep you, only I've just had a very interesting phone call.'

'One of your contacts?'

'Another early riser. He's in the middle of writing a book about the Knights Templar, connecting them to the Masons. That's probably why he saw it straight away.'

Siobhan was in the kitchen now. She checked there was water in the kettle and switched it on. Enough instant coffee in the jar for maybe two or three cups. She had to do a supermarket run one of these days. Crumbs of chocolate on the worktop. She pressed her finger to them, lifting them to her mouth.

'Saw what?' she said.

The Farmer started laughing. 'You're not awake yet, are you?'

'A bit groggy, that's all.'

'Late night?'

'Maybe one Rolo too many. Saw what, sir?'

'The clue. It's a reference to Rosslyn Chapel. You know where that is?'

'I was there not too long ago.' Another case; one she'd worked with Rebus.

'Then maybe you saw it: one of the windows apparently is decorated with carvings of maize.'

'I don't remember.' But she was waking up now.

'Yet the chapel was built before maize was known in Britain.'

' "A corny beginning",' she recited.

'That's right.'

'And the mason's dream?'

'Something you must have noticed in the chapel: two elaborate pillars. One is called the Mason's Pillar, the other the Apprentice Pillar. The story goes, the Master Mason decided to go abroad to study the design for the pillar he was to construct. But while he was away, one of his apprentices had a dream about the way the finished pillar should look. He got to work and created the Apprentice Pillar. When the Master Mason returned, he was so jealous he went after the apprentice and bludgeoned him to death with a mallet.'

'So the mason's dream ended with the pillar?'

'That's right.'

Siobhan went through the story in her head. 'It all fits,' she said at last. 'Thanks so much, sir.'

'Mission accomplished?'

'Well, not quite. I've got to go.'

'Call me some other time, Siobhan. I want to hear how it ends.'

'I will. Thanks again.'

She ran both hands through her hair. *A corny beginning where the mason's dream ended.* Rosslyn Chapel. It was in the village of Roslin, about six miles south of the city. Siobhan picked up her phone again, ready to call Grant . . . But then she put it down. Over at the laptop, she sent an e-mail to Quizmaster:

The Apprentice Pillar, Rosslyn Chapel.

Then she waited. She drank a cup of weak coffee, using it to wash down two paracetamol. She went into the bathroom and had a shower. She was rubbing her hair dry with a towel when she walked back into the living room. There was still no message from Quizmaster. She sat down again, chewed her bottom lip. They hadn't needed to go to Hart Fell: the name had been enough. In less than three hours, time would be up. Did Quizmaster want her to go to Roslin? She sent another e-mail:

Do I stay or do I go?

Again she waited. The second cup of coffee was weaker than the first. The jar was empty now. If she wanted anything else to drink, it would have to be camomile tea. She wondered if Quizmaster could have gone somewhere. She got the feeling he would take a laptop and mobile with him wherever he went. Maybe he'd even run it twenty-four/ seven, just like she'd been doing. He'd want to know when messages came through.

So what was he playing at?

'Can't risk it,' she said out loud. One final message: *I'm going to the chapel.* Then she went to get dressed.

She got into her car, placed the laptop on the passenger seat. She thought again about calling Grant, but decided against it. She'd be all right; she could take any flak he threw at her . . .

. . . you don't want to share. And if that doesn't sound like Rebus, I don't know what does.

Grant's words to her. Yet here she was heading off to Roslin on her own. No back-up, and having alerted Quizmaster that she was coming. Before she'd reached the top of Leith Walk she'd made up her mind. She turned the car in the direction of Grant's flat.

It was just gone eight-fifteen when the phone woke Rebus up. It was his mobile. He'd plugged it into a wall socket last thing, charged it overnight. He slid from the bed and got his feet caught in the clothes strewn across the carpet. Down on hands and knees, he fumbled for the phone, held it to his ear.

'Rebus,' he said. 'And this had better be good.'

'You're late,' the voice said. Gill Templer.

'Late for what?'

'The big story.'

Still on hands and knees, Rebus glanced towards the bed. No sign of Jean. He wondered if she'd gone to work.

'What big story?'

'Your presence is requested in Holyrood Park. A body's been found on Arthur's Seat.'

'Is it her?' Rebus felt his skin suddenly go clammy.

'Hard to judge at this stage.'

'Oh, Christ.' He angled his neck, eyes to the ceiling. 'How did she die?'

'Body's been there a while.'

'Are Gates and Curt on the scene?'

'Expected shortly.'

'I'll go straight there.'

'Sorry to have disturbed you. Not at Jean's by any chance?'

'Is that a wild guess?'

'Maybe call it woman's intuition.'

'Bye, Gill.'

'Bye, John.'

As he was switching off the phone, the door swung open and Jean Burchill walked in. She was wearing a towelling robe and carrying a tray: orange juice and toast, a cafetière full of coffee.

'My,' she said, 'don't you look fetching?'

Then she saw the look on his face and her smile vanished. 'What's wrong?' she asked.

So he told her.

Grant yawned. They'd picked up a couple of beakers of coffee from a newsagent's, but even so he wasn't fully awake yet. His hair was standing up at the back, and he seemed conscious of it, kept trying to press it flat with his hand.

'Didn't get much sleep last night,' he said, glancing in Siobhan's direction. She kept her eyes on the road.

'Anything in the paper?'

He had the day's tabloid – bought along with the coffees – open across his lap. 'Not much.'

'Anything about the case?'

'I don't think so. Relegated to oblivion.' He had a sudden thought, started patting his pockets.

'What?' For a split second, she thought maybe he'd forgotten some vital medication.

'My mobile. Must've left it on the table.'

'We've got mine.'

'Yes, hooked to my ISP: what happens if someone tries calling?'

'They'll leave a message.'

'I suppose so . . . Look, about yesterday . . .'

'Let's pretend it never happened,' she said quickly.

'But it did.'

'I just wish it hadn't, all right?'

'You're the one who was always complaining I—'

'Subject closed, Grant.' She turned to him. 'I mean it. It's either closed, or I take it to the boss – your call.'

He started to say something, but stopped himself, folded his arms across his chest. Virgin AM was playing quietly on the stereo. She liked it; helped her wake up. Grant wanted something newsy, Radio Scotland or Radio Four.

'My car, my stereo,' was all she'd said to that.

Now he asked her to repeat what she'd already told him about the Farmer's call. She did, glad that they were staying off the subject of the clinch.

Grant sipped his coffee while she spoke. He was wearing sunglasses, though there was no sun. They were Ray-Bans, tortoiseshell frames.

'Sounds good,' he said when she'd finished.

'I think so,' she agreed.

'Almost too easy.'

She snorted. 'So easy we almost missed it.'

He shrugged. 'It didn't take any skill, that's what I'm saying. It's the sort of thing you either know or you don't.'

'Like you said, a different kind of clue.'

'How many Masons do you suppose Philippa Balfour knows?'

'What?'

'It's how you found out. How would *she* have worked it out?'

'She was studying art history, wasn't she?'

'True. So she might have come across Rosslyn Chapel in her studies?'

'Possibly.'

'And would Quizmaster have known that?'

'How could he?'

'Maybe she told him what she was studying.'

'Maybe.'

'Otherwise, it's just not the sort of clue she'd have been able to get. Do you see what I'm saying?'

'I think so. You're saying it needed specialist knowledge that the previous clues didn't?'

'Something like that. Of course, there is one other possibility.'

'Which is?'

'That Quizmaster knew damned fine she'd know a little of Rosslyn Chapel, whether she told him what she was studying or not.'

Siobhan saw what he was getting at. 'Someone who knows her? You're saying Quizmaster is one of her friends?'

Grant peered at her over the top of his Ray-Bans. 'Wouldn't surprise me if Ranald Marr turned out to be a Mason, man in his line of work . . .'

'No, nor me,' Siobhan said thoughtfully. 'We might just have to go back and ask him.'

They turned off the main road and drove into the village of Roslin. Siobhan parked the car beside the chapel's gift shop. The door was locked tight.

'Place doesn't open till ten,' Grant said, reading from the notice. 'How long do you reckon we've got?'

'If we wait till ten, not very long.' Siobhan was sitting in the car, checking that there were no new e-mails for her.

'There must be somebody.' Grant banged on the door with

his fist. Siobhan got out of the car and studied the wall surrounding the chapel grounds.

'Any good at climbing?' she asked Grant.

'We could give it a go,' he said. 'But what if the chapel's locked too?'

'What if someone's in there giving it a quick spit and polish?'

He nodded. But then there was the sound of a bolt being drawn back. The door opened and a man stood there.

'We're not open yet,' he said sternly.

Siobhan showed him her warrant card. 'Police officers, sir. Afraid we can't wait.'

They followed him along a path towards the chapel's side door. The building itself was covered with a huge canopy. From her previous visit, Siobhan knew there was a problem with the roof. It had to dry out before work could be done on it. The chapel was small on the outside, but seemed larger inside, a trick of its ornate decoration. The ceiling itself was stunning, even if much of it was green with damp and decay. Grant stood in the central aisle, gawping much as she had done the first time she'd come here.

'It's incredible,' he said quietly, his words echoing back off the walls. There were carvings everywhere. But Siobhan knew what she was looking for, and walked straight towards the Apprentice Pillar. It was next to some steps leading down to the sacristy. The pillar was about eight feet high, carved ribbons snaking down it.

'This it?' Grant said.

'This is it.'

'So what are we looking for?'

'We'll know when we find it.' Siobhan ran her hands over the cool surface of the pillar, then crouched down. Intertwined dragons were coiled around the base. The tail of one of them, twisting back on itself, had left a small nook. She reached in with finger and thumb and brought out a small square of paper.

'Bloody hell,' Grant said.

She didn't bother with gloves or an evidence bag, knew by

now that Quizmaster wouldn't have left anything useful to Forensics. It was a piece of notepaper, folded over three times. She unfolded it, Grant shifting so they could both see what was printed there.

You are the Seeker. Your next destination is Hellbank. Instructions to follow.

'I don't get it,' Grant said. 'All of this, just for *that?*' His voice was rising.

Siobhan read the message through again, turned the paper over. Its other side was blank. Grant had spun on his heels and kicked air.

'Bastard!' he called out, earning a frown from the guide. 'I bet he's having a bloody good laugh, seeing us chasing all over the place!'

'I think that's part of it, yes,' Siobhan agreed quietly.

He turned to her. 'Part of what?'

'Part of the attraction for him. He likes to see us being run ragged.'

'Yes, but he *doesn't* see us, does he?'

'I don't know. I sometimes get the feeling he might be watching.'

Grant stared at her, then walked up to the guide. 'What's your name?'

'William Eadie.'

Grant had his notebook out. 'And what's your address, Mr Eadie?' He started to take down Eadie's details.

'He's not the Quizmaster,' Siobhan stated.

'The who?' Eadie asked, his voice wavering.

'Never mind,' Siobhan said, dragging Grant away by the arm. They went back to the car, and Siobhan started typing an e-mail:

Ready for Hellbank clue.

She sent it, then sat back.

'Now what?' Grant asked. Siobhan shrugged. But then the laptop announced there was a new message. She clicked to read it.

Ready to give up? That's a surer thing.

Grant let out a hiss of breath. 'Is this a clue or a taunt?'

'Maybe both.' Another message came through:
Hellbank by six tonight.

Siobhan nodded. 'Both,' she repeated.

'Six? He's only giving us eight hours.'

'No time to waste then. What's a surer thing?'

'Not a clue.'

She looked at him. 'You don't think it's a clue?'

He forced a smile. 'That's not what I meant. Let's take another look at it.' Siobhan put the message back up on the screen. 'You know what it looks like?'

'What?'

'A crossword clue. I mean, it's not quite grammatical, is it? It almost makes sense, but doesn't.'

Siobhan nodded. 'Like it's a bit strained?'

'If it *was* a crossword clue . . .' Grant pursed his lips. A little vertical crease appeared between his eyebrows as he concentrated. 'If it was a clue, then "give up" could mean "yield", as in yielding meaning. Do you see?'

He fumbled in his pocket, brought out his notebook and pen. 'I need to see it written down,' he explained, copying out the clue. 'It's a classic crossword construction: part of it tells you what you have to do, part is the meaning you'll have if you do it.'

'Keep going. You might start making sense soon.'

He smiled again, but kept his eyes on the words in front of him. 'Let's say it's an anagram. "Ready to give up . . . that's a surer". If you give up – meaning render or use – the letters in "that's a surer", you'll get a word or words meaning a "thing".'

'What sort of thing?' Siobhan could feel a headache coming on.

'That's what we have to find out.'

'If it's an anagram.'

'If it's an anagram,' Grant conceded.

'And what's any of it got to do with Hellbank, whatever Hellbank is?'

'I don't know.'

'If it *is* an anagram, isn't that too easy?'

'Only if you know how crosswords work. Otherwise you'd read it literally, and it wouldn't mean anything at all.'

'Well, you've just explained it and it still sounds like gobbledygook to me.'

'Then aren't you lucky I'm here? Come on.' He tore off a fresh sheet of paper and handed it to her. 'See if you can unscramble "that's a surer".'

'To make a word that means a thing?'

'Word or words,' Grant corrected her. 'You've got eleven letters to play with.'

'Isn't there some computer program we could use?'

'Probably. But that would be cheating, wouldn't it?'

'Right now, cheating sounds fine to me.'

But Grant wasn't listening. He was already at work.

'I was only up here yesterday,' Rebus said. Bill Pryde had left his clipboard back at Gayfield Square. He was breathing heavily as they climbed. Uniformed officers were standing around. They held rolls of striped tape and were waiting to be told whether a cordon was necessary or practical. There was a line of parked cars on the roadway below: journalists, photographers, at least one TV crew. Word had gone around fast, and the circus had come to town.

'Anything to tell us, DI Rebus?' he'd been asked by Steve Holly as he got out of his own car.

'Just that you're annoying me.'

Now Pryde was explaining that a walker had found the body. 'In some gorse bushes. No real attempt to hide it.'

Rebus kept quiet. Two bodies never found ... the other two found in water. Now this: a hillside. It broke the pattern.

'Is it her?' he asked.

'From the Versace T-shirt, I'd have to say yes.'

Rebus stopped, looked around. A wilderness in the middle of Edinburgh. Arthur's Seat itself was an extinct volcano, surrounded by a bird sanctuary and three lochs. 'You'd have a hard job dragging a body up here,' he said.

Pryde nodded. 'Probably killed on the spot.'

'Lured up here?'

'Or maybe just out walking.'

Rebus shook his head. 'I don't figure her for the walking type.' They'd started moving again, getting close now. A cluster of stooped forms on the hillside, white overalls and hoods: all too easy to contaminate a crime scene. Rebus recognised Professor Gates, red-faced from the exertion of the climb. Gill Templer was next to him, not talking, just listening and looking. The scene-of-crime officers were doing a rudimentary ground search – later on, when the body had been shifted, they'd bring in some of the uniforms and start a fingertip search. It wouldn't be easy: the grass was long and thick. A police photographer was adjusting his lens.

'Better not go any further than this,' Pryde said. Then he called for someone to fetch two more sets of overalls. As Rebus started pulling his on over his shoes, the thin material crackled and flapped in the strong breeze.

'Any sign of Siobhan Clarke?' he asked.

'Tried contacting her and Grant Hood,' Pryde said. 'So far, no luck.'

'Really?' Rebus had to hold back a smile.

'Something I should know about?' Pryde asked.

Rebus shook his head. 'Grim place to die, isn't it?'

'Aren't they all?' Pryde zipped up his one-piece and started forwards towards the corpse.

'Throttled,' Gill Templer informed them.

'Best guess at this stage,' Gates corrected her, 'Morning, John.'

Rebus nodded a greeting back. 'Dr Curt not with you?'

'Phoned in sick. He's been sick a lot lately.' Gates was just making conversation while his examination continued. The body lay awkwardly, legs and arms all jutting angles. The gorse bushes next to it must have hidden it well enough, Rebus guessed. Combined with the long grass, you'd need to be closer than eight feet before you'd be able to make out what it was. The clothing helped with the camouflage: light green combat trousers, khaki T-shirt, grey jacket. The clothes Flip had been wearing the day she'd gone missing.

'Parents informed?' he asked.

Gill nodded. 'They know a body's been found.'

Rebus walked around her to get a better view. The face was turned away from him. There were leaves in the hair, and a slug's shimmering trail. Her skin was mauve-coloured. Gates had probably moved the body slightly. What Rebus was seeing was lividity, the blood sinking in death, colouring the body parts nearest the ground. He'd seen dozens of corpses over the years; they never got any less sad, or made him any less depressed. Animation was the key to every living thing, its absence difficult to accept. He'd seen grieving relatives reach out to bodies on mortuary slabs and shake them, as if this would bring them back. Philippa Balfour wasn't coming back.

'The fingers have been gnawed at,' Gates stated, more for his tape recorder than his audience. 'Local wildlife most probably.'

Weasels or foxes, Rebus guessed. Facts of nature you didn't find in the TV documentaries.

'Bit of a bugger, that,' Gates went on. Rebus knew what he meant: if Philippa had fought her attacker, her fingertips might have told them a lot – bits of skin or blood beneath the nails.

'What a waste,' Pryde suddenly said. Rebus got the feeling he didn't mean Philippa's death as such, but the effort they'd expended during the days since her disappearance – the checks on airports, ferries, trains ... working on the assumption that she was maybe – just maybe – still alive. And throughout, she'd been lying here, each day robbing them of possible evidence, possible clues.

'Lucky she was found so soon,' Gates commented, perhaps to comfort Pryde. True enough, another woman's body had been found a few months back in a different part of the park, hardly any distance at all from a popular path. Yet the body had lain there for over a month. It had turned out to be a 'domestic', that handy euphemism when victims were killed by their loved ones.

Down below, Rebus recognised one of the grey mortuary vans arriving. The body would be bagged and taken away to the Western General, where Gates would conduct his autopsy.

'Drag marks on her heels,' Gates was reciting into his tape machine. 'Not too severe. Lividity consistent with body's position, so she was either still alive or only just dead when she was dragged here.'

Gill Templer looked around. 'How far do we need to widen the search?'

'Fifty, a hundred yards maybe,' Gates told her. She glanced in Rebus's direction, and he saw that she wasn't hopeful. Unlikely they'd be able to pinpoint exactly where she was dragged from, unless she'd dropped something.

'Nothing in the pockets?' Rebus asked.

Gates shook his head. 'Jewellery on the hands, and quite an expensive watch.'

'Cartier,' Gill added.

'At least we can rule out robbery,' Rebus muttered, causing Gates to smile.

'No signs of the clothing having been disturbed,' the pathologist commented, 'so you can probably rule out a sexual motive while you're at it.'

'Better and better.' Rebus looked at Gill. 'This is going to be a cinch.'

'Hence my ear-to-ear grin,' she parried solemnly.

Back at St Leonard's, the station was buzzing with the news, but all Siobhan could feel was a dazed numbness. Playing Quizmaster's game – the way Philippa probably had – had made Siobhan feel an affinity with the missing student. Now she was no longer a MisPer, and the worst fears had been realised.

'We always knew, didn't we?' Grant said. 'It was just a matter of when the body turned up.' He dropped his notebook on to the desk in front of him. Three or four pages were covered with anagrams. He sat down and turned to a fresh sheet, pen in hand. George Silvers and Ellen Wylie were in the CID room too.

'I took my kids up Arthur's Seat just last weekend,' Silvers was saying.

Siobhan asked who found the body.

'Someone out walking,' Wylie replied. 'Middle-aged woman, I think. Daily constitutional.'

'Be a while before she takes that route again,' Silvers muttered.

'Was Flip lying there all this time?' Siobhan was looking across to where Grant was busy juggling letters. Maybe he was right to keep working, but she couldn't help feeling a certain distaste. How could he not be affected by the news? Even George Silvers – as cynical as they came – looked a bit shell-shocked.

'Arthur's Seat,' he repeated. 'Just last weekend.'

Wylie decided to answer Siobhan's question. 'Chief Super seems to think so.' As she spoke, she looked down at her desk, and rubbed her hand along it as though wiping off dust.

It hurts her, Siobhan thought . . . even saying the words 'Chief Super' reminds her of that TV appearance and hardens the sense of resentment.

When one of the phones rang, Silvers went to answer.

'No, he's not here,' he told the caller. Then: 'Hang on, I'll check.' He put his hand over the mouthpiece. 'Ellen, any idea when Rebus will be back?'

She shook her head slowly. Suddenly Siobhan knew where he was: he was on Arthur's Seat . . . while Wylie, who was supposed to be his partner, wasn't. She thought of Gill Templer, telling Rebus he was needed there. He'd have gone like a shot, leaving Wylie behind. It looked to Siobhan like a calculated snub by Templer. She would know *exactly* how Wylie would feel.

'Sorry, no idea,' Silvers said into the phone. Then: 'Hang on a sec.' He held the receiver out towards Siobhan.

'Lady wants to speak to you.'

Siobhan crossed the floor, mouthing the word 'who?', but Silvers just shrugged, handed her the phone.

'Hello, DC Clarke speaking?'

'Siobhan, it's Jean Burchill.'

'Hi, Jean, what can I do for you?'

'Have you identified her yet?'

'Not a hundred per cent. How did you know?'

'John told me, then he rushed off.'

Siobhan's lips formed a silent O. John Rebus and Jean Burchill ... well, well. 'Do you want me to tell him you called?'

'I tried his mobile.'

'He might have it turned off: you don't always want interruptions at the locus.'

'The what?'

'The crime scene.'

'Arthur's Seat, isn't it? We were there only yesterday morning.'

Siobhan looked across to Silvers. It seemed like every other person had been on Arthur's Seat recently. When her eyes moved to Grant, she saw that he was staring at his notepad, as if mesmerised by something there.

'Do you know where on Arthur's Seat?' Jean was asking.

'Across the road from Dunsapie Loch and a bit further around towards the east.'

Siobhan was watching Grant. His eyes were on her as he got up from his chair, picking up the notebook.

'Where's that ... ?' The question was rhetorical, Jean trying to picture the location. Grant was holding the notebook out in front of him, but still too far away for her to make out much: jumbles of letters, and then a couple of words circled. Siobhan narrowed her eyes.

'Oh,' Jean said suddenly, 'I know where you mean. Hellbank, I think it's called.'

'Hellbank?' Siobhan made sure Grant could hear her, but his mind seemed to be elsewhere.

'Quite a steep slope,' Jean was saying, 'which might explain the name, though of course the folklore prefers witches and devilry.'

'Yes,' Siobhan said, dragging the word out. 'Look, Jean, I've got to go.' She was staring at the words circled on

Grant's notepad. He'd worked out the anagram. 'That's a surer' had become 'Arthur's Seat'.

Siobhan put down the phone.

'He was leading us to her,' Grant said quietly.

'Maybe.'

'What do you mean, "maybe"?'

'You're saying he knew Flip was dead. We can't know that for certain. All he was doing was taking us to the places Flip went.'

'She turned up dead at this one. And who apart from Quizmaster knew she'd be there?'

'Someone could have followed her, or even chanced upon her.'

'You don't believe that,' Grant said confidently.

'I'm playing devil's advocate, Grant, that's all.'

'He killed her.'

'Then why bother helping us play the game?'

'To fuck with our heads.' He paused. 'No, to fuck with *your* head. And maybe more than that.'

'Then he'd have killed me before now.'

'Why?'

'Because now I don't need to play the game any more. I've come as far as Flip did.'

He shook his head slowly. 'You're saying if he sends you the clue for . . . what's the next stage?'

'Stricture.'

He nodded. 'If he sends it, you won't be tempted?'

'No,' she said.

'You're lying.'

'Well, after this there's no way I'd go anywhere without back-up, and he must know that.' She had a thought. 'Stricture,' she said.

'What about it?'

'He e-mailed Flip . . . *after* she'd been killed. Why on earth would he do that if he'd killed her?'

'Because he's a psychopath.'

'I don't think so.'

'You should get online and ask him.'

'Ask if he's a psychopath?'

'Tell him what we know.'

'He could just disappear. Face it, Grant, we could walk past him in the street and not know him. He's just a name – and not even a real name.'

Grant thumped the desk. 'Well, we've got to do *something*. Any minute now he's going to hear on the radio or TV that the body's been found. He'll be expecting to hear from us.'

'You're right,' she said. The laptop was in her shoulder-bag, still hooked up to the mobile phone. She got it out and set it up, plugging both computer and phone into the floor point for a recharge.

Which gave Grant time enough to start having second thoughts. 'Hang on,' he said, 'we need to clear this with DCS Templer.'

She gave him a look. 'Back to playing by the rules, eh?'

His face reddened, but he nodded. 'Something like this, we need to tell her.'

Silvers and Wylie, who'd been listening intently through-out, had understood enough to know something important was going on.

'I'm with Siobhan,' Wylie said. 'Strike while the iron is hot and all that.'

Silvers disagreed. 'You know the score: Chief Super'll blast the pair of you if you go behind her back.'

'We're not going behind her back,' Siobhan stated, eyes on Wylie.

'Yes we are,' Grant said. 'It's a murder case now, Siobhan. The time for playing games just stopped.' He rested both hands on her desk. 'Send that e-mail, and you're on your own.'

'Maybe that's where I want to be,' she retorted, regretting the words the moment they were out.

'Nice to have a bit of plain speaking,' Grant said.

'I'm all for it,' John Rebus said from the doorway. Ellen Wylie straightened up and folded her arms. 'Speaking of which,' he went on, 'sorry, Ellen, I should have called you.'

'Forget it.' But it was clear to everyone in the room that *she* wouldn't.

When Rebus had listened to Siobhan's version of the morning's events – Grant interrupting now and then with a comment or different perspective – they all looked to him for a decision. He ran a finger along the top of the laptop's screen.

'Everything you've just told me,' he advised, 'needs to be taken to DCS Templer.'

To Siobhan's eyes, Grant didn't look so much vindicated as revoltingly smug. Ellen Wylie, meantime, looked like she was spoiling for a fight with anyone . . . about anything. As a murder team, they weren't exactly ideal.

'Okay,' she said, ready to make at least a partial peace, 'we'll go talk to the Chief Super.' And, as Rebus started nodding, she added: 'Though I'm willing to bet it's not what you would have done.'

'Me?' he said. 'I wouldn't have had the first clue, Siobhan. Know why?'

'Why?'

'Because e-mail's a black art as far as I'm concerned.'

Siobhan smiled, but there was a thread running through her mind: black art . . . coffins used in witches' spells . . . Flip's death on a hillside called Hellbank.

Witchcraft?

Six of them in the cramped office at Gayfield Square: Gill Templer and Bill Pryde; Rebus and Ellen Wylie; Siobhan and Grant. Templer was the only one sitting. Siobhan had printed off all the e-mails, and Templer was sifting through them silently. Finally she looked up.

'Is there *any* way we can identify Quizmaster?'

'Not that I know of,' Siobhan admitted.

'It's possible,' Grant added. 'I mean, I'm not sure how, but I think it's possible. Look at these viruses, somehow the Americans always seem to be able to trace them back.'

Templer nodded. 'That's true.'

'The Met has a computer crime unit, doesn't it?' Grant went on. 'They could have links to the FBI.'

Templer studied him. 'Think you're up to it, Grant?'

He shook his head. 'I like computers, but this is way out of my league. I mean, I'd be happy to liaise . . .'

'Fair enough.' Templer turned to Siobhan. 'This German student you were telling us about . . .'

'Yes?'

'I'd like a bit more detail.'

'Shouldn't be too difficult.'

Suddenly Templer's gaze shifted to Wylie. 'Can you run with that, Ellen?'

Wylie looked surprised. 'I suppose so.'

'You're splitting us up?' Rebus interrupted.

'Unless you can think of a good reason not to.'

'A doll was left at Falls, now the body's turned up. It's the same pattern as before.'

'Not according to your coffin-maker. Different workmanship altogether, I believe he said.'

'You're putting it down to coincidence?'

'I'm not putting it down to anything, and if something else crops up in connection with it, you can start back in again. But we're on a murder case now, and that changes everything.'

Rebus glanced towards Wylie. She was simmering – the transfer from dusty old autopsies to a background check on a student's curious demise . . . it wasn't exactly thrilling her. But at the same time she wasn't going to throw her weight behind Rebus – too busy working on her own sense of injustice.

'Right,' Templer said into the silence. 'For the moment, you'll be going back to the body of the investigation – and yes, I know there's a joke in there somewhere.' She tidied the sheets of paper together, made to hand them back to Siobhan. 'Can you stay behind for a sec?'

'Sure,' Siobhan said. The rest of them squeezed out of the room, glad of the fresher, cooler air. Rebus, however, loitered near Templer's door. He stared across the room to the array of information on the far wall – faxes, photos and the rest. Someone was busy dismantling the collage, now that this was no longer a MisPer inquiry. The pace of the investigation seemed already to have slowed, not from any sense of shock or out of respect for the dead, but because things had changed: there was no need to rush, no one out there whose life they might just possibly save . . .

Inside the office, Templer was asking Siobhan if she'd like to reconsider the liaison position.

'Thanks,' Siobhan replied. 'But I don't think so.'

Templer leaned back in her chair. 'Want to share the reasons with me?'

Siobhan looked around, as though seeking out the phrases that might be hidden on the bare walls. 'I can't think of any offhand,' she shrugged. 'I just don't fancy it right now.'

'I may not fancy asking again.'

'I know. Maybe I'm just too deep into this case. I want to keep working it.'

'Okay,' Templer said, dragging out the second syllable. 'I think that's us finished here.'

'Right.' Siobhan reached for the doorhandle, trying not to read too much into those words.

'Oh, could you ask Grant to pop in?'

Siobhan paused with the door an inch or two open, then nodded and left the room. Rebus stuck his head round.

'Got two seconds, Gill?'

'Just barely.'

He wandered in anyway. 'Something I forgot to mention . . .'

'Forgot?' She produced a wry smile.

He had three sheets of fax paper in his hand. 'These came through from Dublin.'

'Dublin?'

'A contact there called Declan Macmanus. I was asking about the Costellos.'

She looked up from the sheets. 'Any particular reason?'

'Just a hunch.'

'We'd already looked into the family.'

He nodded. 'Of course: a quick phone call, and back comes the news that there are no convictions. But you know as well as I do, that's often just the beginning of the story.'

And in the case of the Costellos, that story was a long one. Rebus knew he had Templer hooked. When Grant Hood knocked, she told him to come back in five minutes.

'Better make that ten,' Rebus added, winking towards the young man. Then he moved three file-boxes from the spare chair and made himself comfortable.

Macmanus had come good. David Costello had been wild in his youth: 'the result of too much money given and not enough attention', in Macmanus's phrase. Wild meant fast cars, speeding tickets, verbal warnings issued where some miscreants would have found themselves behind bars. There were fights in pubs, smashed windows and phone boxes, at least two episodes when he'd relieved himself in a public place – O'Connell Bridge, mid-afternoon. Even Rebus had been impressed by this last. It was said that the eighteen-year-old David had held a record of sorts in the number of pubs he was barred from at the same time: the Stag's Head, J. Grogan's, Davie Byrnes, O'Donoghue's, Doheny and Nesbitt's, the Shelbourne . . . eleven in total. The previous year, an ex-girlfriend complained to police that he'd punched her in the face outside a nightclub on the banks of the Liffey. Templer looked up when she reached that part.

'She'd had a few, couldn't remember the name of the nightclub,' Rebus said. 'Eventually, she let it drop.'

'You think maybe money changed hands?'

He shrugged. 'Keep reading.'

Macmanus conceded that David Costello had cleaned up his act, pinpointing the turnaround to an eighteenth birthday party, where a friend had tried to leap between two roofs for a dare, falling short, plummeting into the alley below.

He wasn't killed. But there was brain damage, spinal damage . . . not much more than a vegetable, cared for round the clock. Rebus thought back to David's flat – the half-bottle of Bell's . . . Not a drinker, he'd thought.

'Bit of a shock at that age,' Macmanus had written. 'Got David clean and sober in no seconds flat, otherwise he might have turned out not so much a chip off the old block as a bloody great boulder.'

Like son, like father. Thomas Costello had managed to write off eight cars, yet never lose his driving licence. His wife Theresa had twice called police to the home when her husband was in a rage. Both times they'd found her in the bathroom, door locked but missing some splinters where Thomas had started attacking it with a carving knife. 'Just trying to get the bloody thing open,' he'd explained to officers the first time. 'Thought she was going to do herself in.'

'It's not *me* that needs doing in!' Theresa had yelled back. (In the margins of the fax, Macmanus had added a handwritten note to the effect that Theresa had twice taken overdoses, and that everyone in the city felt sorry for her: hard-working wife, abusive and lazy husband who just happened to be hugely wealthy through no significant effort of his own.)

At the Curragh, Thomas had verbally abused a tourist visitor and been ejected by stewards. He'd threatened to cut off a bookmaker's penis after the man had asked if Mr Costello might wish finally to settle up his huge losses, losses the bookmaker had been carrying for several months.

And so it went on. The two rooms at the Caledonian made sense now . . .

'Lovely family,' Templer commented.

'Dublin's finest.'

'And all of it covered up by police.'

'Tut tut,' Rebus remarked. 'We wouldn't do that here, would we?'

'Dear me, no,' she said with a wry smile. 'And your thinking on all this is . . . ?'

'That there's a side of David Costello we didn't know

about till now. And that goes for his family, too. Are they still in the city?'

'They went back to Ireland a couple of days ago.'

'But they'll be coming over again?'

She nodded. 'Now that Philippa's been found.'

'Has David Costello been told?'

'He'll have heard. If Philippa's parents haven't said, the media will have.'

'I'd like to have been there,' Rebus said to himself.

'You can't be everywhere.'

'I suppose not.'

'Okay, talk to the parents when they get here.'

'And the boyfriend?'

She nodded. 'But not too heavy . . . doesn't look good with someone who's grieving.'

He smiled. 'Always thinking of the media, eh, Gill?'

She looked at him. 'Could you send Grant in, please?'

'One impressionable young officer coming right up.' He pulled open the door. Grant was standing there, rocking on the heels of his shoes. Rebus didn't say anything, just gave another wink as he passed.

Ten minutes later, Siobhan was getting a coffee from the machine when Grant found her.

'What did Templer want?' she asked, unable to stop herself.

'Offered me liaison.'

Siobhan concentrated on stirring her drink. 'Thought it might be that.'

'I'll be on the telly!'

'I'm thrilled.'

He stared at her. 'You could try a bit harder.'

'You're right, I could.' They locked eyes. 'Thanks for helping with the clues. I couldn't have done it without you.'

Only now did he seem to realise that their partnership truly was dissolved. 'Oh . . . right,' he said. 'Look, Siobhan . . .'

'Yes?'

'What happened in the office . . . I really am sorry.'

She allowed herself a sour smile. 'Afraid I'll tell on you?'

'No . . . it's not that . . .'

But it was, and they both knew it. 'Haircut and a new suit this weekend,' she suggested.

He looked down at his jacket.

'If you're going to be on the box. Plain shirt: no stripes or checks. Oh, and Grant . . . ?'

'What?'

She reached out a finger and slipped it under his tie.

'Keep this plain, too. Cartoon characters just aren't funny.'

'That's what DCS Templer said.' He sounded surprised, angling his head to examine the little Homer Simpson heads which decorated his tie.

Grant Hood's first TV appearance took place that same afternoon. He was seated next to Gill Templer as she read out a short statement concerning the finding of the body. Ellen Wylie watched on one of the office monitors. There wasn't going to be a speaking part for Hood, but she noticed how, as the media all started asking questions, he leaned over to whisper some comment into Templer's ear, the Chief Super nodding a response. Bill Pryde was on Templer's other side, fielding most of the queries. Everyone wanted to know if the corpse was that of Philippa Balfour; everyone wanted to know the cause of death.

'We're not in a position to confirm identity as yet,' Pryde stated, his words punctuated with little coughs. He looked nervous, and Wylie knew the coughs were vocal tics. She'd been the same herself, all that throat-clearing. Gill Templer glanced towards Pryde, and Hood seemed to take this as his cue.

'Cause of death is also yet to be determined,' he said, 'with a post-mortem examination scheduled for late afternoon. As you know, another conference will take place at seven this evening, by which time we hope to have more details available.'

'But the death's being treated as suspicious?' one journalist called out.

'At this early stage, yes, we're treating the death as suspicious.'

Wylie stuck the end of her biro between her teeth and ground down on it. Hood was cool, no doubt about it. He'd changed his clothes: the ensemble looked brand new. Managed to wash his hair too, she thought.

'There's very little we can add right now,' he was telling the media, 'as you'll no doubt appreciate. If and when an identification is made, family have to be contacted and the identification confirmed.'

'Can I ask if Philippa Balfour's family are coming to Edinburgh?'

Hood gave the questioner a sour look. 'I won't deign to answer that.' Beside him, Gill Templer was nodding agreement, marking her own distaste.

'Can I ask Detective Inspector Pryde if the missing persons investigation is ongoing?'

'The investigation's ongoing,' Pryde said determinedly, picking up some confidence from Hood's performance. Wylie wanted to switch off the monitor, but others were watching with her, so instead she got up and wandered down the corridor to the drinks machine. By the time she got back, the conference was ending. Someone else turned off the monitor and put her out of her misery.

'Looked good in there, didn't he?'

She stared at the uniform who'd asked, but there was no malice apparent. 'Yes,' she confirmed. 'He did all right.'

'Better than some,' another voice said. She turned her head, but there were three officers there, all Gayfield-based. None was looking at her. She reached out a hand for her coffee, but didn't pick it up, fearing her trembling would be noticed. Instead, she turned her attention to Siobhan's notes on the German student. She could make a start, busy herself with phone calls.

Just as soon as she got the words *better than some* out of her head.

Siobhan was sending another message to Quizmaster. She'd taken twenty minutes getting it right.

Hellbank solved. Flip's body found there. Do you want to talk?

It didn't take long for him to respond.

How did you solve it?

Anagram of Arthur's Seat. Hellbank the hillside's name.

Was it you who found the body?

No. Was it you who killed her?

No.

But connected to the game. You don't think anyone was helping her?

I don't know. Do you wish to continue?

Continue?

Stricture awaits.

She stared at the screen. Did Flip's death mean so little to him?

Flip's dead. Someone killed her at Hellbank. I need you to come forward.

His reply took time coming through.

Can't help.

I think you can, Quizmaster.

Undergo Stricture. Perhaps we can meet there.

She thought for a moment. *What is the game's goal? When does it end?*

There was no answer. She was aware of a figure standing behind her: Rebus.

'What's Lover Boy saying?'

' "Lover Boy"?'

'You seem to be spending a lot of time together.'

'That's the job.'

'I suppose it is. So what's he saying?'

'He wants me to go on playing the game.'

'Tell him to sod off. You don't need him now.'

'Don't I?'

The phone rang; Siobhan picked up.

'Yes . . . that's fine . . . of course.' She looked up at Rebus, but he was sticking around. When she ended the call, he raised an eyebrow expectantly.

'The Chief Super,' she explained. 'Now that Grant's got liaison, I'm to stick with the computer angle.'

'Meaning?'

'Meaning find out if there's any way of tracing Quizmaster. What do you reckon: Crime Squad?'

'I doubt those buggers could spell "modem", never mind use one.'

'But they'll have contacts in Special Branch.'

Rebus accepted as much with a shrug.

'The other thing I need to do is canvass Flip's friends and family again.'

'Why?'

'Because I couldn't have got to Hellbank on my own.'

Rebus nodded. 'You don't think she did either?'

'She needed to know London tube lines, geography and the Scots language, Rosslyn Chapel and crossword puzzles.'

'A tall order?'

'That's my guess.'

Rebus was thoughtful. 'Whoever Quizmaster is, he needed to know all those things too.'

'Agreed.'

'And to know she had at least a chance of solving each puzzle?'

'I think maybe there were other players . . . not for me, but when Flip was playing. That would put them up against not just the clock, but each other.'

'Quizmaster won't say?'

'No.'

'I wonder why.'

Siobhan shrugged. 'I'm sure he has his reasons.'

Rebus rested his knuckles on the desk. 'I was wrong. We need him after all, don't we?'

She looked at him. ' "We"?'

He held up his hands. 'All I meant was, the case needs him.'

'Good, because if I thought you were trying your usual stunt . . .'

'Which is?'

'Grabbing at every strand and calling it your own.'

'Perish the thought, Siobhan.' He paused. 'But if you're going to be talking to her friends . . .'

'Yes?'

'Would that include David Costello?'

'We already talked to him. He said he didn't know anything about the game.'

'But you're planning to talk to him again anyway?'

She almost smiled. 'Am I so easy to read?'

'It's just that maybe I could tag along. I've got a few more questions for him myself.'

'What sort of questions?'

'Let me buy you a cup of coffee and I'll tell you . . .'

That evening, John Balfour, accompanied by a family friend, made the formal identification of his daughter Philippa. His wife was waiting for him in the back of a Balfour's Bank Jaguar driven by Ranald Marr. Rather than wait in the car park, Marr had driven the car around nearby streets, returning twenty minutes later . – the length of time suggested by Bill Pryde, who was there to accompany Mr Balfour on the uneasy journey to the Identification Suite.

A couple of resolute reporters were on hand, but no photographers: the Scottish press still had one or two principles left. Nobody was going to ask questions of the bereaved; all they wanted was some colour for later reports. When it was over, Pryde gave Rebus a call on his mobile to let him know.

'That's us then,' Rebus told the room. He was in the Oxford Bar with Siobhan, Ellen Wylie and Donald Devlin. Grant Hood had turned down the offer of a drink, saying he had to do a quick crash course in the media – names and faces. The conference had been moved to nine p.m., by which time it was hoped the autopsy would be complete, initial conclusions reached.

'Oh, dear,' Devlin said. He'd removed his jacket, and now bunched his fists into the capacious pockets of his cardigan. 'What a terrible shame.'

'Sorry I'm late,' Jean Burchill said, sliding her coat from her shoulders as she approached. Rebus was out of his chair, taking the coat from her, asking what she wanted to drink.

'Let me buy a round,' she said, but he shook his head.

'My invitation. That makes it my duty to get in the first round at least.'

They had colonised the back room's top table. The place wasn't busy, and the TV in the opposite corner meant they were unlikely to be overheard.

'Some sort of pow-wow?' Jean asked, after Rebus had gone.

'Or maybe a wake,' Wylie guessed.

'It's her then?' Jean asked. Their silence was answer enough.

'You work on witchcraft and stuff, don't you?' Siobhan asked Jean.

'Belief systems,' Jean corrected her, 'but, yes, witchcraft falls into it.'

'It's just that with the coffins, and Flip's body being found in a place called Hellbank . . . You said yourself there might be some connection with witchcraft.'

Jean nodded. 'It's true that Hellbank may have come by its name that way.'

'And true that the little coffins on Arthur's Seat might have been to do with witchcraft?'

Jean looked to Donald Devlin, who was following the dialogue intently. She was still debating what to say when Devlin spoke up.

'I very much doubt there's any element of witchcraft involved in the Arthur's Seat coffins. But you do propose an interesting hypothesis, in that, enlightened though we might think ourselves, we are always ready to invite such mumbo-jumbo.' He smiled at Siobhan. 'I'm impressed that a police detective should be so minded.'

'I didn't say I was,' Siobhan snapped back.

'Clutching at straws then, perhaps?'

When Rebus returned with Jean's lime and soda, he

couldn't help but note the silence which had fallen over the table.

'Well,' Wylie said impatiently, 'now we're all here . . . ?'

'Now we're all here . . .' Rebus echoed, lifting his pint, 'cheers!'

He waited till they'd lifted their own glasses before putting his own to his mouth. Scotland: you couldn't refuse a toast.

'All right,' he said, putting the glass back down, 'there's a murder case needs solving, and I just want to be sure in my own mind where we all stand.'

'Isn't that what the morning briefings are for?'

He looked at Wylie. 'Then call this an unofficial briefing.'

'With the booze as a bribe?'

'I've always been a fan of incentive schemes.' He managed to force a smile from her. 'Right, here's what I think we've got so far. We've got Burke and Hare – taking things chronologically – and soon after them we've got lots of little coffins found on Arthur's Seat.' He looked towards Jean, noticing for the first time that though there was a space on the bench next to Devlin, she'd pulled a chair over from one of the other tables so she was next to Siobhan instead. 'Then, connected or not, we've got a series of similar coffins turning up in places where women happen to have disappeared or turned up dead. One such coffin is found in Falls, just after Philippa Balfour goes missing. She then turns up dead on Arthur's Seat, location of the original coffins.'

'Which is a long way from Falls,' Siobhan felt bound to point out. 'I mean, those other coffins you've got, they were found near the scene, weren't they?'

'And the Falls coffin is different from the others,' Ellen Wylie added.

'I'm not saying otherwise,' Rebus interrupted. 'I'm just trying to establish whether I'm the only one who sees possible links?'

They all looked at each other; no one said anything until Wylie lifted her Bloody Mary and, studying its red surface, mentioned the German student. 'Swords and sorcery, role-playing, ends up dead on a Scottish hillside.'

'Exactly.'

'But,' Wylie continued, 'hard to tie in with your disappearances and drownings.'

Devlin seemed persuaded by her tone. 'It's not,' he added, 'as if the drownings were considered suspicious at the time, and my examination of the pertinent details doesn't persuade me otherwise.' He had taken his hands from his pockets; they now rested on the shiny knees of his baggy grey trousers.

'Fine,' Rebus said, 'then I'm the only one who's even remotely convinced?'

This time, not even Wylie spoke up. Rebus took another long swallow of beer. 'Well,' he said, 'thanks for the vote of confidence.'

'Look, why are we here?' Wylie laid her hands on the table. 'You're trying to convince us to work as a team?'

'I'm just saying all these little details may end up being part of the same story.'

'Burke and Hare to the Quizmaster's Treasure Hunt?'

'Yes.' But Rebus looked like he was believing it less himself now. 'Christ, I don't know . . .' He ran a hand over his head.

'Look, thanks for the drink . . .' Ellen Wylie's glass was empty. She picked her shoulder-bag up from the bench, started getting to her feet.

'Ellen . . .'

She looked at him. 'Big day tomorrow, John. First full day of the murder inquiry.'

'It's not officially a murder inquiry until the pathologist pronounces,' Devlin reminded her. She looked ready to say something, but just graced him with the coldest of smiles. Then she squeezed out between two of the chairs, said a general goodbye, and was gone.

'Something connects them,' Rebus said quietly, almost to himself. 'I can't for the life of me think what it is, but it's there . . .'

'It can be detrimental,' Devlin pronounced, 'to begin

obsessing – as our transatlantic cousins might say – on a case. Detrimental both to the case and to oneself.'

Rebus tried for the same smile Ellen Wylie had just given. 'I think the next round's yours,' he said.

Devlin checked his watch. 'Actually, I'm afraid I'm unable to tarry.' He seemed to find it painful rising from the table. 'I don't suppose one of the young ladies might proffer a lift?'

'You're on my way home,' Siobhan conceded at last.

Rebus's sense of desertion was softened when he saw her glance in Jean's direction: she was leaving the two of them alone, that was all.

'But I'll get a round in before I go,' Siobhan added.

'Maybe next time,' Rebus told her with a wink. He sat in silence with Jean until they'd gone, and was about to speak when Devlin came shuffling back.

'Am I right to assume,' he said, 'that my usefulness is now at an end?' Rebus nodded. 'In which case, will the files be sent back to their place of origin?'

'I'll get DS Wylie to do it first thing,' Rebus promised.

'Many thanks then.' Devlin's smile was directed at Jean. 'It's been a pleasure to have met you.'

'And you,' she said.

'I may pop into the Museum some day. Perhaps you'd do me the honour of showing me round . . . ?'

'I'd love to.'

Devlin bowed his head, and started back towards the stairs again.

'I hope he doesn't,' she muttered when he'd gone.

'Why not?'

'He gives me the creeps.'

Rebus looked over his shoulder, as though some final view of Devlin might persuade him she was right. 'You're not the first to say that.' He turned back to her. 'But don't worry, you're perfectly safe with me.'

'Oh, I hope not,' she said, eyes twinkling above her glass.

They were in bed when the news came through. Rebus took the call, seated naked on the edge of the mattress, uncomfortably aware of the view he was presenting to Jean: probably two spare tyres around his middle, arms and shoulders more fat than muscle. The silver lining was: the view could only be worse from the front . . .

'Strangulation,' he told her, sliding back under the bedclothes.

'It was quick then?'

'Definitely. There's bruising on the neck just at the carotid artery. She probably passed out, then he strangled her.'

'Why would he do that?'

'Easier to kill someone when they're compliant. No struggle.'

'You're quite the expert, aren't you? Ever killed someone, John?'

'Not so you'd notice.'

'That's a lie, isn't it?'

He looked at her and nodded. She leaned over and kissed his shoulder.

'You don't want to talk about it. That's okay.'

He wrapped his arm around her, kissed her hair. There was a mirror in the room, one of those floor-standing models so you could see yourself head to foot. It faced away from the bed. Rebus wondered if that was on purpose or not, but he wasn't about to ask.

'Where's the carotid artery?' she asked.

He placed a finger on his own neck. 'Put pressure on it, the person blacks out in a matter of seconds.'

She felt her neck until she'd found it. 'Interesting,' she said. 'Does everyone except me know that?'

'Know what?'

'Where it is, what it does.'

'I don't suppose so, no. What are you getting at?'

'It's just that whoever did it was in the know.'

'Cops know about it,' he admitted. 'It's not much used these days, for obvious reasons. But there was a time it could make an unruly prisoner manageable. The Vulcan death-grip, we used to call it.'

She smiled. 'The what?'

'You know, Spock on *Star Trek*.' He pinched her shoulder blade. She wriggled free and gave his chest a slap, resting her hand there. Rebus was thinking of his army training, and how he'd been taught attack techniques, including pressure on the carotid . . .

'Would doctors know?' Jean asked.

'Probably anyone who's had medical training would.'

She looked thoughtful.

'Why?' he asked at last.

'Just something from the paper. Wasn't one of Philippa's friends a medical student, one of the ones she was going to meet that night . . . ?'

10

His name was Albert Winfield – 'Albie' to his friends. He seemed surprised that the police wanted to talk to him again, but turned up at St Leonard's at the appointed time next morning. Rebus and Siobhan left him fully fifteen minutes while they got on with other work, then made sure two burly uniforms led him to the interview room, where they left him for a further quarter of an hour. Outside the room, Siobhan and Rebus locked eyes and nodded at one another. Then Rebus pushed open the door forcefully.

'Many thanks for coming along, Mr Winfield,' he snapped. The young man almost leaped from his chair. The window was closed tight, the room stifling. Three chairs – two on one side of the narrow table, one on the other. Winfield had been facing those two empty chairs. Tape recorders and a video recorder were bolted to the wall where it met the table. There were scratched names on the table itself, evidence of time being whittled away by previous occupants called things like Shug, Jazz and Bomber. A No Smoking sign on the wall, defaced with ballpoint pen, and a video camera mounted where wall met ceiling, peering down on proceedings should anyone decide a video record was required.

Rebus ensured his chair-legs made the maximum noise as he scraped them in towards the table. He'd thrown a bulky folder down: no names on it. Winfield seemed mesmerised. He couldn't know it was full of blank sheets of paper borrowed from one of the photocopiers.

Rebus rested his hand on the folder and smiled at Winfield.

'It must have come as a terrible shock.' A quiet voice, soothing, solicitous ... Siobhan sat down beside her thuggish colleague. 'I'm DC Clarke, by the way. This is DI Rebus.'

'What?' the young man said. Perspiration made his forehead shine. His short brown hair came to a widow's peak. There was acne on his chin.

'The news of Flip's murder,' Siobhan continued. 'It must have been a shock.'

'Y-es . . . absolutely.' He sounded English, but Rebus knew he wasn't. Private education south of the border had ironed out all trace of his Scottish roots. Father a businessman in Hong Kong until three years ago, divorced from the mother, who lived in Perthshire.

'You knew her well then?'

Winfield kept his eyes on Siobhan. 'I suppose so. I mean, she was Camille's friend really.'

'Camille's your girlfriend?' Siobhan asked.

'Foreign, is she?' Rebus barked.

'No . . .' The eyes strayed to Rebus, but only for a second. 'No, she's from Staffordshire.'

'Like I said, foreign.'

Siobhan glanced at Rebus, worried he was milking his role. As Winfield stared down at the table-top, Rebus gave Siobhan a wink of reassurance.

'Hot in here, isn't it, Albert?' Siobhan paused. 'You don't mind me calling you Albert?'

'No . . . no, that's fine.' He glanced up at her again, but whenever he did his eyes were drawn towards her neighbour.

'Would you like me to open a window?'

'Wonderful, yes.'

Siobhan looked at Rebus, who pushed his chair back with as much noise as possible. The windows were narrow, fixed high on the external wall. Rebus stood on tiptoe to open one of them, pulling it in three or four inches. The breeze swept over him.

'Better?' Siobhan asked.

'Yes, thanks.'

Rebus stayed standing, over to Winfield's left. He folded

his arms and rested against the wall, directly below the camera.

'Just a few follow-up questions really,' Siobhan was saying.

'Right ... fine.' Winfield nodded enthusiastically.

'So you wouldn't say you knew Flip that well?'

'We went out together ... in a group, I mean. Dinner sometimes ...'

'At her flat?'

'Once or twice. And at mine.'

'You live down near the Botanics?'

'That's right.'

'Nice part of town.'

'It's my father's place.'

'He lives there?'

'No, he's ... I mean, he bought it for me.'

Siobhan looked towards Rebus.

'All right for some,' he muttered, arms still folded.

'I can't help it if my father has money,' Winfield complained.

'Of course you can't,' Siobhan agreed.

'What about Flip's boyfriend?' Rebus asked.

Winfield found himself looking at Rebus's shoes. 'David? What about him?'

Rebus bent down, waved a hand in Winfield's direction. 'I'm up here, son.' He straightened. Winfield held his gaze for all of three seconds.

'Just wondering if you consider him a friend,' Rebus said.

'Well, it's a bit awkward now ... I mean, it *was* awkward. They kept splitting up, getting back together again ...'

'And you took Flip's side?' Siobhan guessed.

'I had to, what with Camille and everything ...'

'You say they kept splitting up. Whose fault was it?'

'I just think they had this personality clash ... you know how opposites attract? Well, sometimes you get the inverse of that.'

'I didn't have the benefit of a university education, Mr

Winfield,' Rebus said. 'Maybe you could spell that out for me.'

'I just mean that they were similar in lots of ways, and that made their relationship difficult.'

'They argued?'

'It was more that they couldn't let an argument lie. There had to be a winner and a loser, no middle ground.'

'Did these disagreements ever turn violent?'

'No.'

'But David's got a temper on him?' Rebus persisted.

'No more so than anyone else.'

Rebus walked over to the table. It only took him a couple of steps. He leaned forward so that his shadow covered Winfield. 'But you've seen him lose the rag?'

'Not really.'

'No?'

Siobhan cleared her throat, a sign that she thought Rebus had hit a wall. 'Albert,' she said, her voice like a balm, 'did you know that Flip liked to play computer games?'

'No,' he said, looking surprised.

'Do you play them?'

'I used to play Doom in first year . . . maybe pinball in the student union.'

'Computer pinball?'

'No, just pinball.'

'Flip was playing a game online, a sort of variation on a treasure hunt.' Siobhan unfolded a sheet of paper and slid it across the table. 'Do these clues mean anything to you?'

He read with a frown, then expelled some air. 'Absolutely nothing.'

'You're studying medicine, aren't you?' Rebus interrupted.

'That's right. I'm in my third year.'

'I bet it's hard work,' Siobhan said, sliding the sheet of paper back towards her.

'You wouldn't believe it,' Winfield laughed.

'I think we might,' Rebus said. 'In our line of work, we see doctors all the time.' Though some of us, he could have added, do our best to avoid them . . .

'I'm assuming you know something of the carotid artery then?' Siobhan asked.

'I know where it is,' Winfield admitted, looking puzzled.

'And what it does?'

'It's an artery in the neck. Actually, there are two of them.'

'Carrying blood to the brain?' Siobhan said.

'I had to look it up in a dictionary,' Rebus told Winfield. 'It's from the Greek, meaning sleep. Know why that is?'

'Because compression of the carotid causes you to black out.'

Rebus nodded. 'That's right, a deep sleep. And if you keep on pressing . . .'

'Christ, is that how she died?'

Siobhan shook her head. 'We think she was rendered unconscious, then strangled afterwards.'

In the silence that followed, Winfield looked wildly from one detective to the other. Then he started rising to his feet, fingers gripping the table's edge.

'Jesus Christ, you don't think . . . ? For pity's sake, you think it was *me*?'

'Sit down,' Rebus ordered. In truth, Winfield hadn't got very far up; it looked like his knees were refusing to lock.

'We know it wasn't you,' Siobhan said firmly. The student fell back on to his chair, nearly toppling it.

'We know it wasn't you because you've got an alibi: you were with everyone else in the bar that night, waiting for Flip.'

'That's right,' he said, 'that's right.'

'So you've nothing to worry about,' Rebus said, backing off from the table. 'Unless you know better.'

'No, I . . . I'm . . .'

'Anyone else in your group like to play games, Albert?' Siobhan asked.

'Nobody. I mean, Trist has a few games for his computer,

Tomb Raider, that sort of thing. But probably everyone does.'

'Probably,' Siobhan admitted. 'No one else in your circle studies medicine?'

Winfield shook his head, but Siobhan could see he was having a thought. 'There's Claire,' he said. 'Claire Benzie. I've only met her once or twice at parties, but she was a friend of Flip's . . . from school days, I think.'

'And she's studying medicine?'

'Yes.'

'But you don't really know her?'

'She's a year below me, and a different specialism. God, that's right . . .' He looked up at Siobhan, then to Rebus. 'Of all the bloody things, she wants to be a pathologist . . .'

'Yes, I know Claire,' Dr Curt said, leading them down one of the corridors. They were in part of the medical faculty at the university, in a block behind McEwan Hall. Rebus had been here before: it was where both Curt and Gates had their teaching offices. But he'd never been to the lecture halls. Curt was leading them there now. Rebus had asked if he was feeling better. Gastric problems, Curt had explained. 'Very pleasant girl,' he said now, 'and a good student. I hope she stays with us.'

'How do you mean?'

'She's only in second year, she could yet change her mind.'

'Are there many female pathologists?' Siobhan asked.

'Not many, no . . . not in this country.'

'It's a weird decision to take, isn't it?' Rebus said. 'When you're that young, I mean.'

'Not really,' Curt mused. 'I was always one for dissecting the frogs at biology.' He beamed a smile. 'And I'd rather treat the deceased than the living: no anxious diagnoses, no expectant families, fewer negligence claims . . .' He stopped at a set of doors and peered through the glass upper half. 'Yes, in here.'

The lecture room was small and antiquated: wood veneer

on the walls, curved wooden benches rising steeply. Curt checked his watch. 'Only another minute or two.'

Rebus peered inside. Someone he didn't know was lecturing to a few dozen students. There were fresh diagrams on the blackboard, and a podium where the lecturer stood brushing chalk from his hands.

'Not a cadaver on view,' Rebus commented.

'We tend to keep those for the practicals.'

'Are you still having to use the Western General?'

'We are, and it's a blessed nuisance with the traffic.'

The autopsy suite at the mortuary was out of commission. Fear of hepatitis allied to a ventilation system past its prime. No sign of funding for a new unit, which meant one of the city hospitals was bearing the brunt of the pathologists' needs.

'The human body is a fascinating machine,' Curt was saying. 'You only really get a sense of that *post mortem*. A hospital surgeon will concentrate on one particular area of the body, but we have the luxury of unlimited access.'

Siobhan's look said she wished he'd stop being so remorselessly cheery on the subject. 'It's an old building,' she remarked.

'Not that old really, in the context of the university. The medical school was based at Old College in earlier times.'

'That's where they took Burke's body?' Rebus added.

'Yes, after he was hanged. A tunnel led into Old College. The bodies were all brought in that way – by dead of night in some cases.' He looked to Siobhan. 'The Resurrection Men.'

'Good name for a band.'

He graced her flippancy with a scowl. 'Body-snatchers,' he said.

'And the skin was flayed from Burke's body?' Rebus went on.

'You know a bit about it.'

'I didn't until recently. Does the tunnel still exist?'

'Part of it.'

'I'd be interested to see it sometime.'

'Devlin's your man.'

'Is he?'

'Unofficial historian of the medical faculty's early days. He's written pamphlets on the subject . . . self-published, but pretty enlightening.'

'I didn't know that. I know he knows a bit about Burke and Hare. He has a theory that Dr Kennet Lovell placed the coffins on Arthur's Seat.'

'Ah, the ones that've been in the papers of late?' Curt frowned in thought. 'Lovell? Well, who's to say he isn't right?' He broke off and frowned again. 'Funny you should mention Lovell actually.'

'Why?'

'Because Claire told me recently she's descended from him.' There was a sound of movement from inside. 'Ah, Dr Easton's finished. They'll all filter out this way; we'd better stand back, lest we're stampeded to death.'

'They're keen then?' Siobhan said.

'Keen to be back in the fresh air, yes.'

Only a few of the students bothered to glance in their direction. Those who did seemed to know who Curt was, some acknowledging him with a bow, smile or word. Finally, with the hall three-quarters empty, Curt went up on to his toes.

'Claire? Could you spare a minute?'

She was tall and thin with short blonde hair and a long straight nose. Her eyes were an almost oriental shape, like tilted almonds. She carried two folders beneath one arm. There was a mobile phone in her hand. She'd been studying it on her way out of the lecture theatre: checking for messages perhaps. She came forwards with a smile.

'Hello, Dr Curt.' Her voice was almost playful.

'Claire, these police officers would like a word.'

'It's about Flip, isn't it?' Her face had fallen, all humour lost to it, and the voice had taken on a sombre tone.

Siobhan nodded slowly. 'A few follow-up questions.'

'I keep thinking maybe it wasn't her, maybe there's been a mistake . . .' She looked to the pathologist. 'Did you . . . ?'

Curt shook his head, but it was less a denial than a refusal to answer the question. Rebus and Siobhan knew Curt had been one of the pathologists at the Philippa Balfour autopsy. The other had been Professor Gates.

Claire Benzie knew it too. Her eyes were still on Dr Curt. 'Have you ever had to ... you know ... on someone you knew?'

Curt glanced in Rebus's direction, and Rebus knew he was thinking of Conor Leary.

'It's not a necessity,' Curt was explaining to his student. 'Something like that happens, you can be excused on compassionate grounds.'

'We're allowed compassion then?'

'The occasional handful, yes.' This put the smile back on to her face, albeit fleetingly.

'So how can I help you?' she asked Siobhan.

'You know we're treating Flip's death as homicide?'

'That's what the news said this morning.'

'Well, we just need your help to clear up a few things.'

'You can use my office,' Curt said.

As they walked, two by two, back down the corridor, Rebus watched Claire Benzie's back. She was holding her folders in front of her, discussing her recent lecture with Dr Curt. Siobhan glanced at him and frowned, wondering what he was thinking. He shook his head: not important. But all the same, he thought Claire Benzie was interesting. The morning her friend's murder is announced, and she's able to attend a lecture, talk about it afterwards, even with two detectives right behind her ...

One explanation: displacement. She was pushing thoughts of Flip aside, replacing them with the routine. Keeping busy to keep from bursting into tears.

Another: she was self-possession itself, Flip's demise a minor intrusion in her universe.

Rebus knew which version he preferred, but he wasn't sure it was necessarily the right one ...

Dr Curt shared a secretary with Professor Gates. They passed through the secretary's office: two doors next to one another, Curt and Gates. Curt turned the doorhandle and ushered them inside.

'I've got one or two things to do,' he said. 'Just close the door after you when you've finished.'

'Thanks,' Rebus said.

But, having brought them here, Curt seemed suddenly reluctant to leave his student alone with the two detectives.

'I'll be fine, Dr Curt,' Claire reassured him, as if she'd understood his hesitation. Curt nodded and left them. It was a cramped, airless room. A glass-fronted bookcase took up one whole wall. It was filled to overflowing. More books and documents covered every bit of shelf space, and while Rebus was sure there was a computer somewhere on the desk, he couldn't place it: more documents, files and folders, learned journals, empty envelopes . . .

'Doesn't throw much out, does he?' Claire Benzie said. 'Ironic when you think what he does to a corpse.'

The statement, so casually made, startled Siobhan Clarke.

'God, sorry,' Claire said, placing a hand over her mouth. 'They should hand out diplomas in bad taste with this course.'

Rebus was thinking of autopsies past: of innards tossed into pails, organs severed and placed on scales . . .

Siobhan was resting against the desk. Claire had dropped into the visitor's chair, which looked like a remnant from a 1970s dining-room suite. Rebus was left with standing in the middle of the floor or taking Curt's chair. He opted for the latter.

'So,' Claire said, placing her folders on the floor by her feet, 'what is it you want to know?'

'You were at school with Flip?'

'For a few years, yes.'

They'd already been through the notes from Claire Benzie's first interview. Two of the Gayfield Square contingent had talked to her, gleaning little.

'You lost touch?'

'Sort of . . . a few letters and e-mails. Then she started her history of art course and I found out I'd been accepted by Edinburgh.'

'You got in touch?'

Claire nodded. She'd tucked one leg beneath her on the chair and was playing with a bracelet on her left wrist. 'Sent her an e-mail, and we met up.'

'You saw her often after that?'

'Not that often. Different courses, different workloads.'

'Different friends?' Rebus asked.

'Some, yes,' Claire agreed.

'Did you keep in touch with anyone else from school days?'

'One or two.'

'And did Flip?'

'Not really.'

'How did she meet David Costello, do you know?' Rebus already knew the answer – they'd met at a dinner party – but was wondering how well Claire knew Costello.

'I think she said something about a party . . .'

'Did you like him?'

'David?' She was thoughtful. 'Arrogant sod, very sure of himself.'

Rebus almost came back with: *not at all like you then?* Instead, he looked to Siobhan, who reached into her jacket for the folded note.

'Claire,' she said, 'did Flip like to play games?'

'Games?'

'Role-playing . . . computer games . . . maybe on the Internet?'

She thought for a moment. Fine, except that Rebus knew you could use a pause to think up some story . . .

'We had a dungeons and dragons club at school.'

'You were both in it?'

'Until we realised it was strictly a boy thing.' She wrinkled her nose. 'Come to think of it, didn't David play at school too?'

Siobhan handed her the sheet of clues. 'Ever seen these before?'

'What do they mean?'

'Some game Flip was playing. What are you smiling at?'

'Seven fins high . . . she was so pleased with that.'

Siobhan's eyes widened. 'Sorry?'

'She came bounding up to me in some bar . . . God, I forget where. Maybe Barcelona.' She looked at Siobhan. 'It's a bar on Buccleuch Street.'

Siobhan nodded. 'Go on.'

'She just . . . she was laughing . . . and she said this.' Claire pointed to the sheet. 'Seven fins high is king. Then she asked me if I knew what it meant. I told her I hadn't the faintest. "It's the Victoria Line," she said. She seemed so pleased with herself.'

'She didn't tell you what it meant?'

'I've just said . . .'

'I mean, about it being part of a quiz clue.'

Claire shook her head. 'I thought . . . well, I don't know what I thought.'

'Was anyone else there?'

'Not at the bar, no. I was getting some drinks in when she came running up.'

'Do you think she told anyone else?'

'Not to my knowledge.'

'She didn't explain any of the others?' Siobhan gestured towards the sheet. She was feeling an intense rush of relief. Seven fins meant she'd been working out the same clues Flip had. Part of her had worried that Quizmaster was setting her new questions, questions specific to *her*. Now, she felt closer to Flip than ever . . .

'Has this game got something to do with her death?' Claire was asking.

'We don't know yet,' Rebus told her.

'And you've no suspects, no . . . leads?'

'We've plenty of leads,' Rebus was quick to assure her. 'Tell me, you said you thought David Costello was arrogant. Did it ever go beyond that?'

'How do you mean?'

'We hear there were some pretty wild fallings-out between him and Flip.'

'Flip could give as good as she got.' She stopped abruptly, stared into space. Not for the first time in his life, Rebus wished he were a mind-reader. 'She was strangled, wasn't she?'

'Yes.'

'From what I've seen on the forensics course, victims struggle. They'll scratch and kick and bite.'

'Not if they're unconscious,' Rebus said quietly.

Claire closed her eyes for a moment. When she opened them, there were tears shining there.

'Pressure on the carotid artery,' Rebus went on.

'Causing ante-mortem bruising?' Claire could have been reading from a textbook. Siobhan nodded an answer.

'Only seems like yesterday we were schoolgirls . . .'

'This was in Edinburgh?' Rebus asked, waiting till Claire had nodded. The first interview hadn't gone into her background, except as it related to Flip. 'Is that where your family live?'

'It is now. But back then, we lived in Causland.'

Rebus frowned. 'Causland?' He knew the name from somewhere.

'It's a village . . . more of a hamlet really. About a mile and a half from Falls.'

Rebus found himself gripping the arms of Dr Curt's chair. 'You know Falls then?'

'Used to.'

'And Junipers, the Balfours' house?'

She nodded. 'For a while, I was more house guest than visitor.'

'And then your family moved away?'

'Yes.'

'Why?'

'My father . . .' She broke off. 'We had to move for his work.' Rebus and Siobhan shared a look: it wasn't what she'd been about to say.

'Did you and Flip ever visit the waterfall?' Rebus asked casually.

'Do you know it?'

He nodded. 'Been there a couple of times.'

She was smiling, eyes losing focus. 'We used to play there, pretend it was our enchanted kingdom. Life Never-Ending we called it. If only we'd known . . .'

She broke down then, and Siobhan went to comfort her. Rebus walked into the outer office and asked the secretary for a glass of water. But by the time he got back with it, Claire was already recovering. Siobhan was crouching by the side of the chair, a hand on her shoulder. Rebus offered the water. Claire rubbed at her nose with a tissue.

'Thank you,' she said, compressing it to the single syllable *kyoo*.

'I think that's plenty to be going on with,' Siobhan was saying. Rebus – who privately disagreed – nodded his compliance. 'You've been a big help, Claire.'

'Really?'

It was Siobhan's turn to nod. 'We might be in touch again later, if that's all right.'

'Fine, whatever.'

Siobhan handed over her card. 'If I'm not in the office, the pager will always find me.'

'Okay.' Claire slipped the card into one of her files.

'Sure you're all right?'

Claire nodded, stood up, clutching her files to her chest. 'I've got another class,' she said. 'Don't want to miss it.'

'Dr Curt tells us you're related to Kennet Lovell?'

She looked at him. 'On my mother's side.' She paused, as if expecting a follow-up question, but Rebus didn't have one.

'Thanks again,' Siobhan said.

They watched as she started to leave. Rebus was holding the door open for her. 'Just one thing, Claire?'

She stopped beside him, staring up. 'Yes?' she said.

'You told us you used to know Falls.' Rebus waited till she'd nodded. 'Does that mean you've not been there recently?'

'I might have passed through.'

He nodded acceptance of this. She made to leave again. 'You know Beverly Dodds though,' he added.

'Who?'

'I think she made that bracelet you're wearing.'

Claire lifted her wrist. 'This?' It looked very much like the one Jean had bought: polished stones drilled and threaded. 'Flip gave it to me. Said something about it being "good magic".' She shrugged. 'Not that I believe in it, of course . . .'

Rebus watched her leave, then closed the door. 'What do you think?' he asked, turning back into the room.

'I don't know,' Siobhan admitted.

'A bit of acting going on?'

'The tears seemed real enough.'

'Isn't that what acting's all about?'

Siobhan sat down in Claire's chair. 'If a killer's hiding in there, it's buried deep.'

'Seven fin high: say Flip didn't come up to her at a bar. Say Claire already knew what it meant.'

'Because she's the Quizmaster?' Siobhan shook her head.

'Or another player,' Rebus said.

'Then why bother telling us *anything*?'

'Because . . .' But Rebus couldn't think of an answer for that.

'I'll tell you what I'm wondering.'

'Her father?' Rebus guessed.

Siobhan nodded. 'There's something she was holding back.'

'So why did her family move?'

Siobhan was thoughtful, but couldn't think of a quick answer.

'Her old school might tell us,' Rebus said. While Siobhan went to ask the secretary for a phone book, Rebus called Bev Dodds's number. She answered on the sixth ring.

'It's DI Rebus,' he said.

'Inspector, I'm a bit pushed at the moment . . .'

He could hear other voices. Tourists, he guessed, probably

deciding what to buy. 'I don't think,' he said, 'I ever asked you if you knew Philippa Balfour.'

'Didn't you?'

'Do you mind if I ask you now?'

'Not at all.' She paused. 'The answer is no.'

'You never met her?'

'Never. Why do you ask?'

'A friend of hers is wearing a bracelet she says Philippa gave her. It looks to me like one of yours.'

'Quite possible.'

'But you didn't sell it to Philippa?'

'If it's one of mine, chances are she bought it in a shop. There's a craft shop in Haddington takes my work, and another in Edinburgh.'

'What's the name of the one in Edinburgh?'

'Wiccan Crafts. It's on Jeffrey Street, if you're interested. Now, if you don't mind ...' But Rebus had already put down the phone. Siobhan was coming back in with the number for Flip's old school. Rebus made the call, putting the speaker on so Siobhan could listen. The headmistress had been one of the teachers during Flip and Claire's time there.

'Poor, poor Philippa, it's terrible news ... and what her family must be going through,' the headmistress said.

'I'm sure they've got every support,' Rebus commiserated, trying to get as much sincerity into his voice as he could.

. There was a long sigh at the other end of the line.

'But actually, I'm phoning in connection with Claire.'

'Claire?'

'Claire Benzie. It's part of the background, trying to build up a picture of Philippa. I believe she and Claire were good friends at one time.'

'Pretty good, yes.'

'They lived near one another, too?'

'That's right. Out East Lothian way.'

Rebus had a thought. 'How did they get to school?'

'Oh, Claire's father usually drove them in. Either him or Philippa's mother. A lovely lady, I do grieve for her so ...'

'Claire's father worked in Edinburgh then?'

'Oh, yes. Some sort of lawyer.'

'Is that why the family moved? Was it to do with his work?'

'Dear me, no. I think they were evicted.'

'Evicted?'

'Well, one shouldn't gossip, but with him being deceased I don't suppose it matters.'

'We'll hold it in strictest confidence,' Rebus said, looking at Siobhan.

'Well, it's just that the poor man made some bad investments. I believe he was always a bit of a gambler, and it looks like this time he went too far, lost thousands . . . his house . . . the lot.'

'How did he die?'

'I think you've guessed. He booked into a seaside hotel quite shortly thereafter, and took an overdose of some kind of tablets. It's quite a tumble after all, isn't it, from lawyer to bankrupt . . . ?'

'Yes, it is,' Rebus agreed. 'Many thanks for that.'

'Yes, I'd better go. I've some sort of curriculum meeting to attend.' Her tone told Rebus this was a regular occurrence, and not one to be savoured. 'Such a pity, two families torn apart by tragedy.'

'Goodbye then,' Rebus said, putting down the phone. He looked at Siobhan.

'Investments?' she echoed.

'And who would he trust if not the father of his daughter's best friend?'

Siobhan nodded. 'John Balfour's about to bury his daughter,' she reminded him.

'Then we'll talk to someone else at the bank.'

Siobhan smiled. 'I know just the man . . .'

Ranald Marr was at Junipers, so they drove out to Falls. Siobhan asked if they could stop and look at the waterfall. A couple of tourists were doing the same thing. The man was taking a photo of his wife. He asked Rebus if he'd take one of the pair of them together. His voice was Edinburgh.

'What brings you here?' Rebus asked, feigning innocence.

'Same thing as you most likely,' the man said, positioning himself next to his wife. 'Make sure you get the wee waterfall in.'

'You mean you're here because of the coffin?' Rebus said, peering through the view-finder.

'Aye, well, she's dead now, isn't she?'

'She is that,' Rebus said.

'Sure you're getting us in?' the man asked worriedly.

'Perfect,' Rebus said, pressing the button. When the film was developed, there'd be a picture of sky and trees, nothing more.

'Wee tip,' the man said, taking his camera back. He nodded towards one of the trees. 'She's the one found the coffin.'

Rebus looked. There was a crude sign pinned to the tree, advertising Bev Dodds's Pottery. A hand-drawn map showed her cottage. 'Pottery for Sale, Teas and Coffees.' She was branching out.

'Did she show you it?' Rebus asked, knowing fine well the answer. The Falls coffin was locked away with the others at St Leonard's.

The tourist shook his head in disappointment. 'Police are holding on to it.'

Rebus nodded. 'So where's your next stop?'

'Thought we'd go look at Junipers,' his wife said. 'Always supposing we can find it. Took us half an hour to find this place.' She looked at Siobhan. 'They don't believe in signposts out here, do they?'

'I know where Junipers is.' Rebus spoke authoritatively. 'You head back down the lane, left through the town. There's a housing scheme on the right called Meadowside. Drive into it and you'll see Junipers just beyond.'

The man beamed. 'Magic, thanks a lot.'

'No problem,' Rebus told him. The tourists waved their goodbyes, eager to be back on the trail.

Siobhan sidled over towards Rebus. 'Completely erroneous?'

'They'll be lucky to get out of Meadowside with four tyres still on their car.' He grinned at her. 'My good deed for the day.'

Back in the car, Rebus turned to Siobhan. 'How do you want to play this?'

'First off, I want to know if Marr's a Mason.'

Rebus nodded. 'I'll handle that.'

'Then I think we dive straight in with Hugo Benzie.'

Rebus was still nodding. 'Which one of us asks the questions?'

Siobhan sat back. 'Let's play it by ear, see which one of us Marr prefers.' Rebus looked at her. 'You don't agree?' she asked.

He shook his head. 'It's not that.'

'What then?'

'It's almost exactly what I'd have said, that's all.'

She turned towards him, held his eyes. 'Is that a good thing or a bad thing?'

Rebus's face cracked into a smile. 'I'm still trying to decide,' he said, turning the ignition.

The gates at Junipers were being protected by two uniforms, including Nicola Campbell, the WPC he'd met on his first visit. A lone reporter had parked his car on the verge across the road. He was drinking something from a flask, watched Rebus and Siobhan draw up at the gates, then went back to his crossword. Rebus wound down his window.

'No more phone taps?' he asked.

'Not now there's no kidnap,' Campbell replied.

'What about Brains?'

'Back at the Big House: something came up.'

'I see there's one vulture.' Rebus meant the reporter. 'Any ghouls?'

'A few.'

'Well, a couple more may be on their way. Who's up there?' Rebus pointed through the gates.

'DCS Templer, DC Hood.'

'Planning the next press conference,' Siobhan guessed.

'Who else?' Rebus asked Campbell.

'The parents,' she told him, 'house staff . . . someone from the funeral home. And a family friend.'

Rebus nodded. He turned to Siobhan. 'Wonder if we've talked to the staff: sometimes they see and hear things . . .' Campbell was opening the gates.

'DS Dickie interviewed them,' Siobhan said.

'Dickie?' Rebus put the car into gear, crawled through the gates. 'That clock-watching wee nyaff?'

She looked at him. 'You want to do it all yourself, don't you?'

'Because I don't trust anyone else to do it right.'

'Thanks very much.'

He took his eyes off the windscreen. 'There are exceptions,' he said.

Four cars were parked in the driveway outside the house, the same driveway Jacqueline Balfour had come stumbling down, thinking Rebus her daughter's abductor.

'Grant's Alfa,' Siobhan commented.

'Chauffeuring the boss.' Rebus guessed that the black Volvo S40 belonged to the funeral home, leaving a bronze Maserati and a green Aston Martin DB7. He couldn't decide which belonged to Ranald Marr and which to the Balfours, and said as much.

'The Aston's John Balfour's,' Siobhan told him. He looked at her.

'Is that a guess?' he asked.

She shook her head. 'It's in the notes.'

'You'll be telling me his shoe size next.'

A maid answered the door. They showed their warrant cards and were ushered into the hall. The maid headed off without saying anything. Rebus had never really seen anyone walking on tiptoe before. No voices could be heard anywhere.

'This place is straight out of Cluedo,' Siobhan murmured, studying the wood panelling, the paintings of Balfours past.

There was even a suit of armour at the foot of the stairs. A stack of unopened mail sat on a table next to the armour. The same door the maid had disappeared through was opening now. A tall, middle-aged and efficient-looking woman walked towards them. Her face was composed but unsmiling.

'I'm Mr Balfour's personal assistant,' she said in a voice not much above a whisper.

'It's Mr Marr we were hoping to talk to.'

She bowed her head to acknowledge as much. 'But you must appreciate that this is an extremely difficult time . . .'

'He won't talk to us?'

'It's not a case of "won't".' She was becoming irritated.

Rebus nodded slowly. 'Tell you what then, I'll just go tell Detective Chief Superintendent Templer that Mr Marr is holding up our inquiry into Miss Balfour's murder. If you could show me the way . . . ?'

She stared daggers at him, but Rebus wasn't about to blink, never mind flinch.

'If you'll wait here,' she said finally. When she spoke, Rebus saw her teeth for the first time. He managed a polite 'thank you' as she headed back towards the door.

'Impressive,' Siobhan commented.

'Her or me?'

'The general combat.'

He nodded. 'Two more minutes, I'd have been reaching for that suit of armour.'

Siobhan walked over to the table and flicked through the mail. Rebus joined her.

'Thought we'd have been opening it,' he said, 'looking for ransom demands.'

'We probably were,' Siobhan answered, studying the postmarks. 'But this is all yesterday's and today's.'

'Keeping the postman busy.' Several of the envelopes were card-sized and black-edged. 'Hope the PA opens them.'

Siobhan nodded. Ghouls again, for whom the death of someone well known was an invitation to become obsessed.

You never knew who'd be sending a condolence card. 'It should be us checking them.'

'Good point.' After all, the killer could be a ghoul, too.

The door opened again. This time, Ranald Marr, in black suit and tie, white shirt, strode towards them, looking upset by the interruption.

'What is it this time?' he asked Siobhan.

'Mr Marr?' Rebus stuck out his hand. 'DI Rebus. I just want to say how sorry we are that we've had to intrude.'

Marr, accepting the apology, also accepted Rebus's hand. Rebus had never joined 'the craft', but his father had taught him the handshake one drunken night, back when Rebus had been in his teens.

'As long as it's not going to take long,' Marr said, pushing for advantage.

'Is there somewhere we could talk?'

'Along here.' Marr led them into one of two hallways. Rebus caught Siobhan's eye and nodded, answering her question. Marr was a Mason. She pursed her lips, looked thoughtful.

Marr had opened another door, leading into a large room filled with a wall-length bookcase and a full-size billiard table. When he flicked on the lights – the room, like the rest of the house, was curtained in a show of mourning – the green baize was illuminated. Two chairs sat against one wall, a small table between them. On the table sat a silver tray laid with a decanter of whisky and some crystal tumblers. Marr sat down and poured himself a drink. He gestured towards Rebus, who shook his head, Siobhan likewise. Marr raised his glass.

'Philippa, God rest her soul.' Then he drank deeply. Rebus had smelt the whisky on his breath, knew this wasn't his first of the day. Probably not the first time he'd made the toast either. If they'd been alone together, they would have exchanged information about one another's home lodge – and Rebus might have been in trouble – but with Siobhan here, he was safe. He rolled a red ball across the table, where it rebounded from the cushion.

'So,' Marr said, 'what is it you want this time?'

'Hugo Benzie,' Rebus said.

The name caught Marr by surprise. His eyebrows lifted, and he took another pull on his drink.

'You knew him?' Rebus guessed.

'Not very well. His daughter was at school with Philippa.'

'Did he bank with you?'

'You know I can't discuss the bank's business. It wouldn't be ethical.'

'You're not a doctor,' Rebus said. 'You just keep people's money for them.'

Marr's eyes narrowed. 'We do a sight more than that.'

'What? You mean lose money for them too?'

Marr leaped to his feet. 'What the hell has this got to do with Philippa's murder?'

'Just answer the question: did Hugo Benzie have his money invested with you?'

'Not with us, *through* us.'

'You advised him?'

Marr refilled his glass. Rebus glanced towards Siobhan. She knew her place in this, was keeping quiet, standing in the shadows beyond the baize.

'You advised him?' Rebus asked again.

'We advised him against taking risks.'

'But he wouldn't listen?'

'What's life without a bit of risk: that was Hugo's philosophy. He gambled . . . and lost.'

'Did he hold Balfour's responsible?'

Marr shook his head. 'I don't think so. Poor bugger just did away with himself.'

'What about his wife and daughter?'

'What about them?'

'Did they bear a grudge?'

He shook his head again. 'They knew what kind of man he was.' He put his glass down on the rim of the billiard table. 'But what's this got . . . ?' Then he seemed to realise.

'Ah, you're still looking for motives . . . and you think a dead man has risen from his grave to seek revenge on Balfour's Bank?'

Rebus rolled another ball across the table. 'Stranger things have happened.'

Siobhan walked forward now, and handed the sheet of paper to Marr. 'You remember I asked about games?'

'Yes.'

'This clue here.' She pointed to the one relating to Rosslyn Chapel. 'What do you make of it?'

He narrowed his eyes in concentration. 'Nothing at all,' he said, handing it back.

'Can I ask if you're a member of a masonic lodge, Mr Marr?'

Marr glared at her. Then his eyes flickered in Rebus's direction. 'I'm not going to dignify that question with a response.'

'You see, Philippa was given this clue to solve, and so was I. And when I saw the words "mason's dream", I had to find a member of a lodge to ask what it meant.'

'And what did it mean?'

'That's not important. What *may* be important is whether Philippa sought help along the same lines.'

'I've already told you, I knew nothing about any of this.'

'But she might have slipped something into the conversation . . . ?'

'Well, she didn't.'

'Any other Masons of her acquaintance, Mr Marr?' Rebus asked.

'I wouldn't know. Look, I really think I've given you enough time . . . today of all days.'

'Yes, sir,' Rebus said. 'Thank you for seeing us.' He held out his hand again, but this time Marr didn't take it. He walked to the door in silence, opened it, and walked out. Rebus and Siobhan followed him back down the hallway. Templer and Hood were standing in the entrance hall. Marr passed them without a word and disappeared through a door.

'What the hell are you doing here?' Templer asked in an undertone.

'Trying to catch a killer,' Rebus told her. 'How about you?'

'You looked good on the telly,' Siobhan said to Hood.

'Thanks.'

'Yes, Grant did bloody well,' Templer said, her attention deflected from Rebus on to Siobhan. 'I couldn't be more pleased.'

'Me neither,' Siobhan said with a smile.

They left the house and got into their respective cars. Templer's parting shot: 'I'll want a report explaining your presence here. And John? The doctor's waiting . . .'

'Doctor?' Siobhan asked, doing up her seat-belt.

'It's nothing,' Rebus said, turning the ignition.

'Has she got it in for you as well as me?'

Rebus turned to her. 'Gill wanted you by her side, Siobhan. You turned that down.'

'I wasn't ready.' She paused. 'You know, this is going to sound daft, but I think she's jealous.'

'Of you?'

Siobhan shook her head. 'Of *you*.'

'Me?' Rebus laughed. 'Why would she be jealous of me?'

'Because you don't play by the rules, and she has to. Because despite yourself, you always seem to get people working for you, even when they don't agree with what you're asking them to do.'

'I must be better than I think.'

She looked at him slyly. 'Oh, I think you know how good you are. At least, you think you do.'

He returned her look. 'There's an insult buried in there somewhere, but I can't quite see it.'

Siobhan sat back in her seat. 'So what now?'

'Back to Edinburgh.'

'And?'

Rebus was thoughtful as he eased the car back down the driveway. 'I don't know,' he said. 'Back there, you'd almost have thought Marr had lost his own kid . . .'

'You're not saying . . . ?'

'Did he look like her at all? I'm useless at that.'

Siobhan thought about it, gnawing her lip. 'Rich people all look the same to me. You think Marr and Mrs Balfour could have had an affair?'

Rebus shrugged. 'Hard to prove without a blood test.' He glanced in her direction. 'Better make sure Gates and Curt keep a sample.'

'And Claire Benzie?'

Rebus gave a wave to WPC Campbell. 'Claire's interesting, but we don't want to rattle her chain.'

'Why not?'

'Because a year or three from now, she could be our friendly local pathologist. I may not be around to see it, but you will, and the last thing you want is . . .'

'Bad blood?' Siobhan guessed with a smile.

'Bad blood,' Rebus agreed with a slow nod.

Siobhan was thoughtful. 'But whichever way you look at it, she has every right to feel pissed off with the Balfours.'

'Then how come she was still friends with Flip?'

'Maybe she was playing a game of her own.' As they drove back down the lane, she kept her eyes open for the tourists, but didn't see them. 'Should we check Meadowside, see if they're all right?'

Rebus shook his head. They were silent once more until they'd left Falls far behind.

'Marr's a Mason,' Siobhan said at last. 'And he likes playing games.'

'So now *he's* the Quizmaster rather than Claire Benzie?'

'I think it's more likely than him turning out to be Flip's father.'

'Sorry I spoke.' Rebus was thinking of Hugo Benzie. Before driving out to Falls, he'd rung a lawyer friend and asked about him. Benzie had specialised in wills and trusts, a quiet and efficient solicitor, part of a large practice in the city. The gambling wasn't common knowledge, and had never interfered with his work. The rumour was, he'd stuck money into Far East start-ups, guided by tip-offs and the financial pages of his favoured daily paper. If this were true, then Rebus couldn't see Balfour's as culpable. Probably all they'd done was channel the money on his instructions, then had to call time when it disappeared up the Yangtze. Benzie hadn't just lost all his money – as a lawyer he could always earn more. To Rebus's mind, he'd lost something much more substantial: his faith in himself. Having stopped believing in himself, it was probably easy to start believing in suicide as an option, and sometime thereafter as absolute necessity. Rebus had been there himself once or twice, with the bottle and the darkness for company. He knew he couldn't leap from a high place: he was scared of heights, had been ever since they'd dropped him from a helicopter during his army days. Warm bath and a razor across the wrists . . . the problem there was the mess, the thought of someone, friend or stranger, confronted with such a tableau. Booze and pills . . . it always came down to those essential drugs. Not at home, but in some anonymous hotel room, discovered by the staff. Just another lonely corpse as far as they'd be concerned.

Idle thoughts. But in Benzie's shoes . . . wife and daughter . . . he didn't think he could have done it, leaving behind a devastated family. And now Claire wanted to be a pathologist, a career filled with corpses and ventilated, windowless rooms. Would each body she dealt with be her father's image . . . ?

'Penny for them,' Siobhan said.

'No sale,' Rebus replied, fixing his eyes on the road ahead.

'Cheer up,' Hi-Ho Silvers said, 'it's Friday afternoon.'

'So what?'

He stared at Ellen Wylie. 'Don't tell me you don't have a date lined up?'

'A date?'

'You know: a meal, some dancing, then back to his place.' He started gyrating his hips.

Wylie screwed up her face. 'I'm having trouble keeping my lunch down as it is.'

The remains of the sandwich were on her desk: tuna

mayonnaise with sweetcorn. There'd been a slight fizziness to the tuna, and now her stomach was sending her signals. Not that Silvers was about to take any notice.

'Must have a boyfriend though, Ellen?'

'I'll call you when desperation takes hold.'

'As long as it's not Friday or Saturday night: my drinking nights, those are.'

'I'll bear that in mind, George.'

'And Sunday afternoon, of course.'

'Of course.' Wylie couldn't help thinking that this arrangement probably suited Mrs Silvers just fine.

'Unless we get some overtime.' Silvers's mind made the switch. 'What do you reckon the chances are?'

'Depends, doesn't it?' And she knew what it depended on: media pressure, forcing the brass to look for a quick result. Or maybe John Balfour, asking another favour, twisting an arm or two. Time was, CID would work seven-day weeks, twelve-hour days on a big case, and be paid accordingly. But budgets were tighter now, along with staffing levels. She'd never seen so many happy cops as the day CHOGM – the Commonwealth Heads of Government Meeting – had rolled into town, bringing with it an overtime jamboree. But that had been a few years back now. Still she caught officers, Silvers among them, muttering the word 'chogm' under their breath, as though it were a talisman. As Silvers shrugged and moved off, overtime probably still on his mind, Wylie turned her attention to the story of the German student, Jürgen Becker. She thought of Boris Becker, her favourite tennis player at one time, and wondered idly if Jürgen might be some relation. She doubted it: a famous relly would have pulled out the stops, like with Philippa Balfour.

And yet what progress had they made? They didn't seem to be any further forward than the day the MisPer inquiry had opened. Rebus had all these ideas, but there was no focus to them. It was as if he reached out his hand and plucked possibilities from some tree or bush, expecting people to swallow them. The one time she'd worked with him before – a body found in Queensberry House, just as they were readying to knock most of it down and start building the parliament – there hadn't been a result. He'd as good as dumped her, refused to talk about the case afterwards. Nothing had come to court.

And yet . . . she'd rather be part of Rebus's team than none at all. She felt she'd burned her bridges with Gill Templer, whatever Rebus said, and she knew it was all her fault. She'd tried too hard, almost to the point of pestering Templer. It was a form of laziness: pushing to be noticed in the hope advancement would follow. And she knew Templer had rejected her precisely because she'd seen it for what it was. Gill Templer hadn't got to the top that way – she'd had to work her damnedest throughout, fighting a prejudice against women officers which was never discussed, never admitted to.

But still there.

Wylie knew she should have kept her head down and her mouth shut. That was how Siobhan Clarke worked; she never looked pushy, even though she was every inch the careerist . . . and a rival – Wylie couldn't help but see her that way. Templer's favourite from the start, which was precisely why she – Ellen Wylie – had begun campaigning overtly and, as it turned out, too strenuously. Leaving her isolated, stuck with a piece of crap like the Jürgen Becker story. On a Friday afternoon, when there'd most likely be no one around to answer her phone calls, reply to her questions. It was dead time, that was all.

Dead time.

Grant Hood had another press conference to organise. He already knew the names to put to faces, had arranged short get-to-know meetings with the 'majors', these being the more reputable journalists, crime reporters of long standing.

'Thing is, Grant,' DCS Templer had confided in him, 'there are some journos we can call our own, in that they're malleable. They'll toe the line, place a story for us if and when we want them to, while holding back stuff we don't want getting out. You already have a foundation of trust there, but it cuts both ways. We have to give them good copy, and they're hoping they get it an hour or two before the oppo.'

'The oppo, ma'am?'

'Opposition. See, they look like a solid mass when you see them in the press room, but they're not. At times they'll cooperate with each other – like sending one of their number on a thankless stake-out. He then shares whatever he gets with the rest of them. They take it in turns.'

Grant had nodded his understanding.

'But in other respects, it's dog eat dog. The hacks who're not in the loop, they're keenest of all, and not likely to be scrupulous. They'll get chequebooks out when it suits, and they'll try to win you over. Not with cash maybe, but with drinks, a bit of dinner. They'll make you feel one of the lads, and you'll start thinking: they're not so bad really. That's when you're in trouble, because all the time they'll be pumping you without you knowing it. You might let drop a hint or a teaser, just to show them you're in the know. And whatever it is you've come out with, you can guarantee they'll print it with knobs on. You'll be "a police source" or "an unnamed source close to the investigation" – that's if they're in the mood to be kind. And if they get anything on you, they'll turn the screws. They'll want chapter and verse, or they'll leave you on the rack.' She'd patted his shoulder, and finished by saying: 'Just a word to the wise.'

'Yes, ma'am. Thank you, ma'am.'

'It's okay to be on genial terms with them all, and you should introduce yourself to the ones who matter, but never forget which side you're on ... or that there *are* sides. Okay?'

He'd nodded. Then she'd given him the list of 'majors'.

He'd stuck to coffee and orange juice in each meeting, and was relieved to see most of the journalists doing likewise.

'You might find the "elders" running on whisky and gin,' one younger reporter had said, 'but not us.'

The meeting after that had been with one of the most

respected of the "elders". He'd wanted nothing more than a glass of water: 'The young ones drink like fish, but I find I can't any more. And what's your tipple of preference, DC Hood?'

'This isn't a formal occasion, Mr Gillies. Please, call me Grant.'

'Then you must call me Allan . . .'

Still Grant couldn't get Templer's warning words out of his head. As a result, he felt he'd come over as stiff and awkward at each get-to-know. Still, one definite bonus was that Templer had arranged for him to have his own office at Fettes HQ, at least for the duration of the inquiry. She'd called it 'prudent', explaining that he'd be talking to journalists every day, and it was best to keep them at a distance from the main investigation. If they happened to drop into Gayfield or St Leonard's for a briefing or even a quick chat, there was no telling what they might overhear or happen to notice.

'Good point,' he'd said, nodding.

'Same goes for phone calls,' Templer had gone on. 'If you want to call a journalist, do so from your office, door closed. That way they're not going to hear anything they shouldn't in the background. One of them phones you and catches you in CID or somewhere, say you'll call them back.'

He'd nodded again.

Thinking back, she'd probably reckoned he resembled one of those nodding dogs, the kind you got in the back of naff cars. He tried to shake the image away, focused on his screen. He was drafting a press release, copies to go to Bill Pryde, Gill Templer and ACC Carswell for their input and approval.

Carswell, the Assistant Chief Constable, was on another floor in the same building. He'd already knocked on Grant's door and come in to wish him good luck. When Grant had introduced himself as Detective Constable Hood, Carswell had nodded slowly, his eyes those of an examiner.

'Well,' he'd said, 'no cock-ups and a result on this, we'll have to see about doing something better for you, eh?'

Meaning a hike to detective sergeant. Hood knew Carswell could do it, too. He'd already taken one young CID officer under his wing – DI Derek Linford. Problem was, neither Linford nor Carswell had any time for John Rebus, which meant Hood would have to be careful. He'd already turned down one drink with Rebus and the rest of the crew, but was conscious that he'd spent some time alone with Rebus in a bar all too recently. It was the sort of thing which, leaked to Carswell, could put a real spanner in the works. He thought again of Templer's words: *if they get anything on you, they'll turn the screws* . . . Another image flashed in front of him, that clinch with Siobhan. He'd have to be careful from now on: careful who he spoke to and what he said, careful who he spent time with, careful what he did.

Careful not to make enemies.

Another knock on the door. It was one of the civilian staff. 'Something for you,' she said, handing over a carrier bag. Then she smiled and retreated. He opened it. A bottle inside: José Cuervo Gold. And along with it, a little card:

Here's wishing you well in your new post. Think of us as sleepy-headed children, who need to be told their daily story. Your news friends, the Fourth Estate.

Grant smiled. He thought he detected the hand of Allan Gillies. Then it struck him: he'd never answered Gillies's inquiry about his favoured drink . . . yet somehow Gillies had got it right. It went beyond guesswork: someone had been talking. The smile left Grant's face. The tequila wasn't just a gift, it was a show of strength. Just then his mobile sounded. He took it from his pocket.

'Hello?'

'DC Hood?'

'Speaking.'

'Just thought I'd introduce myself, since I seemed to miss out on one of the invites.'

'Who is this?'

'My name's Steve Holly. You'll have seen my byline.'

'I've seen it.' Holly's was definitely not one of the names on Templer's list of 'majors'. Her own succinct description of him: 'a shit'.

'Well, we'll be seeing one another at all these press conferences and such like, but I thought I'd just say hello first. Did you get the bottle?'

When Grant didn't reply, Holly just laughed.

'He always does that, old Allan. Thinks it's clever, but you and I know it's just a party trick.'

'Is it?'

'I'm not the sort for rubbish like that, as you'll no doubt have noticed.'

'Noticed?' Grant frowned.

'Think about it, DC Hood.' With that, the line went dead.

Grant stared at the phone, and then it dawned on him. The journalists, all they'd had from him so far were his office phone, fax and pager. He thought hard, and was sure he hadn't given his mobile to any of them. More advice from Templer:

'Once you get to know them, there'll be one or two you really click with – it's never the same combination for any liaison officer. Those really special ones, you might want to let have your mobile number. It's a sign of trust. For the rest, forget it or your life won't be your own . . . and with them clogging the line, how can any of your colleagues hope to contact you? Us and them, Grant, us and them . . .'

And now one of 'them' had his mobile number. There was only one thing for it, he'd have to get it changed.

As for the tequila, that was going with him to the press conference. He'd hand it back to Allan Gillies, tell him he was off the alcohol these days.

He was beginning to think that might not be so far from the truth. There were a lot of changes to be made if he was going to stay the course.

Grant felt he was ready.

The CID suite at St Leonard's was emptying. Officers not involved in the murder case were clocking off for the weekend. Some would work a Saturday shift if it was offered them. Others would be on call, should a fresh case need investigating. But for most, the weekend was beginning. There was a spring in their step; they struck up choruses of old pop songs. The city had been quiet of late. A few domestics, a drug bust or two. The Drugs Squad were keeping their heads down, however, after answering a tip-off: a council house in Gracemount, silver sheeting at an upstairs bedroom window, kept closed all day and night. They'd hurtled in, ready to demolish Edinburgh's latest cannabis supply, and had instead found a teenager's bedroom, newly decorated. His mum had bought a moon blanket instead of curtains, thought it looked trendy . . .

'Bloody *Changing Rooms*,' one of the Drugs Squad had muttered.

There were other incidents, but they were isolated, hardly the stuff of a crime wave. Siobhan looked at her watch. She'd called the Crime Squad earlier, asked about computers. She hadn't even got halfway through her explanation when Claverhouse had said, 'Someone's already on it. We'll send him over.' So now she was waiting. She'd tried Claverhouse again: no answer. He was probably on his way home or to the pub. Maybe he wasn't sending anyone till Monday. She'd give it another ten minutes. After all, she had her own life, didn't she? Football tomorrow if she wanted it, though it was an away match. Sunday she could go for a drive: there were all these places she'd never been – Linlithgow Palace, Falkland Palace, Traquair. A friend she hadn't seen in months had invited her to a birthday party Saturday night. She didn't think she'd go, but the option was always there . . .

'Are you DC Clarke?'

He had a briefcase with him, which he placed on the floor. She was reminded for a second of door-to-door salesmen, cold callers. Straightening, she saw that he was overweight, most of it around the stomach. Short hair, a tuft standing up at the back of his head. He introduced himself as Eric Bain.

'I've heard of you,' Siobhan admitted. 'Don't they call you "Brains"?'

'Sometimes, but to be honest I prefer Eric.'

'Eric it is. Make yourself comfortable.'

Bain pulled over a chair. As he sat, the material of his light blue shirt stretched, opening gaps between buttons at the front, exposing areas of pale pink skin.

'So,' he said, 'what have we got?'

Siobhan explained, while Bain gave her his full concentration, his eyes fixed on hers. She noticed that his breath came in small wheezes, and wondered if there was an inhaler in one of his pockets.

She tried for eye contact, tried to relax, but his size and proximity made her uncomfortable. His fingers were pudgy and ringless. His watch had too many buttons on it. There was hair below his chin which the morning's razor had failed to find.

He didn't ask a single question throughout her speech. At the end, he asked to see the e-mails.

'Onscreen, or printed out?'

'Either will do.'

She took the sheets from her shoulder-bag. Bain moved his chair even closer so he could spread them out on the desk. He made a chronological line, working from the dates at the top of each one.

'These are just the clues,' he said.

'Yes.'

'I want all the e-mails.'

So Siobhan booted up the laptop, connecting her mobile while she was at it. 'Shall I check for new messages?'

'Why not?' he asked.

There were two from Quizmaster.

Game time is elapsing. Do you wish to continue, Seeker?

An hour later, this had been followed by:

Communication or cessation?

'Knows her vocab, doesn't she?' Bain stated. Siobhan looked at him. 'You keep saying "he",' he explained. 'Thought it might help us keep an open mind if I . . .'

'Fine,' she said, nodding. 'Whatever.'

'Do you want to reply?'

She started to shake her head, then changed it to a shrug. 'I'm not sure what I want to say.'

'Be easier to trace her if she doesn't shut down.'

She looked at Bain, then typed a reply – *Thinking about it* – and hit 'send'. 'Reckon that'll do?' she asked.

'Well, it definitely ranks as "communication".' Bain smiled. 'Now let me have those other messages.'

She hooked up to a printer, only to find there was no paper. 'Hell,' she hissed. The store cupboard was locked and she'd no idea where the key was. Then she remembered Rebus's file, the one he'd taken with him when they'd interviewed Albie the medical student. He'd made it look intimidatingly thick by padding it with sheets from the photocopier. Siobhan walked to Rebus's desk, started opening drawers. Bingo: the file was there, the half-ream still tucked inside. Two minutes later she had the history of Quizmaster's correspondence. Bain shuffled the sheets so that everything could fit on her desktop, covering it almost completely.

'See all this stuff?' he asked, pointing to the bottom halves of some of the pages. 'You probably never look at it, do you?'

Siobhan had to admit as much. Beneath the word 'Headers' lay more than a dozen lines of extra material: Return-Path, Message-ID, X-Mailer . . . It didn't mean much to her.

'This,' Bain said, drawing his lips into his mouth to moisten them, 'is the juicy stuff.'

'Can we identify Quizmaster from it?'

'Not straight away, but it's a start.'

'How come some of the messages don't have headers?' Siobhan asked.

'That,' Bain said, 'is the bad news. If a message has no headers, it means the sender is using the same ISP you are.'

'But . . .'

Bain was nodding. 'Quizmaster has more than one account.'

'He's switching ISPs?'

'It's not uncommon. I have a friend who's averse to paying for Internet access. Before the freeserves came along, he'd sign up with a different ISP every month. That way he took advantage of all those "first month free" deals. When time was up, he cancelled and went looking elsewhere. One whole year, he didn't pay a penny. What Quizmaster is doing is an extension of that.' Bain ran his finger down each list of headers, stopping at the fourth line. 'These tell you his ISP. See? Three different providers.'

'Making him harder to catch?'

'Harder, yes. But he must have set up a . . .' He noticed the look on Siobhan's face. 'What?' he asked.

'You said "he".'

'Did I?'

'Would it be simpler if we stuck to that, do you think? Not that I don't appreciate your idea of keeping an open mind.'

Bain thought about it. 'Fine,' he said. 'So, as I was saying, he – or *she* – must have set up a payment account with each one. At least, I'd think so. Even if you're on a month's free trial, they'll usually ask for some details first, including a Visa card or bank account.'

'So they can start charging you when the time comes?'

Bain nodded. 'Everyone leaves traces,' he said quietly, staring at the sheets. 'They just don't think they do.'

'It's like forensics, isn't it? A hair, a fleck of skin . . .'

'Exactly.' Bain was smiling again.

'So we need to talk to the service providers, get them to hand over his details?'

'If they'll talk to us.'

'This is a murder inquiry,' Siobhan said. 'They'll have to.'

He glanced in her direction. 'There are channels, Siobhan.'

'Channels?'

'There's a Special Branch unit deals with nothing but high-tech crime. They concentrate on hard-core mostly, track down the buyers of kiddie porn, that kind of stuff. You wouldn't believe the stories: hard disks hidden inside other hard disks, screen-savers which hide pornographic images . . .'

'We need their permission?'

Bain shook his head. 'We need their *help*.' He checked his watch. 'And it's too late tonight to do anything about it.'

'Why?'

'Because it's Friday night in London too.' He looked at her. 'Buy you a drink?'

She wasn't going to say yes: lots of excuses ready to use. But somehow she couldn't say no, and they found themselves across the road in The Maltings. Again, he placed his briefcase on the floor next to him as they stood at the bar.

'What do you keep in there?' she asked.

'What do you think?'

She shrugged. 'Laptop, mobile phone . . . gadgets and floppies . . . I don't know.'

'That's what you're supposed to think.' He hefted the briefcase on to the bar and was about to snap it open, but then paused and shook his head. 'Nah,' he said. 'Maybe when we know one another a bit better.' He placed it back beside his feet.

'Keeping secrets from me?' Siobhan said. 'That's a fine start to a working relationship.'

They both smiled as their drinks arrived: bottled lager for her, a pint of beer for him. There were no free tables.

'So what's St Leonard's like?' Bain asked.

'Much the same as any other station, I suppose.'

'It's not every station has a John Rebus in it.'

She looked at him. 'How do you mean?'

He shrugged. 'It's something Claverhouse said, about you being Rebus's apprentice.'

'Apprentice!' Even with the stereo blaring, her outburst had heads turning towards them. 'Bloody cheek!'

'Easy, easy,' Bain said. 'It's just something Claverhouse said.'

'Then you tell Claverhouse to stick his head up his arse.'

Bain started laughing.

'I'm not joking,' she said. But then she started laughing too.

After two more drinks, Bain said he felt peckish and what about seeing if Howie's had a table. She wasn't about to say yes – didn't really feel that hungry after the lager – but somehow she found herself unable to say no.

Jean Burchill was working late at the Museum. Ever since Professor Devlin had mentioned Dr Kennet Lovell, Jean had been intrigued. She'd decided to do some investigating of her own, to see if the pathologist's theory could be substantiated. She knew that she could take a short cut by talking to Devlin himself, but something stopped her. She imagined she could still smell formaldehyde on his skin and feel the cold touch of dead flesh when he took her hand. History only brought her in contact with the long-dead, and then usually as mere references in books or artefacts discovered during digs. When her husband had died, his pathology report had made for grim reading, yet whoever had written it had done so with relish, lingering on the liver abnormalities, its swollen and overtaxed nature. 'Overtaxed' was the very word the writer had used. Easy enough, she supposed, to diagnose alcoholism after death.

She thought of John Rebus's drinking. It didn't seem to her to resemble Bill's. Bill would toy with his breakfast, then head out to the garage where he kept a bottle hidden. A couple under his belt before getting into the car. She kept finding evidence: empty bourbon bottles in the cellar, and at the back of the topmost shelf of his closet. She never said anything. Bill went on being 'the life and soul', 'steady and reliable', 'a fun guy', right up until the illness stopped him working, sending him to a hospital bed instead.

She didn't think Rebus was a secret drinker in that way. He just liked to drink. If he did it alone, that was because he didn't have many friends. She'd asked Bill once why he drank, and he hadn't been able to answer her. She thought probably John Rebus had answers, though he would be reluctant to give them. They'd be to do with washing away the world, scouring his mind of the problems and questions he kept stored there.

None of which would make him a more attractive drunk than Bill had been, but then so far she hadn't seen Rebus drunk. She got the feeling he'd be a sleeper: however many drinks it took, and then crashing into unconsciousness wherever he happened to be.

When her phone rang, she was slow to pick it up.

'Jean?' It was Rebus's voice.

'Hello, John.'

'Thought you'd have left by now.'

'I'm working late.'

'I was just wondering if you . . .'

'Not tonight, John. I've a lot I want to get done.' She pinched the bridge of her nose.

'Fair enough.' He couldn't hide the disappointment in his voice.

'What about this weekend: any plans?'

'Well, that was something I wanted to tell you . . .'

'What?'

'Lou Reed at the Playhouse tomorrow night. I've got two tickets.'

'Lou Reed?'

'He could be great, could be mince. Only one way to find out.'

'I haven't listened to him in years.'

'Don't suppose he's learned how to sing in the interim.'

'No, probably not. All right then, let's do it.'

'Where shall we meet?'

'I've some shopping to do in the morning . . . how about lunch?'

'Great.'

'If you've nothing else on, we could make a weekend of it.'

'I'd like that.'

'Me too. I'm shopping in town . . . wonder if we can get a table at Café St Honoré?'

'Is that just along from the Oxford Bar?'

'Yes,' she said, smiling. She thought of Edinburgh in terms of restaurants, Rebus pubs.

'I'll phone and book.'

'Make it one o'clock. If they can't fit us in, call me back.'

'They'll fit us in. The chef's a regular at the Ox.'

She asked him how the case was progressing. He was reticent, until he remembered something.

'You know Professor Devlin's anatomist?'

'Who? Kennet Lovell?'

'That's the one. I had to interview a medical student, friend of Philippa's. Turns out she's a descendant.'

'Really?' Jean tried not to sound too intrigued. 'Same name?'

'No: Claire Benzie. She's related on her mother's side.'

They chatted for another couple of minutes. When Jean put the phone down, she looked around her. Her 'office' was a small cubicle with desk and chair, filing cabinet and bookshelves. She'd stuck some postcards on the back of the door, including one from the Museum shop: the Arthur's Seat coffins. Secretarial and support staff shared a larger outer office just outside her door, but they'd all gone home. There would be cleaners busy elsewhere in the building, and a security guard doing the rounds. She'd wandered all through the Museum at night, never in the least spooked by it. Even the old museum, with its displays of stuffed animals, calmed her. Friday night, she knew the restaurant at the top of the Museum would be busy. It had its own lift, and someone on the door to make sure diners headed straight for it and didn't wander into the Museum instead.

She remembered her first meeting with Siobhan, the story of the 'bad experience'. Couldn't have had anything to do with the food, though the bill at the end could sometimes come as a shock. She wondered if she'd treat herself later. The price of a meal went down after ten p.m.; maybe they could squeeze her in. She touched her stomach. Lunch tomorrow ... it wouldn't hurt her to skip dinner tonight. Besides, she wasn't sure she'd still be here at ten. Her investigation into the life of Kennet Lovell hadn't thrown up a surfeit of information.

Kennet: she'd first thought the name a misprint, but it kept recurring. Kennet, not Kenneth. Born 1807, in Coylton, Ayrshire, making him just twenty-one at the time of Burke's execution. His parents were farming folk, his father having employed Robert Burns's father for a time. Kennet was given an education locally, helped by the local church minister, the Reverend Kirkpatrick . . .

There was a kettle in the outer office. She got up, walked out of her room. Left the door open, so her shadow stretched across the floor. She didn't bother with the lights. Switched the kettle on and rinsed a mug under the tap. Tea-bag, powdered milk. She stood in the semi-dark, leaning against the worktop, arms folded. Through the doorway, she could see her desk and the photocopied sheets, all she'd been able to find so far on Dr Kennet Lovell, who'd assisted at a murderer's autopsy, helped flay William Burke's skin from his bones. The initial post-mortem examination had been undertaken by Dr Monro, in the presence of a select audience including a phrenologist and a sculptor, as well as the philosopher Sir William Hamilton and the surgeon Robert Liston. This was followed by a public dissection in the university's packed anatomical theatre, noisy medical students gathered around like so many vultures, hungry for knowledge, while those without tickets hammered at the doors for entry and fought with police.

She was working from history books: some about the Burke and Hare case, others about the history of medicine in Scotland. The Edinburgh Room at the Central Library had proved helpful as ever, as had a contact at the National Library. Both had done photocopying for her. She'd taken a trip to Surgeons' Hall, too, using their library and database. Hadn't told Rebus about any of this. She knew why: because she was worried. She felt that the Arthur's Seat case was a blind alley, and one down which John, with his need for answers, might go careering. Professor Devlin had been right about that: obsession was always a trap into which you could fall. This was history – ancient history, compared to the Balfour case. Whether the killer had known about the Arthur's Seat coffins or not seemed irrelevant. There was no way of telling. She was conducting this research for her own satisfaction; didn't want John reading anything more into it. He had enough on his plate without that.

There was a noise in the corridor. When the kettle clicked off, she thought no more about it. Poured the water into her mug, dunked the tea-bag a few times, then tipped it into the swing-bin. Took the mug back into her room, leaving the door open.

Kennet Lovell had arrived in Edinburgh in December 1822, aged barely fifteen. She couldn't know whether he'd taken a coach, or walked. It wasn't uncommon to walk such distances in those days, especially if money was an issue. One historian, in a book about Burke and Hare, speculated that Reverend Kirkpatrick had provided for Lovell's journey, and in addition had given him an introduction to a friend, Dr Knox, recently returned from time overseas, during which he had worked as an army surgeon at Waterloo and studied in Africa and Paris. Knox had housed young Lovell for the first year or so of his life in Edinburgh. But when Lovell had started university, the two seemed to have drifted apart, and Lovell moved to lodgings in West Port . . .

Jean sipped her tea and flipped through the photocopied sheets: no footnotes or index, nothing to indicate the provenance of these apparent 'facts'. Dealing as she did with beliefs and superstitions, she knew how hard it could be to sift out hard objective truths from the chaff of history. Hearsay and rumour could find their way into print. Mistakes, only occasionally pernicious, crept in. It galled her that she had no way of checking anything, had for the moment to rely on mere commentary. A case like Burke and Hare had thrown up any number of contemporary 'experts', who believed their testimony to be the one true and worthwhile account.

It didn't mean she had to believe it.

More frustrating still, Kennet Lovell was a bit-player in

the Burke and Hare story, existing only for that one gruesome scene, while in the history of medicine in Edinburgh his role was more negligible still. Large gaps were left in his biography. By the time she'd finished reading, she knew only that he had completed his studies, moving into the field of teaching as well as practising. He had been present at the Burke autopsy. Yet three years later he seemed to be in Africa, combining much-needed medical skills with Christian missionary work. How long he spent there she couldn't say. His reappearance in Scotland came in the late 1840s. He set up a medical practice in the New Town, his clients probably reflecting the wealth of that enclave. One historian's supposition had it that he had been bequeathed the bulk of the Reverend Kirkpatrick's estate, having 'kept in good graces with that gentleman by dint of regular correspondence down the years'. Jean would have liked to see those letters, but nobody had quoted from them in any of the books. She made a note to try tracking them down. The parish in Ayrshire might have some record, or someone at Surgeons' Hall might know. Chances were, they couldn't be recovered, either because they'd perished – been disposed of with Lovell's effects when he'd died – or had gone overseas. An awful lot of historical documentation had found its way into collections overseas – mostly Canada and the US . . . and many of those collections were private, which meant few details of their contents were available.

She'd seen many a trail go cold, frustrated by her inability to know whether some letter or document was still in existence. Then she remembered Professor Devlin, with his dining table crafted by Lovell. Lovell, who according to Devlin was an amateur woodworker . . . She sifted through the papers again, sure that there was nothing in them mentioning this hobby. Either Devlin had some book, some evidence she'd failed so far to find, or else he was myth-making. This, too, she saw all the time: people who 'just knew' that the antique in their possession had once belonged to Bonnie Prince Charlie or Sir Walter Scott. If it turned out she only had Devlin's word for it that Lovell had worked with wood, then the whole notion that he had left the coffins on Arthur's Seat would begin to crumble. She sat back, annoyed with herself. All this time, she'd been working on an assumption that could turn out to be false. Lovell had left Edinburgh in 1832; the boys had stumbled on the cave containing the coffins in June 1836. Could they have gone undetected for so long?

She lifted something from the desk-top. It was a Polaroid she'd taken in Surgeons' Hall – the portrait of Lovell. He didn't look like a man who'd suffered the ravages of Africa. His skin was pale and smooth, his face youthful. She had pencilled the artist's name on the back. She got up and left her room again, opened the door to her boss's office and switched on his light. He had a shelf of thick reference books, and she found the one she needed, turned to the painter's name, J. Scott Jauncey. 'Active in Edinburgh 1825–35,' she read, 'chiefly landscapes, but some portraiture.' After which he'd taken himself to Europe for many years before settling in Hove. So Lovell had sat for the portrait during his early years in Edinburgh, before his own travels. She wondered if such a thing was the luxury it seemed, to be afforded only by the well-off. Then she thought of Reverend Kirkpatrick ... maybe the portrait had been at his request, something to be sent west to the Ayrshire parish, to remind the minister of his charge.

Again, there might be a clue buried deep within Surgeons' Hall, some record of the portrait's history prior to its arrival there.

'Monday,' she said out loud. It could wait till Monday. She had the weekend to look forward to ... and a Lou Reed concert to survive.

Switching off her boss's light, she heard another noise, much closer. The door to the outer office swung open and the lights all came on. Jean took half a step back, then saw it was just the cleaner.

'You gave me a fright,' she said, putting a hand to her chest.

The cleaner just smiled and put a bin-bag down, heading back into the hallway to fetch her vacuum cleaner.

'Mind if I get started?' she asked.

'Go ahead,' Jean said. 'I'm finished here anyway.'

As she tidied her desk, she noticed that her heart was still racing, her hands shaking slightly. All her night-time walks through the museum, and this was the first time she'd been fazed. The portrait of Kennet Lovell stared at her from the Polaroid. Somehow, it seemed to her, Jauncey had failed to flatter his subject. Lovell looked young, yes, but there was a coldness to the eyes, and the mouth was set, the face full of calculation.

'Heading straight home?' the cleaner asked, coming in to empty her bin.

'Might make a pit-stop at the off-licence.'

'Kill or cure, eh?' the cleaner said.

'Something like that,' Jean replied, as an unwanted image of her husband flashed up in her mind. Then she thought of something and walked back to her desk. Lifted her pen and added a name to the notes she'd taken so far.

Claire Benzie.

11

'Jesus, that was loud,' Rebus said. They were back on the pavement outside the Playhouse, and the sky, which had still been light when they'd gone in, was now dark.

'You don't do this sort of thing often then?' she asked. Her own ears were ringing. She knew she was talking too loudly, overcompensating.

'It's been a while,' he admitted. The crowd had been a mix of teenagers, old punks, right up to people Rebus's own age . . . maybe even a year or two older. Reed had played a lot of new material, stuff Rebus hadn't recognised, but with a few of the classics stirred into the pot. The Playhouse: last time he'd been there had probably been UB40, around the time of their second album. He didn't want to think how long ago that was.

'Shall we get a drink?' Jean suggested. They'd been drinking on and off all afternoon and evening: wine with lunch, then a quick one at the Ox. A long walk down to Dean Village and along the Water of Leith. All the way down to Leith itself, with breaks on the way to park themselves on a bench and talk. Two more drinks in a pub on The Shore. They'd considered an early supper, but were still full from the Café St Honore. Walked back up Leith Walk to the Playhouse. Still early, so they'd gone into the Conan Doyle for one, then the Playhouse bar itself.

At one point Rebus had found himself saying: 'I'd have thought you'd steer clear of the drink.' Regretting the remark immediately. But Jean had just shrugged.

'You mean because of Bill? That's not the way it works. I mean, maybe it is with some people, they either become a drunk themselves or they make a pact never to touch another drop. But it's not the booze that's to blame, it's the person using it. All the time Bill had his problem, it didn't stop me indulging. I never lectured him. And it hasn't stopped me drinking . . . because I know it doesn't mean that much to me.' She'd paused. 'What about you?'

'Me?' Rebus had offered his own shrug. 'I just drink to be sociable.'

'And when does it start working?'

They'd laughed at that, and left the subject alone. Now, just gone eleven on a Saturday night, the street was noisy with alcohol.

'Where do you suggest?' Jean asked. Rebus made a show of checking his watch. There were plenty of bars he could think of, but they weren't places he wanted Jean to see.

'Could you stand a bit more music?'

She shrugged. 'What kind?'

'Acoustic. It'd be standing room only.'

She was thoughtful. 'Is it between here and your flat?'

He nodded. 'You know the place is a tip . . .'

'I've seen it.' Her eyes found his. 'So . . . are you going to ask?'

'You want to stay the night?'

'I want you to ask me to.'

'It's only a mattress on the floor.'

She laughed, squeezed his hand. 'Are you doing this on purpose?'

'What?'

'Trying to put me off.'

'No, it's just . . .' He shrugged. 'I just don't want you—'

She interrupted him with a kiss. 'I won't be,' she said.

He ran a hand up her arm, let it rest on her shoulder. 'Still want that drink first?'

'I think so. How far is it?'

'Just up the Bridges. Pub's called the Royal Oak.'

'Then lead me to it.'

They walked hand in hand, Rebus trying his best not to feel awkward. Still he found himself scanning faces they passed, looking for ones he recognised: colleagues or ex-cons, he couldn't have said which he'd like to meet the least.

'Do you ever relax?' Jean asked at one point.

'I thought I was doing a pretty good imitation.'

'I felt it at the concert, bits of you were elsewhere.'

'Comes with the job.'

'I don't think so. Gill manages to switch off. I'd guess most of the rest of CID do too.'

'Maybe not as much as you think.' He thought of Siobhan, imagined her sitting at home, staring into the laptop ... and Ellen Wylie festering somewhere ... and Grant Hood, his bed strewn with paperwork, memorising names and faces. And the Farmer, what would he be doing? Running a cloth slowly over surfaces already clean? There were some – Hi-Ho Silvers; Joe Dickie – who barely switched on when they went to work, never mind switched off at day's end. Others like Bill Pryde and Bobby Hogan worked hard, but left the job in the office, managed the magic of separating their personal lives from their careers.

Then there was Rebus himself, who for so long had put the job first ... because it saved him having to face some home truths.

Jean broke his reverie with a question. 'Is there a twenty-four-hour shop somewhere on the route?'

'More than one. Why?'

'Breakfast: something tells me your fridge won't exactly be an Aladdin's Cave.'

Monday morning, Ellen Wylie was back at her own desk in what everyone in the force referred to as 'West End', meaning the police station on Torphichen Street. Her reasoning was that it would be easier to get work done there, space not exactly being at a premium. A couple of weekend stabbings, one mugging, three domestics and an arson ... these were keeping her colleagues busy. When they passed her, they asked about the Balfour case. She was waiting for Reynolds and Shug Davidson in particular – the pair forming a fearsome double act – to say something about her TV appearance, but they didn't. Maybe they were taking pity on the afflicted; most likely they were just showing solidarity. Even in a city as small as Edinburgh, rivalries existed between stations. If the Balfour investigation shat on DS Ellen Wylie, it was in effect dumping on West End.

'Reassigned?' Shug Davidson guessed.

She shook her head. 'I'm following a lead. It's as easy to do it here as there.'

'Ah, but here you're a long way away from the glamour chase.'

'The what?'

He smiled. 'The big picture, the juicy inquiry, the *centre* of everything.'

'I'm at the centre of the West End,' she told him. 'That's good enough for me.' Earned herself a wink from Davidson and a round of applause from Reynolds. She smiled: she was back home.

It had niggled at her all weekend: the way she'd been sidelined – bumped from liaison and dropped off at the twilight zone in which DI John Rebus worked. And from there to this – a tourist's suicide from years back – seemed yet another snub.

So she'd come to a decision: if they didn't want her, she didn't need them. Welcome back to the West End. She'd picked up all her notes on the way in. They sat on her desk, a desk she didn't need to share with half a dozen other bodies. The telephone wasn't going constantly, Bill Pryde flapping past with his clipboard and nicotine chewing-gum. She felt safe here, and here she could safely reach the conclusion that she was on another wild-goose chase.

Now all she had to do was prove it to Gill Templer's satisfaction.

She was off to a flyer. She'd called the police station in Fort William and spoken to a very helpful sergeant called Donald Maclay, who remembered the case well.

'The upper slope of Ben Dorchory,' he told her. 'The body had been there a couple of months. It's a remote spot. A ghillie happened on the scene; could have lain there years otherwise. We followed procedure. Nothing in the way of ID on the body. Nothing in the pockets.'

'Not even any money?'

'We didn't find any. Labels on the jacket, shirt and such-like didn't tell us anything. Talked to the B and Bs and hotels, checked the missing persons records.'

'What about the gun?'

'What about it?'

'Did you get any prints?'

'After that length of time? No, we didn't.'

'But you did check for them?'

'Oh, aye.'

Wylie was writing everything down, abbreviating most of the words. 'Gunpowder traces?'

'Sorry?'

'On the skin. He was shot in the head?'

'That's right. The pathologist didn't find any burning or residues on the scalp.'

'Isn't that unusual?'

'Not when half the head's been blown away and the local wildlife have been feeding.'

Wylie stopped writing. 'I get the picture,' she said.

'I mean, this wasn't like a body, more a scarecrow. The skin was like parchment. There's a hellish wind blows across that hill.'

'You didn't treat it as suspicious?'

'We went by the autopsy findings.'

'Any chance you can send me the file?'

'If we get a written request, sure.'

'Thanks.' She tapped her pen against the desk. 'The gun was how far away?'

'Maybe twenty feet.'

'You think an animal moved it?'

'Yes. Either that or it was a reflex thing. Put a gun to your head and pull the trigger, there's going to be a recoil, isn't there?'

'I'd think so.' She paused. 'So what happened next?'

'Well, eventually we tried facial reconstruction, then issued the composite photo.'

'And?'

'And nothing very much. Thing was, we thought he was a lot older ... early forties maybe, and the composite reflected that. God knows how the Germans got to hear of it.'

'The mother and father?'

'That's right. Their son had been missing the best part of a year ... maybe even a bit longer. Then we got this call from Munich, couldn't make much sense of it. Next thing, they'd turned up at the station with a translator. We showed them the clothes and they recognised a couple of things ... the jacket, and a wristwatch.'

'You don't sound convinced.'

'To tell you the truth, I'm not. A year they'd been looking for him, going out of their minds. The jacket was just a plain green thing, nothing special about it. Same goes for the watch.'

'You think they managed to convince themselves simply because they *wanted* to believe?'

'Wanted it to be him, yes. But their son was barely twenty ... experts told us we had the remains of someone twice that age. Then the bloody papers went and printed the story anyway.'

'How did all the sword-and-sorcery stuff come into the picture?'

'Hang on a minute, will you?' She heard Maclay put the receiver down next to his phone. He was giving instructions to someone. 'Just past the creels ... there's a hut Aly uses when he's renting out his boat ...' She imagined Fort William: quiet and coastal, with islands off to the west. Fishermen and tourists; gulls overhead and the tang of seaweed.

'Sorry about that,' Maclay said.

'Keeping you busy?'

'Oh, it's always hectic up this way,' he replied with a laugh. She wished she were there with him. After they'd finished talking, she could walk down to the harbour, passing those creels . . . 'Where were we?' he said.

'Sword and sorcery.'

'First we knew about that was when they put it in the paper. The parents again, they'd been talking to some reporter.'

Wylie held the photocopy in front of her. The headline: 'Did Role Game Kill in Highland Gun Mystery?' The reporter's name was Steve Holly.

Jürgen Becker was a twenty-year-old student who lived with his parents in a suburb of Hamburg. He attended the local university, specialising in psychology. He loved role-playing games, and was part of a team who played in an inter-university league on the Internet. Fellow students said that he'd been 'anxious and troubled' during the week leading up to his disappearance. When he left home for that last time, he took a backpack with him. In it, to the best of his parents' knowledge, were his passport, a couple of changes of clothes, his camera, and a portable CD player with maybe a dozen or so discs.

The parents were professionals – the father an architect, mother a lecturer – but they'd given up work to concentrate on finding their son. The story shifted into bold type for its final paragraph: 'Now, two grieving parents know they've found their son. Yet for them the mystery has only deepened. How did Jürgen come to die on a barren Scottish mountaintop? Who else was there with him? Whose was the gun . . . and who used it to end the young student's life?'

'The backpack and stuff, they never turned up?' Wylie asked.

'Never. But then if it wasn't him, you would hardly expect them to.'

She smiled. 'You've been a real help, Sergeant Maclay.'

'Just put that request in writing, and I'll let you have chapter and verse.'

'Thanks, I'll do that.' She paused. 'We've got a Maclay in Edinburgh CID, works out of Craigmillar . . .'

'Aye, we're cousins. Met him at a couple of weddings and funerals. Craigmillar's where the posh folk live?'

'Is that what he told you?'

'Was I being fed a line?'

'Come see for yourself sometime.'

Wylie was laughing when she finished the call, had to tell Shug Davidson why. He came over to her desk. The CID room wasn't big: four desks, doors leading off to walk-in cupboards where they kept old case files. Davidson picked up the photocopied news story, read it through.

'Looks like something Holly made up all by himself,' he commented.

'You know him?'

'Had a couple of run-ins with him. Holly's speciality is blowing a story up.'

She took the article from him. Sure enough, all the stuff about fantasy games and role-playing was kept ambiguous, the text peppered with conditionals: 'may have', 'could be', 'if, as it is thought . . .'

'I need to speak to him,' she stated, picking up the phone again. 'Do you know his number?'

'No, but he's based at the paper's Edinburgh office.' Davidson started back towards his own desk. 'You'll find it in Yellow Pages under "Leper Colonies" . . .'

Steve Holly was still on his way into work when his mobile sounded. He lived in the New Town, only three streets from what he'd recently called in print 'the tragic death flat'. Not that his own place was in the same league as Flip Balfour's. He was at the top of an unmodernised tenement – one of few still left in the New Town. And his street didn't have the cachet of Flip's address. Still, he'd watched the paper value of his flat soar. Four years ago, he'd decided he wanted to live in this part of town. But even then it had seemed beyond his means, until he started reading the death notices in the city's daily and evening papers. When he saw a New Town address, he'd head round there with an envelope marked 'Urgent' and addressed to 'The Owner'. The letter inside was short. He introduced himself as someone who'd been born and raised in whichever street, but whose family had moved away and encountered bad fortune since. With both parents dead, he now wished to return to a street which held such fond memories, and should the owner ever wish to consider selling . . .

And bloody hell, it had worked. An old woman – house-ridden for a decade – had died, and her niece, who was her closest living relative, had read Holly's letter, phoning him that afternoon. He'd gone to look at the place – three bedrooms, a bit smelly and dark but he knew such things could be fixed. Nearly shot himself in the foot when the niece asked which number he'd lived at, but he'd managed to fool her well enough. Then his pitch: all the estate agents and solicitors getting their cut . . . better to agree a fair price between them and cut out the middle-men.

The niece lived in the Borders, didn't seem to know what flats in Edinburgh were fetching. She'd even thrown in a lot of the old lady's furniture, for which he'd thanked her profusely, turfing out the lot his first weekend in residence.

If he sold up now he'd have a hundred grand in his pocket, a nice nest egg. In fact, only this morning he'd wondered about trying something similar with the Balfours . . . only somehow he reckoned they'd know to the last penny what Flip's place was worth. He stopped, halfway up the Dundas Street climb, and answered his mobile.

'Steve Holly speaking.'

'Mr Holly, this is Detective Sergeant Wylie, Lothian and Borders CID.'

Wylie? He tried to place her. Of course! That brilliant press conference! 'Yes, DS Wylie, and what can I do for you this morning?'

'It's about a story you ran three years or so back . . . the German student.'

'Would that be the student with the twenty-foot reach?' he asked with a grin. He was outside a small art gallery, peered in through the window, curious about the prices first, paintings second.

'That's the one, yes.'

'Don't tell me you've caught the killer?'

'No.'

'What then?'

She hesitated; he frowned in concentration. 'Some new evidence may have come to light . . .'

'What new evidence?'

'Right now, I'm afraid I can't divulge . . .'

'Yeah, yeah. Tell me something I don't hear every other day. Your lot always want something for nothing.'

'And your lot don't?'

He turned away from the window, just in time to catch a green Aston revving away from the lights: not too many about, had to be the grieving father . . . 'What's it got to do with Philippa Balfour?' he asked.

Silence on the line. 'Sorry?'

'That's not a very good answer, DS Wylie. Last time I saw you, you were attached to the Balfour case. Are you saying they've suddenly shifted you on to a case which isn't even in the Lothian and Borders remit?'

'I . . .'

'You're probably not at liberty to say, right? Me, on the other hand, I can say whatever I like.'

'The way you made up that sword-and-sorcery stuff?'

'That wasn't made up. I got it from the parents.'

'That he liked role-playing, yes, but the idea that it was some game brought him to Scotland . . . ?'

'Speculation based on the available evidence.'

'But there *was* no evidence of such a game, was there?'

'Highland mountains, all that Celtic myth rubbish . . . just the place someone like Jürgen would end up. Sent out on some quest, only there's a gun waiting for him when he gets there.'

'Yes, I read your story.'

'And somehow it ties in with Flip Balfour, but you're not going to tell me how?' Holly licked his lips; he was enjoying this.

'That's right,' Wylie said.

'It must have hurt.' His voice was almost solicitous.

'What?'

'When they pulled you from liaison. Not your fault, was it? We're like bloody savages at times. They should have prepared you better. Christ, Gill Templer worked liaison for a hundred years . . . she should have *known*.'

Another silence on the line. Holly softened his voice. 'And then they go and give it to a detective *constable*. DC Grant Hood. A shining example. Now there's one cocky little bastard if ever I saw one. Like I say, something like that's got to hurt. And what's happened to you, DS Wylie? You're stuck halfway up a Scottish mountain, scrabbling around for a reporter – one of the enemy – to put you right.'

He thought she'd gone, but then heard something which was almost a sigh.

Oh, you're good, Stevie boy, he thought to himself. You'll have the right address some day, and works of art on the walls for people to gawp at . . .

'Detective Sergeant Wylie?' he said.

'What?'

'Sorry if I hit a nerve. But, look, maybe we could meet. I think I might just have a way to help, even if only a little.'

'What is it?'

'Face to face?'

'No.' The voice hardening. 'Tell me now.'

'Well . . .' Holly angled his head towards the sun. 'Say this thing you're working on . . . it's confidential, right?' He took a breath. 'Don't answer that. We both know already. But say someone . . . a journalist, for want of a better example . . . got hold of this story. People would want to know how he got it, and do you know who they'd look to first?'

'Who?'

'The liaison officer, Detective Constable Grant Hood. He's the one with the line to the media. And if a certain journalist – the one in possession of the leak – happened to . . . well, *indicate* that his source was not a thousand miles from the liaison officer . . . I'm sorry, it probably sounds petty to you. You probably don't want to see DC Hood with a bit of mud on his new starched shirt, or the flak that would head the way of DCS Templer. It's just that sometimes when I start thinking something, I need to go the whole way. Do you know what I'm saying?'

'Yes.'

'We could still have that meeting. I'm free all morning. I've already told you what you need to know about Mountain Boy, but we could talk anyway . . .'

Rebus had been standing in front of Ellen Wylie's desk a full half-minute before she seemed to realise he was there. She was staring towards the paperwork in front of her, but Rebus didn't think she was seeing it. Then Shug Davidson wandered past, slapping Rebus on the back and saying 'Morning, John', and Wylie looked up.

'Weekend that bad, was it?' Rebus asked.

'What are you doing here?'

'Looking for you, though I'm beginning to wonder why I bothered.'

She seemed to pull herself together, ran a hand over her head and muttered something approaching an apology.

'So am I right, was it a bad weekend?'

Davidson was passing again, papers in hand. 'She was fine till ten minutes ago.' He stopped. 'Was it that wanker Holly?'

'No,' Wylie said.

'Bet it was,' Davidson stated, moving off again.

'Steve Holly?' Rebus guessed.

Wylie tapped the newspaper story. 'I had to talk to him.'
Rebus nodded. 'Just watch out for him, Ellen.'

'I can handle him, don't worry.'

He was still nodding. 'That's more like it. Now, do you feel like doing me a favour?'

'Depends what it is.'

'I got the feeling this German student thing would be driving you mental . . . Is that why you came back to West End?'

'I just thought I might get more work done here.' She threw her pen down on the desk. 'Looks like I was wrong.'

'Well, I'm here to offer you a break. I've got a couple of interviews to do, and I need a partner.'

'Who are you interviewing?'

'David Costello and his father.'

'Why me?'

'I thought I'd already explained that.'

'Charity case, am I?'

Rebus let out a long breath. 'Jesus, Ellen, you can be hard work sometimes.'

She looked at her watch. 'I have a meeting at half-eleven.'

'Me too: doctor's appointment. But this won't take long.' He paused. 'Look, if you don't want to . . .'

'All right,' she said. Her shoulders were slumped. 'Maybe you're right.'

Too late, Rebus was having second thoughts. It was as if the fight had gone out of her. He thought he knew the reason, but knew also that there was little he could do about it.

'Great,' he said.

Reynolds and Davidson were watching from one of the other desks. 'Look, Shug,' Reynolds said, 'it's the Dynamic Duo!'

It seemed to take all Ellen Wylie's effort to lift her from her chair.

He briefed her in the car. She didn't ask much, seemed more interested in the passing parade of pedestrians. Rebus left the Saab in hotel parking and walked into the Caledonian, Wylie a couple of steps behind.

The 'Caley' was an Edinburgh institution, a red-stone monolith at the west end of Princes Street. Rebus had no idea what a room cost. He'd eaten in the restaurant once, with his wife and a couple of friends of hers who were honeymooning in the city. The friends had insisted on putting dinner on their room tab, so Rebus had never known the final figure. He'd been uncomfortable all evening, right in the middle of a case and wanting to get back to it. Rhona knew, too, and excluded him from the conversation by concentrating on reminiscences she shared with her friends. The honeymooners holding hands between courses, and sometimes even while they ate. Rebus and Rhona almost strangers to one another, their marriage faltering . . .

'How the other half live,' he said to Wylie as they waited for the receptionist to call the Costellos' room. When Rebus had phoned David Costello's flat, there'd been no answer, so he'd asked around the office and been told that the parents flew into town Sunday evening, and that their son was spending the day with them.

'I don't think I've been inside before,' Wylie replied. 'It's just a hotel, after all.'

'They'd love to hear you say that.'

'Well, it's true, isn't it?'

Rebus got the feeling she wasn't thinking about what she was saying. Her mind was somewhere else, the words just filling spaces.

The receptionist smiled at them. 'Mr Costello's expecting you.' She gave them the room number and directed them towards the lifts. A liveried porter was hovering, but one look at Rebus told him there was no work for him here. As the lift glided upwards, Rebus tried to get the song 'Bell-Boy' out of his head, Keith Moon growling and wailing.

'What's that you're whistling?' Wylie asked.

'Mozart,' Rebus lied. She nodded as if she'd just placed the tune . . .

It wasn't a room after all, but a suite, with a connecting door to the suite next to it. Rebus caught a glimpse of Theresa Costello before her husband closed the door. The living area was compact: sofa, chair, table, TV . . . There was a bedroom off, and a bathroom down the hall. Rebus could smell soap and shampoo, and behind them the unaired smell you sometimes got in hotel rooms. There was a basket of fruit on the table, and David Costello, seated there, had just helped himself to an apple. He had shaved, but his hair was unwashed, lank and greasy. His grey T-shirt looked new, as did the black denims. The shoelaces on both his trainers were untied, either by accident or design.

Thomas Costello was shorter than Rebus had imagined him, a boxer's roll to his shoulders when he walked. His mauve shirt was open-necked, and his trousers were held up with pale pink braces.

'Come in, come in,' he said, 'sit yourselves down.' He gestured towards the sofa. Rebus, however, took the armchair, while Wylie stayed standing. There was nothing for the father to do but sink into the sofa himself, where he spread his arms out either side of him. But a split second later he brought his hands together in a single sharp clap and exclaimed that they needed something to drink.

'Not for us, Mr Costello,' Rebus said.

'You're sure now?' Costello looked to Ellen Wylie, who managed a slow nod.

'Well then.' The father once again arranged his arms either side of him. 'So what can we be doing for you?'

'I'm sorry we have to intrude at a time like this, Mr Costello.' Rebus glanced towards David, who was showing about as much interest in proceedings as Wylie.

'We quite understand, Inspector. You've got a job to do, and we all want to help you catch the sick bastard who did this to Philippa.' Costello clenched his fists, showing he was ready to do some damage to the culprit himself. His face was almost wider than it was long, the hair cut short and brushed straight back from the forehead. The eyes were narrowed slightly, and Rebus guessed that the man wore contact lenses, and was ever fearful of them falling out.

'Well, Mr Costello, we just have some follow-up questions . . .'

'And do you mind me staying while you ask them?'

'Not at all. It may even be that you can help.'

'Go ahead then.' His head snapped round. 'Davey! Are you listening?'

David Costello nodded, ripping another bite from the apple.

'The stage is all yours, Inspector,' the father said.

'Well, maybe I could start by asking David a couple of things.' Rebus made a show of easing the notebook from his pocket, though he knew the questions already and didn't think he'd need to write anything down. But sometimes the presence of a notebook could work a little magic. Interviewees seemed to trust the written word: if you had something in your notebook, then it had probably been verified. Additionally, if they thought their replies were going to be recorded, they gave each utterance more consideration, or else became flustered and blurted out the truth.

'You're sure you won't sit?' the father asked Wylie, patting the space on the sofa.

'I'm fine,' she answered coolly.

The exchange had somehow broken the spell; David Costello didn't look in the least bothered about the notebook.

'Fire away,' he told Rebus.

Rebus took aim and fired. 'David, we've asked you about this Internet game we think Flip might have been playing . . .'

'Yes.'

'And you said you didn't know anything about it, and didn't go much for computer games and such-like.'

'Yes.'

'But now we hear that in your schooldays you were a bit of a whizz at dungeons and dragons.'

'I remember that,' Thomas Costello interrupted. 'You and your pals, up there in your bedroom all day and all night.' He looked at Rebus. 'All *night*, Inspector, if you can believe that.'

'I've heard of grown men doing the same thing,' Rebus said. 'A few hands of poker and a big enough pot . . .'

Costello conceded as much with a smile: one gambling man to another.

'Who told you I was a "whizz"?' David asked.

'It just came up.' Rebus shrugged.

'Well, I wasn't. The D and D craze lasted about a month.'

'Flip played, too, when she was at school, did you know that?'

'I'm not sure.'

'She'd have told you though . . . I mean, the pair of you were into it.'

'Not by the time we met. I don't think the subject ever came up.'

Rebus stared into David Costello's eyes. They were red-rimmed and bloodshot.

'Then how would Flip's friend Claire have got to hear of it?'

The young man snorted. '*She* told you? Claire the Cow?'

Thomas Costello tutted.

'Well, she is,' his son snapped back. 'She was always trying to break us up, pretending she was "a friend".'

'She didn't like you?'

David considered this. 'I think it was more that she couldn't bear to see Flip happy. When I told Flip, she just laughed in my face. She couldn't see it. There was some history between her family and Claire's, and I think Flip felt guilty. Claire was a real blind spot . . .'

'Why didn't you tell us this before?'

David looked at him and laughed. 'Because Claire didn't kill Flip.'

'No?'

'Christ, you're not saying . . .' He shook his head. 'I mean, when I say Claire was vicious, it was just mind games with her . . . just words.' He paused. 'But then maybe that's what the game was, too: is that what you're thinking?'

'We're keeping an open mind,' Rebus said.

'Jesus, Davey,' the father said, 'if there's anything you need to tell these officers, get it off your chest!'

'It's *David*!' the young man spat. His father looked furious, but didn't say anything. 'I still don't think it was Claire,' David added, for Rebus's benefit.

'What about Flip's mother?' Rebus asked casually. 'How did you get on with her?'

'Fine.'

Rebus allowed the silence to linger, then repeated the word back at David, this time as a question.

'You know how mothers are with daughters,' David started to add. 'Protective and all that.'

'Rightly so, eh?' Thomas Costello winked at Rebus, who glanced towards Ellen Wylie, wondering if this would rouse her. But she was staring out of the window.

'Thing is, David,' Rebus said quietly, 'we've reason to believe there might have been a bit of friction there too.'

'How so?' Thomas Costello asked.

'Maybe David can answer that,' Rebus told him.

'Well, David?' Costello asked his son.

'I've no idea what he means.'

'I mean,' Rebus said, pretending to check his notes, 'that Mrs Balfour harboured the thought that you'd somehow poisoned Flip's mind.'

'You must have misheard the lady,' Thomas Costello said. He was bunching his fists again.

'I don't think so, sir.'

'Look at the strain she's been under . . . doesn't know what she's saying.'

'I think she knew.' Rebus was still looking at David.

'It's right enough,' he said. He'd lost all interest in the apple. It hung from his hand, the white, exposed flesh already beginning to discolour. His father gave a questioning look. 'Jacqueline had some notion that I was giving Flip ideas.'

'What sort of ideas?'

'That she hadn't had a happy childhood. That she was remembering it all wrong.'

'And did you think she was?' Rebus asked.

'It was Flip, not me,' David stated. 'She'd been having this dream. She was back in London, back at the house there, and running up and down stairs trying to get away from something. Same dream most nights for a fortnight.'

'What did you do?'

'Looked in a couple of textbooks, told her it might be to do with repressed memory.'

'The boy's lost me,' Thomas Costello admitted. His son turned his head towards him.

'Something bad that you've managed not to think about. I was quite envious, actually.' They stared at one another. Rebus thought he knew what David was talking about: growing up with Thomas Costello couldn't have been easy. Maybe it explained the son's teenage years . . .

'She never explained what that might be?' Rebus asked.

David shook his head. 'Probably it was nothing; dreams can have all sorts of meanings.'

'But Flip believed it?'

'For a little while, yes.'

'And told her mother as much?'

David nodded. 'Who then blamed the whole thing on me.'

'Bloody woman,' Thomas Costello hissed. He rubbed his forehead. 'But then she's been under a lot of strain, lot of strain . . .'

'This was before Flip went missing,' Rebus reminded him.

'I don't mean that: I mean Balfour's,' Costello growled. The slight against his son was still fresh.

Rebus frowned. 'What about it?'

'Lots of money men in Dublin. You get to hear rumours.'

'About Balfour's?'

'I don't understand it all myself: overstretched . . . liquidity ratios . . . just words to me.'

'You're saying Balfour's Bank is in trouble?'

Costello shook his head. 'Just a few stories that they might be headed that way if they don't turn things around. Problem with banking is, it's all about confidence, isn't it? Few wild stories can do a lot of damage . . .'

Rebus got the feeling Costello wouldn't have said anything, but Jacqueline Balfour's accusations against his son had tipped the balance. He made his first note of the interview: 'check Balfour's'.

He'd had a notion himself: to bring up the matter of father and son's wild days in Dublin. But David seemed calmer now, his teenage years in the past. And as for his father, well, Rebus had seen intimations of a short temper. He didn't think he needed a further lesson.

There was silence in the room again.

'Will that do you for now, Inspector?' Costello said, making show of reaching into his trousers and drawing out a pocket watch, flipping it open and snapping it closed.

'Just about,' Rebus admitted. 'Do you know when the funeral is?'

'Wednesday,' Costello said.

It was sometimes the case, in a murder inquiry, that the victim was left unburied as long as possible, just in case some new piece of evidence came to light. Rebus reckoned strings had been pulled: John Balfour again, getting his own way.

'Is it a burial?'

Costello nodded. A burial was good. With a cremation, it wasn't quite so easy to disinter the body should the need arise . . .

'Well,' he said, 'unless there's anything either of you would like to add . . . ?'

There wasn't. Rebus got to his feet. 'All right, DS Wylie?' he said. It was as if she'd been roused from sleep.

Costello insisted on seeing them to the door, shook both their hands. David didn't get up from his chair. He was lifting the apple to his mouth as Rebus said goodbye.

Outside, the door clicked shut. Rebus stood there for a moment, but couldn't make out any voices from within. He noticed the next door along was open a couple of inches, Theresa Costello peering out.

'Everything okay?' she was asking Wylie.

'Everything's fine, madam,' Wylie told her.

Before Rebus could get there, the door had closed again. He was left wondering whether Theresa Costello felt as trapped as she looked . . .

In the lift, he told Wylie he'd drop her off.

'That's okay,' she said. 'I'm walking.'

'Sure?' She nodded, and he checked his watch. 'Your half-eleven?' he guessed.

'That's right.' Her voice died away.

'Well, thanks for all your help.'

She blinked, as though having difficulty taking the words

in. He stood in the main lobby and watched her make for the revolving door. A moment later, he followed her out on to the street. She was crossing Princes Street, holding her bag in front of her, almost jogging. She made her way up the side of Fraser's store, towards Charlotte Square, where Balfour's had its headquarters. He wondered where she was headed: George Street, or maybe Queen Street? Down into the New Town? The only way to find out was to follow her, but he doubted she would appreciate his curiosity.

'Oh, what the hell,' he muttered to himself, making for the crossing. He had to wait for the traffic to stop, and only caught sight of her when he reached Charlotte Square: she was over the other side, walking briskly. By the time he was on George Street, he'd lost her. He smiled to himself: some detective. Walked along as far as Castle Street, then doubled back. She could be in one of the shops or cafés. To hell with it. He unlocked the Saab and drove out of the hotel car park.

Some people had their demons. He got the feeling Ellen Wylie was among them. He was a good judge of character that way. Experience always told.

Back in St Leonard's, he phoned a contact on a Sunday newspaper's business pages.

'How sound is Balfour's?' he asked, no preamble.

'I'm assuming you mean the bank?'

'Yes.'

'What have you heard?'

'There are rumours in Dublin.'

The journalist chuckled. 'Ah, rumours, where would the world be without them?'

'Then there's no problem?'

'I didn't say that. On paper, Balfour's is ticking along as ever. But there are always margins where figures can be buried.'

'And?'

'And their half-year forecast has been revised downwards; not quite enough to give big investors the jitters, but Balfour's is a loose affiliation of smaller investors. They have a tendency towards hypochondria.'

'Bottom line, Terry?'

'Balfour's should survive, a hostile takeover notwithstanding. But if the balance sheet looks murky at year's end, there may have to be one or two ritual beheadings.'

Rebus was thoughtful. 'Who would go?'

'Ranald Marr, I should think, if only to show that Balfour himself has the ruthlessness necessary for this day and age.'

'No place for old friendships?'

'Truth be told, there never was.'

'Thanks, Terry. A large G and T will be waiting for you behind the bar of the Ox.'

'It may wait a while.'

'You on the wagon?'

'Doctor's orders. We're being picked off one by one, John.'

Rebus commiserated for a couple of minutes, thinking of his own doctor's appointment, the one he was missing yet again by making this call. When he put the phone down, he scribbled the name Marr on to his pad and circled it. Ranald Marr, with his Maserati and toy soldiers. *You'd almost have thought he'd lost a daughter* . . . Rebus was beginning to revise that opinion. He wondered if Marr knew how precarious his job was, knew that the mere thought of their savings catching a cold might spur the small investors on, demanding a sacrifice . . .

He switched to a picture of Thomas Costello, who'd never had to work in his life. What must that be like? Rebus couldn't begin to answer the question. His parents had been poor all their lives: never owned their own house. When his father had died, he'd left four hundred quid for Rebus to split with his brother. A policy had taken care of the funeral. Even back then, pocketing his share of the notes in the bank manager's office, he'd wondered . . . half his parents' life savings represented one of his week's wages.

He had money in the bank himself now: did very little with his monthly salary. The flat was paid off; neither Rhona nor Samantha ever seemed to want anything from him. Food and drink, and garage bills for the Saab. He never went on holiday, probably bought a couple of LPs or CDs a week. A couple of months back, he'd thought of buying a Linn hi-fi system, but the shop had knocked him back, told him they'd nothing in stock and would phone him when they had. They'd never phoned. The Lou Reed tickets hadn't exactly stretched him: Jean had insisted on paying for hers . . . and cooked him breakfast next morning to boot.

'It's the Laughing Policeman!' Siobhan called across the office. She was seated at her desk next to Brains from Fettes. Rebus realised he had a big grin on his face. He got up and crossed the room.

'I withdraw that remark,' Siobhan said quickly, holding up her hands in surrender.

'Hello, Brains,' Rebus said.

'His name's Bain,' Siobhan corrected him. 'He likes to be called Eric.'

Rebus ignored this. 'It's like the deck of the Starship *Enterprise* in here.' He was looking at the array of computers and connections: two laptops, two PCs. He knew one of the PCs was Siobhan's, the other Flip Balfour's. 'Tell me,' he asked her, 'what do we know about Philippa's early life in London?'

She wrinkled her nose, thinking. 'Not much. Why?'

'Because the boyfriend says she was having these nightmares, running up and down the London house being chased by something.'

'Sure it was the London house?'

'What do you mean?'

She shrugged. 'Just that Junipers gave me the heebies: suits of armour and dusty old billiard rooms . . . imagine growing up with that.'

'David Costello said the London house.'

'Transference?' Bain suggested. They both looked at him. 'Just a thought,' he said.

'So really it was Junipers she was scared of?' Rebus asked.

'Let's get out the ouija board and ask her.' Siobhan realised what she'd said and winced. 'Worst possible taste, sorry.'

'I've heard worse,' Rebus said. He had, too. At the murder

scene, one of the woolly-suits helping with the cordon had been overheard telling a mate: 'I bet she hadn't banked on that. Get it?'

'It's kind of sub-Hitchcock, isn't it?' Bain said now. 'You know, *Marnie*, that sort of thing . . .'

Rebus thought of the book of poems in David Costello's flat: *I Dream of Alfred Hitchcock*.

You do not die for being bad, you die
For being available . . .

'You're probably right,' he said.

Siobhan read his tone. 'All the same, you still want the low-down on Flip's London years?'

He began to nod, then shook his head. 'No,' he said, 'you're right . . . it's too far-fetched.'

As he moved away, Siobhan turned to Bain. 'That's usually right up his street,' she murmured. 'The more far-fetched it is, the better he likes it.'

Bain smiled. He had the briefcase with him again; still hadn't opened it. After the meal on Friday night they'd said their goodbyes. Siobhan had got into her car Saturday morning and headed north for the football. Didn't bother offering anyone a lift: she'd packed an overnight bag. Found herself a guest house. Good win for Hibs in the afternoon, then a bit of exploring and a spot of dinner. She'd taken her Walkman, half a dozen tapes and a couple of paperbacks with her, leaving the laptop back in her flat. A weekend without Quizmaster: just what the doctor ordered. Except that she couldn't stop thinking about him, wondering if there was a message for her. She'd made sure she was late getting back Sunday night, then busied herself with laundry.

Now the laptop sat on her desk. She was almost afraid to touch it, afraid to give in to the craving . . .

'Good weekend?' Bain asked.

'Not bad. How about you?'

'Quiet. That dinner on Friday was just about the high-light.'

She smiled, accepting the compliment. 'So what do we do now? Get on the blower to Special Branch?'

'We talk to the Crime Squad. They route our request.'

'We can't cut out the middle-man?'

'The middle-man wouldn't like that.'

Siobhan thought of Claverhouse: Bain was probably right. 'Go ahead then,' she said.

So Bain picked up the phone and had a long conversation with DI Claverhouse at the Big House. Siobhan ran her fingers over the laptop's keyboard. It was already connected to her mobile. A phone message had been waiting for her at home on Friday night: her mobile account, wondering if she knew that her usage had suddenly gone up. Yes, she knew all right. With Bain still busy explaining things to Claverhouse, she decided to connect to the Net, just to give her something to do . . .

There were three messages from Quizmaster. The first was from Friday evening, around the time she got home:

Seeker – My patience wears thin. The quest is about to close on you. Immediate response requested.

The second was from Saturday afternoon:

Siobhan? I'm disappointed in you. Your times so far have been excellent. Game is now closed.

Closed or not, he'd come back on Sunday at the stroke of midnight:

Are you busy tracing me, is that it? Do you still want to meet?

Bain ended his conversation and put down the phone. He was staring at the screen.

'You've got him rattled,' he said.

'New ISP?' Siobhan asked. Bain checked the headers and nodded.

'New name, new everything. Still, he's getting the inkling that he's not untraceable.'

'Then why doesn't he just shut down?'

'I don't know.'

'You really think the game's closed?'

'Only one way to find out . . .'

So Siobhan got busy on the keyboard:

I was away all weekend, that's all. Inquiries progress. Meantime, yes, I'd still like to meet.

She sent the message. They went and grabbed coffee, but when they came back there was no reply.

'Is he sulking?' Siobhan asked.

'Or away from his machine.'

She looked at him. 'Your bedroom, is it full of computer stuff?'

'You're angling an invite to my bedroom?'

She smiled. 'No, I was just wondering. Some of these people, they can spend all day and night at a monitor, can't they?'

'Absolutely. But I'm not one of them. Three chat rooms where I'm a regular, maybe an hour or two of surfing when I get bored.'

'What are the chat rooms?'

'Tekky stuff.' He shifted his chair towards the desk. 'Now, while we're waiting, maybe we should take a look at Ms Balfour's deleted files.' He saw the look on her face. 'You know you can undelete files?'

'Sure. We already looked at her correspondence.'

'But did you look at her e-mails?'

Siobhan was forced to admit she hadn't. Or rather, Grant hadn't known it could be done.

Bain sighed and got to work on Flip's PC. It didn't take long. Soon they were staring at a list of deleted messages, both from Flip and to her.

'How far back do they go?' Siobhan asked.

'Just over two years. When did she buy the computer?'

'It was an eighteenth birthday present,' Siobhan said.

'Not bad for some.'

Siobhan nodded. 'She got a flat, too.'

Now Bain looked at her, shook his head slowly in disbelief. 'I got a watch and a camera for mine,' he said.

'Is that the watch?' Siobhan pointed to his wrist.

Bain's mind, however, was elsewhere. 'So we've got e-mails stretching right back to when she first got started. He clicked on the one with the earliest date, but the computer told him he couldn't open it.

'Need to convert it,' he said. 'The hard disk has probably compressed it.'

Siobhan was trying to study what he was doing, but he was going too fast. In no time, they were reading the first e-mail Flip had sent on her machine. It was to her father at his office:

Just testing. Hope you get this. The PC's super! See you tonight. Flip.

'I suppose we need to read them all?' Bain guessed.

'I suppose,' Siobhan agreed. 'Which means converting them one at a time?'

'Not necessarily. If you can fetch me a tea – white, no sugar – I'll see what I can do.'

By the time she got back with the drinks, he was printing out sheets of messages. 'This way,' he said, 'you can be reading them while I'm preparing the next batch.'

Siobhan started chronologically, and it didn't take her long to find something more interesting than gossipy exchanges between Flip and her friends.

'Look at this,' she told Bain.

He read the e-mail. 'It's from Balfour's Bank,' he said. 'Someone called RAM.'

'I'm willing to bet it's Ranald Marr.' Siobhan took the note back.

Flip, Great news that at last you are part of the virtual world! I hope you have a lot of fun with it. You'll also find the Internet a great research tool, so I'm hoping it helps you with your studies . . . Yes, you're right that you can delete messages – it makes space in the memory, and allows your computer to work more quickly. But remember that deleted messages are still recoverable unless you take certain steps. Here's how to delete something completely.

The writer went on to explain the process. At the end he signed himself R. Bain ran a finger down one edge of the screen.

'Explains why there are big gaps,' he said. 'Once he'd told her how to fully delete, she started doing it.'

'Also explains why there are none of the messages to or

from Quizmaster.' Siobhan was sifting through the sheets of paper. 'Not even her original message to RAM.'

'And none afterwards either.'

Siobhan rubbed at her temples. 'Why would she want everything deleted anyway?'

'I don't know. It's not something most users would think to do.'

'Shift over,' Siobhan said, sliding her chair across. She started composing a new e-mail, to RAM at Balfour's Bank. *DC Clarke here. Urgent that you get in touch.*

She added the St Leonard's phone number and sent the message, then picked up a telephone and called the bank.

'Mr Marr's office, please.' She was put through to Marr's secretary. 'Is Mr Marr there?' she asked, her eyes on Bain as he sipped his tea. 'Maybe you can help me. It's Detective Constable Clarke here, CID at St Leonard's. I just sent Mr Marr an e-mail and I was wondering if he'd received it. Apparently we're having some sort of problem at our end . . .' She paused while the secretary checked.

'Oh? He's not? Could you tell me where he is then?' She paused again, listening to the secretary. 'It really is quite important.' Now her eyebrows went up. 'Prestonfield House? That's not far from here. Is there any chance you could get a message to him, asking him to drop into St Leonard's after his meeting? It'll only take five minutes. Probably more convenient than having us visit him at work . . .' She listened again. 'Thanks. And the e-mail did get through? Great, thanks.'

She put the phone down, and Bain, cup drained and binned, applauded silently.

Forty minutes later, Marr arrived at the station. Siobhan got one of the uniforms to escort him upstairs to CID. Rebus was no longer around, but the suite was busy. The uniform brought Marr to Siobhan's desk. She nodded and asked the banker to take a seat. Marr looked around: there were no spare chairs. Eyes were studying him, the other officers wondering who he was. Dressed in a crisp pinstripe suit, white shirt and pale lemon tie, he looked more like an expensive lawyer than the usual visitors to the station.

Bain got up, dragging his own chair round the desk for Marr to sit in.

'My driver's parked on a single yellow,' Marr said, making a show of looking at his watch.

'This won't take long, sir,' Siobhan said. 'Do you recognise the machine.' She tapped the computer.

'What?'

'It belonged to Philippa.'

'Did it? I wouldn't know.'

'I suppose not. But you sent e-mails to one another.'

'What?'

'RAM: that *is* you, isn't it?'

'What if it is?'

Bain stepped forward and handed Marr a sheet of paper. 'Then you sent her this,' he said. 'And it looks like Ms Balfour acted on it.'

Marr looked up from the message, his eyes on Siobhan rather than Bain. She'd winced at Bain's words, and Marr had noticed.

Big mistake, Eric! she felt like screaming. Because now Marr knew that this was the only e-mail they had between himself and Flip. Otherwise, Siobhan could have strung him along, letting him think they had others, seeing whether that bothered him or not.

'Well?' was all Marr said, having read the message.

'It's just curious,' Siobhan said, 'that your first ever e-mail to her should be all about how to delete e-mails.'

'Philippa was very private in many ways,' Marr explained. 'She *liked* her privacy. The first thing she asked me was about deleting material. This was my response. She didn't like the idea of anyone being able to read what she'd written.'

'Why not?'

Marr shrugged both elegant shoulders. 'We all have different personae, don't we? The "you" who writes to an aged relative isn't the same "you" who writes to a close friend. I know that when I'm e-mailing a war-gamer, I don't necessarily want my secretary to read it. She would see a very different "me" from the person she works for.'

Siobhan was nodding. 'I think I understand.'

'It's also the case that in my own profession, confidentiality – secrecy, if you like – is absolutely vital. Commercial subterfuge is always an issue. We shred unwanted documents, delete e-mails and so on, to protect our clients and ourselves. So when Flip mentioned the delete button, that sort of consideration was uppermost in my mind.' He paused, looked from Siobhan to Bain and back again. 'Is that all you wanted to know?'

'What else did you talk about in your e-mails?'

'We didn't correspond for long. Flip was dipping a toe in the water. She had my e-mail address and knew I was an old hand. At first she had lots of questions to ask, but she was a fast learner.'

'We're still checking the machine for deleted messages,' Siobhan led blithely. 'Any idea when your last message to or from her would have been?'

'Maybe as much as a year back.' Marr started getting to his feet. 'Now, if we're quite finished, I really must . . .'

'If you hadn't told her about deleting, we might have him by now.'

'Who?'

'Quizmaster.'

'The person she was playing this game against? You still think that had something to do with her death?'

'I'd like to know.'

Marr was standing now, smoothing his jacket. 'Is that possible, without the help of this . . . Quizmaster?'

Siobhan looked to Bain, who knew a cue when he saw one.

'Oh, yes,' he said confidently. 'It'll take a bit longer, but we'll trace him. He's left enough bits and pieces for us along the way.'

Marr looked from one detective to the other. 'Splendid,' he said with a smile. 'Well, if I can be of further assistance . . .'

'You've helped us enormously already, Mr Marr,' Siobhan said, fixing her eyes on him. 'I'll have one of the uniformed officers show you out . . .'

After he'd gone, Bain pulled his chair back around to Siobhan's side of the desk and sat down next to her.

'You think it's him, don't you?' he asked quietly.

She nodded, staring at the doorway through which Marr had just left. Then her shoulders slumped. She squeezed shut her eyes, rubbed at them. 'Truth is, I haven't a clue.'

'You also don't have any evidence.'

She nodded, eyes still closed.

'Gut feeling?' he guessed.

She opened her eyes. 'I know better than to trust it.'

'Glad to hear it.' He smiled at her. 'Some proof would be nice, wouldn't it?'

When the phone rang, Siobhan seemed in a dream, so Bain answered. It was a Special Branch officer called Black. He wanted to know if he was speaking to the right person. When Bain assured him he was, Black asked how much he knew about computers.

'I know a bit.'

'Good. Is the PC in front of you?' When Bain said that it was, Black told him what he wanted. When Bain came off the phone five minutes later, he puffed out his cheeks and exhaled noisily.

'I don't know what it is about Special Branch,' he said, 'but they always make me feel about five years old and starting my first day at school.'

'You sounded okay,' Siobhan assured him. 'What do they need?'

'Copies of all the e-mails between you and Quizmaster, plus details of Philippa Balfour's ISP account and user names, plus the same for you.'

'Except it's Grant Hood's machine,' Siobhan said, touching the laptop.

'Well, his account details then.' He paused. 'Black asked if we had any suspects.'

'You didn't tell him?'

He shook his head. 'But we could always send him Marr's name. We could even provide his e-mail address.'

'Would that help?'

'It might. You know the Americans can read e-mails using satellites? Any e-mails in the world . . .' She just stared at him, and he laughed. 'I'm not saying Special Branch have that sort of technology, but you never know, do you?'

Siobhan was thoughtful. 'Then give them what we've got. Give them Ranald Marr.'

The laptop told them they had a message. Siobhan clicked it open. Quizmaster.

Seeker – We meet on completion of Stricture. Acceptable?

'Ooh,' Bain said, 'he's actually *asking* you.'

So game isn't closed? Siobhan typed back.

Special dispensation.

She typed another message: *There are questions need answering right now.*

An immediate reply: *Ask, Seeker.*

So she asked: *Was anyone playing the game apart from Flip?* They waited a minute for the response.

Yes.

She looked at Bain. 'He said before that there wasn't.'

'He was either lying then, or he's lying now. Fact that you asked the question again makes me think you didn't believe him first time round.'

How many? Siobhan typed.

Three.

Pitted against each other? Did they know?

They knew.

They knew who they were playing against?

A thirty-second pause. *Absolutely not.*

'Truth or lie?' Siobhan asked Bain.

'I'm busy wondering if Mr Marr's had enough time to get back to his office.'

'Someone in his profession, wouldn't surprise me if he kept a laptop and mobile in the car, just to stay ahead of the game.' She smiled at the unmeant pun.

'I could call his office . . .' Bain was already reaching for the phone. Siobhan recited the bank's number.

'Mr Marr's office, please,' Bain said into the receiver. Then: 'Is that Mr Marr's assistant? It's DS Bain here, Lothian Police. Could I have a word with Mr Marr?' He looked at Siobhan. 'Due back any minute? Thank you.' Then an afterthought. 'Oh, is there any way I could contact him in his car? He doesn't have access to e-mails there, does he?' A pause. 'No, it's okay, thank you. I'll call again later.' He put the phone down. 'No in-car e-mails.'

'As far as his assistant knows,' Siobhan said quietly.

Bain nodded.

'These days,' she went on, 'all you need is a phone.' A WAP phone, she was thinking, just like Grant's. For some reason her mind flashed to that morning in the Elephant House . . . Grant busy on a crossword he'd already completed, trying to impress the woman at the next table . . . She got to work on her next message:

Can you tell me who they were? Do you know who they are?
The reply was immediate.

No.

No you can't or no you don't?

No to both. Stricture awaits.

One final thing, Master. How did you come to choose Flip?

She came to me, as you did.

But how did she find you?

Stricture clue will follow shortly.

'I think he's had enough,' Bain said. 'Probably not used to his slaves talking back.'

Siobhan thought about trying to keep the dialogue going, then nodded her agreement.

'I don't think I'm quite Grant Hood's standard,' Bain added. She frowned, not understanding. 'In the puzzle-solving department,' he explained.

'Let's wait and see about that.'

'Meantime, I can get that stuff PDQ'd to SB.'

'AOK,' Siobhan said with a smile. She was thinking of Grant again. She wouldn't have got this far without him.

Yet since his transfer he hadn't shown the least curiosity, hadn't so much as called to find out if there were some new clue to be solved ... She wondered at his ability to switch focus so completely. The Grant she saw on TV was almost unrecognisable from the one who'd paced her flat at midnight, the one who'd lost heart on Hart Fell. She knew which model she preferred; didn't think it was just professional jealousy. She thought she'd learned something about Gill Templer now. Gill was running scared, terror of her new seniority causing her to dish it out to the juniors. She was targeting the keen and the confident, maybe because she lacked confidence in herself. Siobhan hoped it was just a phase. She prayed it was.

She hoped that when Stricture came through, the busy Grant might spare a minute for his old sparring partner, whether his new sponsor liked it or not.

Grant Hood had spent the morning dealing with the press, reworking the daily news release for later in the day – hopefully this time to the satisfaction of both DCS Templer and ACC Carswell – and fielding calls from the victim's father, angry that more broadcast time wasn't being given to appeals for information.

'What about *Crimewatch?*' he'd asked several times. Secretly, Grant thought *Crimewatch* was a bloody good idea, so he'd called the BBC in Edinburgh and been given a number in Glasgow. Glasgow had then given him a number in London, and the switchboard there had put him through to a researcher who'd informed him – in a tone which said any liaison officer worth their salt would already know – that *Crimewatch* had ended its run and wouldn't be back on air for several months.

'Oh, yes, thanks,' Grant had said, putting down the phone.

He hadn't had time for lunch, and breakfast had been a bacon roll from the canteen, almost six hours ago. He was aware of politics all around him – the politics of Police HQ. Carswell and Templer might agree on some things, but never on everything, and he was poised somewhere between them, trying not to fall too fatally into either camp. Carswell was the real power, but Templer was Grant's boss, she had the means to kick him back into the wilderness. His job was to deprive her of motive and opportunity.

He knew he was coping so far, but only by dint of forgoing food, sleep and free time. On the plus side, the case was now garnering interest from further afield, not just the London media, but New York, Sydney, Singapore and Toronto. International press agencies wanted clarification of the details they had. There was talk of bringing correspondents to Edinburgh, and would DC Hood be available for a short broadcast interview?

In each case, Grant felt able to answer in the affirmative. He made sure he jotted down the details of each journalist, with contact numbers and even a note of the time difference.

'No point me sending you faxes in the middle of the night,' he'd told one news editor in New Zealand.

'I'd prefer an e-mail, mate.'

So Grant had taken those details down, too. It struck him that he needed to get his laptop back from Siobhan. Either that or invest in something more up-to-date. The case could use its own website. He'd send a memo to Carswell, copy to Templer: stating his case.

If he ever got the time . . .

Siobhan and his laptop: he hadn't thought of her in a couple of days. His 'crush' on her hadn't lasted long. Just as well they hadn't taken things any further really: his new job would have driven a wedge between them. He knew they could play down that kiss, until it would seem as if it had never happened. Rebus was the only witness, but if the pair of them denied it, called him a liar, he'd start forgetting, too.

Only two things Grant felt sure of now: that he wanted Liaison permanently, and that he was good at it.

He celebrated with the day's sixth cup of coffee, nodding to strangers in the corridors and on the stairwell. They seemed to know who he was, wanting both to know him and be known by him. His phone was ringing again when he pushed open his door – the office was small, no bigger than the cupboards in some stations, and there was no natural light. Still, it was his fiefdom. He leaned back in his chair, taking the receiver with him.

'DC Hood.'

'You sound happy.'

'Who is this, please?'

'It's Steve Holly. Remember me?'

'Sure, Steve, what can I do for you?' But the tone was immediately more professional.

'Well . . . Grant.' Holly managed to get a sneer into the word. 'I was just after a quote to go with a piece I'm running.'

'Yes?' Grant leaned forward a little in his chair, not quite so comfortable now.

'Women going missing all over Scotland . . . dolls found at the scene . . . games on the Internet . . . students dead on hillsides. Any of it ring a bell?'

Grant thought he'd squeeze the life out of the receiver. The desk, the walls . . . they'd all gone hazy. He closed his eyes, tried to shake his head clear.

'Case like this, Steve,' he said, attempting levity, 'a reporter will hear all kinds of stuff.'

'Believe you solved some of the Internet clues yourself, Grant. What do you reckon? Got to be connected to the murder, haven't they?'

'I've no comment to make on that, Mr Holly. Look, whatever you think you may know, you've got to understand that stories – true or false – can do irreparable damage to an investigation, especially one at a crucial stage.'

'Is the Balfour inquiry at a crucial stage? I hadn't heard . . .'

'All I'm trying to say is . . .'

'Look, Grant, admit it: you're fucked on this one, pardon my French. Best thing you can do is fill me in on the small print.'

'I don't think so.'

'Sure about that? Tasty new posting you've got there . . . I'd hate to see you go down in flames.'

'Something tells me you'd like nothing better, Holly.'

The telephone receiver laughed into Grant's ear. 'Steve to Mr Holly to Holly . . . you'll be calling me names next, Grant.'

'Who told you?'

'Something this big, you can never keep it watertight.'

'So who punched the hole through the hull?'

'A whisper here, a whisper there . . . you know how it is.' Holly paused. 'Oh no, that's right – you *don't* know how it is. I keep forgetting, you've only been in the job five fucking minutes, and already you think you can lord it over the likes of me.'

'I don't know what—'

'Those little individual briefings, just you and your favoured poodles. Stuff all that, Grant. It's the likes of *me* you should be looking out for. And you can take that any way you like.'

'Thanks, I will. How soon are you going to press?'

'Going to try slapping us with a two-eye?' When Grant didn't say anything. Holly laughed again. 'You don't even know the lingo!' he crowed. But Grant was a fast learner.

'It's an interim interdict,' he guessed, knowing he was right. Two i's: a court injunction, halting publication. 'Look,' he said, pinching the bridge of his nose, 'on the record, we don't know that any of the stuff you've mentioned is pertinent to the current case.'

'It's still news.'

'And possibly prejudicial.'

'So sue me.'

'People play dirty like this, I never forget it.'

'Get in the fucking queue.'

Grant was about to put down the phone, but Holly beat him to it. He got up and kicked the desk, then kicked it again, followed by the waste-bin, his briefcase (bought at the weekend), and the corner where two walls met. He rested his head against the wall.

I have to go to Carswell with this. I have to tell Gill Templer!!

Templer first . . . chain of command. Then *she'd* have to break the news to the ACC, who in turn would probably have to disturb the Chief Constable's daily routine. Mid-afternoon . . . Grant wondered how late he could leave it. Maybe Holly would call Templer or Carswell himself. If Grant sat on it till day's end, he'd be in bigger trouble. It could even be that there was still time for that two-eye.

He picked up the phone, squeezed shut his eyes once more in what, this time round, was a short and silent prayer.

Made the call.

It was late afternoon, and Rebus had been staring at the coffins for a good five minutes. Occasionally he would pick one up, examine the workmanship, comparing and contrasting with the others. His latest thought: bring in a forensic anthropologist. The tools used to make the coffins would have left tiny grooves and incisions, marks an expert could identify and explore. If the exact same chisel had been used on each joint, maybe it could be proven. Perhaps there were fibres, fingerprints . . . The scraps of cloth: could they be traced? He slid the list of victims so that it sat in front of him on the desk: 1972 . . .'77 . . .'82 and '95. The first victim, Caroline Farmer, was the youngest by far; the others were in their twenties and thirties, women in the prime of life. Drownings and disappearances. Where there was no body, it was all but impossible to prove a crime had been committed. And death by drowning . . . pathologists could tell if someone were alive or dead when they entered the water, but other than that . . . Say you knocked someone unconscious and pushed them in: even if it came to court, there'd be room for haggling, the murder charge reduced to culpable homicide. Rebus remembered a fireman once telling him the perfect way to commit murder: get the victim drunk in their kitchen, then turn the heat up under the chip-pan.

Simple and clever.

Rebus still didn't know how clever his adversary had

been. Fife, Nairn, Glasgow and Perth – certainly he'd ranged far and wide. Someone who travelled. He thought of Quizmaster and the jaunts Siobhan had taken so far. Was it possible to connect Quizmaster to whoever had left the coffins? Having scribbled the words 'forensic pathologist' on to his notepad, Rebus added two more: 'offender profiling'. There were university psychologists who specialised in this, deducing aspects of a culprit's character from their MO. Rebus had never been convinced, but he felt he was banging his fists against a locked and bolted door, one he was never going to break down without help.

When Gill Templer stormed down the corridor, past the CID suite's doorway, Rebus didn't think she'd seen him. But now she was heading straight for him, her face furious.

'I thought,' she said, 'you'd been told.'

'Told what?' he asked innocently.

She pointed to the coffins. 'Told that these were a waste of time.' Her voice vibrated with anger. Her whole body was taut.

'Jesus, Gill, what's happened?'

She didn't say anything, just swung her arm across the desk, sending the coffins flying. Rebus scrambled from his chair, started picking them up, checking for damage. When he looked round, Gill was on her way to the door again, but she stopped, half turned.

'You'll find out tomorrow,' she said, making her exit.

Rebus looked around the room. Hi-Ho Silvers and one of the civilian staff had stopped the conversation they'd been having.

'She's losing it,' Silvers commented.

'What did she mean about tomorrow?' Rebus asked, but Silvers just shrugged.

'Losing it,' he said again.

Maybe he was right.

Rebus sat back down at his desk and pondered the phrase: there were lots of ways of 'losing it'. He knew he was in danger of losing it too . . . whatever *it* was.

Jean Burchill had spent much of her day trying to trace the correspondence between Kennet Lovell and the Reverend Kirkpatrick. She'd spoken to people in Alloway and Ayr – the parish minister; a local historian; one of Kirkpatrick's descendants. She'd spent over an hour on the phone to the Mitchell Library in Glasgow. She'd taken the short walk from the Museum to the National Library, and from there to the Faculty of Advocates. Finally, she'd walked back along Chambers Street and headed for Surgeons' Hall. In the museum there she'd stared long and hard at the portrait of Kennet Lovell by J. Scott Jauncey. Lovell had been a handsome young man. Often in portraits, the artist left little clues as to the character he was painting: profession, family, hobbies . . . But this was a simple execution: head and upper body. The background was plain and black, contrasting with the bright yellows and pinks of Lovell's face. The other portraits in Surgeons' Hall, they usually showed their subjects with a textbook in front of them, or some paper and a pen. Maybe standing in their library or posed with a few telling props – a skull or femur, an anatomical drawing. The sheer plainness of the Lovell portrait bothered her. Either the painter had had little enthusiasm for the commission, or else the subject had insisted on giving little enough away. She thought of Reverend Kirkpatrick, imagined him paying the artist's fee and then receiving this bland decoration. She wondered if it perhaps showed some ideal of its subject, or if it was the equivalent of a picture postcard, a mere advertisement for Lovell. This young man, hardly out of his teens, had assisted in the Burke autopsy. According to one report of the time, 'the quantity of blood that gushed out was enormous, and by the time the lecture was finished the area of the classroom had the appearance of a butcher's slaughter-house, from its flowing down and being trodden upon'. The description had made her queasy, first time she'd read it. How much more preferable to have died as one of Burke's victims, made insensible with drink and then smothered. Jean stared into Kennet Lovell's eyes again. The black pupils seemed luminous, despite the horrors they'd witnessed.

Or, she couldn't help wondering, *because* of them?

The curator wasn't able to help answer her questions, so she'd asked if she might see the bursar. But Major Bruce Cawdor, while affable and willing, wasn't able to add much to what Jean already knew.

'We don't seem to have any record,' he told her as they sat in his office, 'of how the Lovell portrait came into the College's possession. I'd presume it was a gift, perhaps to defer death duties.' He was short but distinguished-looking, well dressed and with a face shining with good health. He'd offered her tea, which she'd accepted. It was Darjeeling, each cup coming with its own silver tea-strainer.

'I'm also interested in Lovell's correspondence.'

'Yes, well, we would be, too.'

'You don't have *anything*?' She was surprised.

The bursar shook his head. 'Either Dr Lovell wasn't a great man for the pen, or else they've perished or ended up in some obscure collection.' He sighed. 'A great pity. We know so little about his time in Africa . . .'

'Or in Edinburgh, come to that.'

'He's buried here. Don't suppose his grave's of much interest to you . . . ?'

'Whereabouts is it?'

'Calton cemetery. His plot's not far from David Hume's.'

'I might as well take a look.'

'I'm sorry I can't be more help.' He thought for a moment, and his face brightened. 'Donald Devlin's supposed to have some table made by Lovell.'

'Yes, I know, though there's nothing in the literature about an interest in carpentry.'

'I'm sure it's mentioned somewhere; I seem to recall reading something . . .' But try as he might, Major Cawdor couldn't remember what or where.

That evening, she sat with John Rebus in her Portobello home. They ate Chinese takeaway, washed down with cold

Chardonnay for her, bottled beer for him. Music on the hi-fi: Nick Drake, Janis Ian, Pink Floyd's *Meddle*. He seemed wrapped up in his thoughts, but she could hardly complain. After the food, they walked down to the promenade. Kids on skateboards, looking American but sounding pure Porty, swearing like troopers. One chip shop open, that childhood smell of hot fat and vinegar. They still didn't say much, which didn't make them so very different from the other couples they passed. Reticence was an Edinburgh tradition. You kept your feelings hidden and your business your own. Some people put it down to the influence of the Church and figures like John Knox – she'd heard the city called 'Fort Knox' by outsiders. But to Jean, it was more to do with Edinburgh's geography, its louring rock-faces and dark skies, the wind whipping in from the North Sea, hurtling through the canyon-like streets. At every turn you felt overwhelmed and pummelled by your surroundings. Just travelling into town from Portobello, she felt it: the bruising and bruised nature of the place.

John Rebus, too, was thinking of Edinburgh. When he moved from his flat, where would he make his next home? Was there any district he liked better than any other? Portobello itself was fine, pretty relaxed. But he could always move south or west, into the country. Some of his colleagues travelled in from as far as Falkirk and Linlithgow. He wasn't sure he was ready for that kind of commute. Portobello would be okay though. The only problem was, when they walked along the promenade, he kept looking towards the beach, as if expecting to see a little wooden coffin there, like the one they'd found in Nairn. It wouldn't matter where he went, his head would go with him, colouring his surroundings. The Falls coffin was working away at him now. He only had the carpenter's word for it that it had been made by someone else, someone who hadn't made the other four. But if the killer was being *really* clever, wouldn't he have anticipated just that, changing his work habits and tools, trying to dupe them into . . .

Oh Christ, here he went again . . . the same old dance,

reeling around his skull. He sat down on the sea wall, and Jean asked if something was wrong.

'Bit of a headache,' he said.

'Isn't that supposed to be the woman's prerogative?' She was smiling, but he could see she wasn't happy.

'I should be heading back,' he told her. 'Not great company tonight.'

'Do you want to talk about it?' He raised his eyes so they met hers, and she snorted with laughter. 'Sorry, stupid question. You're a Scottish male, of course you don't want to talk about it.'

'It's not that, Jean. It's just . . .' He shrugged. 'Maybe therapy wouldn't be such a bad idea.'

He was trying to make a joke of it, so she didn't push him.

'Let's head back,' she said. 'Bloody freezing out here anyway.'

She slid her arm through his as they walked.

12

By the time Assistant Chief Constable Colin Carswell arrived at Gayfield Square police station on that underlit Tuesday morning, he was out for blood.

John Balfour had bawled him out; Balfour's lawyer had done his damage more subtly, the voice never wavering in its professional and well-educated tones. Still, Carswell felt bruised, and he wanted some measure of revenge. The Chief Constable was remaining aloof – *his* position, his unassailability, had to be maintained at all costs. This was Carswell's mess, one he'd spent all the previous evening busy surveying. He might as well have been exploring a landscape of shrapnel and broken glass, armed only with a dustpan and some tweezers.

The best minds in the Procurator Fiscal's office had pored over the problem and had concluded, in an annoyingly bland and objective way (letting Carswell know that it was no skin off *their* noses) that there was little chance of blocking the story. After all, they couldn't prove that either the dolls or the German student had anything to do with the Balfour case – most senior officers seemed to agree that a connection was unlikely at best – and so would find it difficult to persuade a judge that Holly's information could, once published, be detrimental to the inquiry.

What Balfour and his lawyer wanted to know was why the police hadn't seen fit to share with them the story of the dolls, or the information about the German student and the Internet game.

What the Chief Constable wanted to know was what Carswell intended doing about it.

And what Carswell himself wanted was blood.

His official car, driven by his acolyte DI Derek Linford, drew up in front of a station already crowded with officers. Everyone who had worked or was currently working on the Balfour case – uniforms, CID, even the forensic team from Howdenhall – had been 'requested' to attend the morning meeting. Consequently, the briefing room was packed and stifling. Outside, the morning was still recovering from overnight sleet, the pavement damp and chilling to the feet as Carswell's leather-shod soles stamped across it.

'Here he comes,' someone said, watching as Linford, having opened Carswell's door for him, now closed it and, showing a slight limp, walked back round to the driver's side. There was a sound of folding paper as the fresh tabloids – each copy the same title, each open at the same gathering of pages – were closed and put out of sight. DCS Templer, dressed as though for a funeral, dark lines under her eyes, came into the room first. She whispered something into the ear of DI Bill Pryde, who nodded and tore the corner from a notepad, spitting into it the wad of chewing gum he'd been gnawing for the past half-hour. When Carswell himself walked in, there was a ripple of movement as officers subconsciously corrected their posture or checked their attire for obvious blemishes.

'Is anyone missing?' Carswell called out. No 'good morning', no 'thank you all for coming', the usual protocols forgotten. Templer had a few names for him – minor ailments and complaints. Carswell nodded, didn't seem interested in what he was being told, and didn't wait for her to finish the roll-call.

'We've got ourselves a mole,' he bawled, loud enough to be heard down the corridor. He nodded slowly, eyes trying to take in every face in front of him. When he saw that there were people at the back, out of staring range, he walked up the aisle between the desks. Officers had to shift so he could get through, but left enough room so that there was no possibility he might brush against them.

'A mole's always an ugly little thing. It lacks vision. Sometimes it has big greedy paws. It doesn't like to be exposed.' There were flecks of saliva either side of his mouth. 'I find a mole in my garden, I put down poison. Now, some of you will say that moles can't help it. They don't know they're in someone's garden, a place of order and calm. They don't know they're making everything *ugly*. But they are, whether they know it or not. And that's why they have to be eradicated.' He paused, the silence lingering as he walked back down the aisle. Derek Linford had entered the room as if by stealth and was standing by the door, eyes searching out John Rebus, the two of them recent enemies . . .

The presence of Linford seemed only to spur Carswell on. He spun on his heels, facing his subjects again.

'Maybe it was a mistake. We all make slip-ups, can't be helped. But, by Christ, a lot of information seems to have been pushed to the surface!' Another pause. 'Maybe it was blackmail.' And now a shrug. 'Someone like Steven Holly, he's lower than a mole on the evolutionary ladder. He's pond-life. He's the scum you sometimes see there.' He waved a hand slowly in front of him, as if skimming water. 'He thinks he's made us dirty, but he hasn't: Game's not near over, we all know that. We're a *team*. That's how we *work*! Anyone who doesn't like that can always ask to be transferred back to normal duties. It's that simple, ladies and gentlemen. But just think of this, will you?' He dropped his voice. 'Think of the victim, think of her family. Think of all the upset this is going to cause them. *They're* the ones we're slogging our guts out for here, not the newspaper readers or the scribes who provide them with their daily gruel.

'You might have some grievance against me, or someone else on the team, but why the hell would you want to put *them* – the family and friends, getting ready for tomorrow's funeral – why would *anyone* want to do something like this to people like them?' He let the question hang, saw faces bow in collective shame as he scanned them. Took another deep breath, his voice rising again.

'I'm going to find whoever did this. Don't think I won't. Don't think you can trust Mr Steven Holly to protect you. He doesn't care a damn for you. If you want to stay buried, you'll have to feed him more stories, and more, and more! He's not going to let you rise back up to the world you knew before. You're different now. You're a mole. *His* mole. And he'll never let you rest, never let you forget it.'

A glance in Gill Templer's direction. She was standing by the wall, arms folded, her own eyes scanning the room.

'I know this probably all sounds like the headmaster's warning. Some pupil's smashed a window or daubed graffiti on the bike sheds.' He shook his head. 'I'm talking to all of you like this because it's important we're clear on what's at stake. Talk might not cost lives, but that doesn't mean it should be squandered. Careful what you say, who you say it to. If the person responsible wants to come forward, that's fine. You can do it now, or later. I'll be here for an hour or so, and I can always be reached at my office. Think what's at stake if you don't. Not part of a team any more, not on the side of the angels. But in a journalist's pocket. For as long as he wants you there.' This final pause seemed to last an eternity, nobody coughed or cleared their throat. Carswell slid his hands into his pockets, head angled as though inspecting his shoes. 'DCS Templer?' he said.

And now Gill Templer stepped forward, and the room relaxed a little.

'Don't go getting the holiday mood just yet!' she called out. 'Okay, there's been a leak to the press, and what we need now is some damage limitation. Nobody talks to anybody unless they run it past me first, understood?' There were murmurs of assent.

Templer went on, but Rebus wasn't listening. He hadn't wanted to listen to Carswell either, but it had been hard to block the man out. Impressive stuff really. He'd even put some thought into the image of the garden mole, almost making it work without becoming laughable.

But mostly Rebus's attention had been on the people around him. Gill and Bill Pryde were distant figures, whose discomfort he could almost ignore. Bill's big chance to shine; Gill's first major inquiry as a DCS. Hardly what either of them would have wanted . . .

And closer to home: Siobhan, concentrating hard on the ACC's speech, maybe learning something from it. She was always on the lookout for a new lesson. Grant Hood, someone else with everything to lose, dejection written into his face and shoulders, the way he held his arms across chest and stomach, as though to ward off blows. Rebus knew Grant was in trouble. A leak to the press, you looked at liaison first. They were the ones with the contacts: an unwise word; the drunk and friendly banter at the end of a good meal. Even if not to blame, a good liaison officer might have been all that was needed in the way of Gill's 'damage limitation'. With experience, you'd know how to bend a journalist's will to your own, even if it meant a bribe of some kind: first dibs on some later story or stories . . .

Rebus wondered at the extent of the damage. Quizmaster would now know what he'd probably always suspected: that it wasn't just him and Siobhan, that she was keeping her colleagues apprised. Her face didn't give anything away, but Rebus knew she was already wondering how to handle it, how to phrase her next communication with Quizmaster, supposing he wanted to keep playing . . . The Arthur's Seat coffins connection annoyed him only because Jean had been mentioned by name in the story, cited as 'the Museum's resident expert' on the case. He recalled that Holly had been persistent, leaving messages for Jean, wanting to speak to her. Could she have said something to him unwittingly? He didn't think so.

No, he had the culprit in his sights. Ellen Wylie looked like she'd been wrung out. There were tangles in her hair where she hadn't been concentrating with the brush. Her eyes had a resigned look. She kept staring at the floor during Carswell's speech, and hadn't shifted when he'd finished. She was still looking at the floor now, trying to find the will to do anything else. Rebus knew she'd spoken on the phone with Holly yesterday morning. It had been to do with the German student, but afterwards she'd seemed lifeless. Rebus had thought it was because she was working another dead end. Now he knew different. When she'd walked away from the Caledonian Hotel, she'd been heading either for Holly's office or for some wine bar or café nearby.

He'd got to her.

Maybe Shug Davidson would realise as much; maybe her colleagues at West End would remember how different she'd been after that phone call. But Rebus knew they wouldn't shop her. It was something you didn't do. Not to a colleague, a pal.

Wylie had been unravelling for days. He'd taken her into the coffin case thinking maybe he could help. But then maybe she was right – maybe he'd been treating her as just another 'cripple', someone else who might be bent to his will, do some of the hard graft on something which would always be *his* case.

Maybe he'd had ulterior motives.

Wylie had probably seen it as a way of getting back at all of them: Gill Templer, cause of her public humiliation; Siobhan, for whom Templer still had such high hopes; Grant Hood, the new golden boy, coping where Wylie had not . . . And Rebus, too, the manipulator, the user, grinding her down.

He saw her left with two alternatives: let it all out, or burst with frustration and anger. If he'd accepted her offer of a drink that night . . . maybe she'd have opened up and he'd have listened. Maybe that was all she'd needed. But he hadn't been there. He'd sneaked off to a pub by himself.

Nice one, John. Very smoothly played. For some reason an image came to mind: some old blues stalwart, turning up for 'Ellen Wylie's Blues'. Maybe John Lee Hooker or B. B. King . . . He caught himself and snapped out of it. He'd almost retreated into music, almost got to a lyric that would tide him over.

But now Carswell was reading from a list of names, and Rebus caught his own as Carswell snapped it out. DC Hood . . . DC Clarke . . . DS Wylie . . . The coffins; the German student – they'd worked those cases, and now the ACC wanted to see them. Faces turned, curious. Carswell was announcing that he'd see them in the 'boss's office', meaning the station commander's, commandeered for the occasion.

Rebus tried to catch Bill Pryde's eye as they trooped out, but with Carswell already having exited, Bill was searching his pockets for more gum, his eyes trying to locate his clipboard. Rebus was the tail of this lethargic snake, Hood in front of him, then Wylie and Siobhan. Templer and Carswell at the head. Derek Linford was standing outside the station commander's office, opened the door for them and then stood back. He tried to stare Rebus down, but Rebus wasn't having that. They were still at it when Gill Templer closed the door, breaking the spell.

Carswell was sliding his chair in towards the desk. 'You've already heard my spiel,' he told them, 'so I won't bore you again. If the leak came from anywhere, it came from one of you. That little shit Holly knew way too much.' As his mouth snapped shut his eyes looked up at them for the first time.

'Sir,' Grant Hood said, taking a half-step forward and folding his hands behind his back, 'as liaison officer it should have been my job to damp the story down. I'd just like to publicly apologise for—'

'Yes, yes, son, I got all that from you last night. What I want now is a simple confession.'

'With respect, sir,' Siobhan Clarke said, 'we're not criminals here. We've had to ask questions, put out feelers. Steve Holly could just have been putting two and two together . . .'

Carswell just stared at her, then said: 'DCS Templer?'

'Steve Holly,' Templer began, 'doesn't work that way if he can possibly help it. He's not the brightest bulb in the chandelier, but he's as sneaky as they come, and ruthless with it.' The way she spoke was telling Clarke something, was saying to her that this had all been gone over already. 'Some of the other journos, yes, I think they could take what's out there in the public domain and make something of it, but not Holly.'

'But he did work the case of the German student,' Clarke persisted.

'And shouldn't have known about the gaming connection,' Templer said, almost by rote: another argument that the senior officers had tried out between themselves.

'It was a long night,' Carswell told them, 'trust me. We've been over it time and again. And it still seems to come down to the four of you.'

'There's been outside assistance,' Grant Hood argued. 'A museum curator, a retired pathologist . . .'

Rebus laid a hand on Hood's arm, silencing him. 'It was me,' he said. Heads turned towards him. 'I think it might have been me.'

He concentrated on not looking in Ellen Wylie's direction, but was aware of her eyes burning into him.

'Early on, I was out at Falls talking to a woman called Bev Dodds. She'd found the coffin by the waterfall. Steve Holly had already been sniffing around, and she'd given him the story . . .'

'And?'

'And I let it slip that there'd been more coffins . . . let slip to her, I mean.' He was remembering the slip – a slip Jean had in fact made. 'If she yapped to Holly, he'd have been on a flyer. I had Jean Burchill with me – she's the curator. That might have given him the Arthur's Seat connection . . .'

Carswell was staring at him coldly. 'And the Internet game?'

Rebus shook his head. 'That one I can't explain, but it's not exactly a well-kept secret. We've been shoving the clues at all the victim's friends, asking if she'd asked them for help . . . any one of them could have told Holly.'

Carswell was still staring. 'You're taking the fall for this?'

'I'm saying it could be my fault. Just that one slip . . .' He turned to the others. 'I can't begin to tell you how sorry I am. I let all of us down.' His gaze skirted Wylie's face, concentrating on her hair.

'Sir,' Siobhan Clarke said, 'what DI Rebus has just

admitted could go for any one of us. I'm sure I may have said a little more than I should on occasion . . .'

Carswell wafted his hand in front of him, quieting her.

'DI Rebus,' he said, 'I'm suspending you from active duty, pending further inquiries.'

'You can't do that!' Ellen Wylie blurted out.

'Shut up, Wylie!' Gill Templer hissed.

'DI Rebus knows the consequences,' Carswell was saying. Rebus nodded. 'Someone needs to be punished.' He paused. 'For the sake of the team.'

'That's right,' Carswell said, nodding. 'Otherwise mistrust begins its corrosive influence. I don't think any of us wants that, do we?'

'No, sir.' Grant Hood's voice proved a lone one.

'Go home, DI Rebus,' Carswell said. 'Write your version down, leaving nothing out. We'll talk again later.'

'Yes, sir,' Rebus said, turning and opening the door. Linford was directly outside, and smiling with one side of his face. Rebus didn't doubt he'd been listening. It struck him suddenly that Carswell and Linford might well conspire to make the case against him look as black as possible.

He'd just given them the perfect excuse for getting rid of him for good.

His flat was ready to be put on the market, and he called the selling solicitor and told her so.

'Thursday evenings and Sunday afternoons for viewing?' she asked.

'I suppose so.' He was sitting in his chair, staring out of the window. 'Is there any way I can . . . not be here?'

'You want someone to show the flat for you?'

'Yes.'

'We have people who'll do that for a small fee.'

'Good.' He didn't want to be around when strangers were opening doors, touching things . . . He didn't think he'd make the best salesman for the place.

'We already have a photograph,' the solicitor was saying.

'So the ad could go in the ESPC guide as early as Thursday next.'

'Not the day after tomorrow?'

'I'm afraid not . . .'

When he'd finished the call, he walked into the hall. New light switches, new sockets. The place was a lot brighter, the fresh coats of paint helping. Not much clutter – he'd made three trips to the dump-site on Old Dalkeith Road: a coat-rack he'd inherited from somewhere; boxes of old magazines and newspapers; a two-bar electric fire with frayed cable; the chest of drawers from Samantha's old room, still decorated with stickers of eighties pop stars . . . The carpets were back down. A drinking acquaintance from Swany's Bar had lent a hand, asking if he wanted them nailed at the edges. Rebus hadn't seen the point.

'New owners will turf them out anyway.'

'You should've had these floors sanded, John. They'd've come up a treat . . .'

Rebus had whittled his possessions down until they wouldn't fill a one-bedroom flat, never mind the three he currently possessed. But still he had nowhere to go. He knew what the market was like in Edinburgh. If Arden Street went on the market next Thursday, it could go to a closing date the week after. Two weeks from now, he could find himself homeless.

And, come to that, jobless.

He'd been expecting phone calls, and eventually one came. It was Gill Templer.

Her opening words: 'You stupid bastard.'

'Hi there, Gill.'

'You could have kept your mouth shut.'

'I suppose I could.'

'Always the willing martyr, eh, John?' She sounded angry, tired and under pressure. He could see reasons for all three.

'I just told the truth,' he said.

'*That* would be a first . . . not that I believe it for a minute.'

'No?'

'Come on, John. Ellen Wylie practically had "guilty" stamped on her forehead.'

'You think I was shielding her?'

'I don't exactly take you for Sir Galahad. You'll have had your reasons. Maybe it was simply to piss off Carswell; you know he hates your guts.'

Rebus didn't like to concede that she might be right. 'How's everything else?' he asked.

Her anger was played out. 'Liaison's snowed under. I'm giving a helping hand.'

Rebus bet she was busy: all the other papers and media, trying to play catch-up with Steve Holly.

'What about you?' she asked.

'What about me?'

'What are you going to do?'

'I haven't really thought about it.'

'Well . . .'

'I'd better let you get back, Gill. Thanks for calling.'

'Bye, John.'

As he put the phone down, it started ringing again. Grant Hood this time.

'I just wanted to thank you for getting us off the hook like that.'

'You weren't on the hook, Grant.'

'*I* was, believe me.'

'I hear you're busy.'

'How . . . ?' Grant paused. 'Oh, DCS Templer's been on to you.'

'Is she helping out or taking over?'

'Hard to say at the minute.'

'She's not in the room with you, is she?'

'No, she's in her own office. When we came out of that meeting with the ACC . . . she was the one who looked most relieved.'

'Maybe because she has the most to lose, Grant. You probably can't see that right now, but it's true.'

'I'm sure you're right.' But he didn't sound convinced that

his own survival wasn't more important in the scheme of things.

'Off you go, Grant, and thanks for finding the time to call.'

'See you around some time.'

'You never know your luck . . .'

Rebus put the phone down and waited, staring at it. But no more calls came. He went to the kitchen to make a mug of tea, and discovered he was out of tea-bags and milk. Without bothering with a jacket, he headed downstairs and out to the local deli, where he added some ham, rolls and mustard to the shopping. Back at the main door to the tenement, someone was trying one of the buzzers.

'Come on, I know you're there . . .'

'Hello, Siobhan.'

She turned towards him. 'Christ, you gave me a . . .' She put a hand to her throat. Rebus stretched an arm past her and unlocked the door.

'Because I sneaked up on you, or because you thought I was sitting upstairs with my wrists slashed?' He held the door open for her.

'What? No, that's not what I was thinking.' But the colour was rising to her cheeks.

'Well, just to stop you worrying, if I'm ever going to top myself, it'll be with a lot of drink and some pills. And by "a lot" I mean two or three days' worth, so you'll have plenty of warning.'

He preceded her up the stairs, opened his front door.

'Your lucky day,' he said. 'Not only am I not dead, but I can offer tea and rolls with ham and mustard.'

'Just tea, thanks,' she said, finally regaining some composure. 'Hey, the hall looks great!'

'Take a look around. I may as well get used to it.'

'You mean it's on the market?'

'As from next week.'

She opened a bedroom door, stuck her head round. 'Dimmer switch,' she commented, trying it out.

Rebus went into the kitchen and stuck the kettle on, found two clean mugs in the cupboard. One of them said

'World's Greatest Dad'. It wasn't his; one of the sparkies must have left it. He decided Siobhan could have her tea in it, he'd have the taller one with the poppies and the chipped rim.

'You didn't paint the living room,' she said, coming into the kitchen.

'It was done not so long ago.'

She nodded. There was something he wasn't saying, but she wasn't going to force it.

'You and Grant still an item then?' he asked.

'We never were. And that's the subject closed.'

He got the milk from the fridge. 'Better be careful, you'll be getting a rep.'

'I beg your pardon?'

'Unsuitable men. One of them was staring daggers at me all morning.'

'Oh God, Derek Linford.' She was thoughtful. 'Didn't he look awful?'

'Doesn't he always?' Rebus placed a tea-bag in each mug. 'So, are you here to check up on me or thank me for sticking my neck out?'

'I'm not about to thank you for *that*. You could have stayed quiet, and you know it. If you owned up, it was because *you* wanted to.' She broke off.

'And?' he encouraged her.

'And you'll have some agenda going.'

'Actually I don't . . . not particularly.'

'Then why did you do it?'

'It was the quickest way, the simplest. If I'd bothered to think for a moment . . . maybe I'd have kept my mouth shut.' He poured water and milk into the mugs, handed one over. Siobhan looked at the tea-bag floating there. 'Spoon it out when it's strong enough,' he suggested.

'Yummy.'

'Sure I can't tempt you with a ham roll?'

She shook her head. 'Don't let me stop you.'

'Maybe later,' he said, leading them through to the living room. 'Everything calm at base camp?'

'Say what you like about Carswell, he's a pretty good motivator. Everyone thinks it was that speech of his that made you feel guilty.'

'And they're now working harder than ever?' He waited till she'd nodded. 'A team of happy gardeners with no nasty moles to bother them.'

Siobhan grinned. 'It was pretty bloody corny, wasn't it?' She looked around. 'Where are you going to go when you sell this place?'

'Got a spare room, have you?'

'Depends for how long.'

'I'm just joking, Siobhan. I'll be fine.' He took a gulp of tea. 'So what exactly *does* bring you here?'

'You mean apart from checking up on you?'

'I'm guessing that wasn't all.'

She reached down to place her mug on the floor. 'I got another message.'

'Quizmaster?' She nodded. 'Saying what exactly?'

She unfolded some sheets from her pocket, reached over towards him with them. Their fingers touched as he took them. The first was an e-mail from Siobhan:

Still awaiting Stricture.

'I sent that first thing this morning,' she said. 'Thought maybe he wouldn't have heard.'

Rebus turned to the second sheet. It was from Quizmaster.

I'm disappointed in you, Siobhan. I'm taking my ball home now.

Then Siobhan:

Don't believe everything you read. I still want to play.

Quizmaster:

And go yapping to your bosses?

Siobhan:

You and me this time, that's a promise.

Quizmaster:

How can I trust you?

Siobhan:

I've been trusting you, haven't I? And you always know where to find me. I still don't have the first clue about you.

'I had to wait a while after that. The final sheet came in about' – she checked her watch – 'forty minutes ago.'

'And you came straight here?'

She shrugged. 'More or less.'

'You didn't show it to Brains?'

'He's off on some errand for Crime Squad.'

'Anyone else?' She shook her head. 'Why me?'

'Now that I'm here,' she said, 'I don't really know.'

'Grant's the one with the puzzle mind.'

'Right now he's too busy puzzling over how to keep his job.'

Rebus nodded slowly and re-read the final sheet:

Add Camus to ME Smith, they're boxing where the sun don't shine, and Frank Finlay's the referee.

'Well,' he said, 'you've shown me it . . .' He made to hand the sheets back. 'And it doesn't mean a thing to me.'

'No?'

He shook his head. 'Frank Finlay was an actor – might still be, for all I know. I think he played Casanova on TV, and he was in something called *Barbed Wire and Bouquets* . . . something like that.'

'*Bouquet of Barbed Wire?*'

'Could have been.' He glanced at the clue a final time. 'Camus was a French writer. I used to think it was pronounced "came as" until I heard it mentioned on the radio or the box.'

'Boxing – that's something you know about.'

'Marciano, Dempsey, Cassius Clay before he became Ali . . .' He shrugged.

'Where the sun don't shine,' Siobhan said. 'That's an American expression, isn't it?'

'It means out your arse,' Rebus confirmed. 'You think suddenly Quizmaster's American?'

She smiled, but there was no humour to it.

'Take my advice, Siobhan. Give it to Crime Squad or Special Branch or whoever's supposed to be tracking this arsehole down. Or just e-mail him back telling him to get stuffed.' He paused. 'You said he knows where to find you?'

She nodded. 'He knows my name, that I'm CID in Edinburgh.'

'But nothing about where you live? He hasn't got your phone number?' She shook her head and Rebus nodded, satisfied. He was thinking of all the numbers pinned to Steve Holly's office wall.

'Then let him go,' he said quietly.

'Is that what you'd do?'

'It's what I'd strongly advise.'

'Then you don't want to help me?'

He looked at her. 'Help you how?'

'Copy the clue, do some detecting.'

He laughed. 'You want me in even more trouble with Carswell?'

She looked down at the sheets of paper. 'You're right,' she said. 'I wasn't thinking. Thanks for the tea.'

'Stay and finish it.' He watched her get to her feet.

'I should be heading back. Lots to do.'

'Starting with handing that clue over?'

She stared at him. 'You know your advice is always important to me.'

'Is that a yes or a no?'

'Take it as a definite maybe.'

He was standing now, too. 'Thanks for coming, Siobhan.'

She turned towards the doorway. 'Linford's out to get you, isn't he? Him and Carswell both?'

'Don't fret over it.'

'But Linford's getting stronger. He'll be Chief Inspector any day.'

'For all you know, maybe I'm getting stronger too.'

She turned her head to study him, but didn't say anything, didn't need to. He followed her out into the hall, opened the door for her.

She was on the stairwell before she spoke again. 'Know what Ellen Wylie said after that meeting with Carswell?'

'What?'

'Nothing at all.' She looked at him again, one hand on the

banister. 'Strange that. I was expecting a long speech about your martyr complex . . .'

Back in the flat, Rebus stood in the hall, listening to her footsteps recede. Then he walked to the living-room window and stood on tiptoe, craning his neck to watch her leave the tenement, the door closing with an echo behind her. She'd come here asking for something, and he'd turned her down. How could he tell her that he didn't want her getting hurt, the way so many people he'd let get close to him had been hurt in the past? How to tell her that she should learn her own lessons, not his, and that she'd be a better cop – as well as a better person – at the end of it?

He turned back into the room. The ghosts were faint, but visible. People he'd hurt and been hurt by, people who'd died painful, unnecessary deaths. Not for much longer. A couple more weeks and maybe he'd be free of them. He knew the phone wasn't going to ring, nor was Ellen Wylie about to pay him a visit. They understood one another well enough to render any such contact unnecessary. Maybe one day in the future they'd sit down and talk about it. Then again, maybe she'd never speak to him again. He'd stolen the moment from her, and she had stood there and let him. Defeat once again snatched from the jaws of victory. He wondered if she'd stay in Steve Holly's pocket . . . wondered just how deep and dark that pocket might be.

He walked through to the kitchen, poured Siobhan's and the rest of his tea down the sink. An inch of malt into a clean glass and a bottle of IPA from the cupboard. Back in the living room, he sat in his chair, took pen and notebook from his pocket, and jotted down the latest clue as best he could remember it . . .

Jean Burchill's morning had consisted of a series of meetings, including one heated debate on funding levels which threatened to turn violent, with one curator walking out, slamming the door after him, and another almost bursting into tears.

By lunchtime, she felt exhausted, the stuffiness of her

office contributing to a thumping head. Steve Holly had left two more messages for her, and she just knew that if she sat at her desk with a sandwich, the phone would ring again. Instead, she headed outside, joining the throng of workers released from captivity for the time it took to queue at the baker's for a filled roll or pie. The Scots had an unenviable record for heart disease and tooth decay, both the result of the national diet: saturated fats, salt and sugar. She'd wondered what it was that made Scottish people reach for the comfort foods, the chocolate, chips and fizzy drinks: was it the climate? Or could the answer lie deeper, within the nation's character? Jean decided to buck the trend, purchased some fruit and a carton of orange juice. She was heading into town down the Bridges. It was all cheap clothes shops and takeaways, with queues of buses and lorries waiting to crawl through the traffic lights at the Tron kirk. A few beggars sat in doorways, staring at the passing parade of feet. Jean paused at the lights and looked left and right along the High Street, imagining the place in the days before Princes Street: vendors hawking their wares; ill-lit howffs where business was done; the tollbooth and the gates which were closed at nightfall, locking the city into itself . . . She wondered if someone from the 1770s, somehow transported to the present, would find this part of the city so very different. The lights, the cars might shock them, but not the *feel* of the place.

She paused again on North Bridge, staring eastwards towards where the new parliament site showed no signs of progress. The *Scotsman* had moved its offices down to a shiny new building in Holyrood Road, just across from the parliament. She'd been there recently for a function, standing on the large balcony to the rear, staring out at the immensity of Salisbury Crags. Behind her now, the old *Scotsman* building was being gutted: another new hotel in the making. Further down North Bridge, where it connected with Princes Street, the old Post Office HQ sat dusty and empty, its future apparently still not decided – another hotel, the rumour went. She took a right into Waterloo Place, munching on her second apple and trying not to think of crisps and Kit-Kats. She knew where she was headed: Calton cemetery. As she entered through the wrought-iron gate, she was confronted by the obelisk known as the Martyrs' Memorial, dedicated to the memory of five men, the 'Friends of the People', who had dared in the 1790s to advocate parliamentary reform. This at a time when fewer than forty people in the city had the power to vote in an election. The five were sentenced to transportation: a one-way ticket to Australia. Jean looked at the apple she was eating. She'd just peeled a little sticker from it, announcing its country of origin as New Zealand. She thought of the five convicts, the lives they must have led. But there was to be no counterpart to the French Revolution in Scotland, not in the 1790s.

She was reminded of some communist leader and thinker – was it Marx himself? – who had predicted that the revolution in western Europe would have Scotland as its starting-point. Another dream . . .

Jean didn't know much about David Hume, but stood in front of his monument while she attacked her carton of juice. Philosopher and essayist . . . a friend had once told her that Hume's achievement had been in making the philosophy of John Locke comprehensible, but then she didn't know anything much about Locke either.

There were other graves: Blackwood and Constable, publishers, and one of the leaders of 'the Disruption', which had led to the founding of the Free Church of Scotland. Just to the east, over the cemetery wall, was a small crenellated tower. This she knew was all that remained of the old Calton Prison. She'd seen drawings of it, taken from Calton Hill opposite: friends and family of the prisoners would gather there to shout messages and greetings. Closing her eyes, she could almost replace the traffic noises with yelps and whoops, the dialogue between loved ones echoing back along Waterloo Place . . .

When she opened her eyes again, she saw what she'd hoped to find: Dr Kennet Lovell's grave. The headstone had been set into the cemetery's eastern wall, and was now cracked and soot-blackened, its edges fallen away to reveal the sandstone beneath. It was a small thing, close to the ground. 'Dr Kennet Anderson Lovell,' Jean read, 'an eminent Physician of this City.' He'd died in 1863, aged fifty-six. There were weeds rising from ground level, obscuring much of the inscription. Jean crouched down and started pulling them away, encountering a used condom which she brushed aside with a dock leaf. She knew that there were people who used Calton Hill at night, and imagined them coupling against this wall, pressing down on the bones of Dr Lovell. How would Lovell feel about that? For a moment, she formed a picture of another coupling: herself and John Rebus. Not her type at all really. In the past she'd dated researchers, university lecturers. One brief dalliance with a sculptor in the city – a married man. He'd taken her to cemeteries, his favourite places. John Rebus probably liked cemeteries, too. When they'd first met she'd seen him as a challenge and a curiosity. Even now she had to work hard not to think of him in terms of an exhibit. There were so many secrets there, so much of him that he refused to show to the world. She knew there was digging still to be done . . .

As she cleared the weeds, she found that Lovell had married no fewer than three times, and that each wife had passed away before him. No evidence of any children . . . she wondered if the offspring might be buried elsewhere. Maybe there were no children. But then hadn't John said something about a descendant . . . ? As she examined the dates, she saw that the wives had died young, and another thought crossed her mind: they'd died in childbirth, perhaps.

His first wife: Beatrice, *née* Alexander. Aged twenty-nine.

His second wife: Alice, *née* Baxter. Aged thirty-three.

His third wife: Patricia, *née* Addison. Aged twenty-six.

An inscription read: *Passed over, to be met again so sweetly in the Lord's domain.*

Jean couldn't help thinking that it must have been some meeting, Lovell and his three wives. She had a pen in her pocket, but no notepad or paper. She looked around the cemetery, found an old envelope, torn in half. She brushed dirt and dust from it and jotted down the details.

Siobhan was back at her desk, trying to form anagrams from the letters in 'Camus' and 'ME Smith', when Eric Bain came into the office.

'All right?' he asked.

'I'll survive.'

'That good, eh?' He placed his briefcase on the floor, straightened up and looked around. 'Special Branch get back to us yet?'

'Not that I know of.' She was scoring out letters with her pen. The M and E had no space between them. Did Quizmaster mean them to be read as 'me'? Was he saying his name was Smith? ME was also a medical condition. She couldn't recall what the letters stood for . . . remembered it being called 'yuppie flu' in the newspapers. Bain had walked over to the fax machine, picked up some sheets and sifted through them.

'Ever think to check?' he said, sliding two sheets out and putting the rest back next to the machine.

Siobhan looked up. 'What is it?'

He was reading as he approached. 'Bloody marvellous,' he gasped. 'Don't ask me how they did it, but they did it.'

'What?'

'They've traced one of the accounts already.'

Siobhan's chair fell back as she got to her feet, hands grabbing at the fax. As Bain relinquished it, he asked her a simple question.

'Who's Claire Benzie?'

'You're not in custody, Claire,' Siobhan said, 'and if you want a solicitor, that's up to you. But I'd like your permission to make a tape recording.'

'Sounds serious,' Claire Benzie said. They'd picked her up at her flat in Bruntsfield, driven her to St Leonard's. She'd been compliant, not asking questions. She was wearing jeans and a pale pink turtleneck. Her face looked scrubbed, no make-up. She sat in the interview room with arms folded while Bain fed tapes into both recording machines.

'There'll be a copy for you, and one for us,' Siobhan was saying. 'Okay?'

Benzie just shrugged.

Bain said 'okey-dokey' and set both tapes running, then eased himself into the chair next to Siobhan. Siobhan identified herself and Bain for the record, adding time and place of interview.

'If you could state your full name, Claire,' she asked.

Claire Benzie did so, adding her Bruntsfield address. Siobhan sat back for a moment, composing herself, then leaned forward again so her elbows were resting on the edge of the narrow desk.

'Claire, do you remember when I spoke to you earlier? I was with a colleague, in Dr Curt's office?'

'Yes, I remember.'

'I was asking you if you knew anything about the game Philippa Balfour had been playing?'

'It's her funeral tomorrow.'

Siobhan nodded. 'Do you remember?'

'Seven fins high is king,' Benzie said. 'I told you about it.'

'That's right. You said Philippa had come up to you at a bar . . .'

'Yes.'

'. . . and explained it to you.'

'Yes.'

'But you didn't know anything about the game itself?'

'No. I hadn't a clue till you told me.'

Siobhan sat back again, folded her own arms so that she was almost a mirror-image of Benzie. 'Then how come whoever was sending Flip those messages was using your Internet account?'

Benzie stared at her. Siobhan stared back. Eric Bain scratched his nose with his thumb.

'I want a solicitor,' Benzie said.

Siobhan nodded slowly. 'Interview ends, three-twelve

p.m.' Bain switched off the tapes and Siobhan asked if Claire had anyone in mind.

'The family solicitor, I suppose,' the student said.

'And who's that?'

'My father.' When she saw the puzzled look on Siobhan's face, the corners of Benzie's mouth curled upwards. 'I mean my stepfather, DC Clarke. Don't worry, I'm not about to summon ghosts to fight my corner . . .'

News had travelled, and there was a scrum in the corridor when Siobhan came out of the interview room, just as the summoned WPC was going in. Whispered questions flew.

'Well?'

'Did she do it?'

'What's she saying?'

'Is it her?'

Siobhan ignored everyone except Gill Templer. 'She wants a solicitor, and as chance would have it there's one in her family.'

'That's handy.'

Siobhan nodded and squeezed her way into the CID office, unplugging the first free phone she came to.

'She also wants a soft drink, Diet Pepsi for preference.'

Templer looked around, eyes fixing on George Silvers. 'Hear that, George?'

'Yes, ma'am.' Silvers seemed reluctant to leave, until Gill shooed him out with her hands.

'So?' Gill was now blocking Siobhan's path.

'So,' Siobhan said, 'she's got some explaining to do. It doesn't make her the killer.'

'Be nice if she was though,' someone said.

Siobhan was remembering what Rebus had said about Claire Benzie. She met Gill Templer's gaze. 'Two or three years from now,' she said, 'if she sticks with pathology, we could end up working side by side with her. I don't think we can afford to be heavy-handed.' She wasn't sure if she was copying Rebus's words verbatim, but she knew she was pretty close. Templer was looking at her appraisingly, nodding slowly.

'DC Clarke's got a very good point,' she told the surrounding faces. Then she moved aside to let Siobhan past, murmuring something like 'Well done, Siobhan' as they were shoulder to shoulder.

Back in the interview room, Siobhan plugged the telephone into the wall and told Claire it was 9 for an outside line.

'I didn't kill her,' the student said with quiet confidence.

'Then everything's going to be okay. We just need to find out what happened.'

Claire nodded, picked up the receiver. Siobhan gestured to Bain, and they left the room together, the WPC taking over the watch.

Out in the corridor, the scrum had melted away, but the hubbub from inside the CID office was loud and excited.

'Say she didn't do it.' Siobhan spoke quietly, her words for Bain's ears only.

'Okay,' he said.

'Then how could Quizmaster be tapping into her account?'

He shook his head. 'I don't know. I mean, I suppose it's possible, but it's also highly unlikely.'

Siobhan looked at him. 'So you think it's her?'

He shrugged. 'I'd like to know who the other access accounts belong to.'

'Did Special Branch say how long it would take?'

'Maybe later today, maybe tomorrow.'

Someone walked past, patted both of them on the shoulder, gave a thumbs-up as he bounced down the corridor.

'They think we've cracked it,' Bain said.

'More fool them.'

'She had the motive, you've said so yourself.'

Siobhan nodded. She was thinking of the Stricture clue, trying to imagine it composed by a woman. Yes, it was possible; of course it was possible. The virtual world: you could pretend to be anyone you liked, either gender, any age. The newspapers were full of stories about middle-aged paedophiles who'd infiltrated children's chat rooms in the guise of teens and pre-teens. The very anonymity of the Net was what attracted people to it. She thought of Claire Benzie, of the long and careful planning it must have taken, the anger fermenting ever since her father's suicide. Maybe she'd started out wanting to know Flip again, wanting to like and forgive her, but had found rising hatred instead, hatred of Flip's easy world, her friends with fast cars, the bars and night clubs and dinner parties, the whole lifestyle enjoyed by people who'd never known pain, never lost anything in their lives that couldn't be bought again.

'I don't know,' she said, running both hands through her hair, pulling so hard that her scalp hurt. 'I just don't know.'

'That's good,' Bain said. 'Approach the interview with an open mind: textbook stuff.'

She smiled tiredly, squeezed his hand. 'Thanks, Eric.'

'You'll be fine,' he told her. She hoped he was right.

Maybe the Central Library was the right place for Rebus. Many of the customers today seemed to be the dispossessed, the tired, the unemployable. Some sat sleeping in the more comfortable chairs, the books on their laps mere props. One old man, toothless mouth gaping, sat at a desk near the telephone directories, his finger running ponderously down each column. Rebus had asked one of the staff about him.

'Been coming in here for years, never reads anything else,' he was informed.

'He could get a job with Directory Enquiries.'

'Or maybe that's where he was fired from.'

Rebus acknowledged that this was a good point, and got back to his own research. So far he'd established that Albert Camus was a French novelist and thinker, the author of novels such as *La Chute* and *La Peste*. He'd won the Nobel Prize and then died while still in his forties. The librarian had done a search for him, but this was the only Camus of note to be found.

'Unless, of course, you're talking street names.'

'What?'

'Edinburgh street names.'

Sure enough, it turned out that the city boasted a Camus Road, along with Camus Avenue, Park and Place. No one seemed to know whether they were named after the French writer; Rebus reckoned the chances were pretty good. He looked up Camus in the phone book – by luck the old man wasn't using it at the time – and found just the one. Taking a break, he thought about walking home and getting his car, maybe taking a drive out to Camus Road, but when a taxi came by he hailed it instead. Camus Road, Avenue, Park and Place turned out to be a little quartet of quiet residential streets just off Comiston Road in Fairmilehead. The taxi driver seemed bemused when Rebus told him to head back for George IV Bridge. When they hit a traffic hold-up at Greyfriars, Rebus paid the taxi off and got out. He headed straight into Sandy Bell's pub, where the afternoon crowd hadn't yet been swollen by workers on their way home. A pint and a nip. The barman knew him, told a few stories. He said that when the Infirmary moved to Petty France, they'd lose half their trade. Not the doctors and nurses, but the patients.

'Pyjamas and slippers, I'm not joking: they walk straight out the ward and in here. One guy even had the tubes hanging out his arms.'

Rebus smiled, finished his drinks. Greyfriars Kirkyard was just around the corner, so he took a wander in. He reckoned that all those Covenanting ghosts would be pretty miserable, knowing a wee dog had made the place more famous than they had. There were tours up here at night, stories of sudden chill hands clamping shoulders. He recalled that Rhona, his ex, had wanted to be married in the kirk itself. He saw graves covered with iron railings – mortsafes, protecting the deceased from the Resurrection Men. Edinburgh seemed always to have thrived on cruelty, its centuries of barbarism masked by an exterior by turns douce and strict . . .

Stricture . . . he wondered what the word had to do with

the clue. He thought it meant being tied up, something along those lines, but realised that he wasn't sure. He left the kirkyard and headed on to George IV Bridge, turning in to the library. The same librarian was still on duty.

'Dictionaries?' he asked. She directed him towards the shelf he needed.

'I did that check you asked for,' she added. 'There are some books by a Mark Smith, but nothing by anyone called M. E. Smith.'

'Thanks anyway.' He started to turn away.

'I also printed you out a list of our Camus holdings.'

He took the sheet from her. 'That's great. Thank you very much.'

She smiled, as if unused to compliments, then looked more hesitant as she caught the alcohol on his breath. On his way to the shelves, he noticed that the desk by the telephone directories was vacant. He wondered if that was the old guy finished for the day; maybe it was like a nine-to-five for him. He pulled out the first dictionary he found and opened it at 'stricture': it meant binding, closure, tightness. 'Binding' made him think of mummies, or someone with their hands tied, held captive . . .

There was a clearing of the throat behind him. The librarian was standing there.

'Chucking-out time?' Rebus guessed.

'Not quite.' She pointed back towards her desk, where another member of staff was now positioned, watching them. 'My colleague . . . Kenny . . . he thinks maybe he knows who Mr Smith is.'

'Mr who?' Rebus was looking at Kenny: barely out of his teens, wearing round metal-framed glasses and a black T-shirt.

'M. E. Smith,' the librarian said. So Rebus walked over, nodded a greeting at Kenny.

'He's a singer,' Kenny said without preamble. 'At least, if it's the one I'm thinking of: Mark E. Smith. And not everyone would agree with the description "singer".'

The librarian had gone back around the desk. 'I've never heard of him, I must confess,' she said.

'Time to widen your horizons, Bridget,' Kenny said. Then he looked at Rebus, wondering at the detective's wide-eyed stare.

'Singer with The Fall?' Rebus said quietly, almost to himself.

'You know them?' Kenny seemed surprised that someone Rebus's age would have such knowledge.

'Saw them twenty years ago. A club in Abbeyhill.'

'Real noise merchants, eh?' Kenny said.

Rebus nodded distractedly. Then the other librarian, Bridget, gave voice to his thoughts.

'Funny really,' she said. Then she pointed to the sheet of paper in Rebus's hand. 'Camus' novel *La Chute* translates as "The Fall". We've a copy in the Fiction section if you'd like one . . .'

Claire Benzie's stepfather turned out to be Jack McCoist, one of the city's more able defence solicitors. He asked for ten minutes alone with her before any interview could begin. Afterwards, Siobhan entered the room again, accompanied by Gill Templer who, much to his visible annoyance, had ousted Eric Bain.

Claire's drink can was empty. McCoist had half a cup of lukewarm tea in front of him.

'I don't think we need a recording made,' McCoist stated. 'Let's just talk this through, see where it takes us. Agreed?'

He looked to Gill Templer, who nodded eventually.

'When you're ready, DC Clarke,' Templer said.

Siobhan tried for eye contact with Claire, but she was too busy with the Pepsi can, rolling it between her palms.

'Claire,' she said, 'these clues Flip was getting, one of them came from an e-mail address which we've traced back to you.'

McCoist had an A4 pad out, on which he'd already written several pages of notes in handwriting so bad it was like a personal code. Now he turned to a fresh sheet.

'Can I just ask how you came into possession of these e-mails?'

'They ... we didn't really. Someone called Quizmaster sent Flip Balfour a message, and it came to me instead.'

'How so?' McCoist hadn't looked up from his pad. All she could see of him were blue pinstriped shoulders and the top of his head, thinning black hair showing plenty of scalp.

'Well, I was checking Ms Balfour's computer for anything that might explain her disappearance.'

'So this was *after* she'd disappeared?' He looked up now: thick black rims to his glasses and a mouth which, when not open, was a thin line of doubt.

'Yes,' Siobhan admitted.

'And this is the message you say you've traced back to my client's computer?'

'To her ISP account, yes.' Siobhan was noticing that Claire had looked up for the first time: it was that use of "my client". Claire was looking at her stepfather, studying him. Probably she'd never seen his professional side before.

'ISP being the Internet service provider?'

Siobhan nodded her answer. McCoist was letting her know that he was up on the jargon.

'Have there been subsequent messages?'

'Yes.'

'And do they belong to the same address?'

'We don't know that yet.' Siobhan had decided he didn't need to know more than one ISP was involved.

'Very well.' McCoist stabbed a full stop on the latest sheet with his pen, then sat back thoughtfully.

'Do I get to ask Claire a question now?' Siobhan asked.

McCoist peered at her over the top of his glasses. 'My client would prefer to make a short statement first.'

Claire reached into the pocket of her jeans and unfolded a sheet of paper which had obviously come from the pad on the table. The writing was different from McCoist's scrawl, but Siobhan could see scorings-out where the lawyer had suggested changes.

Claire cleared her throat. 'About a fortnight before Flip

went missing, I loaned her my laptop computer. She had some essay she was writing, and I thought it might help her. I knew she didn't have a laptop of her own. I never got the chance to ask for it back. I was waiting until after the funeral to ask her family if it could be retrieved from her flat.'

'Is this laptop your only computer?' Siobhan interrupted.

Claire shook her head. 'No, but it's linked to an ISP, same account as my PC.'

Siobhan stared at her; still she didn't make eye contact. 'There was no laptop in Philippa Balfour's flat,' she said.

Eye contact at last. 'Then where is it?' Claire said.

'I'm assuming you still have the proof of purchase, something like that?'

McCoist spoke up. 'Are you accusing my daughter of lying?' She wasn't just a client any longer . . .

'I'm saying maybe it's something Claire should have told us a bit earlier.'

'I didn't know it was . . .' Claire began to say.

'DCS Templer,' McCoist began haughtily, 'I didn't think it was Lothian and Borders Police policy to accuse potential witnesses of duplicity.'

'Right now,' Templer shot back, 'your stepdaughter's a suspect rather than a witness.'

'Suspected of what exactly? Running a quiz? Since when was that an offence?'

Gill didn't have an answer for that. She glanced in Siobhan's direction, and Siobhan thought she could read at least a few of her boss's thoughts. *He's right . . . we still don't know for sure that Quizmaster has anything to do with anything . . . this is* your *hunch I'm going with, just remember that . . .*

McCoist knew the look between the two detectives meant something. He decided to press his point.

'I can't see you presenting any of this to the Procurator Fiscal. You'd be laughed back down the ranks . . . DCS Templer.' Putting the stress on those three letters. He knew she was newly promoted; knew she'd yet to prove herself . . .

Gill had already regained her composure. 'What we need

from Claire, Mr McCoist, are some straight answers, otherwise her story's looking thin and we'll need to make further inquiries.'

McCoist seemed to consider this. Siobhan, meantime, was busy making a mental list. Claire Benzie had the motive all right – the role of Balfour's Bank in her father's suicide. With the role-playing game, she had the means, and luring Flip to Arthur's Seat would give the opportunity. Now she suddenly invented a loaned laptop, conveniently missing . . . Siobhan started another list, this time for Ranald Marr, who'd warned Flip early on about how to delete e-mails. Ranald Marr with his toy soldiers, second-in-command at the bank. She still didn't see what Marr would have gained from Flip's death . . .

'Claire,' she said quietly, 'those times you went to Junipers, did you ever meet Ranald Marr?'

'I don't see what that's—'

But Claire interrupted her stepfather. 'Ranald Marr, yes. I never really knew what she saw in him.'

'Who?'

'Flip. She had this crush on Ranald. Schoolgirl stuff, I suppose . . .'

'Was it reciprocated? Did it go further than a crush?'

'I think,' McCoist said, 'we're straying somewhat from the—'

But Claire was smiling at Siobhan. 'Not until later,' she was saying.

'How much later?'

'I got the feeling she was seeing him pretty much up till she went missing . . .'

'What's all the excitement?' Rebus asked.

Bain looked up from the desk he was working at. 'Brought in Claire Benzie for questioning.'

'Why?' Rebus leaned down, reached into one of the desk's drawers.

'Sorry,' Bain said, 'is this your . . . ?'

He was making to get up, but Rebus stopped him. 'I'm

suspended, remember? Just you keep it warm for me.' He closed the drawer, not having found anything. 'So what's Benzie doing here?'

'One of the e-mails, I got Special Branch to trace it.'

Rebus whistled. 'Claire Benzie sent it?'

'Well, it was sent from her account.'

Rebus considered this. 'Not quite the same thing?'

'Siobhan's the sceptical one.'

'Is she in with Benzie?' Rebus waited till Bain nodded. 'But you're out here?'

'DCS Templer.'

'Ah,' Rebus said, no further explanation needed.

Gill Templer burst into the CID office. 'I want Ranald Marr brought in for questioning. Who wants to fetch him?'

She got two volunteers straight away – Hi-Ho Silvers and Tommy Fleming. Others were trying to place the name, wondering what it could have to do with Claire Benzie and Quizmaster. When Gill turned round, Siobhan was standing behind her.

'That was good work in there.'

'Was it?' Siobhan asked. 'I'm not so sure.'

'How do you mean?'

'When I talk to her, it's like I'm asking her things she *wants* to be asked. It's as if *she's* in control.'

'I didn't see that.' Gill touched Siobhan's shoulder. 'Take a break. We'll let someone else have a shot at Ranald Marr.' She looked around the room. 'The rest of you, back to work.' Her eyes met those of John Rebus. 'What the hell are you doing here?'

Rebus opened another drawer, this time pulling out a pack of cigarettes and shaking them.

'Just came to collect a few personal items, ma'am.'

Gill pursed her lips, stalked out of the room. McCoist was in the corridor with Claire. The three started a short discussion. Siobhan approached Rebus.

'What the hell *are* you doing here?'

'You look shattered.'

'I see your silver tongue's as rusty as ever.'

'Boss told you to take a break, and as luck would have it, I'm buying. While you've been busy scaring wee lassies, I've been doing the important stuff . . .'

Siobhan was sticking to orange juice, and kept playing with her mobile: Bain was under strictest orders to call her if and when there was news.

'I need to get back,' she said, not for the first time. Then she checked the mobile's display again, just in case the battery needed recharging or the signal had been lost.

'Have you eaten?' Rebus asked. When she shook her head, he came back from the bar with a couple of packets of Scampi Frics, which she was devouring when she heard him say:

'That's when it struck me.'

'When what struck you?'

'Christ, Siobhan, wake up.'

'John, I feel like my head's about to explode. I honestly think it might.'

'You don't think Claire Benzie's guilty, that much I understand. And now she says Flip Balfour was getting her end away with Ranald Marr.'

'Do you believe her?'

He lit another cigarette, wafted the smoke away from Siobhan. 'I'm not allowed an opinion: suspended from duty till further notice.'

She gave him a dirty look, lifted her glass.

'It's going to be some conversation, isn't it?' Rebus asked.

'What?'

'When Balfour asks his trusted compadre what the cops wanted him for.'

'Think Marr will tell him?'

'Even if he doesn't, Balfour's sure to find out. Funeral tomorrow should be a jolly affair.' He blew more smoke ceilingwards. 'You going to be there?'

'Thinking of it. Templer and Carswell, a few others . . . they'll be going.'

'Might be needed if a fight starts.'

She looked at her watch. 'I should head back, see what Marr's been saying.'

'You were told to take a break.'

'I've had one.'

'Phone in if you really feel the need.'

'Maybe I'll do that.' She noticed that her mobile was still attached to the connector which, were the laptop not back at St Leonard's, would have given her access to the Net. She stared at the connector, then up at Rebus. 'What were you saying?'

'About what?'

'About Stricture.'

Rebus's smile widened. 'Nice to have you back with us. I was saying that I spent all afternoon in the library, and I've worked out the first bit of the puzzle.'

'Already?'

'You're dealing with quality here, Siobhan. So, do you want to hear?'

'Sure.' She noticed that his glass was almost empty. 'Should I . . . ?'

'Just listen first.' He pulled her back on to her seat. The pub was maybe half full, and most of the drinkers looked like students. Rebus reckoned he was the oldest face in the place. Standing by the bar, he might have been taken for the owner. At the corner table with Siobhan, he probably looked like a seedy boss trying to get his secretary tipsy.

'I'm all ears,' she told him.

'Albert Camus,' he began slowly, 'wrote a book called *The Fall*.' He slid a paperback copy from his coat and placed it on the table, tapping it with one finger. It wasn't from the library; he'd found it in Thin's Bookshop on his way to St Leonard's. 'Mark E. Smith is the singer with a band called The Fall.'

Siobhan frowned. 'I think I had one of their singles once.'

'So,' Rebus went on, 'we have *The Fall* and The Fall. Add one to the other and you get . . .'

'Falls?' Siobhan guessed. Rebus nodded. She picked up the book, examined its cover, then turned it to read the blurb on the back. 'You think maybe that's where Quizmaster wants to meet?'

'I think it has to do with the next clue.'

'But what about the rest of it, the boxing match and Frank Finlay?'

Rebus shrugged. 'Unlike Simple Minds, I didn't promise you a miracle.'

'No . . .' She paused, then looked up at him. 'Come to think of it, I didn't think you were that interested.'

'I changed my mind.'

'Why?'

'Ever sat at home watching paint dry?'

'I've been on dates where it would have been preferable.'

'Then maybe you know what I mean.'

She nodded, flicking the pages of the book. Then a frown appeared on her forehead, she stopped nodding, and looked up at him again. 'Actually,' she said, 'I don't have the faintest idea what you mean.'

'Good, that means you're learning.'

'Learning what?'

'John Rebus's own patented brand of existentialism.' He wagged a finger at her. 'That's a word I didn't know till today, and I've got you to thank.'

'So what does it mean?'

'I didn't say I knew what it meant, but I think it's got quite a lot to do with choosing *not* to watch paint dry . . .'

They went back to St Leonard's, but there was no news. Officers were practically bouncing off the walls. They needed a breakthrough. They needed a break. A fight had to be broken up in the toilets: two uniforms who couldn't say how it started. Rebus watched Siobhan for a few minutes. She went from one huddle to another, desperate to know things. He could see she was having trouble holding on: a head full of theories and fancies. She, too, needed the breakthrough, the break. He walked up to her. Her eyes were glistening. Rebus took hold of her arm, escorted her outside. She resisted at first.

'When did you last eat?' he asked.

'You bought me those Scampi Fries.'

'I mean a hot meal.'

'You sound like my mum . . .'

The short walk led them to an Indian restaurant on Nicolson Street. It was dark and up a flight of stairs and mostly empty. Tuesday had become the new Monday: a dead night on the town. The weekend started on Thursday as you planned how to spend your pay, and ended with a quick pint after work on the Monday so you could pick over the highlights just past. Tuesday, the sensible option was to go home, keep what cash you had.

'You know Falls better than I do,' she said now. 'What landmarks are there?'

'Well, the waterfall itself – you've seen that – and maybe Junipers – you've been there.' He shrugged. 'That's about it.'

'There's a housing scheme, right?'

He nodded. 'Meadowside. And there's a petrol station just outside town. Plus Bev Dodds's cottage and a few dozen commuters. Not even a church or a post office.'

'No boxing ring then?'

Rebus shook his head. 'And no bouquets, barbed wire or Frank Finlay House.'

Siobhan seemed to lose interest in her food. Rebus wasn't too worried: she'd already dispatched a mixed tandoori starter and the bulk of her biryani. He watched her take out her phone and try the station again. She'd called once already: no one had answered. This time someone did.

'Eric? It's Siobhan. What's happening there? Have we got Marr yet? What's he saying?' She listened, then her eyes met Rebus's. 'Really?' Her voice had risen slightly in pitch. 'That was a bit silly, wasn't it?'

For a second, Rebus thought: suicide. He drew a finger across his throat, but Siobhan shook her head.

'Okay, Eric. Thanks for that. See you later.' She ended the call, took her time placing the phone back in her bag.

'Spit it out,' Rebus said.

She scooped up another forkful of food. 'You're suspended, remember? Off the case.'

'I'll suspend you from the ceiling if you don't cough up.'

She smiled, put the fork down, food untouched. The waiter took a step forward, ready to clear the table, but Rebus waved him back.

'Well,' Siobhan said, 'they went to pick up Mr Marr at his detached home in The Grange, only he wasn't there.'

'And?'

'And the reason he wasn't there was, he'd been told they'd be coming. Gill Templer called the ACC, said they were picking up Marr for questioning. The ACC "suggested" they phone Mr Marr beforehand, as "a courtesy".'

She picked up the water jug, tipped the dregs into her glass. The same waiter started forward, ready to replace the jug, but Rebus waved him back again.

'So Marr did a runner?'

Siobhan nodded. 'Looks like it. His wife says he took the call, and two minutes later when she went to look for him, he wasn't there and neither was the Maserati.'

'Better stick one of the napkins in your pocket,' Rebus suggested. 'Looks like some egg needs wiping from Carswell's face.'

'I can't imagine he'll have fun explaining to the Chief Constable,' Siobhan agreed. Then she watched a grin light up Rebus's face. 'Just what you needed?' she guessed.

'Might help take some of the heat off.'

'Because Carswell will be too busy covering his own arse to find time to kick yours?'

'Eloquently put.'

'It's the college education.'

'So what's happening about Marr?' Rebus nodded towards the waiter, who took a hesitant step forward, unsure if he'd suddenly be expelled again. 'Two coffees,' Rebus told him. The man made a little bow and moved off.

'Not sure,' Siobhan admitted.

'Night before the funeral, could be awkward.'

'High-speed car chase . . . stop and arrest . . .' Siobhan was imagining the scenario. 'Grieving parents wondering why their best friend is suddenly in custody . . .'

'If Carswell's thinking straight, he'll do nothing till the funeral's over. Could be Marr will turn up there anyway.'

'A fond farewell to his secret lover?'

'If Claire Benzie's telling the truth.'

'Why else would he run?'

Rebus stared at her. 'I think you know the answer to that one.'

'You mean if Marr killed her?'

'I thought you had him in the frame.'

She was thoughtful. 'That was before this happened. I don't think Quizmaster would run.'

'Maybe Quizmaster didn't kill Flip Balfour.'

Siobhan nodded. 'That's my point. I had Marr in the frame for Quizmaster.'

'Meaning she was killed by someone else?'

The coffees arrived, and with them the ubiquitous mints. Siobhan dunked hers in the hot liquid, quickly hoisting it into her mouth. Without being asked, the waiter had brought the bill with their coffees.

'Split it down the middle?' Siobhan suggested. Rebus nodded, took three fivers from his pocket.

Outside, he asked how she was getting home.

'My car's at St Leonard's: need a lift?'

'Nice night for a walk,' he said, looking up at the clouds. 'Just promise me you *will* go home, take a break . . .'

'Promise, Mum.'

'And now that you've convinced yourself that Quizmaster didn't kill Flip . . .'

'Yes?'

'Well, you don't have to bother with the game any more, do you?'

She blinked, told him she supposed he was right. But he could see she didn't believe it. The game was *her* part of the case. She couldn't just let it go . . . He knew he'd have felt the same way.

They parted on the pavement, Rebus heading back to the flat. When he got in, he called Jean, but she wasn't at home. Maybe another late night at the Museum, but she wasn't answering there either. He stood in front of his dining table, staring at the case notes there. He'd pinned some sheets to the wall, detailing the four women – Jesperson, Gibbs, Gearing and Farmer. He was trying to answer a question: why would the killer leave the coffins? Okay, they were his 'signature', but that signature had not been recognised. It had taken the best part of thirty years for someone to realise that there even *was* a signature. If the killer had hoped to be identified with his crimes, wouldn't he have repeated the exercise, or tried some other method: a note to the media or the police? So say they weren't a signature as such; say his motive had been ... what? Rebus saw them as little memorials, holding meaning only for the person who'd left them there. And couldn't the same be said for the Arthur's Seat coffins? Why had the person responsible not come forward in some form? Answer: because once found, the coffins had ceased to have meaning for their creator. They'd been memorials, never meant to be found or associated with the Burke and Hare killings ...

Yes, there were connections between those coffins and the ones Jean had identified. Rebus was wary of adding the Falls coffin to the list, but he felt a connection there, too – a looser connection, to be sure, but still powerful.

He'd checked his answering machine, just the one message: his solicitor, concerning a retired couple who would show the flat to potential buyers, relieving him of the burden. He knew he'd have to take his little collage down before then, hide everything away, do some tidying ...

He tried Jean's number again, but there was still no answer. Stuck a Steve Earle album on: *The Hard Way*.

Rebus didn't know of any other ...

'You're lucky I didn't change my name,' Jan Benzie said. Jean had just explained how she'd called every Benzie in the phone book. 'I'm married to Jack McCoist these days.'

They were sitting in the drawing room of a three-storey townhouse in the city's west end, just off Palmerston Place. Jan Benzie was tall and thin, and wore a knee-length black dress with a sparkling brooch just above her right breast. The room reflected her elegance: antiques and polished surfaces, thick walls and floors muffling any sound.

'Thank you for seeing me at such short notice.'

'There's not much I can add to what I told you on the phone.' Jan Benzie sounded distracted, as if part of her was elsewhere. Maybe that was why she'd agreed to the appointment in the first place . . . 'It's been rather a strange day, Miss Burchill,' she said now.

'Oh?'

But Jan Benzie just shrugged one shoulder and asked again if Jean would like something to drink.

'I don't want to keep you. You said Patricia Lovell was a relation?'

'Great-great-grandmother . . . something like that.'

'She died very young, didn't she?'

'You probably know more about her than I do. I'd no idea she was buried at Calton Hill.'

'How many children did she have?'

'Just the one, a girl.'

'Do you know if she died in childbirth?'

'I've no idea.' Jan Benzie laughed at the absurdity of the question.

'I'm sorry,' Jean said, 'I know this must all sound a bit ghoulish . . .'

'A bit. You say you're researching Kennet Lovell?'

Jean nodded. 'Would your family have any of his papers?'

Jan Benzie shook her head. 'None.'

'You've no relatives who might . . . ?'

'I really don't think so, no.' She moved an arm towards the occasional table next to her chair, lifted her cigarette packet and eased one out. 'Do you . . . ?'

Jean shook her head and watched Jan Benzie light the cigarette with a slim gold lighter. The woman seemed to do everything in slow motion. It was like watching a film at the wrong speed.

'It's just that I'm looking for some correspondence between Dr Lovell and his benefactor.'

'I didn't even know there was one.'

'A kirk minister back in Ayrshire.'

'Really?' Jan Benzie said, but Jean could tell she wasn't interested. Right now, the cigarette between her fingers meant more to her than anything else.

Jean decided to plough on. 'There's a portrait of Dr Lovell in Surgeons' Hall. I think maybe it was executed at the minister's behest.'

'Is that so?'

'Have you ever seen it?'

'Can't say that I have.'

'He had several wives, Dr Lovell, did you know that?'

'Three, wasn't it? Not so many, really, in the scheme of things.' Benzie seemed to grow thoughtful. 'I'm on my second husband . . . who's to say it'll stop there?' She examined the ash at the end of her cigarette. 'My first committed suicide, you know.'

'I didn't.'

'No reason why you should.' She paused. 'Don't suppose I can expect the same of Jack.'

Jean wasn't sure what she meant, but Jan Benzie was studying her, seeming to expect some reply. 'I suppose,' Jean said, 'it would look a bit suspicious, losing two husbands.'

'And yet Kennet Lovell can lose three wives . . . ?'

Jean's thinking exactly . . .

Jan Benzie had risen to her feet, walked over to the window. Jean took another look around the room. All the artefacts, the paintings and framed photographs, candlesticks and crystal ashtrays . . . she got the feeling none of it belonged to Benzie. It had come with her marriage to Jack McCoist, part of the baggage he brought.

'Well,' she said, 'I'd better be going. Sorry again to have . . .'

'No trouble,' Benzie said. 'I hope you find what you're looking for.'

Suddenly there were voices out in the hall, and the sound of the front door being closed. The voices began ascending the staircase, coming closer.

'Claire and my husband,' Jan said, sitting back down again, arranging herself the way an artist's model might. The door burst open and Claire Benzie stormed into the room. To Jean's eye, she bore no physical resemblance to her mother, but perhaps that was partly down to her entrance, the way she crackled with energy.

'I don't bloody care,' she was saying. 'They can lock me up if they want, throw away the bloody key!' She was pacing the room as Jack McCoist walked in. He had his wife's slow movements, but they seemed merely the result of fatigue.

'Claire, all I'm saying is . . .' He leaned down to peck his wife's cheek. 'What a bloody awful time we've had,' he informed her. 'Cops crawling over Claire like lice. Is there *any* way you can control your daughter, darling?' His words died as he straightened and saw they had a visitor. Jean was rising to her feet.

'I really should be going,' she said.

'Who the hell's this?' Claire snarled.

'Ms Burchill is from the Museum,' Jan explained. 'We've been talking about Kennet Lovell.'

'Christ, not her as well!' Claire tossed her head back, then dropped on to one of the room's two sofas.

'I'm researching his life,' Jean explained for McCoist's benefit. He was pouring himself a whisky at the drinks cabinet.

'At this time of night?' was all he said.

'His portrait's hanging in some hall somewhere,' Jan Benzie told her daughter. 'Did you know that?'

'Of course I bloody did! It's in the museum at Surgeons' Hall.' She looked at Jean. 'Is that where you're from?'

'No, actually . . .'

'Well, wherever you're from, why don't you piss off back there? I'm just out of police custody and—'

'You will *not* speak like that to a guest in this house!' Jan Benzie yelped, springing from her chair. 'Jack, tell her.'

'Look, I really should . . .' Jean's words were swamped as

415

a three-way argument started. She backed away, heading for the door.

'You've no bloody right . . . !'

'Christ, anyone would think it was *you* they interrogated!'

'That's still no excuse for . . .'

'Just one quiet drink, is that too much to . . .'

They didn't seem to notice as Jean opened the door, closing it again behind her. She walked down the carpeted stairs on tiptoe, and opened the front door as quietly as she could, escaping into the street, where, finally, she let out a huge breath of air. Walking away, she glanced back towards the drawing-room window, but couldn't see anything. The houses here had walls so thick, they could double as padded cells, and it felt like that was just what she'd escaped from.

Claire Benzie's temper had been something to behold.

13

Wednesday morning, there was still no sign of Ranald Marr. His wife Dorothy had called Junipers and spoken to John Balfour's PA. She was reminded in no uncertain terms that the family had a funeral to see to, and that the PA didn't feel able to disturb either Mr or Mrs Balfour further until some time thereafter.

'They've lost a daughter, you know,' the PA said haughtily.

'And I've lost my fucking husband, you bitch!' Dorothy Marr spat back, recoiling ever so slightly afterwards as she realised it was probably the first time she'd used a swear-word in her adult life. But it was too late to apologise: the PA had already put down the phone and was informing a lesser member of the Balfour staff not to accept any further calls from Mrs Marr.

Junipers itself was full of people: family members and friends were gathering there. Some, having travelled far, had stayed the previous night, and were now wandering the many corridors in search of something resembling breakfast. Mrs Dolan the cook had decided that hot food would not be seemly on such a day, so her usual vapour trail of sausage, bacon and eggs or pungent kedgeree could not be followed. In the dining room sat an array of cereal packets and preserves, the latter home-made but not including Mrs Dolan's blackcurrant and apple, which had been Flip's favourite since childhood. She'd left that particular jar back in the pantry. Last time anyone had eaten some, it had been Flip herself on one of her infrequent visits.

Mrs Dolan was telling her daughter Catriona as much, as Catriona comforted her and handed over another paper handkerchief. One of the guests, sent to inquire whether coffee and cold milk might be available, put his head round the kitchen door, but withdrew again, embarrassed to be witnessing the indomitable Mrs Dolan brought low like this.

In the library, John Balfour was telling his wife that he didn't want 'any bloody police thickos' at the cemetery.

'But, John, they've all worked so hard,' his wife was saying, 'and they've asked to be there. Surely they've as much right as . . .' Her voice died away.

'As who?' His voice had grown less angry, but suddenly colder.

'Well,' his wife said, 'all these people we don't know . . .'

'You mean people *I* know? You've met them at parties, functions. Jackie, for Christ's sake, they want to pay their respects.'

His wife nodded and stayed quiet. After the funeral, there would be a buffet lunch back at Junipers, not just for close family but for all her husband's associates and acquaintances, nearly seventy of them. Jacqueline had wanted a much smaller affair, something that could be accommodated in the dining room. As it was, they'd had to order a marquee, which had been installed on the back lawn. An Edinburgh firm – run by another of her husband's clients, no doubt – was doing the catering. The lady owner was busy out there now, supervising the unloading of tables, cloths, crockery and cutlery from what seemed a never-ending series of small vans. Jacqueline's small victory so far had been to widen the circle of invitees to include Flip's own friends, though this had not been without its awkward moments. David Costello, for example, would have to be invited, along with his parents, though she'd never liked David and felt he held the family in mild distaste. She was hoping they would either fail to turn up, or would not linger.

'Silver lining, in a way,' John was droning on, hardly aware of her presence in the room. 'Something like this, it binds them all to Balfour's, makes it harder for them to make a move elsewhere . . .'

Jacqueline rose shakily to her feet.

'We're burying our daughter, John! This isn't about your bloody *business*! Flip's not part of some ... commercial transaction!'

Balfour glanced towards the door, making sure it was closed. 'Keep your voice down, woman. It was only a ... I didn't mean ...' He slumped on to the sofa suddenly, face in his hands. 'You're right, I wasn't thinking ... God help me.'

His wife sat down next to him, took his hands and lowered them from his face. 'God help both of us, John,' she said.

Steve Holly had managed to persuade his boss at the paper's Glasgow HQ that he needed to be on the scene as early as possible. He'd also, knowing the geographical illiteracy rampant in Scotland, managed to persuade him that Falls was a lot further away from Edinburgh than was actually the case, and that Greywalls Hotel would make an ideal overnight stop. He hadn't bothered explaining that Greywalls was in Gullane, and consequently wasn't much more than a half-hour's drive from Edinburgh, or that Gullane, as the crow flew, wasn't exactly between Falls and Edinburgh. But what did it matter? He'd had his overnighter, joined by his girlfriend Gina, who wasn't really his girlfriend but just someone he'd dated a few times over the previous three months. Gina had been keen, but had worried about getting to work the next morning, so then Steve had fixed a taxi for her. He knew how he'd wing it, too: he'd say his car broke down and he'd used the taxi himself to get back to town ...

After a fabulous dinner and a walk around the garden – designed by someone called Jekyll apparently – Steve and Gina had made ample use of their ample bed before sleeping like logs, so that the first they knew of it, Gina's cab was waiting and Steve had to tuck into breakfast alone, which would have been his preference anyway. But then the first disappointment: the newspapers ... all of them broadsheets. He'd stopped in Gullane and bought the competition on his way out to Falls, leaving them on the passenger seat and flicking through them as he drove, cars flashing and tooting at him as he took more than his share of road.

'Bollocks!' he'd yelled from his window, giving each sheep-shagger and country bumpkin the finger as he got on the mobile, wanting to make sure Tony the photographer was primed for the cemetery shoot. He knew Tony had been out to Falls a couple of times to see Bev, or 'the Potty Potter' as Steve had come to call her. He thought Tony reckoned he was in there. His advice had been simple: 'She's a nutter, mate – you might get a shag, but two-to-one you wake up with your old wotsit sliced off and lying beside you in the bed.' To which Tony had laughed and said he just wanted to persuade Bev into some 'art poses' for his 'portfolio'. So when Steve got through to Tony this morning, his first words, as usual, were:

'Got her on your potter's wheel yet, mate?'

Then, also as usual, he started laughing at his own joke, which was what he was doing when he happened to glance in the rearview and caught the cop car up his bahooky, lights flashing. No idea how long it had been there.

'Have to call you back, Tony,' he said, braking and pulling on to the verge. 'Just make sure you get to the church on time.'

'Morning, officers,' he said, stepping out of the car.

'And a good morning to you, Mr Holly,' one of the uniforms said.

Which was when Steve Holly remembered he wasn't exactly flavour of the month with the Lothian and Borders Police.

Ten minutes later, he was back on the road, the cops tailing him to prevent, as they'd put it themselves, 'further infractions'. When his mobile went, he thought about not answering, but it was Glasgow, so he mirror-signal-manoeuvred back on to the verge and took the call, watching the cops stop ten yards back.

'Yes?' he said.

'Think you're a clever little bastard, don't you, Stevie Boy?'

His boss.

'Not right this second, no,' Steve Holly said.

'Friend of mine plays golf in Gullane. It's practically *in* Edinburgh, you turd. And the same goes for Falls. So any notion you had of turning that little trip round as expenses can now be stuck well and truly up your arse.'

'No problem.'

'Where are you anyway?'

Holly looked around at fields and dry-stane dykes. There was the distant drone of a tractor.

'I'm scoping out the cemetery, waiting for Tony to turn up. I'll head to Junipers in a couple of mins, follow them to the church.'

'Oh aye? Care to confirm that?'

'Confirm what?'

'*That outright fucking lie that just tripped off your tongue!*'

Holly licked his lips. 'I don't follow.' What was it, did the paper have a tracking device fixed to his car?

'Tony phoned the picture editor not five minutes ago. The picture editor who happened to be standing next to my bloody desk. Guess where your missing photographer was calling from?'

Holly said nothing.

'Go on, take a wild stab, because that's what I'm going to take at you next time I see you.'

'The cemetery?' Holly said.

'That your final answer? Maybe you want to phone a friend.'

Holly felt his anger rise: best defence was attack, right? 'Look,' he hissed, 'I've just given your paper the story of the year, scooped every competitor you've got, bar none. And this is how you go and treat me? Well, stuff your miserable paper and stuff *you*. Get someone else out here to cover the funeral, someone who knows the story the way I do. Meantime I think maybe I'll be making a couple of calls to the competition – on my time, my phone bill. If that's okay with you, you chiselling bastard. And if you want to know why I'm not at the cemetery, I'll tell you. It's because I've been stopped by a couple of Lothian's finest. They won't let me shake them off now I've gone and shat on them in print. You want the patrol car's licence plate? Give me a second, maybe they'll speak to you themselves!'

Holly shut up, but made sure he was breathing hard into the mouthpiece.

'For once,' the voice from Glasgow eventually said, 'and maybe they should carve this on my tombstone, I think I may actually have heard Steve Holly tell the truth.' There was another pause, and then a chuckle. 'We've got them worried then?'

We . . . Steve Holly knew he was home and dry.

'I've got what looks like a permanent escort, just in case I'm thinking of taking a hand off the wheel to pick my nose.'

'So you're not driving as we speak?'

'Up on the verge, indicators going. And, with all due respect, boss, that's another five minutes I've just wasted talking to you . . . Not that I don't always enjoy our little tête-à-têtes.'

Another chuckle. 'Ah, fuck it, bit of steam needs to be let off now and then, eh? Tell you what, put that hotel through to accounts, okay?'

'Right, boss.'

'And get your raggedy arse back on the road.'

'Ten-four, boss. This is the shining sword of truth, signing off.' Holly cut the call, exhaled heavily, and did what he'd been told to do: got his raggedy arse back on that road . . .

The village of Falls had neither church nor cemetery, but there was a small, little-used church – more the size of a chapel, really – just off the road between Falls and Causland. The family had picked the spot and arranged everything, but secretly those friends of Flip's who'd been able to attend thought the tranquillity and isolation out of keeping with Flip's character. They couldn't help feeling she'd have wanted something livelier, somewhere in the city itself, where people walked their dogs or went for a Sunday stroll, and where, in darkness, lively biker parties and furtive couplings might take place.

The graveyard here was too neat and compact, the graves too old and looked after. Flip would have wanted wild, straggling creepers and mosses, briar bushes and long wet grass. But then, when they considered, they realised she wouldn't care one way or the other, because she was dead and that was the end of it. At that moment, perhaps for the first time, they were able to separate loss from numb shock, and to feel the pangs of a life left incomplete.

There were too many people for the church. The doors were left open so that the short service could be heard outside. The day was cool, the ground heavy with dew. Birds played in the trees, agitated at this unique invasion. Cars lined the main road, the hearse having discreetly pulled away, heading back to Edinburgh. Liveried drivers stood beside several of the vehicles, cigarettes in hands. Rollers, Mercs, Jags . . .

Nominally, the family had worshipped in a city church, and the minister had been persuaded to lead the service, though he was used to seeing the Balfours only at Christmas, and then not for the past two or three years. He was a thorough man, who had checked his script with the mother and father, asking solicitous questions whose answers would help him bulk out Flip's biography, but he was also bemused by the attentions of the media. Being used to encountering cameras only at weddings and christenings, when one was pointed in his direction for the first time, he gave a beaming smile, only afterwards realising the inappropriateness of his action. These were not carnationed relatives but journalists, keeping their distance from the solemnities and their lenses trained only so far. Though the graveyard itself could be viewed clearly from the roadway, there'd be no photos of the coffin being lowered, or the parents by the graveside. Permission had been granted for one photograph only: of the coffin being carried from the church.

Of course, once the mourners were off church property, they would be reckoned fair game again.

'Parasites,' one of the guests, a Balfour's client of long standing, had hissed. All the same, he knew he'd be buying more than one paper next morning, just to see if he figured in any of the spreads.

With the pews and side aisles being crammed, the police officers present kept their own distance, to the back of the crowd at the church doors. Assistant Chief Constable Colin Carswell stood with hands clasped in front of him, head slightly bowed. Detective Chief Superintendent Gill Templer was next to Detective Inspector Bill Pryde, just behind Carswell. Other officers were further off still, patrolling what grounds there were. Flip's killer was still out there, and so, if the two could be differentiated, was Ranald Marr. Inside the church, John Balfour kept turning his head, examining each face as if looking for someone. Only those who knew the workings of Balfour's Bank guessed who this missing face belonged to . . .

John Rebus was standing by the far wall, dressed in his good suit and a long green raincoat, its collar up. He kept thinking how bleak the surroundings were: typical bare hillside dotted with sheep; dull yellow gorse bushes. He'd read the noticeboard just inside the churchyard gate. It told him the building dated back to the seventeenth century, and that local farmers had raised the contributions necessary for its construction. At least one Templar grave had been found inside the low stone wall, leading historians to believe that a former chapel and burying place must have rested on this site.

'The headstone from this Templar grave,' he'd read, 'can now be seen in the Museum of Scotland.'

He'd thought then of Jean, who, walking in a place like this, would notice things he couldn't see, telltale signs from the past. But then Gill had come towards him, face set, hands deep in pockets, and had asked what he thought he was doing there.

'Paying my respects.'

He'd noticed Carswell move his head slightly, noting Rebus's presence.

'Unless there's a law against it,' he'd added, walking away.

Siobhan was about fifty yards from him, but so far had acknowledged his presence only with a wave of her gloved hand. Her eyes were on the hillside, as if she thought the killer might suddenly reveal himself there. Rebus had his doubts. As the service ended, the coffin was carried out, and the cameras began their short work. The journalists present were studying the scene carefully, jotting mental paragraphs, or else speaking very quietly into mobile phones. Idly, Rebus wondered which service they were using: he still couldn't get a signal out here on his.

The TV cameras, which had recorded the exit of the pall-bearers from the church, switched off and hung from their cameramen's arms. There was silence outside the church-yard walls as within, broken only by the slow crunching of feet over gravel and the occasional sob from a mourner.

John Balfour had one arm around his wife. Some of Flip's student friends were hugging each other, faces buried in shoulders and chests. Rebus recognised faces: Tristram and Tina, Albert and Camille ... No sign of Claire Benzie. He spotted some of Flip's neighbours, too, including Professor Devlin, who had come bustling up to talk to him earlier, asking about the coffins, whether there'd been any progress. When Rebus had shaken his head, Devlin had asked how he was feeling.

'Only, I sense a certain frustration,' the old man had said.

'That's how it is sometimes.'

Devlin had studied him. 'I wouldn't have taken you for a pragmatist, Inspector.'

'I've always found pessimism a great comforter,' Rebus had told him, moving away.

Now, Rebus watched the rest of the procession. There was a smattering of politicians, including the MSP Seona Grieve. David Costello preceded his parents out of the church, blinking at the sudden light, digging sunglasses from his breast pocket and slipping them on.

Victim's eyes catching the likeness of the killer . . .

Anyone looking at David Costello would see only their own reflection. Was that precisely what Costello wanted them to see? Behind him, his mother and father walked their separate and very distinct walks, more like nodding acquaintances than spouses. As the crowd lost its shape, David found himself next to Professor Devlin. Devlin stuck out a hand for David to shake, but the young man just stared at it, until Devlin withdrew and patted his arm instead.

But now something was happening . . . A car arriving, door slamming, and a man dressed casually – woollen V-neck and grey slacks – jogging up the road and in through the churchyard gates. Rebus recognised an unshaven and bleary-eyed Ranald Marr, guessed at once that Marr had slept in his Maserati, saw Steve Holly's face crease as he wondered what was going on. The procession had just reached the graveside when Marr caught it up. He walked straight to the front and stood in front of John and Jacqueline Balfour. Balfour released his grip on his wife, hugged Marr instead, the gesture returned. Templer and Pryde were looking to Colin Carswell, who made a motion with his hands, palms down. Easy, he was saying. We go easy.

Rebus didn't think any of the reporters had noticed Carswell; too busy trying to make sense of this curious interruption. And then he saw that Siobhan was staring into the grave, eyes flickering to the coffin and back, as if she could see something there. All at once, she turned her back on proceedings and started walking between the tombstones, as if searching for something she'd dropped.

'For I am the Resurrection and the Life,' the minister was saying. Marr was standing beside John Balfour now, eyes on the coffin and nothing else. Off to one side, Siobhan was still moving between the graves. Rebus didn't think any of the reporters could see her: the mourners formed a barrier between her and them. She crouched down in front of one stubby gravestone, seemed to be reading its inscription. Then she rose to her feet again and moved off, but more slowly now, without the same sense of urgency. When she turned, she saw that Rebus was watching her. She flashed him a quick smile, which for some reason he didn't find reassuring. Then she was on the move again, round to the rear of the mourning party, and out of his immediate sight.

Carswell was muttering something to Gill Templer: instructions on how to deal with Marr. Rebus knew they'd probably let him leave the churchyard, but insist on accompanying him immediately afterwards. Maybe they'd head to Junipers, do the questioning there; more likely, Marr wouldn't be seeing the marquee and the finger buffet. Instead, it would be an interview room at Gayfield and a mug of greyish tea.

'Ashes to ashes . . .'

Rebus couldn't help it; found the first few bars of the Bowie tune bouncing through his head.

A couple of the reporters were already preparing to head off, either back to the city or up the road to Junipers, where they could make a tally of the invited guests. Rebus slipped his hands into the pockets of the raincoat, started a slow patrol of the churchyard's perimeter. Earth was raining on to Philippa Balfour's coffin, the last rain the polished wood would ever feel. Her mother sent a cry up into the sky. It was carried by the breeze towards the surrounding hills.

Rebus found himself standing in front of a small headstone. Its owner had lived from 1876 to 1937. Not quite sixty-one when he died, missing the worst of Hitler, and maybe just too old to have fought in the First World War. He'd been a carpenter, probably serving the surrounding farms. For a second, Rebus remembered the coffin-maker. Then he went back to the name on the headstone – Francis Campbell Finlay – and had to suppress a smile. Siobhan had looked at the box in which lay the remains of Flip Balfour, and she'd thought: boxing. Then she'd looked at the grave itself and realised that it was a place where the sun didn't shine. Quizmaster's clue had been leading her right here, but it was only once she'd arrived that she'd been able to work it out. She'd gone looking for Frank Finlay, and found him. Rebus wondered what else she'd found when she crouched in front of the headstone. He glanced back to where the mourners were departing the churchyard, the chauffeurs stubbing out their cigarettes and preparing to open car doors. He couldn't see Siobhan, but Carswell himself had taken Ranald Marr to one side so they could have a discussion, Carswell doing the talking, Marr responding with resigned nods of the head. When Carswell put out his hand, Marr dropped his car keys into it.

Rebus was the last to leave. Some of the cars were making three-point turns. A tractor-trailer was waiting to get past. Rebus didn't recognise the driver. Siobhan was standing on the verge, leaning her arms on her car roof, in no hurry. Rebus crossed the road, nodded a greeting.

'Thought we might see you here,' was all she said. Rebus leaned one of his own arms on the roof. 'Get a bollocking, did you?'

'Like I told Gill, it's not against the law.'

'You saw Marr arriving?'

Rebus nodded. 'What's the story?'

'Carswell's driving him up to the house. Marr wants a couple of minutes with Balfour to explain things.'

'What things?'

'We're next in line.'

'Doesn't sound to me like he's about to confess to murder.'

'No,' she said.

'I was wondering . . .' Rebus let the utterance fade.

She tore her eyes away from the spectacle of Carswell attempting a three-pointer in the Maserati. 'Yes?'

'The latest clue: Stricture. Any more ideas?' Stricture, he was thinking, as in confinement. There was nothing in life quite as confining as a coffin . . .

She blinked a couple of times, then shook her head. 'What about you?'

'I did wonder if "boxing" might mean putting things in boxes.'

'Mmm.' She looked thoughtful. 'Maybe.'

'Want me to keep trying?'

'Can't do any harm.' The Maserati was roaring down the road, Carswell having applied just too much pressure to the accelerator.

'I suppose not.' Rebus turned to face her. 'You heading on to Junipers?'

She shook her head. 'Back to St Leonard's.'

'Things to do, eh?'

She took her arms off the car roof, slid her right hand into the pocket of her black Barbour jacket. 'Things to do,' she agreed.

Rebus noticed that she held the car keys in her left hand. He wondered what was in that right-hand pocket.

'Ca' canny then, eh?' he said.

'See you back at the ranch.'

'I'm still on the blacklist, remember?'

She took her hand out of her pocket, opened her driver's-side door. 'Right,' she said, getting in. He leaned down to peer through the window. She offered him a brief smile and nothing more. He took a step back as the car came to life, wheels sliding before finding tarmac.

She'd done just what he'd have done: kept to herself whatever it was she'd found. Rebus jogged to where his own car was parked and made set to follow.

Driving back through Falls, Rebus slowed a little outside Bev Dodds's cottage. He'd half expected to see her at the funeral. The interment had brought with it a number of sightseers, though police cars each end of the road had dissuaded the casual intruder. Parking space was at a premium in the village, too, though most Wednesdays he had the feeling there'd be room to spare. The potter's makeshift sign had been replaced with something more eye-catching and professionally made. Rebus pushed a little harder on the accelerator, keeping Siobhan's car in view. The coffins were still in the bottom drawer of his desk. He knew Dodds wanted the one from Falls back in her possession. Maybe he'd be charitable, pick it up this afternoon and drop it off Thursday or Friday. One more excuse to visit the ranch, where he could have another go at Siobhan – always supposing that was where she was headed . . .

He remembered there was a half-bottle of whisky under his driver's seat. He really did feel like a drink – it was what you did after funerals. The alcohol washed away death's inevitability. 'Tempting,' he said to himself, slotting home a cassette tape. Early Alex Harvey: 'The Faith Healer'. Problem was, early Alex Harvey wasn't too far removed from late Alex Harvey. He wondered how big a part alcohol had played in the Glasgow singer's demise. You started making a line of booze deaths, it would just refuse ever to come to an end . . .

'You think I killed her, don't you?'

Three of them in the interview room. An unnatural hush outside the door: whispers and tippy-toes and phones snatched up almost before they could ring. Gill Templer, Bill Pryde, and Ranald Marr.

'Let's not jump to conclusions, Mr Marr,' Gill said.

'Isn't that what you're doing?'

'Just a few follow-up questions, sir,' Bill Pryde said.

Marr snorted, not inclined to grace such a remark with anything more.

'How long did you know Philippa Balfour, Mr Marr?'

He looked to Gill Templer. 'Since she was born. I was her godfather.'

Gill made a note of this. 'And when did the two of you start feeling a physical attraction for one another?'

'Who says we did?'

'Why did you leave home like that, Mr Marr?'

'It's been a very stressful time. Look,' Marr shifted in his chair, 'should I have a lawyer present, do you think?'

'As you were informed earlier, that's entirely up to you.'

Marr thought about it, then shrugged. 'Proceed,' he said.

'Were you having a relationship with Philippa Balfour?'

'What sort of relationship?'

Bill Pryde's voice was a bear-growl. 'The sort her dad would string you up by the balls for.'

'I think I take your meaning.' Marr looked as though he was thinking through his answer. 'Here's what I will say: I've spoken to John Balfour and he has taken a responsible attitude to that conversation. The talk we had – whatever I said to him – has no bearing on this case. And that's pretty much it.' He sat back in his chair.

'Fucking your own goddaughter,' Bill Pryde said disgustedly.

'DI Pryde!' Gill Templer said by way of warning. Then, to Marr: 'I apologise for my colleague's outburst.'

'Apology accepted.'

'It's just that he has a bit more trouble hiding his revulsion and contempt than I do.'

Marr almost smiled.

'And as to whether something does or does not have "bearing" on a case is up to us to decide, wouldn't you say, sir?'

Colour rose to Marr's cheeks, but he wasn't going to take the bait. He shrugged merely, and folded his arms to let them know that, so far as he was concerned, the discussion was now at an end.

'A moment of your time, DI Pryde,' Gill said, angling her head towards the door. As they stepped out of the room, two uniforms stepped in to stand guard. Officers were already homing in, so Gill pushed Pryde through the door marked 'Ladies', and stood with her back against the door to deter the curious.

'Well?' she asked.

'Nice place,' Pryde said, looking around. He walked over to the washbasin and fished the waste-bin out from beneath, spitting his venerable collection of gum into it and pulling two fresh sticks from their packet.

'They've stitched something up between them' he said at last, admiring his features in the mirror.

'Yes,' Gill agreed. 'We should have brought him straight here.'

'Carswell's blooper,' Pryde said, 'yet again.'

Gill nodded. 'You think he confessed to Balfour?'

'I think he probably said something. He's had all night to come up with the right way of saying it: "John, it just happened . . . it was a long time ago and just the once . . . I'm so sorry." Spouses say it all the time.'

Gill almost smiled. Pryde spoke as if from experience.

'And Balfour didn't string him up by the balls?'

Pryde shook his head slowly. 'The more I hear about John Balfour, the less I like him. Bank's looking like going down the toilet, house filled with account-holders . . . his best friend walks up and says, in so many words, that he's been getting his end away with the daughter, and what does Balfour do? He does a deal.'

'The pair of them keeping quiet, keeping the lid on it?'

It was Pryde's turn to nod. 'Because the alternative is scandal, resignation, public fisticuffs and the collapse of all they hold dearest: namely, cold hard cash.'

'Then we'll be hard pushed to get anything out of him.'

Pryde looked at her. 'Unless we push him really hard.'

'I'm not sure Mr Carswell would like that.'

'With respect, DCS Templer, Mr Carswell couldn't find his own arse if it didn't come with a label marked "Insert tongue here".'

'That's not the sort of language I can countenance,' Gill said with something approaching a grin. There was pressure on the door from outside, and she yelled for whoever was there to stop it.

'I'm desperate!' a female voice called back.

'Me too,' Bill Pryde said with a wink, 'but maybe I should head for the more rudimentary shores of the Gents'.' As Gill nodded and began to open the door, he took a final, wistful look round. 'Though it'll be in my thoughts from now on, believe me. A man could get used to luxury like this . . .'

Back in the interview room, Ranald Marr had the look of someone who knew he'd soon be back behind the wheel of his Maserati. Gill, unable to bear such palpable smugness, decided to play her last card.

'Your affair with Philippa, it lasted quite a while, didn't it?'

'God, are we back to that again,' Marr said, rolling his eyes.

'Fairly common knowledge, too. Philippa told Claire Benzie all about it.'

'Is that what Claire Benzie says? I seem to have been here before. That little madam would say anything to hurt Balfour's.'

Gill was shaking her head. 'I don't think so, because knowing what she did, she could have used it at any time: one call to John Balfour, and she'd have blown the whole secret wide open. She didn't do that, Mr Marr. I can only assume it's because Claire has some principles.'

'Or she was biding her time.'

'Maybe so.'

'Is that what this boils down to: my word against hers?'

'There's the fact that you were keen to explain to Philippa how to erase e-mails.'

'Which I've also explained to your officers.'

'Yes, but now we know the real reason why you did it.'

Marr tried staring her out, but it wasn't going to work. He couldn't know that Gill had interviewed more than a dozen killers in the course of her CID career. She'd been stared at by eyes filled with fire, eyes turned insane. He dropped his gaze and his shoulders slumped.

'Look,' he said, 'there's one thing . . .'

'We're waiting, Mr Marr,' Bill Pryde said, sitting as straight in his chair as a kirk elder.

'I . . . didn't tell the whole truth about the game Flip was involved in.'

'You haven't told the whole truth about anything,' Pryde interrupted, but Gill quietened him with a look. Not that it mattered; Marr hadn't been listening.

'I didn't know it *was* a game,' he was saying, 'not back then. It was just a question . . . maybe a crossword clue, that's what I thought.'

'So she did bring one of the clues to you?'

Marr nodded. 'The mason's dream. She thought I might know what it meant.'

'And why would she think that?'

He managed the ghost of a smile. 'She was always overestimating me. She was . . . I don't think you've been getting anything like the whole picture of the kind of person Flip was. I know what you saw at first: spoilt little rich kid, spending her university days gazing at a few paintings, then graduating and marrying someone with even more money.' He was shaking his head. 'That wasn't Flip at all. Maybe it was one side to her, but she was complex, always capable of surprising you. Like with this puzzle thing, on the one hand I was dumbstruck when I heard about it, but on the other . . . in many ways it's *so* much like Flip. She would take these sudden interests, passions in things. For years, she'd been going to the zoo once a week on her own, just about *every* week, and I only found out by chance, a few months back. I was leaving a meeting at the Posthouse Hotel and she was coming out of the zoo, practically next door.' He looked up at them. 'Do you see?'

Gill wasn't at all sure that she did, but she nodded anyway. 'Go on,' she said. But it was as though her words had broken the spell. Marr paused for breath, then seemed to lose some of his animation.

'She was . . .' His mouth opened and closed, but soundlessly. Then he shook his head. 'I'm tired and I want to go home. I have some things I need to talk about with Dorothy.'

'Are you okay to drive?' Gill asked.

'Perfectly.' He took a deep breath. But when he looked at her again, tears were welling in his eyes. 'Oh, Christ,' he said, 'I've made such an utter balls-up, haven't I? And I'd do it again and again and again if it meant I had those same moments with her.'

'Rehearsing what you're going to say to the missus?' Pryde said coolly. Only then did Gill realise that she alone had been affected by Marr's story. As if to stress his point,

Pryde blew out something approaching a bubble, which popped with an audible clack.

'My God,' Marr said, almost with a sense of awe, 'I hope and pray I never grow a skin as thick as yours.'

'You're the one shagging his pal's daughter all these years. Compared to me, Mr Marr, you're a fucking armadillo.'

This time, Gill had to draw her colleague from the interview room by his arm.

Rebus walked through St Leonard's like the spectre at the feast. The feeling was, between Marr and Claire Benzie, they'd get something. Surely to hell they'd get *something*.

'Not if you haven't worked for it,' Rebus muttered. Not that anyone was listening. He found the coffins in his drawer, along with some paperwork and a used coffee beaker someone too lazy to find a bin had placed there. Easing himself into the Farmer's chair, he drew the coffins out and laid them on his desk, pushing aside more paperwork to make room. He could feel a killer slipping through his fingers. Problem was, for Rebus to get a second chance would mean some new victim turning up, and he wasn't sure he wanted that. The evidence he'd taken home, the notes pinned to his wall – he couldn't fool himself, it didn't amount to evidence at all. It was a jumble of coincidence and speculation, a thin gossamer pattern created almost from air, the merest flutter of breath beginning to snap its tensed threads. For all he knew, Betty-Anne Jesperson had eloped with her secret lover, while Hazel Gibbs had staggered drunkenly on the bank of White Cart Water and slipped in, knocking herself unconscious. Maybe Paula Gearing had hidden her depression well, walking into the sea of her own volition. And the schoolgirl Caroline Farmer, could she have started a new life in some English city, far from small-town Scottish teenage blues?

So what if someone had left coffins nearby? He couldn't even be sure it was the same person each time; only had the carpenter's word for it. And with the autopsy evidence, there

was no way to prove any crime had been committed at all
. . . not until the Falls coffin. Another break in the pattern:
Flip Balfour was the first victim who could definitely be said
to have perished at the hands of an attacker.

He held his head in his hands, felt that if he took them
away it might explode. Too many ghosts, too many ifs and
buts. Too much pain and grieving, loss and guilt. It was the
sort of thing he'd have taken to Conor Leary once upon a
night. Now, he didn't think he had anyone to turn to . . .

But it was a male voice which answered Jean's extension.
'Sorry,' the man said, 'she's been keeping her head down
lately.'

'You're busy over there then?'

'Not particularly. Jean's off on one of her little mystery
trips.'

'Oh?'

The man laughed. 'I don't mean a bus tour or anything.
She gets these projects going from time to time. They could
set off a bomb in the building and Jean would be the last to
know.'

Rebus smiled: the man could have been talking about *him*.
But Jean hadn't mentioned that she was busy with anything
outside her normal work. Not that it was any of his
business . . .

'So what's she up to this time?' he asked.

'Mmm, let me see . . . Burke and Hare, Dr Knox and all
that period.'

'The Resurrectionists?'

'Curious term that, don't you think? I mean, they didn't
do much resurrecting, did they, not as any good Christian
would understand it?'

'True enough.' The man was annoying Rebus; something
about his manner, his tone of voice. It even annoyed him
that the man was giving information away so easily. He
hadn't even asked who Rebus was. If Steve Holly ever
managed to contact this guy, he'd have everything he could
possibly want on Jean, probably down to her home address
and phone number.

'But she really seemed to be focusing on this doctor who carried out the post-mortem on Burke. What's his name again . . . ?'

Rebus remembered the portrait in Surgeons' Hall. 'Kennet Lovell?' he said.

'That's right.' The man seemed slightly put out that Rebus knew. 'Are you helping Jean? Want me to leave her a message.'

'You don't happen to know where she is?'

'She doesn't always confide in me.'

Just as well, Rebus felt like saying. Instead he told the man there was no message, and put down the phone. Devlin had told Jean about Kennet Lovell, expounding his theory that Lovell had left the coffins on Arthur's Seat. Obviously she was following this up. All the same, he wondered why she hadn't said anything . . .

He stared at the desk opposite, the one Wylie had been using. It was piled high with documents. Narrowing his eyes, he rose from his desk and walked over, started lifting piles of paper from the top.

Right at the bottom were the autopsy notes from Hazel Gibbs and Paula Gearing. He'd meant to send them back. In the back room of the Ox, Professor Devlin had specified that they should be returned. Quite right, too. They weren't doing anyone any good here, and might be lost forever or mis-filed if allowed to be smothered by the paperwork generated by Flip Balfour's murder.

Rebus placed them on his own desk, then cleared all the extraneous paperwork on to the desk one along. The coffins went back into his bottom drawer, all except the one from Falls, which he placed in a Haddow's carrier bag. Over at the photocopier, he lifted a sheet of A4 from the tray – it was the only place in the whole CID suite you could ever find spare paper. On it he wrote: COULD SOMEONE PLEASE SEND THESE ON AS SPECIFIED, PREFERABLY BY FRIDAY? CHEERS, J.R.

Looking around, it struck him that although he'd followed

Siobhan's car into the car park, there was no sign of her now.

'Said she was headed down Gayfield Square,' a colleague explained.

'When?'

'Five minutes ago.'

While he'd been on the phone, listening to gossip.

'Thanks,' he said, sprinting out to his car.

There was no quick route to Gayfield Square, so Rebus took a few liberties with traffic lights and junctions. Parking, he couldn't see her car. But when he dashed indoors, she was standing right there, talking to Grant Hood, who was wearing what looked like another new suit and looking suspiciously tanned.

'Been out in the sun, Grant?' Rebus asked. 'Thought that office of yours at the Big House didn't have so much as a window?'

Self-consciously, Grant put a hand to his cheek. 'I might have caught a few rays.' He made a show of spotting someone across the room. 'Sorry, got to . . .' And he was off.

'Our Grant's beginning to worry me,' Rebus said.

'What do you reckon: fake tan or one of those sun bed studios?'

Rebus shook his head slowly, unable to decide. Glancing back, catching them watching him, Grant butted into another conversation, as if these were the people he'd wanted to speak to. Rebus eased himself up on to a desk.

'Anything happening?' he asked.

'Ranald Marr's already been released. All we got out of him was that Flip *did* ask him about that masonic clue.'

'And his excuse for lying to us . . . ?'

She shrugged. 'I wasn't there, so I can't say.' She seemed jumpy.

'Why don't you sit down?' She shook her head. 'Things to do?' he guessed.

'That's right.'

'Such as?'

'What?'

He repeated the question. She fixed her eyes on him. 'Excuse me,' she said, 'but for an officer under suspension, aren't you spending an awful lot of time in the office?'

'Something I forgot, I came to retrieve it.' As the words came out, he realised he *had* forgotten something: the Falls coffin, still in its carrier bag at St Leonard's. 'Is there maybe anything *you've* forgotten, Siobhan?'

'Such as?'

'Forgetting to share your find with the rest of the team.'

'I don't think so.'

'You did find something then? At Francis Finlay's grave?'

'John . . .' Her eyes were avoiding his now. 'You're off the case.'

'Maybe so. You, on the other hand, are on the case but off your trolley.'

'You've no right to say that.' She still wasn't looking at him.

'I think I have.'

'Then prove it.'

'DI Rebus!' The voice of authority: Colin Carswell, standing twenty yards away in the doorway. 'If you'd be so kind as to spare me a moment . . .'

Rebus looked at Siobhan. 'To be continued,' he said. Then he got up and left the room. Carswell was waiting for him in Gill Templer's cramped office. Gill was there too, standing with arms folded. Carswell was already making himself comfortable behind the desk, eyes showing dismay at the amount of clutter accumulated since his last visit.

'So, DI Rebus, what can we do for you?' he asked.

'Just something I had to pick up.'

'Nothing contagious, I trust.' Carswell offered a thin smile.

'That's a good one, sir,' Rebus said coldly.

'John,' Gill interrupted, 'you're supposed to be at home.'

He nodded. 'It's hard though, with all these exciting developments.' His eyes stayed on Carswell. 'Like warning Marr he was about to be picked up, and now I hear he was allowed ten minutes with John Balfour before we interviewed him. Good calls, sir.'

'Sticks and stones, Rebus,' Carswell said.

'You name the time and place.'

'John . . .' Gill Templer again. 'I don't think this is going to get us anywhere, do you?'

'I want back on the case.'

Carswell just snorted. Rebus turned to Gill.

'Siobhan's playing a wild card. I think she's back in touch with Quizmaster, maybe for a meet.'

'How do you know?'

'Call it an educated guess.' He glanced towards Carswell. 'And before you make some gag about intelligence not being my strong point, let me agree with you. But on this, I think I'm right.'

'He's sent another clue?' Gill was hooked.

'At the churchyard this morning.'

She narrowed her eyes. 'One of the mourners?'

'It could have been left any time. Thing is, Siobhan's been wanting a meeting.'

'And?'

'And she's standing around in the Inquiry Room, just biding her time.'

Gill nodded slowly. 'If it was a new clue, she'd be busy trying to work it out . . .'

'Hang on, hang on,' Carswell broke in. 'How do we know any of this? You saw her pick up some clue?'

'The last one was leading us to a particular grave. She crouched in front of the headstone . . .'

'And?'

'And that's when I think she picked up the clue.'

'You didn't see her do it?'

'She crouched down . . .'

'But you didn't see her do it?'

Sensing another confrontation brewing, Gill stepped in. 'Why don't we just bring her in here and ask her?'

Rebus nodded. 'I'll fetch her.' He paused. 'With your permission, sir?'

Carswell sighed. 'Go on then.'

But out in the Inquiry Room, there was no sign of

Siobhan. Rebus walked the corridors, asking for her. At the drinks machine, someone said she'd just gone past. Rebus quickened his pace, hauled open the doors to the outside world. No sign of her on the pavement; no sign of her car. He wondered if she'd parked further away, looked to left and right. Busy Leith Walk one way, and the narrow streets of the New Town's east end the other. If he headed into the New Town, her flat was five minutes away, but instead he went back indoors.

'She's gone,' he told Gill. Catching his breath, he noticed Carswell was missing. 'Where's the ACC?'

'Summoned to the Big House. I think the Chief Constable wanted a word.'

'Gill, we've got to find her. Get some bodies out there.' He nodded towards the Inquiry Room. 'It's not like they're setting the world on fire in here.'

'Okay, John, we'll find her, don't worry. Maybe Brains knows where she's gone.' She lifted the receiver. 'We'll start with him . . .'

But Eric Bain seemed as elusive as Siobhan. He was known to be somewhere in the Big House, but nobody knew exactly where. Meantime, Rebus tried Siobhan's home number and mobile. He got her answering machine at the former, a recorded message at the latter, telling him the phone was in use. When he tried five minutes later, it was still in use. By that time, he was using his own mobile, walking downhill to Siobhan's street. He tried her buzzer, with no response. Crossed the road and stared at her window for so long that passers-by started looking up too, wondering what he could see that they couldn't. Her car wasn't parked kerbside, nor was it in any of the surrounding streets.

Gill had already left a message with Siobhan's pager, asking for an urgent call-back, but Rebus had wanted more, and eventually she'd agreed: patrols would be on the lookout for her car.

But now, standing outside her flat, it struck Rebus that

she could be *anywhere*, not just inside the city boundary. Quizmaster had taken her to Hart Fell and Rosslyn Chapel. No telling where he'd choose for a rendezvous. The more isolated it was, the more danger Siobhan was in. He felt like punching himself in the face: he should have dragged her into that meeting with him, not given her the chance to do a runner . . . He tried her mobile again: still engaged. Nobody made a call that long on their mobile, way too expensive. Then, suddenly, he knew what it was: her mobile was hooked to Grant Hood's laptop. Even now, she could be telling Quizmaster she was on her way . . .

Siobhan had parked her car. Two hours yet till the time Quizmaster had suggested. She reckoned she could lie low till then. The pager message from Gill Templer had told her two things: one was that Rebus had told Gill everything; two, that if she ignored Gill's order, she'd have some explaining to do.

Explaining? She was having trouble doing that even to herself. All she knew was that the game – and she knew it wasn't *just* a game; was something potentially much more dangerous – but all the same it had gotten to her. Quizmaster, whoever he or she turned out to be, had gotten to her, to the extent that she could think of little else. The daily clues and puzzles, she missed them, would gladly take on more of them. But more than that, she wanted to *know*, know everything there was to know about Quizmaster and the game. Stricture had impressed her, because Quizmaster had to have suspected that she would be present at the funeral, and that the clue would only start making sense to her at Flip's graveside. Stricture indeed . . . but she felt the word applied to her, too, because she felt bound by the game, tied to it and to identifying its creator. And at the same time she felt almost smothered by it. Was Quizmaster present at the funeral? Had he – or *she* (remembering Bain's advice to keep an open mind) – seen Siobhan pick up the note? Maybe . . . The thought made her shiver. But then, the funeral had been announced in the media. Maybe Quizmaster had found out that way. It was the nearest cemetery to Flip's home; a good chance she'd be interred there . . .

None of which explained why she was doing what she was doing, going out on her own fragile limb like this. It was the sort of stupid thing she regularly chastised Rebus for. Maybe Grant had decided it for her, Grant who had shown himself a 'company player', with his suits and his tan, looking good on TV – good PR for the force.

One game she knew she didn't want to play.

Many times she'd crossed the line, but always crossing back again. She'd break a rule or two, but nothing important, nothing career-threatening, and then hop back into the fold. She wasn't a born outsider in the way she sensed John Rebus was, but she'd learned that she liked it on his side of the fence, liked it better than becoming a Grant or a Derek Linford . . . people who played their own games, doing anything it took to keep in with the men who mattered, men like Colin Carswell.

At one time, she'd thought maybe she could learn from Gill Templer, but Gill had become just like the others. She had her own interests to protect, whatever that took. In order to rise, she'd had to take on the worst attributes of someone like Carswell, while wrapping her own feelings inside some sort of reinforced box.

If rising through the ranks meant losing a part of herself, Siobhan didn't want it. She'd known as much back at the dinner in Hadrian's, when Gill had hinted at things to come.

Maybe that was what she was doing out here, out on her limb – proving something to herself. Maybe it wasn't really about the game and Quizmaster so much as it was about *her*.

She moved in her seat so she was facing the laptop. The line was already open, had been since she'd got into the car. No new messages, so she typed in one of her own.

Meeting accepted. See you there. Siobhan.

And clicked on 'send'.

After which, she shut down the computer, disconnected

the phone and powered it down – battery needed a boost anyway. She placed both beneath the passenger seat, making sure they weren't visible to pedestrians: didn't want someone breaking in. When she got out of the car, she made sure all the doors were locked, and that the little red alarm button was flashing.

Just under two hours to go now; a little time to kill . . .

Jean Burchill had tried calling Professor Devlin, but no one ever answered. So finally she wrote him a note, asking him to contact her, and decided to deliver it by hand. In the back of the taxi, she wondered what the sense of urgency was, and realised it was because she wanted to be rid of Kennet Lovell. He was taking up too much of her waking time, and last night he'd even infected her dreams, slicing the meat from cadavers only to reveal planed wood beneath, while her colleagues from work watched and applauded, the performance turning into a stage show.

If her research into Lovell was to progress, she needed some kind of proof of his interest in woodwork. Without that, she was at a dead end. Having paid the driver, she stood in front of the Professor's tenement, note in hand. But there was no letter-box. Each flat would have its own, the postman gaining entry by pressing the buzzers until someone let him in. She supposed she could slip the note under the door, but reckoned it would lie there ignored, along with all the junk mail. So instead, she looked at the array of buzzers. Professor Devlin's just said 'D. Devlin'. She wondered if he might be back from his wanderings, and pressed the buzzer. When there was no answer, she looked at the remaining buttons, wondering which one to pick. Then the intercom crackled.

'Hello?'

'Dr Devlin? It's Jean Burchill from the Museum. I wonder if I can have a word . . .'

'Miss Burchill? This is somewhat of a surprise.'

'I've tried phoning . . .'

But the door was already signalling that it was no longer locked.

Devlin was waiting for her on his landing. He wore a white shirt, the sleeves rolled up, with thick braces holding up his trousers.

'Well, well,' he said, taking her hand.

'I'm sorry to bother you like this.'

'Not at all, young lady. Now just you come in. I'm afraid you'll find my housekeeping somewhat lacking . . .' He led her into the living room, cluttered with boxes and books.

'Separating the wheat from the chaff,' he informed her.

She picked up a case and opened it. It contained old surgical instruments. 'You're not throwing it out? Perhaps the Museum would be interested . . .'

He nodded. 'I'm in contact with the bursar at Surgeons' Hall. He thinks perhaps the exhibition there might have room for one or two pieces.'

'Major Cawdor?'

Devlin's eyebrows lifted. 'You know him?'

'I was asking him about the portrait of Kennet Lovell.'

'So you're taking my theory seriously?'

'I thought it was worth pursuing.'

'Excellent.' Devlin clapped his hands together. 'And what have you found?'

'Not a great deal. That's really why I'm here. I can't find any reference in the literature to Lovell having an interest in carpentry.'

'Oh, it's a matter of record, I assure you, though it's many years since I came across it.'

'Came across it where?'

'Some monograph or dissertation . . . I really can't recall. Could it have been a university thesis?'

Jean nodded slowly. If it had been a thesis, only the university itself would hold a copy; there'd be no record in any other library. 'I should have thought of that,' she admitted.

'But don't you agree he was a remarkable character?' Devlin asked.

'He certainly lived a very full life . . . unlike his wives.'

'You've been to his graveside?' He smiled at the idiocy of the question. 'Of course you have. And you took note of his marriages. What did you think?'

'At first, nothing . . . but then later, when I thought about it . . .'

'You began to speculate as to whether or not they had been assisted on their final journey?' He smiled again. 'It's obvious, really, isn't it?'

Jean became aware of a smell in the room: stale sweat. Perspiration was shining on Devlin's forehead, and the lenses of his spectacles looked smeared. She was amazed he could see her through them.

'Who better,' he was saying, 'than an anatomist to get away with murder?'

'You're saying he murdered them?'

He shook his head. 'Impossible to tell after all this time. I'm merely speculating.'

'But why would he do that?'

Devlin shrugged, his shoulders stretching the braces. 'Because he could? What do you think?'

'I've been wondering . . . he was very young when he assisted at Burke's autopsy; young and impressionable maybe. That might explain why he fled to Africa . . .'

'And God alone knows what horrors he encountered out there,' Devlin added.

'It would help if we had his correspondence.'

'Ah, the letters between himself and the Reverend Kirkpatrick?'

'You don't happen to know where they might be?'

'Consigned to oblivion, I'd wager. Tossed on to the pyre by some descendant of the good minister . . .'

'And here you are doing the same thing.'

Devlin looked around him at the mess. 'Indeed,' he said. 'Selecting that by which history shall judge my small endeavours.'

Jean picked up a photograph. It showed a middle-aged woman, dressed for some formal function.

'Your wife?' she guessed.

'My dear Anne. She passed away in the summer of nineteen seventy-two. Natural causes, I assure you.'

Jean looked at him. 'Why should you have to assure me?'

Devlin's smile faded. 'She meant the world to me . . . *more* than the world . . .' He clapped his hands together again. 'What can I be thinking of, not offering you something to drink. Tea perhaps?'

'Tea would be wonderful.'

'I can't promise any sense of wonder from PG tea-bags.' His smile was fixed.

'And afterwards, maybe I could see Kennet Lovell's table.'

'But of course. It's in the dining room. Bought from a reputable dealer, though I admit they couldn't be categorical about its provenance – *caveat emptor*, as they say, but they were fairly persuasive, and I was willing to believe.' He had taken his glasses off to give them a polish with his handkerchief. When he slipped them on again, his eyes seemed magnified. 'Tea,' he repeated, making for the hallway. She followed him out.

'Have you lived here long?' she asked.

'Ever since Anne passed on. The house held too many memories.'

'That's thirty years then?'

'Almost.' He was in the kitchen now. 'Won't be a minute,' he said.

'Fine.' She started to retrace her steps back to the living room. The summer of '72, his wife had died . . . She passed an open doorway: the dining room. The table filled almost the whole space. A completed jigsaw lay on top of it . . . no, not quite complete: missing just the one piece. Edinburgh, an aerial photograph. The table itself was a plain enough design. She walked into the room, studied the table's surface of polished wood. The legs were sturdy, lacking any ornamental flourishes. Utilitarian, she thought. The incomplete jigsaw must have taken hours . . . days. She crouched down, seeking the missing piece. There it was: almost completely hidden beneath one of the legs. As she reached

447

for it, she saw that the table boasted one nice, secretive touch. Where the two leaves met in the middle, there was a central element, and into this a small cupboard had been inserted. She'd seen similar designs before, but not from as far back as the nineteenth century. She wondered if Professor Devlin had been duped into buying something from much later than Lovell's period . . . She squeezed into the narrow confines so that she could open the cupboard. It was stiff, and she almost gave up, but then it clicked open, revealing its contents.

A plane, set-square and chisels.

A small saw and some nails.

Woodwork tools.

When she looked up, Professor Devlin was filling the doorway.

'Ah, the missing piece,' was all that he said . . .

Ellen Wylie had heard reports of the funeral, how Ranald Marr had suddenly turned up and been embraced by John Balfour. The talk at West End was that Marr had been brought in for questioning but then released.

'Stitch-up,' Shug Davidson had commented. 'Somebody somewhere's pulling strings.'

He hadn't looked at her as he'd said it, but then he hadn't needed to. He knew . . . and she knew. *Pulling strings*: wasn't that what she'd thought she was doing when she met with Steve Holly? But somehow *he'd* become the puppeteer, making her the marionette. Carswell's speech to the troops had cut into her like a knife, not just nicking the skin but radiating pain through her whole body. When they'd all been called into the office, she'd half hoped her silence would give her away. But then Rebus had stepped in, taken the whole thing upon himself, leaving her feeling worse than ever.

Shug Davidson knew it . . . and though Shug was a colleague and mate, he was also a friend of Rebus's. The pair of them went way back. Now, every time he made some remark she found herself analysing it, seeking the sub-text.

She couldn't concentrate, and her home station, which she'd seen so recently as a refuge, had become inhospitable and alien.

Which was why she'd made the trip to St Leonard's, only to find the CID suite all but deserted. A suit-carrier, hanging from one of the coat pegs, told her that at least one officer had been at the funeral, returning here to change back into work clothes. She guessed Rebus, but couldn't be certain. There was a plastic bag beside his desk, one of the coffins inside. All that work, and no case to show for it. The autopsy notes were sitting on the desk, waiting for someone to follow the instructions left on them. She lifted the note from the top, sat down in Rebus's chair. Without really meaning to, she found herself untying the ribbon which held the notes together. Then she opened the first file and started to read.

She'd done this before, of course; or rather, Professor Devlin had, while she'd sat by his side taking note of his findings. Slow work, yet she realised now that she'd enjoyed it – the notion that there might be some case hidden in the midst of those typewritten pages; the sense of working on the edge of things, a not-quite-investigation; and Rebus himself, as driven as the rest of them put together, biting down on a pen as he concentrated, or furrowing his brow, or stretching suddenly, unlocking his neck. He had this reputation as a loner, yet he'd been happy to delegate, happy to share the work with her. She'd accused him of pitying her, but she didn't really believe that. He did have a martyr complex, but it seemed to work for him . . . and for everyone else.

Skimming the pages now, she realised finally why she'd come: she wanted to apologise in some way he'd understand . . . And then she looked up and he was standing not four yards away, watching her.

'How long have you been there?' she asked, dropping a couple of the pages.

'What are you up to?'

'Nothing.' She picked up the sheets. 'I was just . . . I don't know, maybe one final look before it all went back into the storeroom. How was the funeral?'

'A funeral's a funeral, no matter who they're burying.'

'I heard about Marr.'

He nodded, walked into the room.

'What's wrong?' she asked.

'I was hoping Siobhan might be here.' He walked over to her desk, hoping for some clue . . . something, *anything*.

'I wanted to see you,' Ellen Wylie said.

'Oh?' He turned away from Siobhan's desk. 'Why's that then?'

'Maybe to thank you.'

Their eyes met, communicating without words.

'Don't worry about it, Ellen,' Rebus said at last. 'I mean it.'

'But I got you into trouble.'

'No, you didn't. I got myself into trouble, and maybe made things worse for you too. If I'd stayed quiet, I think you'd have spoken up.'

'Maybe,' she admitted. 'But I could have spoken up anyway.'

'I didn't make it any easier, for which I apologise.'

She had to stifle a smile. 'There you go again, turning the tables. It's *me* who's supposed to be saying sorry.'

'You're right; I can't help it.' There was nothing on or in Siobhan's desk.

'So what do I do now?' she asked. 'Talk it through with DCS Templer?'

He nodded. 'If that's what you want. Of course, you could just keep quiet about it.'

'And let you take the flak?'

'Who says I don't like it?' The phone rang and he snatched at it. 'Hello?' Suddenly his face relaxed. 'No, he's not here right now. Can I take a . . . ?' He put the receiver down. 'Someone for Silvers; no message.'

'You're expecting a call?'

He rubbed a hand against the grain of the day's stubble. 'Siobhan's gone walkabout.'

'In what sense?'

So he told her. Just as he was finishing, a phone on one of the other desks started ringing. He got up and answered it. Another message. He got a pen and a scrap of paper and started writing it down.

'Yes . . . yes,' he was saying, 'I'll stick it on his desk. No promises when he'll see it though.' While he'd been on the phone, Ellen Wylie had been flicking through the autopsy stuff again. As he put the receiver down, he saw her lower her face towards one of the files, as though trying to read something.

'Old Hi-Ho's popular today,' he said, placing the telephone message on Silvers's desk. 'What's the matter?'

She pointed to the bottom of the page. 'Can you read this signature?'

'Which one?' There were two, at the foot of an autopsy report. Date to the side of the signatures: Monday 26 April, 1982 – Hazel Gibbs, the Glasgow 'victim'. She'd died on the Friday night . . .

Typed beneath the signature were the words 'Deputising Pathologist'. The other signature – marked 'Chief Pathologist, City of Glasgow' – wasn't much clearer.

'I'm not sure,' Rebus said, examining the squiggle. 'The names should be typed on the cover-sheet.'

'That's just it,' Wylie said. 'No cover-sheet.' She turned back a few pages to confirm this. Rebus came around the desk so he was standing next to her, then bent down a little closer.

'Maybe the pages got out of order,' he suggested.

'Maybe.' She started going through them. 'But I don't think so.'

'Was it missing when the files arrived?'

'I don't know. Professor Devlin didn't say anything.'

'I think the Chief Pathologist for Glasgow back then was Ewan Stewart.'

Wylie flicked back to the signatures. 'Yep,' she said, 'I'll go with that. But it's the other one that interests me.'

'Why?'

'Well, maybe it's just me, sir, but if you sort of screw your eyes shut a little and take another look, isn't it just possible it says Donald Devlin?'

'What?' Rebus looked, blinked, looked again. 'Devlin was in Edinburgh back then.' But his voice dropped off. The word *Deputising* floated into view. 'Did you look through the report before?'

'That was Devlin's job. I was more like a secretary, remember?'

Rebus put his hand to the back of his neck, rubbed at the knot of muscle there. 'I don't get it,' he said. 'Why wouldn't Devlin say . . . ?' He grabbed the phone, hit 9 and punched a local number. 'Professor Gates, please. It's an emergency. Detective Inspector Rebus here.' A pause as the secretary put him through. 'Sandy? Yes, I know I *always* say it's an emergency, but this time I might not be stretching the truth. April nineteen eighty-two, we think we've got Donald Devlin assisting an autopsy in Glasgow. Is that possible?' He listened again. 'No, Sandy, eighty-two. Yes, April.' He nodded, making eye contact with Wylie, started relaying what he was hearing. 'Glasgow crisis . . . shortage of staff . . . gave you your first chance at being in charge here. Mm-hm, Sandy . . . is that your way of saying Devlin was in Glasgow in April nineteen eighty-two? Thanks, I'll talk to you later.' He slammed the phone down. 'Donald Devlin was *there*.'

'I don't understand,' Wylie said. 'Why didn't he say something?'

Rebus was flicking through the other report, the one from Nairn. No, neither pathologist was Donald Devlin on that occasion. All the same . . .

'He didn't want us to know,' he said at last, answering Wylie's question. 'Maybe that's why he removed the cover-sheet.'

'But *why*?'

Rebus was thinking . . . the way Devlin had returned to the back room of the Ox, anxious to see the autopsies consigned once more to history . . . the Glasgow coffin, made of balsa wood, cruder than the others, the sort of thing you might make if you didn't have access to your usual supplier, or your usual tools . . . Devlin's interest in Dr Kennet Lovell and the Arthur's Seat coffins . . .

Jean!

'I'm getting a bad feeling,' Ellen Wylie said.

'I've always been one for trusting a woman's instincts . . .' But that was just what he *hadn't* done: all those times women had reacted badly to Devlin . . . 'Your car or mine?' he said.

Jean was rising to her feet. Donald Devlin still filled the doorway, his blue eyes as cold as the North Sea, pupils reduced to black pinpoints.

'Your tools, Professor Devlin?' she guessed.

'Well, they're not Kennet Lovell's, dear lady, are they?'

Jean swallowed. 'I think I'd better be going.'

'I don't think I can let you do that.'

'Why not?'

'Because I think you know.'

'Know what?' She was looking around her, seeing nothing helpful . . .

'You know that *I* left those coffins,' the old man stated. 'I can see it in your eyes. No use pretending.'

'The first one was just after your wife died, wasn't it? You killed that poor girl in Dunfermline.'

He raised a finger. 'Untrue: I merely read about her disappearance and went there to leave a marker, a *memento mori*. There were others after that . . . God knows what happened to them.' She watched him take a step forward into the room. 'It took some time, you see, for my sense of loss to turn into something else.' The smile trembled on his lips, which glistened with moisture. 'Anne's life was just . . . *taken* . . . after whole months of agony. That seemed so unfair: no motive, no one to be found guilty . . . All those bodies I'd worked on . . . all the ones after Anne died . . . eventually I wanted some suffering to go with them.' His own hands stroked the table's edge. 'I should never have let slip about Kennet Lovell ... a good historicist would naturally be unable to resist looking into my claim further, finding disturbing parallels between past and present, eh, Miss Burchill? And it was *you* ... the only one who made the connection ... all those coffins over all that time ...'

Jean had been working hard at controlling her breathing. Now she felt strong enough not to hang on to the table. She released her grip on its edge. 'I don't understand,' she said. 'You were helping the inquiry ...'

'Hindering, rather. And who could resist the opportunity? After all, I was investigating *myself*, watching others do the same ...'

'You killed Philippa Balfour?'

Devlin's face creased in disgust. 'Not a bit of it.'

'But you left the coffin ... ?'

'Of course I didn't!' he snapped.

'Then it's been five years since you last ...' She sought the right words. 'Last *did* anything.'

He'd taken another step towards her. She thought she could hear music, and realised suddenly that it was *him*. He was humming some tune.

'You recognise it?' he asked. The corners of his mouth were flecked white. ' "Swing Low, Sweet Chariot". The organist played it at Anne's funeral.' He bowed his head a little and smiled. 'Tell me, Miss Burchill: what do you do when the chariot won't swing low enough?'

She ducked, reached into the cupboard for one of the chisels. Suddenly he had hold of her hair, pulling her back up. She screamed, hands still scrabbling for a weapon. She felt a cool wooden handle. Her head felt like it was on fire. As she lost her balance and started to fall, she stabbed the chisel into his ankle. He didn't so much as flinch. She stabbed again, but now he was dragging her towards the door. She half rose to her feet and added her momentum to his, the pair of them colliding with the edge of the door, spinning out of the room and into the hall. The chisel had fallen from her grasp. She was on her hands and knees when the first blow came, spinning white lights across her vision. The whorls in the carpet seemed to form a pattern of question marks.

How ridiculous, she thought, that this was happening to her . . . She knew she had to get back on to her feet, start fighting back. He was an old man . . . Another blow made her flinch. She could see the chisel . . . only twelve feet to the front door . . . Devlin had her by the legs now, hauling her towards the living room . . . His grasp of her ankles was like a vice. Oh, Christ, she thought. Oh, Christ, oh, Christ . . . Her hands flailed, seeking purchase, or any instrument she could use . . . She screamed again. The blood was roaring in her ears; she couldn't be sure she was making any noise at all. One of Devlin's braces had come free, and his shirt-tail was hanging out.

Not like this . . . not like this . . .

John would never forgive her . . .

The area around Canonmills and Inverleith was an easy enough beat: no housing schemes, plenty of discreet wealth. The patrol car always made a point of stopping at the gates to the Botanics, just across from Inverleith Park. Arboretum Place was a double-width road which saw little traffic: perfect for the officers' mid-shift break. PC Anthony Thompson always provided the flask of tea, while his partner, Kenny Milland, brought the chocolate biscuits – either Jacob's Orange Club or, as today, Tunnock's Caramel Wafers.

'Magic,' Thompson said, though his teeth told him otherwise: there was a dull ache from one of his molars whenever it came into contact with sugar. Having not been near a dentist since the 1994 World Cup, Thompson wasn't enthusiastic about any future encounter.

Milland took sugar in his tea; Thompson didn't. That was why Milland always brought a couple of little sachets and a spoon with him. The sachets came from a burger chain where Milland's elder son worked. Not much of a job, but it had its perks, and there was talk of a significant step-up for Jason.

Thompson loved American cop films, everything from *Dirty Harry* to *Seven*, and when they stopped for their break he sometimes imagined that they were parked outside a doughnut stand, in baking heat and searing glare, with the radio about to burst into life. They'd have to leave their coffee and burn some rubber, giving chase to bank robbers or gangland killers . . .

Not much chance of either in Edinburgh. A couple of pub shootings, some pre-teen car-jackers (one of them a friend's son), and a body in a skip, these comprised the highlights of Thompson's two decades on the force. So when the radio did burst into life, detailing a car and driver, Anthony Thompson did a double-take.

'Here, Kenny, doesn't that one fit the bill?'

Milland turned and looked out of his window at the car parked next door. 'I don't know,' he admitted. 'Wasn't really listening, Tony.' He took another bite of biscuit. Thompson, however, was on the blower, asking for a repeat of the licence plate. He then opened his door and walked around the patrol car, staring down at the front of the neighbouring vehicle.

'We're only parked bloody next to it,' he told his partner. Then he got on the blower again.

The message was relayed to Gill Templer, who sent half a dozen officers from the Balfour team out to the area, then spoke to PC Thompson.

'What do you reckon, Thompson: is she in the Botanic Gardens or Inverleith Park?'

'It's for a meeting, you say?'

'We think so.'

'Well, the park's just this big flat space, easy to spot someone. The Botanics has its nooks and crannies, places you could sit down for a chat.'

'You're saying the Botanics?'

'But it'll be closing soon . . . so maybe not.'

Gill Templer expelled breath. 'You're being a big help.'

'The Botanics is a big place, ma'am. Why not send the

officers in there, get some of the staff to help? Meantime my partner and me can take the park.'

Gill considered the offer. She didn't want Quizmaster scared off . . . or Siobhan Clarke for that matter. She wanted both of them back at Gayfield Square. The officers who were already on their way would pass for civvies from a distance; uniforms would not.

'No,' she said, 'that's okay. We'll start with the Botanics. You stay put, in case she comes back to her car . . .'

Back in the patrol car, Milland gave a resigned shrug. 'You can't say you didn't try, Tony.' He finished his biscuit and screwed up the wrapper.

Thompson didn't say anything. His moment had come and gone.

'That mean we're stuck here?' his partner asked. Then he held his cup out. 'Any more tea in that flask . . . ?'

They didn't call it tea in the Du Thé café. It was a 'herbal infusion': blackcurrant and ginseng to be precise. Siobhan thought it tasted all right, though she was tempted to add a spot of milk to cut the sharpness. Herbal tea and a finger of carrot cake. She'd bought an early edition of the evening paper from the newsagent's next door. There was a photo of Flip's coffin on page three, held aloft by the pall-bearers as they left the church. Smaller photos of the parents and a couple of celebs whose presence Siobhan had failed to notice at the time.

All of this after her walk through the Botanics. She hadn't meant to walk the entire length, but somehow had found herself at the eastern gate, next to Inverleith Row. Shops and cafés just along to the right, by Canonmills. Still time to spare . . . She'd thought of fetching her car, but had decided to leave it where it was. She didn't know what parking was like where she was headed. Then she remembered that her phone was tucked under the passenger seat. But by then it was too late: if she walked back through the Botanics, then either drove or walked back here, she'd have missed the meeting time. And she couldn't be sure how patient Quizmaster would be.

Her decision made, she left the paper on her table at the café and headed back towards the Botanics, but passing the entrance, staying on Inverleith Row. Just before the rugby ground at Goldenacre she took a right, the path turning into more of a track. Dusk was fast arriving as she turned a corner and approached the gates of Warriston Cemetery.

No one was answering Donald Devlin's buzzer, so Rebus hit all the others at random until someone responded. Rebus identified himself, and was buzzed into the tenement, Ellen Wylie right behind him. She actually passed him on the stairs and was first at Devlin's door, thumping it, kicking, pressing his bell, and rattling the letter-box.

'Not promising,' she admitted.

Rebus, who had caught his breath, crouched in front of the letter-box and pushed it open. 'Professor Devlin?' he called. 'It's John Rebus. I need to talk to you.' On the downstairs landing, one of the doors opened and a face peered up.

'It's okay,' Wylie assured the nervous neighbour. 'We're police officers.'

'Ssh!' Rebus hissed. He put his ear to the open letter-box.

'What is it?' Wylie whispered.

'I can hear something . . .' It sounded like the low mewling of a cat. 'Devlin didn't have any pets, did he?'

'Not that I know of.'

Rebus put his eyes to the letter-box again. The hallway was deserted. The door to the living room was at the far end, open a few inches. The curtains looked to be closed, so that he couldn't see into the room. Then his eyes widened.

'Holy Christ,' he said, getting to his feet. He stood back and launched a kick at the door, then another. The wood complained, but didn't give. He slammed his shoulder into it. No effect.

'What?' Wylie said.

'There's someone in there.'

He was about to take another run at the door when Wylie stopped him. 'Together,' she said. So that was what they did. Counted to three and hit the door at the same time. The jamb made a cracking sound. Their second assault split it, and the door opened inwards, Wylie falling through it so that she landed on all fours. When she looked up, she saw what Rebus had seen. Almost at floor level, a hand had attached itself to the living-room door and was trying to open it.

Rebus ran forward, pushed through the gap into the living room. It was Jean, bruised and beaten, her face a smear of blood and mucus, hair matted with sweat and more blood. One eye had swollen and was completely closed. Flecks of pink saliva flew from her mouth as she breathed.

'Jesus Christ,' Rebus said, dropping to his knees in front of her, eyes running over the visible damage. He didn't want to touch her, thought there might be bones broken. He didn't want her to hurt more than she already did.

Wylie was in the room now, too, surveying the scene. It looked like half the contents of the flat lay strewn across the floor, a bloody trail showing where Jean Burchill had crawled her way to the door.

'Get an ambulance,' Rebus said, voice trembling. Then: 'Jean, what did he do to you?' And watched her one good eye fill with tears.

Wylie made the call. Halfway through, she thought she heard a noise out in the hall: the nervous neighbour grown nosy perhaps. She stuck her head out, but couldn't see anything. She gave the address and stressed again that it was an emergency, then cut the call. Rebus's ear was close to Jean's face. Wylie realised she was trying to say something. Her lips were swollen, and teeth looked to have been dislodged.

Rebus looked up at Wylie, eyes widening. 'She says, did we catch him?'

Wylie caught the meaning at once, ran to the window and pulled the curtains back. Donald Devlin was scurrying across the road, dragging one leg and holding his bleeding left hand out in front of him.

'Bastard!' Wylie yelled, making for the door.

'No!' Rebus's voice was a roar. He got to his feet. 'He's mine.'

As he bounded downstairs two at a time, he realised Devlin must have been hiding in one of the other rooms. Waited till they were busy in the living room and then slipped out. They'd interrupted him. He tried not to think of what Jean's fate would have been if they hadn't . . .

By the time he reached the pavement, Devlin had disappeared from view, but the splashes of bright blood were as clear a trail as Rebus could wish for. He caught sight of him crossing Howe Street, making for St Stephen Street. Rebus was gaining, until the uneven pavement caught him, sending him over on one ankle. Devlin might be in his seventies, but that didn't mean much: he'd have the strength and determination of the possessed. Rebus had seen it before during a chase. Desperation and adrenaline made for a fearful mix . . .

Still the drops of blood showed the way. Rebus had slowed, trying to keep the weight off his twisted ankle, pictures of Jean's face filling his mind. He punched numbers into his mobile, got the sequence wrong the first time and had to start again. When the call was answered, he yelled for assistance.

'I'm keeping the line open,' he said. That way, he could let them know if Devlin suddenly flagged a taxi or boarded a bus.

He could see Devlin again now, but then he turned the corner into Kerr Street. By the time Rebus got to the corner, he'd lost him again. Deanhaugh Street and Raeburn Place were straight ahead, busy with pedestrians and traffic: the evening trawl home. With so many people around, the trail was harder to follow. Rebus crossed the road at the traffic lights and found himself on the road-bridge which crossed the Water of Leith . . . There were several routes Devlin could have taken, and the trail seemed to have stopped. Had he crossed towards Saunders Street, or maybe doubled back along Hamilton Place? Resting one arm on the parapet, taking the weight off his ankle, Rebus happened to look down at the river flowing sluggishly below.

And saw Devlin on the footpath, heading down-river towards Leith.

Rebus lifted the phone and called in his position. As he was doing so, Devlin looked back and saw him. The old man's pace quickened, but then suddenly slowed. He came to a stop, the other people on the path making a detour round him. One seemed solicitous, but Devlin shook away the offer of help. He turned back and stared at Rebus, who was walking to the end of the bridge, taking the steps down. Devlin hadn't moved. Rebus called in his position again, then put the phone in his pocket, wanting both hands free.

As he walked towards Devlin, he saw the scratches on his face, and realised that Jean had been giving almost as good as she got. Devlin was studying his bloodied hand as Rebus stopped six feet away.

'The human bite can be quite poisonous, you know,' Devlin told him. 'But at least with Miss Burchill I'm sure I needn't be concerned about hepatitis and HIV.' He looked up. 'Something struck me, seeing you on that bridge. I suddenly thought: they don't have anything.'

'What do you mean?'

'Any evidence.'

'Well, we can always make a start with attempted murder.' Rebus slipped a hand into his pocket, brought out the phone.

'Who are you going to call?' Devlin asked.

'Don't you want an ambulance?' Rebus held the phone up, took a step forwards.

'Just a couple of stitches,' Devlin commented, examining the wound again. Sweat dripped from his hair and the sides of his face. He was breathing hard, wheezily.

'You don't make the grade as a serial killer any more, do you, Professor?'

'It's been some time,' he agreed.

'Was Betty-Anne Jesperson the last?'

'I'd nothing to do with young Philippa, if that's what you're asking.'

'Someone stealing your idea?'

'Well, it wasn't exactly mine in the first place.'

'Are there any others?'

'Others?'

'Victims we don't know about.'

Devlin's smile broke open some of the cuts on his face. 'Isn't four enough?'

'You tell me.'

'It seemed ... satisfactory. No pattern, you see. Two bodies not even found.'

'Just the coffins.'

'Which might never have been connected ...'

Rebus nodded slowly, didn't say anything.

'Was it the autopsy?' Devlin asked at last. Rebus nodded again. 'I knew it was a risk.'

'If you'd told us at the start you'd carried out the Glasgow post-mortem, we wouldn't have thought anything of it.'

'But back then, I couldn't know what else you might find. Other connections, I mean. And by the time I saw you weren't going to come up with anything, it was too late. I could hardly say "Oh, incidentally, I was one of the pathologists", not after we'd already been through the notes ...'

He dabbed at his face with his fingers, finding blood issuing from the cuts. Rebus held the phone a little closer.

'That ambulance ... ?' he offered.

Devlin shook his head. 'In good time.' A middle-aged woman made to pass them, eyes widening in horror as she saw Devlin. 'A stumble down the steps,' he reassured her. 'Help is on its way.'

She quickened her pace away from the scene.

'I think I've said more than enough, don't you, DI Rebus?'

'Not for me to say, sir.'

'I do hope DS Wylie doesn't get into trouble.'

'For what?'

'Not keeping a closer eye on me when I was studying the autopsy reports.'

'I don't think she's the one that's in trouble here.'

'Uncorroborated evidence, isn't that what we're dealing with, Inspector? One woman's word against mine? I'm sure I can find some plausible motive for my fight with Miss Burchill.' He studied his hand. 'One might almost call me the victim. And let us be honest, what else do you have? Two drownings, two missing persons, no evidence.'

'Well,' Rebus corrected him, 'no evidence apart from this.' He held the phone a little higher. 'It was already on when I took it from my pocket, connected to our comms centre down in Leith.' He put the phone to his ear. Glancing back over his shoulder, he saw that uniformed officers were making their way down the steps from the bridge. 'Did you get all that?' he asked into the mouthpiece. Then he looked at Devlin and smiled.

'We record every call, you see.'

The animation left Devlin's face, his shoulders slumping. Then he turned on his heels, preparing to run. But Rebus's arm snaked out, gripping him hard by the shoulder. Devlin tried to wrestle free. One foot slipped off the walkway and he started to fall, his weight pulling Rebus with him. The two men landed heavily in the Water of Leith. It wasn't deep, and Rebus felt his own shoulder connect with a rock. When he tried standing up, his feet sank to the ankles in mud. He was still holding on to Devlin, and as the bald head appeared from below the surface, missing its spectacles, Rebus saw again the monster who had battered Jean. He reached out his free hand to the Professor's neck and forced him back under. Hands flew up, splashing, wrestling air. Fingers clawing at Rebus's arm, clutching at his jacket lapel.

He felt as calm as he ever had in his life. The water lapped around him, icy but somehow soothing, too. There were people on the bridge, staring down, and officers wading into the water nearby, and a pale lemon sun spectating from above a bruised cloud. The water seemed cleansing to him. He couldn't feel his twisted ankle any more, couldn't feel anything much. Jean would recover, and so would he. He'd move out of Arden Street, find somewhere else, somewhere nobody knew about . . . maybe near water.

His arm was wrenched from behind: one of the uniforms.

'Let go of him!'

The cry broke the spell. Rebus released his grip, and Donald Devlin rose spluttering and choking into the daylight, watery vomit dribbling from his chin . . .

They were loading Jean Burchill into the ambulance when Rebus's mobile started ringing. One of the green-suited paramedics was explaining that they couldn't rule out spinal or neck damage, which was why they'd strapped her to a stretcher and placed braces around her head and neck.

Rebus was staring at Jean, trying to take in what was being said.

'Shouldn't you answer that?' the paramedic asked.

'What?'

'Your phone.'

Rebus lifted the mobile to his ear. When he'd struggled with Devlin, it had dropped on to the walkway. It was scratched and chipped, but at least still working. 'Hello?'

'DI Rebus?'

'Yes.'

'It's Eric Bain here.'

'Yes?'

'Is something the matter?'

'Quite a lot, yes.' As the trolley slid home into the back of the ambulance, Rebus looked down at his sodden clothes. 'Any sign of Siobhan?'

'That's why I'm calling.'

'What's happened?'

'Nothing's happened. It's just that I can't reach her. They think she's in the Botanics. There are half a dozen men out there looking for her.'

'So?'

'So there's news about Quizmaster.'

'And you're bursting to tell someone?'

'I suppose so, yes.'

'I'm not sure you've got the right person, Bain, I'm a bit tied up right now.'

'Oh.'

Rebus was inside the ambulance now, seated across from the trolley. Jean had her eyes closed, but when he reached for her hand, his pressure was returned.

'Sorry?' he said, having missed what Bain had just said.

'Who should I tell then?' Bain repeated.

'I don't know.' Rebus sighed. 'Okay, tell me what it is.'

'It's Special Branch,' Bain said, the words streaming out. 'One of the e-mail addresses Quizmaster was using, it traces back to Philippa Balfour's account.'

Rebus didn't understand: was Bain trying to say that Flip Balfour had been Quizmaster . . . ?

'I think it makes sense,' Bain was saying now. 'Taken with Claire Benzie's account.'

'I'm not getting you.' Jean's eyelids were fluttering. A sudden jolt of pain, Rebus guessed. He lessened the pressure on her hand.

'If Benzie did lend her laptop to Philippa Balfour, we've got two computers in the same place, both used by Quizmaster.'

'Yes?'

'And if we rule out Ms Balfour as a suspect . . .'

'We're left with someone who had access to both?'

Silence for a moment, and then Bain: 'I think the boyfriend's back in the frame, don't you?'

'I don't know.' Rebus was having trouble concentrating. He ran the back of his hand across his forehead, feeling perspiration there.

'We could always ask him . . .'

'Siobhan's gone to meet Quizmaster,' Rebus said. Then he paused. 'She's at the Botanics, you say?'

'Yes.'

'How do we know?'

'Her car's parked right outside.'

Rebus thought for a second: Siobhan would know they

were looking for her. Leaving the car in full view was too big a giveaway . . .

'What if she's not there?' he said. 'What if she's meeting him somewhere else?'

'How can we find out?'

'Maybe Costello's flat . . .' He looked down at Jean. 'Look, Bain, I really can't do this . . . not right now.'

Jean's eye opened. She mouthed something.

'Hang on, Bain,' Rebus said. Then he lowered his head to Jean's.

'Fine . . .' he heard her slur.

She was telling him she'd be okay; that he had to help Siobhan now. Rebus turned his head, his eyes meeting those of Ellen Wylie, who was standing on the roadway, waiting for the doors to close. She nodded slowly, letting him know she'd stay with Jean.

'Bain?' he said into the mobile. 'I'll meet you outside Costello's flat.'

By the time Rebus got there, Bain had climbed the winding stairs and was standing outside Costello's door.

'I don't think he's home,' Bain was saying, crouching down to look through the letter-box. A chill ran up Rebus's spine, remembering what he'd seen when he'd peered into Devlin's flat. Bain got to his feet again. 'No sign of . . . Jesus Christ, man, what happened to you?'

'Swimming lessons. I didn't have time to change.' Rebus looked at the door, then at Bain. 'Together?' he said.

Bain stared back at him. 'Isn't that illegal?'

'For Siobhan,' Rebus said simply.

They hit the door together on the count of three.

Inside, Bain knew what he was looking for: a computer. He found two in the bedroom, both of them laptops.

'Claire Benzie's,' Bain guessed, 'and either his own or someone else's.'

The screen-saver had been activated on one computer. Bain accessed Costello's ISP and opened the filing cabinet.

'No time to try for a password,' he said, almost to himself

more than Rebus. 'So all we can read are the old messages.' But there were none to or from Siobhan. 'Looks like he wipes as he goes,' Bain said.

'Or else we're barking up the wrong tree.' Rebus was looking around the room: unmade bed, books scattered across the floor. Notes for an essay on the desk next to the PC. Socks, pants and T-shirts spilled from the chest of drawers, but not from the top drawer. Rebus limped over, opened it slowly. Inside: maps and guidebooks, including one about Arthur's Seat. A postcard of Rosslyn Chapel and another guidebook.

'Right tree,' he remarked simply. Bain got up, came to look.

'Everything the well-dressed Quizmaster could need.' Bain went to reach into the drawer, but Rebus slapped his hand away. 'No touching.' He tried sliding the drawer out further. Something was sticking. He took a pen from his pocket and dislodged it: an Edinburgh A–Z.

'Open at the Botanics,' Bain said, sounding relieved. If that's where David Costello was, they'd have cornered him by now.

But Rebus wasn't so sure. He was examining the rest of the page. Then he looked over towards Costello's bed. Postcards of old gravestones . . . a small framed photo of Costello with Flip Balfour, with another headstone just coming into the frame. They'd met at a dinner party . . . breakfast next morning and then a walk in Warriston Cemetery. That was what Costello had told him. Warriston Cemetery was just across the road from the Botanic Gardens. Same page of the A–Z.

'I know where he is,' Rebus said quietly. 'I know where she's meeting him. Come on.' He ran from the room, hand already reaching for his mobile. The detectives who were wandering around the Botanics, they could be at Warriston in two minutes . . .

'Hello, David.'

He still had his funeral clothes on, including the sunglasses. He grinned as she walked towards him. He was just sitting there, legs swinging from the wall. He slid down and was suddenly standing in front of her.

'You guessed,' he said.

'Sort of.'

He looked at his watch. 'You're early.'

'You're earlier.'

'I had to recce, see if you were lying.'

'I said I'd be on my own.'

'And here you are.' He looked around again.

'Plenty of escape routes,' Siobhan said, surprised by how calm she was. 'Is that why you chose it?'

'It's where I first realised I loved Flip.'

'Loved her so much you went and killed her?'

His face fell. 'I didn't know that was going to happen.'

'No?'

He shook his head. 'Right up until the moment I had my hands round her throat . . . even then I don't think I knew.'

She drew in a deep breath. 'But you did it anyway.'

He nodded. 'I suppose I did, yes.' Looked up at her. 'That's what you wanted to hear, isn't it?'

'I wanted to meet Quizmaster.'

He opened his arms. 'At your command.'

'I also want to know why.'

'Why?' He framed his lips into an O. 'How many reasons do you want? Her yah friends? Her pretensions? The way she kept teasing and picking fights, looking to break us up just so she could watch me crawling back?'

'You could have walked away.'

'But I *loved* her.' When he laughed, it was as if acknowledging his own foolishness. 'I kept telling her that, and you know what she told me back?'

'What?'

'That I wasn't the only one.'

'Ranald Marr?'

'That old goat, yes. Since before she left school. And still at it, even when *we* were together!' He stopped, swallowed. 'Enough motivation for you, Siobhan?'

'You vented your anger on Marr by disfiguring that toy soldier, and yet Flip . . . Flip you had to *kill*?' She felt calm, almost numb. 'That doesn't seem quite fair to me.'

'You wouldn't understand.'

She looked at him. 'But I think I do, David. You're a coward, pure and simple. You say you didn't know you were going to murder Flip that night – that's a lie. You had it planned all along . . . and afterwards you were Mr Calm, speaking to her worried friends not much more than an hour after you'd killed her. You knew *exactly* what you were doing, David. You were Quizmaster.' She paused. He was staring into the middle distance, soaking up every word. 'Something I don't understand . . . you sent Flip a message after she died?'

He smiled. 'That day at her flat, while Rebus was watching me and you were working on her computer . . . he told me something, said I was the only suspect.'

'You thought you'd try throwing us off the scent?'

'It was just supposed to be that one message . . . but when you replied, I couldn't resist. I was as hooked as you were, Siobhan. The game had us both.' His eyes sparkled. 'Isn't that something?'

He seemed to expect an answer, so she nodded slowly. 'Are you thinking of killing me, David?'

He shook his head briskly, irritated by the assumption. 'You know the answer to that,' he spat. 'You wouldn't have come otherwise.' He walked over to a low headstone and rested against it. 'Maybe none of it would have happened,' he said, 'without the Professor.'

Siobhan thought she must have misheard. 'Which one?'

'Donald Devlin. First time he saw me afterwards, he guessed I'd done it. That's why he came up with that story, someone loitering outside. He was trying to protect me.'

'Why would he do that, David?' It felt strange using his name. She wanted to call him Quizmaster.

'Because of everything we talked about ... committing murder, getting away with it.'

'Professor Devlin?'

He looked at her. 'Oh yes, he's killed too, you know. Old bugger as good as said so, daring me to be like him ... maybe he was just too good a teacher, eh?' He ran his hands over the headstone. 'We had these long talks on the stairwell. He wanted to know all about me, my early days, the angry days. I went to his flat once. He showed me these cuttings ... people who'd disappeared or drowned. There was even one about a German student ... '

'That's where you got the idea?'

'Maybe.' He shrugged. 'Who knows where ideas come from?' He paused. 'I helped her, you know. She was dead impressed, all those clues ... pulling her hair out until I came along ... ' He laughed. 'Flip was never much good with computers. I gave her the name Flipside, then sent the first clue.'

'You turned up at the flat, told her you'd solved Hellbank ... '

Costello nodded, remembering. 'She wasn't going to go with me until I promised to drop her off afterwards ... She'd just kicked me out again – final this time, she'd piled my clothes on a chair – and after Hellbank she was heading off for a drink with all those bloody friends of hers ... ' He screwed his eyes shut for a moment, then opened them and blinked, turning his head to face Siobhan. 'Once you're there, it's hard to go back ... ' He shrugged.

'There never was a Stricture?'

He shook his head slowly. 'That clue was all for you, Siobhan ... '

'I don't know why you kept going back to her, David, or what you thought the game would prove, but one thing I do know: you never loved her. What you wanted was to control her.' She nodded at the truth of this.

'Some people like to be controlled, Siobhan.' His eyes were staring into hers. 'Don't you?'

She thought for a moment ... or tried to think. Opened

her mouth and was about to speak, but a noise interrupted. He snapped his head round: two men approaching. And two more fifty yards beyond them. He turned slowly back to Siobhan.

'I'm disappointed in you.'

She was shaking her head. 'Not my doing.'

He leaped from the headstone, hurtled towards the wall, his hands reaching the top, feet scrabbling for purchase. The detectives were running now, one yelling, 'Stop him!' Siobhan just watched, rooted to the spot. Quizmaster . . . she'd given him her word . . . One of his feet had found a half-inch of ledge, pushing up . . .

Siobhan threw herself at the wall, grabbed the other leg with both hands and pulled. He tried kicking her off, but she held on, one hand reaching up towards his jacket, trying to haul him back. Then they were both flying backwards, his the only cry. His sunglasses seemed to float past her in slow motion. She was watching them when she hit the ground. He landed heavily on top of her, the air exploding from her lungs. She felt pain as her head connected with the grass. Costello was on his feet and running, but two of the officers had him, wrestled him back on to the ground. He managed to slide his head round so he was looking at Siobhan, the two of them only a couple of yards apart. Hatred filled his face, and he spat in her direction. The saliva hit her on the chin and hung there. Suddenly she didn't have the strength to wipe it off . . .

Jean was asleep, but the doctor assured Rebus she'd be fine: cuts and bruises, 'nothing time can't heal'.

'I very much doubt that,' he told the doctor.

Ellen Wylie was there by the bedside. Rebus walked over and stood beside her. 'I wanted to say thanks,' he told her.

'For what?'

'Helping break down Devlin's door, for one thing. I'd never have done it on my own.'

Her reply was a shrug. 'How's the ankle?' she asked.

'Ballooning nicely, thank you.'

'A week or two on the sick,' she said.

'Maybe more, if I swallowed any of the Water of Leith.'

'I hear Devlin took a good few gulps himself.' She stared at him. 'Got a good story prepared?'

He smiled. 'You offering to tell a lie or two on my behalf?'

'Just say the word.'

He nodded slowly. 'Problem is, a dozen witnesses could say otherwise.'

'But will they?'

'We'll just have to wait and see,' Rebus said.

He limped along to A&E, where Siobhan was having a couple of stitches put into a head wound. Eric Bain was there. The conversation stopped as Rebus approached.

'Eric here,' Siobhan said, 'was just explaining how you worked out where I'd be.' Rebus nodded. 'And how you gained entry to David Costello's flat.'

Rebus made an O with his lips.

'Mr Strongarm,' she went on, 'kicking in a suspect's door without authority or any sniff of a warrant.'

'Technically,' Rebus told her, 'I was on suspension. That means I wasn't a serving officer.'

'Making it even worse.' She turned to Bain. 'Eric, you're going to have to cover for him.'

'Door was open when we got there,' Bain recited. 'Botched break-in, probably . . .'

Siobhan nodded and smiled at him. Then she gave Bain's hand a squeeze . . .

Donald Devlin was under police guard in one of the Western General's private rooms. He'd half drowned in the river and was now in what the doctors were calling a coma.

'Let's hope he stays there,' ACC Colin Carswell had said. 'Save us the expense of a prosecution.'

Carswell hadn't said anything at all to Rebus. Gill said not to worry: 'He's ignoring you because he hates making apologies.'

Rebus nodded. 'I've just seen a doctor,' he told her.

She looked at him. 'So?'

'Does that count as my check-up . . . ?'

David Costello was in custody at Gayfield Square. Rebus didn't go near. He knew they'd be cracking open a few bottles of whisky and cans of beer, sounds of celebration drifting into the room where Costello was being questioned. He thought of the time he'd asked Donald Devlin whether his young neighbour was capable of killing: *not cerebral enough for David*. Well, Costello had found his method all the same, and Devlin had protected him . . . the old man sheltering the young.

When Rebus went home, he took a tour of his flat. It represented, he realised, the only fixed point of his life. All the cases he'd worked, the monsters he'd encountered . . . he dealt with them here, seated in his chair, staring out of his window. He found room for them in the bestiary of his mind, and there they stayed.

If he gave this up, what would be left? No still centre to his world, no cage for his demons . . .

Tomorrow he'd call the solicitor, tell her he wasn't moving.

Tomorrow.

For tonight, he had new cages to fill . . .

14

It was a Sunday afternoon of sharp, low sunlight, the shadows impossibly long and skewed into an elastic geometry. Trees bowed by the wind, clouds moving like oiled machines. Falls, twinned with Anguish . . . Rebus drove past the signpost, glanced towards Jean, quiet in the passenger seat. She'd been quiet all week; slow to answer her phone or come to the door. The doctor's words: *nothing time can't heal* . . .

He'd given her the option, but she'd decided to come with him. They parked next to a sparkling BMW. There were traces of soapy water in the gutters. Rebus pulled on the hand-brake and turned to Jean.

'I'll only be a minute. You want to wait here?'

She thought about it, then nodded. He reached into the back for the coffin. It was wrapped in newspaper, a front-page headline by Steven Holly. He got out of the car, leaving his door open. Knocked on the door of Wheel Cottage.

Bev Dodds answered. She had a smile fixed to her face and a frilly apron tied across her chest.

'Sorry, not a tourist,' Rebus said. Her smile faded. 'Doing a roaring trade in tea and buns?'

'What can I do for you?'

He lifted up the parcel. 'Thought you might like this back. It's yours, after all, isn't it?'

She parted the sheets of newsprint. 'Oh, thanks,' she said. 'It really *is* yours, isn't it?'

She wouldn't look at him. 'Finders keepers, I suppose . . .'

But he was shaking his head. 'I mean, you made it, Ms Dodds. This new sign of yours . . .' He nodded in its direction. 'Care to tell me who made it? I'm willing to bet you did it yourself. Nice piece of wood ... I'm guessing you've a few chisels and such-like.'

'What do you want?' Her voice had grown chilly.

'When I brought Jean Burchill here – there she is in the car, and she's fine by the way, thanks for asking – when I brought her here, you said you often went to the Museum.'

'Yes?' She was staring over his shoulder, but averted her gaze when Jean's eyes met hers.

'Yet you'd never come across the Arthur's Seat coffins.' Rebus affected a frown. 'It should have clicked with me right there.' He stared at her, but she didn't say anything. He watched her neck redden, watched her turn the coffin in her hands. 'Still,' he said, 'brought you some extra business, eh? But I'll tell you one thing ...'

Her eyes were liquid; she brought them up to meet his. 'What?' she asked, voice cracking.

He pointed a finger at her. 'You're lucky I didn't tag you sooner. I might have said something to Donald Devlin. And then you'd look like Jean back there, if not a damned sight worse.'

He turned away, headed back to the car. On the way, he unhooked the 'Pottery' sign and tossed it into the gutter. She was still watching from her doorway as he started the ignition. A couple of day-trippers were approaching along the pavement. Rebus knew exactly where they were headed and why. He made sure to turn the steering-wheel hard, running the sign over, front and back tyres both.

On the way back into Edinburgh, Jean asked if they were going to Portobello. He nodded, and asked if that was okay with her.

'It's fine,' she told him. 'I need someone to help me move that mirror out of the bedroom.' He looked at her. 'Just until the bruises have healed,' she said quietly.

He nodded his understanding. 'Know what I need, Jean?'

She turned towards him. 'What?'

He shook his head slowly. 'I was hoping you might tell me ...'

Sexual repression and hysteria are what Edinburgh is all about.

Philip Kerr, 'The Unnatural History Museum'

Afterword

Firstly, a big thank-you to Mogwai, whose 'Stanley Kubrick' EP was playing in the background throughout the final draft of this book.

The collection of poetry in David Costello's flat is *I Dream of Alfred Hitchcock* by James Robertson, and the poem from which Rebus quotes is entitled 'Shower Scene'.

After the first draft of this book was written, I discovered that in 1999 the Museum of Scotland commissioned two American researchers, Dr Allen Simpson and Dr Sam Menefee of the University of Virginia, to examine the Arthur's Seat coffins and formulate a solution. They concluded that the most likely explanation was that the coffins had been made by a shoemaker acquaintance of the murderers Burke and Hare, using a shoemaker's knife and brass fittings adapted from shoe buckles, the idea being to give the victims some vestige of Christian burial, since a dissected *corpus* could not be resurrected.

The Falls is, of course, a work of fiction, a flight of fancy. Dr Kennet Lovell exists only between its pages.

In June 1996, a man's body was found near the summit of Ben Alder. He'd died of gunshot wounds. His name was Emmanuel Caillet, the son of a French merchant banker. What he was doing in Scotland was never ascertained. The report, produced from autopsy and scene-of-crime evidence, concluded that the young man had committed suicide. But there are enough discrepancies and unanswered questions to persuade his parents that this is not the real solution . . .

THE FALLS

© Rankin

ABOUT IAN RANKIN

Ian Rankin, OBE, writes a huge proportion of all the crime novels sold in the UK and has won numerous prizes, including in 2005 the Crime Writers' Association Diamond Dagger. His work is available in over 30 languages, home sales of his books exceed one million copies a year, and several of the novels based around the character of Detective Inspector Rebus – his name meaning 'enigmatic puzzle' – have been successfully transferred to television.

Introduction to DI John Rebus

The first novels to feature Rebus, a flawed
but resolutely humane detective, were not an
overnight sensation, and success took time
to arrive. But the wait became a period that
allowed Ian Rankin to come of age as a writer,
and to develop Rebus into a thoroughly
believable, flesh-and-blood character straddling
both industrial and post-industrial Scotland;
a gritty yet perceptive man coping with his
own demons. As Rebus struggled to keep
his relationship with daughter Sammy alive
following his divorce, and to cope with the
imprisonment of brother Michael, while all the
time trying to strike a blow for morality against
a fearsome array of sinners (some justified and
some not), readers began to respond in their
droves. Fans admired Ian Rankin's re-creation
of a picture-postcard Edinburgh with a vicious
tooth-and-claw underbelly just a heartbeat away,
his believable but at the same time complex
plots and, best of all, Rebus as a conflicted man
trying always to solve the unsolvable, and to do
the right thing.

As the series progressed, Ian Rankin refused
to shy away from contentious issues such as
corruption in high places, paedophilia and illegal

immigration, combining his unique seal of tight plotting with a bleak realism, leavened with brooding humour.

In Rebus the reader is presented with a rich and constantly evolving portrait of a complex and troubled man, irrevocably tinged with the sense of being an outsider and, potentially, unable to escape being a 'justified sinner' himself. Rebus's life is intricately related to his Scottish environs too, enriched by Ian Rankin's attentive depiction of locations, and careful regard to Rebus's favourite music, watering holes and books, as well as his often fraught relationships with colleagues and family. And so, alongside Rebus, the reader is taken on an often painful, sometimes hellish journey to the depths of human nature, always rooted in the minutiae of a very recognisable Scottish life.

The Oxford Bar – Rebus and many of the characters who appear in the novels are regulars of the Ox – as is Ian Rankin himself. The pub is now synonymous with the Rebus novels to the extent that one of the regular medical examiners called in to assist with investigations is named after the pub's owner, John Gates.

Edinburgh plays an important role throughout the Rebus
novels; a character itself, as brooding and as volatile as
Rebus. The Edinburgh depicted in the novels is far short of

the beautiful city that tourists in their thousands flood to
visit. Hidden behind the historic buildings and elegant
façades is the world that Rebus inhabits.

For general discussion regarding the Rebus series

How does Ian Rankin reveal himself as an author interested in using fiction to 'tell the truths the real world can't'?

———

There are similarities between the lives of the author and his protagonist – for instance, both Ian Rankin and Rebus were born in Fife, lost their mothers at an early age, have children with physical problems – so is it useful therefore to think of John Rebus and Ian Rankin as each other's alter egos?

———

Could it be said that Rebus is trying to make sense in a general way of the world around him, or is he seeking answers to the 'big questions'? And is it relevant therefore that he is a believer in God and comes from a Scottish Presbyterian background? Would Rebus see confession in both the religious and the criminal sense as similar in any way?

———

How does Ian Rankin explore notions of Edinburgh as a character in its own right? In what way does he contrast the glossy public and seedy private faces of the city with the public and private faces of those Rebus meets?

How does Ian Rankin use musical sources – the Elvis references in *The Black Book*, for instance, or the Rolling Stones allusions in *Let It Bleed* – as a means of character development through the series? What does Rebus's own taste in music and books say about him as a person?

What do you think about Rebus as a character? If you have read several or more novels from the series, discuss how his character is developed.

If Rebus has a problem with notions of 'pecking order' and the idea of authority generally, what does it say about him that he chose careers in hierarchical institutions such as the Army and then the police?

How does Rebus relate to women: as lovers, flirtations, family members and colleagues?

Do the flashes of gallows humour as often shown by the pathologists but sometimes also in Rebus's own comments increase or dissipate narrative tension? Does Rebus use black comedy for the same reasons the pathologists do?

Do Rebus's personal vulnerabilities make him understanding of the frailties of others?

How does the characterisation of Rebus compare to other long-standing popular detectives from British authors such as Holmes, Poirot, Morse or Dalgleish? And are there more similarities or differences between them?

THE FALLS

Flip, a 20-year-old art history student, is missing after joining a compulsive interactive internet game. A tiny doll in a coffin is discovered at a place called Falls, a companion perhaps to the mysterious eight surviving real-life Arthur's Seat coffins from 1836 (and maybe also to several others found in recent years).

And soon the police realise that a while back the body of Jürgen, another student also keen on interactive games, was found on a remote Scottish hillside; while the other recently discovered dolls in coffins can be linked to a series of apparent suicides that may now have to be regarded as cases of murder.

Rebus doesn't know what to make of the computer angle that seems to be commanding so much of the investigation, and so it is left to DC Siobhan Clarke to step into the breach, although she soon finds herself facing a series of ever more demanding challenges as she embarks on a life-or-death role-playing treasure hunt orchestrated by an enigmatic Quizmaster.

As Siobhan turns down a promotion and Rebus ignores instructions to see a doctor, the pair find themselves in bad odour with their new boss, DCS Gill Templer (who has history with Rebus), as they become gripped by a complex set of clues that may turn out instead to be mere distractions.

Ian Rankin shows Siobhan coming of age as a detective in *The Falls*, played out against the poignancy of Rebus's understanding that technology is now taking over in many investigations and that a technophobe such as himself may be the last of a dying breed unless, of course, the drink gets to him first.

Discussion points for *The Falls*

There's a new love interest for Rebus. Does he treat her better than previous partners?

David Costello comments that the Scots can be overly reductive – such as Old Town versus New, Catholic versus Protestant, east coast versus west – is this true in Ian Rankin's interpretation, or is it, as Rebus responds, 'an attraction of opposites'?

How does Ian Rankin make Donald Devlin, formerly Professor of Forensic Medicine, seem so creepy?

Curator Jean Burchill suggests, '*Aren't we all curious about the things we fear?*' Would Rebus agree?

Rebus claims that his enjoyment of police work is essentially voyeuristic and cowardly: '*He concentrated on the minutiae of other people's lives, other people's problems, to stop him examining his own frailties and failings.*' How true is this?

'*He didn't think he'd go quietly. They'd have to pull him screaming and kicking . . .*' Why isn't Rebus looking forward to retirement?

'*"Such a beautiful city," she* [Jean] *said. Rebus tried to agree. He hardly saw it any more. To him, Edinburgh had become a state of mind, a juggling of criminal thoughts and baser instincts . . . It was a crime scene waiting to happen.*' Is Rebus unable now ever to see the beauty of the city?

Might Rebus regard Father Conor Leary's death as symbolic in some ways of his own looming retirement?

Why does Siobhan reject the Press Liaison job?

'*She had a gut feeling, but it was dangerous to depend on those: she'd seen Rebus screw up more than once on the strength of a gut feeling for someone's guilt or innocence.*' Would Siobhan agree, though, that perhaps 'gut feelings' are integral to Rebus's manner of policing?

When Siobhan says, '*Let's play it by ear, see which one of us Marr prefers,*' what is Rebus's response?

What does the reader feel about Rebus's treatment of the tourists he and Siobhan encounter at Falls?

Does the constantly missed doctor's appointment become something of a running joke?

Discuss whether Siobhan is correct in believing that Gill Templer is 'running scared' since her new promotion?

How does Ian Rankin pun with 'losing it'?

Is Rebus right to take the blame for DS Ellen Wylie's error of judgement?

Is Rebus often a 'willing martyr'?

Big Ger Cafferty doesn't feature in *The Falls* – is he missed?

All Orion/Phoenix titles are available at your local bookshop or from the following address:

> Mail Order Department
> Littlehampton Book Services
> FREEPOST BR535
> Worthing, West Sussex, BN13 3BR
> *telephone* 01903 828503, *facsimile* 01903 828802
> *e-mail* MailOrders@lbsltd.co.uk
> (Please ensure that you include full postal address details)

Payment can be made either by credit/debit card (Visa, Mastercard, Access and Switch accepted) or by sending a £ Sterling cheque or postal order made payable to *Littlehampton Book Services*.
DO NOT SEND CASH OR CURRENCY

Please add the following to cover postage and packing

UK and BFPO:
£1.50 for the first book, and 50p for each additional book to a maximum of £3.50

Overseas and Eire:
£2.50 for the first book plus £1.00 for the second book and 50p for each additional book ordered

---

BLOCK CAPITALS PLEASE

name of cardholder ....   *delivery address*
                                                          (if different from cardholder)

address of cardholder ....

....

....

postcode ....   *postcode* ....

☐ I enclose my remittance for £.....................

☐ please debit my Mastercard/Visa/Access/Switch (delete as appropriate)

card number ☐☐☐☐☐☐☐☐☐☐☐☐☐☐☐☐

expiry date ☐☐☐☐   Switch issue no. ☐☐

signature ....

prices and availability are subject to change without notice